A COMMUNITY UNDER SIEGE

Sociology
533

CHICANO STUDIES RESEARCH CENTER
UNIVERSITY OF CALIFORNIA
MONOGRAPH NO. 11

EDITOR: Oscar R. Martí

SERIES EDITORS: Carlos Vélez
Ray Rocco

CONTRIBUTING EDITOR: Dianne Vozoff

CARTOGRAPHER: Noel Díaz

A COMMUNITY UNDER SIEGE:

A CHRONICLE OF CHICANOS EAST OF THE LOS ANGELES RIVER 1945–1975

by

Rodolfo F. Acuña

CHICANO STUDIES RESEARCH CENTER PUBLICATIONS
UNIVERSITY OF CALIFORNIA LOS ANGELES
MONOGRAPH NO. 11

Library of Congress Cataloging in Publication Data

Acuña, Rodolfo.
    A community under siege.

    (Monograph / Chicano Studies Research Center, Publications, University of
California, Los Angeles ; no. 11)
    1. Mexican Americans—California—East Los Angeles—Politics and
government. 2. Mexican Americans—California—East Los Angeles—Economic
conditions. 3. Mexican Americans—California—East Los Angeles—Social conditions.
4. East Los Angeles (Calif.)—Politics and government. 5. East Los Angeles (Calif.)—
Economic conditions. 6. East Los Angeles (Calif.)—Social conditions. 7. American
newspapers—California—East Los Angeles—Indexes. I. Title II. Series: Monograph
(University of California, Los Angeles. Chicano Studies Research Center.
Publications) ; no. 11.
F869.E18A28   1984   979.4'93   83-26197
ISBN 0-89551-066-9

Design by Serena Sharp

Typeset by Freedmen's Organization

Printed in the United States of America

*To my father, Francisco Acuña
and to Dr. Ernesto Galarza,
a pioneer in the struggle
against the bulldozers.*

CONTENTS

PREFACE

East Los Angeles is the largest and best known Chicano community in the United States. Social scientists have identified East Los Angeles with the Sleepy Lagoon case, the Pachuco Riots, the East L.A. school walkouts, and the 1970 Chicano Moratorium. East Los Angeles is where the Chicano journalist Ruben Salazar was killed, where lowriders cruised Whittier Boulevard. It is where media has depicted Chicanos as crazed, violent gang members, chronically unemployed, and unemployable. Outside of these notorious stereotypes, however, not much is known about the community's history or about the special interests that control its destiny.

The roots of Mexicans in the area east of the Los Angeles River are deep. They lived in Paredón Blanco (White Bluffs), what is today Boyle Heights, since the 1830s. This settlement was later displaced by more affluent colonials in the 1880s. Mexicans did not return in significant numbers until the 1920s, when Civic Center development west of the river displaced thousands of them. The dispossessed migrated across to Maravilla, just south of the Belvedere Township. This began a mass migration into the area. East Los Angeles spread to include unincorporated territories —Belvedere, Maravilla, and City Terrace—as well as Boyle Heights. Today, East Los Angeles often refers to any Mexican barrio in or around the Civic Center.

This book is a chronicle about the Mexican experience in East Los Angeles. It does not include the history of Jews, Japanese, Armenians, or Blacks who lived and struggled in the communities east of the Los Angeles River. The reason for the omission is that the chronicle's focus is limited to a period, from 1945 to 1975, when Mexicans were the area's overwhelmingly dominant ethnic group. This chronicle also excludes other important Mexican American communities, such as Lincoln Heights, which border Boyle Heights and have historically shared public services and territory. For instance, while Hazard Park is in Lincoln Heights, it is used by residents of Boyle Heights and is strongly identified with both communities.

The narrowness of the chronicle was dictated primarily by that of its research sources. Essentially, this book synthesizes the articles in two weekly newspapers, the *Eastside Sun* and the *Belvedere Citizen*, from 1945 to 1975. Its purpose is to narrate the pattern of concerns of East Los Angeles residents as reflected by their news sources. In addition to the two weeklies, also used were the Edward R. Roybal Collection at the Special Collections Library at the University of California at Los Angeles, and the Roybal News Clipping Files. Admittedly, while these sources generated considerable data, they do not represent a total picture. The feeling of everyday life is excluded and could have been included only through an extensive and expensive oral history project that was beyond the resources of this researcher. Moreover, the newspapers often put much more emphasis on gangs and violence than on the tribulations and accomplishments of people who sought to survive in a community that was under siege. For example, child care was an issue that was only scantily reported. Unfortunately, newspapers reflect the interests of advertisers, who are often more concerned with addressing and controlling the symptoms rather than the causes of poverty. It is hoped that future works will fill the gaps left by this chronicle, and a more balanced and comprehensive picture of East Los Angeles will emerge.

The pattern of events in the *Sun* and the *Citizen* dictated the title, *Community Under Siege: A Chronicle of Chicanos East of the Los Angeles River, 1945–1975.* It is the story of a community's effort to preserve territorial integrity, to defend the residential character of their community against efforts to convert the land to a higher utility use. The two weekly newspapers printed conflicting versions of this struggle: the *Citizen* painted these encroachments as progressive, while the *Sun* portrayed them as an invasion by bulldozers.

Although *Community Under Siege* focuses on the territory east of the Los Angeles River, control of its future has always resided in downtown Los Angeles. Throughout its growth and successive changes in principal production—from agriculture to commerce to industry—Los Angeles has become one of the nation's commercial and industrial centers. Its power elites have worked at the city's core to accumulate capital within the city and the county. It has been in downtown Los Angeles that they have concentrated and coordinated their wealth and their power. Throughout expansion, the downtown ruling class controlled state, city, and county politics. They manipulated elected and appointed officials to determine land use in Los Angeles.

Population density, the proximity to the Civic Center and the widening division of labor changed the utility of Eastside land. At one time, it was convenient to the downtown interests to maintain East Los Angeles as a large reserve labor pool. But as production changed, so did the utility of the land. Increasingly, use was measured in terms of exchange value. Elites—the *Los Angeles Times* and the Chamber of Commerce among them—pressured city and county authorities to make the land in and around the Civic Center more productive. Consequently, in the 1950s, Los Angeles entered a period of super-development, expropriating and using land more intensively, extracting higher taxes, turning higher profits. The Eastside was on the periphery of this development; it seemed only a matter of time before it, too, would fall prey to the bulldozers.

Banking, insurance, realty, and oil companies, as well as other commercial and industrial interests, continue to control the downtown core. A *Los Angeles Times* article, dated 25 April 1982, showed that, despite a national recession, downtown L.A. is booming. Land values have risen from $8.00 a square foot in 1969 to over $200 a square foot in 1982. For tax purposes, the downtown property is estimated at $3.1 billion. Real value, however, is probably much greater. The *Times* also pointed to a high degree of monopolization: 75 of the 7,975 parcels of land accounted for more than one-third of the tax evaluation. Downtown investors are in turn very active in city and county politics, dominating local government planning and land commissions that determine how land will be used.

Hopefully, later studies will more intensively study the link between the downtown capitalists and East Los Angeles, as well as other Chicano communities in urban centers throughout the Southwest. *Community Under Siege*'s principal purpose is to encourage scholars to study East Los Angeles, particularly land use in the area. Today, this territory, like others throughout the Southwest, is in danger of extinction.

Support from many sources facilitated the preparation of this chronicle. Appreciated is the Chicano community, whose sacrifices have made this work possible. Perhaps the groundwork laid in *Community Under Siege* will help it to withstand the assault. Acknowledged is a grant from the Ford Foundation that made possible the financial support of three students during the summer of 1976 and the purchase of a microfilm camera. Special thanks go to Evelyn Escatiola, an able assistant throughout the microfilming of the *Sun*. The assistance of the late Joseph Eli Kovner, publisher of the *Sun*, was invaluable, as was that of the East Los Angeles County Library. Also important was the help of Congressman Edward R. Roybal, his staff, and my colleague, Jorge García, who made the filming of Roybal's press clippings possible. My gratitude to Howard Shorr, an expert on the history of Boyle Heights, whose careful reading and extensive criticisms significantly contributed to the completion of this chronicle. Also important is Guadalupe Compeán, upon whom I relied heavily in straightening out many of my ideas on urban planning. Thanks to Dianne Vozoff, who edited this work and displayed unusual dedication, to Noël Diaz for his cartographic research, and to Dr. Oscar R. Marti for his technical and editorial supervision of the project. Always supportive was the Chicano community at California State University, Northridge, to whom I am again indebted. Thanks to Ricardo Romo, Mauricio Mazón, Luis Arroyo, Ray Rocco, Victor Vallejo, Ricardo Chabrán, and Carlos Vélez for reading my rough manuscript. Lastly, as always, I am indebted to my father, Francisco Acuña, and to my sons, Walter and Frank.

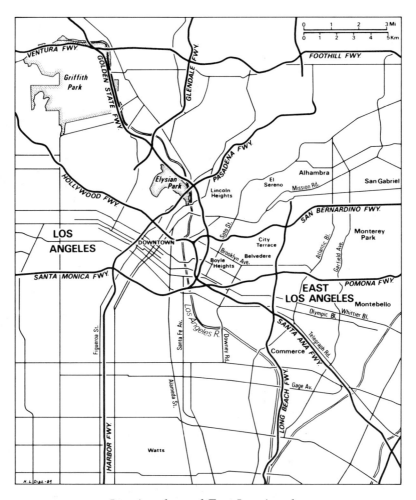

Los Angeles and East Los Angeles

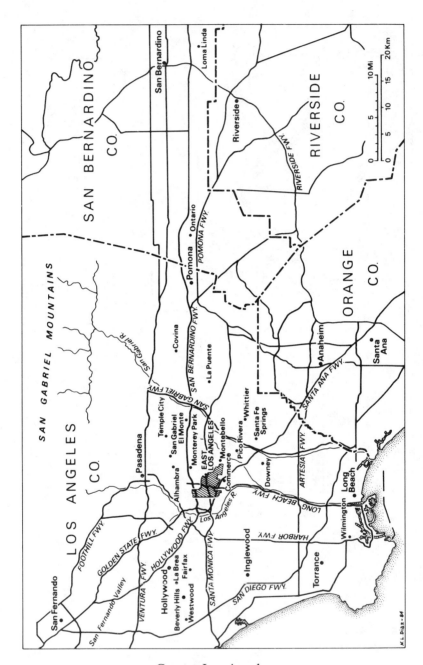

Greater Los Angeles

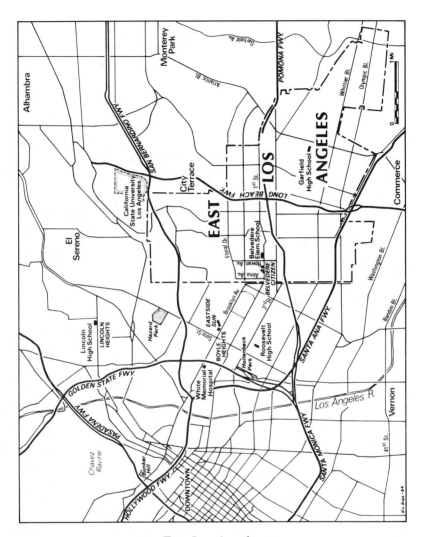

East Los Angeles

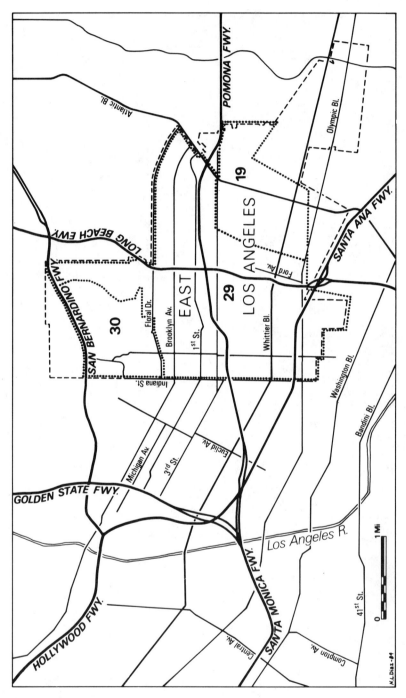

East Los Angeles Congressional Districts

PART I

The Chronicle

1

Early Siege and Escape to the East: An Introduction

Although numerous sources were consulted for this chapter, the following were especially helpful: Robert Gottlieb and Irene Wolt's *Thinking Big. The Story of the* Los Angeles Times, *Its Publishers and Their Influence in Southern California* (New York: 1977); Hubert Howe Bancroft, *History of California*, volumes 1–3 (San Francisco: 1884, 1885); Albert Camarillo, *Chicanos in a Changing Society* (Cambridge: 1979); Robert M. Fogelson, *The Fragmented Metropolis: Los Angeles 1850 to 1930* (Cambridge: 1967); Richard Griswold del Castillo, *The Los Angeles Barrio 1850–1890* (Berkeley: 1979); and Ricardo Romo, *The East Los Angeles Barrio* (Austin: 1983). Central to the study were articles in the *Eastside Sun* and *Belvedere Citizen*. Microfilm copies of these newspapers are deposited in the East Los Angeles County Public Library. The *Sun* holdings, known as the Joseph Eli Kovner Collection, deal exclusively with Chicano articles in that newspaper.

The first siege of Los Angeles began on September 4, 1781, when el Pueblo de Nuestra Señora le Reina de Los Angeles del Río de Porciúncula (the town of Our Lady Queen of the Angels of the River Porciuncula) was established as a colonial Spanish outpost. An estimated 5,000 California Indians lived in the Los Angeles basin when 44 Spanish subjects of mixed bloods—Indian, Black, and Spanish—established a farming community that authorities hoped would lessen colonial Spanish dependence on Mexico's interior and help consolidate Spanish control of California.

Los Angeles expanded slowly. By 1786, only eight of the 11 original male heads of family remained. Four years later, however, the Spanish colony increased to 139, producing more grain than any of the missions, except for one in nearby San Gabriel. Native Californian Indians were hired as laborers and exploited as a class.

By the turn of the century, the Los Angeles population reached 315. The Spanish crown had granted land to private individuals for ranching, and some 11,500 horses and cattle roamed present-day Los Angeles. During the next 30 years, Los Angeles' population increased to just under 1,000. Control of the Los Angeles River was critical. In 1810, a dispute over water rights developed between the pueblo and the San Fernando mission friars when the latter dammed the river and cut off water the pueblo needed for survival. After a legal battle, the pueblo's right to river waters was confirmed.

Los Angeles' economy changed slowly. At the turn of the century, the sea otter and the China trade brought foreign ships to California's shore. The Spanish Empire prohibited trade along the coast, which frustrated early exchanges between Spanish subjects and foreign traders. Contraband, however, flourished. Needless to say, little industry was developed or encouraged during this period.

Encouraged by Mexico's independence, whalers and hide traders arrived more frequently during the 1820s. Growth of the factory system in New England, especially the shoe industry in Massachusetts, created a demand for hides and tallow. This led to the formation of a dominant class of rancheros.

The Mexican government secularized the missions in 1834, putting California's most fertile land into private hands and freeing nearly 15,000 mission Indians to be exploited as laborers. Many authorities believed that secularization would attract settlers from Mexico's interior. However, the migration never materialized. Instead, a small number of ranchers further monopolized the land.

Los Angeles officially became a city in the mid-1830s. By 1836, 2,205 Mexicans lived in Los Angeles. The Mexican population was not confined to the plaza area and spread in all directions. Some moved across the river to what was called Paredón Blanco. The land east of the bluffs was used as public pasture land. José Rubio cultivated his vineyards on the east side of the river and later Francisco López planted his orchards above them. A small Mexican settlement dominated the area until the 1880s.

Definite class divisions developed between the Californios and the newly arrived Mexican colonists who did the manual labor and were perjoratively called *cholos*. This gap between the two classes increased as California further incorporated into the U.S.'s market economy. By the mid-1840s, many ranchers and merchants, who comprised no more than three percent of California's population, looked more to the Atlantic Coast than to Mexico City as the key to their progress.

By the time that U.S. imperialist expansion incorporated California, Mexicans were firmly rooted in Los Angeles. The war brought about changes, and California officially became part of the United States in 1848. James Marshall's chance finding of gold on the American River* in northern California that year caused an invasion of 100,000 Anglo-Americans, which produced a dramatic transformation in California and Los Angeles. For instance, the local Catholic church underwent a restructuring. Prior to the Anglo-American conquest, the priests and prelates had been Spaniards or Mexicans. After the conquest, Mexican priests were replaced with Spanish, French, and Italian clergy to cater to the elites. In 1873, Bishop Taddeus Amat told his congregation that the Church was "the main support of society and order, which imperatively demands respect for legitimate authority and adjuration to legitimate laws." By 1876, the newer St. Viviana's Cathedral served Anglo-Americans, while the placita** was attended by poor Mexicans.

---

*Francisco López had discovered gold just north of the San Fernando Mission in 1842.

**A nickname for the church in front of the plaza.

Land use patterns also changed. During the Mexican period, the rancheros had been exempt from taxes and had an abundance of involuntary labor. Under the Anglo-American system, rancheros were forced to compete on a market economy that favored capital over land interests. As a consequence, the rancheros' holdings shifted to Anglo-American ownership. This process was accelerated by ruthless land laws and by the collapse of the cattle market during the 1850s and 1860s. Finally, production in Los Angeles shifted form cattle to agriculture.

Anglo-Americans dominated the city council. The city inherited nearly 10,000 acres in *ejidos* and *propios* (common and municipal lands) which, under Mexican law, were not to be sold. Under the Americans, this public land did not have a high exchange value and was considered unproductive because its utility was limited. The city council, using the excuse that public lands did not generate tax revenues, sold the common and municipal lands. The development of this and other land within the city was unregulated throughout the 19th century.

After 1848, Mexicans lived in the area just south of First Street. However, as the poor increased in number, they spread to the plaza area. By the 1860s, this area was a slum, occupied mainly by Mexicans and Chinese. Saloons and brothels cluttered Sonora Town, as this section was pejoratively called by Anglo-Americans. Mexicans comprised about three-quarters of the city's population, but a dramatic transformation was underway.

Changes also took place east of the river. In 1868, George Hansen and William Moore surveyed Paredón Blanco, which became Boyle Heights in the 1870s. It was renamed after Andrew Boyle, the first Anglo-American to reside on the Eastside. Boyle bought land between the river and the mesa bluff for $3,000 an acre. He purchased the higher, unirrigated land on the mesa for 25¢ an acre. The arrival of the Southern Pacific in the mid–1870s and the Santa Fe Railroad in the 1880s made Boyle Heights more attractive. In 1876, 35 acres were subdivided. By the 1880s, the area was a suburb of Los Angeles, with 300 to 400 businessmen and their families living there. Few Mexicans now resided in the Heights, an exclusive community. The Evergreen Cemetery was reserved for its ruling elite. The Occidental Presbyterian University was also housed in Boyle Heights until the mid-1910s.

Meanwhile, Mexicans became a minority in Los Angeles by the 1870s. They reacted to defend their status. For example, between 1850 and 1870, no fewer than ten Spanish language newspapers were published. Although they mainly addressed themselves to the more affluent Californios, they did express concerns about the usurpation of their culture, their loss of political power, and their increased inequality. Mexicans also formed *mutualistas*, mutual aid societies, that offered loans and medical and life insurance to their members. Repatriation societies were organized in the 1850s. Mexicans reacted to the increased violence toward them. Social bandits such as Juan Flores revolted and racial tension often escalated into conflict. A definite ethnic consciousness developed.

As the white population increased, so did the pattern of Mexican segregation. Inferior roads and public and medical facilities blighted the Mexican barrios. City authorities were unsympathetic and blamed the 1877 smallpox epidemic on the Mexicans' unsanitary habits rather than on an unsanitary water supply and lack of sewerage. By 1874, municipal ordinance confined brothels to the Mexican section. This law was not changed until 1909. Class divisions increasingly developed along racial and ethnic lines, with Mexicans remaining socially, politically, and, most of all, economically unassimilated.

In 1880, Los Angeles' population reached 11,183; five years later, it was nearly 20,000. Farm acreage increased a hundredfold. Potable water, a gas works, a telegraph system, railroad connections, sewerage, paved public roads, and an electric car line were all part of Los Angeles city—that is, of the Anglo-American sections. As the city modernized, the Mexican community dwindled. New commercial enterprises and a few factories crowded what little residential space was available to Mexican residents. According to historian Robert M. Fogelson, "unsuccessful Americans, unassimilated Chinese, and unadjusted Mexicans still lived in rented rooms in dilapidated and overcrowded adobes and shacks amid rundown hotels, gambling dens, and houses of prostitution near the old Plaza."

The few Mexicans east of the river were skilled craftsmen or merchants, employed in service occupations such as saddle making, butchery, and gardening. In the 1880s, only 12 percent of the

Mexican population lived outside the barrio. Consequently, three decades after the Anglo-American conquest, Mexicans were effectively segregated and unequal.

During the late 19th century, the flood of white Americans arriving from the eastern states further overwhelmed the Mexican population. Real estate boomed and the construction of homes, railways, roads, and other public works attracted non-skilled Mexican workers to Los Angeles. Small colonies also grouped near the railway maintenance yards, the brickyards, and the agricultural areas.

After the turn of the century, the Mexican population moved north of Third Street, near Aliso Street, and then slowly into what is now known as the Belvedere area of East Los Angeles. While Main Street remained the most popular corridor for Mexicans, a shift was underway. New stores, residences, movie houses, and small businesses displaced hundreds of Mexican families from the Plaza's northwestern section. At the same time, population growth elsewhere encouraged construction of financial institutions and stores. In the process, city and county bureaucracies expanded—and bulldozers razed the downtown section to make room for new buildings to house the bureaucrats.

Downtown interests, including the *Los Angeles Times*, promoted commercial and industrial expansion. Water had ensured population growth, which in turn meant commerce. Under Harrison Gray Otis, who had acquired the *Times* in the 1880s, and his son-in-law, Harry Chandler, the newspaper became a major downtown power and was at the forefront of development of downtown space. They were heavily involved in real estate speculation.

Between 1900 and 1920, the Mexican population expanded in Belvedere, where the Teatro Maravilla on Mednik Street became the community's entertainment center. Mexican restaurants, grocery stores, barber shops, and small businesses still operated in the Plaza area. But a commercial center on First Street, north of Indiana Street, challenged Plaza merchants. The escape to the east was logical, since the land had little utility for developers. It lay at the end of the Yellow Street Car Line,* in an area devoted to cemeteries.

---

*The two main electric street car lines serving Los Angeles were the Red and the Yellow systems.

Aside from downtown development, the Mexicans' eastern movement was accelerated by an internal population growth. The Southwest's rapid modernization promoted heavy migration of Mexican workers to the region. In Los Angeles, the demand for cheap labor encouraged Mexicans to move to the area.

Generally, Mexicans did the pick-and-shovel work and did not have ready access to American institutions. Largely ignored by organized labor, they formed their own organizations and collectively struggled to improve work conditions. In 1903, they struck the Pacific Electric railway, forming the Unión Federal Mexicana. Moreover, increased opposition to Mexican dictator Porfirio Díaz brought large numbers of exiles into the city and county. By 1906, the Partido Liberal Mexicano (PLM), the major opposition group, made Los Angeles its headquarters. The Plaza served anarchists, socialists, and nationalists as a forum to call attention to worsening conditions in Mexico and to the inequality of Mexicans locally.

During the 1910s, large numbers of Mexicans arrived in Los Angeles, escaping the bitter fighting and violence of the Mexican Revolution. Their arrival aggravated congested housing conditions. Their choice of residence was mostly restricted to existing barrios. The Plaza district remained the most popular port of entry. Job discrimination forced many Mexicans to work for below-subsistence wages. Mexicans generally remained isolated from the mainstream labor movement and continued to rely on their own resources. They formed organizations such as Jornaleros Unidos (United Laborers) in 1910 to 1911 and sporadically struck local employers. Meanwhile, World War I increased discrimination towards Mexicans, who were accused of being pro-German. Living conditions were stark throughout the decade. In 1914, although Mexicans comprised five percent of Los Angeles, 11.1 percent of the deaths were Mexican. A 1919 survey showed that they lived in deplorable housing, with almost four out of every five families living in quarters without baths. Infant mortality was three times higher than among whites.

By the 1920s, Chandler had amassed a fortune of between $200 million and $500 million. His prosperity and Los Angeles' growth were tied to developments such as the construction of the new harbor and the opening of the Panama Canal. During the first 30 years of the 20th century, Los Angeles' population increased from 102,000 to 1,200,000. Officially, fewer than 100,000 Mexicans lived in Los Angeles in 1930. In reality, however, the figure was probably closer to 200,000. The Chandler growth strategy was an important cause in the Mexican eastward movement.

As the Civic Center area developed, soaring property values and skyrocketing rents forced more Mexicans to leave the Plaza area. Slum conditions threatened to depress the holdings of the downtown powers. De facto segregation of Mexicans was the rule. Still, between 1910 and 1930, poor Italians, Slavs, Japanese, and Anglo-Americans competed with Mexicans for "Sonora Town" housing. In 1924 and 1925, some 140,000 rats invaded the area, causing an outbreak of bubonic plague that claimed five lives. In addition to housing congestion, traffic jams were now more frequent in downtown Los Angeles, reflecting the city's increased centralization.

Also by this decade, the high cost of living and rents in the Civic Center accelerated exodus to the east and, by 1929, slightly over 30,000 Mexican Americans lived in the Belvedere area. Belvedere Gardens, situated on East First Street, had been a 1,000-acre Eastside dairy and vegetable farm. By the mid-1920s, the Janss Investment Corporation, founded in 1901 by Dr. Peter Janss, had subdivided over 100,000 acres, including Westwood, where the University of California at Los Angeles was built. Belvedere Gardens was the company's first subdivision. The strategy was to sell lots for low down payments, creating syndicates to establish townships, banks, commercial centers, and an infrastructure of public utilities. The Janss Corporation was interlocked with the downtown ruling elite.

Meanwhile, rapid urbanization created still other barrios. As manufacturers moved to the suburbs in search of cheap land, Mexican labor followed. A common practice among Mexicans was to rent a plot of land and erect shacks. These shanty towns could be found in the outskirts of Whittier, Montebello, and El Monte.

El Hoyo Maravilla, located east of Rowan and south of Brooklyn Avenue, was situated in an arroyo. A flash flood in the 1920s swept houses off their foundations and drowned a number of residents. Later, a miniature middle class, comprised of small merchants and professionals, developed among Mexicans there. The area also grew organizationally. Mutual aid societies were popular. The Confederación de Sociedades Mexicanas, established in 1926, united the numerous *mutualistas*. In that same year, the Liga Cultural Mexicana established a library in Belvedere.

Relations between Mexicans and police deteriorated during this period. The case of Aurelio Pompa became a symbol of the injustice of the legal system. Pompa, an immigrant from Caborca, Sonora, was convicted of murdering a racist foreman who had physically and mentally harassed him. Mexicans claimed that Pompa shot the Anglo-American in self-defense. They formed a defense committee to have his life spared. In spite of an intensive campaign that included a 12,915-signature petition to the governor of California and a request for clemency by Mexican President Alvaro Obregón, Pompa was executed. The Mexican community in Los Angeles led a large demonstration, protesting what they considered the racism and inequality of the system.

A leadership struggle developed. Mexican businessmen east of the river forming organizations such as the Mexican Chamber of Commerce to challenge the Plaza merchants' popularity. The Comité de Beneficencia Mexicana was founded in 1931 by José Solorzano, an employee of the Southern Pacific. The Comité de Beneficencia performed important charitable work during the Depression years, establishing, among other projects, a free medical clinic.

Some leaders attempted to incorporate East Los Angeles. Vernon incorporated in 1905, Alhambra in 1915, Monterey Park in 1916, and Montebello in 1920. A 1925 incorporation effort in East Los Angeles failed when leaders withdrew the petition. In 1931, East Los Angeles again attempted to incorporate but county supervisors squelched the move. Two years later, voters turned down the incorporation by a 8,439-to-462 margin. Business interests had actively opposed the drive.

Events in Mexico continued to influence the community in Los Angeles and throughout the United States. The *cristero** movement was active in Los Angeles. In 1928, the Hijas de María sponsored a religious procession. Six years later, over 40,000 people turned out for a procession to honor *Cristo Rey* (Christ the King).

In the 1930s, the downtown Union Railroad Station was finally constructed, displacing more Mexicans and Chinese. Dur-

---

*A Catholic movement in Mexico, with followers in the United States, protesting the Mexican government's so-called persecution of Catholics.

ing the repatriation drive of that decade, local police and immigration authorities conducted dragnets throughout the community. The Comité de Beneficencia Mexicana assisted the repatriation of victims. Meanwhile, a festival was held in Mexico City to aid the Los Angeles *colonia*'s underprivileged Mexican children.

Capital and power continued to centralize in the hands of the downtown elite. These forces were divided, however, as to where the new Civic Center would be located. The *Times* wanted the center near its buildings on First and Broadway, while others favored the Southside, to which direction much of the downtown development had switched. In the end, the *Times* triumphed, largely because of its influence over the county supervisors. Meanwhile, the company purchased the property at First and Spring and offered to sell the Broadway property to the county. While the *Times* lobbied local officials, its old property, including the Chandler publications' obsolete equipment, was appraised at $1.8 million. Naturally, the *Times*' heavy-handed manipulation touched off a fury, especially when it was learned that another appraiser estimated the *Times* property at only $600,000. The *Times* barred no holds and used confidential police files to smear its adversaries. After a prolonged struggle, the Chandlers received $1.6 million and the right to salvage their old equipment. Eventually, Chandler's $54 million Civic Center development program was completed. It included the "improvement" of Olvera Street, which used convict labor, and later the completion of Chinatown just north of Olvera.

In the 1930s, a consortium of corporations, including General Motors, Standard Oil of California, Firestone Tire and Rubber, Phillips Petroleum, and others, purchased city transit systems throughout the country and then destroyed them. In 1938, encouraged by the Automobile Club of Southern California and the *Los Angeles Times*, the consortium entered Los Angeles and destroyed the rapid transit system. Simultaneously, the ruling elite promoted its freeway philosophy, which had grave consequences on land use east of the Los Angeles river. Freeways ultimately displaced ten percent of the area's inhabitants.

Meanwhile, the downtown elite consolidated. Its network included the Chamber of Commerce, the All Year Club, the California Club, the Jonathan Club, and, to a lesser extent, the Los Angeles Athletic Club. Informally headquartered in the Jonathan

Club, these forces promoted downtown development. Led by Harry Chandler, Chamber of Commerce president Bryan Hanna, Pacific Mutual Life Insurance executive Asa Call, and lawyer Sam Haskins of Gibson, Dunn, and Crutcher, the downtown elite set the tone throughout the 1930s. They controlled local governments, and, more importantly, they controlled the chief of police and the county sheriff. Their policies also determined land use adjacent to the downtown core, which significantly affected newfound Mexican American communities east of the Los Angeles River.

The California Planning Act of 1929 required counties to create planning commissions and design regional master plans. Los Angeles City and County led most of the state in implementing master plans. Through the Regional Planning Commission and other committees, the supervisors controlled the county's unincorporated areas. Meanwhile, the Los Angeles mayor, with city council approval, appointed members to the City Planning Commission. These appointments centralized planning at the city and county levels. Business, corporate, and banking leaders dominated the commissions. Ordinary citizens were virtually excluded.

The influence of merchants on Brooklyn Avenue and First Street increased during the 1930s. For the most part, Boyle Heights merchants had catered to a Jewish clientele. But during the 1930s, Mexicans moved into the Heights in larger numbers, living among the polyglot comprising the area. The Whittier Street area was just beginning to develop. Mexican Americans were a minority in the merchants' associations east of the river. They owned primarily small businesses such as mortuaries, butcher shops, barber shops, beauty parlors, and mom-and-pop stores.

In 1941, the Mexican American population in California reached 354,432. In Los Angeles City, Mexicans officially approached 100,000. Boyle Heights was a port of entry for Mexican Americans, as it had been for the Jews, Armenians, and Japanese before them. Even City Terrace, once the area's Beverly Hills, felt the Mexicans' presence. Mexican Americans and white senior citizens also lived in Bunker Hill and Chávez Ravine.

The public and private sectors increasingly built facilities east of the river. Sears, Roebuck & Co. owned a large complex in Boyle Heights, as did the *Los Angeles Times*, which also had warehouses there. Los Angeles county located its general hospital on the periphery of Boyle Heights, and Los Angeles city built public housing units in Aliso Village, Pico Gardens, and the Estrada Courts. The county eventually completed the Maravilla Housing Projects in the eastern part of the Belvedere township. The Federal Housing Act of 1937 had encouraged public housing, with the federal government granting state governments sizeable subsidies. Moreover, federal legislation gave municipalities the power to condemn private property for public use. State authorities began construction on the San Bernardino Freeway in 1943 and the Santa Ana in 1947. These served as arteries for the Southland's first freeway, the Pasadena, which had been completed in 1940.

In the mid-1940s, the Jewish exodus from Boyle Heights to the Fairfax area accelerated. Blacks moved into public housing in the flats and the once large Japanese population was now small, having been removed during World War II. The Wynerwood Apartments, built in 1939, were for middle-income renters and generally refused minorities.

The *Los Angeles Times* changed its coverage of Mexican Americans during the war years, shifting "from 'fiesta' and 'old California culture' stories, glorifying a mythical past, to negative accounts of the 'zoot suit' symbol." The communities east of the Los Angeles River were the target of racist reports that made East Los Angeles the symbol of the *pachuco*, the Mexican American gang member. Newspaper accounts exaggerated the extent of gang activity, since less than three percent of the 30,000 school-age Mexican Americans in Los Angeles belonged to gangs. Drug abuse was not a problem in 1943; only 12 Mexican Americans were arrested on drug charges. Nevertheless, the local newspapers stereotyped Mexican American youths as gang members and law breakers.

The daily newspapers did not report Mexican American participation in the war effort or the inordinate number of Mexican American draftees or volunteers. Instead, the press dwelled on stereotyping Mexican youth. The excesses of the Los Angeles press have been well documented elsewhere, especially its extent in coverage of the Sleepy Lagoon case (1942) and the Pachuco Riots (1943).

By the end of World War II, the segregation pattern for Mexicans and other minorities in Los Angeles was rutted. The postwar years saw a population boom and structural changes in the

residential pattern of their community. Population density intensified demand for land around the Civic Center, with the property east of the river becoming even more attractive to developers.
Freeway construction, meanwhile, was displacing thousands of
Mexican Americans. To this end, the downtown capitalists
formed the Greater Los Angeles Plan, Inc. (GLAP) and led efforts
to redevelop Bunker Hill and other older sections of Los Angeles.

During the post-war years, fewer Russian Jews remained in
Boyle Heights and City Terrace, and most white residents migrated to midtown and West Los Angeles. By 1950, the Heights
was no longer the integrated community that it had been in the
past. And it began to rival Belvedere-Maravilla as the community
with the heaviest concentration of Mexicans.

THE CHRONICLE BEGINS: 1930–1945

The *Belvedere Citizen* and, to a lesser extent, the *Civic Center
Sun* (later the *Eastside Sun*) offer some insight into the lack of
political, social, and economic visibility of Mexicans from 1930
to 1945. While a sizeable Mexican population lived east of the
river, these newspapers printed little of any substance concerning this community. The *Citizen* circulated mainly in the
Belvedere-Maravilla area, which had the county's largest Mexican concentration. When it published stories about this minority, the *Citizen* usually portrayed them as the butt of a joke or
as drunk and disorderly. For instance, on 3 August 1934, the
Citizen reported: "Story In Nude Not Confirmed, But Good
Yarn." Police had found an intoxicated Black man and a Mexican woman nude and asleep in each other's arms. On 29 October
1934, the *Citizen* published another story and bannered: "Crazy
Mexican Shoots Three, Killing Girl."

During 1934 and 1935, the *Citizen* reported that the Mexican
Chamber of Commerce, the Spanish American Aviation Club, the
Independent Club of Southern California, and the Silver Star Club
had some 250 members. Alisha A. Holguín led the Independent
and the Silver Star Clubs. He appeared to be a political broker,
with his former club making political endorsements. In June 1935,
the *Citizen* reported that 30,000 members of Roman Catholic societies marched in the Los Angeles Corpus Christi procession in
opposition to the Mexican government's anticlerical politics. A

year later, the *Citizen* wrote that the Belvedere Coordinating Council of agencies and business associations had a Spanish division.

Although these few positive accounts appeared, most articles portrayed Mexicans as a problem. The *Citizen* catered to Belvedere merchants and their interests. Judging from *Citizen* coverage, juvenile delinquency was a major concern. It did, understandably, impact strongly on merchants. In December 1936, the *Citizen* commented that the Mexican Chamber of Commerce was working with Mexican juveniles, adding that "the preponderance of juveniles are of that nationality."

Very little attention was paid to Mexican American political involvement during the second half of the 1930s. Mexican American businessmen and professionals participated in the Belvedere Coordinating Council and the Mexican Chamber of Commerce. Generally, Anglo-Americans occupied leadership posts in these organizations as well as in school and church groups.

Beginning with issues from 1937, a few copies of the *Civic Center Sun* are available. The *Sun* had catered to the Jewish merchants in the downtown and Boyle Heights areas and rarely covered Mexican Americans. However, the transformation of Boyle Heights was underway, with Jews and white Americans abandoning the area to Mexicans. In the process, the community deteriorated. In August 1937, Leo M. Kovner, brother of Joseph, the *Sun*'s publisher, chastised the city of Los Angeles for not cleaning the Temple Street district (west of the river) as thoroughly as it had in the past. Kovner charged that services were not provided equally to all sections of the city.

In 1939, the *Citizen* reported property owner opposition to a housing project in Belvedere. W.A. Pixley, spokesman for the East Los Angeles Property Owners' Protective League, said that the group objected to the low-rent units because they would be tax exempt. Public housing supporters countered that the real reason behind opposition was that property owners did not want to have poor Mexicans living next to them. The Protective League denied this charge. The property owners met on March 30 in an attempt to obtain an injunction against low-cost public housing construction on the 67 acres east of Mednick Avenue. Slum clearance had become popular because federal grants created construction jobs.

The *Citizen* rarely tackled police brutality cases. An exception was in August 1939, when it reported: "Sanchez Boy Dies from Bullet Wound." The article stated that a bullet fired by a motorcycle police officer shot at the sidewalk ricocheted off the pavement and killed Gustino Sánchez. Eduardo Quevedo, a spokesman for the National Congress of Spanish Speaking People, vehemently condemned the incident.

In 1938, the *Sun* reported: "Zoning Quietly Altered." The Bunker Hill Owners and Improvement Association had changed the zoning there from R-1 to R-4. This suggests that the owners knew that developers would be buying their land, since an R-4 zoning permitted multiple dwellings and drove up land values. Bunker Hill's deterioration was mentioned by the *Sun*, which called for the construction of public housing there. In March 1940, the Ramona Gardens Housing Project broke ground. On 4 April 1940, Joseph Eli Kovner noted this transformation and scolded the Brooklyn Avenue merchants for allowing a once thriving community to deteriorate. The publisher chastised them for not maintaining their stores and accused the merchants of having their hearts in Fairfax, La Brea, West Adams, and Hollywood.

Interestingly, a series of articles on "The Background of the History of California" by Deputy Sheriff Ed Durán Ayres appeared in the *Sun* in 1940. The articles are noteworthy because they contradict the deputy sheriff's report in 1942 to the Los Angeles grand jury in which he attributed the Mexicans' violent behavior to their Aztec heritage. In the *Sun* articles, Durán Ayres called the Aztec Eagle 100 percent American and lauded the virtues of Mexican culture.*

By the 1940s, the *Citizen* reported increased Mexican American involvement in Democratic party politics. Rito Madrid, Salomón Durán, Mary Louis Arroyo, and Celia Luna led the Young Democrats (YDs). The YDs opposed the Federal Housing Project because it did not pay a fair price to the homeowners whose houses were condemned by authorities.

In November 1940, Local Board 203, a predominantly Mexican American induction board, was ready to draft residents.

---

*These articles lend support to the theory that it was really the sheriff's department, not Durán Ayres, who wrote the report to the grand jury.

Through 1941, the *Citizen* weekly reported the induction of Mexican Americans. In January 1941, 43 males were drafted from Belvedere and the surrounding areas, 34 of whom were Mexican Americans.

During 1941, the Aliso Village Housing Project broke ground. Meanwhile, the Maravilla project, which included 500 units, was built at a cost of $2 million. Even at this time, the Maravilla Housing Project was referred to as the "Mexican Project."

Most of the *Citizen's* 1942 files are missing. Consequently, its coverage of the Sleepy Lagoon case is not available. The 1943 coverage is scant and limited to reports on servicemen. The *Citizen* did not fully report on the Zoot Suit Riots, either. It made only superficial editorial comment, condemning both sides. On one hand, the *Citizen* stated that there was no room for hoodlums or vigilantes; on the other, it reported that the police had lost control. It condemned the beating of Roy Hernández, an upstanding youth who, according to the editor, was attacked solely because he was Mexican. Hernández had suffered a broken nose. The *Citizen* did not mention domestic tension during 1944. It did report on the activities of the Madres del Soldado Hispano Americano (Mothers of the Spanish American Soldier). The names of war casualties and deaths were printed. In October, the newspaper mentioned that the Sleepy Lagoon defendants had been released.

The *Sun* did not begin publishing regularly until December 1945. Meanwhile, the *Citizen* itself changed in its coverage of Mexican Americans. Some substantive articles appeared, such as a March 16 report that Eduardo Quevedo had appeared before a U.S. Senate Hearing on equal employment opportunities for Mexican Americans. The *Citizen* reported in August 1945 that the First Mexican Baptist Church held its 22nd annual convention and that Mrs. Elisa Ríos headed the Mexican Feminine Society of Southern California. It also reported that, during the war, many Mexican American women joined the work force and that a movement for day-care centers developed in East Los Angeles.**

La Casa del Mexicano, a community center, was dedicated in May. The event was sponsored by the Mexican Federation of

---

**Guadalupe Compeán, *Implementation Report: Child-Care in Boyle Heights* (unpublished), City of Los Angeles, Department of City Planning, October 11, 1982.

Belvedere and the Mothers of the Spanish American Soldier. East Los Angeles City College opened and began by operating out of Garfield High School. In the years that followed, this college would profoundly affect the education of returning Mexican American veterans.

The war overseas ground to a halt in September and both newspapers regularly reported news of dead and returning veterans. Belvedere's returning GIs found many problems awaiting them. The area had few paved streets or concrete sidewalks, and the county was literally dumping unwanted facilities there. Before the end of 1945, for example, the county announced that a new juvenile detention home would be built in Belvedere. The news enraged the First Street merchants, who in turn influenced the *Citizen*. The newspaper wrote a scathing denunciation of the proposed facility in the midst of residential housing. Belvedere residents questioned why this facility was not projected for the Westside or elsewhere in the county.

SUMMARY

By the end of the War, the tone of the siege was established. Even before the Mexican American population had settled east of the Los Angeles River, interests in the downtown core determined the eventual fate of that community. Development moved a sizeable portion of the Mexican population from the Plaza area to Boyle Heights and unincorporated East Los Angeles. Mexican Americans lacked the capital and political power to influence important decisions such as zoning and freeway construction. Moreover, by the 1920s, the network of businessmen, bankers, real estate developers, and powers like the *Los Angeles Times* was firmly entrenched. This "tidewater" occupation of power centers gave this group an advantage that pioneer capitalists have always enjoyed. The absence of a committed English-language press left working-class Mexicans vulnerable to the schemes of the downtown ruling class. During this period, the press was either hostile to or ignored the interests of the people east of the river. The *Citizen* clearly demonstrated that its interests were aligned with the merchant class along First Street. The few available issues of the *Sun* did indicate a latent populist tendency. But generally, even this paper ignored the Mexican American community.

2

The Beginning of the Siege East of the River: 1946–1953

This chapter relies mainly on the *Belvedere Citizen* and the *Eastside Sun*. Microfilm copies of these newspapers are on file at the East Los Angeles County Public Library. The articles are listed chronologically in the second part of the book. The year-by-year chronicle in the body of the text is a synthesis of these articles. The same format is followed throughout the book. In addition to these newspaper articles, the Edward R. Roybal Newspaper Scrapbooks were microfilmed by Jorge García, a professor at California State University, Northridge, and myself. Two reels, comprising the Roybal Newspaper Scrapbooks, are in the East Los Angeles County Public Library. Also researched was the Edward R. Roybal Collection, which is at the University of California, Los Angeles, Special Collections Library. This collection is invaluable in understanding the 1950s and the process of urban renewal. It has countless pamphlets, newspaper articles, and letters. Also helpful was Robin Fitzgerald Scott, "The Mexican American In Los Angeles, 1920–1950," Ph.D. dissertation, University of Southern California, 1971. For background on national events in the 50s, see Douglas T. Miller and Marion Nowak, *The Fifties: The Way We Really Were* (New York: 1979); and Eric F. Goldman, *The Crucial Decade and After: America, 1945–1960* (New York: 1960).

The mid-1940s brought high expectations. It was a period of homecoming for the veterans who wanted to forget the hunger of the Depression and the sacrifices of the war. Over 12 million men and women were demobilized. The spending of their savings spurred prosperity and the creation of a consumer society. The runaway economy was brought under partial control by the creation of the Office of Price Administration (OPA), which placed a ceiling on the prices of goods, wages, and, most of all, rents. The return of massive numbers of veterans and the baby boom worsened housing problems, with many citizens calling for the construction of additional public housing to alleviate the poor's plight. The stimulus of GI and Federal Housing Administration (FHA) loans met the needs of the middle income people. Prefabricated housing materials and tract homes stimulated housing construction. Subsidized urban freeways made these housing tracts more accessible and thus more appealing.

The post-war period also increased the division of labor. Population density led to the growth of bureaucracies, big business, and networks that brought structural changes to society. Once begun, this self-generating development made it increasingly difficult for groups with little power or resources to reach—much less influence—government.

Tests and credentials played an important and sophisticated role in justifying class and racial stratification. The "organization" became the by-word—and the "organization" was the corporation. Between 1940 and 1960, self-employment dropped from 26 to 11 percent. At the same time, the number of small businesses that failed or merged with the giants increased. Many white American males became "organization men." Racial minority members remained marginal to this process. Even by the end of 1953, Mexican Americans as a group were economically weak and politically powerless. This was at a time when government increased its assistance to big business in support of the growth philosophy. The consequences of this support would impact with particular force and use in the barrios.

This period in American history has been called the "Fabulous Fifties" and "Happy Days." (Perhaps this has something to do with the increase in television sets—from 7 million in 1946 to 50 million in 1960.) But when the facts are examined, the period from 1946 to 1953 is better characterized as the "Age of Fear." In 1947, President Harry S. Truman launched the Cold War by issuing the Truman Doctrine. The United States assumed a "mobilized posture." That same year, Truman issued Executive Order 9835, which initiated the loyalty oath for federal employees and encouraged witch hunts to root the "reds" out of government. Also this year, Congress passed the Taft-Hartley Act, which eroded many of the gains that labor had made during the 1930s.

In the next year, a communist coup in Czechoslovakia and a Soviet blockade of Berlin increased American xenophobia and chauvinism. Red-baiting, charging that someone was a communist or communist-sympathizer, became common. In 1949, Soviet test explosion of an atomic bomb and Mao Tse-tung's victory in China drove American anti-communism to irrational proportions. When the Korean War began the next year, demagoguery reached a new low. That year, Senator Joseph McCarthy claimed to have a list of 205 "reds" in the U.S. State Department. He used the House Un-American Activities Committee (HUAC) as his private Office of the Holy Inquisition. Protected by congressional immunity, he made vicious and unfounded accusations that his victims could not disprove in court because of the Senator's privilege.

Historian journalist Theodore White has claimed that "decent conservatives" helped destroy McCarthy in 1954. However, others have charged that both liberals and conservatives did not question McCarthy's values as much as his tactics, which were clumsy and ineffective. And polls in the early 1950s show that 58 percent of Americans favored destroying communism at any cost, even if it meant that innocent people would be hurt. To the end, 36 percent of the public supported McCarthy.

The McCarthy era had far-reaching implications and impacted on Chicanos at the local level. Like other citizens, Mexican Americans were subjected to loyalty oaths that questioned their patriotism. Many progressives who were in a position to assist Mexican Americans in their quest for equality were purged out of government and trade unions. Moderates were reluctant to voice humanistic or civil libertarian sentiments for fear of being labeled communists, and Theodore White's "decent conservatives" supported the McCarran Act, which victimized all citizens, especially immigrants. Unfortunately, in the United

States, conservatives have earned a history of being more concerned with their own economic freedom than with national equality or justice.

Shallow slogans such as "I like Ike" did not make the 50s very fabulous for Eastside Chicanos, who were affected by the times. This chapter chronicles the response of returning veterans and their efforts to achieve equality. Many Chicanos were not prepared to return to their pre-war status of second class citizenship, and a growing emergence of ethnic consciousness took place.

Belvedere-Maravilla remained the community with the highest concentration of Chicanos in the county. Even so, by 1950, Boyle Heights was challenging it for this distinction. The period from 1946 to 1953 set the stage for the rest of the decade, and while the *Sun* and the *Citizen* did not note the structural changes taking place in society, they did express local concerns and interests. These can be categorized as land use, civil rights, efforts to enter mainstream politics, merchant concern over juvenile delinquency, and individual and organizational response to McCarthyism.

THE CHRONICLE
1946

The Latin American Civic and Cultural Committee dedicated an 18-foot granite shaft at Brooklyn Avenue and Indiana Street to Mexican American veterans. The *Eastside Sun* had begun publication early in December of the previous year. The *Sun* was still a Brooklyn Avenue advertising sheet and generally ignored Mexican Americans throughout the year. The *Belvedere Citizen* had continuously published for over ten years in Belvedere-Maravilla and was firmly entrenched, politically and economically, in the area.

The juvenile hall site was pending and Belvedere residents opposed its construction. Their motto was "Keep Belvedere for Homes—Not Juvenile Halls." They circulated petitions throughout East Los Angeles. Under community pressure, the supervisors relented, and the county constructed the new juvenile detention facility in a non-residential sector.

On March 8, 1946, the *Citizen* wrote: "Betrayed in High Places." The editorial exposed the plans to up-zone Bella Vista and Montebello Park from residential to industrial use. The editor cautioned that the First Street merchants wanted residential housing to keep pace with industrial development. Factory workers lived outside East Los Angeles and did not spend their wages in the community. The *Citizen* expressed dissatisfaction with the county supervisors, especially their zoning policies.

The army barracks for veteran families were moved into the Maravilla Housing Project in 1946, providing housing for 144 families. By June, 100 homeless veterans and their families moved into these units. The *Citizen* did not report much detail on this veteran housing project.

Civic, business, and professional groups in Belvedere discussed the growing problem of juvenile delinquency. Proposals were made for an East Los Angeles youth center. Most of the coverage was in the *Citizen*, since the *Sun* continued to focus on issues related to the Brooklyn Avenue merchants. Moreover, there was little political coverage in either newspaper regarding Mexican Americans.

In August, the Latin American Civic Action Committee held a meeting at which Carey McWilliams spoke. However, no further detail of this organization appeared. The Fiestas Patrias were held during Cinco de Mayo and on September 16, and, as usual, the local newspapers reported the events.

The *Citizen* also reported the case of Eugene Montenegro, 13, who was shot and killed by a sheriff's deputy. Deputy H.H. Hodges allegedly saw Montenegro coming out of a window with a knife in his hand. The deputy allegedly ordered the youth to drop the knife. When he ran from the officer, Montenegro was shot and killed. Parents and friends protested the Los Angeles grand jury's decision, which found the killing to be a justifiable homicide.

1947

The *Citizen* reported on events at the Maravilla Housing Project, while the *Sun* covered the Aliso Village and Ramona Gardens Projects. Rent prices were a major issue and evictions of tenants earning over $3,000 a year were threatened. The federal guidelines tied eligibility to the renter's salary. This would have disqualified many of the project's residents. Los Angeles suffered a housing shortage and this requirement would have impacted on a substantial number of families. The *Belvedere Citizen* reported: "Maravilla Project Residents Council Seeks Supervisors Aid As Eviction Date Nears." The *Sun* echoed: "Aliso Village Council Declares 'No Forced Transfers.' "

On August 22, the *Sun* announced a fiesta sponsored by the Mexican American Civil Rights Organization. Margo Albert, prominent Mexican American screen star and wife of actor Eddie Albert, chaired the program. Proceeds went to combat discrimination and police brutality.

The First Street merchants, concerned about vandalism and theft, pressured the sheriff's department to do something about the menace. The sheriff's department announced a "war" on juvenile delinquency, stepping up its night patrols and strengthening enforcement of the county's anti-loitering ordinances.

In January, the *Citizen* announced: "Edward R. Roybal Seeks Councilman's Post in the 9th District." Although this campaign was heated and led to the founding of the Community Service Organization (CSO), neither weekly adequately covered Roybal's ultimately unsuccessful bid for the city council.

An interesting link existed between white liberals and Mexican American political activists in Boyle Heights. This was a period when Jews and whites fled the Heights and Mexican population increased. The Jewish community had many people who were concerned with human rights and saw the lack of access by Mexicans to protective institutions as undemocratic. Many white liberals joined the Progressive Citizens of America (PCA) and later signed up with the Independent Progressive Party (IPP), which supported Henry Wallace's candidacy for president. The PCA sponsored a legal clinic and actively supported civil rights causes in East Los Angeles. Judging from the *Sun's* coverage, the PCA's activity centered in Boyle Heights-Hollenbeck.

By mid-November, an Eastside chapter of the IPP, which drew heavily from labor, fraternal, and civic groups, was founded. The Mexican American surname most mentioned in IPP activities was Larry Perrea. Another name closely associated with this movement was attorney Richard Ibañez, later a Superior Court Judge. However, outside of these persons, few Mexican Americans occupied leadership roles in IPP. (Primarily, Jews and white Americans dominated.) In December, a mass IPP rally was held in the Shrine Auditorium. The *Sun* gave the event heavy coverage. For the remainder of the year, few Mexican American names were listed as IPP leaders in the announcement of meetings and conferences.

The *Citizen* was the more conservative of the two weeklies, reporting more on the activities of professional and business organizations in the Belvedere Township. These included the Belvedere Business and Professional Men's Association, the Mexican Chamber of Commerce, and the Belvedere Coordinating Council.

On July 7, the new sheriff's juvenile facility was opened in the hills of Eastern Avenue. On August 29, the *Citizen* reported the adoption of the Loyalty Oath requirement for Los Angeles County employees. The *Citizen* scarcely commented on community activism. As a result, this information must be pieced together. For instance, on November 26, the *Citizen* announced: "Juan Candia Elected President of Mexican American Movement." MAM was a Mexican American youth organization established in the early 1930s to encourage young men and women to pursue professional careers. The article did not give background information about this organization. The *Citizen's* last article of the year reported that 5,000 people marched in the annual Virgen de Guadalupe parade. The event drew some 30,000 spectators.

1948

In January, the new East Los Angeles Junior College campus moved from its temporary headquarters at Garfield High School to its present location near Atlantic Boulevard and Floral. Some 800 families faced eviction in the East Los Angeles housing projects. Delinquency remained a problem and, in the first two months of the year, the *Citizen* and First Street merchants pressured the sheriff to get tougher on vandals and gangs. The merchants complained that the sheriff was not doing enough to curb these problems. Significantly, up to this point there was infrequent reference in other newspapers to gangs.

The *Sun* devoted considerable space to the Independent Progressive party. It is apparent from this coverage that the IPP cultivated Mexican American candidates to a greater degree than the two major political parties. For instance, José Ramón Chávez ran for the assembly and received the IPP's support. Chávez, a member of Local 9 of the Congress of Industrial Organizations (CIO), and vice-chair of the IPP's Los Angeles County Central Committee, campaigned on a liberal platform. He condemned racial and religious discrimination and police brutality. He called for the right of labor to organize and denounced the Taft-Hartley Act. Chávez also supported the state of Israel. In short, he supported all of the issues popular with Jewish liberals of the day. Yet, he lost the Democratic party primary. When he ran as the IPP candidate in the November runoffs, he lost again.

On April 2, the *Sun* reported the murder of Agustín Salcido, 17, by Los Angeles Police Officer William Keyes. The *Sun* reported that this was the fourth shooting involving Keyes in the past 18 months. Salcido had been at a local bar when Keyes and his partner, E. R. Sánchez, arrested the youth. They took Salcido to "an empty locked building" and shot him to death. Keyes claimed that Salcido had attempted to sell the officers stolen watches, an allegation that was later disproved. The *Sun* demanded that Assistant District Attorney William Simpson try Keyes for first degree murder. When the district attorney's office did not take any action, the *Sun* was vehemently critical. The Community Service Organization, the Mexican American Civil Rights Congress of America, the Furniture Workers, CIO, and PAC all demanded justice for Salcido. Finally, Judge Stanley Moffat accepted the complaint. In response, the Los Angeles daily press viciously attacked the judge by red-baiting him. Later, when the district attorney reluctantly prosecuted Keyes, critics charged that the district attorney purposely allowed the presiding judge, C. C. McDonald, to declare Keyes not guilty on a technicality. The judge maintained that the proper evidence had not been submitted.

Progressives condemned the high incidence of police brutality. Attorney Richard Ibañez was a leading spokesman. The *Sun* covered Ibañez's unsuccessful race for the Superior Court, reporting that he had considerable support and that a rally in his honor would draw 10,000 people.

The *Sun* regularly published stories on protest rallies, which included a variety of issues, ranging from the condemnation of the Jack Tenney Committee to attacks on the Loyalty Oath. The coverage indicates that most Mexican American organizations took an accommodationist position. On April 2, for instance, the *Citizen* reported that Lewis Walker, George Cisneros, Leo Lozano, and Manuel Ochoa had been elected officers of the new League of United Latin American Councils (LULAC) chapter. Three weeks later, this group denounced communism. LULAC, like other mainstream Mexican American organizations, went to great lengths to convince others of its patriotism.

The Community Service Organization (CSO) took a middle path, working on issues and avoiding direct politics. For example, it doubled Mexican American voter registration in East Los Angeles. The CSO, a grassroots organization, had been founded in April with the help of the Steelworkers Union and volunteers from Roybal's unsuccessful city council campaign. The organization heavily involved itself in human rights issues as well as in the promotion of civic improvement. The group grew from 25 members to more than 3,000 members over the following three years. In 1948, the CSO educated the community in solutions to dirt roads, unemployment, poor education, and inadequate housing.

News of business and professional groups filled the *Citizen*. Unfortunately, not much background material was given to the township's organizations. For example, the Comité de Beneficencia Mexicano, a mutual aid society, sponsored a fund raising drive for the Casa del Mexicano, a community center. The *Citizen* covered the event, but did not give any background on the organization itself. The article listed Dr. José Díaz as chair of the Comité. The *Citizen* also reported on a meeting of the Mexican American Press group, headed by Francisco Villagrán and Rafael Trujillo. The issue of narcotics received some attention. The Belvedere Coordinating Council apparently took the lead in informing the public about this and other issues confronting the township.

1949

Edward R. Roybal again announced his candidacy for the 9th Councilmanic District. Most progressive organizations, including the IPP, endorsed Roybal. An enthusiastic cadre of volunteers supported Roybal, and he was elected by a 2-to-1 margin. Almost immediately, Roybal became involved in controversy. By an 8-to-6 vote, the city council vetoed a fair employment practices plan for city employees. Roybal led the fair employment practices forces, who accused the city council of racial bigotry in not passing the ordinance.

In May, the first reference appeared on the Asociación Nacional México Americana (ANMA), an organization led locally by Antonio Luna. ANMA was closely affiliated with trade unions, including the Union of Mine, Mill, and Smelter Workers (UMMSW), and the Congress of Industrial Organizations (CIO). ANMA had been founded in May 1949 in Grant County, New Mexico. Alfrcdo Montoya, of the El Paso local of the UMMSW, headed ANMA nationally. ANMA was involved in civil rights issues and publicly opposed the Immigration and Naturalization Service (INS) raids, claiming that the INS justified the raids and abusive treatment because of high unemployment. The organization held its founding convention on the 20th of October. Montoya served as its first president. The *Sun* listed Ralph Cuarón, Julia Luna Mount, and others as local ANMA officers.

The Civil Rights Congress remained active. In April, it sponsored a rally to protest the policy of jailing suspects without the right of bail. The Eastside Labor Youth Council protested the trial of 12 national communist leaders and took a stand against racism and police brutality. Racial classification was protested by many Mexican American organizations that objected to the use of "Mexican" as a classification for race. In 1949, the Armed Forces prohibited the use of this "adjective" for classifying the race of Mexican American personnel.

The CSO launched a voter registration drive, setting a goal of 10,000 Latin Americans. Other organizations were also active. For instance, the Mexican American Movement, a youth organization dedicated to promoting education for Chicano youth, functioned under the leadership of Angel Cano. The Mexican Chamber of Commerce celebrated its silver anniversary. The two weeklies reported on these and other organizations. However, the coverage was in bulletin board fashion, merely announcing events.

City Terrace residents, meanwhile, protested the granting of a permit for a dump site in their community. And, although fortunes continued to be amassed for people outside the community from the operation of dump sites, the weeklies made little comment on the process. Residents accused the board of supervisors of favoritism and corruption in the granting of permits.

The passage of the Redevelopment Act of 1949 intensified competition for the land east of the Los Angeles River. Under this law, the Belvedere Township became eligible for slum clearance funds and community redevelopment monies. The *Citizen* consistently championed redevelopment while the *Sun* opposed it. A plan for the Belvedere-Maravilla area was approved by the Regional Planning Commission. The plan generated considerable interest. The Maravilla Property Owners Association held a special meeting to listen to the Regional Planning Commission report. Manuel López and Jesse Cortez formed the Marianna Redevelopment Association for the purpose of slum clearance and developments. CSO chair Henry Nava was involved in discussing the plan.

1950

The Asociación Nacional México Americana had close ties with labor and with the IPP. For instance, Virginia Ruiz, national secretary of ANMA, was a delegate to the Independent Progressive Party Convention in Chicago. There were countless examples in which ANMA cooperated with labor groups and the IPP to condemn police brutality. When deputies broke up a baby shower at the home of Mrs. Natalia Gonzales, the Maravilla chapter of ANMA circulated a petition listing grievances against the sheriff's department. This drive was so effective that the state senate formed an interim committee on crime and corruption to investigate the abuse of power at the Gonzales home. IPP leaders Virginia Ruiz and John Forrester condemned the sheriff's department's intimidation of the Mexican American community.

Councilman Edward R. Roybal, while criticizing the communists for attempting to sabotage the Korean War effort, opposed the current red hysteria. Roybal won the hearts of liberals by opposing the city council majority, who proposed the registration of communists. The council, by a 13-to-1 margin, passed a law making it mandatory for communists to register with police authorities and forbidding them the right to own guns. Roybal, although a new councilman, denounced the measures as "thought control'' and stated that it left the public at the mercy of ''biased crackpots.'' For his courage, Roybal was honored by *Fortnight* magazine in its November 13 edition.

Nativists were also active at the county level, where supervisors passed a law similar to the city's. Henry Steinberg, 38, a member of the Communist party, challenged the constitutionality of the ordinance and was arrested for failure to register. Meyer B. Marion, justice of the peace for the Belvedere Township, held the ordinance unconstitutional. On appeal, Marion's decision was upheld.

Roybal also led the fight for rent controls at heated meetings in the city council. In July, the city council entertained motions to decontrol rents, which would drive rents upward. Representatives of the Apartment House Association and the Small Property Owners League lobbied council members. The council voted 10-to-4 for decontrol. The controversy soon heated up, and near riots resulted in the council chambers. In the autumn, President Harry S. Truman flatly declared that Los Angeles would not decontrol rents.

Many Mexican American veterans used their GI Bill loans to buy homes. Much of the housing that Mexican Americans could obtain was segregated. The *Citizen* ran an advertisement on September 28 that warned: ''Chicano GIs Beware.'' The advertisement told GIs of Mexican descent that these rancho homes, which promised the romantic life, were a hoax.

Tensions between the sheriff's department and the community increased. Sheriff Eugene Biscailuz ordered his reserves to enforce the curfew laws. Los Angeles newspapers agitated the public, portraying Mexican American youths as hoodlums. Even the old Los Angeles *Daily News*, considered liberal, ran an inflammatory article on May 6: ''Councilman Has Plan To Curb Punks.'' Councilman Kenneth Hahn stated that ''these boys have gone beyond counsel, reason, or psychological approach . . . the time has come for discipline.'' Roybal opposed Hahn's night-stick approach and recommended a conference to discuss the gang problem. Roybal wrote an article for the *Los Angeles Mirror* on May 22 headlined: ''Dead End Movies Spur Wolf Packs, says Roybal.'' In the article, he pointed out that gang crime had decreased by five percent since the year before and that the economy prompted gang activity. Just as the coverage of the Zoot Suit Riots had inflamed the public from 1942 to 1943, the newspapers in 1950 inflamed readers, creating stereotypes such as "wolf pack." The council and the press were anxious to give the LAPD the power to spank the "rat packers," as they called them. Supervisor Anson Ford agreed with Roybal, stating that police officers should "not fall into the error of determining punishment by popular hysteria."

The annexation of East Los Angeles' prime sections threatened the community. Monterey Park moved to annex the area surrounding East Los Angeles Junior College. East Los Angeles residents opposed the move. In the ensuing years, eastsiders often reacted to threats of annexation by threatening to incorporate East Los Angeles. Consequently, the Belvedere Property Owners Association listened to Dr. Adolph Overveen's plans to submit incorporation papers. Residents were aware that East Los Angeles was vulnerable to annexation by bits and pieces. Some eastsiders believed that the best way to bring about civic improvements to the Belvedere Township was to incorporate. No further mention was made of the Overveen plan.

1951

Joe Kovner and the *Sun* led the fight for rent controls, attacking the rent gougers. Citywide, tenants rallied at City Hall to oppose rent increases. The *Sun* also condemned the proposed annexation of 33 acres of East Los Angeles by Monterey Park. The Boyle Heights Weekly reported that the Independent Progressive party criticized Harry Jaffe, owner of the Wynerwood Apartments, for not renting to minorities.

Roybal appeared at a defense rally for civil rights causes with actress Ann Sheridan, football hero Kenny Washington, and leaders of various civil rights organizations. Roybal was also active in attempting to improve police–community relations. The councilman helped form the "Committee of 21." Sponsored by Mayor Fletcher Bowron, the committee was designed to meet with police periodically. Police authorities, however, refused to participate.

Roybal was re-elected by a 3-to-1 margin in April. This race was interesting because the enemies of the councilman ran Irving Rael against him in an effort to split the Mexican and Jewish-American vote. On March 31, the *Los Angeles Times* refused to endorse Roybal. In contrast, the *Times* endorsed reactionary incumbent Ed Davenport for the 12th Councilmanic District. Davenport was abrasive and abusive. Moreover, he was the puppet of real estate interests. The *Los Angeles Times* made decontrol an election issue during the 1951 elections.

In 1949, Mayor Fletcher Bowron had championed low-cost public housing, signing a $100 million agreement with the federal government that would affect 48,000 families. The city council approved the contract by a 12-to-1 vote. This arrangement involved 213.6 acres that had been designated for public housing projects. Bunker Hill and Chávez Ravine were part of this package. Although they were west of the Los Angeles River, both were communities with heavy Mexican American populations. Roybal staunchly supported public housing, which at the time was supported by a majority of the city council as well. The city, in fact, was ready to implement the contract. By May 1951, the City Housing Authority purchased the first sites in the Bunker Hill area. However, changes began to take place in 1951 that would result in a dramatic attitudinal transformation on the part of the council and the public towards public housing. By this year, downtown realtors, businessmen, and other leaders joined to oppose it. The *Los Angeles Times*, the leader of this opposition, labeled public housing "socialistic." Considering the McCarthy hysteria of the day, this was an explosive charge. Much to the credit of Roybal, he did not abandon his principles.

The *Sun* reported that on May 18 and 19, Mexican American leaders met in El Paso, Texas, to form the American Council of Spanish-Speaking People. Prominent leaders, including Dr. George I. Sánchez, Fred Ross, Tony Ríos, and Ignacio López, attended the conference. The new organization elected Tibo J. Chávez, Lieutenant Governor of New Mexico, as its first president. The American Council was intended to function as an umbrella organization for groups such as the Alianza Hispano Americana, the Community Service Organization, the League of United Latin American Councils, and the American GI Forum. It worked closely with these groups, representing the victims of civil rights violations and educational segregation. The American Council of Spanish-Speaking People represented the mainstream community, which followed the lead of trade unions. It favored restricting undocumented workers under the belief that they took jobs away from citizens and also handicapped trade union organization. The council openly supported American institutions. It advocated working within the system and made it clear that it was not radical.

In contrast, ANMA represented the left. Its members were involved in groups such as El Sereno Defense Organization, which raised funds for police abuse victims. ANMA sought to raise the community's consciousness as to its rights. ANMA's eastside chapter opened its office on July 28.

Police-community relations deteriorated. Despite community criticism of the police, the Los Angeles press and most politicians blindly supported the LAPD. Davenport, for instance, introduced a motion to authorize police road blocks to stem juvenile delinquency. Roybal denounced this as a "thoughtless, unnecessary, un-American measure that is going to cause a great deal of friction between the police department and the community."

During the early part of the year, the county supervisors considered a permit for a dump site in East Los Angeles just north of East Los Angeles Junior College. Eastsiders protested that this dump, along with the 75-acre dump site in City Terrace, would give East Los Angeles the dubious distinction of housing one of the state's largest dump sites. The Neighborhood Improvement Committee, led by Bertha Villescas of the CSO, and the City Terrace Improvement Association mobilized community opposition to encroachment.

The Monterey Park city fathers moved to annex East Los Angeles Junior College and the 300 acres to the north of the campus, stating that they wanted to forestall the granting of a dump site permit. Rallies were held to voice opposition to the dump and annexation but, in April, Monterey Park annexed the 300 acres north of the college. The Monterey Park City Council then granted the permit to the dump site operators. According to the *Citizen*, this site became the "world's largest dump." In August, the Monterey Park authorities granted the dump operators a zoning change so that they could begin operations.

The territory east of Indiana Street underwent a political reorganization in 1951. At the time, two separate courts served Belvedere and the rest of East Los Angeles. Under the reorganization, the two parts were consolidated with the city of Montebello, and the entire area became known as East Los Angeles. The consolidation eventually broke down divisions between different parts of East Los Angeles.

1952

Both the *Citizen* and the *Sun* reported the return of Korean War veterans, dead and alive. 1952's first article on Mexican Americans was titled: "Bodies of Three ELA Heroes Back from Korean War." Throughout the year, these weeklies repeated similar stories.

Police–community relations were tense. The first case which received notoriety was the so-called "Bloody Christmas" affair of 1951. The incident occurred west of the river but involved Mexicans throughout the county. Reportedly, six youths were arrested at a bar on Christmas evening. When the officers dragged one of them from the bar and began beating him, the others came to the victim's defense and were arrested for assault on the officers. They were taken to the Central Jail, where gangs of officers beat the youths so severely that they had to be taken to an emergency hospital. A public outcry resulted over the incident. Police Chief William Parker, however, refused to discipline the officers. Meanwhile, the victims were tried. Although Judge Joseph Call convicted them, he condemned the vicious police attacks and recommended an FBI investigation. As a result of Call's actions, a grand jury investigation was conducted on the eight officers. Finally, they were convicted on felony charges.

Another case was that of CSO's Tony Ríos and Alfredo Ulloa, who were arrested when they questioned two men assaulting a third. The two assailants turned out to be police officers—Fernando Najera, 31, and George K. Kellenberger, 33—who were in civilian clothes. Ríos and Ulloa were taken to the police station, where officers severely beat them and then charged them with resisting arrest. Numerous rallies were held to support Ríos, who was a board member of the Council of Spanish-Speaking People, the Comité de Beneficencia Mexicana and the California Federation of Civic Unity.

On March 17, the police relations unit of the Los Angeles Conference on Community Relations issued a report to the Los Angeles Police Commission. The conference, comprised of 33 multi-racial organizations, included the American Federation of

Labor, the Congress of Industrial Organizations, the Social Action Committee of the Episcopal Diocese of Los Angeles, the Urban League, the CSO, and the Jewish Community Relations Council. It was formed in 1947 to deal with the police abuse of minorities, but from the beginning LAPD stifled communication between itself and the conference. The conference was especially disturbed by the increase in civil rights violations.* Regarding the "Bloody Christmas" case, the conference complained that the LAPD's Internal Affairs Division took 54 days to conclude its report, and had taken no action at all until Judge Call demanded a grand jury investigation.

In the report, the conference's attorney, Everett M. Porter, reviewed the history of police-community relations since 1947. The mayor appointed a committee, headed by George A. Beavers, to determine causes of poor relations between police and the community and to recommend solutions. The committee disclosed the two major problems. The first was the public's attitude toward the police; the second was the police department's attitude toward the Mexican American community. According to the report, many police officers believed that "complaints are motivated by ulterior un-American and political ends."

Porter reviewed the Joe Solis case. On September 21, officers stopped Solis and told him that he resembled a suspect at large. Officers took him to the police station, where he replied "yes" to a question. The officer responded, "Say 'Yes, sir,' to me!" and struck Solis, knocking him to the floor and kicking him. Officers refused to accept a complaint lodged by Solis's father. By the end of the year, a grand jury report severely criticized Chief Parker and the LAPD in the handling of police brutality cases.

ANMA fought the McCarthy era hysteria, cooperating with the National Committee for the Protection of the Foreign Born to protect Mexicans from deportation and harassment by the Immigration and Naturalization Service. ANMA was also the only national Chicano organization opposing the Korean war. ANMA held its national conference July 12 through 13 in El Paso, Texas. The delegates encouraged Mexican Americans to join trade

---

*Armando Morales, ¡*Ando Sangrando! I am Bleeding. A study of Mexican-American Police Conflict,* (Los Angeles: 1971) p. 21, points out that between 1948 and 1956, the CSO's Civil Rights Committee handled approximately thirty-five police brutality investigations.

unions, to struggle for their civil liberties, and to condemn deportations.

The Civil Rights Committee of the CSO, headed by Ralph Guzmán, fought the 1952 Walter-McCarran Act, a law that codified U.S. Immigration regulations. The legislation's main goal was to protect the "purity" of the essentially northern European origins of the U.S. population. The Walter-McCarran Act set up the mechanism to hunt and deport "illegals." It also provided for the deportation of naturalized citizens who were suspected of ever having belonged to an organization on the attorney general's list. Many Americans, including President Harry S. Truman, objected to the law because it was an ex post facto act that made naturalized citizens second-class. Other discriminatory aspects of the Walter-McCarran Act were that it continued discrimination against Asians and required comprehensive loyalty checks for those visiting the country even for a short time. It also terminated the citizenship of any naturalized citizen who lived outside the U.S.A. for five or more years.

The *Citizen* reported the Belvedere Veteran's Housing Project would close unless more interest was shown in veteran housing. Meanwhile, the CSO pushed its sidewalk project that called for the building of cement walkways in Belvedere-Maravilla. With some 3,000 members in Los Angeles County alone, the CSO had become the largest Mexican American organization in California. It championed civil rights, neighborhood improvement, labor relations, education, naturalization, and voter registration.

Public housing remained a controversial issue. In the city council, anti-public housing forces were led by Councilman Ed Davenport and John Holland. The debates over public housing were among the stormiest in the council's history. The Chamber of Commerce, the real estate lobby, and the Small Homeowner's Association financed the publicity against public housing. The first two groups belonged to the Greater Los Angeles Plans Incorporated (GLAP), which had been formed in 1945 to push for the downtown core's redevelopment.

Roybal and L. E. Timberlake vigorously supported public housing. Ernest Debs supported it at first but later changed his mind. The controversy in the council centered around the $100 million contract the city had signed with the federal government in 1949 to build public housing units. In February, Councilman Earle

Baker cautioned that ''public housing was going down the road to socialism.'' In the following months, opponents portrayed public housing as a communist conspiracy. These tactics were effective and council members breached the contract. Proponents appealed this action to the California Supreme Court, which found that the contract was valid and reinstated it.

The downtown elite and the anti-public housing councilmen were furious. They enlisted the support of the state legislature, pressuring the Federal Housing Administration (FHA) to cancel the contract in order to circumvent the court ruling. Ernest Debs, Kenneth Hahn, and Lee Warburton were among those presenting the request to the Federal Housing Authority. Debates intensified; charges and counter-charges were hurled. During one session, it took council president Harold Henry 45 minutes to restore order.

Anti-housing forces constantly attacked the City Housing Authority (CHA). Ultimately, the downtown elite took its fight to the public, presenting the facts in a way to persuade voters to give them a mandate. The *Los Angeles Times* pushed for the contract's repeal. The campaign was vicious, with opponents smearing public housing advocates and the *Times* and its allies committing extensive funds to repeal the contract. In June, the voters turned down public housing. The CHA had already purchased land in the Chávez Ravine area, and the council demanded that it be turned over to the city. The CHA refused and the downtown elite's puppets in the council launched an all-out attack on the CHA. Ed Davenport threw a tantrum in the city council, charging that ''reds'' worked in the CHA. During this period, Davenport became so disruptive that Roybal offered to sit Davenport down, whereupon Davenport accused Roybal of threatening him with a knife. Davenport later made light of the charge, stating that he had not meant it literally. The war between downtown forces and the CHA raged throughout the year.

1953

Roybal ran unopposed in 1953. The community showed concern over drug abuse and gang activity problems. Conferences and studies were conducted to learn how widespread the use of drugs was in East Los Angeles. Juvenile delinquency was still a major problem. Police rounded up 13 members of the Kern Street gang for the alleged shooting of Esperanza Saucedo, 15, during a gang-related fight. Saucedo was paralyzed by injuries sustained in the shooting.

The Korean War hostilities ended in July and an economic recession beset the nation. As is the case during all recessions, economic crisis surfaced a latent nativism. The press and the public always find scapegoats for the system's structural defects. The daily Los Angeles press announced the "wetback" invasion, easily making scapegoats of undocumented workers.

The *Sun* defended the undocumented workers' human rights and condemned the excesses of the Walter-McCarran Act. The paper called this act a major threat to the community. The CSO exposed hardships caused by Walter-McCarran and offered legal relief to its victims. In the Belvedere area, ANMA was very active in agitating the community against this law. Sylvia Cuarón, ANMA's Southern California Region secretary, was quite visible in this fight. The CSO also promoted assistance for the elderly and educated the community on the baby adoption process.

The *Sun*'s determination to keep the Eastside residential became a crusade. Joseph Kovner wrote scathing editorials, condemning the Golden State Freeway and the resultant bulldozing of residential and business sections in Boyle Heights. In November, a rally was organized to protest freeway encroachments. In the following month, another rally was held at the Second Street Elementary School. Leaders vowed that Boyle and Hollenbeck Heights would not be divided.

Ralph Guzmán wrote a series of interesting articles in the *Sun*, articulating the Mexican American community's frustrations. The articles offer some insight into the philosophy of the Mexican American activists of the times. A June 18 article, "Let's Get the Story Straight," condemned distortions of facts made by the Los Angeles press. Guzmán wrote that when a Mexican American youth had been accidentally killed by a car, the daily press had labeled it a gang killing within just a few hours. On June 25, Guzmán accused Los Angeles newspapers of purposely vilifying East Los Angeles in order to sell newspapers. According to Guzmán, the downtown press described East Los Angeles as a gang-ridden, narcotics-infested area where sadistic crimes and drunken brawls were commonplace. Guzmán countered these accusations. He pointed to the positive things that were happening on the Eastside, mentioning especially a CSO-sponsored conference on youth problems.

On November 19, Guzmán condemned the press-generated Mexican American gang hysteria and labeled the coverage "yellow journalism." In December, Guzmán told of the press' and the courts' reactions to an incident that had occurred on Seventh and Broadway. A man had intervened in a fight between one man and two Mexican American youths. The two boys beat this man and he subsequently died. Immediately, the press called it a "Mad Dog Slaying." In reality, the man had a physical ailment and had not died from the blows sustained in the fight. Guzmán cautioned his readers that they should not allow the 1940s to return. On December 17, he wrote: "When teenagers in other parts of the city go astray, the newspapers call it juvenile delinquency, but when Eastside kids wander from the straight-and-narrow they are immediately tagged as 'rat packs,' 'mad dogs,' and 'Bloodthirsty Hoodlums.' "

On September 17 and 24, Guzmán had condemned the sheriff deputies' beating of Máximo Bustillos, 28, on May 2, and David Hidalgo, 15, on May 8. Guzmán wrote: "It is no secret that for years law and order in the Eastside of Los Angeles County has been maintained through fear and brutal treatment of prisoners." On October 1, he demanded a review of the sheriff's department, comparing conditions in East Los Angeles with those of the Wild West. He expressed his belief that the reason why some law enforcement agencies had failed to become more democratic was that citizens had a traditional reluctance to criticize the "wearers-of-the-badge."

Anti-Mexican American sentiment was rampant. Some newspapers openly called for vigilante action. Guzmán's last editorial of the year labeled 1953 a year of super-patriots, freeways, yellow journalism, and teen-age crime.

Aside from numerous articles on the Walter-McCarran Act, Guzmán also exposed the injustices of "Operation Wetback" and the massive roundup of Mexicans. In an editorial, Guzmán chided U.S. Attorney General Herbert Brownell for threatening to send troops to the border. Although Guzmán was against the entry of undocumented Mexican workers, he sympathized with their plight. "First of all," he wrote, "the Mexican peasants are forced to come to this country because they are hungry." On October

15, he described the plight of thousands of hungry Mexicans on the border across from Presidio, Texas. U.S. growers, angry that Mexico wanted better wages for *braceros*, frustrated the signing of the bracero contract. Guzmán also castigated Brownell. "A few weeks ago," he wrote, "Herbert Brownell, the U.S. Attorney General, wanted to shoot wetbacks crossing into the United States, but farmers fearing the loss of cheap labor market complained bitterly and Brownell changes [sic] his mind." Guzmán did not like the bracero program because he felt that it hampered unionization of agricultural labor.

The county made further plans to encroach on East Los Angeles. The County Grand Jury recommended that a women's prison be built in Belvedere. The county also sought a site for its Civic Center in East Los Angeles to house its new municipal courts there. In June, groundbreaking ceremonies took place for the new Civic Center in Belvedere.

The First Street merchants, worried about narcotics and vandalism, pressed the sheriff's department for additional protection. The Belvedere associations, meanwhile, sponsored workshops and conferences and encouraged agencies to do more in the field of narcotics and youth. The Los Angeles district attorney defended the sheriff's department. He said that it was doing a good job, considering that it was under-staffed. Los Angeles District Attorney Ernest Roll stated that a gang problem existed because 70 percent of the gang members were from broken homes. The sheriff's department itself enlarged its crime prevention units and its basic car plan.

Neither weekly fully captured the importance of East Los Angeles Junior College to residents east of the river. For many returning GIs who had been tracked into non-academic courses by the public school, ELA College gave some hope. Many were exposed for the first time to political issues and became involved. Dr. Helen Bailey was especially active with students. In March, she helped sponsor a Spanish-Speaking People's Education Conference.

SUMMARY

While Mexican Americans had spread throughout the county by 1945, the highest concentration remained just east of the Los Angeles River. The post-war period saw the final forging of the

East Los Angeles community, which was increasingly second and third-generation. Returning veterans had high expectations and many involved themselves in organizations such as the Community Service Organization (CSO), a group that was instrumental in electing Edward R. Roybal to the city council in 1949. Many second-generation Mexican Americans also involved themselves in other political organizations, including the Democratic party and the Independent Progressive party.

The coverage in the *Citizen* suggests that business associations, such as the Belvedere Coordinating Council and the Mexican Chamber of Commerce, were more active in East Los Angeles than in Boyle Heights. Juvenile delinquency was an issue in both areas and additional efforts were made to work with youth and to discuss drug abuse. The sheriff's department and the First Street merchants pushed a basic car plan, which was intended to convert gangs into clubs. Police brutality and police–community relations remained concerns. The press stereotyped the area as gang-infested and violence-ridden. This portrayal made the community more vulnerable to slum clearance programs because it depersonalized the people of the area. The *Sun* was outspoken in its defense of the community. A marked transition had taken place in this newspaper and, from 1946 forward, coverage on Mexican Americans progressively increased.

The *Sun*'s major concern was land use. Because of federal intervention, massive land clearance was becoming increasingly profitable. The land east of the river was particularly vulnerable because it was close to the all-important Civic Center. According to the developers' standards, the area was old and the community was poor, making it perfect for renewal. In 1952, the chances of East Los Angeles surviving as a residential area were limited.

Roybal was the sole Mexican American representative. He opposed the downtown powers and supported unpopular issues. Undoubtedly, his career suffered. Often, he alone defended civil liberties and the interests of the poor against the developers. His participation at the local level was crucial during these years.

3

The Battle of City Hall: 1954–1959

This chapter is based on the *Citizen* and the *Sun*. The Edward R. Roybal Newspaper Scrapbooks and the Edward R. Roybal Collection were heavily relied upon. Robert Gottlieb and Irene Wolt, *Thinking Big* (New York: 1977), and Douglas T. Miller and Marion Nowak, *The Fifties: The Way We Really Were* (New York: 1975), are useful reference tools.

The Eisenhower years brought high unemployment, frequent economic recessions and two near depressions (one in 1953 and one in 1958). These were also years in which many Americans started to move to the suburbs. For Mexican Americans, however, it represented a time of a different kind of change. Whereas much of American society indulged itself in reading about personal alienation and loneliness, most Mexican Americans struggled to gain the status and material achievements that the rest of society already enjoyed. It was a time when many Americans worried about racism in the South but ignored its existence in their own communitics. To most Amcricans, racism and discrimination and poverty appeared non-existent and to talk about them as issues seemed un-American.

The 1950s saw many Mexican Americans move from Texas to the Midwest and to California. For Mexican nationals, a favorite port of entry was Los Angeles, and it became the Mexico City of the north. The 50s were also a period of rapid urbanization, with Los Angeles County's Mexican American population increasing to nearly 600,000 by 1959. During this time, California challenged Texas as the state with the heaviest concentration of Mexicans.

Mexican Americans experienced a growth in the membership of their mainstream organizations, including the American GI Forum, the League of United Latin American Councils, and the Community Service Organization. The McCarthy era suffocated radicalism, rooting out radicals and liberals from the Congress of Industrial Organizations (CIO). By 1954, Independent Progressive party members once more joined the Democratic party. And while Mexican Americans themselves did achieve dominance on the Eastside, they found themselves to be increasingly isolated from progressives in other parts of Los Angeles.

The majority of the society was not sympathetic to the plight of minorities in the United States. Many regarded all Mexican Americans, who had a high percentage of immigrants, as aliens. Certainly the impact of the Walter-McCarran Act fell more severely on them than on other groups. In fighting the excesses of the Walter-McCarran Act, a small sector of organizationally active Mexican Americans worked closely with groups such as the Committee for the Protection of the Foreign Born and the American Civil Liberties Union. During the 1950s, Mexican

American organizations grew closer to the mainstream civil rights movement. Suits to end the school segregation of Mexicans had been brought in the 1930s. *Méndez vs. Westminister School District*, 1945, was a landmark case, supposedly ending the de jure segregation of Mexican Americans. Although Mexicans had struggled since the 19th century against racism and segregation, their fight was not rooted in the Black movement. Rather, it was an independent stream that eventually merged with that of Blacks and other minorities.

The events of the 1950s overshadowed the Mexican American civil rights struggle while at the same time influencing it. *Brown vs. Topeka Board of Education*, 1954, signalled the renewal of a non-violent street movement to gain human rights for Black Americans. The drama of the events that followed drew more attention than the similar movements of other groups. Essentially, the struggle for equality in the United States has been perceived as a Black-White phenomenon. Blacks were a national minority, whereas Mexican Americans were considered a regional problem. More importantly, Blacks had a higher population ratio and had been a continuous part of U.S. history since 1619.

Blacks were active during the 1950s. Contrary to popular belief, considerable Black–White tension existed outside the South. In Chicago alone, between 1945 and 1954, there were nine race riots. Blacks were anything but docile. In 1956, the Reverend Martin Luther King Jr. was jailed in Montgomery, Alabama, during a bus boycott. In 1957 and 1958, federal troops were reluctantly sent to Little Rock, Arkansas, to ensure the safety of Black children attempting to attend white schools. Two mild civil rights acts were passed in 1957 and 1960. But for the most part, Americans believed that racial injustice was confined to the redneck South and could not exist throughout the whole United States.

The Mexican struggle for civil rights during this period was not as dramatic. Rather, it was part of the everyday living process. One of the main research problems is that this history of struggle was not recorded. But it is a myth that nothing was happening in the Chicano communities east of the Los Angeles River in the 1950s.

World War II and then the Korean War had impacted strongly on Mexican Americans. The passage of federal fair employment legislation improved access to employment opportunities for a few. Throughout the 1950s, Mexican Americans pressured state and local government to pass similar ordinances. The GI Bill also made it possible for some to secure better homes and/or education. Unfortunately, neither the *Sun* nor the *Citizen* adequately covered education problems.

Federal intervention before and after World War II benefitted the poor in obtaining low cost housing. As the 50s progressed, however, programs for the poor became increasingly unpopular and were seen as socialistic. Not only in Los Angeles, but throughout the whole United States, urban renewal programs victimized the poor, who were concentrated in the inner-city and most likely to be non-white. Slum clearance became an excuse to move people out of their dwellings and roll the bulldozers in. In the period from 1954 to 1959, the battle against these bulldozers was the main struggle of Mexican Americans in and around the Eastside.

THE CHRONICLE
1954

The gang problem was in all probability blown out of proportion by the daily press. It consumed more space than any other issue. The *Sun* responded to the downtown newspapers' sensationalized coverage of the gang situation in East Los Angeles. On January 7, Ralph Guzmán angrily wrote: "It is becoming more and more difficult to walk through the streets of Los Angeles and look Mexican!" A week later, Guzmán observed: "Basically, Eugene Biscailuz' idea to curb the kid gangs is the evening 'roundup,' a well known western drive." Eastsiders never denied that gangs existed; they resented, however, the inordinate attention given to gangs in the press and the methods used to solve the problem.

It is important to note that gangs are part of the American urban scene and not unique to the Eastside. In the 1950s, the community was concerned and sought solutions. The Belvedere Coordinating Council discussed whether or not car clubs were a viable alternative. An all-out effort was made in Belvedere to enlist businesses to sponsor the car clubs so that gangs could be transferred into clubs.

The sheriff's department announced a three-point program to curb juvenile delinquency. The plan called for five roving squad cars to patrol the barrios, establishment of a new juvenile unit, and formalization of a constructive youth program. Critics of the police approach pointed out that the area lacked playgrounds, parks, and recreational facilities. Ultimately, the sheriff's department did incorporate the car club program into its strategy.

Supervisor John Anson Ford addressed a mass meeting of car clubs, and businessman Reynaldo Ochoa devoted a great deal of time to the movement. A league was formed, with car clubs such as the Road Knights, the Los Angeles Drifters, and Wolfhounds joining the new federation. The membership of some of the car clubs included both females and males. They were involved in community activities. For instance, the East Los Angeles Federation sponsored a special Christmas give-away project. The East Los Angeles Youth Council, headed by Mary Bustamante, coordinated youth groups to meet regularly with other youth councils in Los Angeles County. In spite of these efforts, however, gang activity continued in Belvedere and Boyle Heights and little evidence exists that the programs had ameliorated the problem.

The Catholic Youth Organization, founded by Bishop Bernard J. Sheil in 1930, sponsored a four-point plan that included a basic car program. Two of the more prominent CYO clubs were the Road Knights and the Starlighters. The CYO concentrated its efforts in the white-fence barrio in Boyle Heights. Cleland House also sponsored a youth program.

Youth conferences and friendship festivals were common during 1954. In the fall, a small group of Mexican American students organized a conference at the University of California at Los Angeles (UCLA), sponsoring a conference titled "Mexican Americans: A Sleeping Giant." Fernando del Río chaired the conference and Councilman Roybal was the featured speaker.

By 1953, "Operation Wetback" had been launched by the Immigration and Naturalization Service (INS). During this year, INS intensified harassment. Nationwide, 1,035,282 Mexicans were allegedly deported. In Los Angeles, the sheriff's department assisted the INS in the roundups.

Ralph Guzmán condemned the hypocrisy of the INS and U.S. authorities in their relationship with Mexico. Guzmán wrote that bracero program contract negotiations between Mexico and the United States had broken down because U.S. authorities refused to make concessions to Mexico as to the wages and conditions that the Mexican braceros worked under. In an effort to coerce

Mexico into accepting its terms, the INS opened the border and allowed undocumented Mexican workers to flood across the border. This was an arrogant U.S. violation of international law. Guzmán concluded that while the INS referred to undocumented workers as a menace, conducting massive roundups and deporting hundreds of thousands of them, it opened its borders capriciously to serve grower interests.

On February 18, Guzmán reviewed the bracero program and the problems of the 1950s. On March 4, he listed the abuses of the bracero program and accused United States farmers of basing their prosperity on cheap Mexican labor. Guzmán wrote that farmers paid braceros as little as 25 cents an hour. He again condemned the press for distorting the theme of the "Wetback Invasion." He also referred to the Truman Commission on Migratory Labor, which had convened on June 3, 1950, but he did not critique the commission's work.

The brutality of the roundups stunned conservative *Sun* columnist John F. Méndez, who called the "wetbacks" innocent victims of inhumane treatment. Méndez blamed the bracero program for the mass migration of Mexicans to the United States. But neither the *Sun* nor the *Citizen* covered "Operation Wetback" to the degree that the event warranted.

Simultaneously, trade unions were very active in the struggle against the Walter-McCarran Act. Fueled by the anti-communism hysteria of the McCarthy era, the act made second-class citizens out of naturalized citizens. Even the most conservative Mexican American organizations actively opposed Walter-McCarran. The Mexican American Chamber of Commerce, led by Armando Torres, offered help to the victims. Both the *Sun* and the *Citizen* opposed the Act.

The *Sun* supported Councilman Edward R. Roybal for California lieutenant governor. On August 18, *Fortnight* magazine ran an article titled "L.A. Councilman from the Wrong Side of the Tracks." The article reported that Roybal represented a district in which only 16,000 of 87,000 voters were Mexican American. Roybal won elections in spite of opposition from the Los Angeles political machine. His popularity went beyond the Mexican American communities. He alone voted in the city council to oppose the attempts of Forest Lawn Cemetery interests to re-zone property in the San Fernando Valley. During his early career, he had uncovered that the *Los Angeles Times'* property was under-assessed. During his campaign for lieutenant governor, Roybal opposed the Central Valley Project, again stepping on the toes of the *Los Angeles Times*. Roybal won the Democratic party primary but lost in the general election. His campaign, however, united the numerous Mexican American communities throughout California.

CSO was active throughout the year, holding registration drives, sponsoring candidate forums, and expanding its citizenship classes. When it held its first national convention, 150 delegates attended. The housing shortage in the Eastside was somewhat alleviated and, by July 1, the Belvedere Veterans Housing Project was closed.

The *Citizen* was very involved in the development of the Belvedere area. *Citizen* publisher Albert L. Barney was appointed to the County Housing Commission by Supervisor John Anson Ford. This commission determined land use in unincorporated East Los Angeles. Ford was opposed by Councilman Ernest Debs in his reelection bid. Both Roybal and Joe Chávez, president of the Latin American Protective League, supported Ford. The Eastside was badly in need of a symbol. It received bad press, and it was victimized by the stereotype that Mexicans did not value education. In 1954, East Los Angeles mourned the death of 19-year-old Armando F. Castro, a star miler and honor student at East Los Angeles Junior College, who was stabbed to death when he attempted to break up a fight at a party. Councilman Roybal and East Los Angeles Junior College professor Dr. Helen Bailey helped to establish the Armando Castro Memorial Scholarship Award. Castro became the symbol of what Mexican Americans could be and how senseless violence suffocated this hope. The Castro Scholarship Committee received considerable coverage through the 1950s.

1955

In January, the East Los Angeles Youth Council launched a campaign to find jobs for teens. This council also took part in the Sixth Annual Countywide Conference of Youth Councils. The Catholic Youth Organization celebrated its 25th Anniversary, honoring Miss Carmen Lucero of Mahar House and Luisa Rehr of Pico Rivera. Arnold Martínez served as master of ceremonies. On March 25, a conference on the Educational Problems of Mexican American students was held at UCLA. Roybal was the featured speaker.

Meanwhile, 25,000 people attended a Friendship Festival. The *Citizen* continued to cover the car clubs. For instance, when the East Los Angeles Car Club Federation of Social and Car Clubs sponsored a Christmas food program to help the needy, the *Citizen* ran an article on December 22 giving special credit to Sam Nevada, a service station operator at 3400 East First Street. The Eastside Boy's Club opened on October 14.

Public facilities in the Belvedere area still lagged and many organizations sought a remedy. Meanwhile, the supervisors approved $97,259 in improvements for Belvedere Park and opened a senior citizens service club. When civic organizations learned of secret plans to upzone parts of Belvedere to M-4, which would pave the way for more intense industrial use, they opposed the scheme. The City Terrace women's committee continued its fight against the expansion of the dump there.

Relations between police and the Eastside community remained strained. Neither weekly newspaper reported the case of Phillip Brito. On January 1, Brito was arrested in front of the "Cafe Cafetal" on East First. He had been drinking. The LAPD officers took him to the First and Hill Street Police Station. There another officer boarded the patrol car and escorted Brito to Lincoln Heights. In a dark lot, the officer who had last boarded the vehicle brutally beat Brito, knocking him unconscious. When he awakened, Brito was told that if he said anything, he would get more of the same. He was booked.

No further mention was made of the Asociación Nacional México Americana in either the *Sun* or the *Citizen*.

In March, CSO delegates approved a new constitution at its Second National Convention. The CSO conducted citizenship classes, graduating some 3,000 Angelinos. In recognition, the CSO received a citation from the Daughters of the American Revolution. The CSO also championed fair employment and offered community education classes in first aid and other subjects. Mrs. Pauline Holguín was appointed executive secretary of the Los Angeles section. Holguín had formerly served as secretary for the International Ladies Garment Workers Union, Local 384. The

CSO also collected donations for the flood victims of Tampico, Mexico.

The Beneficencia Mexicana of Los Angeles sponsored activities at the Casa del Mexicano. Patterned after Japanese and Jewish-American organizations, the Council of Mexican American Affairs (CMAA) was organized in 1955 (some sources say 1953) to promote leadership and develop participation in community affairs. Organizers wanted to establish a clearing house for information. Joe A. Vargas, María Ford, Carlos Terán, and Agustín Serrato were among the charter members.

1956

The Belvedere Democratic Club was led by Tony Ponce. Trini and Manuel Aragón also participated. Ray Mora's weekly column in the *Sun*, "Politics," reported on Mexican Americans in Democratic party politics. Mora chaired the 19th Congressional District Democratic Central Committee. He also headed the "Elect Ed Elliot to Assembly Committee." Frank Guzmán, president of the Eastside Young Democrats, attended the Chicago Democratic party convention.

The CSO opened its annual membership drive. It challenged the denial of rental privileges to non-citizen residents. The County Housing Authority had banned aliens, although Congress had eliminated this exclusion. The CSO sponsored hearing tests for children. It also conducted voter registration drives, and even managed to register hospital patients who lived in the district. Throughout the year, the CSO expanded. A CSO chapter was even organized in Phoenix, Arizona.

At its second annual affair in January, the CMAA gave awards to numerous Latino leaders. The Beneficencia Mexicana, los Caballeros, the Mexican Chamber of Commerce, the Veterans of Foreign Wars (Obregón Post), the Sociedad Fraternal Mexicana, the Club Durango, the Club Jaliciense, the Latin American Golfers Association, the Pan American Optimists, the Club Social del Río, the Romanos, and the Sons and Daughters of New Mexico all participated in the CMAA's scholarship dinner.

The CMAA organized numerous conferences and conducted various community studies. In February, the CMAA sponsored a Conference on the Education of Mexican Americans. Its housing committee, headed by Arthur Rendón, completed a case study on housing discrimination and sponsored a conference at which some 60 delegates supported national legislation to end housing discrimination.

The East Los Angeles Youth Council established the Youth Employment Services (YES) as a possible solution to the gang problem. The *Citizen* reported on youth education conferences, including the Congress of Youth Coordinating Councils on April 21 and the ''East Los Angeles Looks Ahead'' conference held on May 19. The latter was chaired by Alex Zambrano and conducted workshops on topics ranging form juvenile delinquency to educational opportunities.

In February, the Los Angeles State College dedicated its new campus. In May, it conducted its First Institute of American Problems, which explored the problems of Mexican Americans. Councilman Roybal spoke at the event, as did Dr. Edward Lamas, president of the Southern California Council of Mexican American Relations. Dr. Julian Nava's name first appeared in connection with a study conducted in Puerto Rico by Roger Baldwin, founder of the American Civil Liberties Union. Baldwin represented the Marshall Trust Fund, which made grants to the Texas GI Forum and the Council for Spanish-Speaking People in order to advance Mexican American civil rights causes. The *Sun* reported that the David Hidalgo case against the sheriff's department had been settled for $40,000. The CSO and the Alianza Hispano Americana had brought the case. The *Sun* also covered the case of Lawrence Amaya, 31, and Dan Casias, 38, who on May 20 were pistol whipped by a plain clothes INS officer. Amaya and Casias were charged with assault on a federal officer.

Ralph Guzmán spoke at the Eastside Jewish Community Center's Forum regarding the effects of the Walter-McCarran Act. Assemblyman Edward Elliot lectured on the same topic to the Federation of Spanish-American Voters. Elliot also condemned the Taft-Hartley Act and discriminatory insurance practices.

Generally, the attitude of elected officials toward civil rights was apathetic. The board of supervisors, for instance, delayed passage of a fair employment practices ordinance. Supervisor John Anson Ford wanted to create a Committee on Human Relations but the other supervisors opposed him. This proposal generated considerable support among progressive labor groups and minorities.

The *Citizen* reported on January 12 that ground had been broken for construction of a 2,200-unit housing tract just north of East Los Angeles Junior College. These units generated windfall tax revenues to Monterey Park, which had recently annexed the land. The *Citizen* also reported the construction of new homes for Mexican Americans in the San Fernando Valley and noted that this would add to the pull to the outskirts. Similar housing tracts had been and were being constructed in Pico Rivera, La Puente, and Covina to attract returning Mexican American Korean War veterans.

The County Regional Planning Commission approved a zoning change along the north side of the Santa Ana Freeway from approximately Atlantic to Indiana, changing the area from residential to manufacturing. On April 20, the Long Beach Freeway link was opened. Zoning was a major concern and the Belvedere business community advocated forming a chamber of commerce to help defend the community against arbitrary changes. Alex Zambrano led efforts to establish a welfare planning council in East Los Angeles.

1957

Edward R. Roybal won re-election. Politically, Roybal was the lone advocate of a fair deal for Mexican Americans east of the river. Ralph Guzmán was appointed to the American Civil Liberties Union board of directors. Guzmán also worked for relief to victims of the Walter-McCarran Act. The East Los Angeles Chapter of the ACLU gave local victims free legal services.

The *Sun* printed a series on the Walter-McCarran Act proceedings against longtime East Los Angeles resident Tobías Navarrette. The INS charged that Navarrette had been a communist during the 1930s. He appealed the deportation order to the Board of Immigration proceedings. The government called three witnesses who testified that they had seen Navarrette at a Communist party meeting almost 20 years before these proceedings. These informers also accused Navarrette of attending meetings of the Spanish-Speaking People's Congress during the 1930s. The testimony of the witnesses were contradictory and questionable, according to the *Sun*. The court ruled that the testimony did not establish fact of membership. As it turned out, the informers had been paid for their testimony. Moreover, they had themselves been deported and expected to be readmitted as a reward for their cooperation.

The CSO elected James J. Rodríguez, an official of the Butchers Union, to chair the organization. In August, the CSO announced a civic community improvement program for East Los Angeles. According to the *Citizen*, Fred Ross, the West Coast director of the Industrial Areas Foundation, and César Chávez, an IAF field representative, were involved in developing this program.

The CSO built an impressive record in its first ten years, promoting civil rights causes, opposing freeway displacement, and fighting discrimination. It sponsored forums to discuss police practices and politics, and conducted house meetings to involve community members. It also protested the new driver's license tests as discriminatory toward Latinos. In July, during its ten-year anniversary, the CSO honored past presidents Edward R. Roybal, Henry Nava, Anthony Ríos, Gilbert Anaya, and J. J. Rodríguez.

The American GI Forum received considerable coverage. The Forum's Ladies Auxiliary was headed by Ramona Morín, one of the most visible Mexican American women during the decade. It pressured local officials to name a local park after a Mexican American war hero, organized a conference on juvenile delinquency, and, with other organizations, pushed for the appointment of a Mexican American judge.

The CMAA functioned as a catalyst, uniting various community organizations and leaders. Tennis star Pancho Gonzales was elected to the board of directors of this organization, which had a reputation of admitting only leaders.

The Alianza Hispano Americana elected Enrique Nava of San Gabriel to its board of directors. Eddie Montano was elected president of the East Los Angeles Youth Council. The youth council's YES program for youths continued to operate, filling an important void.

Mexican American leaders gathered at the Casa del Mexicano to elect a Mexican American to the school board. Calling itself the East Los Angeles Committee for Better Civic Government, the group selected Plutarco García as its candidate for the Los Angeles City School Board of Education. When García lost the primary elections, Mexican American activists, led by Roybal, formed the Eastside Mary Tinglof Committee to support her for the board seat.

The Castro Scholarship Committee planned fund raising activities. A coalition of United Latin American Clubs sponsored the events that netted $3,810 for scholarships. A film was produced about the life of Armando Castro. The film told about the athlete scholar and how his life had been lost breaking up a senseless fight. That same year, six students from the University of California at Los Angeles formed the Council for Mexican American Education. These UCLA students founded a youth council panel and raised scholarship money for Mexican Americans who wanted to enter education.

The weeklies continued to report the news of social and car clubs. Groups like the Young Men's Christian Association, the Young Women's Christian Association, and the CYO sponsored these activities. On February 28, the *Citizen* ran a photo of the Panthers Club and, on June 27, it published a photo of the Royal Lancers. Many clubs were affiliated with the East Los Angeles Youth Council.

Neither the *Citizen* nor the *Sun* reported much on gang activities. On January 24, the *Citizen* noted that the district attorney was investigating brutality charges against Deputy Sheriffs Robert A. Chaney and Kenneth Y. Shirley. The two deputies had arrested Robert Salava, 27, in front of his home. Salava had a bad arm as the result of a 1946 accident. When Salava refused to put his arms behind his back, the deputies grabbed his arm and fractured it. Salava was charged with assault.

The sheriff's department clamped down on curfew laws. On March 21, the *Citizen* reprimanded deputies for firing shots at a narcotics suspect, charging that the bullets threatened a small boy's life. A *Citizen* reporter, Ron Cardiel, wrote a series of articles about the sheriff's department's night patrol. Cardiel accumulated his material while riding in a patrol car. His stories gave an exaggerated picture of Belvedere at night and made the deputies look like the stars of "Dragnet."

Three hundred and seventy drug-related bookings occurred at the Hollenbeck Station. The *Citizen* ran a series of articles by John Ackers titled "Narcotics: A Primer on Drug Addiction." A 1957 grand jury report declared narcotics out of control.

On January 3, Joseph Eli Kovner strongly condemned the destruction caused by the freeways. He especially lamented the displacement of people. On November 14, he criticized the debris caused by the San Bernardino, Santa Ana, and Golden State freeways. According to Kovner, the highway authorities had a total disregard for Eastsiders' rights. Kovner attacked construction of the Pomona Freeway and encouraged his readers to organize. The motto was "Pomona Freeway Planners, Don't Tread On Us." The *Citizen*, in contrast, did not criticize the construction of this freeway; it merely reported that the Belvedere Chamber of Commerce would discuss the issue at its January 28 meeting. The chamber named a committee to study the effects of the freeways.

Roybal met with county officials and expressed concern about the dislocation caused by projected parkways. As a result of Roybal's talks and community pressure, the freeway route was altered. However, the controversy did not end and another hearing on the Pomona route took place on October 18 at East Los Angeles Junior College.

Condemning the Chávez Ravine giveaway, Kovner wrote an October 24 editorial asking: "Will Boyle Heights be the next site of the N.Y. Yankees?" The ordinance authorizing the transfer of Chávez Ravine to Walter O'Malley passed the Los Angeles City Council and Mayor Norris Poulson immediately signed it. Chávez Ravine had been named after Julián Chávez, a laborer who arrived in Los Angeles from New Mexico in the early 1830s, settled in the ravine, and was granted the land by the Los Angeles *ayuntamiento* (city council) before his death in 1879. As the city expanded, it surrounded the ravine, which was mostly inhabited by Mexican families. In June 1957, *Frontier* magazine described Chávez Ravine as it was:

> The history of Chavez Ravine, since 1953, is the story of a helpless minority whose rights were indifferently brushed aside by a city administration responding to the real estate lobby.
>
> When Los Angeles was a young city, the rolling hills of Chavez Ravine were left undeveloped as the town spread out in the flatlands below. Without sewers, water facilities, or improved streets, Chavez Ravine became a haven principally for Mexican Americans and Mexican nationals, many of whom grazed sheep and cattle on green hills as early as 1900. A minority group with no political power, they were unable to get municipal services that would make the area a normal residential district. As the years went on, jerry-built shacks dotted the area. This naturally choice location, with hills

looking down on Elysian Park on two sides and a view of the expanding city on another, became a blighted area.

In 1949, the city contracted with the federal government to build 3,360 low-income rental units in Chávez Ravine. Only 40 percent of the ravine had housing and it was a logical site for public housing. However, real estate interests wanted the land for development. Supported by the *Los Angeles Times*, these interests pressured the city to breach the contract with the federal government. After a vicious and distorted campaign conducted by the *Times*, voters decided against public housing.

In 1953, anti-public housing forces had purged Mayor Fletcher Bowron, supporting Norris Poulson, a *Los Angeles Times* puppet, against him. The campaign coverage was lopsided, with the *Los Angeles Times* giving Poulson 1,019 inches of space versus 219 inches to Bowron.

From 1949 to 1951, the City Housing Authority, a state agency, had conducted condemnation proceedings, condemning some 160 acres. This was protested by Chávez Ravine residents. In 1951, after voters had rejected public housing, the city presured CHA to sell its land to the city, which it eventually did. By 1957, the city held deed to 185 acres in the ravine. The city had paid $1,179,203.87 for the land it obtained from the CHA, who earlier had paid $5,500,000.

Throughout the struggle, many hoped that the ravine would at least be converted into a recreational area. However, in 1956, Mayor Norris Poulson, with the downtown elite's support, set in motion a conspiracy that would bring a major league baseball team to Los Angeles. Poulson held secret talks with Brooklyn Dodgers owner Walter O'Malley. Although the formal announcement was not made until 1957, a deal was struck. In 1956, Mayor Poulson announced that a new stadium must be built in order to attract a major league baseball team to Los Angeles. It seemed to be common knowledge that a stadium would not be built in Wrigley Field, since that facility was in a Black area. On October 25, 1956, at a meeting of the Junior Chamber of Commerce, the mayor stated that he favored private construction of the new stadium. A day later, Dodgers owner Walter O'Malley sold Ebbetts Field in Brooklyn, New York for $3,000,000. The terms called for a $300,000 down payment. Two days later, Poulson announced that Chávez Ravine would be the ideal site for a baseball stadium. He stated, however, that the city, along with the Recreation and Parks Department, would have to build roads to make the area more accessible. On January 15, 1957, the Ebbetts Field sale was closed. On February 21, O'Malley purchased Wrigley Field for $300,000.

Although several other major league teams were interested in Los Angeles, Poulson flew to Vero Beach, the Dodgers' spring training site, and dealt exclusively with O'Malley. By May, the city council joined Poulson in steam-rolling the deal. O'Malley, in a secret memorandum, demanded 400 to 600 acres of downtown property. He also wanted the land to be tax-free for 200 years. On October 7, the city council passed a resolution to deed the Brooklyn Dodgers 315 acres in the Chávez Ravine. The council also agreed to up-zone the area to C-3, a change that would have allowed commercial development that was hardly necessary for baseball. The Dodgers, in return, would deed Wrigley Field to the city. The deal was expedited through the City Planning Commission, whose commissioners Poulson had appointed. The Committee to Save Chavez Ravine For People attempted to stop the deal and members circulated petitions against it.

Interest mounted as to what higher office Roybal would seek. In July, Councilman Ernest Debs declared his candidacy for the 3rd Supervisoral District. The councilman had many supporters in East Los Angeles. The incumbent, John Anson Ford, had decided not to run. Ford was a close friend to Roybal. When Ford announced that he would not seek re-election, Roybal announced his own candidacy.

The Los Angeles county supervisors were still intent on granting a dump site permit in Monterey Park. The County Planning Commission granted a zoning variance, making way for the dump. City Terrace residents appealed this decision and mobilized support. By default, they won: although dump site owners received permission to build the dump from the Monterey Park City Council and were granted a zoning variance, the dump was finally ordered closed because it caused pollution.

The East Central Area Welfare Planning Council was founded in 1957 by the Community Chest. This group was part of the county-wide Welfare Planning Council, Los Angeles Region, which coordinated three other councils. The East Central Council held its first installation of officers at the beginning of the year. Virginia Hedges was installed as its first president; Mel Janapol and Frank X. Paz were listed as first and second vice-presidents. The organization's objective was to unite all community associations, public agencies, business leaders and other sectors of the community under a coordinating body to study mutual problems and to take common stands. By April, fifty-four private and public agencies had joined the council.

The Eastside Planning Council focused on aid to youth and improvement of health and recreation services. This council approved a plan to expand Laguna Park and investigated the possibility of other civic improvements. While its recommendations were merely advisory, they carried considerable weight because of the group's leadership's influence. On April 25, the council held an area-wide committee on the "Status and Needs of Youth." The planning council vigorously protested the closing of health and welfare facilities in East Los Angeles and planned to document the need for these agencies to continue operation. Through the council's intervention, two extended day-care centers and one library remained open. The council also established an East Los Angeles Beautiful Committee, which sponsored a clean-up program. In the fall, council members discussed a study of health services. By the middle of December, the group began its own health survey. The *Citizen* and Eastside leaders believed that the council would give the community the necessary muscle to defend the area's interests. In the end, however, council members represented their own self-interests more than the community's.

In Belvedere, the construction of sidewalks, curbs, and gutters remained community issues. The Maravilla-Belvedere Property Owners Association invited Roybal and attorneys Rudolph Victoria and Hank López to their meetings. Alex Zambrano was highly active in housing matters. Pressure was placed on the supervisors for civic improvements such as new street lights, the widening of Eastern Avenue, and sidewalk construction.

1958

Unemployment worsened during the so-called "Happy Days." In March and April, manufacturing employers in Los Angeles and Orange counties laid off some 8,600 workers. Economic retrenchment took place in all industries, especially in auto, rubber, non-electrical machinery, fabricated metals, and apparels—all industries with heavy Mexican American participation. The unemployment rate hit 7.3 percent, the highest since April 1949, when it was 10.3 percent.

On January 2, the *Citizen* announced that Governor Knight had appointed attorney Carlos Terán to the newly created East Los Angeles Municipal Court. This appointment represented a victory for the Belvedere community and eastsiders planned a banquet in honor of the new judge. Meanwhile, Terán was elected president of the East Central Welfare Planning Council.

Knight received an enthusiastic reception at a Mexican Chamber of Commerce banquet, which was attended by 1,500 people. In March, the CMAA held a banquet honoring Terán and actor Anthony Quinn. Terán also spoke at a GI Forum scholarship banquet.

Attorney Henry López ran for the secretary of state post, receiving the endorsement of the California Democratic Council. Anthony Quinn served as his honorary chair. Although López campaigned hard, he did not receive adequate support from the Democratic party or its candidate for governor, Edmund G. Brown, Sr. Democrats swept state executive offices—that is, except for López, who lost by some 18,000 votes. Racism among white voters was clear. Moreover, many Mexican Americans blamed the Los Angeles County Registrar of Voters for an undercount.

Roybal's candidacy for the board of supervisors was probably the most important race for Mexican Americans in the period from 1945 to 1975. For Mexican Americans in unincorporated East Los Angeles, it signaled an opportunity to have direct representation. Roybal would check land-grab schemes that were changing land use east of the Los Angeles River. Outgoing Supervisor John Anson Ford endorsed Roybal. The primary field narrowed to Roybal and Debs. Even before the election, Debs was reported to have a "huge campaign chest." Rumor was that much of his money came from real estate developers. He was, after all, one of urban renewal's main boosters.

During the campaign, Roybal took controversial stands. For instance, he opposed Proposition 18, the state's so-called right-to-work referendum, which was strongly supported by the *Los Angeles Times*. The Eastside supported Roybal. There were, however, defections. In the last days of the campaign, a smear letter, signed by Plutarco García and falsely using Carlos Terán's name, was released to the press. It alleged that Terán did not support Roybal.

Tony Ponce, prominent in Belvedere circles, defected to Debs because the latter promised to appoint a Mexican American field deputy. As expected, the *Los Angeles Times* supported Debs, endorsing him on November 3. Roybal had earned the wrath of the *Times* because of his opposition to Bunker Hill, Chávez Ravine, and Proposition 18. Debs, on the other hand, had been head of the City Council Planning Committee since 1947 and had a pro-development philosophy.

On the first ballot, Roybal led by 393 votes, 139,800-to-139,407. Then the county voter registrar stated that a 12,000-vote error had been made. After four recounts, Debs won 141,011, to 128,994. Both the *Sun* and the *Citizen* charged the county registrar of voters, Benjamin S. Hite, with irregularities. The *Los Angeles Daily Press* excused the error as a mix-up. Hite himself blamed it on "clerical errors." Mexican Americans were not so sure. Nineteen precinct forms were missing for several days.

Debs expressed complete confidence in Hite during the four recounts. The *Citizen's* Committee for Fair Elections investigated the irregularities. Grace Davis headed the committee that included Roger Johnson, Roybal's campaign manager. The county grand jury refused to investigate charges of "excessive challenging" and intimidation of Mexican American voters at the polls. Many eastsiders and Anglo-American politicians maintain to this day that the powers in Los Angeles did not want Roybal in office and conspired to keep him out. The state assembly rackets subcommittee conducted hearings shortly after the election. Debs appeared before the committee and denied charges that from 1943 to 1954 he had aided the re-zoning schemes of real estate interests associated with William Camp, the dump site tycoon, who allegedly had ties with organized crime. Special interests donated substantial funds to Debs, which he used in his supervisorial campaign. Debs denied peddling his influence to these developers.

The Debs election was confirmed on November 25. His parting speech reaffirmed his devotion to the Bunker Hill deal, stating, "I hate the slums and the people who make money in the slums." However, Debs neglected to mention the private interests who made profits in redeveloping slums or where the people who lived in the slums went after they were removed. Debs immediately appointed Anthony Alvarez Ponce as one of his four deputies. Meanwhile, the Committee for Fair Election in the 3rd Supervisorial District was supported by Ignacio Lozano of *La Opinión*. Neither the *Sun* nor the *Citizen* reported on the outcome of this effort, which eventually died out.

Estevan Torres, education and political action director for Chrysler Auto Workers Local 230, led a political and voter education drive in East Los Angeles. The CSO was active in voter registration and there was the usual rhetoric about the Mexican American potential.

The CSO was the leading Mexican American organization during 1958. Tony Ríos was elected CSO president. Besides voter registration, the CSO· conducted citizenship classes. It also discussed the Walter-McCarran Act and opposed unfair INS deportations.

The GI Forum took the initiative in pressing supervisors for a park in Belvedere. It also became active in politics and sponsored a candidates' night. In May, the forum held its first state convention, choosing Los Angeles for the event. At this convention, delegates also decided to hold the forum's national convention in Los Angeles. During its state convention, the forum adopted resolutions against the importation of labor (e.g., the bracero program). It also resolved to favor fair employment legislation. In October, the forum hosted Texas State Senator Henry B. González. Throughout the year, Raúl Morín continued as one of the forum's main spokespersons.

The *Citizen* and *Sun* differed on urban renewal. Arthur J. Baum, publisher of the *Citizen*, was elected chair of the Regional Planning Commission. Kovner and the *Sun* criticized this commission.

The *Citizen* opposed a study by the County Planning Commission that recommended construction of a jail in Belvedere, which required the displacement of 460 families. Property owners and Supervisor Ford opposed the proposed jail site. Ford suggested that Chávez Ravine be used instead. The East Central Welfare Planning Council also lobbied against the jail's construction in Belvedere. The jail site issue surfaced at the same time that the drive for a new Belvedere park gained momentum. The *Citizen*'s attitude was summed up in a story headline: "Take Homes from

Families to Make Room for Prisoners.'' The Parks-not-Prisoners Committee was formed in May. The supervisors appointed an advisory committee to recommend an appropriate location.

In July, Belvedere received another shock. The board of supervisors approved plans for a girls' detention home in East Los Angeles. The community immediately reacted by opposing this potential encroachment. Simultaneously, an advisory subcommittee recommended that the central jail be built in East Los Angeles, targeting Belvedere-Maravilla for a possible site. Property owners vehemently opposed this move and protested to the supervisors. A confrontation was averted when the full committee did not select Belvedere.

The County Planning Commission approved the Pomona Freeway's proposed route through Belvedere. No significant organized opposition to the Pomona Freeway was evident. In Boyle Heights, citizen groups protested the Golden State Freeway. The *Sun* did an adequate job of covering these events and informing its readers about land encroachments. The Golden State was the fourth of five freeways to mar Boyle Heights.

In October, the Welfare Planning Council listened to the results of a "Mental Health Survey Report" by Dr. Louise Seyler. The council reviewed committee reports of community concern. George Russell of the Bank of America chaired its Urban Renewal Committee. Judge Carlos Terán presided over the council.

In an April 10 editorial, Kovner wrote: "Land Hungry Group Wants Piece of Boyle Heights." Kovner warned that Leland J. Fuller intended to build a $20 million medical and shopping center in Boyle Heights. Fuller, a resident of Boyle Heights since 1946, headed the Boyle Heights Urban Renewal Committee. Kovner investigated this group, but could not find any such organization at the address on the letterhead; it was not even listed with the telephone company.

Kovner, concerned over a recent report that called Boyle Heights a slum area, contacted Roybal, who assured him that the classification pertained only to city inspections. Kovner was suspicious, believing that the classification might justify Boyle Heights' urban renewal. The *Sun* publisher wrote that the residents had endured poverty, unemployment, police harassment, and the freeways—and that now they were expected to accept the encroachment of urban developers and White Memorial Hospital. Kovner protested the "Boyle Heights Invasion." And on May 1, he published a letter from Fuller to Mayor Poulson regarding housing, hospital expansion, and commercial development.

Boyle Heights' proximity to the civic core made the land prone to redevelopment schemes. On April 14, Roybal received a letter from Dr. T. Gordon Reynolds, M.D., an associate professor of Medical Evangelists (affiliated with White Memorial), who complained that he could not find adequate housing near the college. Reynolds assured Roybal that this was "a very big problem indeed" for himself and the residents and interns on 24-hour call. He added that Boyle Heights should be redeveloped for two reasons: first, it was one of the city's oldest sections and consequently rundown; second, "our new freeways will all pass this section and unless we redevelop this section our visitors will enter our fair city receiving one of the most unfavorable impressions imaginable as they pass through the ragged back-yard fences, the broken down garages and the sight of sagging kitchen doors."

In May, Kovner wrote: "The Story Behind the Story of Boyle Heights Urban Renewal Committee Landgraft." Seven days later, the *Sun* publisher added that the new shopping and housing center proposed by Fuller would not create jobs, would not raise the standard of living of the community, would not provide more and better housing, and would not eliminate a blighted area. According to Kovner, developers would erect sterile cells for transient hospital workers. He stressed that in the end residents would be removed, adding that many of these people's homes were fully paid for and that, if displaced, these people could not find similar housing elsewhere. They would be, he pointed out, at the mercy of the banks and savings and loan associations.

In the *Citizen*, John F. Méndez published a form letter sent to him from the business agent of the College of Medicine of White Memorial. The letter stated the college's intentions to expand so that it would be better able to serve people. The business agent wrote that White Memorial wanted to purchase the property directly without having to use the "Right Of Eminent Domain," a law passed by California that provided for the condemnation of property for necessary expansion by institutions serving the public interest.

Although G. T. Anderson, president of the College of Medical Evangelists, denied any association between the College of Medical Evangelists and Leland J. Fuller, it was obvious that the two were linked together. On June 5, Kovner asked: "Is There a Hospital Town in Boyle Heights' Future?" The publisher explained that Boyle Heights had always provided a community for its residents, especially for its senior citizens, and he feared that this was now in jeopardy. Boyle Heights property owners fought the encroachments. Their motto was "Remember Bunker Hill."

On June 12, Kovner exposed Sears, Roebuck & Co.'s interest in urban renewal. He quoted from a booklet published by Harry N. Osgood, director of the urban renewal division of Sears, which gave the ABC's of the Sears urban renewal strategy. The booklet clearly stated that Sears supported urban renewal because it wanted to protect its investment and because growth of slums around its property threatened its interests. The *Sun* also published a letter from Sears to its executives that expressed the company's "great economic and civic interest in urban renewal . . ." and concern that the area's blighted condition provoked an "alarming rate of juvenile delinquency and crime." The letter reminded Sears executives that "we cannot afford the corollary effects of unrest, blight and slum formation around our stores. . . ."

In this same editorial, Kovner linked Mayor Norris Poulson to urban renewal. Poulson had created a Citizen's Urban Renewal Advisory Committee to which he appointed persons compatible with his philosophy on "development." In his editorial, Kovner asked if it were a crime to be in a low-income group and questioned why Sears had never complained about the number of liquor stores and bars in Boyle Heights. Finally, Kovner questioned the government's definition of a slum.

On July 31, Kovner wrote: "I Need an IBM Machine." In this editorial, he explained that the supervisors had condemned 480 Belvedere homes north of Brooklyn between McDonnell and Mednick Streets. Kovner also linked the San Bernardino Freeway expansion to the Boyle Heights Urban Renewal Committee. He claimed that the net effect of these activities was the dispersal of thousands of people. The Property Owners Committee for the Preservation of Boyle Heights, which was under the leadership of John F. Méndez, held mass meetings during this period.

By the end of the year, Kovner reported that Fuller and his Boyle Heights Urban Renewal Committee had withdrawn its application to the city to designate the area an urban renewal district. Kovner warned that the siege would continue.

Redevelopment of sections of Boyle Heights was part of the city's master plan since the early 1940s. The Department of City Planning in 1944 designated 325 acres bounded roughly by the Pomona and Santa Ana parkways and the Prospect Park area. The plan called for the elimination of most local roads with added recreational facilities. Originally, Prospect Park was targeted for public housing. However, the entire southwest quadrant was reserved for the White Memorial Hospital. (Eventually, half that quadrant was occupied by the hospital complex.) Density was to be expanded from 32 persons per acre to 41. By 1950, plans were revised and the acreage impacted called for 87 acres.

Two other areas scheduled for redevelopment by 1950 were Ficket Hollow (Whittier Blvd., Marietta, 8th Street, Boyle) and Concord-Bernal Hollow (Concord, 4th, Lorena, Santa Ana Freeway, Marietta, Whittier, Mott).

In October 1958, the City of Los Angeles became so blatant in its dealings in Bunker Hill that DeWitt McCann resigned from Poulson's urban renewal committee. "As a direct result of the Bunker Hill situation," McCann said, "I don't want to be responsible for taking one man's private property through the use of eminent domain and giving it over to another private individual for his private gain." Attorney Phil Silver charged that Bunker Hill distorted the development act and had no legal precedent.

Events leading to the McCann resignation are a study in the abuse of power.

Before structurally changing Bunker Hill's land use, authorities justified the demolition by classifying Bunker Hill as a blighted area. The section encompassed 73.31 acres and included 404 buildings, 346 of which were residential. A city report labeled Bunker Hill as riddled with crime and vice and plagued by juvenile delinquency and severe health problems. The average per annum income in the area was $1,618 and apartments rented for $30.00 per month. Real estate interests described Bunker Hill as a fire trap.

The downtown powers lobbied the city council to make Bunker Hill land available to developers. The power to condemn land, for the use of private developers, had been given to the local government by Title I of the Housing Act of 1949. Moreover, Title I gave cities substantial federal assistance in slum clearance and redevelopment. By 1958, the federal government was allocating between one and two billion dollars annually for this purpose. It also gave free technical assistance for redevelopment.

Los Angeles, along with other municipalities, had lobbied the federal government for broader powers in the use of eminent domain. Under the 1949 law, the city was not specifically granted the right to expropriate land from one individual so that another could profit. The Housing Act of 1954 broadened the provisions of Title I. The act authorized federal assistance for slum and urban blight prevention through rehabilitation and condemnation of blighted and deteriorated areas. It authorized similar assistance for the clearance and redevelopment of slums. In sum, the 1954 act initiated urban renewal, broadening the objective from clearance of slums to area redevelopment and rehabilitation. In 1954, the U.S. Supreme Court reaffirmed the right of Congress and the state legislatures to use the power of eminent domain for anything it wished, provided it was for the "public good."

In 1956, an amendment to the Housing Act liberalized Title I even further, authorizing payments to individuals, families, and business concerns for moving expenses and property loss resulting from urban renewal. A year later, another amendment increased the size of capital grants for urban renewal, and FHA loans were extended to private developers. In the process, the practical criterion for receiving federal aid for slum clearance changed from using land for public use to using it for public good. Strictly speaking, the land also did not have to be a slum area. This allowed city planning to seize homes or other private property from "Citizen A" to resell to private "Citizen B" at below cost. Redevelopment was no longer confined to the use of eminent domain for public use. In a letter to Roybal on September 24, 1957, William H. Claire, assistant executive director of the California Redevelopment Agency, described urban renewal as the "cooperative effort of government and private enterprises to eliminate existing and prevent future blight in urban areas." The definition of blight was almost always left up to local government. Redevelopment was defined as the acquisition, relocation, demolition, site preparation, and land disposition for rebuilding in accordance with officially approved plans. Both urban renewal and redevelopment were part of the same process.

In 1954, under the joint leadership of Mayor Norris Poulson, Councilman Ernest Debs, and CRA director William T. Seson, Jr., the city applied for a grant to fund Bunker Hill's redevelopment. The *Los Angeles Times* conveniently forgot that three years prior it had called public housing "creeping socialism." The paper praised the leadership of the city council, which approved the application, 14-to-1, on November 15.

The initial Bunker Hill plan called for a $40 million cat-and-mouse game. An estimated $33 million of the money needed to purchase and develop the land would come from a federal loan. The city would contribute $7 million, and then it would sell the developed property to real estate developers, who would pay an estimated $19 million. This money would then be repaid to the federal government, which, in turn, would forgive the remaining $14 million. In other words, developers would receive a $21 million subsidy.

The CRA planned to build 20,000 units in tower-type apartments designed for a higher rent class. The downtown powers, including Pacific Mutual Insurance, already owned property in the affected area and pushed redevelopment. The plan's approval did not end the controversy, and Roybal consistently opposed the deal. The committee, opposing Bunker Hill redevelopment, encouraged residents to "Resist the Rape of our Downtown Community," as a pamphlet stated. The Downtown Businessmen's Association conducted a well-financed campaign, advocating Bunker Hill's redevelopment and contending that the Hill was "an integral part of the city of Los Angeles, and of Downtown in particular." On September 14, the *Christian Science Monitor* dubbed redevelopment in Los Angeles the "Battle of Bunker Hill."

The arguments against the project were essentially three. First, the project was chiefly a tax subsidy to private developers. Second, it was an abuse of eminent domain, using it to take away one individual's property for the profit of another. Lastly, it was an abuse of the Redevelopment Act, which stated that federal funds could be used only in cases where the project could not be accomplished without public intervention.

By 1958, Bunker Hill development costs jumped to $65,545,691. Land sales were projected to generate $42,785,000, leaving a balance of $22,764,691. The federal government would forgive $15,176,461, and the city would assume the rest. Developers were also eligible for low-interest-guaranteed FHA loans. The downtown powers were impatient to begin their $300 million redevelopment program and greatly resented hearings on the matter.

Along with Bunker Hill redevelopers, supporters of the Chávez Ravine deal pushed for a voters imprimatur of the project. Meanwhile, the *Los Angeles Times* pushed Proposition 18,* and Roybal ran for supervisor. After a heated campaign and considerable manipulation of the news coverage, the voters turned down Proposition 18 and approved the Dodger deal.

Exactly how much the Dodger giveaway cost is not known. However, the city certainly could have attracted a major league baseball team without the gigantic subsidy to O'Malley. For instance, in a similar situation, San Francisco kept control of its land, floated a $5 million bond issue, built a stadium and parking lot on less than one-third of the acreage given to the Dodgers, and then paid the bond issue from the revenues received. In contrast, Los Angeles gave the Dodgers 315 acres outright, which was an estimated $6 million subsidy. Attorney Phil Silver pointed out that baseball was a business and that the property was not for public use. Silver also found objectionable the gift to the Dodgers of oil rights.

The *Los Angeles Times* and the downtown powers took the issue to the voters. On June 3, people went to the polls, after having been bombarded with pro-downtown propaganda. Trade unions were convinced that the deal would create jobs. Taxpayers' committees were formed to promote a "yes" vote on Proposition B. (" 'B' is for baseball. A 'yes' vote is for the kids!")

A voter breakdown by regions on the table below reveals that the minority areas voted for the proposition, while many of the more affluent districts voted against it.

Channel 11, owned by the *Los Angeles Times*, ran baseball specials just before the elections. A Dodger telethon featured Joe E. Brown, Debbie Reynolds, Carmen Cavallero and Ronald Reagan. To many, free baseball in L.A. was here to stay.

---

*This proposition was a union-busting measure which would make California an open-shop state.

VOTER RESPONSE BY COUNCILMANIC DISTRICT*

		Yes	No
1st	(San Fernando Valley)	26,609	27,140
2nd	(San Fernando Valley)	22,236	25,533
3rd	(San Fernando Valley)	22,756	31,429
4th	(Wilshire area)	22,736	21,152
5th	(Wilshire-Westwood)	27,000	23,929
6th	(Westchester Area)	24,260	23,283
7th	(San Fernando Valley)	23,347	26,425
8th	(South Central Section)	24,678	14,364
9th	(Eastside)	24,625	11,138
10th	(West-Central Area)	27,205	18,718
11th	(Pacific Palisades)	20,948	20,876
12th	(Downtown)	20,204	12,954
13th	(Silver Lake—Lincoln Heights)	18,817	19,187
14th	(Eagle Rock Area)	20,439	26,264
15th	(Harbor District)	22,524	18,333
		348,384	321,724
	Absentee	3,299	4,174
	Total	351,683	325,898

1959

On January 8, Kovner began a series of articles on urban renewal and Poulson. Kovner criticized the mayor's remarks made at a December 30, 1958, Town Hall luncheon. "If you are not prepared to be part of this greatness (urban renewal)," Poulson had said, "if you want Los Angeles to revert to pueblo status . . . then my best advice to you is to prepare to resettle elsewhere. . . ." Kovner accused the East Central Area Welfare Planning Council of being Poulson's tool, stating that the urban renewal committee was dominted by pro-renewal people. For example, George Russell, the manager of the local Bank of America branch, chaired the planning council's urban redevelopment committee. What especially angered Kovner was that this body had surveyed the residents' at-

---

*The Los Angeles Times, July 2, 1958.

titudes towards the condition of their homes. The survey, according to Kovner, was biased and posed questions whose answers would appear to justify renewal in Boyle Heights.

The survey had not been sent out by Russell but by another member of the committee, N. E. Surbaugh, manager of Sears, Roebuck & Co. Kovner had already exposed Sears' interest in urban renewal. A report by Councilman James C. Corman quoted David D. Herferd of Sears in Los Angeles: "Six-hundred billion dollars of our national wealth is in cities. In these cities, slums take 45 percent of the local budget and contribute 6 percent of local income. Sears, Roebuck's California tax bill is 10 percent of Sears' total tax bill." According to Sears, its business future depended on healthy urban areas. According to Corman, "all Sears management personnel must have a broad and uniform concept of urban renewal. Sears conducts regional workshops to discuss urban renewal." Corman added, "They [Sears] are actively participating in the urban renewal program."

In addition to Russell and Surbaugh, Edwin J. Remboldt of White Memorial, and J. E. Nesbitt of Pacific Telephone and Telegraph served on the committee. The men represented special interests and pushed urban renewal. Sears had actively supported the freeway construction and, through its influence, freeways did not disturb the company's complex near Olympic and Soto. Neither was the *Los Angeles Times* building on Boyle disturbed. According to Kovner, Russell supported the designation of Boyle Heights as an urban renewal district. Moreover, the Bank of America had boosted Proposition 18. Property owners protested Sears' survey, demanding that it be stopped. Roybal intervened and the survey was terminated. Speaking before the Property Owners' Committee for the Preservation of Boyle Heights, the councilman said, "I want no Bunker Hill here." He did agree that a study dealing with the Eastside's problems was needed.

Surbaugh, who was new to the area, stated that he had wanted solely to determine how much the freeways contributed to the deterioration of Boyle Heights housing and that he had not intended to justify urban renewal. Kovner responded by stating that if Surbaugh were unfamiliar with Boyle Heights, then he should not have plunged the council into such a controversy. Kovner again attacked Sears' ABC booklet on urban renewal. He chided Surbaugh, warning him that Boyle Heights would not become another Bunker Hill because the residents' life savings were tied up in their homes.

On March 5, Kovner criticized the difference between force and freedom in land acquisition for public purposes. He suggested that in order to avoid the fate of Bunker Hill, perhaps it would be better for Boyle Heights to secede from Los Angeles and to incorporate as Franklin Delano Roosevelt City.

On June 25, Kovner again condemned the survey. He called the *Times*'s anti-inflation program phoney, especially since the prosperity of both the *Times* and the city depended on government spending. Kovner singled out government spending in Bunker Hill and Chávez Ravine as examples of the *Times*'s hypocrisy. The *Sun* publisher called urban renewal a "Cold War," naming Ann Street, Sawtelle, Bunker Hill, Temple, Monterey Hills, Naomi, Standord, and Trinity—where a collective of 50,000 persons were being displaced—as the front lines.

The *Citizen*'s perspective on the Welfare Planning Council differed from the *Sun*'s. *Citizen* publisher Art J. Baum was very active in community affairs and had considerable land and investments in East Los Angeles. He chaired the County Planning Commission and favored the planning council, which conducted studies on topics such as health and urban renewal. These studies greatly influenced government policy. The *Citizen*'s coverage of the planning council was more complete than the *Sun*'s. For example, it wrote that in addition to Russell, Surbaugh, and Remboldt, the three other planning council members of the Urban Renewal Committee were Marie Melton of Belvedere Hospital, John Nixon, and Dean Hardin of the All Nations Community Center. This information allows the reader to put together a more complete picture of interests. For instance, the Eastside All Nations Foundation was a Protestant social service agency. George Russell was chair of its finance committee. In fact, Russell was extraordinarily active: he was treasurer of the planning council and a member of the Big Brothers, the Red Cross, and the Community Chest.

To depress local property values as low as possible, the city refused to issue building permits to residents in Bunker Hill. The Community Redevelopment Agency director ordered Gilbert Morris, superintendent of Building and Safety, to not enforce the building and safety codes in order to keep the property value low.

Due to this negligence, a four-story apartment building at 300 South Figueroa Street collapsed, almost killing the 200 residents. Councilman Roybal accused Poulson of playing politics with human lives.

The siege of Chávez Ravine continued and, on May 14, Kovner reported that sheriff's deputies bodily removed the Arechiga family from its home. Immediately, the family's two houses were demolished. Kovner singled out the *Times* and the *Los Angeles Mirror* for distorting the Arechigas' efforts to keep their homes. In an emotional city council session, protestors hurled insults at Councilwoman Rosalind Wyman for her part in the siege.

The Arechigas were merely a symbol. Other families in Chávez Ravine had undoubtedly lost as much as they had. However, the Arechigas made the last dramatic stand. The CHA had condemned the Arechiga property in 1951 to make room for public housing. The Arechigas had fought the condemnations but, in 1953, a superior court judge ruled against the family, appraising their two houses and three lots at $10,500 (a private appraiser had valued the property at $17,500). Eviction proceedings began in 1957 and the eviction was ordered in 1959.

In May, the bulldozers entered the ravine. Manuel, 71, and Avrana, 66, along with two of their daughters and five grandchildren, resisted. Joined by friends and relatives, the Arechigas attemped to stop the bulldozers, which finally levelled their homes of 36 years. Councilman Roybal was present. "This is not morally right and is very cruel," he said. "I will bring it up in City Council on Monday in an effort to determine why this decision to move these people was so abruptly put out." As she was bodily removed, Mrs. Arechiga shouted in Spanish, "Why don't they play ball in (Mayor) Poulson's backyard—not ours!" The family pitched tents near their homes, stating that they did not have other housing. Trespass notices were handed to them but the Arechigas refused to leave. Finally, under threats that their grandchildren would be taken from them because of a violation of health laws, the Arechigas left.*

The television coverage definitely affected public opinion. Viewers watched as authorities dragged the Arechigas from their homes. Roybal vehemently defended the Arechigas, likening the

---

*Previous efforts to evict the Arechigas in August 1957 had failed.

city's actions to those of the Spanish Inquisition and Nazi Germany. Meanwhile, the Chandler publications feared that public opinion had turned against the Dodgers.

The press launched a relentless media attack on the Arechigas. On May 13, the *Times* branded the Arechiga supporters agitators and attacked Roybal for misrepresenting the facts. The daily claimed that the Arechigas had lived tax free on their property since 1953 and condemned the whole affair as "television dramatics." The *Mirror-Times* headlined: "Evicted Chavez Family Owners of 11 Homes. Property Valued at $75,000." According to the Chandler papers, the Arechigas were frauds who made a fortune on rents while claiming poverty. The *Times* described the Arechiga struggle as "patently dishonest."

Poulson commended the *Mirror* on May 14: "If I have any sympathy for the Arechigas at all, it is for the children—the youngsters who were forced into ramshackle living conditions for hypocritical reasons." Councilwoman Wyman, who lived in Bel-Air, expressed her opinion: "Naturally, I was surprised to learn that the Arechigas have extensive land holdings. It was represented to the City Council that these people were not only homeless, but very poor. I hope that they will make arrangements to move into one of their properties as soon as possible."

The Arechigas' so-called extensive holdings were as follows: a house in City Terrace, with a mortgage payment of $90 per month, which was rented for $60; a house in Los Angeles, rented to a daughter; three houses belonging to another daughter and her husband; two houses owned by another daughter; a house in Santa Fe Springs owned by a daughter; three Chávez Ravine houses, one of which was condemned and another that was owned by their son. These children were all adults. Nevertheless, public opinion was changed dramatically and the press manufactured rumors that the evictees had been coached. But the May 21 letter from Roybal to Mrs. Leone Thornberg indicated the councilman's feelings:

> The Arechiga property, including three lots, zone C-2, and two houses, was appraised at $17,500, but the Court awarded them $10,500, ignoring the value placed on the property by a trained appraiser. The Arechigas do not feel that $10,500 is adequate compensation for three lots within a stone's throw from the City Hall, and frankly, I agree with them.

Roybal concluded, "I think the disclosures do not justify the actions of the sheriff or the city." In a May 22 letter to Mrs. G. Brown, Roybal wrote: "The fact that the family and in-laws of the elder Arechigas have homes is not pertinent. Certainly the homes of my relatives do not belong to me."

A postscript to the Dodger deal: on April 6, 1962, after he was no longer in office, Poulson boasted that he had professionally orchestrated the Dodger deal by using an emotional promotion. Revealing his secret dealings with O'Malley, he acknowledged that he had been supported by John Gibson, Roz Wyman, and downtown businessmen to promote the deal.

Meanwhile, the *Citizen* and the *Sun* differed on whether the East Los Angeles incorporation was necessary. Kovner strongly opposed incorporation, while the *Citizen* apparently supported it. On June 4, the *Citizen* reported that the Belvedere Chamber of Commerce would discuss the incorporation issue. The City of Commerce had petitioned to incorporate and, apparently influenced by this move, a Belvedere-East Los Angeles group also filed a petition to incorporate. This incorporation group was headed by prominent Anglo-Americans. The move was partially in response to efforts to annex areas of East Los Angeles by cities of Monterey Park, Montebello, and Alhambra. If the City of Commerce incorporated, then East Los Angeles would be surrounded by cities wanting to annex it in bits and pieces.

The incorporation of East Los Angeles gained momentum. The Western Opinion Research Center reported that 75 percent of Belvedere residents favored incorporation. Petitions were circulated by a group called the Citizen's Committee for Incorporation of East Los Angeles. Bill Sutherland, a property owner, served as chair. Sal López, a realtor, Ray Mora, a Democratic party activist, Leopoldo Sánchez, an attorney, and Manuel Veiga, Jr., a mortician, served on the committee and helped to prepare a feasibility study. If successful in its efforts to incorporate, East Los Angeles would become the fifth largest city in the county. The group had 50 days to gather the necessary signatures. Manuel Aragón, president of the Belvedere Democratic Club, joined the drive.

Residents of City Terrace held meetings on the proposed incorporation. City Terrace still had a high percentage of Anglo-American and Jewish property owners, who were expected to oppose incorporation of East Los Angeles. Meanwhile, the California State Board of Equalization released a study demonstrating that East Los Angeles would have enough income to operate independently. The county supervisors seemed supportive in the initial stages. During this period, the *Citizen* gave relatively little coverage to the drive itself. In November, a hearing was held to discuss the incorporation of the City of Commerce.

Kovner's reaction to incorporation was cool. On June 18, the *Sun* reported: "Kovner Reports Incorporation Move . . . See No Real Need to Make E.L.A. into a City." Kovner downplayed the drive for "home rule," stating that citizens already had a voice in governmental and police services. According to Kovner, incorporation would result in financial hardships for residents. A possible explanation for Kovner's opposition was that his heart was always in Boyle Heights; he did not understand the sense of community east of Indiana Street and perhaps feared this move since cityhood for East Los Angeles would have effectively separated it from Boyle Heights.

On July 30, Kovner wrote "Anatomy of a Steam Roller," complaining that real estate interests promoted the promise of "home rule" and "lower taxes." The *Sun* charged that this was political steamrolling spearheaded by Frank Winston and Bill Sutherland. In August, Kovner again named Bill Sutherland as the man behind incorporation, attributing support for incorporation to the fear of annexations by Downey and the City of Commerce. Kovner claimed that Downey was annexing land that nobody wanted and that the City of Commerce was not even a city. Kovner concluded by stating that he had spoken to Roybal who, according to Kovner, was not impressed by incorporation efforts.

Mexican Americans wanted representation on the Los Angeles City School Board of Education. They supported Mrs. Lucy Baca, who was active at the county and state levels in the Parent Teachers Association. She also served as vice president of the East Central Area Welfare Planning Council and of the School Board's Office Number 3. Mexican Americans joined the "Committee for Better Schools," which was attacked by racist elements. James Cruz and Ramona Morín co-chaired the East Los Angeles Better Schools Committee. The election was at large, which meant that it included all of the city of Los Angeles and a substantial portion of the county. Baca forced Charles Reed Smoot into a runoff but lost on May 26, 201,065-to-176,825.

Dr. Paul M. Sheldon released a study on Mexican American student dropouts. The study showed that 47 percent of the Mexican American high school students dropped out in their sophomore year. Ironically, *Sun* columninst John F. Méndez blamed parents for not sacrificing enough for their children.

Ground was broken for the new Utah Medical Clinic, which cost $150,000. The name of Eugene Obregón, a Mexican American Congressional Medal of Honor winner, was approved for the new East Los Angeles Park. The supervisors also approved a contract for a park in City Terrace. Meanwhile, Belvedere street improvements lagged behind the rest of the county.

The Council of Mexican American Affairs established a house of delegates to coordinate the different Mexican American organizations. Judge Terán served another term as the CMAA's president.

The group heavily involved itself in youth problems. It issued a report recommending a state youth commission to sponsor research on youth problems. The report was signed by Arthur Rendón, Carlos A. Terán, Ralph Poblano, and Theodore Rodríguez, all of whom belonged to the CMAA's Committee on Youth. The report stated that, in 1957, 21 percent of the arrested youths in Los Angeles City were Latinos and that "unlawful behavior on the part of young people represents a social failure that challenges all the resources of society." Edmund G. Brown, Sr., a candidate for governor in 1958, had endorsed the proposal but, once in office, did little to push it. In 1959, the CMAA's recommendations were incorporated into Assembly Bill 24. The association proceeded to lobby for adoption of this bill.

Mexican American political expression was channeled through the Democratic party. James Cruz, an official of the Brick and Clay Workers Union, was appointed to the Los Angeles County Democratic Central Committee as a representative from the 40th Assembly District. The city council approved the appointment of Dr. R. J. Carreón to the Los Angeles City Police Commission. By the end of the year, the state FEPC opened an office in East Los Angeles. Former Los Angeles Supervisor John Anson Ford headed the unit. The political influence of Mexican Americans, however, had not increased during the Eisenhower years. Ed Roybal remained the community's sole representative in the county of Los Angeles.

SUMMARY

Too many assumptions have been made about the Eisenhower years. Some historians have concluded that nothing much happened, that it was a period of high unemployment following an unsuccessful war. In the case of Mexican Americans in East Los Angeles, however, the Eisenhower years were full of activity as the community struggled against the Walter-McCarren Act and "Operation Wetback." The *Sun* and the *Citizen* offer insights into efforts of the Community Service Organization and other groups to protect the civil liberties of the victims. Unfortunately, coverage of "Operation Wetback" and the bracero program was spotty in both weeklies. In fact, both publications appeared to be divorced from the nation's entire civil rights movement. For instance, only scant references were given to the *Brown* case of 1954.

Urban renewal was a national trend that affected the urban poor throughout the United States. In essence, the developers in large urban centers had carte blanche to redevelop large sections of the cities. The designation of certain areas as "blighted" became a prelude to removal of the "problem." Through this procedure, developers realized huge fortunes at public expense. Unlike the case of public housing, rent for the new units were far beyond the poor's means. Under the guise of alleviating and removing blight, urban renewal became a subsidy for the rich.

Bunker Hill was a blatant example of urban renewal abuse. However, the most sensational instance of robbing from the poor to give to the rich was Chávez Ravine. The poor in the ravine did not have a chance against the combined powers of government and the ruling elite. The home-field advantage did not favor Chávez Ravine residents, whom the *Los Angeles Times* vilified for defending their homes.

The role of the downtown elites—large corporations such as Sears and the *Los Angeles Times*—and their manipulation of area-wide citizen groups has yet to be fully explored. Neither has the impact of the freeway systems on redevelopment schemes in and around East Los Angeles been researched to the extent it warrants. The *Sun*, ever concerned with issues of importance to Boyle Heights, displayed marked hostility toward redevelopment. The *Citizen*, which was focused primarily on unincorporated East Los Angeles, took an often less vocal approach to the issue. Thus, we have a much clearer picture of the redevelopment siege in Boyle Heights than in East Los Angeles. Further research is crucial. Additionally, a major study of the *Citizen*'s publishers—and their financial interests—would lend insight into the process and consequences of redevelopment.

In general, the *Sun*'s coverage was not as complete as the *Citizen*'s, which employed a larger and more professional staff. But Kovner's paper was more accessible to community organizations, which used the *Sun* as a sort of community bulletin board. For example, the *Citizen*'s coverage of youth was more extensive than the *Sun*'s. Apparently, merchants and residents in Belvedere were much more active than those in Boyle Heights in attempting to find solutions to the gang problem. The Belvedere Coordinating Council, the East Los Angeles Youth Council, and various community agencies did impressive work in establishing the Federation of Social and Car Clubs and in attempting to find employment for youth.

Edward R. Roybal became a legend in his own time. He was the only city politician who consistently fought urban redevelopment, condemned police brutality and championed civil rights. His unsuccessful 1958 supervisorial race left many unanswered questions about the election's honesty as well as about the power of the downtown ring. Excluding his victories, the community remained politically powerless.

Despite community powerlessness, however, expectations increased. For example, Carlos Terán's appointment to the municipal court was almost pathetic, because eastsiders, hungry for a hero, treated it as a coronation. Nevertheless, it was evident by the end of 1959 that a community was emerging. And coverage in both the *Sun* and the *Citizen* pointed to much clearer patterns of concern than at the beginning of the Eisenhower years.

4

The Sleeping Giant: 1960–1962

This chapter is based on the same sources as Chapter 3. At this point, a reading of the articles in the *Sun* and the *Citizen* listed in the second half would be of value. The Roybal Newspaper Scrapbooks are also packed with information. Materials at the UCLA Special Collections Department are not as beneficial because they essentially cover Roybal's career in the city council.

Movement had begun long before the 1960s in the communities east of the Los Angeles River. Since the early 1950s, Mexican Americans had symbolized their political potential by calling themselves the "sleeping giant." For some Mexican Americans, this image kindled hope. For others, it was a threat that the Mexican Americans would no longer tolerate being ignored. Essentially, it represented an emerging awareness of the group's growing numbers. Many believed that this growth would be followed by increased participation in the nation's institutions.

The impact of national politics on the communities east of the Los Angeles River has not been fully explored. The Black confrontations of the 1950s undoubtedly influenced many Mexican Americans, as did Fidel Castro's successful Cuban Revolution in 1959. Moreover, the fight against renewal projects that destroyed more housing than they rebuilt politicized many Chicano activists. As mentioned in the previous chapter, the 1950s had been anything but "Happy Days." There was the Black civil rights struggle. The National Committee for a Sane Nuclear Policy (SANE) marched to "Ban the Bomb." And the New Left emerged, adding to the radicalization of Americans. In 1960, the creation of the Student Nonviolent Coordinating Committee (SNCC) and later, the emergence of the Students for a Democratic Society (SDS), broke with the conformity of the 1950s. In all, the 60s saw an escalation of the sit-ins and non-violent direct activity that shook America.

The effect that John F. Kennedy's 1960 presidential campaign and the Viva Kennedy clubs had on the communities east of the Los Angeles River has not been well researched. It is true that Kennedy's campaign committee was the first to nationally recognize the voting potential of Mexican Americans. It is also true that the Kennedy people, along with Chicano activists, helped to organize a regional network of Viva Kennedy clubs. Nevertheless, there had been independent Mexican American activism before this time. The CSO and other Chicano organizations had registered voters in the late 40s and early 50s. Additionally, the Mexican American Political Association had been established in 1959. The narrowness of the Kennedy victory only dramatized the importance and future potential of the Mexican Americans in the United States.

It is important to recognize that registration drives and attempts toward political organization had pre-dated Kennedy in the area east of the river. Political scientist Ralph Guzmán* points out that, in the early 1950s, the Los Angeles Community Service Organization (CSO), along with other groups, maintained the Los Angeles Chicano community's voting strength at above 150,000 registered voters on a year-by-year basis. In the late 1950s, this effort suffered when the Industrial Areas Foundation, led by Saul Alinsky, withdrew funds and full-time organizers from CSO. This caused a decline in voter registration. In a study of 14 selected census tracts in Los Angeles County, Guzmán found that registration was 17,948 voters in 1958, 18,588 in 1960, 18,187 in 1962, and 13,989 in 1963 (representing a 23.1 percent drop from 1958). Guzmán attributes the drop to an absence of continuous commitment to Chicano voter registration. In Los Angeles County, registration had to be kept up on a year-by-year basis because failure to vote in the general election resulted in the registered voter being dropped form the rolls. The gap resulting from the withdrawal of CSO funds was, for a time, filled by the Viva Kennedy effort and the Roybal campaign for Congress in 1962. However, a vacuum soon followed.

Failure to reach the expectations of 1960 and refusal of the "Sleeping Giant" to awaken did a great deal to shake the Chicano community. Once the 1960 election was over, President Kennedy did not deliver on his pre-election promises and very little patronage filtered down. In California, specifically, there was discontentment with Governor Edmund G. Brown, Sr., whose campaign promises were also forgotten. Surely the publication of the 1960 census, which left little doubt that Mexicans were deprived, added to the frustration. In California, there was a gap for Spanish-surnamed males in education: Anglos had a median of 12.2 years of school completed, non-whites 10.6, and Latinos 8.6. Moreover, if they lived in Los Angeles County, only about five percent of Spanish-surnamed males worked in professional or technical occupations; the vast majority were in blue collar or service occupations.

Research indicates that Mexican American nationalism increased during the early 1960s. Many activists were frustrated by the lack of attention paid to them. Some were also disgruntled by the attention given to Black Americans. And, as mentioned,

---

The Political Socialization of the Mexican American People (New York: Arno Press, 1976), pp. 212–213.

discontented Mexican Americans had attempted to lessen their dependence on the Democratic party by forming MAPA in 1959. Increasing numbers became involved in that organization, engaging themselves in political, rather than social and cultural solutions. The victories of Leopoldo Sánchez for the municipal and then superior court, and the victories of John Moreno and Phil Soto for the assembly, were part of this process. However, in spite of this new political activism, the weeklies demonstrate that the community's main fights still remained the nitty-gritty local battles that most scholars have ignored.

Between 1960 and 1962, urban renewal remained a major threat, even though it reportedly was changing under a liberal administration. Interwoven with urban removal were the annexations of parts of East Los Angeles by surrounding cities. Eastsiders supported incorporation of East Los Angeles as a city. First, it was a means of defending territorial integrity. Second, it was a means of achieving "home rule."

As Mexican American political activism increased, police–community relations worsened. Efforts were made to ameliorate the tension through annual institutes sponsored by the National Conference of Christians and Jews. But the heart of the problem was the reaction of political leaders like Police Chief William Parker, who viewed Mexican Americans and other minorities as second-class citizens. As the civil rights movement gained momentum nationally, Mexican Americans became more conscious of their rights. The success of anti-colonial wars in the Third World unsettled social control at home. Therefore, the rise of Fidel Castro and the U.S.'s inability to control him stiffened the resistance of men like Parker to change at home. As minorities became increasingly assertive, the Parkers reacted with increasing hostility.

THE CHRONICLE
1960

On January 21, Joseph Eli Kovner criticized Congressman Chet Holifield for not being concerned with where and how federal funds were spent. Kovner sarcastically called the congressman a liberal. At the crux of the conflict were urban renewal abuses, which Holifield and other politicians condoned. These politicians either favored or had a stake in redevelopment. Some did not want to alienate the powerful trade unions that had an interest in large building programs which urban renewal made possible. Holifield and other elected officials were also rumored to have made fortunes in enterprises such as dump sites.

On February 11, Kovner again sounded the alarm: "The Bulldozers are Coming, Confiscations Under Urban Renewal." In the *Sun*, Robert M. Angier, chair of the Committee for Public Morality, warned against the evils of urban renewal. Councilman Edward R. Roybal took a more cautious view, remaining adamant against blatant expropriations like Chávez Ravine and Bunker Hill but also admitting that the area had problems. Kovner attended luncheons with other newspaper editors and publishers to discuss urban renewal. He appeared to be the sole publisher opposing uncontrolled redevelopment. The *Sun* vowed that Boyle Heights would not become another Bunker Hill. Kovner wrote that Bunker Hill homeowners were forced to pay taxes while awaiting removal. They could not improve their property, since improvements added value to their homes. According to Kovner, this project had already displaced 20,000 persons.

In January 1960, the *Citizen* reported on Monterey Park's attempt to annex some of the most desirable sections of East Los Angeles. Monterey Park wanted prime residential and industrial property, which would increase its tax base.

Meanwhile, the Citizens Committee of Residents of Belvedere-East Los Angeles announced an incorporation plan that adopted the Lakewood Plan. The Lakewood Plan had sparked interest in incorporation throughout the county of Los Angeles. In 1939, there were 45 cities in the county; from 1939 to 1945, no new cities were incorporated. Then, in 1954, Lakewood became a city under a unique arrangement that allowed it to buy municipal services from the county. The arrangement was crucial for many small communities. The Lakewood Plan sparked an incorporation fever throughout Los Angeles County. By July 1957, 23 new communities were or had just recently been involved in incorporation proceedings.

The Belvedere-East Los Angeles Committee drew up new boundaries. These included the area from Atlantic Boulevard to Indiana Street and Floral Drive to Telegraph Road. Excluded from this new plan were Bella Vista and City Terrace since, by law, the 1960 plan had to differ from the 1959 proposal. The committee members planned to annex the excluded territories later.

Incorporation supporters promised not to raise property taxes in the event that East Los Angeles became a city. The group was renamed "Citizens Committee for the Incorporation of East Los Angeles." On the whole, *Citizen* coverage was supportive. On March 3, the publication explained the advantages of incorporation. Advocates began a petition drive to obtain the 6,000 signatures necessary to place the initiative on the ballot.

The citizens committee, comprised of prominent real estate and lay people, had five goals: 1) civic improvements with no new taxes; 2) new job opportunities for residents; 3) elimination of air pollution; 4) improvement of community spirit and cooperation; 5) home rule for residents. According to the *Citizen*, the First Street merchants favored incorporation. But some opposition developed among the Whittier Street merchants and outright hostility came from the Atlantic Boulevard sector of the Eastside business community.

The *Citizen* printed a county report listing the income and expenses that the new city would incur. According to the *Citizen*, the new city would accumulate an initial $500,000 surplus. The Belvedere Chamber of Commerce endorsed incorporation in early May. On July 21, the *Citizen* endorsed incorporation, stating that September 16 was the target date for East Los Angeles' independence. The *Citizen* criticized many East Los Angeles residents for being too lazy to vote for self-government.

On July 28, the *Citizen* supported incorporation in another editorial. This article named Joseph Galea as chair and Ricardo Rubio as vice-chair of the citizen committee and reported that the committee planned to formally file incorporation papers the following week. The proposed city would encompass 3.8 square miles. According to the *Citizen*, Fr. William G. Hutson of the Catholic Youth Organization was the main force behind incorporation. (Hutson had assisted in the incorporation of Pico Rivera in the 1950s.) Henry Porras and F. Fernández Solís were also active on the citizen committee. By mid-August, the petitions phase was completed and the county officials examined the signatures. On September 1, the *Citizen* reported: "Cityhood for East L.A. In Other Hands: Measure to Go on Ballot, Public Hearings Tuesday Morning." The supervisors ordered a hearing for October 20. Heated debates took place on the proposed boundaries. The

Atlantic Street merchants, alledgedly anti-Mexican, did not want to be included in the proposed Mexican American city. The *Citizen* reported that the new city would consist of 17,000 dwellings and have a population of 57,000. The property tax evaluation would be $27,661,000. The hearings were postponed until December.

The East Los Angeles Improvement Association led opposition to incorporation. Supervisor Ernest Debs supported incorporation and denied that "gangster elements" were involved with the drive. A decision on incorporation was again delayed until January 1961. The *Sun* was surprisingly quiet about incorporation.

The *Sun* and the *Citizen* also reacted differently to racist remarks made by Los Angeles Police Chief William Parker on January 26 before the U.S. Civil Rights Commission. Parker was asked to explain why 40 percent of the arrests involved Blacks and 28 percent involved Mexican Americans. "Some of these people [Mexicans] were here before we were," he responded, "but some are not far removed from the wild tribes of Mexico." Parker further testified that you could not "throw the genes out of the question when you discuss behavior patterns of people." While it had at first requested an explanation from Parker, the Los Angeles City Council retreated when Parker appeared before it explaining that he had not meant "wild tribes" and that what he had intended to say was that some elements had not assimilated as quickly as he wished.

When Roybal insisted that Parker apologize, the police chief refused. He alleged that his statement had been made in the past tense and referred to his use of "wild" as "regrettable." In a television interview, Parker blamed his remarks about Latinos on the provocation of a "Negro Commissioner."

The Mexican American Citizen's Committee of Los Angeles, led by Frank X. Paz, demanded that Parker be fired. The committee held a meeting on February 7 at the Casa del Mexicano. Meanwhile, Parker involved himself in running verbal battles with California Attorney General Stanley Mosk over the police chief's unlawful bugging of activists' telephones.

Edmundo González of the Mexican Consul addressed a strong letter to Parker on January 28, 1960, protesting "a statement which [was] . . . derogatory to the Mexican people." González conceded that the quote had appeared in only one of the local daily newspapers and that Parker possibly had been misquoted. The consul then gave the chief a history lesson, explaining that Mexicans were proud of their Indian heritage. "Disclaiming, like you, any special knowledge of sociology," he added, "I for one am inclined to believe that crime among Latin Americans in California's major cities is not linked with 'wild Indian tribes,' but rather with the reasons outlined in Governor Brown's report to the same U.S. Commission on Civil Rights, discrimination and lack of opportunities." González concluded that he objected to the LAPD's use of "Mexican" to describe a race of people.

Parker's actions prompted five hundred Eastside residents to attend a protest rally. The Community Service Organization (CSO), the Federation of Spanish-American Voters, the League of United Latin American Councils (LULAC), the GI Forum, the Young Democrats, the Associated Mexicans of California, the Mexican Chamber of Commerce, the National Association for the Advancement of Colored People, the ACLU, and the Unión Cívica of Wilmington, among others, attended the rally. The body demanded Parker's censure. Police Commissioner Dr. R. J. Carreón, however, refused to participate and criticized the unauthorized use of his name. Carreón added that he had listened to Parker's explanation, accepted it, and wanted the matter dropped.

The *Citizen* published "Editorial of Pride and Prejudice" by John P. Ackers, who commented that nothing could be achieved by firing Parker. He labelled the chief's statement "anthropological ignorance" and urged that "ignorance" could not be destroyed through violence. Criticizing the committee, Ackers wrote: "We think that this committee is in danger of further strengthening the already strong prejudice in the minds of both Anglos as well as Mexicans—the notion that Latins can't control their tempers." The *Citizen* reported that 14 of the 15 council members accepted Parker's explanation and that Roybal alone refused.

Roybal remained insistent and Councilman John Gibson called him out of order. Roybal questioned the police crime wave statistics. He conceded that there was an increase in crime, particularly in juvenile delinquency and narcotics. But he explained that what was not mentioned was that the Hollenbeck precinct had a concentration of 20.1 persons per acre, University division 21.6, and Newton 19.2—and that all three surpassed other LAPD precincts. Considering the heavy concentration of people in these areas, Roybal concluded that crime was not out of proportion.

The daily newspapers supported Chief Parker. On February 1, the *Los Angeles Herald* wrote: "It is unfortunate that such a furor has been [made]. . . over a remark by Chief of Police William H. Parker before the United States Commission." The editorial said that Parker had been quoted out of context: "We believe that Councilman Edward Roybal made a mountain out of a molehill and brewed a tempest in a teapot when he raised the issue of Chief Parker's remark before the City Council." The *Herald* called the incident "regrettable."

On February 9, the *Los Angeles Times* wrote: "Demagoguery Loses a Round." The editorial read: "The most offensive kind of demagoguery in the United States, which suffers from all kinds, is the manipulation of minorities for political purposes." The *Times* attacked Roybal for his behavior in the city council, accusing him of inciting citizens of Mexican descent in order to unite them behind a "hate figure." The *Times* praised Parker.

As in the case of the Arechiga family of Chávez Ravine, the press intentionally manipulated public opinion against Mexican Americans and distorted the issue. Roybal received bags of hate mail. "You attack Chief Parker," one postcard began, "yet he has every reason to rate the Mexican way down because so many are dope peddlers, dope users, thieves, baby gangsters, etc."

In spite of the controversy over crime and the tensions between the police and the Mexican American community, relatively little was reported about these issues in either the *Sun* or the *Citizen*. At a June press conference at the Biltmore Hotel, a number of organizations announced a conference to deal with the police abuse. The ACLU, the NAACP, and members of the Mexican American community called for a police review board. They criticized the present system which referred such cases to the Bureau of Internal Affairs. The police department simply could not accurately investigate itself. In July, two hundred persons attended the conference at the Sidney Hillman Labor Hall, endorsing plans for a Model Police Review Board.

As early as March 1, these organizations had proposed an ordinance to create a police practices review board. The ACLU helped formulate the review board ordinance. Captain Edward Davis, vice president of the Los Angeles Fire and Police Department Protective League, called the proposal "shocking." Davis red-baited its supporters, calling them communists. "It is interesting to note," Davis added, "that some of the promoters of the scheme are people who are attempting to set aside the conviction of Morton Sobell, convicted of conspiracy to commit espionage against the government of the United States. Sobell was convicted with Julius and Ethel Rosenberg. The plan's promoters were also against loyalty oaths for public employees." Davis went so far as to tie the ACLU to organized crime and gangster Mickey Cohen. Davis called the movement to establish police boards a national conspiracy and linked the leaders to the Communist party.

On July 21, the *Citizen* reported that the sheriff's department would enforce juvenile curfew laws. The CSO conducted a police misconduct survey. Unfortunately, little more of substance was printed on the topic or on the results of the survey.

Compared to previous years, news coverage on youth was sparse. Dr. Paul Sheldon, a professor at Occidental College, had conducted a study on the Mexican American dropout. Because generally so little had been published on the Mexican American in education, the study attracted considerable attention. Sheldon was invited to address numerous community organizations about his conclusions.

In his column, "Pan American Panorama," John F. Méndez wrote about a campaign to prevent Mexican Americans from dropping out. Henry López spoke on the problem at a meeting of the Community Fund for Education. Non-Mexican American organizations, including the Ebell Club, discussed the education of Latin American citizens.

Youth conferences were held by agencies such as the East Central Area Welfare Planning Council. And the Castro scholarship remained a symbol of the still unfulfilled potential of Mexican American youth.

On the political front, Governor Edmund G. Brown Sr. appointed Carlos Terán to the superior court. Some 300 persons attended Terán's induction ceremony, with a usual round of testimonials following. Soon after, the governor spoke at a CMAA testimonial for Terán. Ricardo Montalbán participated, along with 600 other guests. Terán spoke at a White House Youth Conference and soon afterwards accepted a trophy on behalf of East Los Angeles Community Chest volunteers. Eastside expectations were expressed in a September 1 letter to the *Citizen* stating that Mexican Americans had previously been ignored as voters and that this would no longer be the case.

Terán's municipal court vacancy caused a scurry for that office. The judicial campaign was covered almost exclusively by the *Citizen*. Six attorneys, including Joseph Galea and Leopoldo Sánchez, filed for the seat. Many East Los Angeles residents were livid when Brown appointed attorney Howard Walshok to fill Terán's unexpired term. Many Mexican Americans felt that Brown had betrayed them. When the California Democratic Council met in Fresno on April 22 through 25, they formed the Mexican American Political Association and elected Councilman Roybal as the first chair. Among those who participated were César Chávez, Ingacio López, and J. J. Rodríguez.

Meanwhile, Walshok campaigned for a full-term municipal court seat on the issue of narcotics control. The primary narrowed the field to Walshok and Leopoldo Sánchez. Although Sánchez led by 453 votes, he did not receive a majority of the votes. In the ensuing runoff, Sánchez enjoyed the support of the Mexican American community; the only defection of note came from attorney John Argüellos, who supported Walshok. Anglo-American organizations, including the East Los Angeles/Montebello Bar Association, also endorsed Walshok. Nevertheless, Sánchez upset Walshok for the municipal seat.

One of the truly amazing realities about East Los Angeles is how quickly political wounds healed. The *Sun* and most Mexican American organizations had vehemently condemned the Dodger deal two or three years previously. But in February, the GI Forum was already considering sponsoring a Dodger-Mexican All-Star baseball game. By 1960, Supervisor Ernest Debs also appeared to be forgiven. He appointed Félix Ontiveros to the County Human Relations Commission. Ontiveros was the past president of the Mexican Chamber of Commerce, the Beneficencia Mexicana, the Pan American Optimist Club, and the Council of Mexican American Affairs.

Moreover, although Brown had not kept his campaign promise to appoint Mexican Americans in any significant number, the Mexican American Political Association formed another in a long series of advisory committees to the governor. Meanwhile, the CMAA invited Brown to keynote its October 20 banquet.

The Council of Mexican American Affairs was still active, finalizing plans for a house of delegates. In June, its officers were elected from among 17 organizations. The CMAA's approach was to hold banquets honoring prominent citizens in order to raise money to support issues. The CSO managed to register 35,589 Latino voters. Herman Gallegos was elected national chair of this hard-working organization.

Most eastsiders supported the Democratic party presidential candidate, John F. Kennedy, and formed Viva Kennedy clubs. The CSO reported that it expected 100,000 Mexican Americans to vote in California. U.S. Senator Dennis Chávez from New Mexico campaigned for the Viva Kennedy clubs. The Kennedy campaign, meanwhile, supported Leopoldo Sánchez in his successful bid for the municipal court.

Eastsiders packed the East Los Angeles College football stadium to support Kennedy. Organized labor's Committee of Political Education (COPE) financed activity east of the river. When Kennedy was elected, Mexican Americans understandably expected attention from the new president, especially since Latino voters had heavily supported him. The narrow victory also demonstrated the impact of the Latino vote—a bloc that had been ignored for many years.

The East Central Area Welfare Planning Council was the most influential association in East Los Angeles. County supervisors ordered a master plan for the county. In addition, they approved plans for the new East Los Angeles court house building.

According to the coverage in the two weeklies, citywide drug abuse was a major problem. Many residents felt that narcotics had reached crisis proportions and demanded a no-parole policy for second offenders. Governor Brown recommended Nalline tests for addicts, predicting that this would eliminate narcotics violations. A narcotics conference was held in the Eastside on February 11. In April, the governor named Attorney Arthur Alarcón to head the State Narcotics Commission.

1961

Throughout 1961, freeway construction continued at a rapid pace. At the end of 1960, California acquired right-of-way for the Pomona Freeway and, in 1961, began widening the San Bernardino Freeway. These projects meant the displacement of thousands of eastsiders.

On March 2, Kovner editorialized: "Give Me Land . . . Lots of Land." The publisher was angry at a letter sent to residents by the Great Western Development Corporation, offering $18,000 to homeowners if they would sell. Kovner accused Great Western of attempting to panic residents into selling their property. Roybal echoed that the real objective of local redevelopment was to depress property values in East Los Angeles and Boyle Heights. In this way, outside interests could convert the Eastside into a skid row and eventually purchase the land cheaply. He also attacked Loma Linda University's plans to expand its Boyle Heights campus.

In Boyle Heights, Kovner criticized the rezoning of Fourth and Soto Streets to make room for the Safeway Market Center. Meanwhile, the Community Redevelopment Agency proceeded to finalize the redevelopment of Bunker Hill. Technically, the CRA used its power to waive federal requirements as to local funding. By the end of June, 1961, the CRA had relocated a total of 150 residents and businesses. Other controversial programs included Ann Street, Temple Street, Monterey Hills, and the Naomi-Trinity-Stanford projects.

On January 12, the board of supervisors agreed to let the voters decide the issue of incorporation. At a meeting of the Lady of Lourdes' Holy Name Society, Supervisor Frank Bonelli stated that "the effort of East Los Angeles is a step in the awakening of the sleeping giant."

Leading the drive for incorporation were attorneys Joseph Galea and Leopoldo Sánchez, sales executive Richard Rubio, Roman Catholic priest William Hutson, real estate man George Gibson, venetian blind manufacturer Henry Porras, and CYO executive secretary Joe Vargas. Apparently, the supervisors and Art Baum, former owner of the *Citizen*, had changed their minds about supporting incorporation: on January 8, 1961, the *Los Angeles Times* identified Baum as the unofficial leader of the anti-incorporation forces. Baum stated that he was not against incorporation but that he did not approve of the new strategy. For example, he objected to the exclusion of City Terrace and the section east of Atlantic Boulevard to the Montebello line.

The 1961 incorporation sparked interest, once the measure qualified for the ballot. The supervisors set a special election for

April 25. East Los Angeles had 13,301 registered voters. Seventeen candidates filed for the city council. Armida Tellez and Josephine Woods were among those who qualified for the seats. The *Citizen* ran a weekly "Know Your Council Candidates" column with a biography of each of the candidates.

Incorporation supporters bitterly attacked the AFL-CIO's Committee of Political Education (COPE) for not endorsing cityhood for East Los Angeles as it had for the City of Commerce. Many Mexican Americans believed that COPE wanted to protect business and commercial interests and that labor leaders feared a Mexican American majority in East Los Angeles would upset its pro-construction policies. They charged that COPE wanted a master plan for East Los Angeles to encourage construction in the area. This would provide jobs for union members, who were not necessarily Mexican American. The GI Forum and most Mexican American organizations endorsed cityhood and home rule, which by this time was a popular appeal. To this end, the citizens' committee endorsed Frank Solis, Josephine Woods, Tim Mestas, Louis J. Kerpec, and William Ramírez for the city council.

In counterattack, COPE alleged that the incorporation would lead to substandard wages for police and fire personnel. Ironically, however, the fire department supported incorporation. A partial explanation for COPE's opposition was that unions generally preferred to deal with larger units. William Bassett, secretary-treasurer of the Los Angeles Federation of Labor, and George O'Brien of the International Brotherhood of Electrical Workers, led the opposition. J. J. Rodríguez and his secretary, Eileen Hernández, supported the federation's leadership and opposed incorporation. Robert M. Angier, chair of the Committee for Public Morality, called incorporation a trap, fearing that developers would gain more control of the area. The *Citizen* gave considerable coverage to the drive in the waning days of the election.

The *Sun* ran an editorial: "Let's go over Briefly the Danger of Incorporating ELA Into a City: Vote No!" When 46.3 percent of the voters turned out, the final results were 2,563 for incorporation, and 2,844 against—incorporation of East Los Angeles failed by only 281 votes. The top vote-getters were Frank Solis and Armida Tellez, who received 2,919 and 2,409, respectively.

Critics of incorporation charged that one of the important factors contributing to the effort's defeat was the internal division within the citizen's committee. According to critics, many members were more concerned with their own political careers than with cityhood. During the election, the issue of home rule was obscured by internal fights between the candidates. This apparent opportunism contributed to community disenchantment. Opposition to cityhood by county officials also caused voter confusion, as did consolidation of many precincts. Moreover, leaders made the mistake of not attracting prominent business, intellectual, and labor people. The Whittier Boulevard Merchants Association openly opposed incorporation. Some even alleged that Father William Hutson's participation caused controversy. Certainly, opponents availed themselves of the opporutnity to interject the issue of religious domination of the Eastside.

Another impediment was the suspect role of the supervisors. Although Ernest Debs was supposedly neutral, many critics claimed that he worked behind the scenes against this particular drive. The Los Angeles County Regional Planning Commission also opposed incorporation. This partially explained Baum's opposition, since he was a prominent member of the commission and had close ties with Debs. In addition, Elizabeth Snyder, past chair of the Democratic State Central Committee, worked openly against home rule for East Los Angeles.

Roybal's position on the city council was secure, his candidacy never threatened. His reports to his constituency were published in both the *Sun* and the *Citizen*. Some politicos expected Roybal to receive a high level appointment in the Kennedy administration. In March, Roybal announced that $7 million in public works was slated for the 9th Councilmanic District. As expected, he easily won his re-election bid.

In the Los Angeles mayoral race, Norris Poulson was challenged by Sam Yorty, who was then a liberal. Poulson symbolized the Dodger deal and urban renewal. Moreover, he was the *Los Angeles Times'* man in city hall. The *Sun* did not endorse a candidate in the mayoral race. Neither candidate received a majority in the primary, which necessitated a runoff. On June 14, the *Sun* announced: "Fighting Yorty Beats Out Mayor Poulson."

Educators spoke at the Belvedere Coordinating Council meeting about the growing problem of the defacement of school property. Graffiti was a growing concern among business leaders and residents and surfaced as a topic at the meeting of the East

Los Angeles Civic Association. In February, a panel discussed Mexican American youth at the National Conference of Christians and Jews.

Youth and unemployment were popular topics reported by the weeklies. The State Department of Employment announced that East Los Angeles would be part of a gigantic employment study. The CMAA remained at the forefront and explored the possibility of creating youth work opportunities.

A teachers' institute was held at Griffith Junior High School. More and better recreational facilities were recommended as a possible solution to growing juvenile delinquency. Professional interest also increased in the area of narcotics. From the coverage, it is not clear whether this notoriety was induced by conditions in the Eastside or reflected national concerns. On February 11, 500 people attended an Eastside citizens conference on narcotics. Recommended solutions included the treatment of addicts as an alternative to punishment. Several more conferences on narcotics were held in the next months. The dialogue involved a large cross section of the Eastside's professional leadership at a November conference.

The election of Leopoldo Sánchez to the East Los Angeles municipal judiciary represented a victory for the Eastside. Sánchez had bucked the political establishment and won. He made the usual rounds of testimonials. At a luncheon for Governor Edmund Brown, Sr., Sánchez received a standing ovation. The *Sun* printed the full text of the judge's speech, in which he had praised the governor for his legislative record but admonished the Democratic party for not supporting Mexican American candidates. Sánchez specifically criticized the governor for his own dismal record in appointing Mexican Americans to important posts and his lack of support for Latino candidates.

The speech did not go by without controversy. Reynaldo Ochoa wrote a letter to the *Sun*, stating that he found Sánchez's remarks shocking. Ochoa wrote that he was proud to be an American and that positions should go to the best qualified person, regardless of ethnic background. Robert Arambula replied to Ochoa, rebuking him for implying that Sánchez was an agitator. He stated the Mexican Americans were not asking the governor to look solely at national ancestry but at ancestry combined with qualifications. Arambula labeled Ochoa's letter a gross misrepresentation of the facts.

Many Mexican Americans had expected President Kennedy to appoint Judge Carlos Terán to an envoy post. When this did not materialize, disenchantment set in. Locally, Yorty appointed Richard Tafoya to his staff. Statewide, MAPA pressured the governor to appoint Mexican Americans to office. Increasingly, MAPA became the vehicle for political expression among activists who also maintained membership in other community associations. This political organization took an interest in zoning questions and other community issues. Its 40th Assembly District chapter was one of its most progressive, closely aligning itself with labor groups. For example, it supported Local 26 of the Longshoremen & Warehousemen's Union in a lockout by McLaughlin Distributors.

Despite its importance, political reapportionment did not receive sufficient coverage in either the *Sun* or the *Citizen*. Democratic incumbents gerrymandered assembly and congressional districts to ensure their own elections. Belvedere-East Los Angeles was divided into three assembly districts and three congressional districts.

In June, Roybal declared his intention to run for Congress. The councilman believed that Mexican Americans needed representation at the national level. Dr. Francisco Bravo was appointed to the Los Angeles Police Commission.

The GI Forum sponsored awards banquets and other community events and hosted candidates for various local, state, and federal offices. Nationally, César Chávez headed the CSO, which specialized in protecting the rights of non-citizens and lobbied a pension bill to extend benefits to them. After successfully lobbying this bill through the legislature, CSO held seminars to educate non-citizens as to their rights under the new law. CSO also held a reception for Henry B. González, who had recently been elected U.S. Congressman from Texas. Finally, the CMAA launched a drive to raise $50,000 for operating expenses. This drive was endorsed by the Los Angeles County Federation of Labor.

Protests against the use of eminent domain to acquire land for Obregón Park continued. Two hundred people attended meetings and heard Debs promise a "fair deal" for the property owners, stating that the park site had been selected before he became supervisor. Residents circulated petitions opposing the condemnation of homes to build the park. Robert Carbajal pleaded that more information should be furnished to the community concerning the construction of public projects. Property owners were also concerned about massive rezoning plans for East Los Angeles. While homeowners opposed this rezoning, merchants and realtors supported it.

The Community Council for Greater East Los Angeles was formed after the incorporation effort failed. The council opposed massive rezoning by the County Planning and Zoning Commission. Meetings were held and attracted hundreds of community people. They vehemently opposed the rezoning of residential property and the condemnation of hundreds of homes to build the seven-acre Obregón Park.

Richard Rubio headed the community council, which met in October to discuss the possibility of another incorporation drive. That same month, Rubio was appointed to the County Planning Commission. This suggests a possible link between the planners and incorporation supporters. Meanwhile, the residents east of Atlantic Boulevard voted against annexation to Montebello.

1962

Zoning hearings were held pursuant to applications for massive zone changes from R-2 to R-3 in East Los Angeles. Community protests forced the Los Angeles Planning Commission to defer to ruling on the proposed changes. Meanwhile, the county studied population changes and how they would affect the area.

Kovner's nemesis, George Russell, was elected president of the East Central Area Welfare Planning Council. Russell's election indicated a definite council bias toward urban renewal. Plans for Obregón Park proceeded rapidly and, by April, one-half of the land parcels had been purchased.

The East Central Area Planning Committee issued a report on housing and economic development. This committee should not be confused with the East Central Area Welfare Planning Council, established in 1957. The committee was established in 1962 as part of the County of Los Angeles' Regional Planning Division.

Dr. E. Sheldon Dunlap chaired this new group, which encompassed roughly the same area as the council but dealt specifically with problems of housing, transportation, and other neighborhood concerns.

Like the council, the committee took a regional approach to area-wide problems. It coordinated the efforts of many small cities and parts of Los Angeles city and county and conducted population and land use studies. It reviewed general and master plans for zoning, transportation, and public utilities data and it assessed guides for future development. The committee centralized regional planning because the expansion of the 1950s had permitted industrial and residential land use to take place side by side. Moreover, the committee contended, the area experienced a loss in population because of land use changes from residential to commercial/industrial uses. This trend was intensified by freeway expansion through densely settled residential areas.

White Memorial Hospital and its affiliate, Loma Linda University, pushed a scheme to make massive zone changes in Boyle Heights in order to expand its Loma Linda University Medical School campus. The Los Angeles City Planning Commission approved rezoning 100 acres of Boyle Heights land. The Committee for the Preservation of Boyle Heights fought the proposed changes. Attorneys Al Song and M. Park represented the preservation committee. Stella Díaz was vice president and the leading spokesperson of the group. The committee circulated petitions and presented them to the City Planning Commission. Members questioned the good faith of the commission, which seemed intent on favoring the interests of White Memorial. On August 8, Roybal called a community meeting at which approximately 100 people confronted a White Memorial representative who insisted that the hospital needed space for parking.

The Temple project was supported by Mayor Sam Yorty. Bordered by Glendale Boulevard, Second Street, and the Harbor and Hollywood freeways, the project was adjacent to Bunker Hill. A high percentage of Mexican American families lived there. The project was still in the planning stage but had been approved by the City Planning Commission. Heated meetings were attended by standing-room-only audiences. At these meetings, residents questioned the constitutionality of urban renewal. The Temple

community had been designated a study area in 1951. Rebecca
Tuck criticized the Community Redevelopment Agency and
blamed the *Los Angeles Times* and the downtown department
stores for the Temple project, saying that they wanted wealthy
customers. Once completed, the rents would increase to $200
and $250 a month. Actual evictions took place during this
controversy.

The most blatant land grab was proposed by Supervisor Ernest
Debs and Councilwoman Rosalind Wyman when they arranged
a swap involving Hazard Park in East Los Angeles for federal land
in West Los Angeles. The plan called for a Veterans Administration hospital to be built near the University of Southern Califor-
nia/Los Angeles County Hospital complex. The city would, in
turn, construct tennis courts for the affluent of West Los Angeles.
Although Yorty criticized Wyman's actions as a publicity stunt,
he supported the swap. Wyman justified the trade by alleging that
few children used the park. Wyman explained that she had not
informed the city council of the plan because of an oversight.
Meanwhile, Roybal and Mexican American organizations such as
the GI Forum opposed the giveaway. Enraged by the proceedings,
Kovner wrote a poem denouncing the treachery of the city council. The struggle for Hazard Park would last for the remainder of
the decade.

A report exposing conditions in the Eastside was released. According to this report, the area was densely populated, had a high
concentration of industry, and enjoyed little green space—all of
which impacted disfavorably on youth and quality of life. Moreover, as in the case of Obregón Park, when a facility was built,
people, not industrial blight, were displaced.

At this time, Monterey Park moved to annex a 100-acre portion of East Los Angeles. Its city council held pre-zoning hearings.
Almost simultaneously, the City of Commerce proposed annexing
eight industrially zoned blocks along Telegraph Road, from Atlantic to Kern. This would yield high tax revenues. The East Los
Angeles Community Council warned the Eastside community of
these annexation threats. Residents also complained about the
pollution that the billboard alley along the Santa Ana Freeway aggravated. By October, Monterey Park was ready to annex 75 acres.
Also by this time, purchase of the land for Obregón Park had been
finalized. Naturally, all this activity caused concern. Not unex-

pectedly, Richard Rubio announced another attempt to incorporate East Los Angeles.

On June 19, Councilman Karl Rundberg introduced a resolution to the Los Angeles City Council, commending the police department and attacking Roybal for supposedly making a "disturbing verbal attack" on Parker. The council and the mayor were staunch Parker supporters. Evidently, Los Angeles politicos and power brokers resented Roybal's defense of police victims. The American Legion withdrew an invitation to Roybal to review a July 4 parade because the councilman supported a group advocating a "Sane Nuclear Policy."

Councilman Edward R. Roybal officially announced his candidacy for the new 30th Congressional District. This generated considerable speculation as to who would run for Roybal's council seat, were he to win the congressional race. Although Roybal had a viable opponent in the Democratic party primary (Loyola University professor William Fitzgerald), he won with the support of the community.

When Roybal won the runoff election in November, the expected scramble for his council seat began. The Mexican American Political Association (MAPA) called a special meeting at the Alexandria Hotel to endorse a candidate for the city council. Roybal presided, Juan Acevedo acted as vice president, Judge Leopoldo Sánchez chaired, and 150 delegates attended the confab. Roybal cautioned that all organizations in the district should participate in the community candidate's selection, since the 9th Council District was no longer Mexican American. (Due to the city council's reapportionment in 1961, Blacks now had a voting edge.) Richard Tafoya received 82 endorsement votes and Josefa Sánchez placed second.

Representatives from labor, Mexican American organizations, property owner groups, and politicos attended the Alexandria Hotel affair. In spite of this wide representation, Kovner criticized the meeting, observing that it was by invitation only and an all Mexican American event. He reported that Roybal had begged delegates not to take the mock vote because it would create dissention.

When Roybal won his congressional seat, he extracted promises from his fellow council members that they would not appoint anyone to fill his seat and instead allow the voters to decide.

Roybal wanted to avoid an open Mexican American–Black fight. By the end of the year, however, rumor had it that council members had forgotten Roybal's words of caution and were planning to appoint a Black to the vacated seat.

Governor Brown was honored by the Mexican American community on May 3 at the Los Angeles Breakfast Club. Brown had successfully defeated Richard M. Nixon for the California governorship. In the election's closing hours, Nixon sent the Mexican American voters a carefully worded letter, inferring that MAPA supported his candidacy. This incident indicates that MAPA had become somewhat important in the political milieu.

Political activity, according to the *Sun* and the *Citizen*, increased and more Mexican Americans ran for political office. John Moreno and Phil Soto were successful candidates for the assembly although other candidates mostly lost in the Democratic party primaries. Generally, however, Mexican Americans were more visible in the County Central Committee.

1962 was also an active year for the CMAA, the CSO, and the GI Forum. The CMAA continued as an issue-oriented organization, holding conferences on employment and other topics of major concern to the residents east of the river. The CSO engaged in important work with the elderly. And the forum elected Judge Sánchez as its president. Significantly, it held a testimonial honoring Mary Orozco of California who, according to the *Sun*, was the first and only Mexican American woman attorney practicing law. Another event of interest was that Eileen Hernández, an organizer for the Pacific Coast International Ladies Garment Workers, was appointed to a top position in the Fair Employment Practices Commission. Further, the Armando Castro Scholarship Committee held its 8th annual fund raising event.

Almost as a footnote, the *Sun* reported on October 4 that Sgt. Jesús Mejía and Sgt. Hector Guevara of the Los Angeles Police Department had spent three months training local police in the Dominican Republic. The officers told of the need for a special school to train police to deal with communists and riots.

SUMMARY

In 1960, the Spanish surname population had increased in Los Angeles County from 311,294 in 1950 to 624,292. About one-fourth of the Latino county population lived in the Eastside.

Overall, the county had a potential of 256,800 Spanish-surname voters. The actual number registered to vote in the county, however, was only about 20 percent. Still, the potential gave hope to activists that the "sleeping giant" would awaken and become a force in county and city politics. The middle-class leadership was not able, however, to convert this political potential into a political reality. Gone was the basic idealism that drove Community Service Organization (CSO) volunteers into the barrios throughout the late 40s and 50s to register literally anyone over 21 who could breathe. According to Professor Ralph Guzmán, MAPA was more inclined to selectively registering precincts that promised the highest returns for selected candidates.

Professional politicians cared little about potential and, although the Mexican American population increased dramatically and deserved representation, incumbents gave little priority to creating Mexican American assembly or congressional districts. In fact, the Los Angeles City Council took the vote away from Mexican Americans by diminishing the percentage of their constituents in the 9th Councilmanic District. This resulted in the loss of Mexican American representation in the council after Edward R. Roybal left for Congress. In fact, the elections of John Moreno and Phil Soto to the assembly in 1962 were made possible by growth of the Mexican American population east of the Boyle Heights-East Los Angeles area and in places like Montebello, Pico Rivera, and Santa Fe Springs.

The election of Leopoldo Sánchez to the municipal and then the superior court was different. He ran in a smaller district where the Mexican American population could maximize its impact. Sánchez had the support of many Mexican American groups, especially the GI Forum. His issues were non-partisan and his candidacy appealed to nationalism.

Roybal had been a formidable force in the city council. His courageous defense against the attacks of Police Chief William Parker demonstrated his importance to Mexican Americans. The city council members and the press were either silent or vehemently supportive of the chief. Roybal's congressional victory was especially significant, since it represented the advance of the only person who had consistently bucked the machine and still won elections.

Old issues such as high unemployment, especially among youth, continued to plague the community. Bunker Hill and

Chávez Ravine entered the annals of lost wars. New encroachments, including the expansion of White Memorial Hospital and the assault on Hazard Park, threatened the Eastside. Councilwoman Rosalind Wyman, who had been a key figure in the Chávez Ravine giveaway, was also heavily involved in the Hazard Park scheme. This is especially important because she and her husband, Eugene Wyman, were leaders in liberal Democratic party politics. Traditionally, this sector had been antagonistic to the downtown elite and the *Los Angeles Times*. In the early 60s, however, they became allies and, over the years, grew even closer.

In sum, the period from 1960 to 1962 did not see an awakening of the "sleeping giant." Rather, it exposed just how vulnerable the community was to the siege by forces outside its borders.

5

A Powerless Community:
1963–1965

Chapter 5 is based on articles in the *Sun* and the *Citizen* as well as on the Roybal Newspaper Scrapbook Collection. Also useful are Reynaldo Macías, et al. *A Study of Unincorporated East Los Angeles* (Los Angeles: 1973), and Howard Schuman, "The Incorporation of East Los Angeles as a Separate City. Problems and Prospects" (Master's Thesis, University of Southern California, 1965). For national politics, see Faustine C. Jones, "External Crosscurrents and Internal Diversity: An Assessment of Black Progress, 1960–1980" (*Daedalus*, Spring 1981) pp. 71–101, and Haywood Burns, "From *Brown* to *Bakke* and Back: Race, Law and Social Change in America" (*Daedalus*, Spring 1981) pp. 219–231.

In 1963, 12.1 percent of non-whites were unemployed versus 4.8 percent whites. It was a year of protest. In just one three-month span, the Department of Justice recorded 1,412 demonstrations. Black discontent moved from the rural South to the cities. Beatings and jailings were common. On August 28, 200,000 Blacks and whites joined in a march on Washington, D.C., listening to Martin Luther King Jr. deliver his "I have a dream . . ." oration. The white and Black freedom riders had joined the crusade, spurred by King's emphasis on love and non-violence. Many followers, however, were becoming disillusioned with token progress, and, during 1963 and 1964, they took to the streets. A new militancy emerged, with "Black Pride" evolving towards the goal of "Black Power."

In the fall of 1963, President John F. Kennedy was assassinated. His death further ignited Blacks and youth in general. Disillusionment at the University of California at Berkeley had been festering since the late 1950s and, in 1964, Berkeley students broke into the headlines. American students did not have a rich history of political activism, yet suddenly white middle-class college students appeared to be in revolt.

Students at Berkeley had been involved in the demonstration against the House Un-American Activities Committee in 1960. They had struggled against racism, the ROTC, nuclear testing, and the Cuban missile crisis. A change had taken place among these white middle-class students: many had become political and were ready for direct action. In growing numbers, they, too, took to the streets.

Many students were influenced by the Student Non-Violent Coordinating Committee (SNCC), which had roots in the civil rights movement. At Berkeley, this group inspired the Free Speech Movement (FSM), led by Mario Savio, and spread to other campuses. Celebrities such as Joan Baez joined the succession of marches and protests.

President Lyndon B. Johnson demonstrated a latent sense of history. Seeking his place in history books and exploiting the memory of the fallen Kennedy and aware of the explosive nature of Black protest, Johnson quickly pushed through the Civil Rights Act and the Economic Opportunity Act in 1964, and the Elementary and Education Act, the Higher Education Act, and the Voting Rights Act in 1965. In 1964, the Twenty-Fourth Amendment to the U.S. Constitution was passed, outlawing the poll tax. That same year, Johnson reached out to become a humanitarian president by borrowing the spirit of Franklin D. Roosevelt's New Deal and announcing his War on Poverty. Within a year, however, shaken by growing criticism and the defection of political cronies, Johnson began to withdraw support from his domestic war and diverted funds to his newly created Model Cities program, which gave more control to local politicians and less "power to the people."

Almost simultaneously, other events greatly affected the nation and East Los Angeles. In August 1964, Johnson alleged that North Vietnam had torpedoed American destroyers in the Gulf of Tonkin. With a mandate from Congress and the public, he began the heavy involvement of U.S. troops in Southeast Asia. U.S. involvement had begun in the early 1950s, when it supported the corrupt dictatorship of Ngo Dinh Diem. After the French withdrawal from Indochina, U.S. involvement increased. Shortly before the death of Kennedy, Diem was assassinated, with U.S. approval, by his generals. In early August, Johnson used the Gulf of Tonkin as an excuse to commit the U.S. to defeat of the Viet-Cong. By 1968, there would be a half million American troops in Indochina. This escalation coincided with a shift in the Black movement, away from a master plan to effect revolution through constitutional changes and towards more direct action.

In August 1965, the Watts Rebellions erupted. Formerly a Chicano barrio, Watts had become a predominately Black area in Los Angeles. It was not the first urban explosion of the times. A year before, the Harlem Rebellions injured 144, and four people were killed in a Rochester, New York, incident. Watts, however, was monumental: 34 were killed, mostly Black (three were Mexican American), whole blocks were burned, and 3,500 adults and 500 juveniles were arrested. The rebellion was suffocated only with the assistance of 14,000 National Guardsmen and 1,600 police.

The causes of the events and the effects that they had on Eastside Mexican Americans have not been adequately documented. One obvious consequence was that Los Angeles media naturally turned its focus further away from local events, lending added attention to the Black movement and the escalating war. Moreover, both Kennedy and Johnson had brought in East

Coast social planners who were overwhelmed by the events of the early decade. Knowing little about Chicanos or other minorities, these planners constructed irrelevant programs to fit familiar models. Additionally, books that were written about poverty addressed mainly the Black condition in the United States. Michael Harrington's *The Other America* spoke principally about Blacks. And, while it discovered poverty for many Americans, it also generated a host of stereotypes such as the "culture of poverty." Mexican American scholars and activists were forced to explode these stereotypes while seeking to forge a reality separate from that of Blacks. They were also forced to fight for access to many of the War on Poverty programs that the government dangled and then quickly withdrew.

Watts held a mixed legacy for Chicanos. At that time, many naively attempted to explain why Mexican Americans did not riot by attributing it to culture. Mexicans, some argued, were not as Americanized as Blacks. They contended that a rebellion like the one in Watts could happen in East Los Angeles once Mexicans became Americanized. Closer to the truth is that, in all probability, the material conditions for rebellion were more developed in Watts than in East Los Angeles. Both communities did suffer from racism and poverty. And, while it is true that Blacks had more resources and professionals as community members, it is also true that the Mexican community was more stable, with owner-occupancy in the Eastside being higher than in Watts. Mexicans migrating into the area found a more familiar community structure than did Blacks moving to Los Angeles from the rural South. Change for Blacks in Los Angeles had been more rapid and more traumatic. At the start of World War II, their county population was 75,000: by the time of the rebellions, this number had increased to 650,000. In short, the anchors of social control were weaker in Watts than in the Eastside.* The *Sun* and the *Citizen* both failed to analyze these conditions and were proud that East Los Angeles was a "peaceful community."

Coverage in both the weeklies indicates that federal programs in the 1960s gave Mexican Americans an illusion of participation. Also, it is clear that a resurgence of Mexican nationalism was reinforced by the symbols of the Black movement. In this milieu,

---

*Milton Viorst, *Fire in The Streets: America In the 1960s* (New York: 1979) p. 310.

César Chávez and his farmworkers strike took on special significance. The weeklies, however, did not cover this important strike as extensively as could be expected.

Although many eastsiders supported civil rights and the antiwar movement, the major concerns reported by the weeklies were local. Eastsiders formed committees to oppose encroachment on park lands. They attempted to achieve self-determination by opposing gerrymandering and by electing Mexican Americans to political office. They fought police brutality. Their ideological spectrum was varied, spanning radical to conservative. Their visions of society differed. They were even concerned with whether they were Americans or Mexican Americans, with or without a hypen.

THE CHRONICLE
1963

The *Citizen* summarized events of the previous year in its weekly column, "Beachcomber." It was a human interest column, summarizing the political gossip in the Eastside. The 9th Councilmanic District race received considerable coverage, with the fights between Mexican American candidates faithfully reported. The *Citizen* ran weekly biographies of the candidates. Richard Tafoya, Josefa Sánchez, and Anthony Serrato were among those featured. Everyone expected an open fight and, as noted in Chapter 4, city council members had promised Roybal that they would allow the voters to decide. However, the city council and Mayor Sam Yorty were feuding and the council members believed that Tafoya, a charter member of the Mexican American Chamber of Commerce, was a Yorty puppet.

In accordance with a rumor begun in December 1962, the council appointed Gilbert Lindsay, a 62-year-old Black, to fill Roybal's unexpired term. According to Roybal, the seat had been offered to David Boubion, Roybal's own administrative aide. Because of personal reasons, Boubion refused the appointment. Roybal publicly criticized the council for reneging on its promise. In effect, the city council had encouraged a Black–Mexican American conflict. After making the appointment, members justified their actions by stating that they were giving the Black community representation. Most political experts, however, believed the Blacks would have gained at least one seat in the up-coming spring election because of the favorable redistricting. The battle lines were thus drawn for the 9th Councilmanic District.

Basically, the full-term race involved Tafoya and Lindsay, since they had the best funded campaigns. Out of 68,114 registered voters in the 9th, 34,986 were Black and 23,114 were Mexican American. Further, voter registration in the 9th was the lowest in the city, largely because many Mexican Americans had not been registered. In contrast, Blacks benefitted from the well-organized and well financed voter registration drives conducted during this period. Many liberals were also sympathetic to the Black struggle, which was reaching national proportions. Mexican Americans, on the other hand, were not included in the early stages of the civil rights movement and were ignored by the media and politicos.

Reaction from the Mexican American community to the Lindsay appointment was bitter. The most pointed statement came from councilmanic candidate Josefa Sánchez. She said that she had believed that the city council would act in good faith but that considering what they had done to Chávez Ravine, Bunker Hill, and Hazard Park, no one should be surprised by the appointment. According to Sánchez, the people were simply too poor at this time to protect themselves against the council. Sánchez was the favorite among many liberals east of the river. However, she had neither a well-financed campaign nor a following among the middle-class political activists who worked the campaigns.

Elsewhere, the Mexican American Political Association failed to endorse a Mexican American candidate, splitting its votes between Sánchez and Tafoya. The reason why MAPA did not endorse anyone was that the votes polarized, with the liberals backing Sánchez and the moderates and conservatives supporting Tafoya. One candidate, Félix Ontiveros, withdrew when Lindsay named him chief deputy. Ontiveros, resident of East Los Angeles for 27 years, proved an asset to Lindsay during the bitter campaign.

Some Mexican Americans seized every opportunity to snub Lindsay. On February 9, Martín Ortiz, executive secretary for the East Central Area Welfare Planning Council, allegedly refused to introduce Lindsay during an Education Conference at Roosevelt High School. This conference was jointly sponsored by the CMAA and the East Central Area Welfare Planning Council. The councilman's supporters protested loudly.

Lindsay opposed combined garbage collection and promised to sweep the streets. He championed senior citizen programs. The *Sun's* coverage definitely favored him. Kovner praised Lindsay's proven leadership and the appointment of Ontiveros as his field representative. Moreover, Lindsay had the support of politically powerful supervisor Kenneth Hahn. A bitter fight raged between Sánchez and Tafoya, with Sánchez calling Tafoya a puppet of Police Chief William Parker. The International Longshoremen's and Warehousemen's Union endorsed Tafoya, as did Roybal. Although the campaign's intensity attracted attention, a light voter turnout was expected. Lindsay won a plurality in the primary but did not receive a majority.

Gilbert Lindsay	11,631
Richard Tafoya	9,096
O.P. Kinkle	1,741
Josefa Sánchez	1,559
Anthony Serrato	620
Ross Valencia	284

In the runoff, Tafoya received solid support from Mexican American organizations. Frank Casado, southern region director of MAPA, Congressman George Brown, Assemblyman Jesse Unruh, and Billy Mills, a Black candidate for the 8th Councilmanic District, all supported him. Tafoya opposed urban renewal and wrapped himself in Roybal's mantle, promising to carry out his programs. Tafoya further urged equal rights for all citizens. Roybal again endorsed Tafoya. So did the *Citizen*. On April 25, Kovner wrote that he had not made up his mind whom to support. Coverage in the *Sun*, however, definitely continued to favor Lindsay.

George Mount, a longtime activist, supported Lindsay and accused Tafoya of favoring urban renewal. Lindsay took a firm stand against urban renewal, while Tafoya opposed only government-imposed urban renewal. Clearly, this issue weighed heavily in Kovner's covert support of Lindsay. On May 26, Kovner headlined: "Lindsay's Deputy HELPS Community: Felix Ontiveros, J. Kovner Work for Progress." This theme was repeated in other *Sun* articles.

Supervisor Ernest Debs endorsed Tafoya. However, the advantage of the incumbency weighed too heavily and Lindsay won the hard-fought race, 16,400-to-13,109. Lindsay delivered a bitter victory statement in which he blasted Yorty, Debs, Roybal, and Unruh for supporting Tafoya. In this election, Billy Mills and Tom Bradley, both Blacks, also won seats in the city council. Consequently, Black candidates won three councilmanic seats, and Mexican Americans were left without representation.

The activism generally associated with the 1960s surfaced boldly in 1963. The intensity of Mexican American numbers east of the Los Angeles River made the community explosive. The 9th Councilmanic District was just one issue. Land use was even more threatening because it was tied to the lack of Mexican American representation. Both the county and the city were committed to so-called development, which made the Hazard Park giveaway that much more probable. During 1963, Kovner frequently attacked the Hazard Park swap. He ran an Independence Day editorial, "Hazard Park Must Not be Swapped for Hospital!" stating that 25 acres would be swapped to build professional-sized tennis courts in affluent West Los Angeles. Kovner singled out Councilwoman Roz Wyman, reminding his readers that Hollenbeck Park already had been chopped up by freeways. He cautioned that the same fate should not befall Hazard Park.

On July 11, Kovner suggested that Wyman and her neighbors donate their West Los Angeles homes for public tennis courts instead of forcing East Los Angeles residents to surrender their park. Letters to the editor expressed both sides of the issue. Some Mexican Americans supported the swap, since the building of a hospital would provide jobs. Parks and Recreation Commissioner Leonard Shane publicly condemned the trade as a land grab. The community was hungry for jobs, and the unions pressured Roybal to support the swap. Even so, he opposed it. But apparently believing the transfer to be a foregone conclusion, he moved to salvage something. On July 11, the *Citizen* reported that the congressman supported the hospital but that he proposed that the city acquire additional land for a park and that he was submitting his plan to the park commission.

Kovner hammered away at the land grab. On August 8, he wrote: "I am not willing to create a park in Westwood or anywhere else at the expense of facilities in another area." The equity of the protests did not deter Wyman, who pressured the Parks and Recreation Department to finalize the deal. She had an ally in department head William Frederickson, Jr. Both weeklies reported the stormy city council sessions. Lindsay motioned, unsuccessfully, that the Veterans Hospital be constructed in Lincoln Hollow. Soon after, the Parks and Recreation Commission authorized a voucher for Commissioner Mel Pierson to go to Washington, D.C., to expedite the Hazard Park swap.

Lindsay vehemently opposed the deal, declaring that "not one square inch of park land will be taken from the 9th Councilmanic District." The council, nevertheless, dispatched a research committee to study the swap. Political maneuvers were evident, and splinter groups within the newly established committee met secretly, excluding both Lindsay and Ontiveros.

On October 3, Kovner accused Bill Frederickson of manipulating the study committee and prejudicing the results in favor of the swap. J. J. Rodríguez, executive secretary of Butchers' Local 563, Dave Fishman Jr., of Local 1348 Painters' Union, and Harold Dune, president of Local 216 United Auto Workers, all supported the swap. They wanted a hospital because of the jobs it would generate. One obstacle stood in the way of the transfer: Hazard Park had an armory for which a new site had to be found. By the end of the year, however, the swap seemed to be a foregone conclusion.

The East Los Angeles Community Council met in February to discuss incorporation. Richard Rubio still headed the group, which was supported by trade unionists, such as Gilbert "Bud" Simpson of the United Packinghouse, Food and Allied Workers. Assemblymen Alfred H. Song and John Moreno endorsed incorporation. Within the council, Rubio represented a moderate element that wanted to build slowly. MAPA became militant on incorporation and called for home rule. Its 45th Assembly District chapter demanded immediate action, stating that the time was ripe. As MAPA emerged as the vanguard of incorporation, Rubio decreased his involvement, blaming the lack of action on the dearth of volunteers. At a meeting between the council, MAPA, and the Eastside Young Democrats, officers were elected to spearhead the incorporation effort. Robert Carvajal became the new president; Whittier merchant Theodore Hall, first vice president; Gil Avila, second vice president; Armida Tellez, third vice president; T. Robert López, fourth vice president; and Rudy Galeano, secretary. Rubio refused to serve as an officer.

The election of Carvajal proved to be unfortunate. He was too much of a maverick. He had been expelled from the Democratic Central Committee for encouraging Mexican Americans not to vote for Edmund G. Brown Sr. because of the governor's non-support of Mexican American candidates and his failure to appoint them to state posts. Carvajal gained popularity for this action but, over the long run, he lacked the consistency and organizational skills needed to bring incorporation before the voters.

When Montebello moved to annex part of East Los Angeles, incorporation took on added significance to community members. That same city had already quietly annexed a small area around Whittier Boulevard and Garfield Avenue. Eastsiders feared that Montebello's actions would encourage other encroachments.

The earlier enthusiasm of MAPA members faded. Division developed within the East Los Angeles Community Council and attendance at the planning sessions dropped. Ray Mora, a long-time Democratic party activist, organized East Los Angeles Property Owners for Incorporation as an alternative to the council. Apparently, differences were resolved and Mora's group was dissolved, with all parties working under the council's leadership. By September, the council filed notice of intent to incorporate and diagrammed the new boundaries. Rubio again refused a leadership post.

Meanwhile, the council ran into another problem: Judge Myer Marion. It had used Marion's name without his authorization and the judge publicly admonished its leaders. Apparently, the council failed to secure Marion's consent before naming both him and Leopoldo Sánchez honorary chairs of the incorporation effort.

Gil Avila assumed the council's top leadership position. Avila, a MAPA member, was too young and inexperienced to handle the various factions that had developed within the council. Carvajal had completely dropped out and moved to Pomona. Some members alleged that he had been bought off. Initially, the deadline for delivery of the petitions was December 6, which made unity essential. The council failed to meet this deadline, but supervisors granted it an extension.

Land use remained East Los Angeles' number one problem. The East Central Area Welfare Planning Council forecast an increase in multiple dwellings in the Eastside and, apparently, approved of this trend. The term *slum renewal* crept more frequently into print. On a positive note, an amendment to the 1961 Redevelopment Act provided that counties or municipalities with populations over 50,000 and an excess of six percent unemployment were eligible for low-interest loans. Roybal supported this form of development assistance.

Planning changes for freeways and the widening of East Los Angeles streets were approved. Master planning was more in the news. The *Citizen* pushed the concept of planned development, and the East Central Area Welfare Planning Council released its fifth annual report on the area's redevelopment, indicating this growth pattern.

Both the *Sun* and the *Citizen* frequently reported Democratic party functions. J. J. Rodríguez chaired the Mexican American Citizens Committee of California, which complained that Latinos were bypassed in political appointments. Arthur Alarcón, the governor's highest ranking Mexican American appointee, responded that "the governor does not make judicial or other appointments on the basis of race, color, or creed." This brought an immediate response from Judge Leopoldo Sánchez, who accused Alarcón of inferring that no qualified Mexican Americans were available. Sánchez pointed out that of some 6,000 appointments made by the governor, less than 30 were to Mexican Americans. Alarcón then met with Dr. Francisco Bravo, Sánchez, Rodríguez, and Mary Orozco. The group accused Pat Brown of breaking campaign promises to Mexican Americans. Despite the group's indignation, it called a truce. The meeting, however, did not produce results; the governor did not alter his appointment pattern. It also became clear that Mexican American political activists would not pressure the governor sufficiently to force results. Without having to make tangible commitments, Brown was invited to address MAPA's annual convention.

Brown did appoint attorney John Argüelles to the East Los Angeles Municipal Court. Many Mexican Americans alleged that this appointment was a political payment to Argüelles for his support of an Anglo against Leopoldo Sánchez.

On December 26, the *Citizen* printed an ethnic survey released by Brown's office. The study revealed that 89,904 Caucasians worked for California, while 5,469 Blacks, 3,190 Asians and

2,409 Mexican Americans were state employed. Mexican Americans did not fare much better in the county, where they numbered less than 2,000 employees out of a work force of approximately 41,000.

The *Citizen* covered a variety of community events and organizations, including the Mexican American Women's League, whose leaders were Ramona Morín and Francisca Flores. The Mexican American Republican Association also held meetings. In addition, *Los Hambriados*, a Mexican American middle-class organization, held its festivities on August 11 to raise funds for orphans in Mexico. Raúl Morín published the second edition of *Among the Valiant*, a study of the role of the Chicano during World War II and the Korean conflict. Both the *Sun* and the *Citizen* reported job mobility in the Eastside, citing, for instance, that Joe Maldonado was named director of the East Los Angeles Youth project.

The Community Service Organization and the Council on Mexican American Affairs worked in the community and sponsored various events. But neither organization received the coverage that it had in previous years, despite the fact that local Spanish language station KMEX–TV reportedly reached 200,000 homes by 1963. Lack of publicity also plagued the GI Forum, which re-elected Judge Leopoldo Sánchez to chair its local chapter. The Beneficencia Mexicana continued its activities at the Casa del Mexicano. Finally, the first printed reference to the Mexican American Lawyers Association (MALA) appeared during this period. Herman Sillas headed this organization, which worked primarily with Chicano law students.

Congressman George Brown reported on new immigration bills and their possible impact on the community. The only voice hostile to the new laws was that of Delfina Varela, director of the Mexican American Social Services. According to Varela, the new regulations made it more difficult for Mexicans to enter the United States. She accused the Kennedy administration and the U.S. Department of Labor of attempting to severely limit the legal flow of Mexican immigrants to the United States in order to create a labor shortage. This would allow the Department of Labor to justify extension of the bracero program. Varela contrasted the treatment of Mexicans to that of Cubans, stating that while the INS harassed Mexicans without papers, the federal government was paying anti-Castro Cubans $500 a month to live in the country. During this period, the bracero program extension was defeated in the House of Representatives, 171-to-158.

The *Sun* commented on articles written by *Los Angeles Times* reporter Rubén Salazar. Salazar was one of the first journalists from a major daily newspaper to use the term Mexican American. Many *Sun* readers objected to the term, stating that they were Americans. Racial tensions increased noticeably. The *Sun* reported that Supervisor Ernest Debs convened a conference to avert the spread of racial tensions.

The shambles created by the Walter-McCarran Act were still being cleared up in the 1960s. The *Sun* reported the case of José Gastelum, 53, who had entered the United States when he was ten years old. Thirty-six years later, the Immigration and Naturalization Service attempted to deport him for political reasons. The Los Angeles Committee for the Protection of the Foreign Born defended Gastelum. After a long hearing, the U.S. Supreme Court vindicated him by a 5-to-4 vote.

Both the *Sun* and the *Citizen* began to increase coverage of youth and education. The Council of Mexican American Affairs and the Los Angeles City Schools' Council on Human Relations co-sponsored a conference on "Education and the Mexican American" at Roosevelt High School. Four East Los Angeles high schools were selected for a special "dropout" pilot program. Assemblyman John Moreno sought to relieve the financial burdens of local school districts by proposing special funding bills. Assemblyman Alfred Song also sponsored special funding during the fall session to help alleviate the dropout problem.

New programs directed at non-English-speaking students were implemented, with added emphasis placed on vocational training programs. These programs sought solutions to dropout and school overcrowding problems. The *Sun* frequently pressured school authorities to solve these problems. Consequently, Eastside schools received a larger share of the school bond issue.

On August 9, a Mexican American Education Opportunities Conference was held, and Chris Ruiz, a social worker, spoke on the dropout problem. Delegates were especially concerned about racism in the schools. Meanwhile, the Mexican American Ad Hoc Education Committee was formed by the County Human Relations Commission. This group attracted educators and grassroots people throughout the county to discuss schools and Mexican American students.

The Department of Labor granted $500,000 to an experimental youth program that provided jobs for Eastside residents between the ages of 16 and 21. The Youth Employability Project was endorsed by the East Central Area Welfare Planning Council as well as by other community organizations. There was hope that the project would furnish a solution to the increased unemployment of Mexican American youth.

Closely related to unemployment were drug abuse and gang activity. These two problems had always received a great deal of coverage. At a meeting of the Equal Opportunity Foundation, George Borrell spoke, and participants saw movies about gangs and discussed the problem. The Belvedere Coordinating Council discussed narcotics and explored possible remedies. On February 17, KMEX-TV aired a panel discussion on narcotics and gangs.

The county initiated a group guidance program that was administered by the probation department. City and county police authorities did not support the program, contending that it coddled gang members. And at one point in the controversy, the county supervisors even suspended the program. Congressmen George Brown, Edward R. Roybal, and Augustus Hawkins endorsed the program at a news conference and accused police of harassing youth. County government also began to allocate more funds to youth programs. The County Human Relations Commission worked with youth, co-sponsoring a conference with Dr. Helen Bailey and East Los Angeles Junior College. It brought youth leaders and workers together. The work of the commission in increasing awareness among youth at this time cannot be overemphasized.

In the fall, the *Citizen* announced that the county supervisors had assigned a committee to study juvenile delinquency problems. The East Central Area Welfare Planning Council urged more youth projects. Meanwhile, research documented the lack of recreational facilities and parks in the Eastside, prompting labor unions to support construction of two new parks in the area. Ironically, Los Angeles pressed to consummate the Hazard Park deal with the federal government.

In August, two confrontations between police authorities and Eastsiders indicated growing tensions in the community. On August 8, the *Citizen* wrote: "Angry Crowds Attack Four Lawmen Here." In one incident, two sheriff's deputies had arrested a youth in the Maravilla Housing Project. When a large crowd assembled, the arresting officers released the suspect. In the second incident, two California highway patrolmen arrested a Mexican American youth in City Terrace for a minor infraction. As a crowd of 200 people surrounded them, the CHP officers panicked and called for back-up units. Soon, 20 units arrived, exacerbating the potential explosiveness of the scene.

Vice President Lyndon B. Johnson addressed a Mexican American conference in East Los Angeles. Present were Chicano leaders from throughout the county. Dionicio Morales coordinated the conference which dealt with equal opportunities for Mexican Americans. Leaders voiced displeasure with government agencies. Johnson countered the demands for minority promotions, stating that this would not solve the discrimination problem. Mexican American participants verbally attacked Anthony Celebrezze, secretary of Health, Education and Welfare, for his ignorance of Mexican Americans and their problems.

The year closed as the nation mourned the assassination of President John F. Kennedy, the man who had initially raised the Eastside community's expectations.

1964

As the year began, the deadline for incorporation petitions approached. A sufficient number of signatures had not been secured and county supervisors granted another 30-day extension. Teamster Local 414 contributed $500 to the drive, but supporters could not obtain the required signatures. Only 3,500 of the 6,000 required signatures were collected. Gil Avila publicly criticized the Eastside community for its apathy.

In one of his first 1964 editorials, Kovner reviewed the dangers of urban renewal, concluding that it remained a clear and present threat. On January 16, he related the history of Eastside park development, pointing out that much of government encroachment had been on park land. Kovner urged the people to unite to stop the state highway commission from building more freeways and to attend freeway expansion hearings. Even as the *Sun* publisher warned the public, the San Bernardino Freeway was widened and more residents were displaced.

On August 13, the *Citizen* reported that the County Regional Planning Commission was preparing to release a three-year study that would establish a master plan for East Los Angeles. The East

Central Area Welfare Planning Council, founded in 1961, issued a statement defending freeway construction as important to progress in East Los Angeles. This action was in line with the policies of the county, which, at the time, facilitated suburban commuting. By the end of the year, the master plan was submitted for discussion.

More coverage on Mexican American women was published. Audrey Rojas Kaslow was appointed to the California Fair Employment Practices Commission. Mrs. Linda M. Benítez, a member of the executive board of the Los Angeles County Central Committee, representative from the 40th Assembly District, and founder and director of the Boyle Heights Community Service Center, urged women to participate in politics. She called for 300 Eastside voter registrars. The League of Mexican American Women presented achievement awards to Audrey Rojas Kaslow and to Lena Archuleta, an educator from the Denver public school system. Francisca Flores was the league's spokesperson. Henrietta Villaecusa was named to the International Development Bureau of Latin America, a division of the Alliance for Progress.

The controversial Rumford Fair Housing Act making it illegal to deny rentals on the grounds of sex, color, or religion was passed. Through the initiative process, opponents of the act countered with Proposition 14, placing it on the statewide ballot. Real estate interests sponsored the initiative. Mexican American organizations, including the CMAA, sponsored debates on Proposition 14. Governor Brown opposed the proposition, claiming that it would doom fair housing in California. Sal Montenegro, an Eastside realtor, resigned from the Mexican Chamber of Commerce when the organization did not oppose it.

In spite of Mexican American leadership opposition, a UCLA survey revealed that most grassroots Mexican Americans knew little about the Rumford Act or Proposition 14. Many believed that it was a Black–white issue. Because of heavy advertisement by real estate interests, which erroneously portrayed it as a freedom of choice issue, Proposition 14 was overwhelmingly passed. Fortunately, the California Supreme Court eventually declared the proposition unconstitutional.

The *Citizen* and the *Sun* covered employment problems. Supervisor Ernest Debs conceded that the number of Mexican Americans employed in government was low. A public meeting was held at East Los Angeles College to discuss the special employment problems of Mexican Americans. Later, a survey was released showing that Mexican Americans filed 12 percent of state unemployment claims. The Belvedere Coordinating Council discussed the unemployment problem and placed more emphasis on training. Richard Tafoya was named director of an East Los Angeles job-finding staff.

During the year, the Fair Employment Practices Committee (FEPC) was active in informing Eastsiders of their rights. FEPC representative Rafael Vega spoke to many groups, including various coordinating councils. Despite newspaper coverage, the FEPC received general criticism from Eastsiders. While the agency did advocate employment rights for Mexican Americans, it did not have a significant number of Mexican Americans on its own staff.

Unemployment among youth was high and, as in 1963, this caused problems and concerns. Unemployment, according to many Eastsiders, was reaching crisis proportions. Although job discrimination was a factor, complaints against employers were infrequent among Mexican Americans. According to the FEPC, Mexican Americans had filed only 199 complaints, while Blacks had filed 90 percent of the complaints. This lack of participation deepened Mexican American alienation from most civil rights agencies. According to many Mexican Americans, these agencies serviced primarily Blacks.

The FEPC published a study documenting that Mexican Americans lagged behind the rest of the population in jobs, income, and education. State civil service opportunities were available to Latinos. Community leaders, however accused the FEPC of tokenism. Meanwhile, the FEPC published a pamphlet, ''Sí Se Puede,'' which encouraged Spanish-speaking youths to seek higher education. This agency later praised the Bank of America for making good progress toward hiring minorities.

The *Citizen* reported that the average Eastside family income was about $6,000. A State Office of Employment study stated that the agency placed 150,000 persons in non-farm jobs and that 27.3 percent of the persons were ethnic minorities. The study added that Mexican Americans were one and one-half times more prone than Whites to be unemployed.

The FEPC published a pamphlet showing that, in 1960, Mexican Americans comprised 9.1 percent of Calfiornia's population, compared to 7.2 percent in 1950, and that Blacks accounted for

5.6 percent of the state population. Also, a majority of the Mexican American population had acquired less than an eighth-grade education. This data forced the FEPC to recognize the special needs of the Spanish-speaking citizenry, and the agency promised to work harder to improve the status of California's Latinos. Meanwhile, the GI Forum and other groups discussed the problems accentuated by the findings. The pamphlet was important because it gave activists data that was not easily accessible at the time and thus helped raise the consciousness of many Mexican Americans.

J. J. Rodríguez was named to the President's Committee on Equal Employment Opportunities. Other Mexican American appointments followed but the community was dissatisfied and growing impatient. At FEPC hearings, MAPA leaders Eduardo Quevedo and Bert Corona lambasted the FEPC for ignoring Mexican American problems and concerns. Carlos Borja, Hector Abeytia, and Dr. Manuel Guerra also spoke at the FEPC hearings.

The civil rights movement in general, and the passage of the 1964 Civil Rights Act specifically, spurred community involvement. The Economic Opportunity Act of August 20, 1964, created the war on poverty, which impacted on poor communities and called for the "maximum feasible participation." Nationally, the war on poverty was put under the Office of Economic Opportunity. It encouraged competition between Blacks, Mexican Americans, and white bureaucrats, each wanting control of their portion of the windfall funds that suddenly came to the communities. Locally, Joe Maldonado was named director of the Youth Opportunities Board (YOB). This agency would consolidate with other groups under its network umbrella, eventually becoming the funding agent for the city and county.

The Youth Training and Employment Program (YTEP) emerged as another important agency in East Los Angeles. Among other functions, YTEP gave college training grants to youth. Like many other agencies, YTEP was involved in the competition for the federally allocated funds. There was considerable competition for control of these funds. Mayor Sam Yorty supported the YOB, while others favored the East Central Welfare Planning Council as a broad economic agency responsible for coordinating and funding programs. The Equal Opportunities Foundation was also considered.

The Hazard Park deal still lingered in 1964. Kovner again editorialized against the Hazard Park swap. Both Edward R. Roybal and George Brown favored a compromise in which the veterans would assume 20 acres and the remaining acreage would be used as a park. Roybal and Brown conceded that a hospital was a good idea, since its construction would attract $22,628,000 for the area. Proponents called Hazard Park an ideal location for a hospital. Kovner was not satisfied and remained staunchly opposed to the giveaway. Meanwhile, the city moved quickly and condemned the park land in order to facilitate the exchange.

Kovner unexpectedly accepted the compromise, writing: "Kovner Publication Wins Fight to Save Hazard Park Aided by Councilman Lindsay and Felix Ontiveros, Deputy Councilman, Congressman Roybal and Field Representative Alex Garcia." However, Kovner proved to be over-optimistic; victory was not as close as it seemed. The swap promoters tried to finalize negotiations for construction of the hospital. Contractors would receive a $22 million contract to build a ten-story VA facility, and there would be hundreds of jobs for union members. Apparently, Kovner realized that too much was at stake and settled for the compromise: building the Kennedy Playground on the remaining seven acres. The support of U.S. Attorney General Robert Kennedy was sought to expedite the deal.

Kovner wrote Roybal an open letter. "How long will it take for the JFK playground to be built?" he asked. "Why isn't the community involved?" The Parks and Recreation Commission accepted the Hazard Park proposal. The playground would include surplus tanks and other war equipment. Meanwhile, Congress cleared the way for construction of the hospital.

The contradictions of the Hazard Park situation were obvious. While the East Central Area Welfare Planning Council called for more parks in the Eastside, the city council was giving away a park already in the area. Many residents did not accept the compromise. J. Patricio Sánchez led a protest, denouncing any compromise. The group broadened its attacks and criticized the Recreation and Parks Commission for not repairing the poor facilities at Fresno Park.

In Belvedere, problems of another source aroused community activists. By autumn, the county had purchased enough land for the construction of Obregón Park. This new recreational facility caused bad feelings because homes had been condemned to make possible its construction. Opponents pointed out that the county could have used the junkyards or run-down industrial areas instead of residential facilities.

Encroachment on Eastside property continued during 1964. Félix Ontiveros warned that property on Whittier Boulevard, between Boyle and Lorena Streets in Boyle Heights, was being condemned for commercial development. The *Sun* in part blamed this on the East Central Area Welfare Planning Council, which, according to Kovner, was the major redevelopment force in the area east of the Los Angeles River. The two weeklies continued to differ in relation to the council but agreed on the negative effects of the freeway. On July 16, the *Citizen*, for instance, bannered an article: "Is it hill or a dirt road? No . . . it's the Pomona Freeway . . ." The newspaper was concerned about the dislocation that the freeways caused. Freeways often separated children from their schools. The tunnels constructed to ensure safe pedestrian safety were often as dangerous as the freeways, providing a shelter for crime.

Police-community relations received more coverage in both the *Citizen* and the *Sun*. The special law enforcement committee to the County Human Relations Commission issued a report reviewing the LAPD's practices. The report was critical of the police and sheriffs. The CMAA also investigated cases of police brutality. One of the more dramatic cases was that of a blind Mexican American, Yolanda Medina, 18, who was jailed along with four other family members. She was booked at the Sybil Brand Institute. The confrontation occurred in front of her parents' home and involved California Highway Patrol officers Don A. Newman and Don Johnson. While the officers cited Yolanda's brother, George Medina, 21, and his friend, Jimmy Martínez, 20, the latter ran to the Medina home, returning with George's mother, Armida Medina. Other family members, including Yolanda and her father, Max, rushed onto the scene and an altercation ensued. Police arrested Yolanda, accusing her of being intoxicated because she was swaying. Yolanda was blind and had trouble finding her way about in the commotion. Police officers ridiculed her and looked for needle marks on her arms. Max and George Medina and Jimmy Martínez were acquitted of assault charges. Yolanda and her mother were tried separately. The outcome of this trial was not reported. In May, tensions between police and Mexican Americans were aired at public hearings.

In a bid for Mexican American re-election votes, President Lyndon B. Johnson met with Mexico's President Adolfo López Mateos during the 1964 political season. The *Citizen* covered this meeting between the two presidents. The encounter was important, since it began a pattern that would emerge in other presidential elections. At the 1964 meeting, in all probability, the two chief executives discussed the bracero program, which expired that year.

On the political front, Chicanos were powerless. Although Assemblyman Moreno was active in the Democratic party and chaired a panel on Mexican Affairs at the party's minority conference, the party itself did not adequately support him. In the 51st Assembly District, the Anglo establishment supported John Fenton against Moreno, as did two of the Anglo mayors within the district. Adding to Moreno's problems was the candidacy of Dionicio Morales, who also filed for the 51st and thereby split the Mexican American vote. Morales was well-known in the community. Fenton received 16,089 votes, Moreno 12,904, Morales 4,485 and Luis Zaoien 628 votes.

Another example of Mexican American powerlessness was the 40th Democratic Primary, in which attorney Tony Bueno ran against incumbent Ed Elliot. The *Sun* printed an article: "Is it Nationalistic to Support a Mexican American in the 40th District in the Primary Election of 1964?" However, both the *Sun* and the Democratic party conveniently ignored an ostensible party policy of keeping Mexican Americans powerless. The Democratic party resented nationalism among Mexican Americans and questioned their voting against party incumbents. Interestingly, party members did not question gerrymandering of the Mexican American community or the fact that Anglo incumbents protected themselves at the expense of Mexican American representation.

Consistently, the Democratic party machine and organized labor supported their own self-interests. For instance, the Los Angeles County Federation of Labor frequently supported non-Mexican American candidates and issues, and many Mexican American labor officials and activists endorsed Anglo candidates. This created confusion. An example was Gonzalo Molina, who endorsed Ed Elliot over Tony Bueno. This is not to say that these endorsements went unchallenged. In Molina's case, Francisca Flores, a prominent activist, levied sound criticism.

George H. Mount, husband of Julia Luna Mount and himself a MAPA activist, criticized MAPA for endorsing only Mexican American candidates. He supported Al Song for the assembly because Song actively opposed urban renewal.

Another controversial race was the Evelle Younger–Vincent S. Dalsimer battle for Los Angeles district attorney. More liberal elements in MAPA supported Dalsimer, while old-time *Mapistas*, led by Eduardo Quevedo, backed Younger. The conservative faction sent out a letter signed by nine MAPA officers endorsing Younger. Because six of these officers were from newly created chapters, Dalsimer partisans charged a violation of MAPA rules. Younger won the election, adding to intra-organizational conflict between liberals and conservatives. Congressman George Brown surveyed his constituents to determine which issues concerned them most. In 1964, he had them list their concerns in the order of their importance. Approximately 12,000 respondents listed their priorities as follows:

PERCENTAGE OF RESPONDENTS
CONSIDERING PROBLEMS MOST PRESSING

Unemployment	50.0%
Juvenile Delinquency, Narcotics, and Crime	46.9
Negro Demonstrations	35.2
Racial Discrimination	35.1
Communist Subversion	28.2
Educational Needs	24.6
Rapid Population Increase	21.9
Poverty of Large Proportion of American Citizens	21.5
Cost of Medical Care for the Aged	20.6
Automation	16.2

Unemployment was the number one concern of 57.3 percent of the Democrats (a large proportion of which was Mexican American), whereas only 37.9 percent of the Republicans considered it to be the primary problem. Republicans in the 29th Congressional District listed juvenile delinquency as the top concern, followed by Black demonstrations. Democrats listed juvenile delinquency second and race discrimination third. The results are not indicative of purely Mexican American attitudes, since a majority of the registered voters were non-Mexicans. Significantly, education was not listed as a priority and urban renewal was not even mentioned.

1965

By the mid-1960s, coverage in the weeklies suggested that education was the major issue among Eastsiders. The term "educationally disadvantaged" became more popular. The Los Angeles City Schools approved the Neighborhood Youth Corps plan. Ralph Poblano, president of the CMAA, former school teacher and candidate for Office Number 2 of the Los Angeles Board of Education, stated that the only barrier to Mexican American progress was education. Poblano was endorsed by Assemblyman Ed Elliot. The *Sun* also endorsed Poblano, while the *Citizen* simply covered this board of education race. Poblano was also supported by Dr. Max Rafferty, state superintendent of schools. This endorsement alienated many liberals and Poblano lost the primary to Reverend James Jones, a Black, who then ran against a conservative white incumbent and won.

By summer, the California Association of Educators of Mexican (CAEM) descent was organized. The CAEM soon split into moderate and conservative factions. Phil Móntez and Marcos de León led the moderates; conservatives followed Bill Zazueta and Al Pérez. Moderates bolted the CAEM and formed the Association of Mexican American Educators (AMAE), which held its first state convention in San Diego during December. Three hundred and fifty educators attended.

AMAE saw the hiring of Mexican American teachers as a prerequisite for quality education and set this as their first priority. Other groups also criticized the poor education that Mexican Americans received. Herman Sillas, Dan Fernández, Ray Gonzales, Dr. Miguel Montes, Charles Erickson, and Marcos de León formed the Mexican American Studies Foundation. This group evolved out of the CMAA and the Poblano campaign and became very active in seeking war on poverty funds.

Meanwhile, the Mexican American Ad Hoc Education Committee became the Los Angeles County Mexican American Education Committee (MAEC), with Marcos de León serving as chair.

MAEC had been formed in 1963 as an Ad Hoc Committee to the Los Angeles County Human Relations Commission. Since then, it had functioned as an open forum for Chicanos throughout the county. In 1965, nearly 150 persons attended an MAEC-sponsored conference on "Education and the Mexican American Student." During this period, MAEC was the most community-oriented organization dealing with education.

Operation Headstart programs east of the river began to emerge. Meanwhile, Marcos de León and other educators advocated changes in the educational system. De León characterized the Mexican American as a marginal person, someone with a hamburger in one hand and a taco in the other. According to de León, the solution was a cultural understanding of the Mexican American child. Schools paid little attention to de León and seemed more concerned with the expected windfall of $16 million in poverty funds. Malabar Street Elementary School received $100,000 for a special project.

At UCLA, a comprehensive project on Mexican Americans was funded by the Ford Foundation for an estimated $500,000. The study basically involved an intensive analysis of the 1960 census. A preliminary report by the UCLA project disproved the Mexican American's illusion that education was a panacea.

The Third Annual Mexican American Conference, sponsored by the Los Angeles County Human Relations Commission, was held at Camp Hess Kramer April 9 through 11. Approximately 150 young Mexican Americans attended the seminar. Esther Hansen covered the events at the youth conference for the *Sun*. The theme of the seminar was "The Self-Concept of Mexican Americans." Speakers included Danny Villanueva and Bert Corona. John Ortiz, then a Stevenson Junior High student and later a leader of the 1968 walkouts at Garfield High School, and Gilbert Luján, an artist, participated in the event. Later, a similar conference focusing on adult leadership was held. Ralph Guzmán was the featured speaker. A third Mexican American Leadership Conference was held at the All Nations Camp. Professors Helen Bailey and Frances Pasternak, both of East Los Angeles Junior College, spoke at this conference.

The Los Angeles City Schools expanded its human relations unit, and Arnold Rodríguez was named its Mexican American consultant. Rodríguez, a former industrial arts teacher, served as a consultant for the Youth Opportunities Board (YOB). Jesse Unruh sponsored a bill encouraging schools, through special funding aid, to teach English as a second language.

Criticism of education for Latino children also received more coverage. Articles exposing the deficiencies of the system appeared more frequently. Activists criticized the lack of history classes detailing Mexico's contributions to the Southwest. They charged that school authorities ignored the special needs of Mexican American students.

A rivalry between Blacks and Mexican Americans for war on poverty funds developed. In order to administer funds, the Youth Opportunities Board and the Economic Opportunities Federation of Los Angeles merged into the Economic Youth Opportunities Agency (EYOA). This consolidation took time and, from the start, Mexican Americans accused white and Jewish administrators of favoring Blacks. On February 23, *Citizen* reporter Ridgely Cummings described the behind-the-scenes struggle for Los Angeles' poverty funds.

Meanwhile, Eastside schools were selected to receive special poverty funds. In an effort to win community support, federal and local authorities sent speakers to the various coordinating councils to explain the poverty act. During this period, three key appointments were made to EYOA: Joe Maldonado was named executive director of the new agency, Dennis Fargas would head the Neighborhood Youth Corps, and Opal Jones received authority over the Neighborhood Adult Participation Project (NAPP). In addition, Dr. Ernesto Galarza was named special consultant to the agency.

Throughout 1965, YOB held meetings to generate grassroots support and ensure what the organization called "maximum feasible participation." Early turnouts to these meetings indicated little community support for poverty programs. As expected, Yorty attempted to control city poverty funds and council members opposed him. Yorty's opponents recognized the potential for building a political machine from this new source of patronage. The battle for control resulted in a stalemate that threatened to have the federal funds revoked. In immediate danger was the loss of $2.3 million in summer school program funds for East Los Angeles.

Because of the delay in approving the formation of the new funding agency, the county lost $800,000. When the poverty funds were belatedly received, economic opportunities and summer school projects were hastily implemented. YOB temporarily disbursed these funds. Meanwhile, the Reverend H. H. Brookings, attorney Frank Muñoz, and Tony Tinejero of the Mexican American Action Committee protested the merger of YOB and the Economic Opportunities Federation of Los Angeles.

During this time, the county, the city, and the schools urged that YOB be expanded. To them, expansion meant an additional $23 million in poverty funds. The weeklies reported poverty program events regularly. The East Central Area Welfare Planning Council endorsed candidates for the new poverty board. Los Angeles City planned to hire 1,500 students during the summer for its youth corps program. Meanwhile, congressional hearings conducted in August attracted 500 people. Congressmen evaluated the status of EYOA and the East Los Angeles poverty program.

Also in August, the Watts riots rocked Los Angeles, costing the city an estimated $2 million. Although Mayor Yorty defended police action during the riots, many felt that the police had overreacted. Councilman Billy Mills called for a review of the police. Three Mexican Americans were killed during these riots.

A by-product of the Watts riots was a further shift in control of poverty funds to Blacks. Government placed more emphasis than before on deteriorating conditions for urban Blacks. In turn, many Blacks felt that the poverty programs generally resulted from their civil rights movement and were enlivened by the Watts rebellions. Certainly, these events made apparent the need for funds. However, the process itself had already been put into motion before the rebellions. The war on poverty was not so much a reaction to the civil rights movement as it was President Johnson's attempt to keep minorities loyal to the Democratic party by creating another patronage network. Additionally, Johnson was from Texas and recognized the importance of the Mexican American vote.

The struggle for control of EYOA continued. Mindful that the agency did not represent all sectors adequately, it was recommended that the EYOA board be expanded to 25. By September, both the city and county had appointed representatives to the poverty board. Initialy, EOYA was allocated some $7 million, a sum that hardly satisfied all sectors of the region.

Congressman Roybal charged favoritism in the allocation of funds. Roybal maintained that Blacks received the lion's share of the funds and appointments. Supervisor Ernest Debs asked for poverty aid hearings. Citing the growing economic hardships in East Los Angeles, Debs said that he did not want to aid "Negroes" at the expense of Mexican Americans. Debs pathetically concluded that Mexican Americans had rioted 20 years earlier during the Zoot Suit era and had gained little. Charges of favoritism were echoed by MAPA, LULAC, the GI Forum, Dan Fernández of CMAA, and Dr. Miguel Montes, president of the Latin American Civic Association. The struggle for funds exposed the political weakness of the Mexican American community. Whereas the Black community had three city councilmen, the Mexican American community did not have any representation. White politicians encouraged tensions between the two groups by playing them against each other.

The *Citizen* and the *Sun* regularly covered the poverty programs. By December, Los Angeles had received over $25 million in poverty funds. The influx of money had an immediate effect on volunteer organizations, many of which sought funding for programs formerly operated by volunteers.

Interwoven with the poverty war was the issue of urban renewal. Encroachments by developers and local government continued. Kovner criticized Yorty for encouraging urban redevelopment and was especially critical of the mayor's attempts to stifle the right to appeal zoning, home condemnation, and building, safety, and traffic decisions.

Plans for the $22 million, 1,040 bed, Veterans Administration Hospital in Hazard Park continued. The *Sun's* publisher commented also on the city's encroachment on Elysian Park. Yorty wanted to build a convention center at the expense of park users, alleging that Los Angeles had to have a convention hall and that Elysian Park was conveniently located. Considerable opposition to this land grab scheme developed, and a citizens committee to save Elysian Park was formed. This latest land grab project became an election issue in the city council races of this year.

While Hazard Park is not technically in Boyle Heights, it borders it and Lincoln Heights, and it is used by both communities. The Hazard Park committee, led by J. Patricio Sánchez, Mrs. Isabel Medrano, and N. Steelink, continued to oppose the park swap. Members also criticized the planned use of war equipment in John F. Kennedy Memorial Park. Proponents wanted to stock the park with salvaged tanks, planes, and other surplus war equipment. Committee members protested that it was unhealthy for children to play with instruments of destruction.

Elsewhere, Congress approved the transfer of the Hazard Park armory. In May, the Save Hazard Park Committee picketed Councilwoman Rosalind Wyman's Bel-Air home, calling attention to her part in the park's giveaway. During this time, the City Park and Recreation Department released a proposal that further angered Boyle Height's citizens: a plan for a privately financed Hazard Park Recreation Center. Opponents charged that the city would not make the financial commitment to fund a center— even after it wanted to take most of the park facilities from the community. Patricio Sánchez pointed out that 17 acres in Hazard Park alone were valued at $4.5 million, that the park already had a clubhouse, and that the community was taking a $300,000 to $400,000 loss.

Roybal defended the compromise, stating that the hospital would furnish some 2,000 jobs and would serve many veterans who could not afford to travel 20 miles to the present VA facility in West Los Angeles. The Save Hazard Park group gained support. In August, the committee picketed a meeting at the All Nation's Center, criticizing Roybal's role in the Hazard Park swap. In spite of this public outcry, most participants at the meeting overwhelmingly favored the construction of a hospital.

The Hazard Park committee won a minor victory when two and a half acres were added to Fresno Park. Plans were also announced to make major improvements in other Eastside area parks. Finally, in October, the county broke ground for the controversial Obregón Park. Many observed that either homes or parks were the victims and that rarely were junkyards used to promote the public good.

On January 21, the *Citizen* announced that the master plan for Los Angeles would be released soon and that it would change East Los Angeles. The county planning commission had initiated this study in 1961 and the board of supervisors ordered it to continue research during 1962. As expected, the master plan was controversial. The planners predicted more intensive use of East Los Angeles land, which would eventually have a population of 122,000 residents. The various coordinating councils discussed the plan and community leaders organized meetings to oppose it. Supporting the master plan were prominent Mexican Americans, including Richard Rubio, leader of the first incorporation drive of the 1960s and now vice-chair of the Los Angeles County Planning Commission. Opponents claimed that the master plan was a land grab scheme. Proponents countered that absence of a master plan would facilitate further piecemeal zone changes.

Arthur Montoya, head of the Maravilla-Belvedere Property Owners Association, emerged as the leading spokesperson opposing the master plan. He called it the first step in urban renewal. Montoya organized a meeting that drew more than 900 property owners.

In August, Montoya began a weekly column for the *Sun*, in which he chiefly criticized urban renewal. This column generated community interest and another rally was held in September. Again, some 900 people attended. Montoya wrote stinging articles, focusing his attack on Supervisor Ernest Debs. Apparently, the attacks had effect and Debs temporarily halted the East Los Angeles master plan study.

In a November 11 editorial, Kovner condemned an increase in the property assessments on Eastside property. Arthur Montoya echoed this call for tax relief. Kovner also criticized the expansion of shopping centers in the Eastside, condemning their displacement of people. This was ironic, since the *Sun* depended almost totally on advertising for revenue. Kovner also opposed the upzoning of property on Brooklyn, between Alma and Indiana Streets, to build a three-acre Lucky Market shopping center.

Kovner and the *Sun* continued to monitor the East Central Area Welfare Planning Council. Kovner's editorials contradicted those of the *Citizen*, which not only supported but praised the council. Apparently, a communion of self-interests existed between the council and the *Citizen*. Both supported the redevelopment of East Los Angeles.

Considerable political activity took place during 1965. The courts had ordered a state senate reapportionment. California apportionment of state senatorial districts by county was found to be unconstitutional and the state was ordered to reapportion according to population. This order increased dramatically the Los Angeles representation, from one to 12 senatorial districts. MAPA passed a resolution demanding a Mexican American senatorial district. However, the new plan did not favor East Los Angeles. The state senators excused their neglect, stating that the freeways provided convenient boundaries for the new districts.

Meanwhile, local assemblymen prepared to run for the state senate districts that they had just drawn to favor themselves in the event that they wanted to move up. The Mexican American community vehemently criticized the new plan. Many accused the Democratic party of crass opportunism.

Power struggles were taking place within MAPA. In a letter to the *Sun*, Ignacio López revealed a rift between the followers of Roybal and those of Eduardo Quevedo. The Quevedo faction had established new chapters and was attempting to change the direction of the organization. These wings and others were active at the MAPA convention in 1965. Like Quevedo and Roybal, Assemblyman Jesse Unruh also had supporters at the MAPA convention.

On the political front, Ross H. Valencia and Richard Calderón challenged Lindsay for the 9th Councilmanic District. George H. Mount, in his weekly *Sun* column, "Thought Provoker," offered insights into the race. By far, Calderón was the most viable challenger and his campaign received ample coverage in the *Sun*. He was supported by Mexican Americans, white liberals, and MAPA. Mount was critical, however, of the MAPA southern region endorsing convention because, he claimed, delegates snubbed Lindsay. On April 1, Mount also criticized Calderón campaign workers for pushing the Mexican American line too hard, expressing fear that the campaign might deteriorate into a Black vs. Mexican American skirmish.

Although the *Sun* gave Calderón coverage, Kovner endorsed Lindsay, taking almost every occasion to portray Lindsay and Ontiveros as a team. Kovner also ran articles praising Lindsay's vast political experience. On April 15, George Mount wrote in the *Sun* that Calderón ran a good race but had made the mistake of running against an incumbent with a good record, and therefore, lost.

James Roosevelt, son of Franklin D. Roosevelt, challenged Sam Yorty for city mayorship. Although the *Sun* had vehemently criticized Yorty in the past, it endorsed him now. Kovner accused Rosalind Wyman of attempting to build a political machine by running Roosevelt for mayor. He also admonished Governor Pat

Brown for supporting Wyman in this scheme. The California Democratic Council also came under attack for not protecting the Eastside interests.

MAPA endorsed Roosevelt, as did other liberal elements in the Mexican American community. Ironically, in spite of the negative role Rosalind Wyman played, she and her husband wielded considerable power within the liberal wing of the Democratic party. Her role in the Hazard Park deal allowed Yorty to gain inroads into the community. She was also remembered for her role in the Chávez Ravine giveaway.

Wyman lost in a runoff to Ed Edelman. At the age of 33, she had been in the city council for 12 years. The *Sun* wrote: "Wyman Loses After Home Demonstration," attributing her loss to the stand she took on Hazard Park.

Dr. Francisco Bravo resigned from the Los Angeles Police Commission because of differences with Councilman Tom Bradley. Bravo was a medical doctor who lived and practiced in the Eastside. Because of intelligence and money, Bravo was an independent who wielded political power. About this time, there was a growing alienation between Bravo and the Democratic party.

The *Sun* covered the escalation of the war in Vietnam. The paper and its reporters generally opposed the war. On July 29, Mount praised Congressman Brown for his opposition to the war. Brown conducted a survey to determine his constituents' attitudes toward the war. Out of 13,000 respondents, the results indicated overwhelming support for the war effort:

Expansion of the War	42%
Continue Present Level Without Expansion	12%
Seek Negotiated Settlement	29%
Immediate Withdrawal	11%

In spite of the results, Brown continued his opposition to the war.

Women were very much in the news. The California League of Mexican American Women honored Faustina Solis, special assistant to the state anti-poverty planning office. Ramona Morín, the league's president, and Francisca Flores, its secretary, organized the ceremonies. Twelve other women were honored. At the ceremonies, a moment of silence was observed for Viola Liuzzo, who had been slain by racists in Alabama. On July 17, the league held its constitutional convention. Francisca Flores was the program chair. Also noteworthy were the appointments of CSO members Aileen Hernández to the California Industrial Welfare Commission and Cruz Reynoso to the state FEPC.

Annexation attempts continued. Monterey Park wanted to absorb the area around East Los Angeles College. Both Kovner and Montoya informed the community and brought attention to this and other attempts to steal land from the Eastside.

An item that was to have far reaching consequences appeared during this period. The 1965 Immigration and Nationality Bill passed Congress. News coverage praised the act because it would end a 41-year-old policy of discriminatory quotas based on national origins and would terminate the exclusion of Asians. However, the nativists in Congress had held up final approval and held a series of debates and hearings on the act. Originally, it had not mentioned a quota on immigrants from Western Hemisphere countries. Nativists, however, were alarmed by the increased birth rates in Latin American countries. They feared that immigrants from these countries would flood into the U.S. Since they were poor and of a different race, according to the nativists, they could not be assimilated. When these nativists held up confirmation, President Lyndon B. Johnson compromised and agreed to a quota of 120,000 persons annually from Canada and Latin America. This act would have far reaching consequences in the years to come, when Congress became concerned with Mexican immigration.

SUMMARY

The death of John Fitzgerald Kennedy did not mark the end of his programs. Lyndon B. Johnson took the models of the Eastern planners and initiated his so-called war on poverty. The nationwide program was geared to Blacks. This is not surprising, considering the size and national distribution of the Black population, as well as the regional orientation of the Eastern intellectuals who conceptualized the war on poverty. Few of them knew what a Mexican American was. In Los Angeles, however, the Mexican American population was too large to be ignored. Middle-class

Mexican American activists resented the neglect of their people, especially considering the gravity of their need. Meanwhile, Yorty and the council struggled over control of the poverty funds. Yorty played all sides against each other.

The city council traditionally favored Blacks over Mexican Americans in the redistricting of councilmanic districts. The actions of white liberal council members determined the outcome of the elections in Roybal's old district by appointing Gilbert Lindsay, a Black, to the seat vacated by Roybal when he won the congressional race. This promoted a rivalry between Blacks and Chicanos that carried over into other areas.

The campaign in the 9th Congressional District exposed the absence of a viable Mexican American candidate. Richard Tafoya was a political professional, but his association with Yorty and the establishment encumbered him with too many liabilities. Tafoya polarized the left into neutrality or, even worse, forced them to support Lindsay as the lesser of two evils. During this period, Mexican Americans did not win any major elections in the Eastside. In fact, one of the two assemblymen of Mexican extraction was bested by John Fenton when a third Mexican American candidate split the vote. Ralph Poblano's unsuccessful race for the Los Angeles City School Board of Education paved the way for future races for the post.

Without doubt, education emerged as the principal issue of the mid-1960s. Citizens talked more about the necessity of improving the quality of education. The Los Angeles County Human Relations Commission helped organize the Mexican American Ad Hoc Education Committee in 1963. The committee had an important role in raising community awareness throughout the county. Activists and parents concerned that their children could not read and that there were not enough Mexican American teachers and counselors met and had a forum to articulate their grievances against the schools. They demanded better and more relevant curriculum. In this atmosphere, the Association of Mexican American Educators was formed in 1965, to more effectively advocate community interests from within the system. Meanwhile, youth also became more political; the Camp Hess Kramer Youth Conferences were important in the process.

Land use remained an issue. The city powers continued their drive to swap Hazard Park. The Los Angeles Federation of Labor supported building development without caring about the effects on residents. The interest of organized labor in this instance was jobs, not the social dislocation of Mexican Americans. By the mid-1960s, the master plans for Boyle Heights and East Los Angeles were released. The freeways were widened, facilitating transportation through the Eastside and increasing traffic pollution and dislocation.

The press covered the achievements of women during this period. The Mexican American Women's League was one of the first groups to focus on women. Linda Benítez, a member of the Executive Board of the Los Angeles County Democratic Party Central Committee, called for greater involvement of women in politics.

Many residents were concerned about police-community tensions. Conferences were held to discuss the situation. Arrests almost ignited several confrontations.

In 1965, President Johnson escalated the war in Vietnam. Also in that year, the Immigration and Naturalization Act was passed and, for the first time in U.S. history, a quota was placed on Mexicans entering the country. Both of these events would have far-reaching implications for Mexicans in the 1970s.

6

Rumblings in the Barrio: 1966–1968

Chapter 6 is based on the *Sun*, the *Citizen*, and the Roybal Scrapbook Collection. Also helpful for understanding the period are Rodolfo Acuña, *Occupied America*, 2nd ed. (New York: 1981); Biliana Ambrech, *Politicizing the Poor: Mexican American Community* (New York: 1967); Barrio Planners, Inc., *Nuestro Ambiente: East Los Angeles Visual Survey and Analysis* (Los Angeles: 1973); Fernando Padilla, "Legislative Gerrymandering of California Chicanos" (Ph.D. Dissertation, University of California, Santa Barbara, 1977); Gerald Paul Rosen, "Political Ideology and the Chicano Movement" (Ph.D. dissertation, University of California, Los Angeles, 1972); James Weinstein, *Ambiguous Legacy: The Left in American Politics* (New York: 1975); Milton Viorst, *Fire in the Streets: America in the 1960's* (New York: 1979); Howard Zinn, *A People's History of the United States* (New York: 1980).

A dichotomy between the Mexican American movement and the national civil rights struggle was evident during this period. In terms of organization, Mexican American activism appeared behind its white and Black counterparts, possessing little political rhetoric and few meaningful networks. Throughout the 1950s and 1960s, the radical input that was normal in the Black community was not common in East Los Angeles.

To its credit, the Community Service Organization (CSO) defended the civil liberties of Mexican Americans. It also furthered political education and was involved in large-scale voter registration drives. However, the loss of financial support from the Industrial Areas Foundation (IAF) made it impossible for the CSO to fully sustain its national contacts. Its resources were in no manner equal to those of many of the major Black organizations, which had considerable access to Washington power brokers. Because of this lack of funds, Mexican American efforts were compromised and often seemed uneven and out of synchronization with major national trends.

Both Blacks and whites involved in the civil rights movement had strong ties in the universities. Mexican Americans were almost absent from the campuses. The most important institution of higher learning to eastsiders remained East Los Angeles Junior College. At the four year colleges, they did not have sufficient numbers to influence the mainstream student movement. As late as 1967, there were only some 70 Chicano students at the University of California at Los Angeles. Moreover, Mexican Americans in college often did not have the educational or economic advantages of white student leaders who dominated the forums. Many early Black student leaders also came from lower-middle-class families. Moreover, the tradition of Black colleges had built a small yet effective cadre of activists. The progress of Mexicans and Blacks in higher education, therefore, could not be compared.

By 1966, the civil rights movement was on the decline. For one thing, militancy had caused a backlash among many white supporters. Also, the war in Vietnam had caused a shift in priorities among liberal white students and adults. By the end of the year, the war had resulted in 44,000 casualities and was claiming 500 American lives a month. Annually, $22 billion was committed to the Vietnam war. This is in contrast to the $1.2 billion spent on the war to end poverty at home.

At first, mainstream Black civil rights leaders did not officially oppose the war, fearing that they might jeopardize administration support and financial assistance from private and public sources. They had been consistent in advancing the Black struggle towards equal access to political, economic, and social institutions. Naturally, they were hesitant to divert attention from these goals. Eventually, however, the younger and more militant Blacks forced opposition to the war on moral grounds.

The on-campus anti-war movement became explosive by the late 1960s, when the Selective Service System abolished their long-standing student deferment policy. Contributing to this decision was the constant rise in college enrollments of 18 to 20-year-olds—from 12 percent in 1940 to 50 percent by 1970—and the fact that an inordinate number of servicemen were from poor Black, white, or brown backgrounds.

The core of the energized anti-war movement was comprised of radicals, but the general membership was mainstream liberal. Undoubtedly, many young people, especially the men, joined the crusade because of self-interest and even more were caught up in the popular cause of their generation. For the most part, these young people were middle-class whites who were sympathetic to the Black struggle but knew little and cared less about Third World people.

Although student contributions were meaningful, the early peace movement was kept alive by groups such as the Committee for a Sane Nuclear Policy (SANE), the Catholic Workers, California's Vietnam Victory Committee, and others. These groups organized among white middle-class liberals. The members of these groups were political. By 1967, the anti-war movement was in full swing. In that year, when Martin Luther King Jr. actively joined the mobilizations, the movement took on a new and expanded proportion.

The Eastside had a core of activists who had been involved in progressive movements since the 1930s, predating the Chicano youth movement and its anti-war involvement by some 30 years. The Chicano student movement got its initial push when the Educational Opportunities Programs recruited larger numbers of

Chicanos to the four-year colleges in 1967. Quickly integrated into anti-war and anti-establishment mobilizations, these Chicano students pushed to get more attention paid to their particular ethnic group. The student input reinforced the activist tradition in the Eastside and added energy to the local Chicano movement.

The rage that ignited the Black communities nationally cannot be solely attributed to the increased radicalization of young Black leaders. Some of the most violent urban rebellions occurred in 1967. Throughout the nation, there were a total of 123 minor mob riots. Also that year, major eruptions in Newark and Detroit left 83 people dead, most of them Black. Studies profiling the rebels showed that they were young, Black, and high school dropouts. They were not Black professionals or college students.

Chronic conditions caused the rebellions. Black Americans had suffered tremendous dislocation in the 20th century. In 1910, 90 percent lived in the South, where they worked in agricultural occupations. But by 1965, 81 percent of the cotton in major areas, including the Mississippi Delta, was harvested by machines. From 1940 to 1970 alone, four million Blacks left the Southeastern countryside for cities. In 1965, 80 percent lived in cities. Significantly, 50 percent resided in the northern states. Few institutions of communal social control survived these migrations. Permanent unemployment, poverty, racism, hopelessness, and oppression created a wellspring of rage and eventually drove urban Blacks to the streets.

The rebellions of 1967 encouraged the passage of the Civil Rights Act of 1968. This law prohibited violence towards Blacks and denial of their civil rights, especially at the worksite. However, the act also imposed penalties and a sentence of five years for anyone traveling across state lines or using interstate facilities, including the mails and telephone, "to organize, promote, encourage, participate or carry on a riot." In the late 1960s, Black leader H. Rapp Brown was prosecuted under this law.

The *Sun* and the *Citizen* largely ignored these events, although the *Sun* did emphasize that violence was not the solution and expressed pride that the Eastside was a peaceful community. Also, to its credit, the *Sun* actively opposed the war in Vietnam.

Much of the coverage in both weeklies suggests a heavy involvement of community folk in the war on poverty. This coverage can be explained in part by community leaders understanding the importance of advertising their programs and events in the community papers. Also important was the fact that the war on poverty was a mainstream activity and a general topic. What specific effects the war on poverty had on communities cannot be determined directly from the weeklies' articles. One important reality is that, by 1966, the war on poverty was on the decline.

From the outset, the Community Action Programs (CAPs) were the most controversial projects in the war on poverty. The intention was to create private, non-profit, non-government agencies that had boards comprised of at least one-third local residents. Local politicians soon ended this social experiment. Mayor Sam Yorty was especially critical of community participation, calling it socialistic. Eventually, the CAP structure was replaced by the Model Cities Program, which was essentially controlled by local politicians.

More popular and longer lasting than CAPs were the advisory boards set up by the Office of Economic Opportunity agencies. The Urban Renewal Act of 1954 had required advisory boards, but generally they were comprised of people outside the community and often included individuals who profited from the redevelopment projects. The OEO advisory boards, which were composed of at least one-third community members, represented the first time that the poor were allowed, and even expected, to act in an advisory capacity.

Leaders in the war on poverty wanted to establish organized community power so that the poor could barter their support in exchange for access to institutions and programs that affected government policy. According to Professor Biliana Ambrecht, there were 60 OEO advisory boards in East Los Angeles-Boyle Heights-South Lincoln Heights. A total of 1,520 individuals, 71 percent of whom were from the affected community, participated on the boards. Two-thirds of the numbers were women.

If the programs had any lasting effect, it probably was in raising the consciousness of individual participants. Frustration followed by participation always plays a role in raising awareness. But how much the agencies contributed to the heightening and strengthening of cultural identity prevalent during the times remains unanswered.

Both weeklies covered the problems surrounding the school system. Discontent had been festering since the 1930s. There were numerous horror stories of unsympathetic counselors track-

ing young Chicanos into vocational education, of future doctors
having been routed into woodshop majors. Frustrations climaxed
in 1968 and the schools became battlegrounds. This was the year
of the Eastside blowouts. These school walkouts were important
because they inspired similar walkouts at Latino high schools
throughout the Southwest and the Midwest.

From this year to the early 1970s, youth dominated the
Chicano movement in the Eastside. The two most important
issues became education and the Vietnam War. Unfortunately,
while doing an excellent job in covering the walkouts, both the
Sun and the *Citizen* ignored the involvement of Chicano youth.
A partial explanation for this is that Chicano students created
their own media. In the mid-60s, veteran activist Francisca Flores
had published *Carta Editorial*. By 1967, *La Raza* magazine, the
Chicano Student Movement, and the *Inside Eastside* newspapers
carried Chicano news. While devoting great energy to education
and problems surrounding the war, the more experienced activists
also participated in organizing political campaigns, fighting the
war on poverty, and protesting the constant land encroachments.
They also continued the tradition of advertising programs and
events in the weeklies.

THE CHRONICLE
1966

Both the *Sun* and the *Citizen* explained how the Economic and
Youth Opportunities Agency (EYOA) worked and what it meant
in terms of service to the community. On January 6, the *Sun* ran
an article titled "The Economic and Youth Opportunities Agency:
What is it?" According to this article, the new program was supposed to organize the poor into grassroots groups that would participate in the election of poverty boards. However, while many
activists were suspicious of elections, the community itself apparently lacked interest in the general process. The article also
criticized the actual election mechanism as well as the distribution of funds.

In the Eastside, the EYOA attempted to generate interest in
the elections among Mexican Americans. On February 24, the
Citizen reported that two seats were hotly contested. Even so, the
turnout for the March 3 elections was disappointing.

The war on poverty attracted large sums of money. Both the Black and Mexican American communities were economically depressed and competed for funding. Complicating matters was the lack of guidelines for funds distribution. Federal grants were thrown into a virtual grab bag and the two hungry communities scrambled for the crumbs.

Although Mexican Americans received a few key appointments, white liberals dominated the bureaucracy. The civil rights movement had conditioned white liberals to think in terms of Black and white—and so most of the money was allocated to Black agencies. Finally, in April, a citizen's committee was formed to represent the interests of East Los Angeles in the poverty war.

The most bitter Black-brown conflict involved the Neighborhood Adult Participation Program (NAPP). Opal Jones, a Black, headed the agency. Jones had always been a controversial figure and, in April, the poverty board fired her because of alleged insolence. However, Jones had considerable support in the Black community and was reinstated. By summer, Mexican American NAPP employees complained that Jones was anti-Mexican. Only two of the 13 NAPP agencies served large numbers of Mexicans. Irene Tovar, director of the Pacoima NAPP Center, resigned, citing Jones's harassment and the under-representation of Mexican Americans in NAPP. An ad hoc committee complained that Mexican Americans were receiving "the short end of the stick." Other Mexican American resignations followed. When Gilbert Yañez quit in October, the GI Forum passed a resolution condemning Jones.

Dr. Manuel Guerra and Dionicio Morales charged favoritism toward Blacks in EYOA. Some grew concerned that the Black–brown feud would get out of control. On March 31, Kovner published an editorial criticizing Guerra and Morales and warning about the danger of pitting race against race.

In April, Morales's East Los Angeles Youth Project was expanded. Changes also took place in the Neighborhood Youth Corps (NYC). The NYC phased out 2,000 youngsters, changing its priorities to the recruitment of "hard core"* young people. Shortly after this transition, cutbacks threatened the program. On

---

*Refers to dropouts and the unemployed.

August 4, the *Sun* ran an article: "Neighborhood Youth Corps Facing Cutback in Spite of Resounding Success Here." The cutbacks affected numerous agencies and, in many cases, forced agency workers to mobilize the community. This in many respects wasted energy that could have been used to provide services to the community.

Most agencies suffered continual changes because of shifting EYOA guidelines. Federal authorities also often reduced agency budgets and threatened to defund them altogether. This caused frustration and instability and undermined the efforts of EYOA.

One of the most influential, and at the same time controversial, agencies was the Eastland Community Action Council, which received a $93,515 grant in September. John Serrato was head of this agency. Another important organization was the Youth Training and Employment Project (YTEP), which offered basic skills and training, as well as job development training. On September 2, YTEP opened its facilities in Boyle Heights. On October 20, Fernando Del Río initiated a series of articles in the *Sun* titled "Inside YTEP." By the end of the year, YTEP was also under fire.

The Mexican American Opportunities Foundation (MAOF) opened its offices. Dionicio Morales directed MAOF, which was more enduring and successful than other poverty agencies. MAOF's priority was job training. Regional and national dignitaries periodically visited these many agencies. Sergeant Shriver, brother-in-law of the late President Kennedy, headed the war on poverty nationally. In July, Shriver toured the Eastside poverty facilities, and Daniel Luevano, western director of the Office of Economic Opportunities, visited the Los Angeles area in November.

On December 8, both the *Citizen* and the *Sun* announced a $9.5 million cutback in EYOA funds. These cutbacks impacted on teen posts, which appeared to be the most vulnerable of the new federal programs. Parents and young people picketed the Bellas Artes Teen Post as early as June when cutbacks were announced there. As funds became more limited, Black-brown tensions increased and both groups competed over the remaining funds. According to the July 28 edition of the *Sun*, the war in Vietnam diverted monies needed for domestic programs.

Politics among Mexican Americans was still largely a Democratic party affair. Congressional representatives Edward R.

Roybal, George Brown, and Augustus Hawkins launched a voter-registration drive in November. U.S. Senator Joseph Montoya (D-NM) kicked off this drive in Southern California.

Interwound with politics was the farmworkers' strike. MAPA supported the National Farmworkers Union and pressured Governor Edmund G. Brown Sr. to support it. From this point on, most Mexican American candidates openly supported the farmworkers.

Richard Calderón received the CDC and MAPA endorsements for his bid for the 27th Senatorial District but lost by 311 votes. This election is an example of how the Mexican American vote was split during this period. Cecilia Pedroza and Raúl Morín badly splintered the Mexican American vote. Had they not run, Calderón would have won. Charges were made that the Anglo candidate who won had encouraged Pedroza to enter the campaign.

Gilbert Avila ran for the 45th Assembly District; Eddie Ramírez, for the 28th Senatorial District. MAPA endorsed Ramírez. Phil Ortiz, meanwhile, declared his candidacy for the 51st Assembly District. William Orozco ran as a Republican for the 29th Congressional District and made a strong showing against incumbent George Brown. Many charged that right wing extremists, including Cuban reactionaries, supported Orozco's campaign. Lastly, Pete Díaz and Ed Elliot vied in the 40th Assembly District. The *Citizen*'s "Political Whirl" column covered these races.

MAPA held an endorsing convention in Fresno, June 24-26. The California gubernatorial race pitted Pat Brown against Republican Ronald Reagan. Roybal headed the Viva Brown committee and MAPA also endorsed the incumbent governor. Meanwhile, Dr. Francisco Bravo charged that Brown was not sensitive to Mexican Americans and openly supported Reagan. Brown responded to Bravo by stating that Reagan was against the Mexican American people. Bravo defended Reagan and attacked Brown's record, which J. J. Rodríguez of the butcher's union defended. All of this infighting polarized Mexican Americans and split the vote. Bravo, however, continued to campaign for Reagan, denying that the candidate was anti-Mexican American.

Meanwhile, Bert Corona assumed MAPA's presidency. Lyndon B. Johnson had earlier named Corona to the U.S. Civil Rights Commission. U.S. Senator Joseph Montoya warned Californians that Mexican Americans would suffer in the event that Reagan was elected. César Chávez endorsed Brown and issued a statement charging that Reagan would destroy the farmworker movements. Even Robert Kennedy entered California to campaign for Brown. Reagan, meanwhile, attracted a crowd of almost 2,000 eastsiders when he visited the area. In the end, Pat Brown lost.

In an unprecedented act, the Mexican American Education Committee (MAEC) opposed the school bonds, explaining that Mexican Americans did not receive their fair share of the school funds. In response, the Los Angeles City Schools promised improvements for Eastside schools if the bond issue were passed. Geraldine Ledesma, who headed MAEC, wrote an open letter to Superintendent Jack Crowther, summarizing the Mexican American community's grievances against the school district.

Unemployment hit eight percent in East Los Angeles in 1966. FEPC reports showed that unemployment declined from 12 percent in 1960 to six percent in 1965 among non-whites. In Boyle Heights, City Terrace and East Los Angeles, unemployment declined from nine to eight percent.

Roybal accompanied President Johnson to Mexico. During this trip, Roybal said, the president presented to the congressman and to Senator Ralph Yarborough the idea of bilingual education. Johnson had been a teacher in a predominately Mexican American school in Texas and told Roybal and Yarborough that the students were bright but just did not know the language.

On March 29, 50 Mexican Americans walked out of an Equal Employment Opportunities Commission conference in Albuquerque. The delegates grew angry when they learned that, although they had come to discuss fair employment for Mexican Americans, the EEOC did not have a single Mexican American on its staff. The Albuquerque walkout immediately became a symbol to Mexican Americans.

The *Sun* and the *Citizen* reported a rash of Mexican American appointments. Former deputy sheriff Rose Marie Rodríguez was the first woman named to the district attorney's office as investigator. Richard Alatorre was appointed the educational resource director of the Association of Mexican American Educators' tutorial program. Audrey A. Kaslow was appointed to the State Welfare Board. And Henry Quevedo, son of MAPA's Eduardo Quevedo, took a job in the office of District Attorney Evelle Younger.

On October 20, 26, and 28, Mexican Americans held preliminary meetings for a national conference on Mexican American problems to be sponsored by the White House and the U.S. Department of Labor. The national conference was scheduled for May 4-6, 1967. Also this year, the League of Mexican American Women honored Mrs. Edmund G. Brown, Sr., as well as other women.

The UCLA Mexican American Study Project released data that surprised many Mexican Americans. For instance, the study stated that intermarriage between Anglos and Mexican Americans was increasing. Between 1924 and 1933, only ten percent of all Los Angeles marriages were interracial. In 1963, 27 percent of the marriages in Los Angeles County were between Anglo males and Mexican American women, and 23 percent were between Mexican American men and Anglo women. The study documented that intermarriage was higher in Los Angeles than in San Antonio, Texas, that it was more likely to take place in the third generation, and that the younger men were more likely to intermarry with Anglos than were older Mexican Americans. The report stated that men who had gone through a divorce were more likely to intermarry than men who had never married. The study also suggested that changes were taking place in the U.S. immigration policies toward Mexico and predicted that the United States would move toward stricter control of Mexican immigration.

Kovner criticized that UCLA study, stating that the project portrayed East Los Angeles negatively. Kovner often romanticized the area and objected to its being characterized as deteriorated or blighted. He also feared that this designation would lead to urban renewal. However, in spite of its publisher's personal objections, the *Sun* reported many of the UCLA findings.

Criticism of the police grew more severe. Ed Cray wrote several articles in the *Sun* criticizing police authorities. Kovner himself, however, seemed reluctant to complain about the police. Reacting to strong denunciations of police activity in the Eastside by Dionicio Morales, Ralph Poblano, Ray Gonzales, and Ed Quevedo, Kovner wrote on June 16, "We're part of a peaceful community." The next week, Kovner outlined new police laws and the role of the U.S. Supreme Court in improving justice. It appeared that Kovner recognized that tensions in the Eastside could lead to another Watts.

The Council on Mexican American Affairs was at the forefront of exposing police brutality. In May, CMAA publicly accused the police of abusing the community. The sheriff's department denied this charge.

The Los Angeles City Police Commission met with Mexican American leaders and attempted to lessen tensions. Meanwhile, the ACLU and the CSO jointly opened and operated a police malpractice complaint center in Boyle Heights. The Neighborhood Legal Service Society, Inc., was also funded to provide legal services to the needy.

Police Chief William Parker died in July. As usual, the newspapers forgot his racist comments, dubbing him a "man of integrity."

Kovner enthusiastically supported District Attorney Evelle Younger's "Operation Cool Head" and praised Younger's aide, Bill Herrera. Kovner went out of his way to build bridges with the police. Neither the *Sun* nor the *Citizen* adequately covered the death of a 17-year-old youth who was shot and killed by an LAPD officer.

Hazard Park and Elysian Park communities remained active. The Hazard Park group attended a California beauty conference called by Governor Brown. The theme was "Keeping California Beautiful." The group lobbied Brown and sent a letter to Lady Bird Johnson, asking both parties to help preserve Hazard Park for the community. At the same time, Yorty's proposed giveaway of 63 acres of Elysian Park land in return for a municipal auditorium drew fire. According to Kovner, the land would be used for commercial purposes, which was a violation of the legal and moral purposes of eminent domain. Nevertheless, on January 13, the city council voted 9-to-4 to accept bids for the Elysian Park convention center.

Oil drilling was canceled in Elysian Park and a permanent injunction was sought against further drilling there. Elysian Park was literally up for grabs in the city council. Final approval for the convention center project seemed certain.

Opposition to the Hazard Park deal had delayed the actual transfer of the park. However, most people believed that it was only a matter of time before the park would be lost. The "Save Hazard Park" group was disillusioned when it learned that the armory at Hazard would be transferred to Rose Hill. Almost simultaneously, the city council held hearings on Hazard Park. Experts testified for the need to preserve the park. The hearings were heated and the council delayed a final action until June. Most observers were certain that the park commissioners would strongly support the transfer. Meanwhile, the County Human Relations Commission conducted hearings at which the Save Hazard Park Committee and USC professor Dr. Manuel Servín asked for an investigation of the final contract.

During the beginning of December, the *Sun* reported that the city council approved the land transfer. The stormy city council meeting was picketed by the Save Hazard Park Committee, which vehemently criticized Yorty, Wyman, Edelman, and Debs.

At the council hearings, Mrs. Harold Morton testified that a park in West Los Angeles was needed because the apartments were small and had no backyards. Attorney Joan Martin responded, "You take away their park and wonder why you have to build more prisons. These people around Hazard Park don't have automobiles. Around Westwood they do not have parks, but they have cars and can drive to parks." Nevertheless, Yorty signed the ordinance approving the Hazard Park swap. A PTA study showed that Los Angeles was 12,000 acres short of park land.

Although both the Democratic Party Central Committee and Governor Brown opposed the convention site at Elysian Park, Yorty's people acted with impunity and bulldozers cut roads in Elysian Park hills. Meanwhile, Obregón Park was dedicated on May 28. Although many community leaders supported Obregón Park, the people whose homes were condemned to build the park remained bitter. The homes had been taken, yet dumpsites and junk-yards still marred the area.

The city approved zone changes for the Lucky Market center. At the same time, both city and county planners urged that zoning be more uniform for the sake of "community growth." The county supervisors heard additional proposals for higher density, more commercial land use. The East Central Area Welfare Planning Council was pivotal in these decisions, since its recommendations were supposed to be unbiased. Jim Madrid, elected head of the council, was closely associated with Yorty.

White Memorial Hospital was approved for Medicare and planned major expansion in Boyle Heights. Standard Oil was also given permission to drill for oil in Belvedere Park. Freeway construction rolled on. People opposing further freeway expansion applauded a 1965 California Act that required closer environment control.

The *Citizen* supported urban renewal and, in his October 6 "Beachcomber" column, Alberto "Al" Díaz defended the master plan and the so-called land grabs. He editorialized that he had faith in Supervisor Ernest Debs, who, according to Díaz, was knowledgeable of community needs.

Parents, meanwhile, protested completion of an unsafe freeway overpass. The structure across the Pomona Freeway had become a barrier to pedestrian travel and posed potential danger to children. In an editorial, Kovner encouraged the governor to veto the Beverly Hills Freeway, which was still in the works. In November, Kovner also called for transferring ownership of the housing projects to the tenants.

In the March 31 edition of the *Sun*, Jack Solomon claimed that the rights of minorities were ignored in urban renewal projects. Arthur Montoya attacked county variance and zoning practices. In the fall, he wrote a series of articles on urban renewal and land grab schemes in East Los Angeles. On another front, Ralph Cuarón cautioned Eastsiders about rent subsidies to builders.

In October, Montoya critiqued the master plan and its relation to past and present urban renewal, criticizing the community renewal programs submitted to the supervisors. Montoya warned of attempts to remove a library on Gage and Michigan Streets to make way for "development." Concluding his weekly series on urban renewal on December 15, he alerted the readers to the fact that local authorities were applying for urban renewal grants.

Montoya was an enigma. Progressive on many issues, he was reactionary on others. In a February 24 article, he objected to the use of the label "Mexican American," writing that it should be Americans of Mexican descent.

In May, the California Supreme Court declared Proposition 14, which nullified the Rumford Fair Housing Act, unconstitutional.

Martín Ortiz resigned as director of the East Los Angeles Area Welfare Planning Council. He had been honored for his work with youth. On February 12, the Mexican American Parents Conference, sponsored by the Los Angeles City Schools and the Equal Opportunity Foundation, was held at Lincoln High School. The proceedings were conducted in Spanish and English. The conference issued a ten-point statement of needs, which included the necessity for Mexican American counselors, teachers, and a Mexican history curriculum. Some 1,000 parents attended.

Dr. Miguel Montes, a dentist from San Fernando, was appointed to the California Board of Education. He proved helpful to the interests of Mexican American children. The Fourth Annual Camp Hess Kramer seminar was held for Mexican American youth leaders in April. That same month saw the Office of Urban Affairs of the Los Angeles City Schools sponsor a "Youth Career Conference" at Los Angeles State College. On May 14, the California Association of Educators of Mexican Descent also held a symposium. The topic was "Effectiveness of Programs for Mexican Americans." The Association of Mexican American Educators was also active, and its Greater East Los Angeles Chapter held an installation banquet, with Ralph Guzmán installing the officers.

Learning the English language was reported as the number one problem for Mexican American children. Tutorial programs were popular. And, in the fall, UCLA established an Upward Bound Program.

The Young Citizens for Community Action (YCCA) met throughout the summer at Laguna Park. Vicky Castro was president, Frank Hidalgo, co-chair, and Rachel Ochoa, secretary. By the end of the summer, the group planned a conference on the "Education Dilemma of the Mexican American."

1967

News coverage of the Vietnam War in the weeklies in 1967 suggests increased awareness of Southeast Asia. The protests and contradictions moved to the foreground. David M. Barrón wrote one of the first analyses of the draft for the *Citizen* on March 23: "Draft Policies: How it Affects Latin Youths." According to Barrón, Mexican Americans suffered a disproportionate number of deaths and casualties in Vietnam. For instance, in 1966, Chicanos comprised 41 percent of San Antonio, Texas, but accounted for 62.5 percent of the city's war casualties. Barrón also pointed out that 30.2 percent of all Black males qualified for the draft, while only 18.8 percent of all white males did. On May 25, the *Citizen* published the names of the eight local youths killed in the war. Dan Moreno wrote an article for the *Citizen*: "Vietnam War Killing Close to Home: Eight ELA Youth Dead!" The *Citizen* also covered awards earned by Mexican American servicemen in its "Your Men in Service" column.* Congressman George Brown stated that Mexican Americans in California comprised nine percent of the Los Angeles County population but represented 17.6 percent of the Angelenos killed in Vietnam in 1966. UCLA studies on Mexican Americans reported that, between January 1, 1966, and February 28, 1967, 19.4 percent of the Southwest's casualties were Mexican American, even though this group accounted for only 11.8 percent of the region's population. Based on this data, Mexican Americans made up 23.3 percent of the Marines, 9.1 percent of the Air Force, and 7.3 percent of the Navy casualties. The latter two armed services were significant because they were noncombatant and very selective in recruitment. Mexican Americans entered these branches at a much lower rate. During November, two more Eastsiders were reported killed, bringing the total to 14. One of the dead was a former honor student.

The *Sun* reported a confrontation between peace protestors and police officers at the Century Plaza Hotel as marchers picketed President Johnson on June 23. The police repression was brutal. The Eastside Democratic Club condemned police tactics, blaming the confrontation on police overreaction. Among themselves, city council members disagreed on the police actions. Ed Edelman called for an investigation, while Paul H. Lamport defended the LAPD. The ACLU filed suit against Police Chief Reddin for the police violence at Century City.

Congressmen George Brown and Roybal were the most outspoken critics of the war. Gil García headed the "Comité Pro-Paz," which opened a peace information center. In August, another Eastside committee was organized against the war. Over the next months, volunteers from the East Los Angeles Peace Center canvassed Boyle Heights to fill petitions opposing the war. Eastsiders flocked to peace rallies in San Francisco and Washington, D.C. David Mares headed the Peace Action Center in Los Angeles. The PAC sponsored an October 15 rally in East Los

---

*The *Citizen*'s "Your Men in Service" articles were run weekly and have not been entirely listed in the second part of this book.

Angeles, featuring Black comedian Dick Gregory. In the fall, the Peace and Freedom party was organized. This new party attracted many Eastsiders who were disillusioned with the Democratic party.

In 1967, 28 candidates filed for the Los Angeles School Board race. This race attracted considerable interest. Mexican American candidates made widespread use of the 1960 census data to show how the educational system was failing the community.

In order to avoid splitting their vote, community leaders held an endorsing convention on January 15, 1967. Frank X. Paz, of the GI Forum and MAPA, was interim chair. The convention endorsed Dr. Julián Nava, who attacked the L.A. Schools and called for an expansion of scholastic services. For the most part, however, other candidates did not abide by the rules of the United Council of Community Organizations, which specified that losers would drop out, and announced that they would run anyway.

The school board ethnic survey showed that the school population was 56 percent white, 20.8 percent Black, and 19.2 percent Mexican/Latino. The survey also showed that while 138,210 Latino students attended Los Angeles schools, only 2.7 percent of the teachers (708) had Spanish surnames. At one high school, Roosevelt, most of the 2,304 students were Mexican Americans but only nine teachers were of Mexican extraction. And at Garfield High, where most of the 3,324 students were Mexican Americans, only six Latino teachers were employed.

Without a doubt, Mexican Americans needed representation on the school board. The *Sun* reported on Nava's activities, devoting considerable coverage to his candidacy. The weekly also reported on the convention proceedings and its follow-up work. Officially, MAPA endorsed Nava, although some members felt considerable sentiment for Julia Mount and Dr. Manuel Guerra. Mount was supported by the New Politics group, which later that year became the Peace and Freedom party. She was the only candidate who enthusiastically embraced the anti-war movement. Nava and Dr. Robert Doctor were supported by the Democratic party. Nava, a graduate of Roosevelt High and East Los Angeles Junior College, was an Eastside native and had a Harvard Ph.D. in history.

The *Citizen*'s "Beachcomber" column extensively covered the campaign and, on April 6, the paper printed the results:

Smoot	177,804
Nava	112,965
Bond	25,540
Guerra	21,093
Zimmerman	18,577
Mount	10,723
Landau	7,092

Although incumbent Charles Smoot received a plurality, he did not achieve a majority. Nava won the ensuing runoff.

In the runoff, most Mexican American organizations supported Nava. Through the primary, Richard Calderón managed Nava's campaign and was the de facto campaign manager in the runoff. Many people attribute Nava's ultimate victory to Calderón, who had strong credentials as an activist.

A by-product of the Nava race was the formation of the Congress of Mexican American Unity. Headed by the Reverend Antonio Hernández, Nava's brother-in-law, CMAU's objective was to support Mexican American candidates. The group called for a community endorsing convention in December to select candidates for the 1968 election.

Organizations such as the East Los Angeles Town Hall Meeting, led by actor Mike de Anda, had avoided direct politics until Nava's campaign. Deteriorating conditions in the schools and proposed budget cuts threatened the Eastside further, forcing many Mexican American organizations into the offensive. Nava effectively exploited the budget cuts and the community's frustrations. Many activists, sensing a victory and realizing the urgency of the issue, jumped on the bandwagon.

In the spring, budget cuts in school programs generated considerable reaction. Mass protests were held on March 20 and 28. The East Los Angeles Town Hall Meeting conducted protests at the board of education and held a dance in City Terrace to raise funds for the drive against budget cuts. Forty members of the East Los Angeles group traveled to Sacramento to protest budget cuts and the lack of state support for education. Members attempted to meet with Reagan but the governor refused to see them. Much to their chagrin, the town hall chair apologized to the governor for the group's tactics. The group retracted the apology, which had not been authorized. During this period, the Town Hall held a fund raising dance for Nava's board of education campaign. Not all Eastsiders supported such activities and a small faction of right-wingers in the barrios opposed Nava. The right wing clustered around Orozco, who was so critical of Nava that he refused to introduce him at a Cinco de Mayo celebration. Meanwhile, Smoot also catered to the right wing, alleging that Nava favored "sit-ins." Smoot even refused to appear with Nava on Channel 9, an independent Los Angeles station, on its program, "Feature Page."

Nava scored an upset victory, winning by a 50,000 vote margin. (There was a relatively low turnout in the white and Black precincts, while there were good showings in the Mexican American and Jewish American precincts, both of which voted heavily for Nava.) The Mexican American community was elated with its victory. For the first time in many years, Mexican Americans had a representative on the board of education. MAPA honored Nava. At the event, one of his former teachers, Dr. Helen Bailey, herself a a legend in the Eastside, spoke fondly of Nava as a student. The Nava campaign spent $15,083 in the primary and $73,900 in the runoffs. As a board of education representative, Nava's salary would be less than $12,000 a year.

Governor Reagan, meanwhile, delayed a hearing on the school tax-relief bill. When 15 members of the town hall finally met with the governor, he confronted them angrily. Pounding on the table, he threatened to veto all education bills. Addressing the board of education on August 14, the Eastside group increased its criticism, censuring the board's Office of Urban Affairs.

Governor Reagan's action inflamed the minority communities. Reagan single-handedly attempted to derail the civil rights movement and programs that equalized educational opportunities. The governor wanted to impose a tuition charge at the state universities and colleges. His tuition proposal would have made the University of California the fifth most expensive in the nation. The California PTA pointed out that the state's economy exceeded that of all but five nations in the world and concluded that "we can afford quality schools." Even the normally fiscally conservative Arthur Montoya vehemently criticized Reagan's proposal. Considering the governor's hard-line approach to education, it seemed ironic that he keynoted the Youth Opportunities Scholarship dance in November in East Los Angeles. At a July meeting, in which Nava voted for an increase, the board of education adopted a $640 million budget.

Meanwhile, Roybal introduced legislation to fund bilingual programs. Many supervisors, including Ernest Debs, supported the bill. The Los Angeles City Schools urged its passage and at the time there appeared to be considerable support from many sectors. Articles on the advantages of bilingual education appeared in the *Sun*. By July, the Roybal bill went to the U.S. Senate, where it was sponsored by Ralph Yarborough. Debates were held. A U.S. Senate subcommittee held hearings in Los Angeles on bilingual education June 22 and 23.

On July 8 and 9, the Advisory Committee to the U.S. Civil Rights Commission held hearings on the topics of civil rights, education, and employment problems of Mexican Americans. Bishop James Pike chaired these meetings. Politicians and community folks testified at the hearings and cited the need for more jobs and Mexican American teachers.

The East Los Angeles Library was dedicated on July 27. On October 9, the community activists picketed Euclid Avenue Elementary School, demanding removal of its principal, Dr. Lillian Tallman. Patricio Sánchez headed this band of activists as representative of the United Council of Community Organizations led the protests. At a November 30 board of education meeting, the Educational Issues Coordinating Committee aired grievances and demanded Tallman's removal. Not persuaded, the board gave the principal a vote of confidence.

An ethnic survey of the UCLA student body showed that there were only 303 Mexican Americans enrolled in the university. This represented 1.3 percent of all enrollment.

Various community colleges also held conferences on educational opportunities for Mexican Americans. The Mexican American Student Association (MASA) was formed at East Los Angeles Junior College. Al Juárez, a former Teen Post director, led the group. The Association of Mexican American Educators (AMAE) criticized the teacher training program at California State College, Los Angeles, calling it inadequate. The Los Angeles City Schools repsonded to the unrest by enrolling some of its employees in Spanish classes. The school district also announced a $3.1 millions building program for local schools.

Senior citizens conferences were held in the Eastside, where a senior citizens referral center was established. Amazingly, special programs for almost every sector of society developed during this time.

The CSO Young Adult and Community Development Program was funded by EYOA. Like many established organizations, CSO was able to expand its service because of grants. A bilingual health center was dedicated in East Los Angeles in October. Even the East Central Area Welfare Planning Council coordinated the East Los Angeles Central Area Inter-Agency Youth Services Committee, which was made possible by poverty funding.

The April 28, 1967, issue of *Time* magazine ran "Pocho's Progress," an article that presented a distorted view of East Los Angeles. Roybal called the article an affront to the Mexican American community. Even a local eighth-grade class wrote critical letters to the *Time* editor. Eastsiders called for a boycott of the magazine, which replied to the flood of letters by stating that it had not meant offense.

James Corral of the Mexican American Action Committee (MAAC) joined Vicky Castro of the Young Citizens for Community Action (YCCA) to plan an East Los Angeles Youth Conference. MAAC celebrated its first year as an organization. Soon afterward, James Corral became Assemblyman Walter Karabian's field deputy.

Meanwhile, on May 13, about 200 Mexican American students met at Loyola University and formed a countywide student group, the United Mexican American Students. Its central committee pooled representatives from local universities and colleges. UMAS increased cooperation among Mexican American students and helped them become more political. The Mexican American Youth Conference was again held at Camp Hess Kramer.

The YCCA attended a "heated meeting" with Los Angeles Police Chief Tom Reddin. Nearly 200 community people aired their grievances. The Young Adult Leadership and Community Development Project of the CSO sponsored the session. The fact that Reddin appeared at the meeting was interpreted by the *Citizen* as a favorable sign. It was evident that police authorities were concerned about the long hot summer. District Attorney Evelle Younger pushed his "Cool Head" program and a rally was held at Belvedere Park on July 22. Captain Lorenzo Sánchez, a Vietnam hero, addressed the participants.

In January, Dan Reyes was named the new director of the Eastland Community Action Council. From the beginning, there were problems. After several months, the East Los Angeles poverty board fired Reyes, which caused further divisions. ECAC was controversial in part because its action centers organized residents for the purpose of pressuring government to provide services for the community. In August, ECAC named Fernando del Río to replace Reyes as director.

Shortly after, a special U.S. cabinet report was issued. "The Mexican American: New Focus on Opportunity" showed that, since 1964, 90,000 Mexican Americans had been served by Neighborhood Youth Corps, 34,000 by Headstart, and 50,000 by basic education programs.

Federal funding for hardcore delinquents was in constant jeopardy because many funding agencies considered it to be too controversial. Teen Posts, for instance, could not find sponsors. Further, by the end of the year, many funding agencies were being dismantled. EYOA, therefore, looked for new organizations to direct NAPP and the Teen Post programs.

A demonstration protesting Governor Reagan's medical cuts took place on September 20. The Save Medi-Cal Committee was active in the Eastside. In response to criticism, the state's finance director avowed that Medi-Cal must be—and would be—cut. Governor Reagan showed little sympathy in providing medical care to the poor.

Drug addiction assistance projects remained controversial. When EYOA approved a new narcotics center in Boyle Heights, 175 neighborhood residents protested. Although Councilman Gilbert Lindsay supported local residents, the board of supervisors approved the new narcotics center.

Elsewhere, LULAC and the GI Forum signed a $5 million training contract with the U.S. Department of Labor for Operation SER, a national program that included East Los Angeles. On August 31, the *Citizen* reported that Arthur Fregoso had been appointed job coordinator for the Mexican American Opportunities Foundation. MAOF signed a million-dollar job training contract with the Department of Labor for a special Mexican American agency. Headed by Eduardo Moreno, this bilingual project was very active, sponsoring conferences and other public concern forums. The term "grassroots" became an integral part of the vernacular of all the agencies.

The Hazard Park committee recommended a one-year moratorium on zoning changes and new building permits around Hazard Park and General Hospital. It still sought a restraining order to stop the land swap. City authorities opposed the freeze, but the committee won a victory when it delayed the trade. By this time, it had effectively advertised the plight of the area and an impressive list of community leaders and celebrities supported the park. Meanwhile, accommodationists sought a federal grant to beautify Hazard Park. Ironically, the grant hinged on the construction of a veterans hospital.

Arthur Montoya condemned the Hazard Park swap, tying the master plan and the park deal to redevelopment of the Eastside. Kovner and property owner groups also participated on the Save Hazard Park Committee. As in other incidents of urban redevelopment, the *Sun* was much more outspoken during this battle on issues than the *Citizen*. Meanwhile, the Hazard Park committee picketed and pressured authorities to rescind the transfer order. The Parks Commission apparently played both sides, ignoring the Hazard Park improvement plan in their federal funds bill. The committee continued meeting and holding fund raisers. Their court case was scheduled to reach the superior court by December. The committee demanded that absolutely no compromise be made on the Hazard Park swap. The Save Elysian Park Committee was also busy countering moves to convert that park into a convention center.

Urban development still threatened the community. Unfortunately, activists did not pay as much attention to the threat as they had in the past. The *Sun* and Montoya, however, kept the issue alive. On January 19, Montoya called attention to the Community Analysis Program, which, he said, was the city's new urban renewal bureau. A week later, the *Sun* published a pictorial essay: "Eastside Must Not Repeat Bunker Hill Redevelopment."

Political candidates discussed the master plan. Many claimed that property taxes were skyrocketing because of rezoning and land use potential in East Los Angeles. Property owners protested the land-grab schemes. Manuel Aragón, later deputy mayor of Los Angeles under Mayor Tom Bradley, participated in the Maravilla and Belvedere Property Owners Association. Opponents claimed that the master plan threatened the Belvedere community with extinction.

When Assemblyman Leon Ralph charged that only 25,000 of the estimated 100,000 people displaced in the Watts area had been relocated, Montoya saw a link between this and displacement in

East Los Angeles. On February 2, Montoya and his group held a meeting with the East Los Angeles Improvement Council to discuss solutions. On April 6, Montoya criticized the city's redevelopment agency for its role in Bunker Hill. The displacement of homeowners was an important issue among mainstream politicians, and even the Eastside Republican party condemned urban renewal programs.

Montoya's column in the *Sun* demonstrated the strong communal land use ethic in the Eastside. On August 31, Montoya reviewed the Los Angeles County Building Rehabilitation Program and its activities. Supervisor Ernest Debs defended the Building Rehabilitation Appeals Board which, according to Montoya, usually supported pro-removal decisions.

Montoya listed the communities' chief enemies as HUD, urban renewal, and freeways. On October 26, he wrote that the Edison Company's facility would displace 13 families. Montoya had been fighting the Edison removal project since the spring. He also condemned arbitrary zone changes that benefitted business interests. (The Regional Planning Commission had granted Edison a variance so that the company could begin its projects.)

Both Montoya and Kovner condemned the Los Angeles Goals Program Report, which had been released on November 7. Kovner called the report's program, which favored high-rise buildings, an "anti-kid" project, stating that the real answer was to upgrade, not redevelop. Meanwhile, the county wanted to rehabilitate buildings that it considered to be substandard, reporting that there were 8,775 deteriorating buildings in East Los Angeles.

The *Citizen* paid considerable attention to a scheduled White House conference during which President Johnson had promised to meet with Mexican American leaders. However, worried that Chicano leaders would politically embarrass him by walking out, the president expressed the possibility of canceling the conference. Congressman Roybal took the lead and pressed for the conference. Debs seconded Roybal and urged the president to hold the conference as soon as possible. Claiming credit, Debs soon afterwards announced that the so-called White House conference had been approved.

Community organizations and leaders prepared position papers for the conference, which was scheduled for El Paso, Texas. The event was sponsored by the Inter-Agency Committee of Mexican

American Affairs. MAPA boycotted the October 25–28 event, calling the conference "window dressing." The Eastside GOP went so far as to call the event "political opportunism."

In spite of criticisms, a huge delegation from the Eastside went to El Paso. Both the *Sun* and the *Citizen* extensively covered the event. The *Sun* carried a three-part series featuring Dr. Julián Nava's position paper to the participants. The conference itself coincided with the Chamizal ceremonies between Mexico and the United States, in which the U.S. handed back to Mexico disputed territory in El Paso.

Vicente Ximénez was the key broker. Johnson had appointed Ximénez to the U.S. Equal Employment Opportunities Commission. Meanwhile, Dr. Ernesto Galarza, an economic historian and farmworker organizer in the 50s, led the opposition to the media event. Johnson had not invited César Chávez, Rodolfo "Corky" Gonzales, or Reies López Tijerina—the leading Chicano acitivists of the time—to the conference. Other activists boycotted and picketed the sessions. The dissidents formed a group called La Raza Unida and condemned LBJ for political posturing.

Police-community relations remained strained during 1967. In an attempt to alleviate tensions, an LAPD-Mexican American conference was held on April 22 in Elysian Park. Any optimism that dialogue would lessen tensions ended on May 26, when an LAPD officer shot to death a 17-year-old Mexican American youth at the Ramona Gardens Housing Project. Kovner abandoned his accommodationist position regarding the police and vehemently chastised the LAPD for the shooting.

The death of MAPA leader Eduardo Quevedo marked the end of an era. In many ways, Quevedo's death was symbolic. He had been the charismatic Mexican American politician whose career spanned three generations. It seems more than coincidental that after his death Mexican American youth became increasingly active in the movement.

1968

Without a doubt, 1968 belonged to youth—not only in East Los Angeles, but nationally and internationally as well. One of the first *Sun* articles of the year bannered: "Community Assistance Only Way to Save Teen Posts."

With the escalation of the Vietnam War, funds were reduced and Teen Post directors, consciously or unconsciously, defended their jobs by agitating their clients. They wanted to save their programs, which they believed were badly needed. In many ways, this did encourage youth to become involved. By this time, the Brown Berets, who represented a more militant and conscious sector of youth, had emerged. The precursors of the Brown Berets, the YCCA, had opened the Piranya Coffee House in the fall. The coffee house had attracted many activists, who eventually grouped together as the Brown Berets under the leadership of David Sánchez. Meanwhile, UMAS students at California State College, Los Angeles staged a rally protesting a tuition fee plan and UMAS/UCLA sponsored a symposium featuring Ralph Guzmán and Bert Corona. The topic for discussion was the educational neglect of Mexican Americans.

In January, community leaders increasingly discussed unrest in the schools. Alternative press activists and various community organizations condemned the inferior quality of education afforded Mexican Americans. In February, a college and high school student coalition submitted a 30-page proposal to the Los Angeles City Board of Education. The group threatened a walkout if its recommendations were rejected. American Federation of Teachers Local 1021, aware of school discontent, scheduled a community speakout for March 30. On February 29, another teachers' group met to discuss "Should Mexican American History and Culture Be Taught?" One-third of the audience was Mexican American.

A call for walkouts had appeared in the *Chicano Student Movement* newspaper and *La Raza* magazine as early as the fall of 1967. The basic demand was for better education. High school teacher Sal Castro emerged as the blowout leader.

Teacher reaction was mixed. Yet despite all indicators, most educators were surprised by the East Los Angeles high school walkouts during the first week of March. The normally liberal AFT disclaimed any endorsement of the walkouts. However, some teachers did support the blowouts, stating that teachers should have followed students. Meanwhile, the United Mexican American Students (UMAS) and the Mexican American Student Association (MASA) demanded that the board of education negotiate student demands. Although the walkouts started at Wilson High, the news coverage centered on Garfield, Roosevelt, and Lincoln High Schools. Following the lead of the Chicano schools,

Black students at Jefferson High also walked out. Congressman Roybal was the first politician to publicly support the students' objectives. Martin Luther King was assassinated during this period. This national tragedy drew away daily press coverage of the blowouts, although both the *Sun* and the *Citizen* remained interested.

Numerous community meetings were scheduled. One, sponsored by the East Los Angeles Coordinating Council, was held at Griffith Junior High School and chaired by Judge John A. Argüellos. The agenda was to discuss student proposals.

Based on police overreaction during Roosevelt High walkouts, community leaders met with LAPD Chief Tom Reddin to discuss police irresponsibility during the blowouts. Throughout this period, the CMAA urged officers to adopt a calmer approach and criticized them for abusing students and community supporters. The CMAA also issued a report stating that the schools had ignored proposals for reform. The board of education held an open meeting at Lincoln High on March 26 but little was accomplished. Ironically, the schools asked for more federal support for their programs, using the issue of urban unrest to justify the proposal. Roosevelt High teacher Rudolph Chávez sided with the school administration and criticized titular walkout leader Sal Castro. Chávez accused the school board of ignoring, rather than praising, teachers who had not participated. Carmen Terrazas, another Roosevelt teacher, encouraged the board of education to discipline the dissidents. Walkout opponents made appearances before the board of education at later meetings, bemoaning the elimination of campus controls, grade standards, and other pre-disciplinary measures.

Superintendent Jack Crowther told students that walkouts would not be tolerated. Judge Leopoldo Sánchez criticized the militants at a March 30 speakout, which KCET-TV televised. Sánchez condemned the walkouts as a violation of the law. Even Vicente Ximénez stated that although he supported the goals of the walkouts, he could not support the tactics.

Concerned parents formed the Educational Issues Coordinating Committee. The EICC packed the March 26 School Board meeting at Lincoln High. Tensions continued to run high and 300 members of the community picketed the board of education. The board, however, delayed taking a stand on the student demands. During this period, the term "Chicano" was more freqently used by the press. Many older Mexican Americans, however, considered the term pejorative.

After heated debates, the board approved a secondary school minority administrative internship program. At first, some board members stated that its rules would not allow the selection of principals on the basis of race. Nava played a key role in pushing through the internship plan, as well as other programs. At the board meetings, Nava generally lost his motions. However, he did win occasional concessions, especially in the area of student rights. Parent and community participation in pressing for education reforms broadened during this period. AMAE submitted an extensive education plan to the board of education, which included demands for teaching materials, student counseling, study centers, work study, and a breakdown of staff ethnic composition.

In May, the EICC sponsored a "Walk Through" of the schools because community activists had charged that the school board was taking reprisals against students and teachers. A group walked through area schools to demonstrate parent involvement and concern with the state of education. The committee remained staunch and picketed Lincoln High once more.

The California Advisory Committee to the U.S. Commission on Civil Rights stated that the education of the Mexican American was inadequate and that the "English-speaking oriented school system is indifferent to the needs of the Mexican American student." The Reverend James Pike headed the committee.

As the school semester ended, District Attorney Evelle Younger and the Los Angeles Grand Jury issued secret indictments against student and activist leaders. This move shocked the Chicano community, which rallied around the indicted leaders. Community organizations, progressive politicians, and lay people criticized the indictments.

The Reverend Vahac Madirosian became EICC president. Fund-raisers were held for Sal Castro and the other grand jury defendants. AMAE issued a statement supporting the walkout defendants and affirming the validity of the student grievances. Community groups also discussed the arrests and the educational issues raised by the walkouts.

Incidents of overt racism were abundant. Near the end of the academic year, Lincoln High shop teacher Richard C. Davis responded negatively in a letter to fellow teacher Joe McKnight, who had called for understanding Mexican Americans. Davis charged that Mexican Americans were basically passive and should be happy just to be in the United States. The letter was an irresponsible attack on the intelligence, character, and history of Mexican Americans. EICC members picketed the board of education, demanding that Davis be removed. School authorities publicly defended Davis. A compromise, however, was reached: Mr. Davis voluntarily transferred to another school.

The assassination of Robert Kennedy in June pushed the local news of the indictments into the background. Ironically, the Kennedy campaign committee had contributed large sums of money to the walkout defendants, 13 of whom had been indicted for conspiracy to disturb the peace. Bail was set at $12,500 each. The United Council of Community Organizations appealed for support for the "13." Mervyn M. Dymally, a Black politician, called the D.A.'s action a violation of the Mexican Americans' civil liberties. Dr. Francisco Bravo challenged the district attorney's conspiracy charges. Bravo's letter to Younger appeared in the *Sun* on July 4. The League of United Latin American Citizens Council (LULAC) announced that it would furnish legal assistance to the defendants.

Meanwhile, the board of education discussed the student walkout demands. In later June, the board agreed to abolish the ROTC, to reopen restrooms that had been closed for disciplinary reasons, and to dismiss racist teachers and administrators. J. C. Chambers cast the only dissenting vote and accused the Brown Berets of conducting "guerrilla warfare."

The indictments polarized police-community relations. Letters to the editor complaining about police harassment appeared more frequently in the *Sun*. Judge Leopoldo Sánchez remained adamant in his condemnation of the walkouts. He criticized the East Central Area Welfare Planning Council for supporting the students. "There are problems in the schools involved that need attention and solutions . . ." he said, "but the walkouts were a violation of the law . . ." Surprisingly, the *Citizen* supported the blowouts.

In July, the board approved a report on the walkouts, acknowledging more of the student grievances. In other sectors, tensions increased when Police Commissioner Dr. Reynaldo Carreón removed Sal Montenegro as a hearing officer for the Los Angeles

Police Commission because he supported the "13." Meanwhile, defendant attorneys moved for a dismissal of the charges and initiated legal proceedings to prohibit the prosecutions.

Simultaneously, the EICC pressed the Los Angeles City Schools' Office of Urban Affairs for formal recognition. In the fall, the EICC picketed Lincoln High and demanded that the school board return Sal Castro to his classroom. The board replied that policy did not allow into the faculty anyone charged with a felony. It was evident, however, that while the board took a hard line publicly, it was making concessions. Bilingual classes were started at Roosevelt High, and Mexican American studies classes were initiated at Lincoln.

On September 26, the EICC conducted a sit-in at the board to protest its refusal to reinstate Castro, whom the *Sun* editorially supported. Meanwhile, the board approved a new policy regarding teachers facing criminal charges and was able to reinstate Castro by assigning him non-teaching duties. Nevertheless, the sit-in lasted from September 26 until October 2.

Nine women and 26 men, ranging in age from 15 to 64, were arrested. J. C. Chambers demanded that the board tighten its rules governing sit-ins. Four citizens of Mexican extraction supported Chambers.

School principals tightened restrictions on UMAS and refused to recognize it as a campus club. On October 25, students at Roosevelt walked out again. Los Angeles police overreacted and maced the participants. Sal Castro remained in the spotlight and KNXT-TV ran a three-part report on Castro and the walkouts.

Meanwhile, the "13" challenged the racial composition of the grand jury. Four judges testified that they had not nominated many Mexican Americans to the grand jury. Judge Kathleen Parker stated that in a ten-year period she had interviewed 1,602 nominees and selected only 38 to 40 Spanish-surnamed persons. Judge James Whyte admitted that during this same period he had nominated only one Spanish-surnamed person. Judges Harold W. Schwitzer, Emil Gimpertz, Edward E. Doherty, Joseph Call, and George Dockweiller had never nominated a Latino to the grand jury. The presiding judge in the case denied motions to dismiss and allowed the indictments to stand. Another controversy arose when the defendants attempted to eliminate hearsay evidence and prejudicial remarks from the grand jury transcripts. This maneuver delayed the proceedings.

By this year, young people were heavily involved in the anti-war movement and the formation of the Congress of Mexican American Unity, which met on February 25 to endorse candidates. Over 500 delegates attended the convention, endorsing, among others, James Cruz for the 40th Assembly District, Phil Soto for the 50th Assembly District, Phil Ortíz for the 51st Senate District, and Richard Calderón for the 27th Senate District. Students packed the convention and reacted militantly throughout the proceedings. Undoubtedly, the anti-war movement helped give students a sense of purpose.

Anti-war activists dovetailed the walkouts and, with many blowout participants, became actively involved in the anti-war movement as well. On January 4, the *Sun* published an article titled "Anti-War, Anti-Racism, Anti-Poverty Calif. Democrats Endorse McCarthy for Pres." The *Citizen* echoed, "Two E.L.A. Marines Slain in Viet Ambush, War Dead Toll Reaches 16 As New Year Starts." And on January 18, the Citizen published "Eastside Vietnam War Roll Mounts, Two More Local Youths Lose Lives, Reported as 17th and 18th Casualties of Conflict." Congressman Brown pointed out that out of 623 men from the Southwest killed in Vietnam, 132 had Spanish surnames. While Chicanos represented ten percent of Los Angeles County, they represented 21 percent of its war casualties.

National anti-war activity increased. U.S. Senator Robert Kennedy entered the Democratic party presidential primary in California. Kennedy spoke to walkout leaders, many of whom were incorporated into his campaign. Campaign appearances by Eugene McCarthy and Kennedy helped build an anti-war environment. The Kennedy people contributed $10,000 to the walkout defendants' defense. In June, Kennedy won the California Democratic party primary, but his campaign ended shortly thereafter. Kennedy's assassination contributed greatly to youth's growing disillusionment with the system.

On the national level, César Chávez endorsed Democrat Hubert H. Humphrey at the MAPA convention. In spite of Chávez's support, Chicanos did not enthusiastically support the Humphrey campaign. Richard M. Nixon's victory further alienated Chicano youth from the establishment.

Locally, the November election results were a disaster for Chicano candidates, with only Alex García in the 40th Assembly District scoring a victory. After the election, the Congress of Mexican American Unity attempted to unify Chicano organizations and build towards future campaigns.

The U.S. Congress reacted to increased Chicano militancy by adopting a law-and-order posture. The U.S. Senate and House of Representatives passed a supposed anti-crime bill that negated many previous U.S. Supreme Court pro-civil rights decisions. Meanwhile, many social programs were abandoned. In Congress, the bilingual bill was an on-again/off-again situation. At the state level, a legislative committee cut the California bilingual reading funds.

The 1960s, however, had unleashed latent militancy, and the newspaper coverage gives witness to this activism. When NAPP fired Ben Cortez, MAPA protested. The *Sun* lent considerable coverage to Alicia Escalante, whose East Los Angeles Welfare Rights Organization militantly fought for the rights of welfare recipients. Escalante remained much in the news over the next five years.

The Urban League honored the Brown Berets at its Ghetto Freedom Awards ceremonies. The Brown Berets attempted to change their image and offered Chicano history classes to the community. Nevertheless, the group remained the target of Councilman Art Snyder and other politicians. A Chicano and Puerto Rican conference was scheduled in the Midwest for October 19.

In contrast to the success of the Mexican American Opportunities Foundation, the Eastland Community Action Program ran into problems. Politicians demanded a review of this agency. Press coverage indicated that a shift had taken place, from loose community participation to specific job training. In November, the U.S. Department of Labor announced a $27 million joint business-government effort for East Los Angeles. Manuel Aragón replaced Joe Maldonado as EYOA director. The United Auto Workers organized the East Los Angeles Labor Action Committee to implement community self-help projects. This organization later evolved into TELACU.

The issue of land use was not as dramatic as civil rights or the war because it was not as obvious a threat. The Johnson administration had escalated land encroachments by creating the Department of Housing and Urban Development. HUD sugarcoated redevelopment and won support for its housing programs by involving itself in recruiting minority students to go to college and funding a wide array of social programs. The *Sun* opposed HUD, alleging that it was renewal in disguise.

The Maravilla and Belvedere Park Owners Association, Inc., which Montoya led, was one of the few community organizations to actively oppose the Edison Company's condemnation proceedings against property owners. The association also opposed the master plan and Model Cities program in Belvedere. Both Kovner and Montoya frequently critiqued the new Model Cities program in their *Sun* columns. Almost weekly, Montoya attacked urban renewal, linking it to Model Cities. He organized 300 Eastside property owners who met and characterized the program as urban renewal in disguise. Meanwhile, Mayor Yorty aggressively pursued funding for Model Cities, urging the council to approve his plan and to apply for HUD model neighborhood planning grants. Title I of the Demonstration Cities Act of 1966 made available $965,728. Montoya and his organization vehemently criticized Yorty.

On March 28, Montoya wrote: "Model Cities Not for ELA," and on April 5, Kovner and Montoya labelled HUD a "New Urban Renewal Gimmick." Kovner was alarmed when he learned that Boyle Heights and Lincoln Heights were to be designated Model Cities areas. The *Citizen*'s coverage was almost opposite to that of the *Sun*. It viewed Model Cities as a way of improving housing and living conditions in the Eastside.

Councilman Gilbert Lindsay, a principal booster of Model Cities, ignored criticisms of the program. Despite intense opposition from groups such as MAPA, the council refused to exclude Boyle Heights from the plan. Kovner accused authorities of railroading it through. On April 29, the Maravilla and Belvedere Property Owners Association invited Lindsay and Robert Goe of the Community Redevelopment Agency to answer questions on Model Cities.

All activists did not oppose HUD. In fact, most agency people welcomed it as a new source of funding. War on poverty funds were drying up and the agency people, realizing that HUD was President Johnson's favorite program, knew that it would receive significant financial support. Montoya and Kovner looked at it differently and raised questions about the Model Cities program. They also attacked agencies that cooperated with Model Cities. According to Montoya, Model Cities circumvented the Maravilla and Belvedere Property Owners Association, complying with federal guidelines for community involvement by enlisting the CSO's Tony Ríos. Montoya accused Ríos of helping to get approval of the Model Cities application.

The East Los Angeles Coordinating Committee and the East Central Area Welfare Planning Council also supported Model Cities. Both organizations were pro-development. The *Sun* pointed to the high rents in the Bunker Hill Towers as an example of urban renewal, predicting that the same would happen to the Eastside.

Another controversial HUD program was the Home Owner's Modernization Effort (HOME). HOME was attractive because it offered low-interest loans or outright grants for home improvements. There was, however, a catch: once HOME designated an area as eligible, all homes in that area were required to conform to HOME code regulations, despite the fact that the agency could provide funds only for a small fraction of the houses. Furthermore, HOME maintained no control of the cost or quality of work performed. The mandatory improvements also meant higher taxes to homeowners. Many small contractors had a vested interest and supported HUD.

Montoya had at first liked HOME because of its improvement grants. He was cautious, however, and did not endorse it. On the other hand, Supervisor Ernest Debs from the beginning enthusiastically pushed the program as a low-cost home improvement project and gathered a long and impressive list of politicians who supported it.

Montoya soon changed his neutral stance to one of antagonism towards HOME. His column on August 1, "Montoya Fears HOME Could Hurt 'Propertarios'," prompted a mass rally at Belvedere Junior High on August 8. HUD counterattacked by sending speakers to community organizations, including the East Los Angeles Town Meeting. HOME officials claimed that theirs was a program for the elderly and boasted that 200 senior citizens endorsed HOME.

In an apparent fit of frustration over the HUD campaign, the *Sun* ran an article titled: "We, the People of E.L.A., Demand That Our Complex Communities Be 'Kennedy City'." Kovner almost abandoned hope that city officials would help Boyle Heights. Urban renewal forces, meanwhile, were firmly entrenched in Monterey Hills and elsewhere in the Eastside.

According to Montoya, history was repeating itself. He charged that HOME's code enforcement provisions would work against homeowners. He accused Supervisor Debs of acting as the principal advocate of urban renewal. Federal representatives met with the Maravilla-Belvedere Park Property Owners to discuss the HOME program. Meanwhile, at one of their sessions, the county supervisors unanimously endorsed HOME.

Montoya questioned the hard-sell tactics of HOME officials. At the crux of Montoya's objections was the code enforcement provisions (i.e., the requirements) that were built into the law. Montoya maintained that code enforcement would lead to the condemnation of homes. He took his fight to federal authorities and his column hammered away at code enforcement. Turning his wrath onto both city and county authorities, Montoya demanded, but was refused, a copy of the local HOME application. There was criticism from other sectors, too. For example, on November 21, the Maravilla-Belvedere Park Property Owners met at Ford Elementary School. Also, Tony Ríos criticized the lack of planning in a recent HUD Los Angeles Recreation and Park grant. But, in the end, both HOME and Model Cities programs were adopted and became an established part of East Los Angeles.

In the meantime, Roybal and other Chicano community activists criticized the Hazard Park swap. The initial Hazard Park trial was declared a mistrial but it went once more to the courts on July 18. Finally, in August, the court declared the swap legal. This decision was immediately appealed by the Save Hazard Park Committee. When the committee pressured federal authorities to invalidate the swap, the Veterans Administration agreed to reevaluate the deal. Mayor Yorty became more aggressive, replacing Parks and Recreation Commissioner Francis Lederer with Jim Madrid. According to Kovner, Madrid was Yorty's puppet. He was associated with urban renewal forces and headed the East Central Area Welfare Planning Council.

SUMMARY

1966–1968 was a period of intense activity. The Economic Youth Opportunity Agency (EYOA) administered new and experimental programs. The failure to generate enthusiasm among grassroot Mexican Americans in the Eastside, however, surprised bureaucrats. Funding inconsistencies, blatant neglect of Mexican Americans, and the apparent favoritism towards Black agencies resulted in Mexican American activists vocally criticizing EYOA. The Black–Chicano rivalry for funds and services was most evident in the Neighborhood Adult Participation Project (NAPP), from which numerous Mexican Americans resigned, citing discrimination against Mexicans. At the same time a kaleidoscope of new programs was implemented, including the Neighborhood Youth Corps (NYC), the Youth Training and Employment Project (YTEP), various manpower programs, the Teen Posts, and Headstart. Community volunteer organizations, including LULAC and the GI Forum, became parent agencies, and administed programs such as Operation SER.

During this period, Eastsiders were enthusiastic about the National Farmworkers Union and its grape boycott. However, Mexican Americans did suffer a series of setbacks. Assemblyman Phil Soto was defeated for re-election. Richard Calderón lost the Democratic party primary for a state senate seat by 311 votes. And last, but by no means least, Ronald Reagan was elected governor.

In 1966, unemployment in the Eastside was above the national norm. On March 29, even middle-class Mexican American activists walked out on the EEOC in Albuquerque, protesting unequal opportunities for Chicanos and EEOC insensitivity.

Militancy snowballed. The YCCA evolved into the Brown Berets. The Mexican American Education Committee and the Association of Mexican American Educators also became more vocal at the numerous education and youth conferences. Their constant concern was that Mexican Americans educationally lagged almost two years behind Blacks and almost four years behind whites. There were few Mexican American teachers, counselors, or administrators; classes on Mexican heritage were almost nonexistent. An additional complaint was that Latino students were tracked into non-professional careers. The election of Dr. Julián Nava to the Los Angeles Board of Education was the product of the ferment.

Meanwhile, the Chicano college student population, on whom the anti-war protests had their greatest impact, increased slightly. Anti-war and anti-colonialist rhetoric, as well as the farmworkers and the Black civil rights movements, motivated Mexican American college student chapters on many campuses. This broad-based organization stimulated the establishment of other college groups in 1967. Ultimately, this Mexican American militancy filtered down to the high schools and, in March, 1968, the Eastside school blowouts occurred. Sal Castro, a teacher at Lincoln High, was an inspiration for these student walkouts, as was the emergence of barrio newspapers, which ran articles critical of the system.

Police authorities, afraid that the Eastside could become another Watts, clamped down severely, deploying large numbers of officers to patrol the barrios. Law enforcement authorities wanted to ensure control of these communities. District Attorney Evelle Younger indicted Sal Castro and other walkout leaders on conspiracy charges.

During this period, the Eastside Chicano movement generally ignored the effects that government programs had on local land use patterns. Coverage of the new programs and their possible dangers was left largely to the *Sun*. Kovner's paper portrayed HUD as a Trojan horse capable of completing what overt urban renewal was not able to do in the 1950s and early 1960s.

By the end of 1968, the Great Society's experiment in social engineering had obviously failed. The U.S. Justice Department did not adequately enforce civil rights laws. The revolution of the 1960s proved to be one that did not produce structural changes.

Due to Johnson's faltering commitment to the war on poverty, caused by political opposition to the program within his own party, and the escalation of the war in Southeast Asia, which increasingly diverted funds from social programs, the nation and its leaders lost interest in assuring equality. By the end of the decade, the SDS and Black civil rights movements were on the decline. In contrast, Chicano awareness was just peaking. The turmoil had produced neither a revolution nor fundamental structural changes. However, Chicanos were now more aware of their identity and, like Blacks, had become very nationalistic. Generally, many Chicanos saw their commitments and relationship to the rest of the nation differently. Unfortunately, the political climate changed dramatically with the election of Richard M. Nixon to the presidency in 1968.

7

The Storm Breaks Over East Los Angeles: 1969–1971

In addition to the *Eastside Sun* and the *Belvedere Citizen*, the following sources were used: Rodolfo Acuña, *Occupied America: A History of Chicanos*, 2nd Edition (New York: 1981); Peter N. Carrol, *It Seemed Like Nothing Happened: The Tragedy and Promise of America in the 1970s* (New York: 1982); The Center For Research On Criminal Justice, *The Iron Fist and the Velvet Glove: An Analysis of the U.S. Police*, Revised Edition (Berkeley: 1977); Los Angeles, Department of City Planning, *Boyle Heights Community: Socio-economic Analysis*, n.d.; U.S. Census, 1970; Milton Viorst, *Fire in the Streets: America In the 1960's* (New York: 1979); and Howard Zinn, *A People's History of the United States* (New York: 1980).

The impact of Richard M. Nixon's first three years has been underestimated by many social historians. More than preceding administrations had, Nixon's people assertively appealed to minorities along class lines to divide them and build a network of social control agents. In order to manage them more easily, Nixon's appointees consolidated all Latinos, Puerto Ricans, Cubans, Chicanos, and other Latin Americans into a national minority that the administration called "Hispanic." Nixon the conservative proved more adept than even Johnson the liberal at using the powers of the presidency to political advantage.

Nixon had ignored the minority vote throughout the 1968 campaign. Afterwards, however, he changed his strategy. The 1968 report of the National Advisory Commission on Civil Disorder, chaired by Governor Otto Kerner, asserted that the United States was "moving toward two societies, one Black, one white—separate and unequal." Once scornful of this report, Nixon now realized the threat of confrontations. His strategy was simple: encourage Black and brown capitalism.

The war on poverty was replaced by the Office of Minority Enterprise as the main facilitator of Nixon's minority programs. Since urban violence also affected the corporate structure, business leaders, including David Rockefeller of the Chase Manhattan Bank, involved themselves in encouraging the "Americanization" of the Black and brown middle sectors. During his first three years of office, Nixon tripled loans to minority businessmen. He also increased support to the community development corporations and extended aid to some civil rights leaders. For example, Floyd McKissick and the Congress of Racial Equality (CORE) received a $14 million loan to develop a housing project in North Carolina.

Nixon and his minority brokers preached the gospel of Black and brown capitalism. The rhetoric appealed to extreme nationalists, whose vision of society was limited to replacing whites as the distributors of goods and services. Opportunity was extended through the private sector. Minority leaders were appointed to corporate boards of directors. Organizations such as the Ford Foundation cultivated their Black and brown brokers. Nixon further channeled millions of dollars into urban renewal and employment. In April 1969, inspired by the approaching long hot summer, he channeled $9 million into the Department of Housing and

Urban Development to rebuild riot torn cities. Nixon increased rent subsidies, which benefitted developers and landlords. Finally, through the Emergency Employment Act of 1971, he allocated money to the Office of Economic Opportunity and the Department of Health, Welfare, and Education for jobs. Significantly, the funds were channeled through the faithful.

But Nixon's strategy was one of illusion. Increasing numbers of small enterprises went bankrupt each month. Ultimately, there was little change in the status of Blacks and browns, who had not penetrated the corporate structure. It would take considerably more than sitting next to the ruling class to achieve equal power.

Changes in the economy that began in the mid-1960s manifested themselves during this period. In 1965, inflation was two percent; four years later it climbed to six percent. Corporate profits increased from $33 billion annually in 1963 to $50 billion annually in 1968. Inflation, profits, and government expenditures for "defense" brought changes for which the poor would eventually pay. When Nixon took measures to control inflation, he increased unemployment. By 1966, housing interest rates also began their upward spiral, which further centralized capital. In order to ensure his reelection, Nixon became a social engineer and orchestrated the economy with the help of his friend, Arthur Burns, chair of the Federal Reserve Board.

The Nixon administration also shifted national control of funds to local governments, making block grants for health, law-enforcement assistance, community development, job training, and social services. Control mechanisms to ensure the proper expenditure of these funds were purposely weakened, and Nixon's policies betrayed a marked absence of guidelines. Local authorities were given additional control, and the impacted citizens were left with not even their former illusion of participation.

The Vietnam War diverted not only funds but attention from poverty. The war continued to frustrate and appall Americans. By April 1969, 33,641 soldiers had been killed and 232 institutions of higher learning had been the scenes of anti-war and other demonstrations. An estimated 215,000 protestors took part in the activities. There were 3,652 arrests and 956 suspensions or expulsions. War atrocities—My Lai in March 1968, the incessant bombing of Laos and Cambodia and Vietnam, the shooting by National Guardsmen of four students at Kent State, the publication of Daniel Ellsberg's *Pentagon Papers* in June 1971—heightened American awareness to the horrors of the war.

A 1969 survey showed that 57 percent of the American public favored withdrawal from Southeast Asia. In October of the year, the New Mobilization Committee to End the War in Vietnam executed mass mobilizations that attracted a cross section of the American public. By this time, Chicanos organized mass demonstrations in East Los Angeles as well as throughout the Southwest and Midwest. Eastside police authorities, already frustrated by the civil rights and anti-war movements, reacted violently in their attempts to suffocate this new threat to their authority. The entrance of Chicanos into the anti-war movement brought attention to the plight of the group. Along with Chávez's farmworkers struggle, Chicano anti-war activities heightened awareness of Latinos.

At universities and colleges all across the nation, activist groups demanded ethnic studies programs and admission of more minority students. Their demands were widely—and correctly—associated with the civil rights movement and with the self-awareness process of Third World groups. Activists sought to increase the responsiveness of colleges and universities to the needs and interests of the growing number of minorities. For example, few institutions offered courses in Mexican history or literature. And in Los Angeles, where the need was especially keen, courses to prepare Chicano teachers to educate were nonexistent. In 1969, some such programs were established on local campuses. Interestingly, however, neither the *Sun* nor the *Citizen* devoted much coverage to these successes.

Along with the growing awareness of racial and cultural identity, women's demands became more popular. By 1969, women comprised 40 percent of the entire work force, and Mexican women were entering the labor market at an accelerated pace. The feminist movement predated most other movements in the United States. But until the 1960s, middle-class white women had determined its priorities. The 1960s saw the publication of a host of works about women and feminism. Of these, Betty Friedan's *The Feminine Mystique*, which was first published in the early 1960s, was perhaps the most influential. This book and others raised the consciousness of many women and of some men. Throughout the struggle for civil rights and the anti-war movements, women were an important cadre. As their politicization grew increasingly sophisticated, they began to recognize the contradictions in the division of labor. While at first many feminists dwelt on social equality and freedom, their attention soon shifted to the work-place. In fact, the more political women became, the more their demands shifted from equality of rights to equality of power.

While the *Sun* and the *Citizen* covered the dramatic confrontations between police and community, few articles reported— or seemed even to have discovered—the extent of disruption directed by police authorities during these years. National, state, and local surveillance was commonplace throughout the 1960s. During the Nixon years, it was expanded and refined. Government used research groups and agencies to gather information and exploit naive and altruistic activists.

Rebellions and mass demonstrations encouraged lawmakers to take more direct control and increase police militancy. The Omnibus Crime Control and Safe Streets Act of 1968, for example, created the Law Enforcement Assistance Administration (LEAA), which funded programs, such as the Management Development Center, to improve police control methods. LEAA encouraged the planning and coordination of police efforts to strengthen the internal security network. Between 1969 and 1972, this single agency distributed more than a billion dollars. It apportioned $63 million in 1969, $268 million in 1970, and $700 million in 1972. Attorney General John Mitchell coordinated CIA, FBI, and military spy activities. But the most comprehensive program was J. Edgar Hoover's Counterintelligence Program (Cointelpro), which covertly attempted to destroy popular movements. Coverage in the *Sun* and the *Citizen* reported efforts to control the new militancy east of the Los Angeles River, but the extent of Los Angeles police authorities' surveillance and disruption is only today surfacing.

Also in 1969, census takers swarmed over the country, counting the population and collecting vital statistics for the 1970 report. Although there were obvious flaws in the collection of the data—with a serious undercount of Mexican Americans throughout the nation—an interesting profile of Boyle Heights-East Los Angeles emerged:

	Boyle Heights	East Los Angeles	Los Angeles City	Los Angeles County
Total population	82,000*	105,033	2,816,061	7,032,075
Spanish-surname	83.7 %	87%	18.4%	18.3%
Living same home since 1965	46.6 %	52%	44.2%	45.4%
Under 20 years	43.8 %	43.6%	33%	35.4%
No school	9.2 %	7.3%	1.9%	1.5%
High school education	25.3 %	25.9%	62%	62%
Median years of education	8.0	8.8	12.4	12.4
Median family income	$5,928	$7,622	$10,535	$10,972
Female head of household	24.8 %	21%	16.9%	13.9%
Owner occupied	24.29%	39.2%	39%	46.5%

*The City Planning Figure is 75,926; the two figures differ because the census includes two census tracts in Lincoln Heights.

Source: U.S. 1970 Census and City of Los Angeles, Department of City Planning, Boyle Heights Community Background. Summary, January 1974 and 1970 U.S. Census.

The data suggests that the area east of the Los Angeles River was predominately Chicano, since approximately 95 percent of the Spanish-surname population belonged to that ethnic group. There were other trends. The population was young and only one-fourth had a high school education, in contrast to two-thirds of Los Angeles residents. The median education was a full four years behind the rest. Boyle Heights residents earned approximately 56 percent and East Los Angeles residents 69 percent of what other Angelenos earned. The households were markedly larger, lowering the per capita income. This profile becomes more pronounced when Spanish-surnamed residents in the East Los Angeles area, for example, are compared to others in that same community. The median education of Latino residents was 8.2, and only 21.4% had a high school education. Their median income was $1,095 below the East Los Angeles median. The only positive comparison is residency in the same housing unit, which indicates a degree of stability.

The census demonstrated in concrete terms the vulnerability of Chicanos east of the Los Angeles River. Yet despite this vulnerability, community events and activities, from 1969 through 1971, left a lasting legacy.

THE CHRONICLE
1969

The Eastland Community Action Program (ECAP) was controversial, since it was supposed to organize the poor and ensure their "maximum feasible" participation. In principle, it was supposed to give the people the bargaining power to demand equal access to government. However, the program was so controversial that, during 1968, steps were taken to put ECAP under the control of local politicians.

Frank Veiga acted as chair of ECAP throughout this construction period, during which the EYOA was temporarily put into receivership. Activists argued that the reorganization task force was not responsive to the poor. The Neighborhood Legal Centers had become part of the community life and Manuel Aragón, director of EYOA, stated that his agency would extend its services into unincorporated East Los Angeles and the five surrounding cities. On March 13, the *Citizen* reported that $400 million in grants would be allocated to poverty programs nationally.

Competition between Blacks and browns for funds, caused by the ethnic imbalance of the EYOA staff, was a major source of friction. Armando Chaves, head of the Ad Hoc Committee on Equal Employment for Minority Personnel, stated that only 37 of EYOA's 260 staff members were Mexican Americans. The rest of the personnel included 106 whites, 100 Blacks, and 17 individuals from other ethnic groups. Chicano organizations pressured authorities to bypass EYOA and provide direct funds. Because of this struggle, EYOA's power eroded. Chicanos severely criticized this umbrella organization during the summer months for neglecting barrio programs.

Under Esteban Torres, the East Los Angeles Labor Community Action Committee emerged as the most influential Chicano organization. Together with the United Auto Workers, this committee operated a joint statewide training program. Seven other states had similar projects. Torres himself traveled to Venezuela as a consultant to Latin American trade unionists.

In the fall, Torres also headed the Mexican American Community Programs Foundation, which was affiliated with the East Los Angeles Labor Community Action Committee. The foundation, which served East Los Angeles, Lincoln Heights, and Boyle Heights, received a Ford grant through the Southwest Council of La Raza. In April, the Action Committee changed its name to The East Los Angeles Community Union (TELACU). In October, Martin Castillo, the top ranking Chicano in the Nixon administration, visited TELACU.

The politics of poverty intensified. Patricio Sánchez announced the formation of Barrios Unidos, a task force that would set up a poverty board to serve as an EYOA advisory unit. Barrios Unidos would oversee the elections, which, after a number of postponements, finally were held June 22. The *Sun* portrayed Barrios Unidos as a "grassroots" movement. Politics, however, surrounded the establishment of this group.

The Youth Opportunities Council sponsored a "Jobs for Youth" conference that drew 400 participants. The Mexican American Opportunities Foundation, headed by Dionicio Morales, launched a summer membership drive. The Youth Training and Employment Program (YTEP), one of the oldest surviving organizations, was involved in helping East Los Angeles young people secure employment. When YTEP's Youth Corps funds were slashed, the organization protested to the U.S. Department of Labor. The cutbacks worsened the unemployment crisis among youth. On August 21, Carol Stevens wrote an article in the *Sun* titled "YTEP Funding Might Have Averted Fatal Shooting." The article underscored that young people needed jobs during the summer months, and that without positive outlets they would turn to negative activities.

Arthur Montoya wrote that the $8 million grant to HOME was simply urban renewal in disguise. HOME, as discussed in Chapter 6, was a code enforcement program that subsidized only a small percentage of homeowners. Eastsiders had become dependent on HUD money, and politicians, such as Councilman Gilbert Lindsay, took credit for the influx of HUD funds. Housing needs were very real but HUD's approach made many residents nervous.

Supervisor Ernest Debs defended the HUD programs in general—and HOME in particular.

Both TELACU and the Congress of Mexican American Unity sponsored a meeting on February 20 to discuss the HOME project. Debs refused to attend the meeting because Montoya would participate. In February, Montoya spoke at a California State College, Los Angeles seminar on urban issues. He criticized Debs's press release, which urged expedition of the building rehabilitation program and the demolition of unsafe or substandard structures in East Los Angeles.

By March, Model Cities was ready to name its board members. Authorities of the project repeatedly denied that it was urban renewal, assuring the public that the agency would not take a bulldozer approach in East Los Angeles. On March 13, Montoya criticized the local clergy for not opposing Model Cities and accused it of supporting the program. A week later, Montoya reported that he believed that the clergy had begun to come around. Soon afterwards, however, he bitterly attacked a pro-HOME petition circulated by the "Citizens Affiliated for Urban and Social Action." Montoya accused the Catholic church of culpability for this petition and of organizing Neighborhood Coordinating Councils, which cooperated with Model Cities. Moreover, according to Montoya, Father Hilario Liras and Sister Georgeanna exposed the Catholic church's urban renewal biases at a meeting later in April.

Montoya challenged Debs to meet with the people at an open meeting to discuss Model Cities and HOME. By May, the Model Cities Board was approved and Yorty had appointed four members to the board. It was apparent that the citizen participation phase had ended and that local officials now controlled Model Cities.

On June 19, the *Citizen* warned the community that the East Central Area Planning Council and HUD were gaining increasing influence over Los Angeles Regional Planning. By July, Model Cities received approval for its funding. A month later, the Model Cities Board was functioning and, in October, L. V. Whitehead was named the agency's director.

Montoya called HOME "people enforcers," stating that HOME had the power to file criminal complaints against homeowners who failed to bring property to code. If they did not comply, owners could be forced to sell. Montoya estimated that 305 families would be relocated under the program. Meanwhile, Congressman George Brown issued a statement of concern about the HOME victims. On August 7, Montoya declared that "no other group should speak for us, we are the property owners."

Meanwhile, HOME issued regular press releases acclaiming the homes it rehabilitated in East Los Angeles. The county had a $20 million HOME grant, which was not nearly enough money to meet even minimal needs. Only a few homeowners could possibly receive a $3,000 grant or a loan of up to $14,500 at three percent interest. Coverage of this issue in the *Sun* and *Citizen* differed like day and night. The *Sun* had nothing good to say about HOME and the *Citizen* printed little that was critical.

Meanwhile, Joe Kovner attended the Maravilla-Belvedere Property Owners meetings and vehemently chastised HOME. In his column, Montoya criticized the agency for being undemocratic because it was virtually "government without consent of the governed."

Montoya sponsored a rally in September to organize opposition to HOME. On October 2, he wrote: "We Know How H.O.M.E. Program Will Affect Our Lives; We Oppose It." Montoya again said that HOME only pretended to rehabilitate the area and was actually urban renewal in disguise. He questioned why the streets in East Los Angeles were being widened and why traffic was not simply rerouted. After all, widening meant the removal of people and/or the raising of taxes.

Montoya's attacks on HOME finally produced results. Former assemblyman Ed Elliot retracted his endorsement and, on November 13, Montoya wrote: "Remember Bunker Hill; Model Cities Is Urban Renewal in Disguise." Joining Kovner and Montoya in the crusade against Model Cities was Patricio Sánchez, an old-time Eastside activist who had been active in the EICC and the Save Hazard Park Committee.

The Los Angeles City Council had adopted Model Cities in 1968. A year later, the agency's power was evident. Montoya and his supporters picketed Our Lady of Lourdes in November. According to Montoya, the East Los Angeles Maravilla-Belvedere Park Property Owners Association, Inc. was 5,000 strong and opposed to HOME. Meanwhile, HOME officials claimed that the program had already rehabilitated 71 homes. In a belated vein, the county supervisors finally approved the Indiana-Brooklyn-Alma zone change, benefitting the Lucky Market development.

The Save Hazard Park Committee protested the county's elimination of Camp High Sierra,* which had been used for urban youths. On March 13, the *Sun* published an article titled "Hazard Park . . . That Classic Robin Hood Story in Reverse." The Hazard Park swap included the best portion of the park— rolling hills with a view of the Civic Center. According to the *Sun*, it was incredible that, in days of urban unrest, parks should be eliminated. The paper questioned why the city did not use the junkyards that marred Boyle Heights to make its swap.

Community support for Hazard Park remained resolute. In May, Mayor Yorty unexpectedly requested that the swap be rescinded. The Hazard Park Association called Yorty's move misleading, claiming that Yorty still supported the deal. Congressman Brown reported that the Veterans Hospital project lagged and that Hazard Park appeared safe.

In 1969, a federal law was passed to prohibit the government from using park lands for its developments. The Hazard Park threat, however, was not totally ended. Although the park could no longer be traded, the Parks and Recreation Authority had purposely allowed it to deteriorate. No capital improvements had been made since 1958. Councilman Gilbert Lindsay pressured William Fredrickson, head of the Department of Parks and Recreation, for funds to improve Hazard Park, which was heavily used, especially by local children. The park sponsored a free day camp. In the end, a new deal was completed between the federal government and the city. The compromise allowed tennis courts to be constructed in Westwood but left Hazard Park alone.

Meanwhile, Ramona Gardens residents pushed for a "Vest Pocket Park" plan for their community. Congressman Roybal supported the plan. Unexpectedly, the California Highway Patrol opposed the use of state land for the project and temporarily blocked its acceptance. Residents protested the CHP action and presented its plan to the Public Safety and Highway Department, stressing

---

*Similar moves to eliminate Lincoln Park, which over the years had been reduced to a fraction of its original size, were made recently. Under the leadership of labor organizer Frank López, community activists saved the park. Through these efforts, Plaza de La Raza, a community cultural center, became a reality.

the need for a park. Residents gained support and, by the end of July, the *Sun* reported: "Vest Pocket Park in Ramona Gardens '20 Days' Nearer Being a Reality." On July 31, the *Sun* reported that the Ramona people had won. The Los Angeles Parks and Recreation Commission proceeded with plans for the "Vest Pocket Park."

Community pressure forced the Los Angeles Parks and Recreation Department to service Eastside facilities and proposed funding for their improvements. Park preservation was a major issue, and community residents expressed concern over the master plan for Griffith Park.

Immigration was becoming a major issue in the Chicano community. In June, workshops on the Mexican immigrant were held at the International Institute of Los Angeles. There was little coverage, however, in either newspaper.

Chicanos were becoming more visible in the media. Channel 28, a local public broadcasting station, ran "Canción de la Raza," a soap opera that explored East Los Angeles problems. A California survey reported favorable response to the show. Channel 28 carried other regular programs on Chicanos. Two of its better known programs were "Línea Abierta" and "Ahora." These programs interviewed Chicano activists, including Irene Tovar and Alicia Escalante. They also discussed problems such as immigration and education. The EICC served as an advisory committee to the Ahora show. On April 20, Channel 28 aired "The Invisible Minority," a documentary on Chicanos.

Coverage on the major networks was limited, and what did get on the air was often negative. This was especially true in commercials. Particularly repugnant to Chicanos was the "Frito Bandido," which stereotyped and insulted Mexicans and Mexican Americans. Regular programs depicting the Chicano experience were rare, although Chicanos did appear sporadically on local network public affairs talk shows. When Danny Villanueva was named station manager of KMEX-TV in the fall, many Chicanos hoped that this influential Spanish-language station would become more responsive to community needs.

Unrest among young people remained a major concern. There were not enough classrooms for Eastside students and, on January 9, Kovner asked: "Why Not Build Another Senior High by Ourselves?" Just about this time, Roosevelt High School teacher John

Hogan allegedly called a student a "dirty Mexican" and approximately 600 students walked out when the administration ignored the insult. Also in response, the EICC picketed the school. On January 13, the board of education dismissed the case, claiming that it had insufficient evidence to act. Thirty-five teachers signed a petition supporting Hogan.

As a result of student pressure, East Los Angeles Community College, which at this time was 44 percent Latino, established a Mexican American Studies department. Chris Ruiz was its first director. Roberto Chávez, Dr. Rafael Pérez-Sandoval, and Ray Ceniceros were named to staff the new department. UMAS at California State College, Los Angeles met with community members to discuss the relevance of new courses as well as the community's involvement in curriculum development. Ultimately, a Mexican American Studies department was founded there.

Many activists and community people considered education the key to solving community problems. The board of education recommended adoption of Afro-American and Latin American history textbooks. The board later adopted bilingual mathematics texts, too. Chicanos generally felt that Eastside schools did not receive their fair share of public funds. The city schools offered solutions that were more or less remedial, encouraging teachers to learn Spanish rather than making structural changes in the system. Minority enrollment in the city schools was 46.4 percent of the student population.

Dr. Charles Leyva, an education professor at California State College, Los Angeles, announced a special teacher training program for Chicanos. The board of education appointed two Mexican American principals, William Zazueta and Hilario Peña, to Roosevelt High and Hollenbeck Junior High, respectively. Zazueta had been a principal at Birmingham High in the San Fernando Valley. He refused to transfer to Roosevelt High School, filing discrimination charges against the Los Angeles City Unified School District. A grievance committee eventually voided Zazueta's transfer. Meanwhile, other appointments were made, including that of John León to coordinator of east area elementary schools. The schools also implemented a limited number of Mexican American courses.

Most comments on the schools criticized the quality of education. The *Sun* reported that school authorities constantly warned of the impending financial crisis facing the schools. Secretary of Health, Education, and Welfare Robert Finch promised federal relief for bilingual programs. Dr. Eugene González, assistant state superintendent of schools, spoke at the Bilingual Adult Conference on March 29, advocating bilingual education.

In fact, "bilingual" was becoming one of the most popular words in the community. On February 13, the *Sun* printed: "Bilingual School Students Enjoy Ballet Folklorico." Candidates for all offices urged bilingual teacher recruitment. The East Los Angeles Health Task Force pushed for Spanish-speaking county attendants. A bilingual health conference drew 400 participants at East Los Angeles College on October 25. The schools also implemented bilingual programs which, to many, were a general curative. Meanwhile, the Los Angeles schools increased their activities in this area, establishing a resource center.

Due to considerable community pressure, the schools eliminated group intelligence tests in the first grade. The results of these tests were tragic and alarming: East Los Angeles schools' reading and mathematics scores were the lowest in the Los Angeles Unified School District. Activists pressured the board of education to improve reading scores in Eastside schools.

The board established the Mexican American Education Commission (MAEC). In many ways, this commission institutionalized the EICC. MAEC received opposition from both the right and the left. A group called "Education Through Peace on Campus" protested the creation of MAEC. Some activists believed that the board had co-opted the EICC. At first, 36 members sat on the panel; later, the number was increased to 40. In spite of the formation of MAEC, the EICC continued to operate and generally took more militant stances. In fact, it was involved in a wide range of issues, including the Carlos Martínez case, which involved a student who allegedly beat up a Belvedere Junior High teacher. Supporters claimed that this was a case of mistaken identity and attorney Oscar Acosta defended Martínez. The committee reported regularly to the EICC. Members also discussed the Nuevas Vistas Conference and the progress of *Con Safos* magazine. Finally, EICC members picketed the schools and distributed a leaflet deploring the low reading scores.

At the universities, student groups fought for the special admission of Chicanos. UCLA established an outreach center in East

Los Angeles that offered extension classes in the Centro Universitario. Chicano studies courses were held out of the Centro. UMAS/UCLA sponsored a conference to examine reforms in education, but students criticized UCLA's token efforts in recruiting Chicano students. Meanwhile, UCLA established a recruitment office in East Los Angeles which, according to students, was window dressing. Immaculate Heart College also offered courses on the Mexican American.

On May 22, California State College, Los Angeles/UMAS opened a UMAS Center in East Los Angeles. Soon afterwards, a campus confrontation between administration and Chicano students resulted when students presented a list of demands to the president. Students staged a massive march and camp-in on June 22, in order to publicize their unsuccessful efforts to obtain equal opportunities for Chicanos at the college. Participants included students and grassroots citizens demanding educational reforms.

The protest did not bring immediate concessions. This is not to say that the campaign was a total failure. As a result of pressure, David Boubion was appointed dean of students at California State College, Los Angeles in the fall. Alfred Fernández was appointed director of admissions shortly afterwards. Generally, however, the college went through only the motions of meeting community needs.

The Camp Hess Kramer Mexican American Youth Leadership Conference was held on April 3 through 5. Its theme was "Education: Myth or Reality." By the fall, coverage of youth involvement in anti-war activities increased. Some students circulated a petition for the release of Lt. Everett Alvarez, USMC, a Chicano Vietnam prisoner of war. Many Chicanos, however, refused to sign the petition because Alvarez was an unrepentant military officer, one who did not regret his involvement in the war. On November 18, Rosalio Muñoz, 23, student body president of UCLA, refused induction. On December 20, the Chicano Moratorium Committee staged a march protesting the war. This event marked the entrance of Chicano youth's leadership role in the anti-war movement.

The community criticized the loss of federal funding for the Malabar project, an experimental program that combined bilingual education and reading. Ironically, the Los Angeles Unified School District had sought to expand this experiment.

Politicians and school authorities exploited the issue of bilingual education, which they perceived as another funding source. Critics charged that gifted children in East Los Angeles were shortchanged. These critics alleged that special funds earmarked for East Los Angeles schools were not totally used for that purpose and that monies intended for the Eastside actually supplemented other special funds in more affluent areas. This shifting of funds resulted in inferior education for East Los Angeles.

The walkout cases still were not settled. The "13" petitioned the California Court of Appeals to bar prosecution on charges of conspiracy to disturb the peace. Thirteen of sixteen charges had been dropped, but two counts of "conspiracy to disturb public schools" and "conspiracy to disturb the peace" remained. The "13" won a major victory in winning long trial delays while they explored the constitutional issues in the appeal courts.

The Community Association for Education (CAFE) was formed to protest Sal Castro's removal from Licoln High, calling his transfer to a non-teaching assignment racist. Vahac Madirosian, chair of the MAEC, bitterly clashed with school board member Richard Ferraro over the Castro transfer. In October, a peaceful march was held to support Castro. By the fall, the National Education Association's legal department supported Castro's appeal as well as his fight to keep his teaching credential.

An interesting article appeared in the *Sun* on August 21: "Cultural Nationalism: A Fight for Survival." Purportedly, this was the philosophy of the Chicano student movement. (The article glimpsed into the thinking of the times and should be read in the context of the 1960s, the years of the Mexican American push-out.)

Violence in the barrio worried residents. Tony Ríos, director of CSO, wrote an article, "Violence to Our Barrio Neighbors," for the *Sun* on August 8. Dr. R. J. Carreón, Jr., recently reelected president of the Los Angeles City Police Commission, did not help the problem of violence. His relations with the Chicano community were strained; he represented LAPD interests. Another setback was the appointment of Ed Davis to chief of the LAPD. Meanwhile, Jesús Domínguez was tried for the second time for assault on police officers. The trial resulted in a hung jury. The case had begun on September 1, 1968 when Domínguez, a father of 11 children, inquired about a daughter and niece at a dance. Police severely beat and then charged Domínguez with assault on officers. Even after this second trial, the district attorney did not drop the case and contemplated retrying Domínguez.

In another case, Alfredo Bryan, 16, allegedly shot and killed a police officer in Aliso Village. Authorities shuffled Bryan between the juvenile and adult courts. Police Chief Davis and Governor Reagan pressured the courts to try Bryan as an adult in order to qualify the youth for the death penalty. The case dragged into 1970. Meanwhile, Bryan, while free on bond, was the victim of intense police harassment.

The ACLU released a police maltreatment study, "Law Enforcement: The Matter of Redress." The report underscored increased tension between police and community. Relations were especially strained in the housing projects, and Yorty did not help matters by taking an extreme law-and-order posture. The mayor openly praised the LAPD for keeping militants off the city streets and condoned the use of police force in the minority communities.

The Congress of Mexican American Unity (CMAU) met at the beginning of the year at East Los Angeles Community College to endorse candidates for the college's board of trustees. Three hundred delegates, representing some 40 organizations, attended the endorsing convention. CMAU settled on four candidates. The two most popular were Joe Ortega, an attorney, and Irene Tovar, a community activist from the San Fernando Valley. Tovar was an expected winner. The CMAU also honored the walkout defendants. In spite of this display of unity, however, none of the Chicano candidates were elected to the board.

Just as Parker's "wild tribes" statement had inflamed the Chicano community years earlier, San José judge Gerald Chargin's racist remarks to a Chicano youth caused an uproar in the Eastside community. During the trial of a boy accused of incest, Chargin burst into an intemperate attack against all Mexican Americans, stating that Hitler might have been right in sterilizing society's undesirables. This outburst resulted in the *Sun* receiving a flood of letters to the editor condemning the judge. Most politicians censured Chargin and demanded his ouster. Chargin later apologized for his remarks, but the extreme nature of the act demanded more. Ironically, in contrast to its coverage of the "wild tribes" remark and in spite of the many letters, the *Sun* did not fully cover the Chargin affair.

"Project Intercept" was condemned as an abuse of the Mexican communities on both sides of the border. The border patrol closed the border and cars entering the United States were stopped and subject to an unusually extensive search. The stated purpose was to stop drug traffic. But to Chicanos, this activity was one more case of harassment. During this time, President Nixon ironically declared "National Hispanic Heritage Week." The sincerity of the decree escaped many Chicanos, who protested the virtual closing of the border. Guy Gabaldón, a war hero whose experiences had been made into a feature film, *From Hell to Eternity*, protested "Project Intercept" as racist. Gabaldón wrote that a direct connection existed between illegal drug traffic and the "corrupt, immoral, decadent and bigoted [United States] government." Gabaldón concluded by saying that since he had moved to Ensenada, Mexico, U.S. authorities had harassed him.

Congressman Brown reported that Mexican American deaths in Vietnam had decreased. In 1968, out of 1,637 southwest men killed, 252 had a Spanish surname. Out of 3,446 persons from California killed during the entire war, 601 (17 percent) were Latinos. Dr. Ralph Guzmán stated that Mexican Americans had the highest death rate of any ethnic/racial group in Vietnam. Organized protests against the war intensified, with an anti-war rally scheduled for October 15.

Alicia Escalante clashed with the county supervisors over welfare program cuts. Escalante and other Welfare Rights Association members jammed the board meeting. Debs described their tactics as mob rule. Escalante and Sy Villa gave the supervisors 43 demands, among them a Christmas bonus for welfare recipients. The county supervisors in turn pressured federal authorities for additional funds.

Tom Bradley, a Black city councilman, ran for mayor against Sam Yorty. The Political Action League of Mexican Americans (PALMA) and MAPA endorsed Bradley, as did Congressman Roybal. The *Sun* also endorsed Bradley, while the *Citizen* backed Yorty. Bradley heavily courted the Mexican American community, supporting a farmworkers rally and calling for a Bill of Rights for Chicanos. In the primaries, neither candidate received a majority and Yorty and Bradley were forced into a runoff. Bradley had edged Yorty in the primaries and was expected to win. The Yorty campaign took the low road, exploiting the race issue. Yorty won on May 27 by a 55,000 vote margin and the *Sun* wrote: "Good Grief: Another Four Years of Yorty . . ."

Attorney Martín Castillo was named director of the U.S. Inter-Agency Committee on Mexican American Affairs. Henry Quevedo was also appointed to this agency. Castillo conducted the usual round of inspection tours, stating that the squeaky wheel got the grease. Meanwhile, Romana Bañuelos was elected to chair the Pan American Bank Board.

LUCHA and the Protestant Community Services of the Los Angeles Council of Churches established a caucus to act as a clearinghouse of calm, accurate information on drug-related problems. LUCHA was the most active organization in the field of narcotics. Together with TELACU, LUCHA set up a wood production factory in East Los Angeles. LUCHA's chair, Eduardo Aguirre, also established the Committee for the Rights of the Imprisoned to lobby for prison reforms. Aguirre had begun this organization at San Quentín.

The year closed and neither the *Sun* nor the *Citizen* reported on Católicos Por La Raza. CPLR was under the leadership of Loyola University law student Ricardo Cruz. It picketed the newly constructed St. Basil's Church to draw attention to the fact that the Catholic church, of which Mexican Americans comprised over 60 percent locally, ignored the poverty and injustice suffered by Chicanos. According to the demonstrators, instead of building magnificent church buildings, the Church should take an active role in ameliorating the social, economic, and political deprivation of Latinos*. A violent confrontation resulted, with the police beating and arresting the protestors.

1970

Católicos Por La Raza demonstrations and confrontations at St. Basil's were closely followed, even in the new year. The *Sun* did

---

*Activists continuously cited the leadership role of Black ministers in the Black community, contrasting it to the almost colonial role of the Catholic church in the barrios.

not comment on the events until January 8, when the Congress of Mexican American Unity wrote a letter in support of the group.

On January 22, the *Sun* reported the retirement of Cardinal Timothy McIntyre. Many attributed the prelate's departure to growing criticism. Archbishop Timothy Manning replaced McIntyre.

In February, the *Citizen* published a statement by the Catholic archdiocese defining the Church's role in the community and government and answering CPLR charges of lack of Church involvement to better the material well-being of Mexican Americans. The statement cited the Church's contribution in education, in social and cultural rehabilitation, and in health care, adding that it would be unreasonable for the Church to compete with the state in the field of welfare. Soon after, the Los Angeles Archdiocese announced the formation of an Inter-Parochial Council, which was an outgrowth of the 1969 East Los Angeles Priest's Committee.

Meanwhile, the CPLR defendants went to trial. In two separate trials, 12 were convicted. Gloria Chávez, Larry Hahn, Armando Vásquez, Duane Doherty, Richard Cruz, Richard Martínez, Pedro Arias, Raúl Ruiz, Tony Salazar, José "Karate" Comareño, and Alicia Escalante. Cruz, Salazar, Escalante, Martínez, and Doherty each received four-month jail sentences.

On March 11, another walkout occurred at Roosevelt High in which 75 students broke through a locked gate. Several days of unrest followed, with other Eastside high schools supporting Roosevelt students. Nearly 150 Chicanos walked out at Lincoln and Huntington Park High Schools. At Roosevelt, 33 juveniles and four adults were arrested. David Sánchez, prime minister of the Brown Berets, was arrested the night before the walkout when 250 people marched on the Hollenbeck Police Station.

The Metro Squad, according to Kovner, overreacted at Roosevelt. On March 17, a long and heated meeting between local residents and the LAPD regarding the Roosevelt High confrontations resolved nothing. School authorities, meanwhile, responded by transferring student leaders out of Roosevelt and by calling on parents to assist classroom teachers. MAPA labeled the police tactics as gestapo-like. The Mexican American Education Commission (MAEC) designed grievance procedures for Roosevelt High School students. María Rodríguez, a student, was suspended but later reinstated. Not everyone in the community, however, condemned the police. In April, Rubén Almazán wrote a letter to the *Sun* attacking Sal Castro and saying that white society was not all bad.

On February 16, an inquest probed the hanging of Richard Hernández, 22, at the Los Angeles County Jail on the night that sheriff's deputies booked him. Hernández allegedly committed suicide because he became despondent when he learned that bail could not be raised. Hernández's mother denied that her son was depressed sufficiently to take his own life. Meanwhile, the coroner's jury ruled that Hernández could have died from manual strangulation, since he had a broken rib and internal bleeding. The inquest officer, however, ruled that Hernández had committed suicide. Hernández had bruises, and medical testimony suggested that a choke hold may have been applied. Significantly, Hernández's death marked the third hanging in as many months. His family filed a $2,305,000 claim against the sheriff's office.

According to David Sánchez, 7,000 (according to the *Citizen*, the number was 2,500) people marched in the rain in an East Los Angeles anti-war protest held February 28. Bob Elías, Sal Saucedo, and Rosalio Muñoz spoke at the rally. The growing militancy among Chicanos alarmed police authorities, who intensified operations in the Eastside. On March 19, in testimony before the U.S. Senate Internal Security Sub-Committee, Sgt. Robert Thomas of the Los Angeles Police Department charged that TELACU secretly sponsored violent and/or subversive groups. Thomas called TELACU an umbrella group for these organizations. Police testimony also implicated the Mexican American Opportunities Foundation (MAOF) as possibly violent or subversive. Although Chief Ed Davis sent MAOF a letter of regrets, Davis did not apologize to the numerous other organizations that his agents had redbaited or kept under surveillance.

The community was equally harassed by the Los Angeles County Sheriff's Department. Oscar "Zeta" Acosta, an activist lawyer who was heavily involved in the defense of Chicanos and had spent several days in jail on a contempt of court charge, ran for sheriff. His platform was the establishment of a community review board and the abolition of the sheriff's department. Acosta ran a no-compromise campaign, had no Anglo advisers, and ran strictly as a Chicano candidate. He received more than 100,000

votes, running ahead of Monterey Park Police Chief Everett Holla-
day. But, in the end, incumbent Peter Pitchess won the election
with some 1,300,000 votes.

Meanwhile, tensions built. Joe Montaño, 51, died of an alleged
heart attack while jailed at the Los Angeles sheriff's station. Montaño was arrested when his former wife called the police, alleging that Montaño was violent. Arresting officers handcuffed him
and, when he hesitated in getting into the squad car, they
physically threw him into it. While Montaño's feet were dangling
out of the car, the deputies slammed the door on his legs. Then
the sheriffs beat him. Montaño expired within a half hour of his
arrest. His death was the fifth at the station.

The fund allocations to Chicano students still lagged behind
those of the rest of the community. On April 2, the *Sun* compared
grants received by Chicano Los Angeles high school graduates to
those received by their white counterparts in the San Fernando
Valley. The results are stated on the table below. Considering that
the Eastside schools were larger than the San Fernando Valley
schools and that they were located in economically disadvantaged
areas, these figures demonstrate how Eastside students were
tragically underfunded.

Anti-war sentiment increased, and normally moderate organizations, including MAPA, condemned the Vietnam action. Abe
Tapia, a MAPA leader, ran for the Democratic party primary in
the 45th Assembly District, making the war his number one campaign issue. Tapia received 29 percent of the vote in a district that

LOCAL GRADES SHORT-CHANGED ON FINANCIAL AID

Name of High School	Total Sum	Grades Receiving Aid	Average Amount Per Student
Taft (S.F. Valley)	$ 99,400	3.5%	$ 3,206
Granada Hills (S.F. Valley)	66,140	2.3%	3,150
Birmingham (S.F. Valley)	88,302	6.1%	3,154
Monroe (S.F. Valley)	117,700	5.0%	2,009
Garfield (E.L.A.)	19,085	10.2%	209
Lincoln (E.L.A.)	16,150	15.2%	376
Roosevelt (E.L.A.)	47,789	11.9%	771
Wilson (E.L.A.)	23,670	7.9%	1,023

was only 30 percent Chicano. The vote, according to many analysts, was strictly along ethnic lines, which documented the effects of gerrymandering.

On May 7, Joe Kovner wrote an editorial, "No Gifts for Mother's Day," vehemently criticizing the Vietnam War and its growing casualties. During the first days of May, when Cambodia was bombed, Congressman Roybal protested American intervention there. At Cal State College, L.A., the Cambodia bombings unleashed heated demonstrations. On May 5, pro-Vietnam partisans at San Fernando Valley College, angered by Chicano antiwar demonstrations against Cambodia intervention, burned down the Chicano campus house.

On May 5, a search warrant was presented to Mrs. Quentín Galván Gutiérrez. The name on the search warrant was Pedro González. Police did not permit Mrs. Galván to see the warrant. On the 11th, police arrested and beat Quentín Galván Gutiérrez and almost arrested his daughter when she attempted to intervene. Galván Gutiérrez was released two days later, the victim of a case of mistaken identity. Celia L. De Rodríguez, a Barrio Defense Committee activist, appealed to the U.S. Commission on Civil Rights for relief.

On May 5, 1969, LAPD Officer Thomas L. Parkham, 29, killed Frank González, 14, who had been skipping school but had not committed a crime. Parkham had been suspended twice before for questionable conduct. District Attorney Evelle Younger did not prosecute the officer. A year later, however, federal authorities tried Parkman for violation of González's civil rights. Judge Andrew Hauk, who over the years had consistently displayed antiminority biases, heard the Parkham case. Blacks and Mexican Americans were arbitrarily excused from the jury. Hauk displayed openly hostile attitudes during the trial and the jury found Officer Thomas Parkham not guilty.

The district attorney pressed the prosecution of the 1968 high school walkout and the Biltmore fire defendants. In the spring of 1969, a group of Chicano activists had picketed the Nuevas Vistas Conference sponsored by the California Department of Education at the Biltmore Hotel. Picketers protested the keynote address by Governor Ronald Reagan, whom they labeled as anti-education and anti-minority. During the conference, fires broke out. Defendants in the Biltmore case claimed that police provocateurs lit these fires. The LAPD arrested the demonstrators and charged 13

Chicanos with disturbing the peace. Ten were tried for conspiracy to commit arson. After two years of appeals, the D.A. finally tried the case and the jury acquitted the defendants. One of the original defendants, Carlos Montes, a Brown Beret, did not stand trial at this time. Due to police harassment, he was a fugitive for many years and did not stand trial until the late 1970s, when he was also acquitted.

On the Fourth of July, a demonstration was held at the East Los Angeles substation. The crowd protested the deaths of six Mexican Americans at the substation in the past five months. Sheriffs shot one youth and deputies arrested three juveniles and 19 adults. Meanwhile, demonstrators responded by breaking windows on Whittier Boulevard. Nearly 250 sheriff and CHP deputies suppressed the rebellion.

On July 10, some 500 Chicanos protested police brutality in front of the East Los Angeles sheriff's station. A few weeks later, seven LAPD and San Leandro officers shot and killed two cousins, Beltrán Sánchez, 23, and Guillermo Sánchez, 22, both of whom were undocumented workers. The plainclothes officers broke into the Sánchez apartment and yelled, "Freeze!" The men did not understand the officers, and as a result, one cousin was shot in the bedroom and another while hanging out of a windowsill. The entire incident was another case of mistaken identity. Infuriated, Congressman Roybal pressured the Los Angeles City Police Commission to take action. The Mexican Consul issued a strong statement condemning the shootings, and the community insisted that manslaughter and assault charges be brought against the police officers involved. On the eve of the 1970 Chicano Moratorium, Manuel Alcazar returned to Mexico with the bodies of the Sánchez cousins.

Just prior to the Sánchez killings, Danny Jiménez, 19, was arrested for assault on an officer and resisting arrest. Deputies badly beat Jiménez, a resident of Montebello, when he inquired why sheriff's deputies were mistreating a man. Although a jury voted 11-to-1 for acquittal, the district attorney refused to drop charges until Jiménez signed a probable cause affidavit. In August, a bomb ripped the East Los Angeles Municipal Court.

In El Monte, Esteban Anguiano, 14, Lee Anguiano, 15, and Massey Albert Enciso, 25, were charged on June 18 with intent to commit murder. Enciso was asleep in the garage when police began shooting into the Anguiano home. He pleaded with the officers not to fire because children were in the house. Rosie Anguiano and her eight children fled the house, dodging bullets. The house burned down. One police officer was shot. Considering the amount of confusion, this could have been the result of police crossfire.

In spite of this hostile environment, organizers were optimistic about the Chicano Moratorium of August 29, predicting 50,000 marchers. Numerous organizations, among them the Brown Berets and the CMAU, sponsored the march. Congressman Roybal praised the organizers and supported the moratorium. The *Sun* covered pre-moratorium events on the front page, endorsing the march.

An estimated 20,000 anti-war demonstrators gathered in Belvedere Park. No incidents occurred, although a minor disturbance happened a half block from Laguna Park at the Green Mill Liquor Store, where teenagers stole some soft drinks. It was a hot day and children were playing in the park. The participants attended speeches, watched the folk dances, and listened to music. Sheriff's deputies used the soft drink incident as an excuse to attack the participants, wielding clubs and firing tear gas. The *Citizen* carried an excellent article by María Pacheco, "Eyewitness Account of Scene as Riot Breaks Out at Park." A photo essay accompanied the article. Police aggression caused a rebellion, which resulted in over one million dollars in damages. *Los Angeles Times* journalist and KMEX-TV news director Rubén Salazar, 42, Gilbert Dias, 25, and Lynn Ward, 15, were killed during the riot. Hundreds were arrested and beaten without provocation. Both the *Sun* and the *Citizen* condemned Salazar's murder and police aggression.

Sheriff Peter Pitchess defended his deputies' actions. "Don't forget," he excused, "these deputies were in combat." Pitchess blamed provocateurs, pointing out that officers arrested some 250 rioters who had damaged 128 buildings and wrecked 25 cars. In an editorial, the *Citizen* called for peace and unity. The *Sun*'s coverage was extensive but took a partisan view. On September 6, the *Sun* ran a special article by Carol Infranca titled "What Caused the Riot?"

As a coroner's inquest into the death of Rubén Salazar began, local television stations aired the daily proceedings in their entirety. Simultaneously, a September 16 parade was planned in which an anti-war contingent would march. In order to prevent a bottleneck and to better control the parade, sponsors attempted to lease the East Los Angeles College football stadium. At the last minute, the Los Angeles Community College Trustees denied the parade access to the stadium. The bottleneck occurred as predicted and deputy sheriffs and police attacked the marchers. On September 17, Kovner wrote: "I am sitting here in occupied East Los Angeles while I write this column." A week later, the sheriff's department rebutted Kovner's version of what happened. Meanwhile, the *Sun* condemned a curfew imposed on all East Los Angeles youth as unconstitutional, charging that Chicanos suffered from injustices.

On September 20, the *Sun* published another Carol Infranca article: "Peaceful Parade Ends in Clash." On September 24, Eddie Pardo examined the causes of the confrontation in yet another *Sun* article, "Another View of Sept. 16 ELA Parade." In contrast, the *Citizen* downplayed the September 16 riots entirely.

As the result of considerable pressure, the U.S. Justice Department began considering a federal probe. Symbolically, the county supervisors changed the name of Laguna Park to Rubén Salazar Park. The U.S. Commission on Civil Rights demanded a probe into the East Los Angeles events. And the *Sun* carried a tear-off ballot so that readers could petition for a federal probe into Salazar's death.

The Salazar murder inquest proceeded, painfully slowly. Then the *Sun* carried an eyewitness account, told to George C. Muñoz, of Salazar's death. Gustavo García and A. Tony García, who had been at the Silver Dollar Café, where Salazar's body was found, testified that as they were leaving, sheriff's deputies ordered them to return to the bar. Suddenly, the deputies fired without warning. This testimony contradicted that of the deputies, who claimed they had given warning. The *Citizen*'s coverage of the Silver Dollar testimony was also extensive. Witnesses told how they found Salazar's body. Sheriff Peter Pitchess criticized the media's coverage of the inquest and the circumstances surrounding Salazar's death. Raúl Ruiz, a professor at San Fernando State College and the editor of *La Raza* magazine, also testified on events at the Silver Dollar Café.

On October 24, Kovner wrote that anti-war sentiment was increasing and that even executives "more and more were expressing . . . anti-Vietnam war sentiments." Meanwhile, Thomas Wilson, the deputy who fired the projectile that killed Salazar, testified before the coroner's jury. Attorney Oscar Acosta walked out in disgust. Carol Infranca wrote a lengthy article for the *Sun*, "Deputy Who Fired Projectile Testifies," which was followed on October 4 by another article, "Coroner's Inquest Continues." The inquest jury split 4-to-3 on its recommendations. Four inquest jurors found "death at the hands of another;" the remaining jurors, "death by accident." The jury was, moreover, very critical of the deputy's actions.

In the end, District Attorney Evelle Younger decided not to prosecute Deputy Wilson. Politics weighed in this decision: Younger was running scared for state attorney general. Another candidate, Charles O'Brien, accused Younger of intimidating the media in the Salazar case. Many prominent leaders accused Younger of abdicating his responsibility. Abe Tapia of MAPA and Esteban Torres, president of the Congress of Mexican American Unity, had in July accused Younger of political motives in his handling of the Biltmore and walkout trials. The handling of the moratorium and the inaction of the district attorney in Salazar's death proved to many that Younger wanted to exploit the law-and-order mood of the so-called silent majority. Many activists alleged that Younger had refused to prosecute Wilson because of his own political ambitions. Ironically, the Mexican American Labor Council endorsed Younger for attorney general. Younger won his race—but only after a close contest. Meanwhile, many questions surrounding Salazar's death remained unanswered.

The *Sun* pressed for a federal investigation into the Salazar murder. The U.S. Civil Rights Commission was requested to conduct a probe. In this charged climate, a bombing took place at Roosevelt High. Reportedly, this was related to the events of August 29.

In the spring, the U.S. Civil Rights Commission issued a report, *Mexican Americans and the Administration of Justice in the Southwest*. The report documented the systematic abuse of Mexican Americans by law enforcement authorities and the lack of judicial justice for Chicanos. Another study, by the Equal Employment Opportunities Commission for the Colorado Civil Rights Commission, called the status of Chicanos a "caste system."

The National Moratorium Committee was by this time factionalized. Frank Martínez, who later admitted that he was an agent for the Alcohol, Tobacco, and Firearms Agency of the U.S.

Treasury Department, had become chair of the Moratorium Committee. On November 14, arrests took place at the committee's headquarters. (Many sources claim that Martínez provoked several confrontations). By the end of the year, public pressure forced the LAPD to expand its office in the Eastside to handle complaints of police abuse. Also, the federal grand jury was secretly investigating the August 29 events.

Congressman Roybal called for the resignation of FBI director J. Edgar Hoover, who was quoted in the December 4, 1970, issue of *Time* magazine as saying, "You did not have to worry about a Mexican American or a Puerto Rican with a gun since they were bad shots; however, if they had a knife that was a different story." Not surprisingly, a poll revealed that 44.9 percent of East Los Angeles Mexican Americans felt unequal before the law.

Chicanos strongly protested commercials that stereotyped Mexicans. Eastsiders found the Frito Lay "Frito Bandido" especially offensive. In a *Sun* article "Adios A Frito Bandido," Angel Solis summed up community indignation. The Elgin watch company also advertised that Emiliano Zapata, the Mexican revolutionary hero, robbed to get Elgin watches.

Meanwhile, Younger stunned everyone by proposing that charges against the "13" be dropped. The case had dragged on for two years, winding its way through the appellate syndrome. According to news sources, Younger anticipated an unfavorable decision on the conspiracy charges and wanted to pile on new charges that could not be appealed. Judge George M. Dell refused to drop the charges, stating that he did not want the prosecution to clog the appeal process. The Second California Appellate Court, comprised of Justices Otto Kraus, Clark Stephens, and William Peppy, found that the felony charges based on conspiracy to commit misdemeanors were a violation of the First Amendment guarantees. Suddenly, the long, drawn-out process was ended.

Grumblings from the Judge Chargin case carried over into 1970. A follow-up report was aired on the "Ahora" TV program. Assemblyman Alex García introduced a resolution to impeach Chargin. And although the State Judicial Commission censured Chargin, this amounted to a slap on the hand.

Esteban Torres and TELACU were more visible during 1970. In January, Torres testified before manpower hearings held by the

U.S. Senate Subcommittee on Employment, Manpower and Poverty. He documented the need for more programs in the Eastside. Manpower programs became more important and the Mexican American Manpower Agency (MAMA), made up of 22 organizations, was formed.

Torres also participated in the Congress of Mexican American Unity, which held its convention at East Los Angeles College on February 14 and 15. The convention's theme was "Power Through Unity." The CMAU endorsed candidates for the June election. The convention became controversial when student delegations, which dominated the voting, did not endorse Congressman Roybal because he failed to attend the proceedings. Richard Calderón, candidate for the 29th Congressional District, was an overwhelming favorite of delegates. In its final report, the CMAU issued various resolutions on school reform. The CMAU resolved that Chicanos should control the teaching of their history and culture. Delegates also endorsed LUCHA's People's Resolution (CRI), which dealt with prison reform.

The CMAU elected Torres as its president. MAPA's Bert Corona was Torres's closest rival. The steering committee held its first meeting in March, during which it planned a fundraiser.

TELACU received a grant of $160,000 for economic development and MAOF received $690,000 for a new careers program. Meanwhile, Mexican American entertainers prepared for the April 4 fundraiser at the Sports Arena. Anthony Quinn, Ricardo Montalbán, Vicki Carr, and other celebrities performed at this event.

In May, the CMAU endorsed Roybal. The congressman defeated Father Blase Bonpane in the primary. Dr. Julián Nava ran for state superintendent of schools against Dr. Max Rafferty. Nava accused Rafferty of misapplication of $2 billion in education funds. According to Nava, Rafferty's lack of leadership created hardships for the schools. Nava ran third behind Rafferty and Dr. Wilson Riles, a Black. Although he lost, Nava's votes prevented Rafferty from receiving a majority vote in the primary. This forced a runoff between Rafferty and Riles.

Eastside newspapers covered Richard Calderón's race for the 29th Congressional District. As had happened before, too many Mexican American candidates ran in the primary. This resulted in vote splitting and allowed George Danielson to win the Democratic primary by 1,590 votes.

Arthur Montoya continued his private war against Model Cities and HOME. Of the two programs, HOME was the easier target. Model Cities was simply too diversified and not all of its numerous programs were connected with housing. Thus, it was able to create a constituency. Montoya called for the convening of a Congress of Property Owners Associations. In addition to Model Cities and HOME, Montoya condemned the Pico-Union project, which designated the area west of the Civic Center for urban redevelopment.

Many community activists, ironically, criticized HUD for not doing enough. They called HUD indifferent to street lighting in East Los Angeles alleys. HUD neutralized criticism by recruiting Spanish-speaking college graduates to work as brokers. The agency stressed community service and set up a law and justice telephone line.

Model Cities conducted community meetings at Lincoln Heights which were not as relevant as they had been in the past. Under Nixon, both the war on poverty and Model Cities programs de-emphasized community involvement. Montoya surprised—and distressed—Model Cities officials by being overwhelmingly elected as an East/Northeast area representative to their program. Montoya called for a total change in the federal guidelines in order to give people control. Six hundred people attended the meeting at which Montoya was elected.

As a spokesperson for the East/Northeast area, Montoya met with Mayor Yorty's aides. He wanted the housing allocation clauses removed from the Model Cities application and publicly called for a cessation of Model Cities activities. According to Montoya, Boyle Heights and Lincoln Heights still remained prime targets for redevelopment. As proof, he cited a survey recently conducted by the Community Redevelopment Agency (CRA). Montoya charged that Model Cities was using questionable tactics.

Montoya attacked politicians who supported HOME, singling out Councilman Debs as the main culprit. A recall movement involving Art Snyder made the councilman's support of HOME and Model Cities a major issue. Montoya denigrated Model Cities' "community participation" rhetoric, calling it phony. He cited instances of harassment by HOME inspectors. One of Yorty's aides, Joe Quinn, admitted that Model Cities had the potential to develop into a huge patronage bonanza for the mayor of Los Angeles and the city council. After all, the project attracted $32 million to the city.

Model Cities' financial assistance to the Mexican American Cultural Center at Lincoln Park was welcomed. Frank López, a popular Eastside trade unionist, coordinated Plaza de la Raza, which enjoyed broad community support. The new building at Lincoln Park would be named after Rubén Salazar. In the fall, supporters launched a fundraising drive to complete Plaza de la Raza.

Yorty submitted a plan to Model Cities for more programs. In opposition to the mayor, 200 community folk met at Lincoln High School. This body passed a strong resolution condemning Model Cities. Soon afterwards, a suit questioned the legality of the Model Cities Council in the North/Northeast area.

A series of follow-up meetings were held. Montoya had an attorney present at these meetings to explain legal rights to property owners who were threatened by HOME and Model Cities. The Maravilla-Belvedere Park Property Owners Association again expressed opposition to Model Cities. Montoya wrote: "Resident councils have influence, Yorty has power." On August 20, Montoya listed Eastside Model Cities victims, calling master planning a product of a totalitarian state and asserting that it had no place in a free society. At a East/Northeast Model Cities Neighborhood Residence Council meeting, Councilman Snyder placed Raúl Ruiz and Patricia Borjón, both of *La Raza* magazine, under citizen's arrest after a verbal confrontation during which Snyder attempted to intimidate the two journalists.

Montoya passed out petitions opposing the master plan, which he again charged would displace Eastside residents. At this point, the CMAU, questioning not the program itself but the criteria for funds allocations, sued the city to show evidence of citizen participation in Model Cities. Ultimately, the group gained a court order to halt Model Cities projects. The CMAU claimed inequities in East Los Angeles and Watts programs. The organization objected to the fact that $11 million out of $13 million went to public institutions, while Model Cities allocated only $2.8 million to community organizations spread over 26 projects. An injunction claimed HUD violated its own guidelines. Model Cities denied charges that its program involved urban renewal. Arthur Bastidos, a Model Cities administrator, and Ray Carrasco, a HUD area director, defended the agency. Meanwhile, there was considerable community pressure to lift the injunction because it affected jobs and funding.

Montoya charged that aggressive HOME inspectors harassed homeowners. Model Cities countered by issuing publicity releases claiming that "HUD money was coming to ELA for Clean-up and Repair."

The *Citizen*'s coverage of Model Cities remained positive. The paper announced deadlines and promoted program events. Groups such as the Mexican American Builders organized and, in turn, lobbied for more funds. The *Citizen* reported contract bids for HOME street repairs. By the end of April, the *Citizen* announced the formation of resident councils comprised of Model Cities appointees and representatives elected by residents. According to critics, the councils allegedly rubber stamped development proposals.

CSO filed a complaint against the East Los Angeles workable plan, which had been submitted to HUD's Community Improvement Department, charging that it was inadequate. (It is important to note that workable plans always preceded applications for renewal of an area.) The *Citizen* focused on HOME street improvement. While the *Sun* condemned HOME's destruction of trees, the *Citizen* applauded its planting of trees.

The wide spectrum of funded Model Cities programs held open houses to generate community support. Model Cities also proposed a health assistance and referral center. Although involved in applying for funds, TELACU suprisingly joined the Maravilla and Belvedere Property Owners Association in attacking Model Cities' goals for the Eastside.

In early June, TELACU received a grant for home repairs. The organization also received a $210,000 grant from the Ford Foundation. During this time, United Auto Workers President Leonard Woodcock visited TELACU's mattress factory. Torres enjoyed good relations with the activist community due to his leadership in CMAU, which supported activities of groups such as Católicos Por La Raza. César Chávez also strongly endorsed TELACU.

Drugs remained a leading concern in East Los Angeles. Drug Awareness Week was called at Roosevelt High School from January 12 to 16. A drug deterrence program called the "Happening" began a so-called new approach to youth in East Los Angeles. A narcotics information center was set up on February 12 at El Mercado, in Boyle Heights. Poverty agencies funded a drug treatment clinic in the Eastside. And in November, professional educators sponsored a conference on Drug Abuse to inform the public about the problem's many facets.

Edward "Moe" Aguirre was the leading figure in the ex-convict or *pinto* scene. LUCHA conducted weekly community training sessions, which were coordinated by Roberto Castro. It also formed a statewide council for prisoner's rights and reforms. Inmates at San Quentin prison filed a suit to obtain ethnic news. César Chávez supported CRI's "People Resolution" petition, which was circulated statewide.

The grape strike was won in July, and Chávez moved to the Salinas Valley, where he organized lettuce workers. During his stay there, he was placed in jail for defying a court injunction.

At the federal level, President Richard Nixon vetoed the Health Education Bill, even after his own task force had recommended approval. Ironically, HEW searched for a special assistant on Mexican health problems. And at the state level, Governor Reagan continued his war on the impoverished, attempting to cut legal aid to the poor. His favorite target was the California Rural Legal Assistance program.

A state governor has the power to provide relief to local school districts. When the Los Angeles city schools underwent financial problems in 1970, Governor Reagan turned a deaf ear to their difficulties. Meanwhile, the teachers suffered a sixth year of budget cuts and the no salary increases. They threatened to, and were expected to, strike. In increasing numbers, residents came to realize that Ronald Reagan had a "life and death" power over welfare dependents as well.

At the local level, Councilman Gilbert Lindsay warned Opal Jones of the Neighborhood Adult Participation Project not to engage in politics. Cuts, which would affect four programs, were projected in the Eastside Office of Economic Opportunities (OEO). Ernest Sprinkles had been named to head this agency.

Headstart was one of the few war on poverty programs that remained popular and was supported by politicians. Other programs were in trouble. The city and county assumed direction of the Neighborhood Youth Corps after EYOA dropped the program. Funding was tighter and even Headstart was reduced. The EYOA itself was still under fire for not meeting the needs of the Mexican American community. Matters worsened when it was announced that $1.5 million would be cut from Eastside programs.

At California State College, Los Angeles, the Educational Participation in Communities (EPIC) program was initiated to encourage student community volunteerism. UCLA's Centro still functioned in East Los Angeles. Other colleges continued to recruit in East Los Angeles, and the MECHAs at the various campuses were very active. Off-campus groups also gained momentum. "Stay in the Community and Help Our People" was the motto of one such group, Casa Carnalismo.

Chicano students joined the brotherhood slate at California State College, Los Angeles and, along with other minorities and White radicals, gained control of student government. College campuses in the fall came under fire by Younger, who stated that students should be treated like other community members. On October 1, the *Sun* listed new laws dealing with campus disturbances. It was clear that authorities were moving to suffocate campus militancy.

The Mexican American Education Commission (MAEC) commended the schools for a slight improvement in reading scores. Some activists criticized this as a premature accolade and accused the MAEC of abandoning its independence. In the fall, reading scores were again published by the Los Angeles Unified School District, and *Sun* reporter Carol Infraca wrote an article titled "ELA Elementary Reading Scores Frightening at First Glance."

In a total student population of 654,420, minority enrollment in the Los Angeles City Schools hit 48.4 percent. The school census showed that there were 153,515 Blacks, 136,316 Latinos, 21,942 Asians, and 1,026 Native Americans. Even though Blacks outnumbered Chicanos, the trend toward higher Chicano enrollment was obvious: Black and White enrollment was falling, while the Mexican American population was growing.

The courts ordered the Los Angeles schools to integrate; the board of education approved the order by a 5-to-2 vote. Many eastsiders feared that desegregation would result in loss of special programs at Eastside schools. Nevertheless, a UCLA research center survey refuted that Mexican Americans opposed busing. In fact, 37 percent of the Mexican American community favored busing to achieve integration. The UCLA survey also learned that

57 percent of all Los Angeles Blacks supported busing, while only 15 percent of the city's Whites approved of it. In October, anti-busing forces attacked Superior Court Judge Alfred Gittelson for his order to desegregate.

CSO celebrated its 23rd anniversary, regretting that issues existing in 1947 were the same ones still plaguing the community in 1970. The rights of the foreign born, for example, were still violated. In May, the Immigration and Naturalization Service (INS) was accused of violating the rights of undocumented workers. CSO had been one of the leaders in this struggle throughout the 1950s.

A Chicana Forum was held at Cal State Los Angeles. María Cristina de Penichet, the first woman brain surgeon in Mexico, and Celia Luna Rodríguez of the Barrio Defense Committee were honored.

Dionicio Morales appeared before the Urban League convention and urged the easing of tensions between Blacks and Chicanos. Finally, by the end of the year, the U.S. Census count was almost completed.

1971

Governor Ronald Reagan was still at war with the poor. The director of the California Rural Legal Assistance program asked the governor to please release its funds. Reagan had withheld CRLA funding to punish the agency for defending farmworkers against the abuses of agribusiness. These interests formed the base of the governor's support. The Western Center on Law and Poverty charged that the bottom line in Reagan's harassment of CRLA was that it served the poor, which the governor personally found objectionable. Many feared that all legal assistance to the poor would soon be terminated.

Meanwhile, in testimony before the advisory committee to the U.S. Commission on Civil Rights, Dr. Francisco Bravo stated that both Reagan and former Governor Edmund G. Brown Sr. had failed to live up to promises to appoint more Mexican Americans.

On January 9, a demonstration against the war and police brutality took place in front of Parker Police Center. Protestors called for an end to violence. Throughout the march, police harassed and finally attacked participants. Forty-seven arrests followed. LAPD

Chief Ed Davis said that "White Bolshevik swimming pool communists" manipulated Chicano youth, claiming that the Communist party had switched from Blacks to Chicanos some 15 months prior to the demonstration. Davis also accused the Rev. John Luce of spawning the Brown Berets. Despite the weekend violence, a march was announced for the last day of the month. Alex Cota, head of the Concerned Citizens Committee, called the demonstrators troublemakers.

Meanwhile, the community prepared for the January 31 protest, which was called the "March for Justice." Organizers announced their intent that the march be peaceful. Letters to the *Sun* and *Citizen* urged peace in the community.

Rally organizers coordinated three simultaneous three-day marches from outlying Chicano barrios, meeting in East Los Angeles on the 31st. These occurred without incident. At the rally itself, the participants heard speeches. When it ended, Rosalio Muñoz asked the crowd to disperse peacefully. However, as the demonstrators left, some went to the sheriff's substation to protest police abuses. A riot ensued. Gustavo Montag, Jr., 24, was killed, 50 others were injured, and 88 were placed under arrest. The moratorium organizers were stunned and, at a press conference, Rosalio Muñoz and David Sánchez parried questions.

The attitude of the press changed noticeably. Salazar's death was forgotten and the daily press dwelled on the violence. Sheriff Peter Pitchess effectively manipulated the media, blaming the so-called militants. Pitchess alleged that his deputies had not shot to kill and underscored that this was, afterall, the fifth disturbance. The February 7 issue of the *Sun* published photos of the January 31 rebellions. Four days later, the *Sun* printed a letter from a "disgusted ELA mother," who defended the police and condemned the marchers. José María Sánchez, owner of La Quebradita market, rebutted "Disgusted Mother." Brown Beret prime minister David Sánchez wrote an open letter in the *Sun* titled "Police State in ELA." In March, a grand jury charged Sánchez with draft evasion.

Roybal continued to press for a congressional probe of the East Los Angeles disturbances. Finally, through the efforts of Congressman Roybal, a house judiciary subcommittee in February scheduled a study on police-Chicano relations in Los Angeles. To top things off, a major earthquake followed on the heels of this violence and destroyed many overused East Los Angeles facilities.

The moratorium confrontations were the most dramatic, but not the only, cases of police abuse. In January 1971, the Barrio Defense Committee reported the case of Connie Bustamante and John Márquez, which had occurred on 6 December 1970. The couple had gone to visit Bustamante's brother. There they found her ex-husband and an argument ensued. Mrs. Bustamante and Márquez got into her car and backed out of the driveway. The car windows were fogged. Bustamante heard shouts, which she believed came from her ex-husband. All of a sudden, shots whizzed around the couple in the car. Both Bustamante and Márquez went into shock. Police booked them for assault with a deadly weapon.

The sheriff fired three guards at the central jail who had sprayed 71 inmates with gas. The Civil Service Commission held hearings at which witnesses testified that they had seen the inmates gassed.

Los Angeles Police Chief Davis called March 3 a day of infamy. On that day, a federal grand jury indicted four police officers, three from Los Angeles, and one from San Leandro, for depriving the Sánchez cousins of their civil and constitutional rights the year before. Davis charged that U.S. Attorney General John Mitchell's action was a grandstand play. As a result of pressure from Davis and Yorty, the city council voted to pay the LAPD officers' legal defense before the federal court. Only five councilmen voted against this legal assistance. Chicanos and liberals protested this misuse of taxpayers' money. Roybal praised the grand jury investigation and the officers' indictment and joined in condemning the city council's action. A taxpayers suit was filed against the council. In the Salazar case, the community was not as fortunate; the U.S. Attorney General terminated the probe into the journalist's murder.

On April 15, the *Sun* published an article, "Hollenbeck Lake," recalling the plight of Eastside Mexican Americans. The *Sun* stated that the Eastside was run for Anglos, attacking Snyder for his defense of the police. On April 25, the *Sun* asserted that Councilman Lindsay objected to a $1,400,000 federal grant to teach California police how to behave at demonstrations. Lindsay countered that the money should be spent to teach citizens how to deal with government.

Rosalio Muñoz, David Sánchez, and the Brown Berets turned their attention from anti-war demonstrations to La Marcha de la

Reconquista. Five hundred Latins marched from Calexico to Sacramento. The *Sun* reported that the group was denied the right to use toilet facilities at the Southern Pacific Railroad Station outside of Palm Springs.

Reconquista leaders in the city of San Fernando urged Chicanos to join La Raza Unida party. Muñoz and Mike Heralda requested assistance from *Sun* readers for the marchers. Leaders planned a rally on the steps of the state capitol in August. They also announced a petition drive to recall Governor Reagan. Finally, in mid-August, the marchers reached Sacramento and held their rally.

Roybal asked the U.S. Civil Rights Commission and the U.S. Justice Department to look into the Riverside police killing of Francisco García. García had died at the hands of Riverside police and customs agents in an altercation during which his wife was also wounded. As it turned out, this was yet another case of mistaken identity.

The *Sun* reported that 120 out of 380 complaints against the LAPD were found valid. Ironically, an amendment was passed for higher pension plans for fire and police personnel—largely because of the support of minority voters.

The Barrio Defense Committee scheduled a July 27 vigil for the Sánchez cousins. At the end of July, Casa Carnalismo formed the Free Los Tres Committee. The three were Rodolfo Sánchez, 25, Alberto Ortiz, 22, and Juan Ramón Fernández, 22. Allegedly, the trio had shot and paralyzed undercover officer Robert E. Canales, 30. Canales was a special agent for the Bureau of Narcotics of the Dangerous Drugs Division of the U.S. Justice Department. Casa Carnalismo, to which the three belonged, had sponsored a campaign to clean up drugs in the community. Canales allegedly was dealing in drugs. Police responded to Casa's militancy by breaking into its headquarters. Harassment was so blatant that Councilman Lindsay called for a probe into police abuse. The councilman had met with Carnalismo members. Meanwhile, Los Tres underwent a lengthy trial and, on November 15, were found guilty. Carnalismo then launched a campaign to free the three.

The LAPD officers tried for the violation of the Sánchez cousins' civil rights were acquitted. The *Sun's* Carol Stevens called the acquittal an "unsatisfactory decision," adding that even

The Los Angeles Times criticized the verdict, which made police "accountable to no one but themselves." Stevens wrote that civilians were not criminals until they were proven guilty. Apparently, the court reasoned that the Sánchez had no legal status in the United States because they did not have documents and were not U.S. citizens.

On August 8, a disturbance broke out on Whittier Boulevard. About 600 people participated in this disturbance, which apparently was not politically motivated. On August 29, Whittier merchants commemorated Rubén Salazar's death by closing their businesses. Only a few incidents were reported on this first anniversary of the 1970 Chicano Moratorium.

Meanwhile, the Chicano Liberation Front (CLF) admitted to the theft of rifles from Lincoln High in February 1970. It took responsibility for two bombings at Roosevelt High but disclaimed bombing a Spanish language station. It also took credit for bombing a patrol car at Cal State Los Angeles. The CLF listed its bombings from the past 17 months:

Roosevelt High (twice)
Los Angeles City Hall
U.S. Post Office on East 8th Street
Bank of America on West Pico
Bank of America on Brooklyn Avenue
Bank of America in Monterey Park
Safeway Store on Brooklyn Avenue
Chevron Chemical in East Los Angeles
Department of Public Services on Grand Avenue
Bank of America in Woodland Hills
Shopping Bag Market in Altadena
Atlantic Savings & Loan in East Los Angeles
United California Bank in El Sereno
Patrol car, Lincoln High School
Belvedere Junior High
Montebello High
Pan American Bank in East Los Angeles
Hazard Park Armory Reserve

The CLF criticized David Sánchez of the Brown Berets.

During this period, Superior Court Judge Arthur Alarcón ended six weeks of hearings concerning the Biltmore Hotel affair. The defense contended that Chicanos had been deliberately and systematically excluded from the grand jury. Alarcón found insufficient evidence to support the appeal.

The community pressured the Los Angeles city council to control the police. For the first time in history, a city council committee opened its doors to complaints of the police and fire departments. On September 2, the *Sun* expressed disappointment when only a few residents attended that session. Disappointingly, only five testified before the new Police, Fire, and Civil Defense Committee. Witnesses urged the investigations of police-community relations, police overreactions, and shooting incidents. Gilbert Lindsay appeared to be the only city council member who consistently criticized the LAPD. The Police, Fire, and Civil Defense Committee resumed hearings on September 19, setting up guidelines and scheduling semimonthly public "grievance hearings." Meanwhile, the police commission short-circuited the process by announcing that it would make itself available to the public. Not satisfied, Lindsay underscored a need to control the LAPD, which apparently the commission had failed to do. Many community leaders echoed this sentiment, citing that the LAPD had killed some 800 civilians between 1950 to 1970.

In an apparent public relations effort, the LAPD employed bilingual operators to assist the Spanish-speaking. On December 2, the *Sun* ran an article observing that Davis no longer criticized the press but praised its "objective" reporting—that is, the press lessened its criticism of the LAPD. Police enforcement had been tightened at all levels. J. Edgar Hoover praised Attorney General John Mitchell. "Now I can relax," Hoover said. "Attorney General Mitchell can take over the job and no one will be the wiser."

An apparent pattern emerged. With the decline of Chicano activism, the press covered more gang activity and shootings. The *Sun* reported these events in the last three months of the year: "15-Year-Old ELA Boy Shot, Killed Saturday," "One Youth Killed, Four Wounded in Separate Local Shootings," and "Second ELA Youth Dies in Gang Shooting."

In the May 13 edition of the *Sun*, Angel T. Solis praised youth for questioning unjust laws, stating that young people should protest and struggle vigorously for their rights.

Housing project residents were concerned about the Basic Car Plan and law enforcement authorities' manipulation of the car clubs, which supposedly converted gangs into clubs. The program was not new but press releases made it appear as if it were a fresh approach. The LAPD sponsored a similar program, expanding its boys and girls Explorer Troops.

The poverty programs were under attack and a survival coalition was formed to prevent further cuts. The coalition held a rally on Sunday, January 24. Meanwhile, the Chicano Caucus sought direct funding from the Office of Economic Opportunities. Caucus members accused EYOA of discriminating against Mexican Americans. Tony Ríos of CSO, Abe Tapia of Joint Venture, and Geraldine Ledesma of Community Training and Leadership filled key roles in the caucus. They emphasized that poverty was the number one problem in East Los Angeles. Unemployment among youth in Boyle Heights/East Los Angeles reached 35 percent. Almost all of the unemployed young people had given up hope of finding jobs. The caucus accused EYOA of not recognizing the Chicano community's needs and of being sympathetic to only Blacks. According to the news stories, the Chicano Caucus picked up support of other agencies, which encouraged it to more militantly press its demand for direct funding.

Roybal called the situation a "caste system" and asked for a 90 percent freeze in federal hiring. The congressman stated that Latinos comprised seven percent of the population but only 2.9 percent of the 2.5 million U.S. Department of Health, Education and Welfare employees and only 2.3 percent of the 5,000 U.S. Civil Service Commission employees. Roybal also attempted to form a coalition of Spanish-speaking Americans to lobby for federal funds. To this end, he called the National Coalition Conference for Spanish-Speaking Americans. At this conference, participants organized a national task force to lobby for services for Latinos.

The political situation complicated the conflict between Chicanos and EYOA. Elected officials increasingly relied on federal funds to placate agencies whose employees often supported their candidacies. Generally, Black incumbents supported EYOA and Latinos criticized it. In spite of protest from the caucus, EYOA received its funding by the end of March.

The conflict between Blacks and Chicanos in the EYOA intensified. The ethnic imbalance in EYOA staffing and Chicano awareness of the inequity caused a walkout, led by Rudy Salinas. Of the 74 Spanish-surname staff members, 59 participated. The strikers underscored that only one-fourth of the EYOA employees were Latino. Moreover, other minorities were also underrepresented. For instance, Jim Olguín had been the only Native American working for the agency since 1966. The walkout forced the Office of Economic Opportunity (OEO) to investigate EYOA. It also increased polarization, with the directors refusing to compromise. Battle lines were drawn along racial lines and EYOA's refusal to deal equitably with Chicanos heightened racial divisions at a time when unity was essential.

Chicano employee organizations increased within the local, state, and federal bureaucracies. They grouped along special interest lines. Richard Amador was elected president of the Los Angeles County Manpower Association, which focused on unemployment in East Los Angeles. Chicano city employees formed the Los Angeles City Employees Association. In November, LACEA presented an affirmative action plan to the city council. While the principal function of these groups was affirmative action, they also lobbied for increased services to Chicanos. La Asociación Nacional de Contratistas México Americanos, a Latino contractor association, was organized to lobby for government construction contracts. At the national level, Chicano government employees formed Incorporated Mexican American Government Employees (IMAGE).

The Los Angeles city schools received the largest share of the federal vocational education grants. Nixon's proposed cutbacks would cost California schools an estimated $17 million in federal assistance. The president was dismantling the war on poverty, and many vested interests were threatened. A U.S. Senate subcommittee held hearings on federal aid to Los Angeles during the first week in April. Education, air pollution problems, and unemployment programs were also discussed at these hearings. At the local level, poverty agencies charged that the federal government was insensitive. Neighborhood Youth Corps officials stated that their organization suffered a lack of support from high officials "who don't understand."

EYOA funding for health and drug programs was approved and numerous events were held to inform the public about drug addiction. A heroin detoxification center was established in September. An anti-drug project was expanded at East Los Angeles

College. Chicano agency workers pointed out that addiction patterns among Chicano clients differed from those of Black and of White patients. Additionally, the Labor Department funded a training program for Chicano inmates. Certainly, a greater consciousness about drugs was under way.

Cutbacks in welfare triggered protests. The dismissal of a sympathetic worker caused picketing of the welfare office. The Welfare Rights Organization demanded an investigation of the DPSS for the firing of four other welfare employees. Alicia Escalante was the leader of the welfare rights struggle and, in an August 26 *Sun* article, she wrote that welfare recipients were tired of being exploited. The county, needing to absorb the cuts, reduced allowances for stoves, beds, and refrigerators. Escalante attacked the cutbacks to families with dependent children. She pointed out that training and poverty programs helped only a few and that reductions in the Medi-Cal hurt the poor badly. She asked for an investigation and specifically attacked the State Welfare Reform Act of 1971. Meanwhile, on the state level, Reagan made further cuts, eliminating child-care centers from the state budget. And in Washington, Nixon vetoed a federal bill providing for child care centers.

Land encroachments continued. When Monterey Park held hearings to consider annexing parts of East Los Angeles, Montoya sounded the alarm. Although the Monterey City Planning Commission voted against annexation, the city council refused to accept its recommendation. Immediately, many activists recognized the need to incorporate. While the *Sun* opposed the annexation schemes, it stood firmly against incorporation, calling it a noble but unnecessary effort. Meanwhile, the Monterey Park City Council voted to proceed with the annexations, sending the proposal to the county planning commission, which scheduled public hearings. The Central Committee for Incorporation was organized to coordinate the incorporation of East Los Angeles. Abe Tapia chaired a special committee that prepared a plan to be submitted to the Local Agency Formation Commission (LAFCO). Incorporation enthusiasts attended the annexation hearing and publicly opposed the move. Meanwhile, the county planning commission approved the annexation. Japanese American residents in East Los Angeles, believing that land values would rise if they annexed to Monterey Park, spearheaded the annexation.

In the board of supervisors, Debs made a motion to make the Pomona Freeway the new East Los Angeles boundary. This proposal would have given Monterey Park an even larger area than it had sought. William Orozco, a community college trustee, backed the annexation that would locate East Los Angeles Community College in Monterey Park. The supervisors postponed taking any action and annexation was tabled for another year. In response to these annexation threats, the East Los Angeles Cityhood Committee presented its report. The proposed city would encompass 6.14 square miles and would have 86,490 residents. By the end of the year, calls for home rule grew louder.

In January, a fire gutted the HOME headquarters, causing $130,000 in property damages. Meanwhile, program officials awarded street repair contracts and moved to expand activities. Montoya charged that HOME inspectors made illegal inspections without a court order.

The Community Analysis Bureau of the City of Los Angeles classified Boyle Heights as a blighted area. This designation unsettled many residents, who feared it was the signal for urban renewal. The expansion of Model Cities into non-housing areas was especially noticeable. During this period, Model Cities received funds to provide nearly 1,000 new jobs. Moreover, city council members had veto power over programs in their district. This made them more vulnerable to the charge that they were ward bosses.

The *Citizen* continued to support HOME, publishing glowing accounts from homeowners who had received grants. In May, the HOME program expanded, announcing that its funding totalled $6 million. On June 10, the *Citizen* published a map of the area that the HOME program would service. Apparently the *Citizen* and Debs had formed an alliance to support the program.

In the summer, TELACU received a contract from Model Cities to build low income housing units in Belvedere. On June 24, Montoya charged ties between the Community Redevelopment Agency and HUD. He emphasized that CRA historically had supported and even pushed urban renewal. Montoya also increasingly criticized TELACU and its ties to the supervisor.

TELACU's growth, meanwhile, resembled that of Model Cities. It enjoyed good federal contacts and, in May, Roybal announced a $140,000 federal grant to TELACU from the Office of

Minority Business Enterprise. During this time, TELACU opened its first low income housing project. The organization sponsored Taller Gráfico, which in turn sponsored a California Chicano Art Symposium. Esteban Torres was appointed the director of TELACU during the summer. On December 2, the *Sun* published an article, "Que es TELACU?" and answered its own question by saying that it was a corporation for economic development. TELACU enjoyed the advise of business experts as well as the benefits of considerable HUD money. By the end of the year, TELACU was power in the Eastside.

Lindsay named a 26-member Boyle Heights Advisory Committee to study redevelopment. Advisory committees in the past generally meant that someone wanted the community to rubber stamp a pet scheme. So to many, the councilman's creation of this advisory group meant that the redevelopment of Boyle Heights was near. When the local housing chief stated in November that low income housing had low priority, suspicions were further aroused.

By the end of the year, the city approved plans for Plaza de la Raza. Although the Hazard Park committee had won its fight to retain the park, Yorty continued to propose similar trades. After the February earthquake, he recommended making a deal with the veteran authorities without specifically naming Hazard Park. Fortunately, the Environment Policy Act of 1969 clearly stated the intent of Congress: park land should not be used for federal projects.

In spite of this, similar encroachments took place. The Parks and Recreation Commission planned to phase out the police academy in Elysian Park. This had been mandated by the Elysian Park master plan. The LAPD, however, wanted 21.5 acres of the park for its permanent facilities. Police authorities proposed a charter amendment to allow this transfer.

Power struggles broke out between poverty agencies and their parent volunteer organizations. For instance, there was a clash between the East Los Angeles Health Task Force and its sponsoring agency, the Congress of Mexican American Unity. At the time that the CMAU was on the decline, the task force had increased in influence. The task force had organized a demonstration on the steps of the state capitol to protest Medi-Cal cutbacks, and many of its employees were highly visible. The truth was that the

CMAU really did not have the resources to supervise the task force. The CMAU was comprised of volunteers, while the task force had paid personnel and a defineable constituency. In May, the task force showed its independence by announcing in the *Sun* that it had held board nominations. This had been done without CMAU approval, and the CMAU officers protested the nominations. The task force replied that it had cleared the move with some of the CMAU affiliates that belonged to the board. The task force further asserted that the Department of Health, Education, and Welfare recognized it as a separate legal entity. The task force moved ahead and held elections on May 29.*

The possibility of a favorable reapportionment raised community hopes for more Chicano representation. But when the California Legislature Elections and Reapportionment Committee announced its districts, Chicanos were enraged. State Senator Mervyn Dymally blamed the inadequate redistricting on the 1970 census undercount of Chicanos. However, this explanation was unacceptable and the California Advisory Council to the Civil Rights Commission concluded that the legislature's power in reapportionment should be curtailed because of a conflict of interest.

Meanwhile, the state senate held hearings on reapportionment. Democrats blamed their own blatant opportunism on Reagan, whom they said abetted the lack of Mexican American representation in the state senate. Everyone knew, however, that the Democrats controlled the senate. The legislature conducted additional hearings at which Chicanos opposed the new redistricting plan. Because of this pressure, the state senate included, in name only, a Mexican American district. At this point, the governor exploited the controversy, threatening to veto the plan and attacking the initial omission of a Mexican American state senate district.

The Los Angeles city schools ethnic survey showed that "minority" students now comprised a majority. Minority enrollment reached 50.2 percent, of which 24.1 percent was Black and 21.8 percent Latin. The Chicano student population would skyrocket and, by the end of the 1970s, it would double that of

---

*This case study of the task force is important because it is similar to countless relationships between working agencies and their sponsors in which the child became stronger than the parent.

Blacks and Whites. In February, 30 Mexican American education commissioners resigned in protest of the transfer of Sal Castro and the treatment of Mexican Americans in the schools.

In January, the school board finalized hearings on its decentralization plan, which supposedly would correct the Los Angeles school system's size and unresponsiveness to community needs. Many critics did not accept decentralization. Some urged a slowing down of the plan in order to seriously study its implications. Others believed that a better solution would be to break up this mammoth system entirely. Still others criticized the plan because the proposed districts further dissected Mexican American communities.

Meanwhile, board member J. C. Chambers objected to the showing of *I Am Joaquin* to Los Angeles students, especially in the context of the summer's violence. Chamber apparently believed that Chicano pride had caused the riots.

Community and educators associations actively pressured for more Chicano administrators. In June, the L.A. school superintendent appointed Leonard Pacheco superintendent of 43 area schools. And Hilario Peña was appointed principal of Roosevelt High. Chicanos, however, were not successful in electing community members to the Board of Trustees of the Los Angeles Community Colleges. Dr. David López Lee lost to J. William Orozco.

The reading scores from East Los Angeles schools were released to local newspapers. Both the EICC and the Mexican American Education Commission called the scores inadequate. The MAEC formed a task force to protest the content of textbooks in the schools. This task force condemned the textbook publishers for their inadequate treatment of Mexican Americans. Meanwhile, Mexican Americans again sued the board of education to halt IQ examinations.

Dr. Julián Nava ran for reelection and won easily. He was the only incumbent to win a majority in the primary. Julia Mount ran on the Peace and Freedom party ticket for the 27th Senatorial District. In this race, she took a clear stand against the war in Vietnam. The Peace and Freedom party had counted on the 18-year-old vote, which did not materialize until several years later. David Roberti, a Democrat, won easily.

The most successful race for the newly formed Raza Unida party involved the 48th Assembly District, in which a special election was held in November. After a bitter struggle, Richard Alatorre had defeated Ralph Ochoa for the Democratic party primary.Ochoa was backed by Speaker of the Assembly Bob Moretti, while Alatorre was supported by Assemblyman Water Karabian. Bill Brophy was the Republican nominee, James Blaine ran for the Peace and Freedom party, and Raúl Ruiz was La Raza Unida's candidate. The district was decidedly Democrat and Alatorre was heavily favored. He ran a strong race, with even U.S. Senator Edmund Muskie entering the district to campaign for him. He had his party's support as well as that of the Eastside newspapers. Nevertheless, he lost:

Bill Brophy	16,346
Richard Alatorre	14,759
Raúl Ruiz	2,778
James Blaine	1,108

Democrats called La Raza Unida party a spoiler. Before the end of the election, Alatorre disclosed that he had spent $45,745, Brophy $28,396, Ruiz $2,534, and Blaine $1,735. Although Alatorre attributed his loss to confusion, community discontent with the Democratic party was apparent.

On August 13, the CSO's Young Adult Leadership project marched to the office of Lyman Jones, head of the Los Angeles City Public Library System, to protest the inferior library services to East Los Angeles. The young people questioned Jones about the lack of bilingual personnel, the inadequate facilities in Mexican American barrios and the neglect of the earthquake-damaged Ben Franklin Library in Boyle Heights. The YAL condemned the library system's hiring procedures and the funding of branch libraries based on circulation rather than on service area population.

Media began to pay more attention to women. The Mexican American Opportunity Foundation organized a Mexican American Women's Testimonial Committee, which many other organizations joined. The first national Chicana conference was held in Houston on May 29 through 30. Its theme was "Women for La Raza." On July 1, Francisca Flores wrote an important article for the *Sun*, detailing the historical events preceding this conference.

Flores related the early history of MAPA's women's caucus, which later disbanded, and drew attention to a 1970 Latino conference in Wisconsin that had included a women's workshop. Also in 1970, the Mexican American Issues Conference in Sacramento sponsored a workshop on Chicanas. Participants voted to form La Comisión Feminil Mexicana, an independent organization that was, for the time, affiliated to the National Issues Conference.

By the end of 1971, President Richard M. Nixon prepared to run for reelection. Nixon had appointed Henry M. Ramírez to head the Spanish-speaking Cabinet Committee. He made other Mexican American appointments in the hopes of attracting a high percentage of middle-class Chicano votes.

SUMMARY

Richard M. Nixon assumed the presidency in 1969. While he dismantled the poverty programs, Nixon did not end federal intervention in the economy—he was just more selective in the kind of grants that he allocated. Cutbacks occurred in programs most accessible to Blacks and Chicanos, heightening competition between the two groups. The conflict probably hurt Chicanos more than it did Blacks because the former lacked the organizational networks that the latter community had established over years of involvement in the national scene. In the end, the old game of divide and conquer succeeded once more, and both communities lost.

Another phenomenon within the East Los Angeles political ghetto was the rise of TELACU. Esteban Torres was one of the most active Eastside leaders, controlling TELACU and presiding over the Congress of Mexican American Unity. The East Central Area Welfare Planning Council did not receive as much coverage as it had in the past. Montoya continued to fight HUD and its affiliates, HOME and Model Cities. Coverage in the *Citizen* and the *Sun* continued to contrast during this period.

Also in 1969, the Biltmore Hotel affair occurred, in which Chicanos were accused of setting fires which apparently had been set by police provocateurs while Governor Ronald Reagan spoke at a Nuevas Vistas conference. District Attorney Evelle Younger attempted to pull political mileage out of this incident, as well as out of the walkouts of the previous year. By the end of the year, Chicano activists picketed St. Basil's Church, protesting inequities within the Catholic church. A confrontation followed, resulting in more arrests and prosecutions.

Police brutality was interwoven with international violence. Mexican American "suicides" and "natural deaths" at the central LAPD and sheriff's department jails were frequent—as were community protests of these incidents. Police murders of the Sánchez cousins in the closing days of July 1970 enraged the sensitivities of many in the community. The August 29 Chicano Moratorium, which resulted in Rubén Salazar's death at the hands of police officers, shocked many people east of the river. Coverage in both the weeklies of these events was excellent. However, when three more riots followed the August 29 march, the community became nervous. The lack of clarity surrounding the causes of the confrontations created divisions within the community. During 1970 and 1971, extensive Chicano Liberation Front bombings also rocked and worried the Eastside.

Nineteen-seventy-one was a year that saw political reapportionment at all levels of government. This year also introduced a new political party, La Raza Unida. Party member Raúl Ruiz ran against Democrat Richard Alatorre and Republican Bill Brophy. While Ruiz did not win the election, enough Chicanos voted for him to deprive the Democrat the election. After this, the Democratic party paid more attention to Chicano campaigns than it had in the past.

8

There Ain't No Rainbow Over East L.A.: 1972–1975

The *Sun* and the *Roybal Newspaper Scrapbooks* were consulted for material up to 1975. Microfilm copies of the *Citizen*, however, were available only through 1972. Since the staff would allow me to use originals for only limited periods at a time, research of *Citizen* articles dated later than 1972 proved impossible. For additional sources, see the reference note at the beginning of Chapter 6. For historical background information, read: Rodolfo Acuña, *Occupied America: A History of Chicanos* (New York: 1981); Peter N. Carroll, *It Seemed Like Nothing Happened: The Tragedy and Promise of America in the 1970s* (New York: 1982); and Howard Zinn, *A People's History of the United States* (New York: 1980).

In 1972, Richard M. Nixon enjoyed a landslide victory over Democratic party candidate George McGovern. It was fitting that the Columbia Broadcasting Studios (CBS) produced "All In the Family," featuring Archie Bunker, during the Nixon years. Archie was the silent majority personified. Perhaps, like Archie Bunker, working-class white Americans were frustrated by their increasing lack of social and economic opportunity. This fear and confusion surfaced the nativist phenomenon that has always run deep within the currents of American history. With shrinking opportunities, even low echelon white-collar workers felt the competition from the few minorities who ventured into fields that had always been reserved for whites.

As the decade had rolled in, recession had toyed with the American economy. By 1972, economic retrenchment was firm. From 1971 to 1974, home financing increased 147.9 percent. In 1974, the dollar was worth 65¢ of what it had been seven years before. Between 1964 and 1973, the average inflation rate had been 3.7 percent. For the first five months of 1973, it was 9.5 percent; for the entire year, it was 6.2 percent, with a 14.5 percent rise in the cost of food. Recession hit again in 1974 through 1975 and local property taxes rose, further unsettling the middle-class. More Americans felt angry over the considerable loss of prestige in the Vietnam War. World recriminations against the United States for global atrocities further annoyed the silent majority, who no longer apologized for economic inequality at home.

Many citizens blamed the cost of social and public services for inflation and the unhealthy economy. Other factors, however, were more directly responsible for the problems. From October, 1973 to March of the following year, OPEC nations called an oil embargo. American oil companies used the incident to substantially hike prices. Ultimately, they quadrupled the cost of a gallon of gas. The roots of the oil crisis ran all the way back to the 1950s, when American oil companies decided to cut back on domestic exploration and production in order to maximize profits. These cartels invested large amounts of capital abroad, and, consequently, the nation became increasingly dependent on imported oil. In 1960, 19 percent was imported. By 1970, it had increased to 24 percent. By 1978, it had increased to 38 percent. Sales of American cars also fell by 11 million in 1973 and by another 7 million in 1974. Automobile manufacturing was basic to the

American economy; one out of every six workers was affected by the slide. American auto makers had ignored trends and were tragically out of step with the times. They produced gas guzzlers that were technologically inferior to the smaller European and Japanese models. Moreover, multinational corporations had invested their profits in Taiwan, South Korea, and the Philippines to maximize gains.

Other factors contributing to inflation and higher prices were the policies of the Nixon administration. In September 1972, Earl Butz, Nixon's Secretary of Agriculture, oversold American food surpluses to foreign nations. Simultaneously, in order to ensure high prices for farm goods, growers took huge acreages out of production. In total, five million acres were left fallow. The situation worsened because of bad weather. The shortage of domestic grain drove up the prices of meat and other items and contributed greatly to the overall inflation.

In February 1973, Nixon for the second time devalued the dollar by 10 percent in an effort to stem the dollar drain. Meanwhile, the Archie Bunkers of the country thought that it was un-American to criticize the multinationals—so they blamed minorities for changes that they didn't understand.

For minorities, the times worsened. Their collective upward mobility depended on education, which was conditioned by four additional factors. First, like nineteenth century immigrants, American minorities depended on an expanding economy. Second, that expansion needed to be in industries that employed a labor intensive work force. Third, to penetrate the modern economic structure even modestly, they needed effective affirmative action programs. Lastly, they could not make significant progress without expansion in public sector employment. These four conditions were generally absent in the 1970s. Moreover, on the national front, the Burger Court killed hope of effective affirmative action in education in its *Bakke* decision of 1978. And in California specifically, Propositions 13 and 4 cut public funds. This resulted in cuts in services and employment at all levels of state government.

Domestic and international disruption continued. In 1973, the CIA helped topple the constitutionally elected government of Chilean president Salvador Allende. Also that year, fierce bombing took place in Vietnam. By 1973, 300,000 Americans had been wounded, 56,000 were dead and $140,000 billion had been spent on the war. And internally, COINTEL effectively disrupted the Black Panthers and undermined other popular struggles.

Meanwhile, the Burger Court and the Nixon administration eroded past civil rights gains. Nixon shifted enforcement of school desegregation from the Department of Health, Education, and Welfare to the courts. Access to institutions for minorities was difficult. By 1973, public attention turned from poverty and race to other matters. The administration itself was in trouble, and to ensure Nixon's reelection, aides directed a "plumber's squad" to break into the office of Daniel Ellsberg's psychiatrist in order to obtain damaging information. Later, another group broke into the Democratic party headquarters in the Watergate Hotel in Washington, D.C. Unlike the first group, this one was caught. A year later, in August, Nixon resigned from office and Gerald Ford became president. Symbolically, liberation forces marched into Saigon a year later, ending an era.

From the beginning of the American occupation of Texas in 1836 and the Southwest in 1848, bilingual education has been a priority demand of Mexicans in the United States. In 1968, the Bilingual Edducation Act was passed to allocate funds so that children with limited or no English speaking skills could receive instruction in their native language. Money was made available for bilingual programs, research, teacher training, and other aspects of education. The Office of Bilingual Education was established under the Office of Education and funds were granted through Title VII. It is estimated that by the late 1970s, $200 million had been spent by state and federal governments on bilingual education. This financial commitment generated organizations that supported bilingual education. It also encouraged the publication of bilingual materials and forced schools of education at different universities to seriously look at the education of Chicano children.

In 1974, the U.S. Supreme Court laid down its decision in *Lau vs. Nichols*, stating that the San Francisco School District was out of compliance with Section 601 of the 1964 Civil Rights Act, which prohibited discrimination on the grounds of race, color, or national origins in any program receiving federal assistance. The Court found that the San Francisco schools had failed to furnish instruction to 1,800 Chinese children in their native language.

This decision had far-reaching effects and, for a time, Latinos had the false impression that the *Lau* decision guaranteed bilingual education. In order to assist local school districts to achieve compliance with the dicta of the *Lau* decision, the Department of Health, Education, and Welfare set up Lau centers. These early actions helped cement a network to lobby for bilingual education.

By the end of the mid-70s, the number of Chicano teachers in the schools was visibly larger. Many were sincere advocates for the rights of Chicano children but were limited by their lack of proper political background. Most had not participated in the movement of the 1960s and did not possess a sense of history. To them, bilingual education meant the study of culture, when the reality was that it did not involve politicizing students. This lack of political acumen made these teachers easy targets as the backlash from the Archie Bunkers increasingly threatened bilingual education. By the mid-70s, the promise of *Lau* was fading.

It cannot be denied that progress had been made since the postwar period. There were more Chicanos in government and the professions. In 1965, the community did not have a single national organization. Ten years later, they had ten. Mostly these organizations pushed the special interests of Chicanos, including affirmative action, bilingual education, increased funding, and the like. The Mexican American Legal Defense and Education Fund was notable in the area of defending the legal rights of Mexican Americans nationally.

The National Association for Chicano Studies was formed in the early 1970s. Primarily concerned with scholarly endeavors, this group did not involve itself in advocating the rights of the community. In fact, no association developed in the 70s that effectively reflected the interest of Chicanos in achieving higher education. The Association of Mexican American Educators enjoyed growth, and individual chapters did support community issues. The national organization, however, maintained only a few community ties. Throughout the decade, Chicano studies programs declined in the universities.

Most Chicano gains made in the 1960s eroded in the 70s. Fertility rates remained high among Chicanos—estimated at between 2.2 and 3.5 percent annually. Recession and the changing labor market aggravated already strained economic conditions for the poor. In the mid-70s, fewer unskilled and semiskilled workers were needed. The only jobs that were abundant were those paying below subsistence levels or those in agriculture, where only the most marginal workers were employed. Educational progress in the 1960s had been limited and only one-fourth of the Chicanos east of the river had high school diplomas. In 1975, only about one-third of the Latinos nationally held jobs in expanding industries. The Chicano dropout rate in Los Angeles was about 50 percent, which was almost five times higher than the Black dropout rate.

In 1970, Chicanos had attempted to create their own political institution, La Raza Unida party. The RUP had limited success in Texas and other areas and, in the first years, generated considerable hope and ferment. By the mid-70s, however, many supporters were disillusioned and many of its early leaders became born-again Democrats. The left was fragmented and, as in the case of the last days of the Students for a Democratic Society (SDS) in the late 1960s, a splintering process took place. Marxists of 14 different varieties, nationalists, and anarchists all made each other the enemy.

The farmworkers movements were active in the Midwest and in Texas, Arizona, and other Southwest states. California remained the scene of the largest and most dramatic struggle, since its size and industrialized agriculture demanded a large response. The area east of the Los Angeles River continued to support César Chávez and the farmworkers. Chávez and his followers campaigned actively in the Eastside to defend the rights of farmworkers and to defeat grower-backed state propositions that would have badly damaged unionization efforts. Boycotts were a popular tactic. Grapes, lettuce, Gallo wine, and Safeway Stores were all major targets. Boycotts spread to brand name manufacturers, including Coors and Nestlés, that injured the rights of workers and the community. Growers supported the Teamsters Union in an effort to break the United Farmworkers Union and the period was marked by violent confrontations in the California fields. Industrial peace was achieved for a time with the passage of the California Agricultural Relations Act, which attempted to referee labor-management relations in state agriculture. The weeklies reported some of these events but, in general, they concentrated on covering local events.

By the early 70s, immigration had become important to most Chicano organizations. Since 1968, El Centro de Acción Social

Autónoma-Hermandad de Trabajadores (CASA) organized undocumented workers against exploitation by employers and abuses from the Immigration and Naturalization Service (INS). It followed in the tradition of early *mutualistas* (mutual aid societies) and Chicano organizations of the 1950s in the latter's fight against the Walter-McCarran Act. As the economy worsened, the Archie Bunkers made scapegoats of undocumenteds. Throughout the decade, this nativism became more marked.

Chicanos significantly affected national attitudes and policies towards the undocumented. First, opposition to efforts to send undocumented workers back to Mexico coupled with early research by Chicano scholars forced serious and extensive study of this phenomenon. Second, more time and energy was spent on this issue than any other. This marked a break with the 1950s, when Chicanos followed the lead of trade unionists, who saw undocumenteds as a threat. Third, a handful of Chicano organizations were able to slow down repressive immigration legislation at the local, state, and national levels. Fourth, the issue itself forged bonds between Chicano and Mexican scholars and activists, who in growing numbers pressured Mexican government officials to take a more active role in protecting citizen rights. Significantly, efforts to reinstitute a bracero program were thwarted. Chicanos played a primary role in jarring the conscience of many scholars on both sides of the border, inspiring them to consider the political and economic dimensions of how the international labor market affected immigration.

This chronicle documents that, in the face of national recessions, conditions worsened and the level of activism declined east of the river. As was true in the 1950s, however, changes were under way that would affect future generations. Something was happening in East L.A. Even if activism had slowed down during this period of bad economy and resurfacing bigotry, it had not died.

1972

Coverage in the *Sun* and the *Citizen* about immigration was spotty. The mounting economic recession in Los Angeles caused a backlash in anti-Mexican feelings—especially towards undocumented workers. The INS encouraged the hysteria by issuing unsubstantiated statistics on the gravity of the problem. The phenomenon lacked a good analysis. Arthur Montoya, for example, supported the *Dixon-Arnett* law because of high unemployment among the Chicano.

Montoya's reaction was in contrast to that of most Chicano activists. While there was some anti-undocumented sentiment east of the river, the vast majority of politically active Chicanos denounced the libel and abuses of civil liberties levelled at this sector of society. Chicanos supported a suit against Section 2806 of the California Labor Code (*Dixon-Arnett*), which prohibited employers from knowingly hiring undocumented workers. This law put the onus on employers and encouraged them to discriminate against all brown-looking people. The state supreme court eventually found *Dixon-Arnett* unconstitutional.

Meanwhile, the East/Northeast Model Cities Project funded the "One Stop" Immigration Center, directed by Roberto Armendáriz, which offered a free service to undocumented workers. Centers like this one ameliorated the suffering of those victimized by the massive INS raids. On March 9, the *Sun* published an article titled "Estimate cost of illegal aliens to taxpayers set at $18 billion." The piece was not based on fact, merely reporting INS releases, which distorted the problem in order to generate public support for its policies.

Other groups, such as MAPA and CASA, led the fight against the Rodino bill—a federal version of the *Dixon-Arnett* law. Though the Rodino bill had support in the U.S. Senate, it died when Roybal called for a review of the House version.

The City of Los Angeles dropped its $800 per acre fee to property owners who petitioned for annexation to the city. The purpose was to discourage surrounding areas from joining the city. This move raised speculation that the city wanted to annex East Los Angeles.

There were also some rumors about the redevelopment of Boyle Heights. The Los Angeles City Planning Department was in the process of creating a community plan for Boyle Heights that supplemented the city's master plan. Chicano planners attempted to counteract past policies and to persuade officials to preserve the area's residential character. On January 27, the *Citizen* ran "Planners Report the History of Boyle Heights," an article which gave a brief history of the various ethnic and racial groups that had lived in Boyle Heights. Finally, noting that after World War

II, when the area became predominantly Mexican, former occupants had the land upzoned to R3 for speculative purposes.
Similar stories were run in the weeklies throughout the year.

Also dominating the weeklies was the coverage of Model
Cities and poverty programs. The *Sun* remained the only consistent critic of Model Cities, which was favored by politicians such
as Mayor Sam Yorty. The *Sun* condemned this and tree cutting
programs. Model Cities also seems to have had internal problems.
When it terminated its Med-Ocho contract with the Los Angeles
County-USC Medical Center, residents and employees contacted
Lawrence Whitehead, Model Cities program administrator, and
demanded reinstatement of the contract. The controversy was
complicated by the involvement of Councilmen Gilbert Lindsay,
who favored continuance of the program, and Arthur Snyder, who
opposed Med-Ocho. The feud between Model Cities and the
county had been going on for some time; basically, the program
cost $6 million, of which Model Cities paid 10 percent, yet
demanded considerable control.

Criticisms of Model Cities did not appear to hurt its popularity
and it continued to grow by funding popular programs such as the
Center for Law and Justice. Model Cities awarded scholarships
to medical students and offered the community job development
assistance. Meanwhile, it reviewed proposals and maintained an
aura of community participation. On March 21, 600 supporters
attended Plaza de la Raza's ground-breaking ceremonies for its
new cultural center.

Congressman Roybal appealed to HUD for more low-income
housing, a cause that he had championed for more than 30 years.
In the meantime, the Model Cities Development Corporation
promised to assist East Los Angeles small business interests and
funded the Hispanic Urban Institute. The institute's purpose was
to increase awareness among Los Angeles city school teachers of
Mexican American problems. To this end it conducted in-service
workshops on Mexican American culture and history. Vahac
Madirosian, a leader in the EICC and the Mexican American
Education Commission, administered the institute.

Montoya attacked the newly formed Housing Development
Corporation's designation of East/Northeast Los Angeles and East
Los Angeles as development areas. Montoya saw a definite trend
toward a partnership between local government, private

developers, and finance corporations to reconstruct the area east of the river. This three-way partnership was similar to that which had operated in the downtown area years earlier. The objective, according to Montoya, was the urban renewal of East Los Angeles/ Boyle Heights. Arthur Fregoso, a community representative to Model Cities, also criticized these plans. Joe Kovner sarcastically asked what was in Boyle Heights' future.

Zone changes were indeed taking place in both Boyle Heights and East Los Angeles. Alexander Mann, coordinator of the Save Hazard Park Committee, protested these changes, which were also discussed at the East Central Area Welfare Planning Council meetings.

During this time, HUD won the backing of Latino housing specialists, many of whom supported plans to modernize the area's buildings. On the other hand, some local business people opposed the modern design for a neighborhood center. The Barrio Planners, a group of young Chicano urban planners, also opposed the new development plans. This group had received a $60,000 grant to conduct a study of East Los Angeles.

Meanwhile, homeowners pressured authorities to improve the area, demanding especially the pavement of alleys. Simultaneously, many residents complained that the street improvements were poorly executed and insisted on some form of accountability from contractors. As mentioned one of these improvement projects called for the cutting down of trees. Kovner referred to this controversial project as "Eastside defoliation."

County supervisor Ernest Debs announced that the HOME program was near completion, even though irregularities in its operation were disclosed. Los Angeles District Attorney Joseph Bush criticized HUD's prosecution of an East Los Angeles property owner for refusal to participate in HOME. Bush contended that this prosecution violated the owner's civil rights. Based on his investigation of HOME, Bush called the program an atrocity. He drew attention to several incidents of fraud, including work that was never started, work that was left incomplete, and work that was poorly executed. The district attorney also charged that many homeowners were assessed penalty payments before the work had been completed.

On April 27, Montoya alleged that the Martin Luther King Hospital had killed the federal housing project in the Watts area.

He once more charged that it had become common for nonprofit organizations to cooperate in urban renewal projects. As if to underscore Montoya's allegations, the White Memorial Hospital broke ground for a new addition in Boyle Heights.

The *Citizen*'s coverage of Model Cities remained favorable. Art Bastidos, a spokesman for Model Cities, announced in the *Citizen* that the agency had funded 26 projects. These projects, he said, ranged from reading classes to college scholarships for 192 Cal State Los Angeles students and amounted to over a quarter of a million dollars in the fall alone. Bastidos added that Model Cities involved community people in project planning.

On May 11, the *Citizen* listed Model Cities projects. Among these were the Maravilla Housing Project and special programs for 12 Los Angeles elementary schools. The Los Angeles City Council requested another $26 million for Model Cities programs. Soon after, Model Cities approved a swimming pool for Roosevelt High School.

On August 8, Alexander Mann sent a letter to Dr. Julián Nava, a member of the Los Angeles Unified School Board of Education, complaining that school appraisers were attempting to acquire additional barrio land. Mann recounted the history of urban renewal and questioned the legality of the board's use of eminent domain in this instance—even if it were to establish a child care center.

In Lincoln Heights, groups mobilized against the city's urban renewal plans as outlined in the "Preliminary Master Plan for East/Northeast Los Angeles." Rosalio Muñoz, chair of the National Moratorium Committee, was now involved in the fight against redevelopment. Master plan opponents pressured Councilman Arthur Snyder, who promised that the area would not be renewed in the traditional sense. Because of community pressure, the plan was temporarily withdrawn. Similar spirited protests against master plans took place in other areas.

In September, when the city approved the Model Cities program, Larry Whitehead, director of the program, drew fire. At public hearings, critics charged that Whitehead was not responsive to the community. Gordon Moreno, a resident council member, and the Reverend Vahac Madirosian testified in Whitehead's favor.

Additional problems emerged in the operation of Model Cities. The Mexican American Youth Organization (MAYO) denied that

Model Cities had originated or controlled the youth coordinated services program which conducted a Chicano studies class at the central juvenile hall.

Attorney Richard Hernández, who had been involved in earlier incorporation efforts, was elected head of the Housing Development Corporation. HDC drew fire in Lincoln Heights, where the Committee to Stop House Destruction opposed development and, through democratic elections, gained control of the advisory body. When the Model Cities director in Lincoln Heights was fired, he filed suit. Congressman Roybal attempted unsuccessfully to mediate. Art Snyder proposed that the HDC be placed under the City Housing Authority until the corporation was returned to what he called "responsible" community control. He claimed that the HDC's business affairs were in chaos. In the meantime, the mayor and the city attorney invalidated the recent elections.

TELACU, an organization whose stated goal was self-determination for the community, received $1 million for redevelopment projects in East Los Angeles. Formed in the 1960s to attack the problems of high unemployment, inadequate housing, and the lack of economic development in the Mexican American community, TELACU affiliated the following groups: the Arizona Mothers, Casa Maravilla, Plaza de la Raza, the Federation of Barrios Unidos, El Hoyo Neighborhood Association, the Tenants' Advisory Board of the Maravilla Public Housing Project, Cleland House Senior Citizens, and the Lote Association. According to TELACU, its purpose was "to increase participation in decisions that affect the community. To help start or assist local businesses. To bring more outside resources into East Los Angeles. To help its member agencies with organization and funding. To overcome the standstill in construction of low and moderate housing. To expand recreational and cultural institutions." The Office of Economic Opportunities designated TELACU a community development corporation.

Ground-breaking ceremonies for the Nueva Maravilla Housing Project, for which $10 million in funds were earmarked, took place in November. The contract involved knocking down the existing 30-year-old, 504 unit housing project. First occupancies were scheduled for 1973. Completion of the project was expected to be 1975.

Meanwhile, the Maravilla Neighborhood Development Program elected officers. The corporation's boundaries encompassed 218 acres and stretched from Floral Drive on the north to Third Street on the south, from Mednik Avenue on the east to the Long Beach Freeway on the west. Several other county agencies and community-based organizations were closely affiliated with the TELACU development program. On October 10, the board of supervisors awarded a contract to Joint Venture, Voorheis-Trindle-Nelson, and TELACU to conduct a feasibility study for development of East Los Angeles. The cost of the first stage of redevelopment was estimated between $10 and 24 million; the time frame was six to eight years. To generate support, TELACU held a series of community meetings, out of which evolved the Project Area Committee (PAC), technically an independent community organization.

Meanwhile, TELACU's economic specialists attended business seminars establishing TELACU's expertise in this field. The Maravilla Development Project scheduled hearings in December, which representatives from business and residents of Belvedere-Maravilla attended. A group called the Barrio Associates opposed the TELACU project and sought to delay the hearings. Surprisingly, a rift developed between PAC and TELACU, which attorneys for the two sides settled.

The police's bid for permanent use of Elysian Park for their academy had not been resolved. Lindsay opposed the police, stating that more parks were needed in the Eastside. The LAPD, however, pressured city officials and, when it did not get its way, took the matter to the polls. In November, police encroachment won when the public voted yes to Proposition U.

In August, the County Planning Commission granted Monterey Park more time to initiate proceedings to annex 252 acres of East Los Angeles. The area sought included East Los Angeles Community College. Public meetings were held in Monterey Park on the proposed grab. Unexpectedly, Monterey Park dropped its proposal, but the annexation effort caused a resurgence of another East Los Angeles incorporation drive. Esteban Torres and TELACU formed an ad hoc committee to coordinate the drive and take its proposal to community organizations.

MAOF and the Narcotics Prevention Project honored the East Los Angeles District Attorney's Office. MAOF also sought job opportunities for Vietnam veterans and offered training courses on a wide range of skills, including paralegal services. MAOF received substantial funding from Model Cities. On its tenth anniversary, MAOF presented Aztec Awards to honored community leaders.

In late March, EYOA terminated dissident employees, who immediately filed a suit against the agency. The firings climaxed years of conflict between Black and other minority employees. EYOA drew fire from state and federal authorities also and, during much of the year, the agency limped along. Councilman Gilbert Lindsay avidly supported EYOA. Governor Ronald Reagan, however, agitated the breach between the two minority groups by threatening to cut off funding altogether. By July, the Office of Economic Opportunity began to phase EYOA out of existence.

In September, EYOA received its terminal grant. The group threatened court action but took the money anyway. By the end of the year, EYOA evolved into the Community Action Agency (CAA). Negotiations proceeded to create an entirely new agency to administer Los Angeles poverty funds. During this period, fighting increased considerably between Blacks and other groups. Congressman Roybal demanded a fair share for Chicanos. Eventually, the Greater Los Angeles Area Agency was created as the umbrella organization for poverty programs in Los Angeles.

For all its weaknesses, the war on poverty had encouraged poor people from every sector of society to organize. In January, a group called Unemployed Chicanos de La Raza Unida held a demonstration to dramatize the plight of workers without jobs. The Roman Catholic church formed the Campaign for Human Development to distribute grants to community agencies. Senior citizens formed numerous organizations. And the Parent Involvement for Community Action (PICA) sponsored a parent-teacher conference.

The Los Angeles City Employees Chicano Association held regular meetings that featured speakers such as Assemblyman Jesse Unruh and Councilman Arthur Snyder. Latino engineers organized, offering information to the community and lobbying for affirmative action in engineering. Because of the lack of Chicano librarians, a special Chicano media librarian program began at California State University, Fullerton. In the meantime, community activists J. Alex Cota and Alex Partida attacked Lindsay for not doing enough to push the delayed reconstruction of the Franklin Library in Boyle Heights.

The Mexican American Business and Professional Men's Scholarship Association raised $5,300 for grants to Chicano students. Vicki Carr also gave scholarships to 19 students. Moreover, a growing sense of national unity between Chicanos and other Latinos developed, with many joining the National Council of Spanish-Speaking Organizations.

An ethnic survey of the Los Angeles Unified School District showed that 52.4 percent of the students were minorities—24.9 percent Black, 22.7 percent Latino, and 7.2 percent members of other ethnic groups. During the 1960s, Mexican American population in the county increased from 651,879 persons in 1960 to 1,228,594 in 1970. This represents a 113 percent boom.

LULAC, the GI Forum, and Congressman Roybal filed a landmark suit against the U.S. government, charging employment discrimination against Latinos, who comprised 9 percent of the nation's population but represented only .9 percent of the government's employees. Roybal also supported major reforms of the U.S. Border Patrol.

The National Chicano Health Organization (NCHO) received a grant for career centers. In January, the first Chicano health conference in the Southwest was held in San Antonio, Texas. Its theme was the Chicano consumer. Health was a major concern in East Los Angeles and in other barrios. A study showed that the cancer rate among Eastside women registered two to four times above the national norm. OEO granted East Los Angeles health centers $1.2 million. On August 6, the East Los Angeles Health Task Force sponsored a health fair. Meanwhile, the county supervisors approved a $4 million health center for East Los Angeles.

The Committee on the Administration of Justice held hearings in Los Angeles. Mexican Americans testified before this committee, leveling charges against representatives of the law. On February 3, the *Sun* reported that Eustacio (Frank) Martínez, 23, had admitted at a press conference that he had worked for the Alcohol, Tobacco, and Firearms Division of the Treasury Department. Martínez had been a paid informer in Texas for two years before coming to California, where he infiltrated the National Chicano Moratorium Committee. As its co-chair, he conducted a rumor campaign against fellow co-chair Rosalio Muñoz. With the knowledge of Los Angeles police authorities, Martínez attempted to provoke other incidents. Finally, federal agents ordered Martínez to infiltrate Casa Carnalismo and, when he found nothing wrong, they ordered him to manufacture something. It was at this point that Martínez held a press conference and exposed his former employers.

The Alfred Bryan Defense Committee accused LAPD Chief Ed Davis of harassing and persecuting Bryan. Davis actively pressured the justice system to try Bryan as an adult. In 1969, Bryan, then 16, was to be tried as an adult for the alleged murder of a police officer. His attorney petitioned against this action.

Bryan spent 18 months in isolation at the county jail as he awaited a decision on his petition. Eventually, this petition was granted. A juvenile court found Bryan guilty. However, the California Youth Authority refused to accept him. This further frustrated the process and the case was appealed to the state supreme court. On January 26, the court released Bryan on bail pending this review. LAPD officers hounded Bryan, constantly searching for him in the Pico Gardens Housing project.

In February, Rodolfo "Corky" Gonzales, a national Chicano leader who had been arrested during the 1970 Chicano Moratorium for allegedly carrying concealed weapons, was released from jail.

Nine East Los Angeles organizations united to end barrio gang warfare and set a youth gang conference for December 14. Police, meanwhile, released a survey that showed 72 percent of the Blacks in Los Angeles approved of the LAPD. The sheriff's department continued to push its basic car plan as a solution to the gang problem.

Los Abogados de Aztlán (the Lawyers of Aztlán) was formed. Chicano lawyers and law students in this organization petitioned the state bar to certify Richard Cruz and Mike García, who had been denied certification because of their community involvement. Cruz underwent a lengthy hearing at which Dr. Julián Nava and Bishop Juan Arzube testified on his behalf.

Ricardo Chávez Ortiz hijacked a Frontier Airlines jet en route to Los Angeles. He was unarmed. He demanded the opportunity to address the press because he wanted to tell the public about the plight of Mexicans in Los Angeles. Following Chávez Ortiz's arrest, community organizations, churches, and private citizens secured $35,000 for bail. When Chávez Ortiz entered a not guilty plea, the court conducted extensive hearings on his mental competency, concluding that he was sane. Finally, there was a short trial and the jury took only seven hours to find Chávez Ortiz guilty.

Mexican President Luis Echevarría toured the United States and met with Chicano leaders. Echevarría unexpectedly called for better treatment of undocumented Mexican workers in the United States. Historically, Mexican presidents had been silent on this issue, treating it as an internal U.S. affair.

The state assembly held hearings on police abuse. Former deputy sheriff Preston Guillory testified that sheriff's deputies in East Los Angeles treated local Latinos badly. Guillory stated that residents were harassed and that half the arrests made were illegal.

At this time, two Latino actor/actress associations emerged. JUSTICIA represented the more militant contingencies and NOSOTROS the more moderate. They had similar goals but different tactics. Ricardo Montalbán headed NOSOTROS and Ray Andrade JUSTICIA. Andrade vehemently criticized the movie and television industries. He spearheaded the drive against offensive commercials, including the Frito Bandido series. In July, a bomb went off in Andrade's apartment when he switched on the lights, seriously injuring him. Police accused Andrade of being the victim of his own bomb.

A 9 year-old Chicano faced an assault with a deadly weapon charge. The incident occurred when a police officer stopped the boy's brother, Rudy García, 26, for a traffic violation. Witnesses testified that the turn García had made from his driveway was legal. Also, according to witnesses, the officer became abusive during an argument. This upset the boy, who grabbed his brother's belt and hit the officer.

During this period, a change could be noted in David Sánchez, prime minister of the Brown Berets. In an open letter to "Los Vatos de los Barrios," Sánchez pleaded for a cessation of violence. On June 8, Sánchez wrote another letter, this one describing the death of 14-year-old Teresa García at a carnival in Santa Fe

Springs. He seemed almost melancholy. Even so, he participated in the Brown Beret "occupation" of Catalina Island, claiming that the island still belonged to Mexico under the terms of the Treaty of Guadalupe Hidalgo. Twenty-six Berets took part in the operation. After the incident, internal rifts developed within the Beret organization and Sánchez disbanded the group. However, most members ignored the order and the Brown Berets exist to this day.

In February, the government dropped draft evasion charges against Rosalio Muñoz. On October 19, Kovner advocated the hiring of more Chicano police officers in an article titled "Do we need more cops? Yes! Chicano cops. . . ."

Anti-war demonstrations continued. Police and sheriff repression, however, made it impossible to conduct peaceful assemblies in the Eastside. Chicanos nevertheless continued to protest the war. In April, many joined a march down Wilshire Boulevard to MacArthur Park. The *Sun* asked: "Are Today's 11-year-olds to Fight in 1979?"

The Eastside mural project was expanded this year. The walls at Estrada Courts were among those first painted. Young Chicano artists also displayed their works at art festivals. The theme of much of the mural art was both cutural and political. One of the many groups active in this mural movement was the Little Valley Youth Association. The *Sun* praised the mural movement as a war against graffiti. Professional murals were also commissioned, including a painting of Rubén Salazar at a local hospital. Also this year, the Mechicano Art Center celebrated its first birthday.

The second annual Chicana conference was held April 29 at La Casa del Mexicano. The theme was "Is Society Meeting the Needs of the Chicana?" Marianna Hernández of Cal State Los Angeles and Alicia Escalante led workshops. On September 8, the Chicana Service Action Center opened its doors. La Comisíon Feminil Mexicana Nacional, Inc., funded the action center. La Comisión held its organizing conference on November 18.

The Chicana Welfare Rights Organization (CWRO) opposed the Talmadge Amendment to the Social Security Act. Supposedly, the law would make recipients "earn a check." CWRO charged, however, that the amendment assumed that homemakers had as much chance as men to work outside the home. Moreover, the amendment did not offer women a choice between working as homemakers or working outside the home. Finally, it did not ensure women meaningful jobs. In fact, according to CWRO, the jobs that were generally available amounted to slave labor. CWRO also protested cuts to mothers with dependents in the DPSS and WIN programs.

The Los Angeles school board refused to discontinue its policy of corporal punishment and articles criticizing the schools appeared more frequently in the *Sun*. Significantly, the Los Angeles Board of Education approved a busing program that "transferred" minority students to "safe" schools. Dr. Carolyn A. Sebastian, a University of Southern California professor, released a study showing that "a majority of elementary teachers don't understand Chicano students." According to Sebastian, teachers psychologically damaged Chicano children. In March, the Center on Law and Poverty brought a suit against the schools on behalf of 12 Chicano students to halt testing because it was used to justify tracking.

Ironically, at a time when education was apparently failing all children, and when declining reading scores had become the norm, library services were cut in the schools. East Los Angeles schools were forced to also reduce their Title I programs due to changes in the federal and the Los Angeles Unified School System guidelines. The new regulations eliminated most East Los Angeles schools from Title I. The ramifications were severe. First, students no longer received the special programs that Title I funding made possible. Second, many recently certified Chicano teachers had financed their education through large federal loans, which were forgiven if the teacher taught at a Title I school for at least five years. Cancellation of this program ultimately cost Latino teachers millions of dollars and Latino students a better education.

The U.S. Civil Rights Commission released reports on the educational system's general neglect of Chicanos in the Southwest. These reports detailed how language and cultural conflicts handicapped barrio pupils. Other studies published during this period portrayed bilingual education as the answer to the Chicanos' educational problems. Congress, however, did not properly fund bilingual programs and the Senate was reluctant to make a commitment. Roybal remained the most persistent congressional advocate for bilingual education. At the state level, Governor Reagan vetoed the bilingual bill. In late November, another $5 million bilingual package went to the governor, who decided to postpone any action.

In July, La Raza Unida party sponsored a platform convention in Los Angeles. The RUP opposed both Republican and Democratic candidates. When Senator Ted Kennedy campaigned for Senator George McGovern in East Los Angeles, RUP partisans heckled him. Meanwhile, President Nixon developed a Latino strategy designed to win five percent more of this vote than in 1968. His tactic was to appeal to middle-class Chicanos.

Art Torres ran against Alex García in the Democratic primary. García, the incumbent, campaigned harder than in past elections, hitting at the new regulations that had eliminated the Title I program from most Eastside schools. Torres, in turn, criticized García, stating that the incumbent had opposed a bill that would have protected farmworkers' rights to organize. César Chávez endorsed Torres and actively campaigned for him. In spite of this support, Torres lost to García, 9,558-to-8,943. After this, Torres formed the Community Association for Political Action to advance progressive political causes in the Chicano community.

Meanwhile, Raúl Ruiz qualified as an independent to represent the RUP for the 40th Assembly District and ran against García in the fall runoff. In an unexpected move, the United Teachers of Los Angeles endorsed Ruiz. García refused to appear with Ruiz on several occasions. When he did meet the RUP candidate, he was insulting. He also won the election.

East Los Angeles Chicanos supported the United Farmworkers Union, which changed from an organizing committee to a full-fledged union. In September, the farmworkers increased opposition to grower-sponsored Proposition 22. Passage of 22 would have crippled the union, for it would have made their boycott of grower products illegal. Meanwhile, Secretary of State Edmund G. Brown Jr. brought a suit against the organizers of 22, charging fraud in their circulation of petitions. After a highly emotional campaign, which the *Sun* covered in depth, the voters defeated the proposition.

In the spring, President Nixon illegally pressured the National Labor Relations Board, which had no jurisdiction over the United Farmworkers Union, to order an injunction against the boycott.

Roybal vehemently protested this action and the farmworkers went to the community for support.

Reapportionment was also a problem again this year. Because of their increased numbers, Chicanos naively thought that they would receive a favorable redistricting in the California legislature's plan. Just the opposite happened. The plan was so unfair that even Governor Reagan had to veto it. In fact, the controversy finally went to the courts, since no other resolution was possible in a case of such gross partisanship. And Chicanos fared no better in the city council reapportionment plan. Latinos had applied considerable pressure on the council in an effort to receive a district that would ensure representation for their community. The Chicano population was rapidly approaching 25 percent of the city's population.

Liberals such as Councilman Ed Edelman were caught in a dilemma of conscience. How could they continue to deny Mexican American representation? Edelman drew up a plan that he said would soon ensure Chicano representation on the city council. The plan roughly divided the northeast Los Angeles community, taking Boyle Heights and linking it up with Eagle Rock. Boyle Heights was formerly in Lindsay's district, whereas Eagle Rock had been in Snyder's old district. The new plan also cut Highland Park in half, separating the Atwater district from the new Edelman-created 14th Councilmanic District. Supposedly, this plan would put maverick City Councilman Arthur Snyder on the defensive, forcing him to run in this newly created so-called Mexican American district and making it embarrassingly obvious that the seat had been denied to the Chicano community.

But the Chicano community was not satisfied with the plan and the Mexican American Legal Defense and Education Fund (MALDEF) threatened to sue the city council. "I hate hypocrisy," Snyder wrote, charging that the plan had been drawn up at a secret meeting and that rather than ensuring Chicanos representation, it effectively excluded them. Snyder objected also to the northeast area's arbitrary division, underscoring that even though the new district was 68 percent Mexican American, it was far from a safe bet: 45 percent of the Chicano population was under 18 and 40 percent were noncitizens and could not vote. Although Boyle Heights had a population of 81,159, it was a port of entry for Mexican nationals, and only 13,618 residents were registered to vote. Even in the hotly contested mayoral race of 1969, the voter turnout in Boyle Heights was only 34 percent. Predominantly white Eagle Rock, on the other hand, had only 28,545 residents—but 16,584 of them were registered voters, 77 percent of whom had turned out for the 1969 elections.

Yorty vetoed the redistricting plan but the council overrode his veto and the new 14th Councilmanic District was created. Snyder predicted that he could win easily, since the Edelman plan gave merely the illusion of creating a Chicano district. This prediction proved correct.

The year ended with President Richard Nixon's reelection victory. This was another reason for the apathy and hopelessness that pervaded the 1970s.

1973

The year began with Alicia Escalante serving a jail sentence for her participation in Católicos Por La Raza. In the meantime, *Ms.* magazine honored Escalante. Richard Cruz's hearing before the California Bar drew to a close and, later that year, he won certification from the bar.

The fight against the Rodino Bill, which would prohibit employers from knowingly hiring undocumented workers, continued. A coalition of community organizations planned a series of conferences to educate the community to the importance of the issue. The first meeting was held at St. Joseph's Church in Los Angeles. The proceedings analyzed and condemned the Rodino Bill and attendants discussed the rights of U.S. born children of undocumented workers. CASA took a leading role. A series of similar conferences were repeated throughout the Southwest and Midwest.

In Congress, Roybal opposed the Rodino Bill, stating that it discriminated against Mexicans and Chicanos. Assemblyman Richard Alatorre also characterized the Rodino Bill as discriminatory. Some misunderstanding developed over the farmworker stand on the bill. The UFW supposedly supported the bill, but toward the end of April, Art Torres issued a statement on their behalf, opposing the bill.

Meanwhile, the INS conducted massive roundups of undocumented workers. At a press conference, CASA's Bert Corona
and Soledad Alatorre condemned the inhumanity of the raids. The
pair cited a case in which a woman was apprehended while she
babysat for her grandchildren. On June 21, Reverend Mark Day
wrote an article for the *Sun*. "Immigration raids . . . [treat] people
like dogs," Day wrote, "Nobody's doing anything about it."
Meanwhile, the Mexican American Legal Defense Fund and the
American Civil Liberties Union sued to stop the raids. And the
"One Stop" Immigration Center reported that it had helped 1,235
families.

The blatant disregard for Mexicans' rights encouraged more
organizations to oppose the INS. A rally was held in San Isidro
to stop repression of undocumented workers. CASA continued at
the vanguard against the Rodino Bill and, in September, invited
the public to a barbecue in Lincoln Park. Art Snyder proposed the
licensing of immigration consultants. Chicanos opposed this recommendation, however, since it would curtail already effective
volunteer efforts to assist the undocumented.

In the meantime, public meetings were held to discuss the
ramifications of the East Los Angeles master plan. The county
supervisors conducted hearings at which opponents charged that
the plan called for massive redevelopment of the Eastside. Nevertheless, the supervisors approved the plan. Opponents accused
TELACU of supporting the plan and also alleged that the organization and HUD paid PAC members to attend block meetings.
Esteban Torres admitted to paying PAC members but denied any
conflict of interest. TELACU attacked the opponents of the Neighborhood Development Project, calling them dissidents and
absentee landlords. The community, according to TELACU,
elected PAC members and, in turn, PAC represented the community's interests. TELACU singled out Ray Rodríguez, Rosalio
Muñoz, and Art Montoya as troublemakers.

TELACU had grown to a staff of 85 and employed full-time
attorneys, engineers, accountants, and economists. It also had numerous divisions, including business development and assistance,
business operations and housing, urban development, and manpower. It also had an impressive team of specialists. TELACU
worked directly with the Office of Economic Opportunity and
local governments. It was one of 40 community development cor-

porations in the United States and the only one in Los Angeles County. According to its founder, Esteban Torres, "TELACU is bent on building our own power." That power was dependent upon the construction of an economic base. Since the aftermath of the January 1971 riots, according to Torres, TELACU dedicated itself exclusively to that pursuit because it was tired of violence.

Torres quit the Congress of Mexican American Unity to devote himself completely to building TELACU. He explained that he was disillusioned with CMAU, which had been infiltrated by extremists. He was, therefore, selective about whom he let participate in TELACU. Significantly, Torres said that he had worked as a trade union consultant in Latin America, where he saw what he called disruptive tactics. It was this experience that triggered his dedication to saving TELACU from infiltration. In the quest to build an economic base, TELACU acquired a sizeable interest in redevelopment and the implementation of the master plan.

Opposing the master plan was Rosalio Muñoz and other volunteers, who enlisted the support of many Catholic parishes. Through the churches, they organized mass meetings. Montoya was the other pole: he opposed the plan and worked through the East Los Angeles-Maravilla-Belvedere Park property owners. Montoya scheduled a public rally at Belvedere Junior High on April 10. Five hundred residents attended the meeting to discuss the master plan. On May 17, the *Sun* ran a Muñoz article, "Save the Barrio Now," which discussed how the master plan endangered the existence of East Los Angeles. In his weekly columns, Montoya denounced the master plan and accused TELACU of acting as the tool of urban renewal interests. Bitterness increased and the issue was loudly debated at a supervisors' hearing.

The incorporation of East Los Angeles was also at issue, dovetailing the debate over the master plan. To many Eastsiders, home rule represented a defense against redevelopment. However, who supported and who did not support incorporation was often as unclear as the motives. For example, according to the *Sun*, Ernest Debs pushed the incorporation plan through the County Regional Planning Council. The supervisor was quoted as stating that he supported home rule for East Los Angeles. The *Sun* tied Debs to TELACU, while other sources alleged that differences had developed between the two. It is fact that TELACU later supported Ed Edelman against Debs. All indications are that Debs was initially pro-incorporation and gradually cooled to the idea, finally declaring neutrality. TELACU was clearly the driving force behind the initial incorporation effort and, along with Debs, had supported the master plan. Although Montoya in his column portrayed TELACU as Debs's alter ego, they apparently split company in regards to incorporation. What is true is that TELACU's interests were opposed to those of most boosters of incorporation. At the same time, Kovner and Montoya opposed the master plan and incorporation, while Muñoz and most barrio activists supported it.

Meanwhile, the incorporation plan went to the Local Agency Formation Committee (LAFCO), which had the power to approve or kill the drive. While it vehemently opposed incorporation, the *Sun* did publish countless letters supporting it.

On August 8, Montoya wrote an article, "Facts . . . Not Fancy in ELA City," in which he gave his reasons for opposing incorporation. Basically Montoya supported the interests of the small landowner. In October, when TELACU circulated incorporation petitions, Montoya attacked its motives. He criticized a KNXT editorial supporting incorporation. In essence, Montoya stated that he opposed incorporation because TELACU would gain too much power if East Los Angeles became a city. According to Montoya, this would accelerate the redevelopment of ELA.

While Montoya's efforts on the behalf of small landowners had considerable merit, it could not be denied that many non-resident landlords failed to keep their properties in good repair. The case of Francisco Mendoza, 12, illustrates this point. On November 16, Francisco electrocuted himself when he touched faulty wiring. This accident could have been prevented since that wire had been reported as dangerous to county authorities. At the same time, however, it could not be denied that should massive redevelopment take place, there would be no homes for the area's poor.

The war on poverty limped along. The emphasis had shifted to job training. The East Los Angeles Skills Center boasted a 92 percent job placement rate, but its enrollment was frozen. The federal government also paid increased attention to occupational education at the community college level.

Federal authorities cut funding across the board, which threatened legal aid centers with closure. Nixon's phase-outs produced angry denunciations that he neglected the poor. Meanwhile, congressional Democrats fought reductions in the Office of Economic Opportunity budget. Once again Roybal emerged as the leading spokesperson for the poor. When Nixon cut $29 million from the OEO, he simultaneously escalated the defense budget to the highest level in the country's history.

At the local level, city employees with bilingual skills were paid merit allowances. This additional pay was achieved through the efforts of the Los Angeles City Chicano Employees Association. The Los Angeles County Chicano Employees Association was not as effective and had to sue the county. Meanwhile, the Los Angeles school system expanded its bilingual program as it sought $203,470 in supplemental funds.

Attorneys for Los Tres appealed the conviction of their clients. The Free Los Tres Committee had incorporated itself into CASA and sponsored a march and a rally at the courthouse, with Rodolfo "Corky" Gonzales speaking at the gathering. The committee held another demonstration on May 19. By the fall, the defendants were released on bail while their case was on appeal.

In Aliso Village, a race riot between Blacks and browns erupted during the summer and three persons were killed. The City Housing Authority called for more police and helicopters. The *Sun* did not note any city authority attempts to solve the Aliso Village problems of unemployment, heavy drugs, and general neglect of the project's residents.

Graffiti was out of hand. The state legislature studied spray paint control legislation. A positive alternative remained the mural project, which was promoted in the barrios and housing projects such as the Estrada Courts. Kovner wrote a number of editorials praising these projects. In fact, more attention was paid generally to the murals than to the root causes of graffiti and increased gang violence. On October 18, Kovner described the mural artists' goals and problems. Efforts were made to channel the gangs' energies into beautifying the communities and some gang members helped remove graffiti from public walls. Angel T. Solis wrote about the gang problem in an August 23 *Sun* article, "El Pandillerismo y sus Remedios." According to most experts, gang activity had increased with the worsening of economic conditions.

Tom Bradley ran for the second time against Sam Yorty. Bradley enjoyed the support of Roybal, the *Sun* and most Chicano activists. In May, he upset Yorty and became the city's first Black mayor. Kovner campaigned for Chicano appointments to the city commissions. On August 2, the *Sun* asked: "Will Bradley Chicano advisers committee be able to impress Mayor Bradley that they mean business?" On November 8, the paper more pointedly wanted to know: "Will Mayor Bradley Help Stop Land Grabs?" In this vein, the *Sun* still criticized Model Cities, but ironically, on September 27, Kovner wrote "I Deplore Model Cities Cuts. . . ."

The *Sun* reported that Chicanos had launched a movement to recall Art Snyder. In spite of past criticisms of Snyder, however, the *Sun's* coverage was generally positive to the councilman. Community activists, led almost singlehandedly by Dr. David López Lee, condemned the councilman's pro-development record and made the widening of the streets near Hazard Park an issue in their recall movement. On June 14, the *Sun* ran pro and con articles on Snyder's recall. On June 28, the *Sun* listed the councilman's accomplishments, claiming that Snyder contributed to an increase in construction and services in Boyle Heights and Lincoln Heights. Snyder himself answered critics in direct language and campaigned actively in Boyle Heights, especially in the housing projects. Meanwhile, the recall forces collected 7,500 names on a petition to recall the councilman. Snyder charged misrepresentation in the recall effort, but the courts approved the petitions and set the stage for the recall election in 1974.

A Chicana caucus actively participated in the National Woman's Political Caucus. On April 28, the Mexican American Political Association honored women activists. Chicana opposition to the Talmadge Amendment to the Social Security Act continued. A group called "Madres por Justicia" wrote several articles, published in the *Sun*, opposing the amendment. Alicia Escalante remained the leader of the opposition, with the Los Angeles Chicano Welfare Rights Organization conducting an active anti-amendment campaign. Under Escalante's leadership, a court case was brought against the Talmadge Amendment.

Assemblyman Richard Alatorre addressed the Comisión Femenil. The Semana de la Raza at Cal State, Los Angeles featured information and speakers on incarcerated Chicanas and the Mexican American Resource Association (MARA). The Chicana of the Year banquet held its third annual affair in July. In the late summer, MAPA again honored women activists. In September, the Chicana Service Action Center celebrated its first anniversary. Its services had expanded with a grant from the SER/MAOF Skills Center.

The *Sun's* coverage of the United Farmworkers increased. Volunteers conducted emergency food drives for the farmworkers throughout Los Angeles. In the summer, the Teamsters brutally attacked UFW members in the Imperial Valley. César Chávez appealed for support, picketing the Los Angeles wholesale market, which was the largest in the world. Supporters organized local protests against the Teamsters, condemning the use of violence by the truckers' union. UFW officials also charged that the Teamsters discriminated against Chicano members. By the end of July, the strike had moved to the San Joaquin Valley, where authorities arrested some 1,700 farmworkers and supporters. Meanwhile, Congressman Roybal called for a National Farmworkers Act. In October, the Farm Labor Non-Violence Committee of the state legislature held hearings. Support for creation of a state farm board to end violence in the fields increased.

1974

The year kicked off with Councilman Arthur Snyder's recall election. Kovner predicted a heated race. Richard Calderón and David López Lee were the leading Chicano candidates. César Chávez endorsed Calderón, as did the County Democratic Central Committee and numerous business people in the area. López Lee charged that Snyder was guilty of influence peddling. Kovner vacillated, first writing that Snyder had done a good job and then ultimately endorsing both Calderón and López Lee. Ironically, Montoya criticized the recall election, stating that Mexican Americans should not vote solely on the basis of race. Labor staunchly supported Snyder and the AFL/CIO endorsed him. The recall election failed, 15,575-to-9,647.

On March 21, Kovner wrote "It Was Closer Than You Thought." According to Kovner, Snyder had directed his campaign to those who would vote—senior citizens. Because Snyder's votes came heavily from a selected portion of his constituency, it did not represent a crushing defeat. On April 4, López Lee gave a breakdown, showing that Chicano precincts had supported the recall. Meanwhile, Calderón brought suit against the city council, challenging the reapportionment plan.

Strongly supported by César Chávez, Art Torres ran for the newly created 56th Assembly District and won. Esteban Torres, endorsed by the Mexican American Labor Council, ran for Congress but lost.

Arthur Montoya was still president of the East Los Angeles–Maravilla–Belvedere Park Property Owners Association. Speaking at a Town Hall of California meeting, he expressed his views on urban renewal and incorporation, which he linked to Esteban Torres and development interests. Montoya also attacked the proposed Temple-Urban Renewal Project. Meanwhile, the supervisors received approximately 2,100 letters from homeowners who were opposed to incorporation.

On June 13, Montoya reviewed the history of incorporation. Again, he linked incorporation to TELACU and at this time asserted that Debs controlled the Ad Hoc Committee to Incorporate East Los Angeles (ACIELA). In the July 25 *Sun* article, he charged that East Los Angeles "was not now capable of incorporation." Proponents refuted Montoya, stating that East Los Angeles was losing millions of tax dollars on retail sales and that incorporation would stem the leakage. On September 19, Renaldo Macías of ACIELA wrote an article for the *Sun* in which he laid out a case for incorporation and resounded the theme of home rule. Meanwhile, Richard Polanco, a Maravilla project administrator, accused Montoya of misrepresentation. Montoya charged that the Local Agency Formation Commission report, which he said favored incorporation, had made an $1,574,070 error. Ironically, Montoya's charge had first been made by LAFCO itself in an update of its 1973 figures. LAFCO had never meant this report for public circulation. It had been released to Debs, who apparently made it available to incorporation opponents.

The incorporation election took place on November 5. Encompassing seven square miles, the debated area had 105,033 residents, 90,008 of whom were of Mexican extraction. In 1970, the median resident income was $8,389 per annum and median education background was 8.5 years. In 1974, some 26,110 eastsiders were registered to vote. As Professor Jorge García underscored in a 1977 *La Raza* magazine article, East Los Angeles was in the 3rd Supervisorial District, which had 630,693 registered voters. Consequently, residents could vote for district supervisor but had little collective political power and even less direct representation. At the time of the election, Debs was supposedly neutral. But the alienation between him and Esteban Torres of TELACU was marked. In June, he had stated that incorporation "may [be a] vote for a city without any money to run it." Debs also openly opposed Torres at supervisor hearings. The *Sun*, however, continued to link the two men. Lastly, property tax bills were issued on November 1. These showed tax increases, fueling claims that taxes would increase further in the event of cityhood. Councilman Ed Edelman supported incorporation and was a candidate against Debs for the 3rd Supervisorial District.

After the votes were counted, incorporation lost 3,262-to-2,369. Belvedere had voted solidly for incorporation, but the areas abutting Monterey Park, Montebello and Commerce had solidly turned down the proposition. Many people attributed the defeat to fears that taxes would increase. Current studies, however, point to more complex reasons. And although at the time Kovner and Montoya called incorporation an overwhelming defeat, data suggests that it was closer than first believed. The top vote-getter in this election was Raúl Ruiz, the RUP candidate for city council, who received 1,138 votes.*

The East Los Angeles master plan revived fears of urban renewal. Admittedly, encroachment on barrio land was not as overt as in the 1950s and 1960s. Montoya, however, underscored that the master plan set aside land that was "now occupied by homes" for industrial development. He said that Maravilla and Boyle Heights were prime target areas and claimed that the Maravilla Neighborhood Development group was partial to urban renewal.

In the August 8 *Sun*, Los Angeles city planner Raúl Escobedo asked: "Is Boyle Heights Worth Saving?" He concluded that it was and described community efforts to preserve its residential char-

---

*Data is presently surfacing that police agencies—especially the Los Angeles Police Department—closely monitored this election. The full extent of their interference is not known *at this time*.

acter. Montoya, in turn, charged that the new Los Angeles city master plan menaced Boyle Heights. In the meantime, the East/Northeast Economic Development Corporation and private investors combined to build the City Heights Industrial Plaza. KABC-TV endorsed this venture.

The East Los Angeles Chicana Welfare Rights Organization pressured local agencies, especially DPSS, to be more sensitive and responsive to the community. Congressman Roybal complained about the poor services at the County/USC General Hospital. On other fronts, Alicia Escalante criticized KMEX-TV for its "Operación Navidad," a telethon for gifts for the poor. In an open letter to station manager Danny Villanueva in the February 14 *Sun*, Escalante criticized the program's management. Her letter encouraged numerous response letters to the editor. Escalante also wrote several *Sun* articles on La Causa de los Pobres, openly criticizing slashes in services. Bertha Marshall, president of the Eastside Democratic Club, protested cutbacks in aid to seniors.

The Comisión Femenil Mexicana Nacional, Inc., held its installation banquet on February 8 and went on to establish new chapters. Also this month, Ramona Gardens residents began a campaign to "Stop the Pusher."

On January 8, Judge Robert M. Takasugi dismissed 46 criminal cases in East Los Angeles due to flagrant violations of constitutional rights. In April, Roybal championed an effort to introduce bilingual courts. On March 8 through 10, CASA sponsored a National Immigration Conference and, on August 31, the National Moratorium to Stop Deportations and Repressions held a rally at Belvedere Park.

Padres Unidos, a grassroots parent organization, picketed elementary schools, including Albion and Magnolia, as well as the offices of the United Teachers of Los Angeles. Parents even went so far as to file discrimination suits against the schools.

1975

A recount of the results of the incorporation took place, but the election's outcome remained the same.

Councilman Arthur Snyder claimed that the failure to count undocumented workers in his district resulted in reduced allocations for his district. At another level, Assemblymen Art Torres and Richard Alatorre supported granting undocumented residents services and rights. Community groups also championed the rights of undocumented workers and their families to receive welfare and other services. State Senator Anthony Beilenson successfully sponsored a bill that required court summonses to be available in Spanish and English.

U.S. Senator Edward Kennedy sponsored an amnesty bill for undocumented workers who had established three years of continuous residency. Councilman Snyder supported the so-called reform bill, but Chicano organizations were not so certain. They directed all their energies to stopping the Rodino Bill, which they considered the Mexican community's number one priority. CASA held a press conference to denounce the Rodino Bill as well as to criticize immigration counselors who cheated undocumented workers.

On May 1, Montoya wrote in the *Sun* that he had once opposed the entry of illegal aliens but that the airlifting of thousands of Vietnamese had changed his mind. Meanwhile, the courts invalidated an order that required public agencies to turn over the identities of illegal aliens to the Immigration and Naturalization Service. Without a doubt, the increase in unemployment from 4.6 percent in October 1973 to 6.5 percent in January 1975, together with the recession of 1974, contributed to the steady rise in nativist sentiment.

Meanwhile, Councilman Art Snyder advocated massive federal spending to end the depression. He also announced his candidacy for reelection. Throughout the year, the *Sun* was generous in allowing the councilman space and coverage. In February, Snyder wrote an article in which he described his love affair with Boyle Heights. On May 1, he wrote on the "Legacy of Cinco de Mayo." The *Sun* covered him at the dedication of the new Ben Franklin Library building. Snyder easily won reelection with 11,514 votes, which was 57.84 percent. David López Lee received 3,958 votes, Edward Avila 2,860, and the son of state Senator Alex García 945.

Montoya warned of redevelopment west of Ford Street, from Third Street to City Terrace. He accused Supervisor Ed Edelman, who had recently defeated Debs, of being a major supporter of urban renewal and of being heavily influenced by TELACU. This was an accusation that he often repeated.

Meanwhile, Supervisor Edelman met with the Maravilla redevelopment program director. By this time, TELACU enjoyed influence at all levels of government. The *Sun* reported the attendance of its executive director of economic development at a White House conference on minority businesses. TELACU's ability to lobby in Washington gave it increased influence over other local organizations that lacked the resources to do the same. By the end of May, TELACU opened its development offices in East Los Angeles and simultaneously expanded its business division. Finally, TELACU met with a coalition of East Los Angeles social services and held various community functions, including a testimonial honoring 32 Chicanas.

By the summer, Supervisor Edelman had opened his Eastside offices and partook in talks with redevelopment leaders who wanted to use HUD money to redevelop the López-Maravilla community. Montoya called East Los Angeles a political football between these forces and the community. According to the *Sun*, urban renewal remained East Los Angeles' number one problem. Kovner wrote nostalgically about Boyle Heights, stating that it had always been a haven for the poor. According to Kovner, Boyle Heights' only sin was how close it was to the Civic Center.

Chicano activists were not consistent in their opposition to redevelopment, and Montoya's homeowners association appeared to be the sole group opposing urban renewal. Monterey Park again threatened annexation of the property around East Los Angeles Community College and hearings were held once more. About this time, Snyder proposed a resolution in the city council to annex East Los Angeles to Los Angeles while Montebello made moves to annex Montebello Park in the unincorporate area. This time, however, annexation moves did not produce serious effort to incorporate the area.

As the head librarian for the Los Angeles City Public Library System, Lyman Jones, attended ceremonies for the opening of the Ben Franklin Library in Boyle Heights, petitions were circulated to remove him. Snyder was also in attendance. Antoinette "Toni" Mitchell, herself a librarian, also confronted Jones, whom she accused of staging a political show.

The only real political gains made by the community were the appointments of a few city commissioners. The most prominent was José Sánchez, owner of La Quebradita Market, to the Fire

Commission. Also, Bradley appointed Kovner to the City Human Relations Commission.

In January, the *Sun* published a short piece on congressional failure to extend the Spanish-speaking unit in the Presidential Cabinet. The *Sun* was critical of Watergate and of the Nixon administration's attempts to use Chicanos during the 1972 election.

In the City Human Relations Commission, Kovner championed the fight against redlining in East Los Angeles. Redlining meant that loans were more difficult to obtain and interest rates and insurance rates were higher than in white areas. The commission held hearings on the issue.

More emphasis was paid to the delivery of bilingual services. Congress overrode a presidential veto of the bilingual health program and Assemblyman Richard Alatorre lobbied through a law that mandated state and local agencies to hire bilingual personnel.

Garfield High School, which in the 50s had given a temporary home to the East Los Angeles Community College, lost its accreditation because of poor administration, poor instruction, and poor curriculum.

The Poder Femenil unit of the Comisión Femenil Mexicana sent delegates to Mexico City in July 1975 for the International Women's Year Conference, which was sponsored by the United Nations. Other Eastside women's groups attended. In July and August, Bertha Marshall wrote a series of *Sun* articles on the Mexico City conference. Meanwhile, Francisca Flores's Chicana Service Action Center expanded into a major skills training center.

The murals of East Los Angeles, especially those on the Estrada Courts walls, were featured in *Time* magazine. Kovner reviewed this article in the April 17 *Sun*. Chicano arts were also exhibited widely at this time. In September, the *Sun* ran a special supplement on the murals of East Los Angeles.

SUMMARY

President Richard Nixon won by a landslide in 1972. Within two years, his empire crumbled under the weight of Watergate. This and the end of the Vietnam conflict contributed to the economic recession of the period. Even before Nixon's reelection, the INS and the press generated a hysteria that aliens were invading the United States. The California Dixon-Arnett law and the proposed Rodino Bill activated Chicano organizations to counter this attack.

Considerable coverage appeared in the *Sun* and the *Citizen* during 1972 on Model Cities and HUD. In 1973, a shift in the *Sun*'s coverage became apparent: attention to community Model Cities and poverty agencies became focused primarily on redevelopment and job training. (Also by this time, it had become evident that the *Sun*'s coverage of all topics had greatly decreased.) By 1975, pro-renewal TELACU was the strongest organization east of the river, enjoying political contacts at the local, state, and federal levels. TELACU's service area spanned from Boyle Heights/East Los Angeles to Lincoln Heights.

Police brutality and INS abuses were still reported and the hijacking of an airliner by Ricardo Chávez Ortiz caused interest among activists. However, the news increasingly concerned itself with affirmative action and expanding bilingual services to the community. Also, a wider participation of women was reported. The activities of Francisca Flores and Alicia Escalante were the most frequently mentioned.

On the direct political scene, the Eastside had two more assemblymen, Richard Alatorre and Art Torres, both of whom had benefitted from reapportionment. Representation at the local level, however, still evaded Chicanos. The supervisors ran from too large an area, preventing the maximum impact of the Chicano vote. The Los Angeles City Council reapportionment plan was a disaster, giving only the illusion of creating a Chicano district. Meanwhile, efforts to recall Councilman Arthur Snyder failed, as did the drive to incorporate East Los Angeles.

The lack of local representation, the absence of any mass resistance to developers, and the decline of activism during this period left the community politically weak. Groups such as CASA, La Raza Unida party and MAPA confined themselves usually to single issues, and few organizations dealt with the problem of redevelopment and what form it should take. Even the Association of Mexican American Educators, which benefitted from bilingual education, was surprisingly silent on the pages of the *Sun*. Unemployment, inflation, high rents, and social decay of youth left the community east of the river vulnerable. The general inability of most Chicano organizations to tackle more than one issue destroyed the community's ability to withstand the atavistic siege of anti-minority activity.

9

Epilogue

The epilogue is based on: the *Eastside Sun* through August 1976; the Roybal Newpaper Scrapbooks; The Los Angeles City Department of City Planning, *Boyle Heights Community Plan, Background Reports*, 1974, 1979; and selected articles from the *Los Angeles Times*.

What the future holds in store for the community east of the Los Angeles River cannot be predicted. This study has been largely limited to two weekly newspapers, the *Eastside Sun* and the *Belvedere Citizen*. Definite trends have been suggested, both by the articles listed at the end of this work and by the chronicle itself. Most of the concerns are those of poor people bound together by a common ethnic and racial identity.

Certainly, changes have taken place since World War II. The sheer volume of the Eastside renter class has grown—as has the proportion of undocumented workers. Today, there are fewer homeowner occupants. Usually, they are the older residents who also form part of a large reserve labor pool concentrated east of the Los Angeles River. The trade unionists and semiprofessionals have increasingly moved to the outskirts of the area. And while the total Chicano community has made political gains at the state and federal levels, local representation has proved perpetually elusive. All of this leaves a disappointingly powerless community.

The intense militancy of the period between 1965 and 1973 has remained dormant. After 1973, the *Sun* paid less attention to community events and, by the mid–70s, the paper's physical size reflected the community's relative inactivity. While the *Sun* still championed community concerns, much of its crusading spirit diminished. This was due in part to Kovner's advancing age and to his death in 1977. In great part, however, it was due to the times. In 1976, Kovner alerted the Eastside to annexation moves by Monterey Park and Montebello, both of which had substantial middle-class Mexican American populations. But by this time, even Montoya's *Sun* articles lacked their former zing and this longtime fighter soon retired. Most of all, these new annexation threats did not produce the organized response that had in the past been a battle cry for home rule. Consequently, by June of 1976, Monterey Park annexed East Los Angeles Community College and the surrounding territory, conveniently excluding the Maravilla housing project. This action produced a feeble and unsuccessful law suit. On February 26, 1976, Montoya warned that "the people of East Los Angeles better believe that urban renewal is a reality in your community." From the response, it was apparent that few understood the warning. Supervisor Ed Edelman favored redevelopment as vehemently as had his predecessor, Ernest Debs, and most politicians in the area supported him. Edelman formed a citizens advisory committee to assist the County Planning Department. In the past, the formation of such an advisory committee meant that an area would merely participate in its own demise as a community. There was no reason to think that things would be different this time.*

TELACU's role in the redevelopment of East Los Angeles must be still further researched. During 1976, TELACU worked with redevelopment forces to prepare a comprehensive survey of the area. Apparently, the organization functioned as a mini Model Cities, establishing manpower training programs, CETA programs, and a senior citizens cooperative. The labyrinthine nature of TELACU's activities makes it difficult to evaluate the total impact of its contribution. However, it is certain that social programs must be separated from the impact of TELACU's land use policies.

To this day, housing remains a problem, since most dwellings in the Eastside were constructed before or just after World War II. Meanwhile, the Mexican American and Latino populations in Los Angeles continue to grow—and need for adequate housing grows apace. By 1980, 26 percent of the houses in Boyle Heights were overcrowded, versus 24.7 percent in Watts and 21.5 percent in Lincoln Heights. Also by this year, 29.8 percent of Los Angeles Latinos lived in deteriorated housing versus 2.7 percent of the Black population. The shift in federal land policy to rehabilitation helped owners in the 70s, but to renters it still often means higher rents.†

Edelman is not alone in his pro-development views. Arthur Snyder is a favorite among construction contractors and workers. In the April 2, 1979, *Los Angeles Times*, Bill Boyarsky wrote that the councilman "is backed by organized labor whose leaders appreciate the pro-building stand he has taken as chairman of the

---

*Victor Vallejo of Los Angeles City Planning does not believe that Boyle Heights is in danger of redevelopment because the thrust of the Community Redevelopment Agency (CRA) is to the west.

Also, an important study by Guadalupe Compeán, "The Los Angeles Corporate Center: Its' Probable Impact on North East Los Angeles," (A Client Project, School of Architecture and Urban Planning, University of California at Los Angeles, June 6, 1983), proves considerable land speculation in Belvedere-Maravilla, with large investments being made in the area.

†In spite of the fact that the area had lost prime residential property, East Los Angeles populations increased to 114,000 in 1977. Compared to the population of the area in 1970, this represents a 10 percent growth.

Council's Planning Committee." Land use patterns in Boyle Heights have encouraged developers to look to that area for future development. Although 75 percent of the dwellings were residential in 1974, a mere .3 percent—15 out of 3,824 acres—were zoned for single family occupancy. This pattern had begun in 1946, when a massive rezoning effort took place. This produced a mass exodus of middle-class whites and Jews because they expected that the area would be condemned and their homes torn down and replaced with apartment buildings. This speculation and exodus led to a deterioration of Boyle Heights, since improvement and home loans became more difficult to obtain and insurance rates escalated. Traditionally, as this chronicle has suggested, blight has led to a justification for redevelopment.

For the moment, the community east of the river appears safe. A lull in the economy—in part due to high interest rates and inflation—has tempered federal subsidies to construction and lessened the pressure to redevelop the periphery. However, the lessons of the past 50 years make it almost certain that this state of affairs will not continue. Population density and the proximity to the downtown core make it almost inevitable that unincorporated East Los Angeles and Boyle Heights land will be used more intensely.

In the case of Boyle Heights, the master plan (or community plan, as it is also called) recommends that much zoning be rolled back to reflect actual land use. This concession was the result of community pressure, the early work of Roybal and the *Sun*. However, master plans are subject to change.* Boyle Heights is one of 35 districts that started to draw up community plans in 1965, supposedly setting guidelines for growth, housing expansion, land use, and open space development. The plans, however, are merely advisory; politicians and developers have often dismissed them. Van Nuys, for example, was one of the first communities to begin master plan implementation. Councilman Enani Bernardi criticized the original plan, stating that the city invested $30 to $40 million on plans that appeared to be "gathering dust on the shelves in the Planning Department." A developer underscored that he had little respect for the Van Nuys plans

---

*Similar rollbacks are occurring in East Los Angeles. In a November 13, 1980, letter to the *Sun*, Arthur Montoya warned that the rollbacks reduced the value of property. He charged that the purpose of the rollbacks was to permit developers to pay lower prices for homes that were condemned under eminent domain.

because "although they set standards, they don't have laws backing them. We play by the prevailing zoning laws—that's the real
ball game in this city." What this developer failed to add is that
builders, real estate people, trade unions, and the business community have often dominated the appointments to planning and
zoning commissions. And that they have generally been pro-
development.

The East Los Angeles master plan calls for multiple dwellings
and intensification of land use. The most impacted area will be
Belvedere. In both the Boyle Heights and Belvedere communities,
owner-occupancy has declined. The possibility exists that whites
and middle-class Mexican Americans will return to the territory
and rehabilitate the homes. However, considering the large
numbers of public housing projects, how many will want to live
next door to poor people with problems? Another possibility is the
acquisition of these homes by the occupants themselves. But what
is the feasibility of this happening, given the high interest rates,
inflated property prices and individual income potential?
Moreover, federal programs principally benefit property owners.
For instance, HUD's Homes Opportunities Maintenance Effort
(HOME), funded by a community development block grant,
spends over two-thirds of its $2 million budget on administration.
But given that the eastsiders are mostly renters and that HOME
subsidizes the owners, how many renters benefit from the
program?

The residents east of the river continue to suffer unemployment, overcrowded schools, inadequate housing, and a population
boom. The influx of undocumented workers, the youth of the
residents, and low income status add to the community's political
powerlessness. For example, over 33 percent of Mexican
Americans between the ages of 16 and 20 had dropped out of
school by 1980 versus less than 10 percent of Blacks. The median income of Bolye Heights was almost one-half that of the rest
of the city. And East Los Angeles was even more depressed. In
1977, unemployment ran 17.3 percent, which was almost twice
the rest of the county.*

This chronicle synthesizes community concerns as they were
reflected in the two Eastside weeklies. It is apparent that the community changed considerably during the first 30 years following

*In 1970, 23 percent of that community earned an annual salary that was below
the poverty line.

World War II. More extensive research is needed in the numerous factors contributing to these changes. The division of labor has increased and a subclass of undocumented workers within the subclass of Mexican Americans now occupies the Eastside. Whether it is to the benefit of the ruling elite to maintain this reserve labor pool in a concentrated area has not been definitely determined. The Eastside problems of unemployment, gangs, and inferior schooling are phenomena created by the system, not by Mexican Americans. These problems form a very real part of the capitalist system.

Extensive research is needed also on the changes that have taken place in the mode of production and the market in Los Angeles over the past 50 years. Future changes in production will, in great part, determine the fate of East Los Angeles, generating further alterations in the utility and value of property. The current conversion from an industrially based economy to high-tech production could have disastrous consequences.

Consider, too, that extensive study must be conducted not only of the city and county's ruling elite, but also of those within the Eastside. The roles of banking institutions and the *Citizen* itself are ripe research prospects.

In all events, the future of East Los Angeles is now at the crossroads. The prospects of Mexicans continuing to occupy this community as it is presently constituted certainly look dismal. For the present, two things are certain. One is that the Eastside situation has resulted from complex patterns and events that are simultaneously local and national. The second certainly is that developers may be digging for gold—but there ain't no rainbow over East L.A.

PART II

The Community Bulletin Boards

The *Eastside Sun* and the *Belvedere Citizen* are community weeklies that depended on advertisers for their existence. They are not
newspapers in the tradition of the *Los Angeles Times* and, from
1945 to 1975, did not reflect what is often called "journalistic ex-
cellence." Purely and simply, news often filled the empty spaces
between ads.

The main contribution of the weeklies through the period was
that they were accessible to the communities who used them.
They would accept announcements of events and/or expression
of views that the Los Angeles dailies ignored. Newspapers such
as the *Los Angeles Times* concentrated on White middle-class
readers. According to one *Times* publisher, the large metropolitan
daily did not concern itself with the interests of the Mexican
American community because Chicanos did not read that
newspaper. Consequently, throughout the period, the dailies reported only the more sensational events on the Eastside and ignored the day-to-day events affecting Chicanos east of the river.
This was the important gap filled by weeklies.

The articles that follow represent most of the items that appeared in the *Sun* (1945–1975) and the *Citizen* (1934–1972). The
more repetitious items and announcements of marriages, deaths
and the like were omitted, since the amount of material included
would have been overwhelming. The East Los Angeles County
Library has the microfilm copy of the selected articles from the
Sun—called the Joseph E. Kovner Collection and the Edward R.
Roybal Newspaper Scrapbook Collection. It also has microfilm of
the *Citizen* to 1972.

These articles are as important as the synthesized chronicle.
They suggest trends and patterns of community concerns and
served as the basis for the narrative of Part I. But this entire project touches only the tip of the iceberg. To learn what really happened, researchers must explore extensively the original sources.
Community Under Seige does not pretend to have made a comprehensive study of the area but to suggest the lack of serious
research on the Eastside.

The limitations of the coverage in the weeklies has been
underscored throughout Part I. The *Sun* did not have the kind of
experienced staff that the *Citizen* enjoyed. Equally important, it
often represented the views of one concerned citizen: Joseph
Kovner. The *Citizen*, ironically the more professional of the two

papers, did not excel in investigative reporting. Both newspapers represented mainstream Democratic party politics and covered only the fringes of activist left thought. Also, their coverage on issues such as police brutality and efforts to ameliorate the situation was uneven. And often they did not give much background information on the organizations mentioned in articles.

The strength of the weeklies is that, when taken together, they represent an interesting dialectic. Joe Kovner was a Jewish American liberal who was concerned initially with the community of Boyle Heights and, to a lesser degree, the unincorporated area of East Los Angeles. With the passage of time, his concern spread to include other parts of the city and county. Until his death, Kovner saw developer encroachment as the major threat to Mexican American communities. Somewhat paternalistic and flamboyant, he nevertheless identified with the area.

The *Citizen* had other interests. This paper concentrated strictly on the unincorporated territory and was more involved with the county and its government than with the city. The *Citizen* functioned as a mini *Los Angeles Times*; progress in this paper was often defined in terms of development. This weekly was a major power broker and, while Kovner was eventually appointed to the city's Human Relations Commission, the publishers of the *Citizen* were appointed to powerful planning groups.

Countless forgotten battles are relived on the pages of the two bulletin boards. The siege of the Eastside and the responses of its citizens come alive. Congressman Edward R. Roybal shines through the articles as a champion in the fight against urban renewal. Without the coverage of the weeklies, the history of Boyle Heights and East Los Angeles may very well have had another interpretation. Their articles serve to refresh the memories of area residents and to document their struggles for the modern researcher. They provide history that cannot be gleaned out of the major dailies or government records. But the purpose of the chronicle and the articles listing is not merely to revive memories. It is to identify and clarify the issues that have shaped the Eastside so that the community will be able to withstand the sieges that will inevitably come.

CIVIC CENTER SUN

1937

AUG 26   "Our Filthy Streets," by Leo N. Kovner

1938

MAY 5   "Death Ends Quarrel at Apartment House"
OCT 13   "Mexican Indigents Repatriation Studied at Conference"
DEC 22   "Zoning Quietly Altered"

1939

APR 24   "Cinco De Mayo Comes to Custer"
MAY 3   "Announcing Festivities"
JUN 1   "The Story of the Civic Center, When Temple Street Was in Her Teens," by I. Krasnow
JUN 22   "Juarez"
SEP 14   "Juarez Starts at Town Theatre"
SEP 28   "Gus Alvarez Tells His Voyage 'Down-Under'," by L.C.R.
DEC 28   "Wages Increase in Los Angeles"

1940

MAR 7   "Bunker Hill Village, Engulfed by Metropolis, Wants Federal Housing Project," by George C. Reeves
MAR 14   "Groundbreaking For Ramona Gardens" March 16, 1940; Housing Authority of LA City
APR 4   "Joseph Kovner's Column," on merchant neglect of community
"Discussion Club To See Film On Farm Worker"
APR 18   "The Background of the History of Calif.," by Deputy Sheriff Ed Duran Ayres
APR 20   "Migratory Labor Plan Announced"
"The Background of the History of Calif.," by Deputy Sheriff Ed Duran Ayres
MAY 2   "Cinco de Mayo Celebrated by Local Mexicans"
"Migratory Problem Challenged By New Program"
MAY 16   "The Background of the History of Calif.," by Deputy Sheriff Ed Duran Ayres
MAY 30   "The Background of the History of Calif.," by Deputy Sheriff Ed Duran Ayres
JUN 6   "The Background of the History of Calif.," by Deputy Sheriff Ed Duran Ayres
JUL 4   "The Background of the History of Calif.," by Ed Duran Ayres
AUG 1   "The Background of the History of Calif.," by Ed Duran Ayres

SEP 12   "Open Forum Defends Alvarez & Moore Beware of Vultures," by
          Mrs. C.L.
          "Anti-Alien Hysteria Challenged"
NOV 21   "Rent Charged in Housing Projects," by U.S. Housing Authority
DEC 19   "Mexican Young Ladies Hold Annual Convention"

1941

MAY 1   "Alvarez and Moore Complete 20 years of Service"
          "Cinco De Mayo to be Celebrated by Many Here"
SEP 18   "Plea to Import 30,000 Mexicans Denied," Western states request
          to Immigration Service
NOV 13   "Father Gonzales Heads New Church at Beaudry"
DEC 11   "Olson Backs Boys Town for Negroes"

1942

FEB 12   "L.A. County Has 1172 Jap Farms"
JUL 30   "Imported Mexicans Must Be Assured Repatriation"

EASTSIDE SUN

1945
DEC 10   First issue, nothing on Chicanos

1946
APR 29   "Carmen Estrada, Raul Sanchez To Wed May 5"
JUL 1   "L.A. Mexicans Honor Heroes"
JUL 22   "Local Boys Make Good"
AUG 23   "Field Workers Carry Good Identification"
DEC 6   "Americans of Mexican Descent, Who Died in World War II, to
          Have Memorial at Indiana and Brooklyn"

1947
MAR 14   "Local Army Office Recruits 13 Youths"
APR 04   "Martinez Fights in Youth Group Tilt at Olympic"
JUN 6   "Torres, Lopez, Escalante, Lewis, Win Awards"
JUN 13   "Aliso Village Council Calls John Gonzales"
JUL 4   "Oil Drilling In Boyle Hights [sic] Decision Due July 29"
JUL 11   "Aliso Village Council Declares 'No Forced Transfers,' " by Milton
          Shields
JUL 25   "Families In Low Rent Projects With 'Excess Income' Will Not Be
          Forced to Move," by Milton Shields
AUG 15   "Olympic Auditorium Censored for Prejudice"
AUG 22   "Fiesta Given by Mexican-American Civil Rights Group"
SEP 5   "Richard Ibanez," on Legal Aid Clinic sponsored by Progressive
          Citizens of America
SEP 19   "Hollywood Arms Against Investigation"
NOV 7   "Latin American War Heroes To Be Honored at the 'Monument' "
          "Eastside Supporters of the IPP to Hold Important Meet"
NOV 14   "Independent Progressive Party Is Launched This Week in
          Eastside"
NOV 21   "Mexican Tipica Band Presents Concert Sunday"
          "Independent Progressives Get Closer to Place on California
          Ballot"
NOV 28   "Petition Effort Goes Into High Gear for IPP," Headquarters of
          Jewish People's Fraternal Order, City Terrace Division
DEC 12   "Mass Rally at Shrine to Stress IPP Theme 'We've Got a Date in
          '48' "

1948
JAN 9   "Cuadra Joins Up To Cut Down Living Costs"
JAN 16   "Carillo [sic] Wants to Further Medical Education"

JAN 23   "New Campus of ELAJC to Open Thurs., Jan 29"
JAN 29   "Annual Inter-Project Council Meeting Held"
          "Rev. Father Luis Vasquez Gets Honor for Youth Work"
FEB 6   "Roosevelt High School Holds Graduation"
FEB 13   "Calderon, Garcia, Navarro, Gonzales Join U.P."
MAR 19   "Art Quesada Is First Catholic Youth Group Entry in Boxing Fest"
          "Eviction Threat Not Ignored By Senate"
MAR 26   "Jose Ramon Chavez Woos IPP Support"
APR 2   "Investigation of Salcido Shooting Is Demanded"
APR 9   "Fight to Avenge Shooting"
APR 23   "Investigation Asked By Local Councilmen of District 44"
APR 30   "Community Leaders Support Civil Rights Congress in
              Condemning Editorial" in the Los Angeles Times, April 14,
              1948.
MAY 7   "Ibanez Deplores Salcido Case Mishandling"
          "Latin American Youth Meet"
MAY 14   "Ibanez For Judge Dance Tonight"
MAY 21   "Chavez Deplores Substitute For Mundt-Nixon Bill"
          "10,000 People to Attend Ibanez Rally Sunday"
MAY 28   "Lopez Says to Vote for Ibanez"
          "Jose Chavez Victory Urged"
JUN 11   "Chavez Still Very Much In Evidence"
JUL 23   "Chavez, Berman Receive High IPP Offices"
          "AJC Requests Action in Salcido Killing"
AUG 13   "Latin American Colony to Hold 'Black and White' Ball"
AUG 20   "La Reina Churubusco Will Rule 'Black and White' Ball"
OCT 1   "Rally to Protest 'Smear' Tactics of Inquisitors"
OCT 8   "Housing Called Principal ELA Health Problem"
OCT 15   "Chavez Discusses Loyalty Check"
DEC 22   "Pancho Gonzales Enters Local Net Tourney"

1949

JAN 11   "Homage and Honor Paid Luzon Hero"
MAR 4   "Nab Addicts as Robber $1000 in Heroin Located"
MAR 18   "IPP Announces Support for Candidate Roybal"
APR 1   "Roybal Favors Police Reform"
APR 8   "Mass Rally for Protest of Jail Without Bail"
MAY 12   "Roybal Demands Action on Public Library . . ."
MAY 19   "Roybal Names Committee to Spur Campaign"
MAY 26   "Mexican Folk Suffering Attack, Says A. Luna," on immigration
              raids
JUN 2   "Roybal Elected Councilman Overwhelming Christensen with
              Almost 2 to 1 Margin in 9th District"
JUN 16   "Eastside Gang Problems," by Joseph Eli Kovner
          "14 Attack Pair With Tire Irons"
JUL 7   "Civic Leaders Attend Police Meet," by Joseph Eli Kovner
JUL 14   "Mass Rally to Be Held Tuesday," on Civil Rights Congress

AUG 18   "Eastside Slums Redevelopment Seen in $100,000,000"
         "FEPC Law Is Topic of Meet Friday"
SEP 15   "Mexican-Americans Celebrate 'Fiesta of Freedom' Sept. 16–18"
SEP 22   "Bravo Scholarship Winner Revealed"
SEP 29   "Late Flash!" City Council rejects FEPC bill 8-to-6
OCT 6   "Roybal Gives Info on New Clubhouse"
OCT 13   "Labor Youth Group Meets On First St"
OCT 20   "Mexican-American National Association Will Hold Founding
         Convention Today"
OCT 27   "Over a Hundred Delegates for Mexican-American National
         Association"
NOV 17   "Roybal Battles for Rezoning of Juvenile Hall"
NOV 21   "Roybal Wins in Move to Find Site for Hall"

1950

JAN 5   "May Co. Asked to End Discrimination in Hiring Mex., Negro,
         Jap.-Americans"
         "Mexican-American National Assoc. to Convene Here"
JAN 19   "Latin-American Voters League to Hold Dance"
JAN 26   "Urge Spanish Speakers to Apply for Fellowship"
FEB 9   "Leo Carrillo Kicks Off YMCA Drive"
FEB 16   "Carlotta Bass Heads Delegates to Chicago," on IPP La Asociacion
         Nacional Mexico Americana
MAR 9   "Open Letter to the Honorable Board of Supervisors"
MAR 30   "Roybal Spurs Drive for Free Medical Care"
APR 13   "Interim Committee on Crime and Correction to Conduct
         Inquiry," on sheriff's department brutality
         "CSO Gets CIO Council Backing"
APR 20   "Minority Groups Intimidation Hit," on Sheriff's Foreign Relations
         Bureau
         "Roybal Speaks at Old Fashioned Election Rally," sponsored by the
         IPP
APR 27   "Roybal Officiates at Evergreen Playground Re-Opening Tonight"
MAY 11   "Larry Simmons, Richard Ibanez Speak Tonight"
MAY 18   "Yanez Asks For Volunteers"
         "Who Are the Wolf Packs?" by Bertha Marshall, on gangs
         "Demos Open Eastside Headquarters"
MAY 22   "Contrast Between Headlines and Facts in Regard to 'Rat Packs',"
         by Joseph Eli Kovner
JUL 27   "Councilman Roybal Hits Communists"
         "Progressive Party Takes Stand on Korea"
         "Crisis in Korea Raises Eastside Recruitments"
AUG 17   "Roybal Speaks As Local Zionists Pledge Tractor"
AUG 31   "Roybal, Aries, Other Notables Attend CSO Fete"
         "Latin Colony's Black and White Ball Due Sunday"
SEP 14   "Ed Roybal Merits 'Badge of Courage'," by Joseph Eli Kovner
OCT 5   "Eastside Notebook," on Margarita Duran

"Walter Wanger, Movie Stars Joan Bennett and Ronald Reagan to Appear Here Tonight," on CSO among sponsors

OCT 12 "Pulpiteer Jose Morales Stills Draws Throngs," on Mexico's Billy Graham

OCT 19 "Order Study of 'Red' Law Court Upset"
"[Carey] McWilliams to Appear at Soto-Michigan"

OCT 26 "Testimonial Dinner to be Held for Roybal"
"Nate Cisneros Represents ELAJC at Confab"

NOV 9 "Local Community Service Organizations Need Funds"

NOV 16 "Los Angeles Police Heroes to be Honored"
"Friends of Beatrice Griffith, Author of 'Americans We,' Hold Benefit at Joy and Jewel"

NOV 23 "Community Service Organization Leads Fight for Improved Conditions in Eastside"
"Roybal Given Honors by Forthnight"

NOV 30 "23 Lawsuits Filed Against Rent Boosts"
"United Nations Inter-Cultural Programs at Soto-Michigan is Talk of Eastside"

DEC 28 "Rent Control Rally to be Held Tonight"
"Eastside Notebook," by Joseph Kovner

1951

JAN 4 "Fight For Rent Curb Restoration," on Eastside Committee to Keep Rent Control
"The Case Against Rent Gouging," by Joseph Eli Kovner

JAN 11 "Annexation of 33 Acres by Monterey Park Also Scored at Mass Meeting," by Joseph Eli Kovner

JAN 18 "Tenants Group to Rally at City Hall"

JAN 25 "Wynerwood Owner Jaffe Hit by IPP" Harry Jaffe paid $5 million for real estate, restricted renting
"Mexican-National Committee, IPP, Aliso Tenants Council, Join in Big Registration Drive"

FEB 1 "Bill Phillips Elected to Head Citizens Committee to Re-Elect Roybal"

FEB 8 "Citizens Committee to Re-elect Roybal to Hold Kickoff Banquet; Dr. Robinson, NAACP Head to MC"
"Roybal Acts to Prevent Hollenbeck Park Lake Drownings"
"Pan-American Panorama," by John F. Méndez (weekly column that is not always cited)

FEB 15 "Jack Y. Berman to Be Keynote Speaker at Roybal Dinner"

FEB 22 "Roybal Dinner Huge Success as Crowd Promises Support"

MAR 8 "Roybal Shares Spotlight with Ann Sheridan, Kenny Washington, Dr. Shelter, in JDA Banquet"

MAR 29 "Pan-American Panorama," by John F. Méndez, on Roybal's work for better police relations

APR 5 "Councilman Whips Foe 3 to 1; In By Mandate," by Joseph Eli Kovner

MAY 17   "Pan-American Panorama," by John F. Méndez, on removal of
              homeowners from Chávez Ravine for new federal housing
MAY 31   "American Council of Spanish Speaking People"
              "New Spanish Speaking Group Formed in Texas"
              "Pan-American Panorama," by John F. Méndez, on American
              Council of Spanish Speaking People
JUN 28   "Roybal Leads Eastside Civic Group Battle to Victory for Aliso
              Village Extension"
              "Pan-American Panorama," by John F. Méndez, on his annoyance
              that some Mexicans speak Spanish loudly in streetcars
JUL 12   "El Sereno Defense Group To Give Dance"
              "Local Opening of A.N.M.A. Set for July 28"
JUL 19   "Our Councilman Speaks," by Edward R. Roybal
JUL 26   "Grand Opening of ANMA Set for Saturday"
              "Our 9th District Councilman Speaks," by Edward R. Roybal
AUG 2   "Pan-American Panorama," John F. Méndez, on speed burner Eddie
              Sanchez with the Washington Redskins for six years
AUG 6   "Ray Hernandez Is Awarded Silver Star"
              "Pan-American Panorama," by John F. Méndez, on American
              Council of Spanish Speaking People
              "Big Mexican Holiday Plans Jell for ANMA"
AUG 9   "New Eastside Headquarters of ANMA to Observe Sept. Sixteenth,
              Mexican Holiday"
AUG 23   "Baltazar Yanez Appointed Aide to District Attorney by Mark
              Keats"
AUG 30   "Our City," by Edward R. Roybal
OCT 11   "Councilman Roybal, Mel Janapol to Speak at Cost of Living
              Conference at Roosevelt High"
OCT 25   "Catholic Youth Organization Settlement Houses and Center to
              Observe National CYO Week"
NOV 29   "New Spanish Speaking Group Makes Strides," on American
              Council of Spanish Speaking People
DEC 13   "Alleged Police Brutality Aired By Board"
              "ANMA Anounces Inaugural Banquet"

1952

JAN 17   "Bodies of Three More ELA Heroes Back from Korean War"
JAN 31   "Mexican-American Assn. to Help Bayard Miners"
FEB 7   "CSO Midwinter Ball Attracts Huge Throng"
              "CSO to Back Rios Fight to Clear Name"
              "Roybal Speaks at Hollenbeck Council Meeting"
MAR 6   "Ponce Will File in Race for Assembly"
              "Councilman Ed Roybal Speaks," on Tony Ríos case
MAR 13   "Civic Leaders (Tony) Rios, (Alfredo) Ulloa Not Guilty"
              "Nacional-Mexico Americano [sic] Fights Deportation Move"
              "Belvedere Citizens Hear Civic Reports at CSO Meet"
APR 10   "Candidates Will Meet With CSO"

1953

APR 9   "Pan-American Panorama," by John F. Méndez, on different labels: Mexican-American, Mexican, Latin American, American of Mexican ancestry

MAY 25 "CSO Urges Age Aid to Aliens," by Joseph Eli Kovner

JUN 4   "Hope Mendoza Gets Immigration Job Appointment," on Congressman Chet Holified and hardships caused by the Walter-McCarran Act

"CSO Lose [sic] Fight for Old Age Assistance—But Starts New Battle"

JUN 11 "Plans Jell In Jobs for Junior Program, Says Louis Diaz"

JUN 18 "Let's Get the Story Straight," by Ralph Guzmán

JUN 25 "Scapegoats East of the River," by Ralph Guzmán

JUL 2   "75 Spanish Speaking Aliens to Be Given Citizenship Classes by CSO in Three Eastside Locations"

JUL 16 Ralph Guzmán on homeless Mexican children

JUL 23 "Elders Citizenship Opportunity," by Ralph Guzmán

JUL 30 "Front Line GI Faces Deportation," by Ralph Guzmán

AUG 6   "Drum Beaters Drown Out School Teacher," by Ralph Guzmán

AUG 13 "No Action Taken on Walter-McCarran Act"

Ralph Guzmán on the Walter-McCarran Act

"Mexican University Professor to Discuss Spanish Influence on Mexican Culture with Local Group"

AUG 27 "Plight of Hungry Wetbacks Told," by Ralph Guzmán

SEP 3   "Hunger Drives Wetbacks Into U.S.," by Ralph Guzmán

"POW Won't Talk," on Sgt. Henry Conteras

SEP 10 "El Cura Hidalgo," by Ralph Guzmán

SEP 17 "Assault, Battery Suits Brought by Community Service Group and CLU Against Sheriff"

SEP 24 "Law and Order Through Brutality?" by R. Cortez Guzmán

"Political Virgins and the Body Politics"

OCT 1   "Route Would Slash Through Residential and Business Districts; Protests Mount," by Joseph Eli Kovner, on $32 million Golden State Freeway

"The Eastside and Police Brutality," by R. Cortez Guzmán

OCT 8   "Anti-Golden State Freeway Sentiment Mounts," by Joseph Eli Kovner

"Senora de Millan Dies: Ambition Unfulfilled," by R. Cortez Guzmán

OCT 15 "Ojinaga, Chihuahua and Wetbacks," by R. Cortez Guzmán

OCT 22 "Catholic Labor School Opens Classes Here"

"Eastside Residents to Protest Freeway at Nov. 6 Rally"

"Eastside Responds to Help Pleas," by Ralph Guzmán

OCT 29 "Dr. [R. J.] Carreon, Jr. Appointed Civil Defense Head"

"The Reactionary Neanderthal Influence," by R. Cortez Guzmán

"Let's Talk About Here," by Joseph Eli Kovner

NOV 5   "Eastside Vet Council to present Flag to Be Flown at Memorial to Mexican-American War Dead"

"Pertinent Facts on CSO Citizenship Classes in Spanish," by
    Joseph Eli Kovner
"Re-Awakened Desires," by R. Cortez Guzmán, on politics
NOV 12 Joseph Eli Kovner editorial on the Golden State Freeway
"The White Man's Way . . . ," by R. Cortez Guzmán, on the death
    of Native American war hero Ira Hayes
NOV 19 "Juvenile Delinquency Investigation," by R. Cortez Guzmán, on
    newspaper hysteria
NOV 24 "Officer Julio Gonzales Transfers as Liaison Between Police Dept.-
    Spanish Speaking Communities"
DEC 3   "Mass Rally Against Freeway December 10 at 2nd St. School:
    Boyle-Hollenbeck Shall Not be Divided is Committee's
    Cry," by Dan Kohn
"United We Stand, Divided We Fall," by Joseph Eli Kovner
"Juvenile Delinquency Major Civic Headache," by R. Cortez
    Guzmán
DEC 10 "2nd Street School Meet Tonight to Fight Freeway"
Ralph Guzmán, on yellow journalism
DEC 17 Ralph Guzmán, on the press and police reaction to Mexican youth
"More Deputies Added to ELA Crime Patrol"
Letter from Mel Janapol supporting the Roybal staff condemnation
    of the press's encouragement of police and public physical
    assault on Mexican American youth
Letter from Edward R. Roybal commending Chief William Parker
    and Capt. James Glavas
"Eastsiders Jam State Freeway Hearings; To Check Alternatives,"
    by Dan Kohn
DEC 24 Ralph Guzmán
"Wolfhounds Fight Juvenile Delinquency," by Ralph Guzmán
DEC 29 "CSO New Year's Ball Promises to be Gala Event of Season"
"Salinas Forms New CSO Unit"
Ralph Guzmán, on the year that passed

1954

JAN 7   Ralph Guzmán, on newspaper agitation
JAN 14 Ralph Guzmán, on sheriff department's tactics
JAN 21 "Ed Roybal May Run for Lt. Governor"
"George Gonzales Wins Presidency of Wolfhounds"
JAN 28 Ralph Guzmán on braceros
FEB 4   "Who is Ralph Guzmán?"
Letter from Rogelio Avila on Guzmán article
FEB 11 "Estrada Courts Open Here"
"Councilman Edward Roybal is Democrats' Choice for Lieutenant
    Governor of California," by Joseph Eli Kovner
FEB 18 "Dickie and Adolfo Garcia to Be Honored by Mexican Chamber of
    Commerce at Statler Hotel"

Ralph Guzmán, on bracero and undocumented workers

"Trade Unions," on the Walter-McCarran Act

FEB 25   "Mexican Vote Holds New Political Power"

MAR 4   "Alvarado Enters 40th District Assembly Race," on Raymund D. Alvarado, Republican Candidate

Ralph Guzmán on braceros and "Wetback Invasion"

MAR 11   "Roybal Rally Set Soon for Joy Theatre"

MAR 18   "Roybal Rally Wednesday at Joy Theatre"

"Holifield Opposed to Bracero Bill and Lower Wage Level"

MAR 25   "Grass-Roots Group [CSO] Holds 1st Nat'l Confab," by Ralph Guzmán

"359 Grads of Citizens Training Classes Here"

"CSO Chapters Mobilize Drive for New Voters"

John Méndez on U.S. Congress giving the President power to recruit Mexican farm workers unilaterally

APR 1   "A Message From Louis Diaz"

APR 8   John Méndez asks for support for Roybal

APR 22   "Planning Meet for Ed Roybal Coalition Called"

MAY 6   "Juan Chacon to Appear at American Hall"

MAY 13   "CSO Candidate Nites Slated May 19, June 2"

"Sacramento, Here He Comes," by Joseph Eli Kovner

"Noted Politico, Jose Chavez, Backs Debs"

"PanAmerican Panorama," by John Méndez, on theme that Mexicans are legally White

MAY 20   "Roybal Dinner May 25 at Swally's"

"Debs, Roybal Honored by 400 in Railroad Rally"

"Gold Star Mothers to Be Honored Memorial Day at Mexican-American Monument, Lorena & Brooklyn"

May 27   "Kovner MC's GOP-Demo Coalition at Swally's; Many Candidates Speak"

"Ernest Debs, Ed Roybal Land Anti-Segregation Law in City Council"

"Memorial Day Rites to Be Held Sun. at Mexican-American Monument," by Andy Valencia

JUN 10   "Roybal, Graves, Yorty, Richards, Holifield & Elliot Look Good for Nov. Election Run-off," by Joseph Eli Kovner

JUN 17   "Pan-American Panorama," by John F. Méndez

JUN 24   "LA Youth, 18, Held in Street Slaying"

"Police Quiz Eight in Youth Dance Slaying"

"Pan-American Panorama," John F. Méndez on undocumented workers

JUL 1   "Eduardo Roybal Triunfara en Noviembre," by Ray Mora

JUL 8   "Pan-American Panorama," by John F. Méndez

JUL 27   "Importantes Convenciones Del Partido Democrata," by Ray Mora

AUG 26   "FEPC Through Democratic Party," by Ray Mora

SEP 16   "Expect 10,000 to Attend Mexican Fiesta"

"Youth for Roybal to Hold Rally Sept. 23"

SEP 23   "Roybal Proposes Help for Overtaxed School Districts"
          "Richard Graves Acclaimed at Parade," by Ray Mora
OCT 14   "Demo Victory Means Better California-Mexico Relations," by Ray
          Mora
OCT 21   "Democrats United—GOP Split," by Ray Mora
          Numerous articles endorsing Roybal appear
NOV 11   "Eastside Panorama," by John F. Méndez
DEC 22   "An Open Letter to the Eastside," by Ray Mora

1955

JAN 6   "Star Miler Slain," on Armando F. Castro, 19
JAN 13   "Castro Memorial"
          "Politics," by Ray Mora, on Committee For An Improved School
          Board
JAN 20   "Castro Fund Set Up to Aid Students"
          "Politics," by Ray Mora
          "Gil Anaya on TV; Expresses CSO Aims"
JAN 27   "Politics," by Ray Mora
FEB 10   "School Segregation of Mexican-American Children in El Centro,
          [Calif.] Schools Challenged in U.S. District Court"
FEB 17   "Roybal Announces Sidewalks to Be Built on Marengo Street"
FEB 24   "Garcia Opens Vigorous School Board Campaign"
          "FEPC and Community Aid, CSO Aim"
MAR 3   "Politics," by Ray Mora
MAR 10   "Golden State Freeway Fight Lost, Roybal in Lone Dissent.
          Sun's Crusade Junked As 'Truck' Freeway Approved"
MAR 17   "Garcia Wants Federal Aid in Classroom . . ."
          "Politics," by Ray Mora
          "CSO 2nd National Convention Approves New Constitution"
MAR 24   "Glass Assumes Leadership of Eastside Business Men to Elect
          Plutarco Garcia"
MAR 31   "Castro Dance to Feature Les Brown"
          "Politics," by Ray Mora
APR 7   "Bill to End Insurance Discrimination Passes Legislature"
          "Politics," by Ray Mora
          "Eastside Panorama," by John F. Méndez, on conference on
          educational problems of Mexican American students held at
          UCLA
APR 14   "Politics," by Ray Mora
APR 21   "Armando Castro Memorial Shrine"
          "Politics," by Ray Mora
          "Armando Castro Memorial Shrine Dance Success"
APR 28   "Roybal Speaks For Minimum Wage," by Joseph Eli Kovner
          "Politics," by Ray Mora
MAY 5   "CSO to Hold FEPC Planning Meet Here"
          "Politics," by Ray Mora
          "A Message from Garcia to the Community"

MAY 12 "Construction of College Begins," on Los Angeles State College
"Politics," by Ray Mora
MAY 19 "Welcome to Friendship Festival Sunday," 25,000 attend
MAY 26 "Politics," by Ray Mora
"Eastside Panorama," by John F. Méndez, on California FEPC bill
to state senate
JUN 2 "State Senate Committee Blocks F.E.P.C."
JUN 23 "Community Service Organization Honored"
"Councilman Ed Roybal Presented with Children Service Award"
JUL 14 "Pauline Holguin Is Executive CSO Secretary"
AUG 4 "Ray Mora Elected Chairman of 19th CDC"
"GOP Views from the 40th AD," by Raimund D. Alvarado
AUG 18 "CSO Moves Into New Quarters"
"GOP Views from the 40th AD," by Raimund D. Alvarado
AUG 25 "GOP Views from the 40th AD," by Raimund D. Alvarado
SEP 16 "Mexican Independence Day to Be Celebrated Here for Gigantic
Sept. 16 Parade"
SEP 29 "Speaker for CSO Is NAACP L.A. Prexy"
OCT 6 "Holifield, Roybal Disagree"
"Roybal Eyes Ford's Post"
OCT 20 "CSO to Offer Aid Class"
NOV 10 "Politics," by Ray Mora, on Walter-McCarran Act
DEC 1 "L.A. State College to Open in City Terrace Feb. 1, 1956"
DEC 8 "Mexican Welfare Committee Sponsored Benefit"
DEC 29 "Boyle Heights Strikes Oil Gusher Comes Up at Fourth and Breed
Streets"

1956

JAN 12 "Politics," by Ray Mora, on the Belvedere Democratic Club
FEB 2 "Roybal Announces Approval of Sketch of New Health Center"
FEB 9 "3000 Greet Adlai in ELA at Laguna"
"C.S.O. Assists 300 Aliens to Register"
"L.A. Sheriffs in $40,000 Brutality Suit"
FEB 16 "I Attend a Meeting Just Before Deadline . . . ," on zoning
FEB 23 "Local Demos Plan Own Early Endorsing Conclave"
"Politics," by Ray Mora
MAR 8 "Richards to Keynote Democratic Convention Here Sat. March 17"
MAR 22 "Politics," by Ray Mora
MAR 29 "Democratic Convention Held Here"
APR 12 "Panorama," by John F. Méndez, on Council of Mexican American
Affairs project to help dope addicts
"Report On Governor's Conference—April 4-5," by Robert L.
Mendoza, Chairman, Youth Employment Committee
"[Fernando de la Pena] Wins Castro Scholarship"
MAY 3 "Ida Lupino To Speak at CSO Annual Awards Dinner"
"Roybal, Elliot Speak at Lincoln"
MAY 10 "Armando Castro 'Scholar' Dance Shrine, May 26"
"Objectives of CMAA"

" 'Gangs to Clubs' Is Just One of Many Workshops Planned for
        'ELA Look Ahead' Confab"

MAY 17   "Council of Mexican-American Affairs Gives Housing Committee
        Reports to Eastsiders"

MAY 23   "Council of Mexican-American Affairs Housing Committee
        Reports," by Joseph Eli Kovner, on case studies of
        discrimination

JUN 28   "Politics," by Ray Mora, on Tony Ponce, candidate for Los
        Angeles County Democratic Central Committee

JUL 19   "CM & AA Seeks Funds"

JUL 26   "Ray Mora Re-elected Chairman 19th Cong. District Dem.
        Council"

AUG 9   "Federation of Spanish-American Voters Meet at Pontrellis Hall,"
        on Walter-McCarran Act and other discriminatory laws

AUG 16   "UCLA Housing Survey"

AUG 23   "Frank Guzman Addresses YDA Conclave at Chicago Democratic
        Convention"
        "Amaya, Casias Trial Focuses on Eastside"

SEP 6   "Ray Mora Appointed Chairman of 19th C.D. Richards Campaign"

SEP 13   "Mexican Independence Day Sept. 16 Parade to End at Belvedere
        Park"
        "Armando Castro Story on Du Pont Cavalcade"

SEP 20   "El Grito Echoes by 20,000 Open Mexico Freedom Fete"

SEP 27   "Galaxy of Star-Studded Talent to Appear at Community Service
        Org. Picnic Sunday"

OCT 4   "Roybal Seeks Answer to $64,000 Query"
        "Mora Appointed CD Chairman"

OCT 11   "Guzman Opens Four Forum Lecture Series on Walter-McCarran
        Act at Eastside Center"
        "Award Castro Fund"

OCT 18   "Serrato Warns Oil Production Must Be Upped," by John F.
        Méndez, on CSO

OCT 25   "Elliot to Speak at Carpenter's Hall"
        "CSO News Letter"

NOV 1   "CSO To Help Voters, Legal Advice, Rides"

NOV 8   John F. Méndez

NOV 15   "CSO Made Sure Hospitalized People Voted"

DEC 13   "New Health Center for This Area Now a Reality as Roybal, Debs,
        Aid in Ground Breaking Ceremony"
        "Eastside Committee for Better Civic Govt. to Hold Conference"
        "[John Anson] Ford Heads Advisory Group of CMAA"

DEC 20   "Southland Panorama," by John F. Méndez, on Mexican American
        population of Texas

1957

JAN 3   Joseph Eli Kovner, on destruction by freeways

JAN 10   "Guzman Gets High ACLU Post"

JAN 24   John F. Méndez on CMAA banquet
JAN 31   "Officers Elected for Community Organization; Rodriguez Prexy"
FEB 7   "Standout Personalities of Mexican-American Community to Be
             Honored at Banquet"
          John F. Méndez
FEB 21   "Castro Memorial Scholarship Fund Dance Soon"
FEB 28   "ELA Youth Council Has New Officers"
          "CSO Slates Discussion on Education"
          "GI Barrister, Gus Garcia to Speak Here"
MAR 7   "Cash Awards to Youngsters by Mexican-Amer. Affairs Council"
MAR 14   "Will Roybal Be Asked to Run for United States Senator?" by
             Joseph Eli Kovner, Part I
          "CSO News and Activities"
MAR 21   "Will Roybal Be Asked to Run for United States Senator?" by
             Joseph Eli Kovner, Part II
          "Roybal Campaign Advisors Named" for city council race
MAR 28   "Vote for Ed Roybal for Councilman in Ninth District"
          "Will Roybal Be Asked to Run For U.S. Senator?" by Joseph Eli
             Kovner, Part III
          "Third Annual Armando Castro Dance Underway"
          "Deportation Is Meeting Topic"
APR 4   "Variety Boys Club Stresses 'Juvenile Delinquency' as National
             Boys Club Week opens April 1 to 7"
APR 11   "3rd Annual Armando Castro Memorial Scholarship Dance," by
             Joseph Eli Kovner
APR 25   John F. Méndez on FEPC legislation
          "GI Forum"
MAY 2   John F. Méndez on CSO and free legal aid
          "G.I. Forum Meets to Discuss Mexican-American Representation
             in Althetic [sic] Commission"
MAY 9   "Frank Guzman Reports on Young Democrats Convention"
          "To Attend Boys Club Convention"
MAY 16   "Roybal Named Head of Eastside [Mary] Tinglof Group"
JUN 20   "Armando Castro Fund Story"
JUL 4   "CMAA to Hold Installation and Dinner"
JUL 18   "County FEPC Ordinance Urged"
          "GI Forum Circulates Petition"
JUL 25   "Tobias Navarrette Case," by Joseph Eli Kovner
          "Seek to Avert Closure of Utah Health and Welfare Services in the
             Eastside"
AUG 1   "The Tobias Navarrette Case: U.S. Justice Department, Board of
             Immigration Appeals," by Joseph Eli Kovner
AUG 8   "CSO Launches New Campaign," on Saul Alinsky, Fred Ross, and
             César Chávez
          "The Tobias Navarrette Case, U.S. Department of Justice, Board of
             Immigration Appeals, May 1957," by Joseph Eli Kovner
AUG 15   "The Tobias Navarrette Case," by Joseph Eli Kovner
          "CSO Holds House Meets"

1958

MAY 8   "Boyle Heights Urban Renewal Group Exposed," by Joseph Eli
                Kovner
            "Powers of Government as It Demands Property Owner Sell in
                Following Letter," by Harold Ermsheer, business agent,
                College of Medical Evangelists
            Letters to the editor, critical of White Memorial
            "GI Forum to Hold Night for Candidates"
MAY 15   Joseph Eli Kovner continues to condemn hospital land grabs
            "Courageous Statesman Is With Us"
            "Urban Plan Opposition Reported"
MAY 22   Joseph Eli Kovner on Dr. Leland J. Fuller
            "Law Against Urban Renewal Scheme Here"
JUN 5   "Is There a Hospital Town in Boyle Heights' Future?" by Joseph
                Eli Kovner
            "Holifield, Elliot to Leppek, Law in Elections," on Edward R.
                Roybal versus Ernest E. Debs in November
            "White Memorial Claims No Ties With Renewal"
            "GI Forum Convention Is Big Success"
JUN 12   "Proclamation of the Property Owners Committee for the
                Preservation of Boyle Heights," by Joseph Eli Kovner
            "Sears, Roebuck & Co. Is Talking About You in Boyle Heights!"
            "Without Comment I Give You a Letter to Sears Executives"
JUN 26   "Who's Behind Urban Renewal?" by Joseph Eli Kovner
JUL 3   "What's the Matter, Your Honor, Is It a Crime to Have Lower
                Income?" by Joseph Eli Kovner
JUL 10   "Who's Behind Urban Renewal?" on Mayor Norris Poulson's radio
                speech
            "Tony Rios Is New CSO President"
JUL 17   "Mayor Poulson For Urban Renewal," by Joseph Eli Kovner
            "GI Forum Will Be In L.A. in '59"
JUL 24   "An Observer Writes About Urban Renewal," by Joseph Eli Kovner
            "People in Slums," by Timothy G. Turner
            Ray Mora on Chávez Ravine
JUL 31   "I Need an IBM Machine," by Joseph Eli Kovner
            "Urban Renewal," by Joseph Eli Kovner
            "A Letter Concerning Realignment of the San Bernardino Freeway"
            "MAEC Has 3d Banquet"
AUG 7   "Urban Renewal," by Joseph Eli Kovner
            "Voting Strength of Democratic Minority Grows"
            "GI Forum to Hold Picnic"
AUG 14   "Rundown Area Renewal Seen," by Joseph Eli Kovner
AUG 21   "GI Forum in State Aux. Meet"
AUG 28   "Junior Forum to Hold Discussion"
            "CMAA Makes $50 Grant"
SEP 4   "[Esteban] Torres Named 19th CD Coord. by Auto Workers"
            "Pomona Freeway Route 'Under Construction' "
SEP 11   "Sheriff Biscailuz to Preside Over Gala Independence Parade
                Through Belvedere"
            "GI Forum Begins Big Member Drive"

OCT 2   "Henry Lopez Gets Demo Support Here"
OCT 9   "Aide Quits in Bunker Hill Row"
OCT 16   "Assemblyman Elliot Proposes Eastside University Campus"
         "GI Forum to Fete Texas Senator Henry Gonzales"
OCT 23   "Local Property Owners Group Supports Roybal"
         "Councilman Roybal, Hank Lopez Join Against Proposition 18"
OCT 30   John F. Méndez on Tony Ponce backing Ernest Debs
         "Fanfare Fiesta to Be Given By and For Roybal Supporters"
NOV 20   "Look Into Irregularities in Supervisor Race"
         "Another Setback for Minorities in Bakersfield"
NOV 27   John F. Méndez on Henry Lopez losing by 18,000 votes
DEC 4   "Adopt Pomona Freeway Route"
         "Judge [Carlos] Teran to Speak at Awards Banquet"
         "Bunker Hill Legality Under Fire"
DEC 30   Joseph Eli Kovner on the Boyle Heights Urban Renewal Committee

1959

JAN 8   " 'Resettle Elsewhere,' Says Mayor, 'If You Don't Want Urban
             Renewal!' "
         "East Welfare Planning Council Is Tool of Mayor's Urban Renewal
             Committee . . . ," by Joseph Eli Kovner
         "Milt Nava Runs for Prexy of Mexican Chamber of Commerce"
         John F. Méndez on Tony Ponce, field deputy to Debs
JAN 15   "What Qualifications Does Russell Have to Conduct Survey?" by
             Joseph Eli Kovner
JAN 22   "Property Owners Decide to Send Letters to Halt Eastside Survey,"
             by Joseph Eli Kovner
JAN 29   "Councilman Points Need for New Study on Eastside Problems,"
             by Joseph Eli Kovner
         "Eastside Clubs, Organizations"
FEB 5   "Eastland Savings to Open on 1st St., Roybal President"
FEB 26   Letter from N.E. Surbaugh, Sears, Roebuck & Co., to Ralph E.
             Garcia
         "A Friendly Debate: Surbaugh of Sears, Roebuck & Co., vs. Kovner
             of Kovner Publications," by Joseph Eli Kovner
MAR 5   "Kovner to Speak on Ends of Urban Renewal at Euclid Heights
             Democrats, Public Invited"
         "Force vs. Freedom," by Joseph Eli Kovner
MAR 12   "FDR CITY! Must Boyle Heights Secede from LA to Evade Fate of
             Bunker Hill Community?" by Joseph Eli Kovner
         "Euclid Demo Club Hits Urban Renewal Abuse in Resolution"
         "Resolution on Immigration, the California Democratic Council,"
             on the Walter-McCarran Act
         "Brazen Politics Endangers Lives to Lost Property Taxes"
MAR 19   "Eastside YD's Attend Fresno Demo Confab"
         "John Anson Ford Backs School Slate"
         John F. Méndez

MAR 26 "Guidance Needed for Children Says Lucy Baca"
APR 9 "GI Forum Enters Five in Contest"
    "Variety Boys Club Here Has 5,000 Members, Director Diaz"
APR 16 "Senior Citizen Center to Be Built at Hollenbeck Park"
    "Jimmy Cruz Is Appointed to LA County Demos"
APR 23 " 'Young Land' Sponsored By GI Forum"
    " 'Smear Attacks' on Committee for Better Schools Backed by 'Hate-Peddlers' Says Frank Paz"
    "Comentando," by John F. Méndez
    John F. Méndez, Council for Mexican-American Affairs Dinner
APR 30 "Comentando," by John F. Méndez
MAY 7 "En Homenaje," by José Martinez, on *Cinco de Mayo*
MAY 14 "Calling All Democrats: Call to the Convention of the 40th A.D. Democratic Council"
    "Demo. Governor Appoints Local Residents"
    Joseph Eli Kovner on Arechiga family being bodily removed from Chávez Ravine
MAY 21 "Publicists Launch Castro Fund Dance Campaign," on Armando Castro
    "Whose Law Is It?"
JUN 11 "Shall E.L.A. Become City?"
JUN 18 "Kovner Reports Incorporation Move . . . See No Real Need to Make E.L.A. into City," by Joseph Eli Kovner
JUN 25 "The Mysterious Mr. English, the Bank of America and Thou," by Joseph Eli Kovner
JUL 2 "Dodgers Contract for Ravine Still Not Legit"
JUL 23 "Councilman Roybal Reports to Eastside Constituents"
JUL 30 "CSO Office Open Evenings"
    "Anatomy of a Steam Roller," Joseph Eli Kovner
AUG 6 Joseph Eli Kovner on incorporation
AUG 13 "Joaquin Peter Castillo E.L.A. Pioneer, Dies Had Distinguished Career"
    "Citizens Committee To Save Chavez," by Joseph Eli Kovner
AUG 20 "GI Forum Honors War Heroes Here"
AUG 27 "Name Change Refused by Dept. Public Works. Macy St. Will Not Be Changed to Brooklyn Ave."
    "Roybal Reports to Eastside"
SEP 10 "Pete Pitchess to Be Grand Marshall of Local Mexican Independence Parade"
OCT 15 "Star Studded GI Extravaganza at Carpenter's"
    "Ninth Councilmanic Report on Roybal"
OCT 29 "McCann Proposes 8 Areas for Urban Renewal"
    "GI Forum to Gird for Member's Drive"
    "Urban Renewal Examined," by Joseph Eli Kovner
NOV 5 "Urban Renewal Is Recertified"
NOV 23 "GI Forum to Hold 2nd Awards"
    "Roybal Votes Against 'Friends of Zoo' Nonprofit (?) Group"
    John F. Méndez on Dr. Paul Sheldon's report on dropouts

"Roybal to Welcome Alcor Family as 100,000th Family to Occupy
Housing Authority Units"

DEC 3   "White Memorial Hospital Seeks $300,000 Facility; Eastside Asked
to Help"

1960

JAN 7   "Roybal to Request Fund to Reimburse Whittier Track Work"

JAN 21   "Eastside Demos Invite Educator to Scan Alarming Dropout of
Mexican-American Collegians"

Joseph Eli Kovner on Congressman Chet Holifield

FEB 4   "Dodgers-Mexican Stars Baseball Game Studied by GI Forum"

"Groups Assail Language Used by Chief Parker in Speaking of
'Wild Tribes of Mexico,' " by Joseph Eli Kovner

FEB 11   "Chief Parker Criticized in Protest Meeting Held Sunday"

"Police Commissioner Carreon Says Name Used Without
Consent"

"The Bulldozers Are Coming Confiscations under Urban Renewal,"
by Joseph Eli Kovner

FEB 25   "CDC Holds Second Issues Conference in Fresno, California"

MAR 10   "Roybal Comments on Crime Reports of East Los Angeles"

MAR 17   "PanAmerican Panorama," by John F. Méndez, on campaign to
keep Mexican-Americans in school

APR 3   "Northeast Health Center Has Bi-lingual Phone"

APR 28   "Roybal Is State Chairman of MAPA"

MAY 12   "Los Angeles GI Forum Hosted State Controller Cranston Monday
Night"

MAY 15   "Henry Lopez Talks on School 'Drop Outs' at CFE"

JUN 9   "Urban Renewal Evil Exposed"

"Sixth Armando Castro Dance"

JUN 12   "Judge Walshock Defeated by [Leopoldo] Sanchez in Primary"

JUN 16   "Roybal Addresses Brooklyn CC on Urban Renewal Problems"

"Police Maltreatment Subject of Conference at Biltmore Hotel"

JUN 19   "Roybal Announces Issuance of Mexican Commemorative Stamps"

"Population Figures Means Reapportionment"

AUG 25   "New Group to Aid Gov. on Mexican-American Problems," on
formation of Mexican American Political Association

"Viva Kennedy Clubs Open Headquarters on E. First St."

SEP 18   "Over 100,000 Mexican-Americans Registered to Vote"

SEP 25   "Area-wide Banquet Given by Council Mexican-American"

SEP 28   "Kovner Attends Urban Renewal Luncheon with Many Other L.A.
Editors and Publishers"

OCT 6   "Dennis Chavez to Campaign in California for Viva Kennedy
Clubs"

OCT 13   "Councilman Edward Roybal Reports to Community"

OCT 20   "Leo Sanchez Honored at Cranston Meeting"

OCT 27   "Women Unite for Sanchez"

DEC 1   Joseph Eli Kovner
DEC 22   Joseph Eli Kovner on Bunker Hill

1961

JAN 5   "Projects to Keep Rapid Pace Here," on widening of the San
         Bernardino Freeway
JAN 12   "New Locale for GI Forum"
         "Paul Sheldon," by Joseph Eli Kovner
         "Councilman Edward R. Roybal Reports"
FEB 12   "Payan Files for Council," on incorporation
FEB 19   "9th District News Letter," by Edward R. Roybal
MAR 2   "Give Me Land . . . Lots of Land," by Joseph Eli Kovner
MAR 23   "Roybal Charges 'Redevelopment' Aim to Depress Property Values
         in East Los Angeles and Boyle Heights Area"
MAR 30   "Union Denies Bias; Opposes Incorporation"
         "Bands Set for Armando Castro Dance April 30"
         "More Groups Come Out for Roybal"
APR 2   "Roybal Endorsed by Eastside Sun; No Mayor Backing"
APR 9   "Castro [Scholarship] Fete Helps Local Students"
APR 16   "Incorporation Trap," letter by Robert M. Angier, Chair of the
         Committee for Public Morality
APR 20   "Let's Go Over Briefly the Danger of Incorporating ELA into City;
         Vote No!" by Joseph Eli Kovner
APR 23   "These Are the Issues Tues, April 25: ELA Incorporation—For or
         Against . . . Choice of 5 Council Candidates"
         "Eastside Sun ELA Council Recommendations"
APR 30   "Semi-Official Election Results"
MAY 4   " 'Cinco De Mayo' to Be Observed by East L.A. Mexican Colony
         Friday Evening"
         "[Felix] Ontiveros Appointed Noise Abatement Commissioner for
         the City of Los Angeles"
MAY 7   "MAPA to Hold State Confab"
MAY 11   "Unemployment Residents of East LA to Be Part of Gigantic
         Survey, Says McDowell of Local SDE"
MAY 18   "Eastside Youth Conference on Narcotics to Be Held Saturday at
         Roosevelt High"
MAY 25   "COPE Eastside Campaign Headquarters for Poulson in Final
         Mayoralty Drive"
         "About Reapportionment . . . ," by Assemblyman Edward Elliot
JUN 4   "Fighting Yorty Beats Out Mayor Poulson"
JUN 18   "Meeting Recommendations Aim at Alleviating Conditions
         Promoting Narcotics Addiction"
AUG 10   "Ask $50,000 for CMAA"
AUG 17   "MAPA Moves to Support Union in Lockout Fight"
AUG 24   "New Congressional Districts: Candidates Scramble for
         Congressional Seats," by Assemblyman Edward E. Elliott

SEP 28   "Richards Lauds M-A Community"
          "Career Incentive for Youth"
OCT 5   "Las Vegas Attorney John Mendoza to Address GI Forum at
              Reception-Dance"
          "Sanchez Gets Standing Ovation at Pat Brown Luncheon," by
              Joseph Eli Kovner
          "CMAA Labor Committee in Fund Drive"
          "Judge Sanchez Delivers Speech"
OCT 12   "Full Text of Speech by Judge Leo Sanchez at Gov. Brown
              Luncheon"
          "Safeway Stores Look Foreword![sic]"
OCT 19   "Judge Sanchez' Remarks Shocking to Resident," a letter by
              Reynaldo Ochoa
OCT 27   Letter from Robert Arambula to Reynaldo Ochoa
NOV 2   "Frank Paz to Run for Assembly in 48th District"
          "Judge Leo Sanchez Names Christmas Seal ELA Chairman"
          "Jesse Castillo Named Service Officer for Blinded Vets"
NOV 5   Joseph Eli Kovner
NOV 9   " 'Grass Roots' Discussion Heads for Citizens on Narcotics"
          "A Dispassionate Viewpoint," by Joseph Eli Kovner, on use of
              term "Mexican-American"
NOV 16   "[Arthur] Alarcon to Speak at Conference"
          "Brooklyn Chamber of Commerce Hears Dionicio Morales," by
              Joseph Eli Kovner
          "Loma Linda University to Expand in Eastside"
          "Narcotics Conference: Governor's Aide Listed as One of Main
              Speakers"
NOV 20   "CSO Hears from Texas"
NOV 30   "Will Lou Diaz Be Democratic Candidate for Secretary of State?"
              by Joseph Eli Kovner
          "Annual Guadalupe Procession Shows Strong ELA Devotion"
          "Group Fights Communism"
DEC 21   "Hollenbeck Police Station Plans Approval by Public Works Board"
          "Casa del Mexicano Is to Be Scene of Christmas Party for Over
              3000 Kids"

1962

JAN 11   "ELA-Belvedere Demo Club Plans Tardeada"
          "Diaz Considered for Key Posts"
JAN 25   "Jim Cruz and Linda Benitez, Active Leaders from 40th A.D. Hold
              Key Post at Fresno Confab"
          "[John] Moreno to Run for Assembly"
FEB 8   "Councilman Roybal Runs for Congress"
FEB 15   "Brooklyn Chamber of Commerce Starts Scholarship Fund. Coun-
              cilman Roybal, Felix Ontiveros, Al Nafero, Joe Kovner to Be
              'Trustees of Merchants' Our Philanthropic Project"
          "R. Poblano Is President of CMAA"

"[Tony] Bueno Officially Kicks Off Hot Campaign at Alexandria Hotel"

"CSO to Honor Elder Citizens"

"Candidates to Speak for ELA Democrats Sun"

FEB 22   "*Warning By Police Department*: Parents Responsible for Kids Defacing ES Buildings by Use of Spray Paint in Cans"

MAR 11   "Eastside Sun Endorses Ed Roybal for Congress at 30th CD Convention Today"

"Roybal Seeks Support of Delegates"

MAR 15   "Open House at Ed Roybal Headquarters"

MAR 22   "Moreno Leads List in Balloting for Assembly"

MAR 29   Letter from Francisco Bravo, M.D., Police Commissioner

APR 5   "*A CMAA Project*: Employment Problems Facing Mexican Americans Will Be Topic of Eight Workshops at Garfield"

"Judge Sanchez Urges Citizens Planning to Vote in Primary to Qualify before Aug. 12th"

"Frank Solis Files for Congress"

APR 26   "Brown to Be Honored by Spanish-Speaking Community: Testimonial Dinner Set for May 3rd at Breakfast Club"

"Spanish-Speaking Senior Citizens Can Learn What Governmental Services Are Available for Them"

MAY 3   "P.M. Garcia Manager of Campaign"

MAY 10   "MAPA Endorses Prop A, B, C"

"In 40th AD Dr. Bravo Endorses Antonio Bueno"

"CSO Honors Maria D. Lang"

MAY 17   "Rocket Roybal to Congress Dance to Be Held May 26"

MAY 24   "Endorses Roybal—New 30th District," by Joseph Eli Kovner

"Raul Morin and Wife, Ramona, Team Up to Run for Democratic Committee in 45th"

MAY 27   "Cranston Backs Roybal"

JUN 5   "[Tony] Bueno Issues Election Statement"

JUN 21   "5 out of 7 Kovner Publications Endorsed Candidates Make Democratic Central Committee"

JUN 28   "Bill Zazueta Heads Roosevelt Alumni Assoc."

JUL 12   "CMAA Annual Banquet to Honor Alarcon New Executive Secretary for Governor Brown"

JUL 19   "Jim Cruz Wins Top Demo Spot"

JUL 26   "Letter and Map Reveal Scheme of White Memorial Hospital Change or Neighbor to Obtain Mass Zoneing [sic] Homes"

"*100 Acre Site*: Council Ok's Prezone of ELA Area Property"

"Hazard," a poem by Joseph Eli Kovner

"Protesting Hazard Park Swap"

AUG 2   "Victory Won in Rezoning War with White Memorial Hospital"

"Petitions Submitted to the City Planning Commission at Hearing Held Monday, July 30, Room 361-A, at City Hall"

AUG 9   "Good Faith of White Memorial Questioned by Property Owners"

"Full Text of Rezoning Hearing of White Memorial at Meeting"

AUG 16   Joseph Eli Kovner

AUG 23 "Conclave Called to Embark on Long Range Planning Boyle
          Heights Property Owners Association"
        "Citizens Aroused by Freeway Right-of-way neglect"
AUG 26 "Richard Calderon Appointed by Roybal"
AUG 30 "Pontrellis Hall Jammed with Property Owners Intent on Holding
          on to Homes"
SEP 9   "City Hall Tuesday at 2 p.m."
SEP 13 "I Speak before LA City Council on Loma Linda University
          Rezoning"
OCT 4   "Returning LA Officers Riot School Need," on LAPD training of
          Dominican Republic police; anti-communist tactics
OCT 11 "Loma Linda Drops Plans for Expansion Here"
        "Mexican American Comm. Backs John Gibson Jr."
OCT 18 "Texas Congressman Henry Gonzales to Appear at Belvedere Park
          Saturday at 5 p.m.; Music Entertainment on Top"
        "[Cecilia] Pedroza Is PP Director"
OCT 25 "Joe Jimenez Candidate for Assembly 40th District Says Incumbent
          Here Infrequently"
        Joseph Eli Kovner on opening of ELA Halfway Home
NOV 1   "President Kennedy Endorses Edward Roybal for Congress"
NOV 15 "Roybal Thanks Citizens for Their Support"
        Joseph Eli Kovner on history of Boyle Heights
        "MAPA Deplores Election Misrepresentation"
        "Educationally Deprived"
NOV 18 "Joseph Anthony Garcia-Mijares III Creditable Rep for LAPD"
NOV 29 "William H. Workman Boyle Heights Pioneer . . . ," by Joseph Eli
          Kovner (continued)
        "Felix Ontiveros Files for 9th D. Council Seat"
DEC 6   "William H. Workman . . . Boyle Heights Pioneer," by Joseph Eli
          Kovner (continued)
        " 'Roshamon' " Drama at the Alexandria Hotel," by Joseph Eli
          Kovner
        "CSO Noticias"
DEC 13 "Against Yorty's Renewal Program"
        "For Yorty's Renewal Program"

1963

JAN 3   "Fernando Del Rio Spearheads Felix Ontiveros Drive for
          Councilman at Lorena St. Home"
        "Loma Linda Shares in Nursing Training Grant"
        Letter from Howard Willenberg on the Roybal seat
JAN 10 "[Robert] Baca Heads ELA Demos Club"
        "Gilbert Lindsay Files to Fill 9th CD Vacancy"
        "Ontiveros Files for 9th Council"
        Letter from George Mount, candidate for the 9th CD
JAN 17 "Delfino Varela, Shepherd to New Americans"

MAY 2   "Councilman Gilbert Lindsay Takes Strong Stand Against Urban
              Renewal"
           "Dick Tafoya Unalterably Opposed to Government Imposed Urban
              Renewal"
MAY 5   "Cinco de Mayo Dance to Be Held by MAPA"
MAY 23   "Roybal and Debs Endorse Richard Tafoya for City Council 9th
              District"
MAY 26   "*Lindsay's Deputy Helps Community*: Felix Ontiveros, J. Kovner
              Work for Progress"
MAY 30   "Lindsay Wins 9th CD Over Tafoya," by Joseph Eli Kovner
           "Eastside Area Gets Large Share of School Bond Issue"
JUN 6   "Debs Calls for Conference to Avert Spread of Racial Tensions;
              100 to Meet"
           "Top Bands Slated for Armando Castro Dance"
JUN 20   "$500,000 Grant for Experimental Project in ELA to Train Jobless
              Youth between Ages 16 and 21"
           "Jose Gastelum Free of Mexico Deportation"
JUN 27   "Jose Gastelum Vindicated"
JUN 30   "House Defeats 'Bracero' Program"
JUL 4   "Hazard Park Swap Opposed by 40th MAPA"
           "Al Perez Is Roosevelt High Alumni Prexy"
           "Hazard Park Must Not Be Swapped for Hospital!" by J.E.K.
JUL 11   "Hazard Park," by Joseph Eli Kovner
           "Civil Rights Meet by CSO at St. Mary's"
           Letters to editor giving the pros and cons of the Hazard Park swap
JUL 18   "Here's Lindsay's Stand on Hazard," by Joseph Eli Kovner
           "Here's Roybal's View on Hazard," by Joseph Eli Kovner
           "[Delfino] Varela Raps Ban on Bracero"
JUL 25   "Don't Let Them Take Hazard Park Away from Boyle Heights.
              Protest Land Grabs"
           "Commissioner Leonard Shane Is Against Hazard Park and Land
              Grab"
           "Dr. Francisco Bravo, Georgiana Hardy to Speak at VP Conclave"
AUG 1   "Joe Maldonado Named Head Youth Project"
AUG 8   "Mexican-American Community Educational Opportunities
              Conference to Be Held Aug. 9"
           Joseph Eli Kovner on Hazard Park
           "Wyman Urges Recreation Dept. to Consumate Proposed Trade
              with Hazard Park 'Land Deal' "
           Letter from Fernando del Río discussing Public Law 78
           "Johnson Meets Leaders"
AUG 15   "Lieutenant Dave Arroyo to Retire from Hollenbeck Div."
           Letter from William Frederickson, Jr. on proposed trade of land in
              Westwood area for Hazard Park
           "To: All Interested Residents of Boyle Heights," by Joseph Eli
              Kovner
AUG 29   "GI Forum Slates Seminar on Political Education"
SEP 5   "The Truth vs. Roberts Rules of Order," by Joseph Eli Kovner, on
              Hazard Park.

SEP 12   "Job Opportunies Program Established by Station KWKW"
SEP 19   "Ontiveros Suggests VA Hospital Be Built in Lincoln Hollow at
          Boyle Heights Meeting"
          "Temple Urban Renewal Project"
SEP 22   "Park Swap Problems Force Trip," on Hazard Park
SEP 26   " 'Not One Square Inch of Park Land Will Be Taken from the 9th
          Councilmanic District' Says Councilman Gilbert Lindsay,"
          by Joseph Eli Kovner
          "East L.A. Area Tries Again to Be City"
OCT 3   "East Los Angeles Project for Jobless Youth to Open"
          Joseph Eli Kovner on Hazard Park
OCT 10   "Hazard Park Stays in Boyle Heights," by Joseph Eli Kovner
          "CMAA to Present Annual Awards Dinner November 2"
OCT 24   "Ghouls of All Sizes Cavort at MAPA Halloween Party"
OCT 31   "Gonzalo Molina New Field Rep." to Edward Elliot
          Joseph Eli Kovner: Letter from J. J. Rodríguez, executive secretary
          of Butchers Local 563, Dave Fishman, Jr., Local 1348 of the
          Painters' Union, and Harold Dunne, president of Local 216
          of the United Auto Workers, to William Frederickson,
          director of Los Angeles City Parks and Recreation, on Hazard
          Park
NOV 7   "CSO's National Board to Meet at Santa Monica"
NOV 14   "Councilman Lindsay Wants Committee Formed to Prepare Policy
          on Urban Renewal to Avoid 'Mental Unrest' of Citizens"
NOV 21   "M.A.P.A. Elects Officers"
          "250 Mexican-American Youth Leaders at Confab"
DEC 5   "Homeowners Assn. Opens Drive for 500,000 Signatures to Kill
          BH Freeway Plan"
DEC 12   "Congressman Roybal Reports from Washington"
DEC 26   "Special Employment Problems of Mexican-American to hearing at
          ELAJC"

1964

JAN 2   "Mexican-American Employment Ratio Too Low, Says Debs"
JAN 9   "Special Employment Problems of Mexican-Americans to Hold
          Public Meeting at ELAC"
          Joseph Eli Kovner on urban renewal
JAN 16   "Mexican-Americans File 12% of All Unemployment Claims"
          "Maldonado Appointed Director YOB"
          "Rafael Vega, FEPC Member Speaks to Coordinating Council"
          Joseph Eli Kovner on the history of park development
JAN 23   "Cultural History of Mexican-American People a New Class at
          Roosevelt Adult School"
          "Cong. Joseph M. Montoya to Be Honored Sat., Feb. 1"
          "Los Democratos Promueven Una Conferencia En Los Derechos
          Minoritarios"
JAN 30   "Seguira La Lucha Contra La Discriminacion En Alojamientos"
          "MAPA Aids in Fight to Get Soto Traffic Signals"

FEB 6   "El Proyecto De Entrenamiento De Empleos De Los Jovenes" by
           Angelo Vasquez Basco
FEB 13   "George Saiki, Richard Hernandez Appointed as Mayor Yorty's
           New Administrative Assistants"
           "Juan Acevedo Elected as [Los Angeles chapter] GI Forum
           Chairman"
FEB 20   "ELA to See LBJ, Lopez Mateos"
           "Mexican-Americans to Present United Front at CDC," by Joseph
           Eli Kovner
           "Tafoya Appointed Supervisor of ELA Job Finding Staff"
           "Convencion De Democratas En Long Beach Llama La Atencion
           De ELA Comunidad," by Angelo Vasquez Basco
FEB 27   "Senior Citizens Dinner at Park Huge Success," on Club Latino
           Americano for Senior Citizens of Laguna Park
           "Felix Ontiveros, Rep. To Councilman Lindsay Warns of
           Condemnation of Homes in MI Zone"
           Joseph Eli Kovner on gerrymandering and the State Highway
           Commission
           "More Women in Politics"
           "Gonzalo Molina Elected to Chairmanship of the 30th Delegation
           to CDC"
MAR 5   "CMAA Presents Rumford Debate at Institute"
           "Consuelo Rodriguez Runs for 40th County Demo Central
           Committee"
           "Manuel Guerra MC for Quevedo Testimonial"
           "Is It Nationalistic to Support a Mexican-American in the 40th
           Assembly District in the Primary Election of 1964?"
           "Oportunidades En Puestos Electorales Para Mexico-Americanos,"
           by Angelo Vasquez Basco
MAR 12   "Luis R. Diaz Reappointed to CIW by Gov."
           "La Comunidad en Desfile," by Angelo Vasquez Basco
MAR 19   "Josefina Quezada Mexican Artist to Exhibit Here"
           "Ernie Sanchez of East L.A. Sets Example for School Dropouts"
           "$22,628,000 for Hazard Park Vet. Hospital"
           "Hazard Park Story," by Joseph Eli Kovner
APR 2   "Question of What Lies Ahead for Hazard Park Rec Facilities to Be
           Aired at Wabash-CT CC"
           "No Endorsement Is Decision of MAPA 40th"
           "Congressman Ed Roybal Reports From Washington"
           "Nueva Proteccion Para El Consumidor"
           "Opportunities Project Taps Hidden Potential of Boyle Heights and
           ELA Jobless Youth"
           Letter from George H. Mount supporting Al Song
APR 9   "MAPA Backs Ed. Ramirez, Geo. Brown"
           "[Frank] Solis Files for Judge in ELA District"
           "Counselor Cisneros Stresses Development of 'Whole Person' in
           Working with Jobless Youth"

"Cruz Named VC of County Demo Group"
Letter from Joseph Eli Kovner to Congressman Edward R. Roybal
JUL 30   "Roybal Charges Discrimination," by Ester Hansen
"Mexican Americans Lag in Jobs, Income, Schooling, According to
     FEPC Study"
"Special Opportunities for State Civil Service Jobs for Spanish
     Speaking Citizens"
AUG 13   "Governor Charges Supporters of Proposition 14 Seek to Wipe Out
     Equality of Housing in Calif."
"Ontiveros Battles to Save Victims of Home Condemnation"
AUG 20   "Sterilization in Failure to Provide Cases as a Violation of 8th
     Amend."
"J. J. Rodriguez Charges MCC of 'Profiteering in Bigotry' "
"J. Montenegro R. E. Broker Resigns MCC"
AUG 27   *Si-Se Puede . . .* " on FEPC Booklet
SEP 3   "Sterilization in a Penal Statute as Violation of the 8th
     Amendment," by Phil Silver
"No Racial Discrimination in Hwy. Patrol"
SEP 6   "Tobias Nararrette, E.L.A. Humanitarian, Is Dead," by George H.
     Mount
SEP 10   "ELA Pastor Greets LBJ"
SEP 14   "Roybal & Soto Leaders for Local Group Against No. 14"
SEP 24   "L.A. Policeman Suspended for Selling Political Literature While
     on Duty"
"Yorty Joins 'War on Poverty' "
"FEPC Report Indicates that Bank of America Makes Good
     Progress in Hiring Minorities"
OCT 1   "Battle Raging Over War on Poverty"
OCT 8   "ELA Job Training, Acosta Heads Project"
"Local Civic Leaders Head Spanish Speaking Californians
     Committee for President Johnson"
OCT 15   "Charter New ELA Bank"
OCT 22   "Ortega Elected Association V.P." of Los Angeles City Employees
     Association
OCT 29   "Disparity in Minority Hiring"
"Roybal Keynotes Student Meeting"
"Ontiveros Arranges Meet with Frederickson; Consider Problem of
     Playground Rehabilitation"
"Mexican-Amer. Gets U.S. Atty Appointment"
NOV 5   "Congressman Ed Roybal Wins . . ."
"J. J. Rodriguez Sworn In on Johnson's Employment Com."
NOV 12   "Lindsay, Ontiveros Help Local Chamber of Commerce Alleviate
     Hazards of Bad Intersection"
"Charge State Agencies with Discrimination"
NOV 19   "Tony Rios Says Bracero Plan Is 'Servitude' "
NOV 22   "Elliot Says Plans Made for State to Expedite Anti-Poverty
     Program"

FEB 18   "Calderon Criticizes Move of Employment Office on Job Referral
                Positions"
           Joseph Eli Kovner on the Los Angeles Welfare Planning Council
           "Youth Opportunities Board Adds Administrative Assistant"
           "Elliot Endorses Ralph Poblano"   ·
           "The Thought Provoker," by George H. Mount, on the Vietnam
                War
FEB 25   "Neighborhood Youth Corps Program Starts"
           "Mayor Yorty Can Stifle People's Appeal Rights," by Joseph Eli
                Kovner
           "Some Answers to Administrators' Questions on Minority Youth
                Council," by Ruth B. Love
           "Youth Opportunities Board Fills Three Top Positions"
           "The Thought Provoker," by George H. Mount, on the Vietnam
                War
MAR 4   "[Richard] Calderon Urges Independent Investigation"
           "IL & WU Give Endorsement to Calderon"
           "Elliot War on Poverty Bills Move in Legislature"
           "Fiesta for Poblano Set Here Sunday"
           "GI Forum Installs New Officers"
           "The Thought Provoker," by George H. Mount
MAR 11   "Elysian Park Must Be Saved for Recreation Area"
           "MAPA OK's R. Calderon for Council"
           "$22 Million VA Hospital Set," on Hazard Park
           "Roosevelt Offers Drop Out Program"
           Joseph Eli Kovner on eminent domain and freeways
           "The Thought Provoker," by George H. Mount
           "War on Poverty and 'How it can Be Waged Here' Is CSO Topic
                Sunday"
           "Labor Gives Calderon an Endorsement"
           "Keep Your Asphalt Out of Beautiful Elysian Park"
MAR 18   "The Thought Provoker," by George H. Mount
           "CLR Fetes Calderon"
           "Roybal Announces April Bid on Vets Hospital"
           "21 Aliso Village Women Gather to Invest in Future"
           "Dr. Guerra Resigns Race in Favor of Poblano"
           "County Plans Exhibit Center in Elysian Park"
           "Assemblyman Tom Carrell Introduces Bill Expunging Arrest
                Entries Where No Conviction Has Occurred: Backed by DA
                Evelle Younger"
           "Oral Interviews Should Be Re-evaluated . . . Calderon"
MAR 25   "Supreme Court Jurist Says 'Elysian Park Should Be Saved for
                Children in Years to Come' "
           "[Richard] Calderon Raps Lindsay on Elysian Park Giveaway"
           Joseph Eli Kovner endorses Ralph Poblano
           Letters on Elysian Park
           "The Thought Provoker," by George H. Mount
APR 1   "64 Youth Placed on Jobs by ELA YTEP"

"The Thought Provoker," by George H. Mount, on Calderón
  campaign workers pushing Mexican issue too hard
Joseph Eli Kovner endorses Sam Yorty for Mayor and Lindsay for
  the 9th Councilmanic District
"Gilbert H. Lindsay Has Government Experience Covering Over 30
  Years"
"Felix Gutierrez Elected Pres. at Cal State"
"Poblano Says Property Owner Carries Unfair Tax Load at Malabar
  St. School Rally"
"Elysian Park Convention Center: Nine Out of Thirteen
  Candidates for 13th District Council Opposed to Giveaway"
"Assemblyman Vincent Thomas Announces Support of Ralph
  Poblano in School Board Race"
"Authorization of Use of 2,900 Mexican National Farm Workers
  Requested of Secty. of Labor"
APR 4   "We Endorse Ralph Poblano"
APR 8   Joseph Eli Kovner accuses Rosalind Wyman of building political
  machine
"UCLA Offers Classes in Mexican-American Values"
"Third Annual Mexican-American Conference to be Held at Camp
  Hess Kramer April 9, 10, 11"
Letter from Citizens Committee to Save Elysian Park
"Report from Washington," by Edward R. Roybal
"The Thought Provoker," by George H. Mount
APR 15   "All Nation's Camp Selected for Mexican Amer. Leadership
  Camp"
Letter from Ralph Poblano thanking voters
"Describe Events at Youth Confab," by Esther Hansen
"The Thought Provoker," by George H. Mount
"GI Forum Endorses Dr. [Ernesto] Galarza"
APR 22   "Councilman Lindsay Announces Street Improvement Plans for
  Boyle Heights"
"The Thought Provoker," by George H. Mount
"GI Forum Installation Banquet"
APR 29   "The Thought Provoker," by George H. Mount
"Club Latino-Americano to Honor Mothers"
"Meeting of Hazard Group to Be Held"
MAY 6   " 'War on Poverty' Open Forum at Roosevelt High"
"Calderon Thanks Voters"
"Taxes, Discrimination, Jobs, Rate High in Congressman's Poll"
"The Thought Provoker," by George H. Mount
MAY 13   Letter from J. Patricio Sanchez, Mrs. Isabel Medrano, and Mr. N.
  Steelink on Hazard Park
"CSO Patio Party on Hubbard St."
"The Thought Provoker," by George H. Mount
MAY 20   "Anti-Poverty Program LA Youth Opportunities Board to Seek
  Massive Federal Grant"
"Brown Strives for Mexican-American Representation"

JUL 8   "Historic Sixth St. Bridge Is Marked for Demolition; to Build New
Pedestrian Crossing Soon"
"City Council Considers Joint Powers Agreement to Create EYOA
Coordinating Body"
"The Thought Provoker," by George H. Mount
"Mexican-Americans Honored," on California Association of
Educators of Mexican descent
"FEPC Service Established in ELA"
"Reapportionment Revolt," by Assemblyman Edward Elliot
"Congressman Ed Roybal Reports from Washington"

JUL 15   "NAPP Poverty Program Has Total Grass-Roots Approach"
"L.A. Community Service Organization Honors Members
Appointed to FEPC and State Industrial Welfare
Commission"
"Conciliation Big Factor in FEPC Role"

JUL 22   "William Acosta, YTEP Manager to Resign Post"
"Drive to Hire 37,000 Mexican-Americans by Farm Labor Serv."
"Frontal Attack on Problems of Children and Adults Who Have
English-Speaking Difficulty"

JUL 29   "Councilman Gilbert Lindsay Moves City Council Closure of Dirty
Brooklyn-Breed Tunnel"
"Bad Example Set If LA Loses Elysian Park"
"Save Hazard Park Group to Meet . . ."
"Anti-Poverty Congressional Hearing in East Los Angeles and
Watts Saturday, Aug. 7"
"Estudio de Planeacion de la Comunidad del Este de Los Angeles"
"Govt. Operation Headstart Is 'Total Success' "
Joseph Eli Kovner on Arthur Montoya
"Top Mexican Investigator Vows Cooperation with D. A. Younger"
"The Thought Provoker," by George H. Mount, on the Vietnam
War

AUG 5   "Anti-Poverty Sub-Committee Holds Public Hearing Sat."
"Two Views on Anti-Poverty War," by U.S. Senator George
Murphy and Rep. Edward Roybal
"Save Hazard Park Committee Gains Members"
"Younger Appoints [Henry H.] Peralez as City District
Investigator"
Arthur Montoya on meeting of Maravilla & Belvedere Property
Owners Association
"The Thought Provoker," by George H. Mount

AUG 12   "500 Attend [anti-poverty] Hearing," by Esther Hansen
"Judge Sanchez to Install Metro MAPA Officers"
"The Thought Provoker," by George H. Mount
"Save Hazard Park Pickets at Poverty Committee Meeting"
"Youth Corps Jobs Boom in ELA Area, Says Joe P. Maldonado"
Arthur Montoya

AUG 19   "Let's Get L.A. Police Officers to Walk Their Beats; Automation is
Greatest Cause of Loss of Communication with People in an
Area"

Arthur Montoya
"The Thought Provoker," by George H. Mount
"Debs Asks Poverty Aid Hearings"

AUG 26   "Fair Anti-Poverty Share for Mexican-Americans Economic
Hardships Faced by ELA Neighbors"
"Three Mexican-Americans Killed in Southland Riots"
"Hazard Park Effort Continues"
"Economic Youth Opport. Agency in Operation"

SEP 2   "Immigration and Nationality Act Expected to Pass"
"Riot Area Anti-Poverty Expenditures"

SEP 9   "Unequal Distribution of Poverty Funds Charged. Congressman
Roybal calling for equality"
"Poverty Area Representatives Chosen for Recently Formed
Economic Youth Opport. Agency"
"District Attorney Younger's Report on the August Riots"

SEP 16   "County Poverty Program Gets $7,401,339 Boost"
"R. Guzmán to Speak on Leadership"

SEP 23   "Policy Statement of So. Cal. Community Relations Conference
Subject; the Los Angeles Police Department . . . Recent
Riots"
"Better Pico & Aliso Police Relations Scanned"
"Three Chosen as New E & U Opportunities Representatives by
L.A. Board of Education"
"*Confab on War on Poverty at Hess Kramer*"
"Equal Opportunities Demanded by Rep. Roybal in House"

SEP 30   "War on Poverty Reaches Mexican-American Community Declares
Director Joe P. Maldonado"
"Committee to Draft Richard Calderon as Candidate for Assembly
District Seat"
Arthur Montoya criticizes the master plan
"State, County, Federal Affairs Committee Opposes Freeway
Through Westside"
"Strong Protest Against Proposed [Beverly Hills] Freeway"
"Demo State Committee Activists"

OCT 3   "Honor Dr. Francisco Bravo and Dr. Reynaldo Carreon Jr. at
Banquet, Monday, October 25"

OCT 7   "Robert Kennedy to Make First LA Appearance in Two Years"
"Debs Orders Halt to ELA Community Planning Study"
"Discrimination Charged by Mexican-American Leaders"
" 'Boot Strap' Program to Offer Leadership Plan to Mexican-
Americans," on speakers Dr. Ernesto Galarza and Marcos De
León
"Study of 'Headstart' to Be Focused on Mexican-Americans"
" 'Stop and Frisk' is Law Question," by Ed Gray
Arthur Montoya on master plan for ELA
Joseph Eli Kovner
Letter from Edward Serrato on Save Hazard Park

OCT 10   "YWCA Launches Experimental Program with Young Girls from
Hard-Core Poverty Areas"

OCT 14   "Immigration Bill Signed into Law by President Johnson"
         "Elogia Roybal la Nueva Ley De Immigraction [sic] Que Firmo
            LBJ"
         "Police Reforms to Be Discussed," by Mike Hannon
OCT 21   "Job Corps Recruitment Underway Here; 23 Accepted"
         Arthur Montoya on annexation
OCT 24   Arthur Montoya on annexation
OCT 28   "Roybal Announces $1,000,000 Grant to ELA Area"
         "Federal Grant of $5,948,690 Expands Neighborhood Youth Corps
            In-School Program"
         "Community Action Organizations Meeting for ELA Area Will Be
            Held at Casa del Mexicano"
         "Assemblyman Philip Soto Asks Attorney General Lynch to Stop
            Discrimination Law Enforced"
OCT 31   Arthur Montoya
NOV 4   "Low Income Group Hardest Hit by Tax Increases"
         "Congressman Brown to Hold Open House at New Branch Office
            in East Los Angeles"
         "Importante Conferencia Educacional de Educadores Mexico-
            Americanos"
NOV 11   "Eastside Increase on Property Assessments Told," Kovner editorial
         "More on $1 Million Federal Grants for ELA Poverty Area"
         "Mexican-American Appointments by Gov. Brown Cited"
         Arthur Montoya on master plan
         "Dangers Probed in Funneling Federal Funds to Disadvantaged"
NOV 18   "Roybal Gets $2,000,000 Grant for Teen Training"
         "Anti-Poverty Grant Approved by Gov. Brown: $1,045,158 to Be
            Concentrated on ELA"
         Arthur Montoya on taxes in ELA
NOV 25   "Chamber of Commerce Busy in Crash Program to Supply Jobs in
            Underprivileged Areas"
         "Mexican-American Students Not Being Reached Effectively"
         "Immigration Reform calls attention to discriminatory phase of
            bill"
         Arthur Montoya on tax relief for ELA
DEC 2   "Food Stamp Program to Aid Local Area Families"
         "New Officers Voted in Greater ELA Chapter of [Mexican
            American] Educators Association"
DEC 9 $2.2 Million Received for Teen Post Program"
         "New Latin American Community Office Opened at City Hall,"
            by Mayor Sam Yorty
         "$8 Million Poverty Grant Latest Funding Brings to Total
            $25,665,997 for LA"
         "Association Tells Plans to Improve Education"
DEC 12   "Ode to Hollenbeck Park," by Joseph Eli Kovner
DEC 16   "More Freeways Not Answer to Transportation Problem Says
            Councilman in Opposition to Proposed Beverly Hills
            Freeway"
         "Sanchez Elevated to Superior Court by Gov. Brown"

"Mexican-American Teachers Not Being Used Enough in New
Educational Programs"

"Educationally Disadvantaged Funds Approved by State; Program to
Begin February 1"

"New Eligibility Standards Set for Neighborhood Youth Corps"

"New Quarters for Save Hazard Park Committee"

"Roybal Announces $100,000 Federal Grant for Special Education
in East Los Angeles"

"Few Braceros Will Be Needed for 1966 Says New Farm Labor
Report"

"Poor to Be Given Vote on War on Poverty Board"

DEC 30   "Mexican-American Parent Conference Sat., Feb. 12 at Lincoln
High School"

"The Mexican-American in California," by Eugene Gonzales,
Assistant Superintendent of Public Instruction, State of
California

"Disrespect Toward Police Criticized by Official," by Cartha De
Loach, Assistant Director of the FBI

"[George] Murphy criticizes Wirtz's Farm Labor Program"

"Roybal Inspects Fenner Canyon Job Corps Center During Recent
San Gabriel Mountain Storm"

"Mexico's True Contribution to Pacific Southwest Ignored"

1966

JAN 6   "Maravilla-Belvedere Property Owners Association, Inc. to Hold
First Meeting of Year"

"Rev. Ramon Garcia Being Considered for Public State Monument
Post," by Mike Banuelos, Jr.

"Minority Job Seekers Heard on Job Testing Practices"

"Philip Toia New Project Manager of East LA Youth Training-
Employment Plan"

"LA Economic and Youth Opportunities Agency"

"Nuevo Centro de YOC en el Valle de San Fernando, Calif."

"Se Escuchan Las Quejas De Las Minorias Sobre Pruebas De
Empleo"

Letter from A. J. Maytorena, Save Hazard Park Committee, to
Mayor Samuel Yorty

"Breaking the Language Barrier," by Evelle J. Younger

"The Economic and Youth Opportunities Agency: What Is It?"

JAN 13   "Public Park Land Grabs by Mayor Yorty Opposed: *63 Acres of
Elysian Park to Be Given Away Today If 'Blank Check'
Center Oked*"

"Hazard Park Destruction Also Contemplated for Vet Hospital"

"Anti-Poverty Elections Postponed to March 1st"

"Sixty Teachers Urgently Needed for M-A Headstart Pre-School
Program in Jan."

"Non-Profit Corporation Opened to Provide Neighborhood Legal
Services to Those in Need"

"40th A. D. MAPA to Enforce Consumers Boycott Against Sellers
of Delano Grapes"

"Mexican-American Parents Conference to Reach 'Forgotten
Families in Area' "

"Voting Districts Announced for March 1st Anti-Poverty Board
Elections by Poor"

"Boyle Heights: East of the River Prior to and after the Turn of
the Century," by Curt Hyans

"Eastside Democratic Club to Elect Delegates and Alternates to
CDC Convention"

"U.S. Moves Toward Stricter Control of Mexican Immigration"

"Major Victory in Control of Freeway Planning by a 1965 Act of
Legislature"

JAN 20   "Calif. Jesuits Serve Mexican Labor Center"

"Congressman Roybal, Brown and Hawkins to Initiate Joint Vote
Registration Drive in Districts"

"County Librarians Trying to Get ELA Library"

"LA Mexican Chamber of Commerce to Install Officers"

"Los Angeles 12,000 Acres Short of Park Land, Says PTA"

Arthur Montoya

"Save Hazard Group Attends California Beauty Conference"

"Complete Voting Action on New Human Relations Bureau to Be
Decided by Council Tuesday"

JAN 27   "Poverty Board Elections Are Floundering in ELA"

"2000 Youths Phased Out of NYC in Attempt to Reach Hard-Core
Poor"

"Pan American National Bank Names Two Directors to Board"

"Elysian Park Convention Center Being Railroaded Through the
City Council"

"Martin Ortiz Honored for Outstanding Service to Youth of
Mexican-American Descent"

"Congressman Ed Roybal Reports from Washington on 'State of
Union' Message"

Arthur Montoya

"Oil Lease at Elysian Park Cancelled-Seek Permanent Injunction
Against Drilling"

FEB 3   "Elysian Park Up for Grabs Again in City Council"

"Operation Headstart to Help 8,800 Beginning February 15"

"Mexican-American Parents Conference at Lincoln High"

"Lauds MAPA on Work on Farm Strike"

FEB 10   "Mexican-American Parents Meet Will Draw 1000"

"Honor Police Officer Julio Gonzales"

"Language Is a Key"

"Mexican-American Education Committee to Los Angeles City
Schools Superintendent Jack Crowther"

"More on the Proposed 'Steal' of Eastside Parks and Neglect of
  Facilities"
Arthur Montoya
Joseph Eli Kovner
FEB 17   "Officer J. Gonzales Marked 'Choice' at Testimonial"
"Morin in State Senate Seat Race"
"Elysian Park Put Off Again"
Arthur Montoya
"Mexican-American Education Committee Demands on Proposed
  Bond Issus [sic]"
FEB 24   "Julio Gonzales Saluted as LAPD's 'Ambassador of Good Will' at
  Special Luncheon"
"Anti-Poverty Board Candidates Seek Votes in March 1st
  Elections"
"Dymally Protests Freeway Intrusion Through District"
"Neighborhood Youth Corps Moves to Extend Out-of-School
  Program for Jobs"
"El Estudiante Mexico-Americano Es Un Estudiante Olvidado," by
  F. Móntez
Arthur Montoya takes issue with the label "Mexican-American"
Letter from Geraldine Ledesma, chair of the Mexican American
  Education Committee, to Jack Crowther
"Candidate for Economic and Youth Opportunities Agency"
"Massive 'Get Out Vote' Campaign Launched for Anti-Poverty"
"Al Hernandez, Cand. Dist. No. 2 Poverty Board States Position"
"Approve 50 Candidates for Anti-Poverty Board Election"
"El Diputado Roybal Dice"
MAR 3   "Calderon Seeks 27th Senate Seat Here"
"Citizens Com. Critical of Yorty"
"Dr. Miguel Montes Begins Duties on State B of E"
"Eastside Democratic Delegates to CDC Conference Return with
  Renewed Enthusiasm"
"UTEP Programs Offer Youth Basic Skills, Plus Job Training"
Arthur Montoya on property taxes
MAR 10   Letter from Michael Aguilar of Belvedere condemning the "I made
  it" attitude
"Senator Montoya (D-N.M.) Launches Mexican-American Voter
  Registration Campaign in Southern California"
"Are Police Law Enforcers or Upholders in America," by Ed Cray
"Education In Eastside Area"
MAR 17   Letter form John R. Serrato on the police
MAR 24   "False Rumors and Inflammatory Remarks to Incite Violence Must
  Cease," by Joseph Eli Kovner
"Save Hazard Park Meeting at All Nations Set for March 25"
"Calderon Receives CDC Endorsement for 27th Senatorial
  District"
"People's Rights; the Escobedo Case," by Ed Cray
MAR 31   "Dionicio and Dr. Guerra Do Not Pit Race Against Race!" by
  Joseph Eli Kovner

"Minority Rights in Urban Renewal Programs Being Overlooked,
 says Solomon," by Jack Solomon
APR 7   "Eddie Ramirez to Run in 28th Senatorial Race"
         Letter from Mary Sparkuth on the CSO convention in Hanford
APR 10   "First Mexican-American Bank Opens Tonight to the Public with a
         Grand Party Fiesta"
APR 14   "Elysian Park Grab Being Pulled Through in Spite of Taxpayers'
         Objection"
APR 21   "Can An 'Outraged Citizenry' Save Its 'Beloved Park'?"
         "Calderon Lauds Walkout Delegates in Albuquerque"
         "Report from Camp Hess Kramer," by Victoria Lewis
         "Youth Career Conference at Cal State L.A. April 30th"
         "East of the River Before and After the Turn of the Century," by
         Curt Hyans
APR 28   "Expert Witnesses to Testify for Preserving Hazard Park Today at
         City Hall Meeting"
         "Roybal Joins in President's Delegation"
         "Convention Center in Elysian Park Recommendation to Go to the
         City Council this June"
         "MAPA Endorses Candidates"
         "Un Seminario Especial Investiga: Mexicoamericanos en
         Transicion"
         "East of the River Before and After the Turn of the Century," by
         Curt Hyans
         Arthur Montoya
MAY 5   "Cal State to Hold Symposium May 14 on Effectiveness of
         Program for Mexican-Americans"
         "Governor Brown Speaks at MAPA Dinner in Compton as Farm
         Workers Fight for Union"
         "L.A. Councilmen Critized [sic] for Overspending, and Overlooking
         Preservation of Park Lands"
         "Roybal Congratulates Israel State on 18th Year of National
         Independence"
         "Promete Brown Nuevas Leyes De Proteccion A Los Campesinos"
         "Invitan Al Publico A Participar En Simposio Mexico-americano"
         Letter from George Mount on an anti-Black incident that occurred
         outside a fundraiser for Ed Perez
MAY 8   "Calderon, Candidato a Senador En El Dist. 27, Apoyado Por El
         C.D.C."
MAY 12   "[California State] Supreme Court Says Prop. 14 Unconstitutional"
         "Agreement Reached on New Plan for County-Wide Anti-Poverty
         Program"
         "Death Penalty Discriminatory to the Poor"
MAY 19   "Democratic Central Committee and Governor Brown Oppose
         Elysian Park Convention Site"
         "Improvements on ELA Elementary Schools if School Bond Issue is
         Passed"
MAY 26   "Improvements of Elementary Schools in ELA," Part II
JUN 2   "Roybal Will Vote for Calderon"

JUN 9   "Are Some Citizens Manhandling Police, or Is it Vice Versa?"
           "Calderon Loses by 311 Votes"
           "County Human Relations Hears Save Hazard Group"
JUN 16   "1000 Jobs to Cool the Hot, Hot Summer"
           "We're part of a peaceful community," by Joseph Eli Kovner
JUN 23   "U.S. Supreme Court and New Police Laws . . ." by Joseph Eli
           Kovner
           "MAPA Endorsing Convention at Fresno 24, 25, 26 Expected to be
           Hotly Contested"
JUN 30   Arthur Montoya on variances and zoning
JUL 7   "Corporation Formed to Direct Youth Training and Employment
           Project [YTEP] in East LA"
           "Does this seem like deterioration?" by Joseph Eli Kovner
           "Investigation of Final Contract on Hazard Park Requested"
JUL 14   "Teen Post Program May Be Left Underfunded: *Teen Post Budget
           Not Met Says EYOA*"
           "Mex. American Study Project"
JUL 21   "Chief Parker Dies; City Mourns Passing of Man of Integrity"
           "Hearing on Hazard Park Wed. July 27"
           "Settlement in Sight on Dispute between Grape Grower and Farm
           Labor"
           "UCLA Mexican-American Study"
           "El Singular Proyecto 'Ser' Ayudara A Los Mexico-americanos De
           California"
           Arthur Montoya on Chief William Parker
JUL 28   "Negotiations Underway to Forestall Cutback of Neighborhood
           Youth Corps"
           "Controller Cranston Reveals Birch Society Abounds with Anti-
           Catholics and Racists"
           "Recomendacion Favorable A Los Padres De Escolares"
           "Poverty Could Be Eliminated with Funds Used in Undeclared Viet
           Nam War"
JUL 31   "Congressman Ed Roybal Reports on Freedom-of-Informaion if
           Passed"
AUG 4   "Roybal Spurs 'Viva Brown' Committee"
           "Alex Garcia Accused of 'Bad Faith' in Park Swap"
           "MAPA State President Quevedo Charges Reagan's Agriculture
           Committee 'Phoney Front' "
           " 'Viva Brown' Committee Formed By Mexican-Americans"
           "Save Hazard Park Committee Raises $447"
           "Neighborhood Youth Corps Facing Cutback in Spite of
           Resounding Success Here"
           "Dr. Francisco Bravo Pro Reagan"
           Arthur Montoya on traffic signals
AUG 11   "Outgoing MAPA President to Be Given Banquet"
AUG 18   "Elysian Park Road Cut in Hill Opposed"
           "6,000 Braceros OK'd for 1966 Tomato Harvest"
           Joseph Eli Kovner on Hazard Park and Elysian Park

"Arthur Montoya Says . . ."

"Mexican-American Elected New Democratic Party Secretary for So. California"

AUG 25   "Hazard 'Blue Ribbon' Group Get Roybal OK"

"ELA Youths Plan a Critical Community Action Meeting August 30, at Laguna Park," on Young Citizens for Community Action (YCCA)

"Vista Seeks Spanish Speaking Volunteers"

"Progress is Being Made for East Los Angeles Young Adult Leadership"

SEP 1   "Gov. Brown Here Fri.: Gov. Brown to Officiate at New YTEP on Breed St. Friday Morning, Sept. 2"

"LAPD Shoots Fleeing Youth, 17"

" 'Reagan Against Mexican-American People'—Brown"

SEP 8   "Charge Right-Wing Extremist Influence in [William] Orozco Campaign"

"Pat Brown Gets Eastside Welcome But Must Listen to Demands!"

SEP 15   "Roybal to Urge Saving Hazard Park at City Council: *Congressman Roybal to Attend Meeting at City Council on Fate of ELA's Hazard Park*"

"Dr. Francisco Bravo Makes Statement Defending Reagan"

Arthur Montoya

SEP 22   "Ben Franklin Library Here Celebrates 50th Year"

"J. J. Rodriguez Takes On Dr. Bravo in Rebuttal to Statements Against Brown"

"US Grants Money to Anti-Poverty Group: *Eastland Community Action Council Gets $93,515*"

SEP 29   "Expose ELA Urban Renewal Land Grab Scheme," by Arthur Montoya

"Ad Hoc Committee to Win War on Poverty Sends Telegram to Sargent Shriver, Claiming Mexican American Gets Short End of Stick"

"The Story of Centro Hispano"

OCT 6   "Dick Tafoya Appointed New YTEP Project Director Here"

"Cesar Chavez States that California Farm Workers Will Support Gov. Brown"

"El Llamado Bert Corona," by Angel T. Solis

Joseph Eli Kovner

"Operation Cool Head," by District Attorney Evelle Younger

"New Housing Law Means Urban Renewal and Grab for ELA," by Ralph Cuaran [sic]

OCT 13   "Senator Joseph Montoya Speaks to Group on Plight of Mexican-Americans if Reagan Wins"

"Inside YTEP," by Fernando del Río

"Sen. Montoya Praises Cong. Brown, Roybal"

Arthur Montoya on master plan and urban renewal land grab

OCT 20   "El Sereno A.L. Post Enrolls First Viet Nam Vet"

"Viva Reagan, Joins Demos for Reagan"

"Fund Raising for Candidate for Assemblyman Peter Diaz, Friday, October 21"

"Reagan Would Stop Farm Worker Movement Says Cesar Chavez Today"

"Inside YTEP," by Fernando del Rio

"Chavez y Brown"

Arthur Montoya prints copy of the urban renewal grant

OCT 27   Arthur Montoya on urban renewal

NOV 3   "Pete Diaz Could Upset Ed Elliot in 40th Dist."

"No Ya Basta," by Angel T. Solis, endorsing Brown

"League of Mexican-American Women Honor Mrs. Brown and others"

Letter from Ignacio S. López condemning the Foundation for Mexican-American Studies and the Mexican G.I. Forum

Arthur Montoya, Part IV in an eight-part series condemning an application for a community renewal program submitted to the Board of Supervisors

NOV 10   "Luevano on ELA," by Daniel M. Luevano, on the Office of Economic Opportunities

Arthur Montoya, Part V in urban renewal series

Letter from the California Soccer Football Association to Gilbert Lindsay, Part I

NOV 17   California Soccer Football Association to Lindsay, Part II

"Let the Tenants in Housing Projects Take Over Ownership," by Joseph Eli Kovner

Arthur Montoya on urban renewal

"They Always Speak Spanish, Bunco Schemes Rampant This Time of the Year"

NOV 24   "Grass Roots Legal Aid for the Poor"

"36 New Businesses to be Organized from East LA Small Business Loan Program"

DEC 1   "Hazard Park Up for Final Grabs Today: Final Vote on Hazard Park Transfer Dec. 1st at City Council Chambers"

"Mrs. LBJ Asked to Intercede on Unfair Hazard Park Swap"

Arthur Montoya, Part VII

"Salvemos el Parque Hazard," by Angel T. Solis

"Mobilizacion General En Pro Del Parque Hazard, Hoy"

"Inside YTEP," by Fernando del Río

DEC 8   "War on Poverty Funds to Be Cut by $9.5 Million"

"Hazard Park"

DEC 15   Arthur Montoya, Part VIII

DEC 18   "Intermarriage Rising for Mexican-Americans Says Report"

1967

JAN 5   "Roybal New 'Grand-pop' "

"Racial Bias in Employment, Housing Complaints Can Now Be Filled at State Center"

"Save Elysian Park Committee Receives Wide Recognition"

"Day Care Homes Needed Desperately in This Area"

Arthur Montoya on urban renewal

JAN 8   "Property Owners Meeting"

JAN 12   "Suit Filed Against Los Angeles to Save Park Restraining Order
Object of Immediate Importance in Suit to Save Hazard
Park"

"MAOF Hosts Past Boxers at Dinner"

"Karabian Names [Ben] Estrada as Aide"

"GI Forum to Give Dinner for Dr. Montes"

"Roybal Urges Use of Equal Employment Commission Office"

"Discriminacion Contra Los Mexicoamericanos"

Joseph Eli Kovner reports on 40th A.D. vote and Felix and Sally
Ontiveros

JAN 19   "Depriving Less Affluent Students of Higher Education Unfair
Solution to Budget"

"L.A. Congressmen Support NAPP Final Shuffle"

"Julia Mount to Run for Board of Education"

Arthur Montoya on the Los Angeles City urban renewal program
and the Community Analysis Program (CAP)

"More on Nava"

JAN 26   "Eastside Must Not Repeat Bunker Hill Redevelopment Mistake,"
a pictorial editorial

"Unimmunized Seven-year-old Dies from Diphtheria"

"Save Hazard Park Group Meets Tonite"

"LA Youth Agencies Meet to Discuss Problems and Issues"

Letter from Dr. Manuel Guerra charging that the Convention of
Community Organizations was rigged

Arthur Montoya on the County Committee on Community
Improvement

"Dr. Nava Committee to Meet January 30th for Board of Education
Race"

"Richard Alatorre Joins County Staff, Assigned to Delinquency
Prevention"

"NAPP of Boyle Heights to Hold Meeting Monday in Ramona
Gardens"

JAN 29   "Community Endorsement on Board of Education"

FEB 2   "Master Planning Skyrocketing Property Taxes Because of
Rezoning and Use Potential, Accuses O'Neill, Candidate for
Council in 14th District"

"Dr. Julian Nava, Board of Education Candidate, to Speak February
7"

Arthur Montoya on master plan and Hazard Park

"Endorsing Convention of United Council of Community
Organizations"

FEB 5   "Property Owners Meeting"

FEB 9   "Maria Medina Victim of Hit-and-Run Driver at 4th & Fickett"

"$1,000,000 in Poverty War Funds to be Deposited in Pan
American National Bank"

"Governor Refuses to Budge on Budget Cuts and Tuition"

"Report of Convention at Casa del Mexicano"

Arthur Montoya on urban renewal

Letter from John R. Hang, Coordinator for Board of Education
     Campaign, on New Politics candidate Julia Luna Mount and
     the anti-war issue

FEB 16   "California's Economy Exceeds All but Five Nations; We Can
     Afford Quality Schools," by the California Teachers
     Association

Arthur Montoya on the Maravilla and Belvedere Park Property
     Owners Association

FEB 23   Arthur Montoya on *Los Nietos* urban renewal program

"Candidates for School Board . . . Nava and Doctor Special Guests
     at Bradley Open House"

"[Charles] Galindo Speaks at Optimist Group on Common Sense
     in Los Angeles Education"

Letter from Matt Glernier answering Dr. Manuel Guerra

"Community Meeting with Congressman Roybal Feb. 24th
     Sponsored by CSO"

FEB 26   "Program Development Specialist Needed for Organizing
     Residents"

"Pico Rivera Youth New Vista Volunteer with Migrant Workers"

MAR 2   "Eastside Community to Protest Park Trade Sale: Hazard Park
     Group Wins First Round in Legal Battle to Stop Park
     Trading"

"Former East LA Student Dr. Nava Returns as Speaker"

Arthur Montoya on East Los Angeles Improvement Council

"Fiesta en Beneficio del Candidato Dr. Julian Nava"

MAR 9   "Nava and Doctor, Candidates for LA Board of Education at All
     Nations Center, March 17"

Arthur Montoya on urban renewal

MAR 12   "Property Owners Meet"

MAR 16   "Another East LA Town Meeting March 20 to Stop School Cuts,"
     by Carol Stevens

"CSO to Celebrate 20th Anniversary; CSO Honors Friends at
     Dinner-Dance"

"2,700 New Jobs for Disadvantaged Workers in New Manpower
     Program"

"Victory for Nava Predicted"

"MAPA Endorses Four Candidates for School Board at Convention"

"Declaracion del Doctor Julian Nava"

Arthur Montoya on Ronald Reagan budget and Hazard Park

MAR 23   "Community Asked to Show Support Against ELA School Budget
     Cuts in Another Mass Protest Meeting Monday Night March
     27," by Carol Stevens

"Julio Gonzales Named to California Youth Authority by Gov.
     Reagan"

"EYOA Approves Plan to Create 2000 Jobs in ELA Area"

"[Daniel] Luevano to Speak at CSO Reunion Celebration"

"LA Garment Industry Needs 4,000 New Employees"

MAY 4   "Governor Reagan 'Ducks' ELA Town Meeting Group in Sac." by
           Carol Stevens
         "Wrath of ELA Directed at 'Time' Magazine"
         "ELA Community Hits Back at Mexican-American Smear by Time
           Magazine," Statement by Cong. Edward R. Roybal
         "Carta de Ralph Guzman A Joseph Kovner," on *Time* magazine
           article
         "Respuesta de Debs a Time"
         Arthur Montoya on City of Monterey Park's proposed annexation
           of the Maravilla area
MAY 7   "Maravilla Threatened by New 'Master Plan'," by Arthur Montoya
MAY 11   "A Town Meeting Denies Apology to Governor—Asks for Meet,"
           by Carol Stevens
         "Bill Orozco Refuses to Introduce Dr. Nava at Cinco de Mayo
           'Plaza Day' "
         "Enough Smoke Seen to Warrant Investigation of Zoning
           Commission"
         "8th Grade History Class Answers Time Magazine"
         "Plan ELA Youth Conference"
         "Public Interest Mounting in Getting Dr. Nava Elected to School
           Board"
         "Raul Morin: Among the Valiant," an obituary
         "More Letters on 'Time' Article," by Joseph Eli Kovner
         "Nava Replies: Let's Discuss Education"
         "Smoot Claims Rival Must Favor Sit-ins"
         "Philip Montez Coordinates Civil Rights Commission"
         "Una Arma Valida: El Boicot," by Angel T. Solis
         "Demonstracion Del Comite 'Pro-Nava' "
         "Protestas del Dr. Nava Por Unas Reducciones Al Sistema Escolar"
         Arthur Montoya on Monterey Park annexation
         "Mexican-American Conference Dialogue Among Collegians at
           Loyola University May 13"
         Arthur Montoya, more on Monterey Park annexation
MAY 14   "Maravilla Amenzada Por Nuevo Plan Maestro," by Arthur
           Montoya
MAY 18   "ELA Town Meeting Will Join in B of E Cutback Protest," by
           Carol Stevens
         "Senator Kennedy Visits East Los Angeles YTEP"
         "Orozco Explains Refusal to Introduce Dr. Nava"
         Letter to the editor protesting *Time* article
         Arthur Montoya on Monterey Park Planning Commission
         "U.S. Is Capital of the Military Mind," by Cong. George Brown,
           Jr.
         "La Lucha por la Educacion," by Angel T. Solis
         "Carta del Deputado Federal George E. Brown a 'Time' "
MAY 21   "Walk-Out at [Opal] Jones Meeting"
MAY 25   "Town Meetings Dance Sunday for Nava, B of E Formalizes Cuts"

"We Endorse Dr. Nava for Board of Education"

"Parks Commission Ignores Hazard Park Improvement Plan in Federal Funds Bill"

"United Council Delegates Walk Out of Meeting with NAPP Officials," by Patricio Sanchez

"State Board of Education Opposes Repeal of Rumford Act"

Letter from Mark Davidson, TV Channel 9 "Feature Page," concerning Charles Reed Smoot's refusal to appear with or subsequent to Nava

"Golpe a la Educacion"

"Porque Julian Nava?" by Gonzalo Molina

MAY 28   "Vote for Dr. Nava for Board of Education, Office No. 3, Wed. May 31"

JUN 1   "Governor Reagan Holding Up Hearing of School Tax Relief Bill," by Carol Stevens

"Railroad Through Brooklyn Ave. Opposed by Entire Community and Brooklyn C of C"

"Public Relations Is a Two Way Street!" by Joseph Eli Kovner

Concerning the L.A.P.D.-Mexican American Conference at Elysian Park

Arthur Montoya on Monterey Park and the master plan

JUN 4   "Dice," by Arthur Montoya

JUN 8   "Sweeping Victory for Dr. Nava, Board of Education"

"Dr. Julian Nava Wins Election 50,000-Plus Victory in Board of Education Office No. 3," by Carol Stevens

"Civil Rights, Education, Employment of Mexican-American Hearings June 8-9"

" . . . Quincy Jones' . . . Fund-Raising . . . Hazard Park June 10"

"A New Law Provides Bilingual Instruction When Advantageous to Students"

Arthur Montoya on Maravilla and master plan

Letter to the editor on *Time* Magazine reply

"Educacion Bilingue En California"

JUN 15   "Governor Loses 'Cool' and Pounds Fist in ELA Town Meeting Confrontation Monday. Threatens Veto of All Education Bills," by Carol Stevens

"Vicente T. Ximenes New Commissioner of Equal Opportunities Commission"

"Federal Funds Will Provide Schooling for Disadvantaged Youngsters this Summer"

"Julio Gonzales Testimonial Banquet June 19 at Los Angeles Police Academy"

Arthur Montoya on zoning and master plan

"Debs Aboga por los Mexicoamericanos Ante una Comision de Derechos Civiles"

"Hearings on Bilingual Bills June 22-23; Public Urged to Attend at Supervisors"

"El 'No' de Reagan," by Angel T. Solis

JUN 22   "School 'Beefs' Meeting Fri. and Annex of ELA 'Briefing' Mon."
by Carol Stevens

"Pot Luck Picnic for Dr. Nava at Hazard Park for His Birthday
June 25"

"East LA Peace Committee to Join Protest June 23rd Anti-Vietnam
Demonstration"

Arthur Montoya on master plan and Monterey Park

"ELA Speaks Out for More Jobs and Better Teachers"

"Senala [George] Brown Que El Numero De Mexicoamericanos
Muertos En Vietnam Es Demasiado Elevado"

"Congressman Brown Reports High Ratio of Deaths in Vietnam
[for] Mexican-Americans"

JUN 29   "Look at Crowd Control Methods Asked by Edelman," on LAPD
actions at Century Plaza

"Some Personal Opinions about the Century Plaza Confrontation"

"Edelman Calls for Look at Police Force"

Arthur Montoya on Monterey Park annexation

"New Foundation Being Started to Help Mexican American
Retarded Children"

"June 23 a Dark Day in Los Angeles because of Police Violence:
ACLU"

Letter from Alfred H. Song, State Senator, on the Monterey Park
annexation

"El Abuso de la Fuerza," by Angel T. Solis, on Century Plaza

"Bilingual Problems Discussed at Senate Hearing Saturday"

JUL 6   " 'Wrong-Way' Reagan Hits Local Taxpayer with Biggest 'Butched-
up' Calif. Budget"

"Dr. Nava to be Honored at 8th Annual So. MAPA Meet"

"Con. Roybal Presents Bilingual Bill to U.S. Senate Subcommittee
in Los Angeles"

"Guest Editorial: East L.A. College Professor Recalls Dr. Nava as
Student," by Dr. Helen Miller Bailey

"Eyeball to Eyeball," by George H. Mount, on Century Plaza
confrontation

Arthur Montoya on master plan and Monterey Park

JUL 13   "Open Letter to Los Angeles City Councilmen," on Century Plaza
incident

"General Public Meeting on Way Poverty Funds are to Be Spent,
this Friday, July 14"

"New York Leaders to Attend MAPA Convention this Friday in
Riverside"

"Algunas Opiniones Personales Sobre La Confrontacion Del
Century Plaza"

"Raul Morin Memory to be Honored with 'Morin Memorial
Square' Resolution"

Letter from Alex Montalvo, Eastside Democratic Club, on the
police overreaction at Century City

"MAPA Convention Opens Tomorrow at Riverside"

Art Montoya on urban renewal

SEP 21   "City School Board Restores Drastic Budget Cut"

Art Montoya on urban renewal

SEP 28   "Dr. Nava, B of E Member to Visit Youth Training and
        Unemployment Projects"

"Million Dollar Small Business Loan Approved for El 'Mercado de
        Los Angeles' "

"Educational Group to Picket Euclid Ave. School Oct. 9"

Arthur Montoya: a letter from Ernest E. Debs on Building
        Rehabilitation Appeals Board

"Police Rally in E.L.A. Oct. 15 Dick Gregory"

OCT 1   "Save Medi-Cal Committee Urgently Needs Members from
        Mexican-American Community"

OCT 5   "Tafoya Helps Save 'Homepower' Youth Program"

"Peace Action Council of SC Sponsor Giant Rally Oct. 15"

OCT 12   "Roybal Clarifies Euclid Avenue School Problem"

" 'Medi-Cal Must and Will Be Cut' Rallying Cry of California
        Director of Finance"

"Demandas Mexico-Americanos A Lyndon B. Johnson"

OCT 19   Arthur Montoya on Edison Electric Company facility at Rowan and
        Folson Avenues

OCT 26   "Hazard Park to Reach Superior Court Dec. 4"

"Conservative Republican Group Objects to El Paso Conference,"
        by Jud Leetham

NOV 2   "Chief Reddin Creating Better Community Dialog [sic]"

"Roybal Hails Action on Bilingual Legislation"

NOV 9   "L.A. 'Goals' Fiasco at Casa Del Mexicano"

"The War Against People in the 90th Congress," by Carol Stevens

"Dr. Nava Testifies at El Paso Convention on Mexican-American
        Affairs" Part I

"Dr. Nava Testifies at El Paso Convention on Mexican-American
        Affairs," Part II

"EYOA to Hold Meetings to Discuss War on Poverty in LA
        County"

"Informara Sobre La Conferencia Del El Paso, Texas"

"Priority on Mexican Americans El Paso Conference Urged"

Arthur Montoya on arbitrary zoning changes for businesses

NOV 16   Joseph Eli Kovner on Los Angeles Goals Program presentation

Arthur Montoya

"Anti-War Committee to Give Reports on Washington Rally and
        San Francisco Vote"

NOV 23   "Dr. Nava Testifies at El Paso Convention on Mexican-American
        Affairs," Part III

"Yorty Blames Freeways for Disrupted LA Neighborhoods"

NOV 30   "One Hundred and Seventy-Five Residents and Property Owners of
        Enchandia Street and Vicinity; Protest Opening of Narcotics
        Project"

"County Human Relations Sponsor Youth Group Discussion Dec.
3"
Letter to the editor on narcotics center
DEC 7   "Roybal Supports Big Peace . . . Drive in LA"
DEC 14   "Seek No Compromise on Hazard Park"
"B of E Supports Euclid Ave. School Principal, Acknowledges
Inadequacies"
"No Compromise on Hazard Park, Save H P Association Replies to
KNX-TV Editorial"
Art Montoya
"Peace March December 17 in Torrance"
"Discussion on Mexican-American and Vietnam War"
DEC 21   "Bilingual Bill Passes on Last Session Day"
"$1.7 Billion Poverty Bill Passed Until Next July"
"Peace and Freedom Party," by George Mount
"Aliens Can Get Medicare"
"Police Aid in New Career Program of EYOA and City"
DEC 28   "16 ELA Boys Graduate as Law Enforcement Explorers"
"Boyle Heights Beautiful . . ." by Joseph Eli Kovner
"Peace and Freedom Party," by Linus Pauling
"School Board Approves Plans for $3.1 Million in East LA School
Projects"
"County Pressing Rehabilitation of ELA Substandard Buildings"

1968

JAN 4   "Community Assistance Only Way to Save Teen Posts, Says
Elkin," by Carol Stevens
"No Goals to Los Angeles Goals program!"
"Anti-War, Anti-Racism, Anti-Poverty Calif. Democrats Endorse
McCarthy for Pres."
"Federal Bilingual Bill of Critical Importance to 4,000,000 Students
in Natio [sic]"
JAN 11   "Pacheco Assigned to New ELA Educational Complex"
"Bridge Over Boyle Heights?"
" 'Educational Happening' at Piranya Coffee House, Jan 17"
JAN 18   Arthur Montoya on the Edison Company
"United Mexican-American Students Protest Fee Increase as an
Injustice"
JAN 25   "Protest Tuition Hike at Cal-State"
"Battle Plans Drawn to Keep Remaining Teen Posts Going," by
Carol Stevens
Arthur Montoya on the Edison Company dispute
FEB 1   Joseph Eli Kovner on David Sánchez of the Brown Berets
"Let's Get Organized," by Mike De Anda
Letter from Robert Sánchez, a senior at Roosevelt High School,
stating that Mike de Anda expressed racist views

Letter from David Santiago to Capt. Guindon, Hollenbeck LAPD,
   complaining about police harassment
"Drop out Guidance Program at Garfield and Roosevelt"

FEB 8   "Congress of Mexican-American Unity Meets Sunday, February
   25"
Arthur Montoya on the master plan and Model Cities
"Mexican-Americans Desire More Representation in Reagan
   Government Says POLARA"
Letter accusing George Brown of being a communist

FEB 15   "Boyle Heights Rejects 'Model Cities' Scheme"
Joseph Eli Kovner on Model Cities Program
"New Police Organization of Latin-American Officers Holds First
   Meeting This Week"
"Congress on M-A Unity Meets February 21"
"Judge [Benjamin] Vega Elected as Presiding Judge of ELA"
Arthur Montoya on the Model Cities Program
"El Congreso de Unidad Mexico-American sigue Organizando Su
   Gran Convencion"
"Convencion Designatoria," by Angel T. Solis

FEB 22   "Congress of Mexican-American Unity Convention Sun. Feb. 25"
"UMAS Holds Symposium"
"Support Spreading for Student B of E Proposal," by Carol Stevens
Arthur Montoya on urban renewal
"12 New Police Officers . . . More Needed Now"

FEB 29   "Calderon 'Peoples Choice' for Senator at Confab"
"Calderon, Cruz Selected by Community Caucus"
Letter from Gonzalo Molina withdrawing from the 40th A.D. race
Letter from Alex Garcia refusing to withdraw
"Community 'Speak-out' Mar. 30 Sponsored by AFT Local 1021
   Subject: ELA Education"
"The Shot Heard Around the World," by Carol Stevens
"CMAA Says Mexican-American Community Should be Involved
   in Planning of Police Program"
Arthur Montoya on the master plan, Monterey Park and Model
   Cities
"Congressman Brown Reports New High Ratio of Deaths in
   Vietnam for Mexican-Americans"

MAR 7   "ELA High School Students Press for Better Education, Facilities"
"Arthur Montoya Says . . . Don't be fooled by the Model Cities
   Program"
"Friendship Fiesta March 17 Sponsored by Hollenbeck LAPD"
"Police Questionnaire to Be Published Next Week"
"MAPA Endorses Convention Choices at 40th Meeting"
Letter from Isidore Serrato on substandard services in Hazard Park
"AFT Not Part of Walkout"
"Students Walkout at Garfield, Roosevelt and Lincoln High
   Schools"

"Chavez to End Fast on Reaffirming Non-Violence"
"LA Law Schools Seek Mexican-American Students"
"Name [Philip] Montez to Head U.S. Civil Rights Unit"
"Y Otra Vez La 'Reurbanizacion' "
MAR 10 Arthur Montoya
MAR 14 "Students of Roosevelt High Present Solutions to Educate"
"300 Property Owners Vote No on 'Model Cities' "
"Roybal Supports Objective of Student Protest"
"Public Meeting on Student Proposals Held at Griffith," by Carol
     Stevens
Arthur Montoya on Mayor Sam Yorty's Model Cities Program
"Community Inquiry on Crime and Delinquency Begins Today"
"Act One of a Morality Play . . ." by Joseph Eli Kovner, on police
     surveillance of East Los Angeles walkouts
"$250,000 Granted to Opportunity Foundation"
"Roosevelt Presents Solutions to Board of Education on Student
     Grievances"
"Forces at Work Today May Destroy State Colleges"
"Civil Disorder Report Focus Questioned," by Kyle Ogden, 40th
     AD candidate
"Community Speakout March 30"
"MAPA Raps Firing Poverty Worker," by Delfino Varela
"City to Investigate 'Civil Disorder' Report"
"CMAA Urged Calmer Approach by Police"
"Las Protestas Estudiantiles," by Angel Solis
MAR 21 "Board of Education Meeting at Lincoln Auditorium March 26th,"
     by Carol Stevens
"Crowther and Debs Ask for Financial Support on Urban Area
     Schools"
"LAPD Friendship Fiesta at Evergreen Community Success"
"All Nations Supports ELA Students"
Letter to the editor on walkouts
"Citizen Groups Back Student Aims at Board"
"Amplia Discusion De Los Problemas En Ram. Gardens"
Letter in Spanish from Isidore Serrato on subject of saving Hazard
     Park
"George Brown Jr. to Address Eastside Democrats"
"CMAA Recognition Banquet Ambassador Hotel March 23"
MAR 24 "Neighborhood Groups Express Concern on War, Education"
MAR 28 "Community Speak Out for Better Education March 30 at
     Belvedere Jr. High School"
"Hazard Park Trial Gets New Date"
Letter from Helen Aragón, Public Information Officer for the Los
     Angeles City Housing Authority
"Model Cities Not for ELA," by Arthur Montoya
Photograph of Sal Castro
"Board of Education Meeting at Lincoln Accomplishes Little"

"Senator Kennedy Greeted by Enthusiastic Crowds"
"Photo of Brown Berets of Lincoln at Lincoln H.S. B of E
    meeting"
"Old Holenbeck [sic] Police Station May Become Community
    Service Center"
"New Political Education Committee for CSO"
MAR 31   "Meeting at Lincoln," by Carol Kovner
APR 4   "El Mercado Holds Grand Opening Today"
         " 'Model Cities': Fish or Fowl? Montoya and Kovner to Speak on
             New Urban Renewal Gimmick Friday"
         "Parents March to B of E This Afternoon," by Carol Stevens
         " 'Speakout' to Be On TV KCET Channel 28 Tonight"
         "Pide Cooperacion El Depto. Policían 'A La Comunidad' "
         "Anarquia Educacional"
         Arthur Montoya on the word "Chicano"
         "Headstart Boycott by Mothers Tues"
         "Programa De TV Con Los Estudiantes De Ford Blvd"
         "County to Cooperate with 'Model Cities' "
APR 11   "Shame, Shame on you, Oh Mighty City Fathers!" by Joseph Eli
             Kovner
         "Tranquility in Streets of LA Tribute to Doctor King Says Chief
             Reddin"
         "Rights Measure Passes House of Representatives"
         "Martin Luther King '29–'68 Free at Last, Free at Last . . .' "
         "Crime Survey Underway"
         Arthur Montoya on Boyle Heights Model Cities and Councilman
             Gilbert Lindsay
         "Action Council Gets the Action," by John Crowe
         "Participacion de los Padres de Familia en la Educacion"
         "Urgent Need to End National Frustration and Disunity, Says
             Calderon"
         "Labor Secretary Wirtz to Speak at Roybal Dinner"
         "Highlights of Panel in 'Speakout' Discussed"
         "Revisions in Building Plans by School Board"
         "B of E Hears Reactions to Intensive Instruction Begun in Sept."
APR 18   "Secondary Schools Get Minority Administrative Personnel as
             Interns"
         "Local People Organizing for Better Education," by Carol Stevens
         "Choo! Choo! Went the Locomotive, or, Model Cities Is
             Railroaded Through!"
         Arthur Montoya on Model Cities
         "Calderon Headquarters Opening Thursday, April 18"
         "Evaluation Committee at Roosevelt Reports on Adult Activities in
             Community"
         "Peace Corps Gains 'Simpatico' from Spanish-Speaking Americans"
         "CSO Voter Drive Reaches 11,357"
APR 26   "CDC and Bishop Pike Hosts Calderon, Wyatt Fri"

"Sal Castro to Speak at Democratic Dinner"
"Peace Action Walk April 27th"
Arthur Montoya on Model Cities
"Peace Move Says Lt. General North Vietnamese Sincere In"

MAY 2   "Cinco de Mayo Set for Hazard Park Demonstration at U.S. Court
House"
Letter from Alicia Escalante of the East Los Angeles Welfare Rights
Organization
Arthur Montoya on Model Cities
"Two Brown Berets Are Convicted"
"UAW Backs Calderon for State Senate in 27th"
"Educational Issues Committee Sponsors 'Walk Through', " by
Carol Stevens
"Police Aide Program Opens Office in Ramona Gardens"
"Roybal Secures Pledge to Re-Study Park Swap"
"Sargent Shriver to Leave OEO for Ambassadorship"

MAY 9   "McCarthy to Visit El Mercado in E.L.A."
"The Purpose of a Teen Post," by Ron Arkin
"Project Drop-In to Work with 5000 Mexican-American High
Schoolers if Funded"
" 'Viva La Raza' Nite May 10 for Cruz and Calderon"
Arthur Montoya
"La Policia Y La Comunidad"
"Calderon Calls for Increased State Aid to Schools Here"

MAY 16   "Cesar Chavez Gives Strong Support to Calderon"
"Grassroots Approach by Candidate Calderon and Cong. George E.
Brown Jr."
"Issues Committee to Picket Lincoln," by Pat Sanchez
"The Rut of Poverty," by Ron Arkin
Arthur Montoya on Model Cities.
"Bunker Hill Towers, City Urban Renewal in Action, Apartments
Start At?"
"Mexican American College Students Host High Schools"
"Student Walk Out Panel at Speak-out Reports"
"Open House at Hollenbeck LAPD"
Letter from Garfield Blowout Committee
"FEPC—What It Can Do for Spanish-Speaking Citizens on Orderly
Atmosphere"
An open letter to the Mexican American Community from Richard
Du Bois, teacher at Garfield High School
"History of the Police," by Bergen Lee
"Se Da A Conocer 'Lucha' Una Nueva Organizacion"
"Huge MOSAICS Unveiled Wed, at ELA Doctors Hospital"
"Philosophy and Purpose of L.U.C.H.A."

MAY 23   "Artist Honored at Dedication of ELA-DH Mosaics"
"Boyle Heights Beautiful," by Joseph Eli Kovner
"The Ramona Gardens Ass'n," by Ron Arkin

"The Real Truth About Drug Abuse," by Evelle J. Younger
"Parks Commission Closes Camp High Sierra Sends Ghetto
    Youngsters to Saugus"

MAY 26 "100 Picket Lincoln High"
"Dick Calderon Backed by Cesar Chavez"
"We Endorse Calderon"

MAY 30 "Alex Garcia Endorsed by UAW"
"Yorty Hurries Model Cities Along"
"El Camino de McCarthy," by Angel T. Solis
"Quality of Education Criticized at MASA by Don Negrete"
Arthur Montoya on Model Cities

JUN 6   "CMAA Criticizes District Attorney's Office and Grand Jury for
    Secret Indictments"
"Statement by U.S. Senator Gene McCarthy on Arrests of
    Mexican-Americans"
"Kennedy Critically Wounded; Wins Calif."
"On ELA Student Walkouts"
"Heroicas Acciones en Viet Nam de Un Marino de ELA"
"Criticas A La Accion Del Procurador"
"Add: A Fund-Raising Rally for the Defense of Sal Castro and the
    Students, Saturday, June 8"
"Share of Poverty Funds for East Los Angeles"
"Peace and Freedom Party, Paper Organization or a Force in L.A.
    County Politics?" by George H. Mount
"Community Leader Speaks Out on Walk-out Arrest"
"Fund Raising Rally for Sal Castro and Students at Cal State June
    15"
Arthur Montoya
"Association of Mexican American Educators Supports Castro and
    Educational Issues"
"School Arrests Discussed at All Nations"

JUN 13 "Major Reorganization and Decentralization of Schools Announced
    by Mrs. Hardy"
"Letter to the Young People of East Los Angeles on Kennedy's
    Death," by Joseph Eli Kovner
"Anti-Crime Bill with Senate Amendments Goes to President to
    Sign," by Congressman George E. Brown
Letter from Ramón L. Ponce for the United Council of Community
    Organizations, appealing for help. Grand jury indicted 13 for
    conspiracy to disturb peace.

JUN 20 "Montoya Chairs Mass Meeting Tonight at Belvedere, Against
    Model Cities"
"East Central Area Welfare Planning Council Questions Wisdom of
    Walkout Arrests"
"Trevino New Champion of U.S. Open"
"UCLA Project Upward Bound Graduates 90 Students"
"Sacramento Report by Senator Mervyn M. Dymally Civil Liberties
    and the Mexican-American"

Letter from Vincent Rubalcalva on the unequal representation of
Mexican Americans in the service centers advisory
committees

JUN 27 "Low Cost Home Program Gaining Acceptance in ELA"
"Banks in Minority Areas Should Liberalize Loan Requirements"
"Hazard Park Trial Date July 18"
Arthur Montoya

JUL 4 "Francisco Bravo Challenges D.A. on Walkout Conspiracy
Charges"
"Governor Cuts into Higher Education," by Carol Stevens
"LULAC to Provide Legal Aid to Leaders Arrested During School
Walkouts," by David Santiago
"Judge Sanchez Supports HOME Program, ELA"
Arthur Montoya on home improvement grants
"We the People of E.L.A. Demand That Our Complex of
Communities Be 'Kennedy City' "
Letter from Dr. Francisco Bravo to Evelle Younger
"The Battle of Monterey Hills Slated for 'Urban Redevelopment' "

JUL 11 "Summer Lecture Series Features Castro, Nava, Cesar Chavez,
Morales"
"LULAC Opens LA District"
"Armando Morales Asks for Police Cooperation"
"Bank of America to Advance $100 Million for Real Estate Loans
in Minority Areas"
Letters on police harassment
"EYOA Reorganized to Meet New Federal Regulations"
"The Heleotrope Incident"

JUL 18 "Court Acted to Drop Charges Against 12 in Student Walkouts"
Letter from Herminia Ramírez to the Save Hazard Park Committee
"CMAA Hd. Start Complaints Now Being Studied"
"Bilingual Reading Program Cut by State Committee"
"Hazard Trial Begins Today"
Arthur Montoya on H.O.M.E.'s modernization effort
"Is Mayor's Job Program for Youth a Big Put-on?"
"Busca Voluntarios El Centro De Estudios Bilingues De E.L.A."

JUL 25 "Citizens Asked to Save Homes"
Letters from Salvador Montenegro and Francisco Bravo regarding
the Police Commission

AUG 1 "Montoya Fears H.O.M.E. Could Hurt 'Propertarios,' " by Arthur
Montoya
"Unity Day Aug. 3-4 Planned for Reform in Corrections"
"EICC Asks for Formal Recognition," by Carol Stevens
"New Eastside Bilingual Study Center at Salesian Hi Opens"
"Brown Berets Hold First Annual Open House Friday"
"McCarthy Apoya El Boicot A Las Uvas De California"
"Councilmen, Now Read This!" by Joseph Eli Kovner

AUG 8 "Mass Rally on H.O.M.E. Tonight at Belvedere Jr. Hi," by Art
Montoya

Joseph Eli Kovner on Sal Montenegro
"Prof. David A. Sanchez Vice Chair EICC"
"Dismissal of Charges on School Walkouts Asked by '13's'
    Attornies [sic]"
AUG 11 "HUD Speakers at ELA Town Meeting"
    "H.O.M.E. for Senior Citizens"
AUG 15 "Code Enforcement in H.O.M.E. Not for Us, Montoya: History
    Repeats Itself," by Art Montoya
    "School Board Begins Purchase of Roosevelt High Land Addition"
    "Brown Berets Offers Community Services"
    "Project SIR [sic] Most Creative Cultural Program Going for Young
    People in the East Los Angeles Area," by Carol Stevens
    Art Montoya on the H.O.M.E. program
    "Hazard Park Decision to Be Appealed to Higher Court"
AUG 22 "214 New Career Positions Closed Out in Dispute Roybal Asks
    Reinstatement"
    "Serie Dramatica 'Cancion De La Raza' En El Canal 28"
AUG 25 "Cal State Opens Centers In East-South-Central L.A."
    "Eastland Community Action Council Asks Guidelines"
AUG 29 "Black & Brown Caucus Members Go to Chicago"
    "Mexican-American Honored at Urban League's Ghetto Freedom
    Awards Ceremony"
    "Seek to Prohibit Prosecution of the '13' "
    Letter from Arthur Montoya to Ernest Debs
SEP 5 Arthur Montoya on the H.O.M.E. program
    Letter from Bonnie López, Brown Beret, to Councilman Art
    Snyder, commenting on the Urban League of Los Angeles
    award to the Brown Berets
    "Youth Training and Employment Project (YTEP) Doing
    Indispensable Job at Grassroots Level"
SEP 12 "Maravilla Property Owners to Hear Federal Reps on H.O.M.E.,"
    by Art Montoya
    "Congressional Approval Expected for National Hispanic Week
    Sept. 15"
    "Mexican-American Opportunity Foundation Invites Community to
    Fiesta Weekend Opening"
    "Open Letter to All Law Enforcement Officials," by John Edgar
    Hoover
    "Maravilla Property Owners Oppose H.O.M.E."
SEP 19 "EICC Picketts [sic] at Lincoln to March all This Week"
    "School Board Upholds Policy on Felony Arrests"
    "Bilingual Classes Now at Roosevelt"
    "Eastland CAP Faces Suspension"
    "Board Approves H.O.M.E. Program"
    "Mexican-American Studies at Lincoln High School"
SEP 26 "There's Room for More at Bilingual Study Center on Soto"
    "Methods Questioned in Selling H.O.M.E. to ELA," by Art
    Montoya

"Fernando De [sic] Rio Resigns from Eastland CAP"
"Hazard Park Appeal Filed"

OCT 3   "Sit-in Demonstrators Await Castro Decision Today: School Board Sit-in Ends Wednesday, Awaits Decision 6 day sit in on Tuesday"

Joseph Eli Kovner on Sal Castro and education
Arthur Montoya on H.O.M.E.
"The Jesus Dominguez Case Discussed by L.A. Peace [and Freedom Party]"
"Brown Berets Hold Class in Chicano History"
"El Caso Dominguez"
"Sal Castro Debe Ser Repuesto," by Angel T. Solis

OCT 10   "Three Pronged Attack on Crime to Begin in ELA"
" 'Sir' [sic] Program Funding Ends Oct. 13; Program Must Continue"
"Ethnic Insult by T.V. Commercial," by Dionicio Morales
"Castro Reinstated as School Board Approves New Policy on Teachers Facing Criminal Charges"
Art Montoya on H.O.M.E.
"Reliance on the Poor," by Tony Rios
"Protestas por Insultos A los Mexicoamericanos"

OCT 17   "Montoya Addresses Humphrey Committee"
"Groundbreaking for 'Inner City Townhouse' Model"
Arthur Montoya
"Principals Vote Against UMAS"

OCT 24   "Dr. Nava Fears Passage of Prop 9 Will Hurt Schooling in ELA"
Arthur Montoya on the H.O.M.E. program
"Chicano History at All Nations Center"
"Farm Workers Number Over One Million"
"Youth Involvement in Solving East L.A. Problems Aim of Antipoverty Programs"

OCT 31   "MAPA to Honor Garcia at Sun Reception"
"Brown Berets Hold New Class Series on Mexican-Amer. History"
"Mace!" by Michael Sánchez, age 15
"City Elementary Teachers Participate in Human Relations Workshop"
"Lincoln Students Go on to College"

NOV 7   "Nixon Wins All! George Brown, Alex Garcia Victors"
"1968 Great Western Livestock Show Will Honor Dr. Francisco Bravo; Selected by Directors"

NOV 14 "Property Owners Are Denied a Copy of H.O.M.E. Application," by Art Montoya
"$27 Million Business-Government Effort for East Los Angeles Disadvantaged Announced by United States Department of Labor"
"Who Are the Mexican Americans among Us?" by Joseph Eli Kovner
"Central UMAS Sponsors Dance," by Michael Sánchez

" 'Cancion de la Raza' Tackles E.L.A. Problems in Continuing TV
Drama"
"Adeline Gomez Cleared of Battery Charges with DA's Help"
"Linea abierta—Immigration"
"The Urban Coalition," by Lee A. Du Bridge

JAN 9   "Why Not Build Another Senior High by Ourselves?" by Joseph Eli
Kovner
"Formation of Minority Studies Dept. at Cal State College L.A."
"Neighborhood Legal Centers Serve Thousands of Poor"
"Dr. Julian Nava to Remain on L.A. School District Board"
"Students Walk-out at Roosevelt," by Michael Sánchez
Arthur Montoya
"The Urban Coalition," by Lee A. Du Bridge

JAN 16 "Bd. of Educ. Ignores Community," by Michael Sánchez
"January 13, 1969 Board of Education Decision"
"Congress of Mexican American Unity Selects 4 Candidates to
Back for Board of Education"
"Leave Our Boats Alone!"
"New Careers Director at MAOF Symbolizes Problems and Hopes"
"Mexican-American Young Power"
"United Mexican-American Students Elect President"

JAN 23 Arthur Montoya on HOME
"Chris Ruiz to Head New East LA College Department"
"Housing Needs in Boyle Heights"
"Four Leading Mexican-American Women in Linea Abierta Panel"
"Hogan Issue Dead?" by Michael Sánchez
" 'Bill of Rights' for Mexican Americans Pledged by Tom Bradley"
"Mexican-American Merit Employment Conference"
"EYOA to Broaden Participation of Poor Community—Aragon"
"Report from Citizens Committee to Save Elysian Park"

JAN 30 "UMAS to Meet at Cal State to Discuss with Community About
Involvement with New Courses," by Richard Santillan
Joseph Eli Kovner
"ELAIP Works on Housing," by R.C.
"Attornies [sic] File Suit Against L.A.; Represent Barba"
"Lindsay Gets Millions from H.U.D. for Three Areas"
"Thirteen Mexican-American Militants Ask California Court of
Appeals to Bar Prosecution on Charges of Conspiracy to
Disturb Peace"
"School Officials Study Possibility of Forming Student Advisory
Board"

FEB 6   "Cranston, Roybal, Garcia to Install MAPA 40th Officers Tonight"
Joseph Eli Kovner
Arthur Montoya on HOME application submitted by Supervisor
Ernest Debs
"Linea Abierta to Explore Job Opportunities in Barrio"
"New Mexican-American Studies at East LA College to be Staffed
with Some New Instructors"

"Cutbacks Made in City Schools Compensatory Education
          Program,"
"Adios Al OEO," by Angel T. Solis
FEB 13   "Hollenbeck LAPD Change Command"
"Reagan Wants to Spend More But in the Wrong Places Says
          Assemblyman Alex Garcia"
Letter from Aliso-Pico Association to Congressman Ed Roybal
"Standard Oil's Mother Goose," by Joseph Eli Kovner
Art Montoya on East Los Angeles Community for Action and
          Congress of Mexican American Unity
" . . . New Careerists to Be Honored at E. Los Angeles College"
"Textbooks in Afro-American—Latin Amer. History Recommended
          for Adoption in City Schools"
"Bilingual School Students Enjoy Ballet Folklorico"
"Mexican-Americans Feel ELA Schools Not Getting Fair Share of
          School Money"
"Graduates from Police Academy," photograph
"The Mexican-American 'Push-Out' "
"Hollenbeck Police Announce Spanish Class"
"Honores a 'Cancion De La Raza' En La Ciudad"
FEB 20   "Art Montoya to Appear in 'Panel' at Cal State Seminar on Urban
          Issues"
"School Officials Warn of Disaster Facing L.A. Schools in Financial
          Crises"
"Youth Speakout in East Los Angeles to Be Sponsored by 'Linea
          Abierta' "
Joseph Eli Kovner
Art Montoya on Debs
"Assemblyman Alex Garcia Expresses 'Bitter Disappointment' at
          Not Being Appointed to Commision [sic] on the Cal."
"Finch Promete Mejorar La Educacion Bilingue"
"Importante Junta Del Comite Raza Pro Tom Bradley"
"[Tom] Quinn Urges Bilingual Teacher Recruitment"
"Assault on Racism"
"[Antonio] Medina Names Executive Director of Cleland House"
"Miss Ophelia Flores Appointed Girls' Vice Principal at Belvedere
          Jr. High School"
FEB 27   "It's Disaster Time, Citizens, Unless New Revenues Are Raised by
          L.A. District"
"Landmark Wrigley Field Is Razed"
Letter from Gary Alexander on saving Hazard Park and Camp High
          Sierra
"Workshops Held for Teachers in Disadvantaged-Area School"
MAR 6   "Group Intelligence Tests Eliminated in First Grade"
"Pupils Help in Planting Trees in Hazard Park"
"[Dionicio] Morales Named Chairman of E.L.A. Manpower Group"
Letter from Art Montoya to Supervisor Ernest Debs on HOME
"MAPA Backs Tom Bradley for Mayor"
"Law School Enrollment for Minority Students Increased"

Art Montoya on HOME
Joseph Eli Kovner on oil drilling
"La Ley Announces Annual Dinner-Dance"
"MAPA Announces School Board Support for Three"
"ELA-LCAC Spurs on the Job Training"
MAR 13   "Hazard Park . . . That Classic Robin Hood Story in Reverse"
Arthur Montoya on clergy's lax attitude toward Model Cities
        program
"Special Commission to Study Mexican-American Education"
"La Ley Announces Annual Dinner-Dance"
"Channel 28 to Televise 'Chicano Crises' Education"
"New Administration Assignments at East Los Angeles Schools"
MAR 20   "Asks Voters to Cast Ballots by Conscience, Not Color"
Arthur Montoya on clergy
"Mexican-American Leaders Support Irene Tovar"
"Agenda for EICC," by Richard Du Bois
"Teacher's Name Misspelled," by Mike Sánchez
"PALMA Endorses Tom Bradley,"
"Ed Roybal Endorses Tom Bradley"
MAR 27   "Vote for Ortega, Tovar, Shields, Barrera, Bennet, Fadem, Ed
        Brown, Jr."
"UCLA UMAS Needs Support to Win Special Entry for Chicanos"
"Centro Universitario to Open Monday in East Los Angeles"
"Death Ratio in Vietnam for Mexican-Americans Lower"
"Agenda for Educational Issues Coordinating Committee," by
        Richard Du Bois
"Cesar E. Chavez endorsed Rabbi Mathew Simon"
"A Mexican American History Course for High School Students"
MAR 30   "We Endorse Tom Bradley"
"Seek to Halt Elysian Park Freeway Plan"
APR 3   "Brown Bills Would Limit President's Power in Vietnam"
"Value of Schools to Be Studied by Mexican-American Confab"
"Barrios Unidos Meeting on Board Selection"
Art Montoya on petition circulated by Citizens Affiliated for Urban
        and Social Action
"Eugene Gonzales Spoke at Bilingual Adult Education Last
        Saturday"
"The Mexican-American's Search for Identity," by Yolanda Araiza
"Record Number of School Employees Learning Spanish"
"Educational Issues Coordinating Council"
"Education: Myth or Reality"
Letter form Bert Corona to Supervisor Kenneth Hahn on the
        expansion of the board of supervisors to include a Chicano
        supervisor
"Assemblyman Alex Garcia Seeks Funding of Bilingual Education
        on Augmented Scale"
"Critical Need to Find Employment for L.A. County Youth to Be
        Attacked"
"Police Academy Grads," photographs

"New Name for E.L.A. Labor Action Committee; to Be Called
   T.E.L.A.C.U."

APR 10   "[Pat] Sanchez Announces 'Barrios Unidos' Task Force Meeting
   Today to Set up Poverty Board"

"United Mexican American Students of U.C.L.A.," by Luis Arroyo,
   Chair of UMAS at UCLA

"Two Hundred Children Help Plant Trees in Hazard Park"

"Fiesta de Los Barrios to Be Held at Lincoln Park May 2–5"

Arthur Montoya prints letter to Ernest Debs inviting him to
   meeting to talk about Model Cities and HOME

"Agenda of the Educational Issues Coordinating Committee, April
   1, 1969, Euclid Heights Community Center, Albertine &
   Whittier, ELA," by Richard Du Bois

"Minority Enrollment Reaches 46.4 Per Cent [sic] in City Schools"

APR 17   "Tapia, State President of M.A.P.A., Tells it Like it Is on 'Tell it
   Like it Is' Confab of Democratic Party for Reform and
   Reorganization Up North," by Abe Tapia

" 'The Invisible Minority' To Air on TV-28 April 20"

"MAPA Meet Will Really Pop"

"Cartoon Books on Mexican-American Heros"

"Drive to Get Teachers of Mexican-American Descent Into
   Teaching"

"Benefit to Help LUCHA"

Arthur Montoya

"2nd Barrios Unidos Committee Meeting Set for Tonight, 7:30"

"Fiesta de los Barrios Seeks Works of Writers and Artists"

"ACLU Police Maltreatment Report Released Last Week"

APR 24   "Group Opposes Mexican American Education Commission: Group
   named 'Education Through Peace on Campus' "

"Tom Bradley Supports Farm Workers Strike at Rally"

Joseph Eli Kovner on the Eastside Sun's new offices

" 'Grassroot Power' Meeting Today of Barrios Unidos"

"Immigration Problems in the Barrio"

MAY 1   "Fiesta de Los Barrios Observes Cinco de Mayo"

Letter from Assemblyman David Roberti to Joseph Eli Kovner in
   response to accusation by Abe Tapia

Arthur Montoya on the Catholic Church and urban renewal

"Treaty Signed by Politicians in 'Little Los Covenants,' Ramona
   Gardens-Murchison," by Mario Hernandez, Jr.

MAY 8   "Hollenbeck Police Will Host Community Next Week"

"Eastside Leaders Join to Support Re-election of Yorty"

Letter from the Monterey Park City Council stating that the
   councilmen opposed the East Los Angeles Community
   College ethnic newspaper called La Vida Nueva, which
   annually used $30,000 of student funds

"Bilingual Ed Application Approved"

MAY 15   "Barrios Unidos Election Open for EYOA Board"

"Social Workers Accuse Professor of Gross Insensitivity"

"MAYAS Sponsor, Ramirez Says They Will Back Bradley All the
        Way to May 27 Runoff Election"
MAY 22   Joseph Eli Kovner on political endorsements
        "Yorty Asks Rescinding of Hazard Park Swap for Land in West Los
        Angeles"
        "Yorty Praises LAPD for Keeping Militants off the City Streets"
        Arthur Montoya on HOME and Model Cities
        "UMAS to Sponsor Student Speakers This Thursday"
        "400 Eastsiders Attend YOC 'Jobs for Youth' Campaign Meeting"
MAY 25   "[Irene] Tovar Leader in Race for Jr. College Trustees"
MAY 29   "Good Grief! Another Four Years of Yorty . . ."
        "Veteran's Hospital Program Lagging But ELA's Hazard Park
        Appears Safe," by Congressman George E. Brown
        "Hazard Park, Art Festival June 6, 7, 8"
        Joseph Eli Kovner on close mayoral race
        Arthur Montoya
        "Senior Citizens to Exchange Ideas with Youth at Cal State LA"
        "Chicanos to Examine Reforms in Education"
        "Roybal Promises Support to Vest Pocket Park Plan in Ramona
        Gardens"
        "Hunger Commission Holds Second of Scheduled 3-Days of
        Hearings"
JUN 5   ". . . Refusal of Bilingual Plan by Washington Protested by East
        LA"
        "Community Fiesta at Hazard Park This Weekend"
JUN 11   "EYOA Community Meeting at All Nations to Plan Future Anti-
        Poverty Services Tonight"
        "Nat. Institute on Police-Community Relations Meet"
        "UMAS Students Propose Changes to Cal State LA
        Administration"
        "Community, College Support Grows for UMAS Proposals to Cal
        State's Greenlee"
        "Census to Identify Ethnic Groups"
        "Yorty Makes Misleading Move on Hazard Park, May 13, Says
        Hazard Park Association," by A.M.
JUN 12   "Drug Abuse Time to Question More Closely 'Where It's At' "
        "Narcotics Abuse: Entire Community's Problem: Narcotics
        Prevention Project Is to Help Youth," by Carol Stevens
        "CAUCUS Aims to Be Source of Non-Hysterical Information on
        Drug-Related Problems"
        "Barrios Unidos Election"
        "Police Malpractice Brochure from ACLU"
        "TELACU Criticizes EYOA's Funding of Summer Program"
JUN 19   "A Free Clinic Sponsored by Brown Berets, Begins Operation"
        "Bible Tale: How Little Ramona Gardens Slew the City Giant of
        Goliath," by Mario Hernández
        "Drug Abuse Prevention Goals of Parents in ELA," by Carol
        Stevens

"Community Urged to Find Jobs for ELA Youth Through YTEP"
"Barrios Unidos Election Sunday Locally"
"Workshops on Mexican Immigrant to Be Held"
"Bradley Asks Vote Rights for Spanish Literates"
"Massive March and Camp-in to Begin Sunday at Cal-State for Educational Opportunity"
"Police Officers Graduation Held," photographs
JUN 26   ". . . Property Owners Meet Tonight," by Arthur Montoya
"UMAS Camp-in Supports Educational Reforms"
Joseph Eli Kovner on the police
"Mrs. Ramona [sic] Banuelos, First Woman Bank Board Chairman in U.S., at Pan American Bank"
"UMAS Camp-in at Cal-State to Show Public Support for EOP"
"Roosevelt and Hollenbeck to Get Mexican-American Principals in September"
"Omission of LA in Bilingual Ed. Unexplained"
"Formal Protest to Department of Labor Cutbacks on Youth Corps at YTEP"
"La Educacion Entre Los Mexicanos," by Angel T. Solis
"Piden Que La Comunidad Tome Parte En Una Lucha"
"Mexican Militants Press Conference," by Mike Sánchez
JUN 29   Letter from Celia L. De Rodríguez and George Mount
JUL 3   "All About the Killing of Schooling for the Poor People," by Carol Stevens
"Ramona Gardens Park Project Blocked by the State Highway Dept."
" 'Location to Where?' Asks Montoya of H.O.M.E. Program Enforcers," by Arthur Montoya
"NYC Cutbacks by Dept. of Labor Protested by ELA: YTEP Enrollees and ELA Residents Demonstrate at Cutbacks of Youth Corps"
"Education for the Deprived Murdered," by Carol Stevens
"Seek Bilingual Education for East Los Angeles"
"Mexican-American Workshop at Immaculate Heart College"
"Food for Grape Strikers"
JUL 10   "Arthur Montoya Discussed Basis for Rehabilitation Grants," by Arthur Montoya
Letters from Ramona Gardens residents
"Ethnic Composition of Area Should Be Represented in Draft Boards, Says Brown"
"School Board Adopts Bilingual Math Books"
JUL 17   "Why Must Authorities Dictate to the People Where & How They Live?" by Arthur Montoya
"This is the Park Ramona Gardens is Trying to Build"
"Result of Law Suit by Legal Aid Foundation Benefits Latin-Americans"
"Ramona Gardens Presents . . . to Highway Dept.," by Mario Hernández

"Fund Shuffling Foists Inferior Education on ELA"
"[Ed] Davis New Police Chief Takes Office"
"Hazard Park Land Swap Rescinded in City Council"
"Sal Castro to Appear on AHORA"
Letter from the Community Advisory Council of Second Street
        Elementary on SB 28 and the Miller Unruh program
        re-evaluation
"Health Needs of the Mexican-American Community as I see
        Them," by Vicente Zapata, Part II
"Delinquency Headaches Growing in LA County," by Jack Johnson
SEP 11   "What Does Director IMUS of HOME Mean When He Whispers
        Sweet Nothings in Our Ears," by Arthur Montoya
Letter from the Domínguez Defense Committee
"Mexican American Education Commission Supports Castro"
"Community Committee on AHORA New TV Program, Asked by
        Education Group"
SEP 18   "H.O.M.E. Program 'Government Without the Consent of
        Governed' " by Arthur Montoya
"250,000 View Mexican Independence Day Parade"
"ELA Health Task Froce Seeks Spanish-Speaking County Hospital
        Attendants"
"MAPA Urges Boycott of Safeway Stores"
SEP 25   "Attend Big Rally-Meeting to Oppose H.O.M.E. Programs Tonight
        at Belvedere Junior Hi [sic]"
"Chicano Studies Offered in ELA's Centro Universitario, An
        Extension of UCLA"
"Operation Intercept Is Not Enough," by Vicente Zapata
"El Teatro Campesino Opens Thurs."
"CMAA Seeking Financial Grant to Implement Research Project"
OCT 2   "We Know How H.O.M.E. Program Will Affect Our Lives; We
        Oppose It," by Arthur Montoya
"Peaceful March to Protest Sal Castro Transfer: ELA Parents Rally
        Oct. 6, in Support of Sal Castro"
"Report to the People on Proposed Bonds for Funding Improve-
        ments for Eastside Parks and Rec. Centers," by Joseph Eli
        Kovner
"Presbyterian Finance Group Deposits Funds in Pan American
        Bank to Assist Minorities"
"Reorganization of LAPD"
"National Hispanic Heritage Week Nixon Proclamation"
"Drugs in Our Community," by Eddie Lopez
OCT 9   "The H.O.M.E. Program, with Pretended Rehabilitation Is Urban
        Renewal in Disguise," by Arthur Montoya
"Judge's Intemperate Outburst Against Mexicans Investigated"
"Adolph Hitler Ideas Still Live in San Jose," by Joseph Eli Kovner
"Telegram Sent to President on Border"
"Sal Castro Harassment Protested"
"Public Hearing on Griffith Park Master Plan"

Letter from Guy Gabaldón to Richard Nixon, dated 28 September
    1969
"Suspension of Judge Asked by Assemblyman Alex Garcia"
OCT 16   "Why Spend Million $ to Widen Streets; Make Them 1 Way,
    Montoya," by Arthur Montoya
"Vietnam Moratorium Asks Nixon to End War Now: Moratorium
    on Vietnam War Begins Organized Dissent"
Letters on Chargin case
"30th Black and White Ball October 18 at Biltmore Hotel"
"Nixon Official Visits ELA to Review Community Self-Help
    Organization"
"Findings Revealed on Health Needs of ELA Community at
    Bilingual Conference"
"Groups Underwriting Police Malpractices Holds Dinner"
OCT 23   "Property Owners Meet Tonight at Belvedere Jr. Hi [sic] School"
"The Genocidal Mr. Yorty," by Carol Stevens
"Treatment of Bryan Questioned," by Roberto Castro
"Bilingual Health Conference at ELAC, This Saturday"
"High Chaparral Cast Guests at MAOF Aztec Awards Banquet
    October 23"
"Dominguez' Second Trial Ends In Hung Jury for Second Time"
OCT 30   "Daniel Lopez Is Appointed Deputy Director in State Human
    Resources Department"
"MAYO Seeks Community Involvement with Casa de Mayo," by
    Carol Stevens
"Conference on Health . . . of East LA Attended by 400 at ELAC"
"NEA Supports Sal Castro in Appeal"
"New Book on Mexican Americans"
Letter from Esteban Torres to EYOA
"Bilingual Education Proposed As Remedy for Low Reading
    Scores," by Louis Negrete
"No MAS Estudiantes"
NOV 6   "Former Assemblyman Elliot Retracts HOME Endorsement, Praised
    by Montoya," by Arthur Montoya
"Sen. Murphy Amendment May Cripple OEO Legal Services to
    Poor," by Congressman George E. Brown
"EYOA hits Protest Today in Civic Center Rally"
"Petitions to President Nixon to Free POW Lt. Everett Alvarez
    Now Being Circulated in ELA," by Carol Stevens
"Moratorium Activities at Cal-State"
"Judge Chargin Apologizes for Court Remarks"
Letter from Herminta R. Lewal, co-chair of the Committee to Save
    Hazard Park to Gilbert Lindsay
"Rally Opposes Poverty War Cutbacks; Raised to Send Delegates to
    the Capital"
"AD HOC Group Asks for Investigation of County Employment of
    Minorities"
"Mexican American Casualties in Vietnam," by Ralph Guzmán

"Chicano History Class Begun By Brown Berets"

"Chargin y Sus Disculpas," by Angel T. Solis

NOV 13   "Remember Bunker Hill; Model Cities Is Urban Renewal in
          Disguise," by Arthur Montoya

"Rosalio U. Munoz to Refuse Draft on Tuesday Morning"

"LUCHA to Set Up Wood Prod. Factory in ELA"

"ELA Divided Up by City Human Relations"

"EICC Leaflets on Reading Distributed"

"Third Fund-Raising Dance for Jesus Dominguez"

"11 De Noviembre," by Angel T. Solis

"ELA Health Service Conference November 22 at Medical Center"

NOV 20   "Detraction of HOME Program Endorsements Subject at Belvedere
          Jr. Hi [sic]"

"Alfred Bryan Faces Death Penalty If Convicted As An Adult," by
          Carol Stevens

"Rosalio Munoz Refuses Draft in Demonstration"

Joseph Eli Kovner on Model Cities

NOV 27   "Committee for the 'Rights of Imprisoned' Meet Thursdays"

Letter from Arthur Montoya on demonstration at Lady of Lourdes
          against HOME program

"More Chicano Nurses Is Goal of Cal State Los Angeles-
          Community Project"

"Lorena St. School—Community Council to Meet Tuesday Night"

"Girls Wanted by LAPD Hollenbeck Division," by Edward Lopez

"¿Education or Crimen del Siglo?" by Arturo Sanchez

"Project at College Seeks Chicano Vietnam Veterans"

DEC 4   "Rally Against Mishandling of Lincoln Heights Jail Project Dec. 7"

"Chicano Moratorium ELA On Vietnam, Saturday, Dec. 20"

"Resolution of the Members and Supporters of the East Los
          Angeles Maravilla-Belvedere Park Property Owners
          Association, Inc. Totalling an Excess of 5,000 people," by
          Art Montoya

Letter from Bill Sánchez, President of MECHA, to John J. Collins,
          President of Moorpark College

"War Makes Beasts of Men," by Angel T. Solis

Letter from Julian Nava to Barry M. Goldwater, Jr. on CRLA

Letter from Gilbert W. Lindsay to William Frederickson,
          Department of Parks and Recreation, on funds to improve
          Hazard Park

"MAPA 40th Dist. Meeting"

"Chris Ruiz to Study Day Care Program"

"School Board Members Charge Mexican-American Education
          Often Shameful"

"Lincoln Park Boathouse Proposed Chicano Art and Cultural
          Center by TELACU"

DEC 11   "We Propose Owners Insist on Being the Master of Our Own
          Destiny," by Arthur Montoya

"Dominguez Case Today 9 a.m."

"Dominguez Demandado Por la Ciudad"

"Labor/Management Relations Rocky at All Nations Center"

Letter from the Director of HOME to Kovner Publications program defending the program and stating that HOME had already rehabilitated 71 houses

"Moratoria de Mexicoamericanos"

"Jesus Dominguez Deserves Support of the Community"

"An Open Letter to George Ingles, Principal at Lincoln High School"

DEC 18   "4,000 Property Owners Have Signed Petitions Against HOME Program," by Arthur Montoya

"Management at All Nations Center Explains Role in Community Action and Service"

"Usted Y La Policia," by Roberto Arguello of the LAPD

DEC 25   "ELA Job Trainee Project Delay to Be Examined"

"Congressmen to Investigate Lincoln Heights Jail for Job Training Project in East LA"

"LA City Housing Authority Charged with Indifference to Public Housing Tenants"

"EYOA Gets $355,000 But OEO Cut Still at $780,000"

"Frito Bandido Stereotype Insult Says Dionicio Morales"

"Active Senior Citizen Helps Maravilla Property Owners"

1970

JAN 1   Letter from Rev. John R. Luce on Sal Castro

Letter from Frank S. López on the Frito Bandido

"Difficulties of Prisoners and Families Described to Assembly Committee"

"Ethnic Studies Library Open"

JAN 8   "Drug Awareness Week at Roosevelt High School"

"Eugene McCarthy Plans Visit to LA to Aid George Brown in Race for US Senator"

Letter from the Congress of Mexican American Unity on Católicos Por La Raza

"Mexican American Studies at Cal State LA Begins Jan. 5"

"EPIC Looking for Community Involvement in Education"

JAN 15   Art Montoya on HOME and Model Cities

"Youths Dig Drug 'Rap Sessions' in Camp Oak Grove"

"Fund Raising Dinner for El Proyecto del Barrio"

"Dominguez Celebration Dance Saturday, Jan. 31"

"Drug Deterant [sic] Program 'The Happening' Begins New Approach to Youth"

"Victor in Correctional Reform at CRC"

"MAOF Apprentice Contract Calls for 10 Week Training"

"Ask Legal Aid to Poor Continued"

JAN 22   "Destruction of Trees for Street Widening Ecologically Unsound," by Arthur Montoya

"No Progree [sic] on Lady Fair's Special Impact Contract on ELA
Says U.S. Dept. of Labor"
"McIntyre Retires as Cardinal"
Letters on urban renewal
"Positive Steps Needed to Reconcile Police and Youth"

JAN 29   "Pico Union, H.O.M.E., Model Cities Programs Hit Mexican-
Americans," by Arthur Montoya
"Nixon Ignores Own Task Force Report Vetoes HEW Education
Bill," by Carol Stevens
"Short Sight of Leaders Create Violence," by Carol Stevens
"Julio Gonzales New Vice Chairman California Youth Authority
Board"
"Colleges Now Recruiting for Mexican-American Students"
"Assemblyman Garcia on Urban Affairs Committee in Assembly"
"Local Librarian Promoted for ELA Service"
"California Rural Legal Assistance Report"

FEB 5   " 'We Are Interested in Convening a Congress of Property Owners
Associations' Montoya," by Arthur Montoya
"Alex Garcia Asks for Judge Chargin Impeachment: Assemblyman
Introduces Resolution to Impeach Judge Chargin"
"[Alfonso] Perez Named Principal at Roosevelt High School"
"Bilingual Special Assistant Sought for HEW on Health of
Mexican-Americans"
" 'Moe' Aguirre Is Down but Not Out . . . He Would Want
LUCHA Continued"
"Second Meeting on Plaza de la Raza February 6"
"Follow-up on Judge Chargin on AHORA"
"Historic Cleland House to Be Demolished After Disastrous
November Fire"
"Chicano Group to Convene for 'Power Through Unity"
"Llamado De MAPA Del 52 Districto"

FEB 12   "Inquest Hearing on Richard Hernandez to Be Held February 16th"
"Unlit Local Alleys in ELA Scene of Anti-Social Activity"
Joseph Eli Kovner on the Congress of Mexican American Unity
"Julian Nava Candidate to Rafferty's Job"
"Roosevelt Offers Mexican History Course for Adults"
Arthur Montoya
"Triunfo de MAPA en Huntington Park"
Letter from Rosalio Muñoz
"Congress of Mexican American Unity Convention Feb. 14–15th"
"Congress of Mexican American Unity Community Convention
Rules and Regulations"

FEB 19   "Maravilla, Belvedere, Boyle Heights Property Owners Meet
Tonight," by Arthur Montoya
"Garfield Complex Accepting Education Proposal: Mini-Grant
Proposals Being Accepted from Community by Garfield
Educational Complex"

"Archdiocese Clarified Church Role in Society in Answer to
Catolicos por la Raza"
"HUD Indifference to Street Lighting Needs in ELA Alleys"
"Chicano and Latino Community Join in March and Rally War
Protest February 28"
"Congressman Roybal Seeks Reelection in House of Rep."
"Un Ex Policia Consignado En el Caso Gonzales"
" 'Rafferty's Negative Influence on Education Must Be Stopped,'
Nava"
"Model Cities Meeting at Lincoln Heights"
"Adios A Frito Bandido," by Angel T. Solis
"Marcha de Protesta por La Guerra de Viet Nam El 28," by Angel
T. Solis
FEB 26   "Chicano Moratorium March and Rally in Eastside Sat., Feb.
28th"
"Reagan Is After 'Life and Death' Power Over Welfare
Dependents"
Arthur Montoya
"Inquest Rules Jail Hanging a Suicide"
Letter from MECHA California State Los Angeles
"Weekly Community Training Sessions Sponsored by LUCHA"
MAR 5   "Montoya Elected Community Chief Over Model Cities Program
Residents Give Him Overwhelming Vote to Represent East/
Northeast Area for Total Local Control; Federal Guidelines
Must be Changed"
Letter from David Sánchez stating that 7,000 people marched in
the rain on February 28 against the war
"Carta Abierta a Todos los Catolicos . . . ," by Pedro Arias
MAR 8   "LAPD Start New Neighborhood Patrol: Understanding between
police and citizens anticipated"
MAR 12   "Parents Opportunity to Meet LAPD on Roosevelt Problems
Tues."
"Montoya Meets with Mayor's Aides as Spokesman for the North,
Northeast Community: Housing and Relocation Clauses
Must Be Removed form Model Cities Application, Montoya
Tells Russell Ames, Administrative Assistant to Mayor
Yorty," by Arthur Montoya
"Roosevelt High School Student Demonstrations Broken Up:
Roosevelt Student Protest," by Celia De Rodriguez
"Permanent Assignments Given to Hollenbeck LAPD in Effort to
Work with Residents"
"Rafferty Accused of Misapplication of Two Billion in Education
Funds"
"TELACU Mattress: A Means of Economic Awakening"
Joseph Eli Kovner on demonstrations at Roosevelt High School
"Esteban Torres New President of Congress of Mexican American
Unity"

APR 12   "Grammar school students plan Earth Day pollution protest," by
         Carol Stevens
APR 16   "He Will Have to Take the Issue of Model Cities Direct to the
         People," by Arthur Montoya
         "Will Gov. Reagan Listen to Los Angeles Teachers?"
         "Hernandez Family Files Claim $2,305,000 Against Sheriff"
         "Roybal and Bonpane to Seek CDC 30th Dist. Endorsement"
         "EYOA Delegation Asks for More State Headstart Funds"
         "Chargin Censure by Judicial Commission"
         Letter from Frank Sifuentes titled "Reflections on a Police Riot at
         Roosevelt in East Los Angeles"
APR 19   "[Herman] Sillas Launches new campaign"
APR 23   "Reagan Must Bear Responsibility for the L.A. Strike," by Carol
         Stevens
         "Some Incumbents Facing Political Suicide on H.O.M.E.
         Positions?" by Arthur Montoya
         "Henry Lopez, Noted Author, to Discuss Chicano Politics"
         "Free Lecture Series Sponsored by LUCHA Every Wednesday"
         "Tuition to Be Raised in LA Archdiocesan Schools"
         "EYOA Not Meeting Needs of Mexican-American Community"
         "30th District Backs Roybal"
         "La Venganza De Los Conservadores," by Angel T. Solis
APR 30   "Congressman Asks for Removal of 'Hitler-Was-Right' Chargin"
         "Cinco De Mayo Observed Throughout Los Angeles"
         "[Snyder] Recall Building Up . . ." by Arthur Montoya
         "Nava, Castro and Sanchez Speakers at 'Semana de Cultura' in Rio
         Hondo"
         "Joe Montano, Fifth Death in ELA Sheriff's Station"
         Letter from Ruben Almanzan defending the LAPD and school
         administrators at Roosevelt High
         "Peticiones de Mecha Y Umas A Chas. Young"
MAY 7   "Reagan Up to Old Tactics of Avoiding Issue in Teacher Strike,
         Says Gonzalo Molina"
         Letters from parents telling of conditions at Lorena Elementary
         " 'Community Participation' " Methods for 'Model Cities' Phony,
         Says Montoya," by Arthur Montoya
         "No Gifts for Mother's Day," by Joseph Eli Kovner
         "Brown, Tapia Endorsed by Chavez"
         "Chicano Brotherhood Slate Brings New Type of Student Body
         Representatives"
         Letter from Richard Hultman answers letters from Frank Sifuentes
         and Ruben Almanzan
         "US Civil Rights Commission Issues Report On Discrimination"
MAY 10   "Cal State LA Students find planned strikes 'close' campus"
MAY 14   "Here are 2 Cases with Names, of Harassment by H.O.M.E.
         Inspectors," by Arthur Montoya
         "School Strike Now Over"
         "CSO Holds 23rd Year Celebration"
         Letter from Charles (Chuck) Pineda on HOME

JUN 22   "Human Relations phase out rejected by Council"
JUN 25   "Suit Questions Legality of Model Cities Elected Councils in
         North/Northeast Area," by Arthur Montoya
         "First Annual Arte de los Barrios"
         Letter from Esteban Torres, President of the CMAU
         "Who is Mayo?" by Joseph Ortiz
         Letter from Richard López asking why others make it and
         Mexicans do not
JUL 2   "Attorney to Explain Legal Rights of All Affected by HOME and
         Model Cities Program," by Arthur Montoya
         "Dr. Nava Elected New LA School Board President"
         "KWKW Airs LUCHA Documentary"
         "D. A. Plans Prosecution of 1968 High School Walkouts and
         Biltmore Arrests"
         "Shift on Grape Strike Seen"
         "Chavez Helps TELACU to Celebrate"
         "Mexican American Education Commission Commends Schools on
         Raising Reading Scores"
         Letter from Joe Sánchez of *La Quebradita* to Kovner thanking him
         for good community coverage on issues ranging from Model
         Cities to the workings of community organizations
         "Welfare Rights Group Says They Are Ready to Take All Jobs
         Available"
JUL 9   "Why Are the Maravilla-Belvedere Park Property Owners Against
         Model Cities Program?"
         "New Bilingual Educational Program at Bridge, City Terrace,
         Second St. Schools"
         "The Beginning and Growth of the Mexican-American Education
         Commission"
         "$95,000 Program to Expand Construction Job Assistance for
         Mexican-American Contractors"
         "Where are the Landmarks of Yesterday?" by Joseph Eli Kovner
         "Bilingual Help on Tax Refunds for Senior Citizens"
JUL 16   "NYC Program Mutilated by New Department of Labor
         Guidelines"
         "Residents Councils Have Influence, Yorty Has Power," by Arthur
         Montoya
         "United Stand and Some Demands," by Joseph Eli Kovner;
         "Mexican American Education Commission Stresses Equal
         Attainment for All Children"
         Open Letter to ELA businessmen regarding the LAPD
JUL 23   "City/County Continues NYC after EYOA Drops Labor Contract"
         "CSO Resolution Outlaws 'Justifiable Murder' "
         "Assemblyman Garcia Calls for Protection of Community from Los
         Angeles Police"
         "I'm Going to My Home Town, Clifton, Arizona," by Arthur
         Montoya
         "Tragic Deaths," on Beltran Sanchez, 23, and Guillermo Sanchez,
         22

"Cong. Roybal Assails Tragic Mistake of LAPD Resulting in Death
of Two Mexican Nationals: DA Presses Charges on 7 Police
Officers with Manslaughter: Congressman Puts Police
Commissioners on the Carpet"
"Felix Ontiveros Warns Localities Who Build," by Joseph Eli
Kovner
"A Second Trial for Danny?" by Celia de Rodriguez
"Investigation Requested on ELA Sheriff's Station Deaths"
"Chicano Health Workers Hold Conference in S.F."
"The Police Commission," by Edward Lopez
"[Dionisio] Morales Suggests Easing Tensions Between Mexican
Americans and Blacks"
"An Eastside Autobiography," Part I

JUL 26   "Cal State LA Opens first College drug information Center"
JUL 30   "Summer School Bill Could Turn Schools Over to Birch Soc."
AUG 6   "Dr. Nava Endorses Niles [sic] in Race for Rafferty's Job"
"Fiesta for Chicano Unity"
"NYC Labor Dep. Guidelines Changed by Request of EYOA"
" 'I am Joaquin' Drama from Poem at Roosevelt"
"UAW's Woodcock Visits TELACU's Mattress Company"
"El Monte Police Shoot-out Victim Held on $50,000 Bail," by
Celia de Rodriguez
"Charges Abandoned Against Sal Castro on '68 Blowout"
AUG 13   "Eastside Autobiography by a Resident of Monterey House"
"Sanchez Families Helped"
"Legislation to Halt Proposed Beverly Hills Freeway Passes," by
Joseph Eli Kovner
"Maravilla-Belvedere Park Prop. Owners to Meet Thurs., Aug. 20"
"Interview with President Elect Luis Echeverria," by Eddie Pardo
AUG 20   "Chicano Art Spotlighted in Centro Library Exhibit Sept."
"Read All About Workable Programs Model Cities and Eastside
Victims," by Arthur Montoya
"Commercial Drug Overproduction Reaching Crisis: Drug
Companies Producing Twice the 'Ups' and 'Downs' Needed
for Medical Purposes"
"NBC Mexican American series," by Joseph Eli Kovner
"Equal Opportunity and Adequate Delivery of Medical Services to
Mexican Americans," by Dr. Francisco Bravo
Letter from Edmund D. Edelman to Kovner on Elysian Park
giveaway
AUG 23   "Cal State LA EOP Performs 'miracle' for Chicano Coed"
AUG 27   "Cong. E. Roybal Lauds Organizers of Anti-Vietnam Moratorium"
" 'Master Planning Belongs in a Totalitarian State, Not in a Free
Society,' Montoya," by Arthur Montoya
"National Chicano Moratorium March Saturday"
"Chicano Moratorium August 29"
"Chicano Moratorium Gets Community Support," by Joseph Eli
Kovner

OCT 15 "El Teatro Campesino Returns to Inner City"

    "D.A. Announces No Prosecution on Salazar Death," by Evelle J. Younger

    "Meet of Police Commissioners Open to Public"

    "Mexican American Community Leaders Support Superior Court Judge Alfred Gitelson"

    "PICA Workshops Now Going at Salazar Park"

    "Sen. Dymally Asks for Investigation into Killing of Newsman Ruben Salazar"

    "Younger Charged by [Charles] O'Brien with Intimidation of Media"

    "Arreola Supervisor on M-A Education Commission"

    "LAPD Answers Allegations"

    "Sheriff Dept. Better Prepared from Standpoint of Weaponry Says Sheriff Peter Pitchess"

OCT 22 "D.A. Charged with Abdication of Responsibility on Salazar Death Case"

    "There Are Questions That Must Be Answered—About Aug. 29 Fracas"

    "Roybal Repeats Plea for Salazar Federal Inquiry"

    "LUCHA-CRI Report Calls for Sweeping Penal Reform"

    "Poll 44.9 Percent of ELA Mexican-Americans Feel Unequal Before the Law"

    "Mexican-American Labor Council gives support to Younger for Att'y General"

    "Fondos Para Educacion Compensatoria"

OCT 29 "School Decentralization in LA Will Proceed Without Having 'Gun in the Back' "

NOV 5 "Barrio Defense Group Charges Law Officials with Genocide"

    "Just Another Form of Instant Urban Renewal," by Arthur Montoya

    Letter from Frank Martínez, Chair of the National Moratorium Committee

    "City Must Show Evidence of Citizen Participation in Model Cities—CMAU Suit"

NOV 12 "Tell Us If Aggressive Inspectors Harass Homeowners," by Arthur Montoya

    "Plaza de la Raza Launches Ruben Salazar Building"

    "P.R. for Model Cities"

    "Minorities Face Job Barriers in Asbestos and Sheet Metal Trades"

    "Conference on Drug Abuse by Professional Educators"

NOV 15 "Vikki Carr devotes portion of earnings for Mexican-American scholarships"

NOV 19 ELA Elementary Reading Scores Frightening at First Glance," by Carol Infranca

    "Police Commission Increases Misconduct Complaint Services"

    "Moratorium arrests Last Sat.," by Carol Stevens

1971

JAN 21   "Survival Coalition calls poor people to mass protest rally Sun."
"Meet tonight to fight annexation of part of ELA to Monterey
    Park," by Art Montoya
"Fast begun as proof of marchers' non-violent intent 31st"
"MP Planning Commission says no to ELA Annexation"
Commentary by Deputy Concilman Felix Ontiveros remembering
    Boyle Heights in the old days
"Chicano Caucus seeks direct OEO funding"
"*Mi Vida Loca En El Barrio*: Social adjustment in a drug-free life,"
    by George Uribe

JAN 28   "ELA Health Task Force march on capital to protest Medi-Cal
    cuts"
"Unemployed Youths in ELA rise to 37% in new EYOA statistics"
"64 Congressmen protest U.S. air war over Cambodia"
"The Police view on ELA demonstrations"
"Sun. march backed by MAPA"
Letter from Rosalio Muñoz, co-chair of the National Chicano
    Moratorium, on the January 31 march
"Bradley supports better representation for Chicanos"
"Bill to bring bilingual doctors up from Mexico"
"In defense of Alex Cota"
Letter from David Sánchez, Co-Chairperson of the National
    Chicano Moratorium
Art Montoya
"Protesta Roybal por la ampliacion de la guerra"
"On 'peaceful' protests," by Eddie Lopez

FEB 4   "Three day march ends with peaceful Chicano Moratorium rally"
"Bill to limit Defense Department buying on non-union lettuce"
" 'Post rally party' at sub-station snowballs into violence: ELA
    scared by 4th outburst in 5 months," by Carol Infranca
"*Press Conference*: Media's questions parried"
Letter from Mario Vásquez supporting UFWOC and César Chávez
"El Domingo fatal"
Art Montoya on the California Rural Legal Assistance

FEB 7   "Pitchess raps 'tragic results' of Chicano Moratorium events," by
    Peter J. Pitchess
"Davis lauds citizens who avoided violence"
Photographs of January 31 demonstration

FEB 11   "Roybal announces congressional probe into ELA disturbances"
"Lack of M-A representation on Senate abetted by Reagan"
"Quake shakes Southland"
"Eastside Democratic Club protests Medi-Cal cuts"
Letter from "A disgusted ELA mother" condemns the marchers
    and defends the police
"Cleaned-up Hazard Park has family program"
"Mexican-American assistant director of OEO appointed by Nixon"
"Reagan signs CRLA short-term grant"
"Pitchess announces dismissal of jail guards"

FEB 14   "HEW and Scientific Affairs Assistant Secretary Visits East Los
          Angeles health agencies"
          "OEO notifies CRLA of six month funding"
          "Peace Corps position available for M-A's"
          "Minority enrollment up to 50.2% in Los Angeles School system"
FEB 18   "A Police proposed Charter Amendment threatens Elysian Park"
          "We all agree the move to incorporate ELA is a noble one,
          but . . ."
          "In Rebuttal to 'Disgusted Mother,' " by Jose Maria Sanchez,
          owner of La Quebradita
          "Student Replies to 'Disgusted Mother' "
          "Aftermath of Violence"
          Letter from David Sánchez, Prime Minister of the Brown Berets,
          titled "Police State in ELA"
          "Mexicans are beautiful," by Micaela Calderon
FEB 25   " 'The young lawyers help us in our struggle,' says Art Montoya"
          "Hazard Park not for 'grabs' "
          "Earthquake closes library"
          Letter from César Chávez
          "La Raza Unida Party to build platform Set"
          "Roybal sees HEW-sponsored bilingual program at Huntington
          Drive School"
FEB 28   "Bill to rescend [sic] Medi-Cal cuts blocked by State Republicans"
          "Julia Orozco, bilingual USC grad, to head East Los Angeles
          library"
MAR 4   "The majority is not silent—Government is deaf," by Art Montoya
          Joseph Eli Kovner on the closure of the Franklin library
          "Four police indicted in July apartment raid," by Carol Infranca
          "A Policeman's Mother Speaks Out"
          "Yorty and Hazard Park," by A. Ramirez and Kyle Ogden
          Letter from Mrs. Martinez, 24, titled "Mr. Sanchez—You Are Not
          a Mother"
          " 'Vida loca' obscure since leaving drugs," by George Yribe
          "ELA YTEP Supports UFWOC's lettuce strike in Delano"
          "Model Cities meeting to begin at jail"
MAR 11   "Emergency immigration conference set for Mar. 26–27 at ELA"
          "School decentralization under consideration," by Carol Infranca
          "Complete So. Cal freeway system could cost $18 billion"
          "Council has five 'no's' on legal aid"
          "The Barrio Free Clinic reopens Mar. 12"
          "The President said . . . ," by Art Montoya
          "Curb sought on weapons of LA Sheriff Dept."
          "Imigracion y la raza se discuten"
MAR 14   "[Julian] Nava opens Eastside campaign headquarters"
MAR 18   "Roybal praises grand jury investigation, indictment of officers"
          "Garcia declared for vacated state seat"
          "M-A Ed Commission resignation still stands"

"Statement of Mexican American Education Commission on Resignation"

"MAPA 40th endorse B of E candidates"

"Raza y la imigracion"

MAR 25   "Molina testifies before State Committee on Reapportionment"

"ELAC and Hollenbeck Park neglected by authorities"

"Security bumping into each other at ELAC," by Carol Stevens

"B of E ok's another decentralization step," by Carol Infranca

"Shall it be clear or muddy waters for Hollenbeck's lake?" by Joseph Eli Kovner

"Immigration conference received wide support"

"B of E Member Sees 'Joaquin' "

"Committee to Save Hazard Park wins"

APR 1   "First Housing Authority Resident Advisory Council holds election"

"Taxpayers suit filed Against City Council"

"Dr. Nava y otros liberales, peligran"

APR 4   "Gonzalo Molina reelected to CDC Board of Directors"

APR 8   "Rehabilitation and prison reform to be discussed at CSLA confab"

"Parks and Rec approves phasing out of Police Academy in Elysian Master Plan"

"Open Hearing on ELA Annexation," by Arturo A. Franz

"Elysian land grab by police slowed, not halted"

"Manuel Ruiz new member of Civil Rights Commission"

"Catholic fund used for 'seed money' projects"

APR 15   "ELA residents watch police copter landing"

"LA Unified to get biggest slice of Federal vocational ed grant"

"Karabian tells of major prison reform plans to aid rehabilitation"

". . . Staff report on ELA annexation"

"Hollenbeck Lake"

"Festival erupts into melee," by Carol Infrance

"Barrio Free Clinic offers blood tests for V.D."

"Senate districts in south show increased population"

APR 18   "NYC related programs suffer support lack from high officials who 'don't understand' "

"Calif. schools to lose more than $17 million in Federal aid under Nixon recommended cutbacks"

APR 22   "Southwest Museum trial ends in 'guilty' verdict for 12 Indians"

"Senator asks spring war protesters not to violate laws"

"Nonviolence in anti-war demonstration urged"

"Hollenbeck Lake Caper"

"PICA [Parent Involvement and Community Action] has important meeting"

"Witnesses Claim they saw inmates gassed"

"Drug Problem," by George Yribe

"Chicano unemployment in ELA discussed"

APR 25   "Angry demonstrations could be eliminated"

APR 29   "Amount of participation in Model Cities should be interesting,"
                by Art Montoya
           "Legislator's reapportionment power should be curtailed, Advisory
                Committee issues report"
           "Commission [Mexican American Population Commission of
                California] issues 1970 Report on Mexican American
                population"
           "Answers Barrio Defense Police Charges," by Joseph G. Velna
           "New Group plans strike against entire Anglo system"
           "My Raza," by Manuel Jesus Rodriguez
           "Aliso Village Demonstration," by Bernard Lambert
MAY 2   "ELAC Sets week long Cinco de Mayo fiesta"
MAY 6   "Anderson 'prods' Justice Dept. and HEW on controlling drugs"
           "Dr. David Lee challenges Orozco to debate Jr. college issues"
           "School dress codes abolished by Los Angeles Board of Education"
           "American Friends Service Committee"
MAY 9   "Population pressures in urban Centers cited as 'immediate'
                problem by Councilman Bradley"
           "Conference will spotlight M-A education programs"
MAY 13   "Educational Issues Conference explores Chicano student Needs"
           "Voter turnout can save community colleges," by Arthur Lee
           "The Real Story behind J. Edgar Hoover," by Carol Stevens
           "Barrio Free Clinic gets dental aids"
           "Sheriff's Dept. to begin own 'basic car plan' "
           "ELA Health Task Force Clears Up Points"
           "CMAU Notice On Past May 8th Meeting"
           LAPD graduate photographs
           "TELACU gets $140,000 in federal funds"
           "Problema que hay que solucionar," by Angel T. Solis
           "[EYOA] Candidates in Area 5 at All Nations"
           Letter from Leonard Castellanos, TELACU Taller Gráfico,
                announcing the California Chicano Art Symposium
           "Picketting of Plaza Center"
MAY 16   "Legislation proposed by Assemblyman Stull, La Corte would
                modify teacher tenure laws"
           "Community relations program announced"
MAY 20   "Do you want common sense or nonsense in community colleges"
           "Filibuster against draft extension to be initiated if all else fails"
           "Determined Chicanos march to Sacramento from Calexico"
           "Judge holds Oxnard accountable for discriminatory pattern in
                schools"
           "Avanza la marcha de Mexicoamericanos"
           "Las becas Salazar fueron donadas . . ."
           "Lopez Lee vs. Orozco," by Angel T. Solis
           Art Montoya on the Catholic school system
           "Task Force nominations closed amid confusion"
MAY 23   " 'Reconquista' marchers 'denied' use of facility," by Carol
                Infranca

"A Real taxpayers revolt is necessary to evoke desperately needed
    tax reform"

"WRO reminds welfare recipients of hearing deadline, procedure"

MAY 27   "Senator Cranston adds his support to cut in size of NATO forces"

"Conservatives tighten grip on school system in LA," by Joseph
    Eli Kovner

"Western Center Refunded"

"Withheld billions adds to unemployment"

"Gang Activities' to be held June 2 topic at Hollenbeck Basic Car
    meeting"

"La marcha de la reconquista"

"Chicano manpower specialists dedicate convention to Salazar"

"ELA Health Task Force election May 29"

"Chicana to be heard from in Houston"

"Root causes of police-community crises must be investigated"
Art Montoya

JUN 3   "Chief Davis commends ethnic communities," by Joseph Eli
    Kovner

"MECHA sponsors canned food and clothing drive for march"
Art Montoya on HOME program

"Euclid Heights Center to host Barrio Housing Seminar Saturday"

"Model Cities Neighborhood Resident Council," a photograph

"Sheriff cites weekend 'teen' party problems"

"Querellas contra LAPA"

"Lincoln Separated in new decentralization"

JUN 6   "ELA Health Task Force to aid health department in today's
    Rubella immunization campaign"

"Yuba City murders point to needed reform in California's migrant
    labor system"

"Sesame, Model Cities on same bill at Euclid"

JUN 10   "Comm. Ortega makes appeal to end defacing of structures"

"City Human Relations Dept. on verge of getting . . ."

"Reconquista marchers arrive," by Carol Infranca

"ELA Health Task Force election"

"Chicano Art exhibit at Bullocks, downtown"
Art Montoya

"Mexican American doctors can now practice under new state
    law"

"Human Relations Budget Cut"

"Senatorial Candidate," on Julia Luna Mount for 27th District

"Hazard Park contract awarded"

"Se Salva importante comision," by Angel T. Solis

"Bomb explodes at Roosevelt High School"

"Chicano woman's rise to independence studied"

JUN 13   "Criminal trials' cost critically examined by California State
    Legislature this year"

"Federal grant given to renovate Hazard Park"

"New merger enlarges legal services for poor"

"Reconquista marchers plan retreat to discuss strategy," by Carol Infranca

JUN 17 "Hazard Park improved with federal-city funds"
"Reconquista marchers plan June 19 rally at San Fernando Park"
"Los documentos secretos," by Angel T. Solis, on the Pentagon Papers
"La marcha de la Reconquista," by Arturo Sanchez
"Pacheco Superintendent of 43 East LA Schools now"
"Garcia cites issues in June 22 election"

JUN 20 *"Alien deportation problems outlined*: Immigration and your rights," by Jorge Licon

JUN 24 "Successful Mujeres Por La Raza Convention held in Houston," by Francisca Flores
"Plaza de la Raza free summer program starts"
"Parochial School Financial Crisis"
"Reconquista speakers urge all to join political party"
"Three separate bombings occur in E. Los Angeles"
"Law scholarships in honor of Ruben Salazar"
"Self-awareness can be key anti-drug weapon," by George Yribe
Art Montoya on redevelopment agency and the federal Department of Housing and Urban Development
"Supervisors of police study of helicopters' utility"

JUN 27 "Human Relations Bureau Hearing slated in final attempt to gain funding for summer"
"Grand jury indicts 31 in welfare fraud case"

JUL 1 "ELA reading scores too low MAEC says"
"U.S. Supreme Court rules 6–3 against Government Publication of Pentagon papers Ok"
"Mexican-American women ponder future role of the Chicana," by Francisca Flores
"El dificil camino," by Angel T. Solis
Art Montoya on encounter with Debs over HOME
"Cardoza appointed to head Affirmative Action program"

JUL 4 "Beilenson charges deceit in welfare reform fight"

JUL 8 "Labor Dept. launches program to help migrant farmworker"
"Legislation disadvantageous to farmworkers blocked. Right to boycott threatened"
"Senatorial Candidate," on Julia Luna Mount
"Infection, abortion Increase among youth," by Francisca Flores
"East LA Task Force receives grant"
"Falla la educacion," by Angel T. Solis
"Dinero para combatir la drogadiccion"
"Relevant classes about Chicano community set"
"Council committee sends anti-DDT bill to floor"
"Mount seeks Senate seat as voice for barrio, women"
"Bilingual education program enters second year in ELA; expands services to include 2nd grade"

JUL 15 "Reagan's veto of $100 million for local schools boomerangs"
   "Barrio woman for State Senator," by Carol Stevens
   "Community Responds to Youth's crisis"
   "A Report from MACF"
   "Vigil to be held for Sanchez cousins' death"
   "Nuestra comunidad," by Angel T. Solis
   "El Pocho"
   Letter from Julia Luna Mount stating that other judges should
    emulate Judge Stanley Moffat's courage in opposing the
    police when seeking justice

JUL 18 "Solicitors collecting Medi-Cal cards stopped by DPSS, East Los
    Angeles Health Task Force"

JUL 22 "Welfare changes discussed at Board meeting"
   "Textbook Task Force charges 'Band-aid' treatment by publishers"
   "East LA Senior Adult Center slates Housing Authority Program"
   "MAOF decries removal of A-A education"

JUL 25 " 'Festival de Artes' talent show for community youth scheduled
    August 4 at East LA College"
   "Lawsuit in offing after Gov. Reagan's veto of bill for Spanish
    language in election booths"
   "Narcotics officer wounded in ELA shooting incident"
   "Unsafe schools target of Roybal legislation"
   "First community housing project opens in East Los Angeles area"

JUL 29 "Owner of car allegedly used in ELA shootings was not involved"
   "Hundreds of community children to display talents: Festival de
    artes scheduled," by Carol Infranca
   "Reconquista Marchers Need Aide"
   "Fast planned by four ELA residents to support UFWOC's lettuce
    boycott"
   "26 member Boyle Heights Advisory group named to aide Planning
    Dept."

AUG 1 "Mexicano Art Center three man show opens"

AUG 5 "Delegation sent to testify against textbooks"
   "Food Stamp advisement centers set up to help ELA residents"
   "Reconquista marchers plan rally on Capitol steps Sat."
   "Lindsay meets with Carnalismo members"
   "Handicapped ELA youngsters get free speech therapy this
    summer"
   "Justice Dept. asked to probe [Francisco] Garcia slaying"
   "Slate drive to recall governor"
   "Nueva orientacion de M.A.P.A."
   "Garcia 'appalled' at Reagan's veto"
   "Barrio Free Clinic needs funds now"
   "Board of Ed forms new committee on community"
   "ELA Big Brothers elect new Advisory Board pres., Gilbert A.
    Moret"
   "New advisory council holds little power," by Art Montoya

"Roybal announces new YMCA minibike project"
"Mechicano Center offers free art classes weekly"
"State Supreme Court casts wary eye at LA's voter-apportioned
    council districts"

AUG 8   "Students probing tax loopholes find $20 million annual loss"
"Sal Castro featured on " 'Let's Rap' television"
"Three-unit college credit given for televised History of Mexico
    series"

AUG 12   "Policeman acquitted in mistake slaying of Mexican Nationals"
"Picketers protest welfare cuts dismissal of worker"
"Unsatisfactory decision in Sanchez case," by Carol Stevens
"Welfare Rights Organization seeks investigation of DPSS firing of
    four welfare employees"
"Marchers reach Sacramento"
"August Basic Car meets to salute local youth"
"Library Protest"
"Esteban Torres new director of TELACU"
"Practicas policiales," by Angel T. Solis
" 'Chicanos' para la Esc de Medicina"
" 'Justicia' seeks end to anti-Chicano racism of Hollywood film
    studios"
"Justicia-KABC reach agreement"

AUG 15   "Emergency employment funds will create 'at least' 25,000 public
    jobs in state"
"Commission to discuss oil issue at public meeting"
"Welfare compromise a start Supervisor [Debs] Says"

AUG 19   "Freeze effect on 'average American' announced"
"ELA residents invited to air complaints on Fire, Police Depts.,"
    by Carol Infranca
"Marchers' Sacramento stay ends"
"ELA YALP demonstrators question head librarian about poor
    services"
"Los Angeles' Chicano employees unite under new association"
"East LA Health Task Force announces Board nominations"
"La congelacion de precios y sueldos," by Angel T. Solis
"Poetry provides new meaning to 'Chicano' "
Open letter from the National Chicano Treasury (Marcha de la
    Reconquista)
"[Richard A.] Hernandez appointed to Los Angeles District
    Advisory Council of SBA"

AUG 26   "Reagan condemned for delaying 48th AD Elections"
"Carnalismo plans strike Sun"
Letter from Jacobo Rodríguez, El Pueblo Community member,
    announcing El Dia del Chicano on August 29
"WRO leader tells other side of welfare issue," by Alicia Ecalante
"Lindsay letter prompts police investigation"
"La comunidad no es 'Pelota' de nadie"

"Welfare rights pide se haga investigacion"
"MAEC received apology from Eastern publisher"
"ELAC anti-drug project gets grant, expands"
"Labor dept. funds training for Chicano prison inmates"
"Media corporation hires first Mexican-American"
"Welfare Reform Act author [Anthony Beilenson] says bill is major
    step forward"
"Racial balances may . . . school transfers—Lindsay"
Letter from the National Chicano Treasury to the community

SEP 2   "Opportunity knocks—community doesn't answer," by Carol
    Infranca
"Citizen's rights when stopped or arrested by police explained"
"East LA stores close in memory of Ruben Salazar"
"August 29 activity"
"Five testify before new Police, Fire Committee"
"Congressmen urge attention to Mexican-American issues"
"Investigation of Police-community . . . actions, shooting incident
    urged"
Letter from Julia Mount, Peace and Freedom candidate

SEP 5   "Court ruling against public school funding hailed by LA school
    superintendent"
"New Captain [to Hollenbeck Division]"

SEP 9   "Barrio Defense Complaint"
"Police Commission VP lauds officers; acquittal decision"
"TELACU alcanza su mayoria de edad, afirma"
"Suggestions from Lindsay how to deal with Police reported"
"TELACU's business successes reported"
"Chicano Employees [LACECA] discuss Affirmative Action
    Program"
"Aptitude test in Spanish now being developed in Southwestern
    states"

SEP 12   "JOBS '70 MAOF launches new employment program"
"Registration at bilingual school starts tomorrow"

SEP 16   "Local clinic offers Heroin detoxification service"
"Free clinic moves"
"La Feria de la Raza starts Sat. at CSLA"
"Different perspective on holiday"
"Police, Fire and Civil Defense hearings resume next Thursday"
"La fiesta de la raza en Cal State"
Letter from Rafael Flores, Director of the National Chicano
    Survival Committee

SEP 19   " 'Project Loophole' students cite California based insurance
    companies' avoidance of tax increase"
"U.S. Justice Dept. tightening controls on certain drugs"

SEP 23   (Entire issue is missing)

SEP 26   "Fair representation for Mexican-Americans urged"
"House prohibits establishment of WW II-like detention camps"

SEP 30   "National Women's Political Caucus to meet Sat."
          "Governor cuts out child care centers in state budget," by Alex
              Garcia
          " 'Preguntada' Oct. 5 features live play 'The Junkie' "
          "New Health educator appointed"
          "Brutality, harassment, perjury charges made against police"
          "New Hollenbeck Captains"
          "Maestros de Nayarit hold monthly meeting"
          "Mayor Yorty signs ordinance enabling city to participate in
              Emergency Employment Act"
          " 'Justicia' examined on KWKW"
          "Tenants' Union forming in Los Angeles Area"
          "Maestros de Nayarit discuss Issues conference"
          "MAPA backs earthquake safety bill for schools"
          "Sixteen local residents assume East LA Model Cities positions"
          "Los Comicios en el 48," by Angel T. Solis
OCT 3   "Hold 4 youths as suspects in fatal shooting of 10 yr.-old"
          "[George] McGovern calls for more Chicano teachers"
OCT 7   "Imbalance in ethnic staffing prompts EYOA Walkout: Chicanos
              Object," by Carol Infranca
          "Fire to be Basic Car meet topic"
          "Thirteen Chicanos certified in film, TV training program"
          "Senate ok's anti-detention camp bill"
OCT 14   "Chicano walkout exposes EYOA irregularities"
          "Creation of East LA district could equalize California Senate"
          "EMPLEO to arrange transportation for Calif. prison inmates
              families"
          "Chief Davis, Lee Trevino join Stars for gold Sun."
          "Fifteen-year-old ELA boy shot, killed Saturday"
          Photos of and statements by candidates for the 48th Assembly
          Joseph Eli Kovner, endorsing Ralph Ochoa for the 48th AD
          "Mexican Chamber of Commerce to honor Consul General of
              Mexico"
          Letter from Rafael Flores titled "Police Chief Challenged"
          "Video tape reading program aides bilingual students at Belvedere"
          "La eleccion del martes," by Angel T. Solis
          "Amenza a la UFWOC una ley propuesta"
          "Ochoa blasts GOP's reapportionment hearings"
          "Federal insurance Commission to probe ghetto problem"
          "Special services program aides low-income, minority students at
              UCLA"
OCT 17   "Feminine touch sought on US Supreme Court"
OCT 21   "Mrs. Banuelos' 'crime' suddenly its big news," by Dionicio
              Morales
          "Patrolman proposes Mexican-American city council district in
              '72"
          "Alatorre, Brophy, Blaine, Ruiz face runoff election: Assembly
              District seat sought"

Joseph Eli Kovner on election post-mortem
"Senate Bill," by Danny Montoya of the UFWOC
Letter from Richard López, disagreeing with the Rafael Flores
    letter
"Police, Fire complaints: New Policy re-evaluated"
"USC's MECHA student protest"
"Post mortem en el 48," by Angel T. Solis
"Distribuye TELACU estampillas"
"Hollenbeck Police hold visitation day Saturday"

OCT 28   "Loophole study shows banks get free car plates"
National task force established by Chicano unity conference"
"Chief Davis criticizes prison passes, early paroles"
Joseph Eli Kovner on the Romana Banuelos case
"Ellsburg to address 'end the war' rally in Los Angeles"
Letter from George Martinez answering the Richard Lopez letter of
    the previous week
"Name co-directors for 'Chicano Pride' Program"

NOV 4   "Freeways Threaten East LA Area," by Art Montoya
"Group Charges Federal Hiring Discrimination"
"ELA Health Fair slated for Sunday"
"EYOA ethnic balance New Committee to study"
"Muskee to campaign here for assembly candidate Alatorre"
"Los Tres del Barrio trial enters third week," by Carol Infranca
"Mexican Americans form government employee group [IMAGE]
"[Los Angeles City] Planning Commission hold night meeting"
"Alatorre guests on KTTV's 'Let's Rap' show tomorrow"
"The Illegal Alien, A Chicano Point of View," by Alfred C.
    Magallanes
"Affirmative Action Program to be presented to City Council"

NOV 7   "Committee passes [reapportionment] bill on state Senate plan"
NOV 11   "Children Ignored, Group Charges"
"Whittier College Chicanos Present Demands"
"State bans hiring of illegal aliens: New Law makes it a
    misdemeanor with minimum fine of $200"
"Chicano students stage silent protest during Senator Muskee's
    press conference," by Carol Infranca
"Alatorre endorsed by State Caucus"
"Commission ok's Hazard Park work"
"Under-employment still haunts East LA barrio"
Art Montoya supports Howard Jarvis constitutional amendment
    petition

NOV 18   "GOP's Brophy Polls Upset Victory," by Carol Infranca
"Price and Wage Restraints Hinder Freedom," by Alan Cranston
"Help is available in Spanish now: Police Department, City Hall,
    both have special telephone lines manned by bilingual
    operators," by Carol Infranca
"Strikers denied retroactive pay provisions by EYOA directors"
"Reflections on the election . . ." by Joseph Eli Kovner

"Traffic violations are no ground for car search, state court rules"

"MAYO to raise funds"

"Roberti to enter farmworker unemployment insurance bill"

"Five Latins hold advisory positions for HEW"

"Investigacion especifica de practicas policiales"

"Refuse CRLA appeal on ability to pay check"

"Labor Dept. funds training school in San Antonio for lower-paid govt. employees"

"Jarvis tax amendment should be signed," by Art Montoya

NOV 21   "Ann St. School cited for success on reading"

NOV 25   "COP-Community Relations viewed"

"Roybal charges Federal Job 'Caste System' "

"Unemployment plagues barrio; Federal anti-poverty agencies other state and local programs provide only 'band-aid relief' "

"Regret Gov.'s veto of housing tenant bill"

"Attorney [Oscar Acosta] for Berets quits"

"Chicano concert set Dec. 11"

"Unemployment still plagues M-A's"

"Siguen su lucha los huelguistas de EYOA"

"Las Palabras de Arthur Montoya"

DEC 2   "Davis Analyzes 'Dynamic' LAPD"

"Council may OK new hiring policy 'Must be LA City resident' "

"Resolution on Reapportionment intro Gonzalo Molina on behalf Brown Caucus-CDC"

"Mayo to mark third year with stage drama"

"Meyer outlines case in 'Los Tres' trial"

"MAFC plans 'child abuse' hearing next Monday"

"QUE ES TELACU?"

Letter from La Casa Carnalismo on Los Tres

Art Montoya on federal spending, the Los Angeles City Council and criticism of the War on Poverty

"Mechicano art exhibit opens at East LA College art gallery"

"Chief Davis praises Hollenbeck Council"

"Residency Proposal Won't Help LA"

"New Reading Program May Be Key"

"Preguntada set for Tues. night. Hundreds expected to attend second ELA Drug Information Fair"

"One Youth killed, 4 wounded in separate local shootings"

"YALP charges in study, Discrimination"

"Senate confirms Mrs. Banuelos as treasurer"

"Community to gain by a 'dream come true' "

"Emergency Employment Act: Chicanos urged to apply for jobs"

"An Open Letter To Chief Ed Davis," by Rafael Flores

DEC 12   "Task Force condemns proposed textbooks," by Carol Infranca

DEC 16   "Nixon's veto of child care tragic," by Carol Stevens

"Council ok's residency requirement, awaits Yorty's decision today"

"Judge [Carlos] Velarde names [sic] to ELA court bench"
"Job Corps assists Spanish-speaking"
"Diciembre, mes de gran actividad en TELACU"
"N.A.M.C. tuvo caso abierto . . ."
" 'Centurions' owes more to Chicanos," by Allen Galvan

DEC 19 "U.S. Tax System Keeps Poor on Bottom," by Alex Garcia
"JUSTICIA urges boycott of films: 'New Centurions' included
    among pictures that ridicule Chicano character, group says,"
    by Carol Infranca
"Farmworkers due in LA"
Letter rebuts López letter
"TELACU Mattress firm gets contract"
"Roybal views program for bilingual children"

DEC 23 "Mexican Americans Sue Board of Education"
"Veteran Job Program Gets Federal Funds"
"Mayor vetoes LA residency plan," by Carol Infranca
"JUSTICIA to boycott 'Big' film"
Art Montoya on bill to expand supervisors
"Rep Roybal asks recount of Spanish-speaking"

DEC 26 "Busch seeks Better Criminal Justice System"
"Citizens may air 'cop' complaints new police commission
    guidelines allow semi-monthly public 'grievance' hearings,"
    by Carol Infranca
"Phase I: 'Plaza' plans ok'd"
"City Parks Dept. keeps supervisor for senior citizen group
    activities"
"Board's ruling draws praise from Snyder"
Letter from E. Villa stating that gangs foster dependence not
    independence

DEC 30. "Nixon veto of OEO Bill called 'contradiction' "
"18-year-olds lose state welfare aid"
"Five children die in apartment fire; gasoline vapors blamed"
"Police chief praises 'objective' reporting"
"Open Letter to Community, Monte Perez asked to resign asks for
    help," by Rebecca Reza Grace
"Bill urges data collection on Latin unemployed"

SPECIAL AUGUST 1971 Los Angeles East Supplement
    •Plaza de la Raza
    •Marcha de la Reconquista
    •El Teatro de la Tierra

SPECIAL NOVEMBER 1971 Los Angeles East Supplement
    •Community Karate
    •MAYO "Inside and Out"
    •Ethnic Studies at Garfield

1972

January

Los Angeles East Supplement on the Mexican Calendar

JAN 6   "Hearings on cops stop, start anew"
          "Garfield Students Enter Computer World"
          "EOP director under fire at Cal-State, LA"
          "A message to Los Vatos de los Barrios," by David Sánchez
          "Pitchess affirms dept.'s minority hiring policy"
          "Greater State, Federal aid sought for methadone maintenance
             program"
          "PICA fue organizada en mayo de 1970"
          "Senior Citizens compose new political force"
JAN 9   "Model neighborhood sponsors program for 12 East Los Angeles
             elementary schools"
          "Snyder urges support for tax code change"
          "Welfare study results released"
JAN 13   "ELA Trees Threatened"
          "Pilot recycling program omits ELA Eastern portion of City not
             included in experimental program to recycle solid waste," by
             Carol Infranca
          "Law, Justice Center schedules open house"
          "Open Letter to Model Cities Program Administrator," by the
             Concerned Residents and Employees of Medocho to Mr.
             Lawrence Whitehead
JAN 16   "Unemployed workers hold demonstration"
          "Yorty Praises ELA Model Neighborhood Area"
JAN 20   "Hunger Conference Scheduled Jan. 26 at USC"
          "Cal. Pupil Expenditures Fall Below Average"
          "Reagan's EOP cut affects 11,000"
          "Free income tax assistance available for East LA residents"
          Letter from Mrs. Julia Mount, President of the Roosevelt Advisory
             Council, to Mayor Yorty
          "Federal, state officials to assist if City Council withdraws from
             EYOA"
          "Torres appointed rep by Senator Roberti"
          "ELA Model Neighborhood meets"
          "Model Cities aid given to medical students"
JAN 23   "School transciency statistics remain up"
JAN 27   "Residency Plan Blow to East LA"
          "Council overrides Mayor's 'Veto' " New ordinance requires all
             future employees to establish residency," by Carol Infranca
          "Police seek Echo Park boy with projectile similar to the one
             which blew up in youth's hand"
          "Courts settle one phase of Cal reapportionment"
          "Population booming Mayor says"
          "Families with dependent children recipients receive raise"

JAN 30   "Equal representation bill becomes law"
FEB 3   "New Model City Plans Proposal," by Art Montoya
          "Corporal Punishment continues," by Carol Infranca
          "Latins air charges against lawmen: Steady stream of Mexican-
              Americans testify before Committee on the Administration
              of Justice," by Carol Infranca
          Joseph Eli Kovner editorial on bad economic conditions
          "Informer relates life as federal investigator"
FEB 10   "Criticism of model cities," a letter from Arthur Fregoso,
              Community Development Representative, to Model Cities
              Program Manager
FEB 17   "Secretive Destruction of ELA Trees Deplored," by Art Montoya
          "Davis criticizes criminal justice," by Carol Infranca
          "Police state desired?" a letter from the Alfredo Bryan Defense
              Committee
          "Local Chicano group [TELACU] criticizes VP"
          "Political association [MAPA] honors publisher"
FEB 20   "Barrio group [TELACU] works toward betterment"
FEB 24   "Crusade members awaiting leader's release"
          "Nine groups unite [Federation of Barrios Unidos] to end wars—aid
              barrios," by Carol Infranca
          "Chief Ed Davis' letter to Court blasted by slayer's attorney"
          "B of E rejects move to abolish commissions"
          Art Montoya on Jarvis Constitutional Convention
          "Unificacion de pandillas," by Angel T. Solis
          "Educacion deficiente para los Mexico-americanos"
          Letter from Alexander Man to Councilman Gilbert Lindsay
              concerning the Hazard Park recreation building
          "Hunger conference urges return to old food stamp regulations"
          "Rate of cancer among ELA women two to four times national
              norms"
MAR 2   "Roybal urges Housing Approval"
          "Erosion of Beauty Funded by Government," by Art Montoya
          "Mayor proposes NYC Sponsorship"
          "Boyle Heights' future?" by Joseph Eli Kovner
          "B of E okays poll on busing minority pupils to 'safe' schools," by
              Carol Infranca
          "United Farm Workers receive union status"
          "ELA Model Cities Starts teacher class"
          "Conference outlines food stamp problems, proposes legislation"
          "Majority of elementary teachers don't understand Chicano
              students"
          "Mechicano Center marks second year"
          "Community Service Organization celebrates silver anniversary"
MAR 5   "Work Incentive program a failure," by Alex Garcia
          "Snyder reacts to EYOA termination"
          " 'Voice of La Raza' picked as one of nineteen best movies"
MAR 9   "Chicanos protest Dixon Arnett Law"

"[INS] Estimate cost of illegal aliens to taxpayers set at $18 billion"

"Terminated EYOA employees file Superior Court suit against agency"

"Cranston introduces bill to halt drain of bilingual funds"

MAR 16   "Lawmen May Face Contempt Charge," by Carol Infranca

"Federally Funded Public Jobs Bill Proposed"

"Law students seek signatures: Petition protests denial of certification by Bar for Chicanos active in barrios," by Carol Infranca

Joseph Eli Kovner on groundbreaking at Plaza de la Raza

"Council approves sponsorship of city of 1972 Youth Corps"

MAR 19   "Bill introduces privileges for prisoner"

MAR 23   "Plaza de la Raza begins first phase"

Letter from Alexander Mann, coordinator of Save Hazard Park Committee, to Warren Dorn on zone change

"Roybal announces his support of United Farm Workers' boycott"

"Education Commission meeting"

"St. Mary's MECHA asks community support," by Hector Sandoval

Art Montoya on Jarvis Amendment

"Chicano Employees to try advisory group"

"Release of suppressed work report urged"

MAR 30   "City, county OK Funds for EYOA, Pending anti-poverty program board approval, the state may free $900,000 for general use"

"LAPD told to seek new academy location"

"Yorty assails lack of Human Relations Bureau in Los Angeles"

"Bill prevents college teens on welfare from being cut off," by Henry C. MacArthur

"Job Development aid offered by Model Cities"

"Majority of Blacks pleased with LAPD"

Art Montoya on Dixon Arnet law

"Farm Workers engage in struggle versus NLRB boycott injunction"

"Winners of Mechicano Art Contest announced"

APR 2   "Mexican-American group sponsors play"

APR 6   "Local Gov't Take-Over of EYOA Deplored," by Carol B. Gil

"Consumer protection agency opens"

"Roybal reacts to boycott"

"East LA, Watts residents pay more for prescription drugs," by Carol Infranca

"Servicios de immigracion para residentes de cuidades [sic] modelo"

Art Montoya

"Landmark Chicano discrimination case to be heard in Washington"

APR 13   "Students Protest EOP Cutbacks"

"Assemblyman Optimistic About Equal Rights"

"Ralph Ochoa withdraws from Assembly race"
"Raza continues to lead anti-war demonstrations"
"Complaints against LAPD result in disciplinary action"
"Hire Chicanos—[Henry] Ramirez"

APR 20   "Hijacker Tells Chicano's Plight Surrenders," by Carol Infranca
"Skyjacker Ortiz released on bail $35,000 posted by ELA
     Community organizations, churches and private parties freed
     local resident," by Carol Infranca
"Model Cities election participation urged"
"IT&T's innovative hiring plan praised by some Latin leaders"
"Probation officers stage protest today"
"Fruto de la desperacion," by Angel T. Solis
"Como realizo Ricardo Chavez Ortiz el asalto aereo"
"Washington visitors learn about ELA"
"One-stop immigration handles many"
"Chicano conference to be held April 29"

APR 23   "Library staff cut hit by Lindsay"

APR 27   "Suit Seeks to Halt School Tests"
"Crisis Day for War on Poverty Approaching"
"Thousands protest Viet Nam war; Chicano contingent leads anti-
     war demonstrators down Wilshire Blvd. to rally at
     MacArthur Park," by Carol Infranca
"Persecution Protested"
"People's Law Day set to expose U.S. Justice"
"Six elementary schools dropped from Federal Title I funding"
"Mayor's law enforcement agencies Boycott State Assembly
     hearing"
Art Montoya
"Mrs. Mount names chair"
"Garcia received MAPA assembly endorsement"
"Street Improvement resented"

APR 30   "Cal State LA received university status"
"Bilingual voting gets assembly approval"

MAY 4   "ELA College Slates Cinco de Mayo Activities"
"Latins harassed, ex-deputy says; Half of arrests made in ELA are
     illegal former Sheriff's deputy tells State Assembly Hearing,"
     by Carol Infranca
"Roybal introduces bill for minority school aid"
"Chicanos 'take over' USC Law Day activities"
"Petition measure tried," by Howard Jarvis
"Medicine Conference slated for college students"
"Rights commission calls Chicano student 'excluded' in report"

MAY 7   "Language barrier overcome by bilingual teaching"
"Demo caucus votes for Viet war end"
"Narcotics prevention program at Roosevelt High picks up steam"

MAY 11   "Thousands protest Vietnam move: 'Die-in' staged at Nixon's L.A.
     headquarters following action to blocade North Vietnam," by
     Carol Infranca

"HUD told of tree cutting"
"Chicano employees hear Unruh"
"Riles boosts State effort on bilingual education"
MAY 14 "Sacramento gets store of protests"
"Spanish voting materials circulated"
MAY 18 "Wallace wounded at Maryland rally," by Carol Infranca
"Affirmative Action Tools Studied"
"Hispanic Center pushes ELA teacher awareness," by Carol
        Infranca
"Birth Control Info. available from agency"
"Plain Talk," by Joseph Eli Kovner
"Chavez Endorses Torres"
Art Montoya on HOME and Ernest Debs
"101 Californians paid no taxes," by Alfred Song
"Breed Students Protest Discrimination"
"LAPD investigates 286 complaints"
"Drop-outs get help at YTEP office"
MAY 21 "Street improvement efforts continue"
MAY 25 "Are Today's 11 year-olds to Fight in 1979?"
"MALDF opposes Council's action," by Carol Infranca
"ELA College president Wells fired by trustees"
"[Art] Torres challenges Garcia"
MAY 28 "Health Department asks for methadone increase"
JUN 1   "Hundreds greet McGovern in ELA: Chicanos on front lines in
        Vietnam, unemployment lines in barrio, hopeful tells
        supporters," by Carol Infranca
"Residents endorse Torres in 40th AD"
"Ortiz pleads 'not guilty' "
"Unemployment attack launched by Roybal"
"Passage of Equal Rights Amendment seen," by Alfred Song
"H.O.M.E. program under DA investigation"
"MALC [Mexican American Labor Council] endorses Bush"
JUN 4   "Torres' support grows as June 6th nears"
JUN 8   "Board Sets Reading Levels for Area Schools"
"McGovern wins June 6 primary"
"Estrada Court youths repaint project walls"
"Police want academy issue on Nov. ballot"
"Six business women attend national conference"
"Painting walls at Estrada Court"
Letter from David Sánchez on the death of Teresa García, 14, at a
        carnival in Santa Fe Springs
JUN 11 "Debs commends camp project"
JUN 15 "Council undecided on Police Academy Fate"
"Banquet Honors Mexican-American Women"
"Classic struggle," by Joseph Eli Kovner
"Class action lawsuit seeks to end wiring of 'faulty homes' "
"Grants benefit non-English speaking children"

"Roybal wins support for Chicano delegates"
"Bill's wisdom Questioned," by Rafael Flores

JUN 18   "LA County Sheriff's present car program"
"Club seniors visit Roybal"

JUN 22   "Court Extends Stop and Search Power," by Carol Infranca
"ELA visit ends Echeverria's US tour: Mexican president
            encourages investments and calls for better treatment of
            migrants," by Carol Infranca
"Torres to continue his campaign goals"
"Local businesswomen attend D.C. meeting"
"La Presencia de Echeverria"
"City of Angels is two-day host of Mexican President, staff"
"Echeverria interviewed by Chicanos in Texas," by Carol Infranca
"[Henry] Ramirez says Spanish woman's cultural role
            misinterpreted"

JUN 25   School's compensatory program to be reviewed"

JUN 29   "Fire casualties up; LAFD Budget Down," by Vickie Hines
"La Raza Unida Party to Write Platform"
"Local construction of library likely," by Carol Infranca
"Coalition gives demonstration to support accused hijacker," by
            Carol Infranca
"Judge Vega attends council on drug abuse"
"9-year-old faces ADW Charge against officer"

JUL 2   "Block phone service aids Chicano community"
"Young people's camp scheduled"
"Senate may fund bilingual education"

JUL 6   "JUSTICIA pres. seriously injured: Explosives in mailbox triggered
            by light switch sends Ray Andrade to hospital," by Carol
            Infranca
"Eastside defoliation," by Joseph Eli Kovner
"City Council revives human relations agency"
"Community Service Organization sets programs"
"Democrats set Chicano Caucus"
"Corrales and Alonzo promoted by state crime fighting agency"
"La Convencion Democrata," by Angel T. Solis
"Chicano group [LACECA] hosts Snyder"
"End to state job discrimination called," by Carol Infanca

JUL 9   "Senate considers bill to protect reporters"

JUL 13   "Half of new firemen required to come from minority groups," by
            Carol Infranca
"Police say Andrade victim of own bomb explosion," by Carol
            Infranca
"ELAC obtains renewal of $150,000 funding"
"Roybal announces OEO local grants"
Letter from R. M. Baron on the García family and the police

JUL 12   "Spanish-speaking youth enter intern program"

JUL 20   "OEO Funds $1.2 million for ELA Health Centers"

"Jury selected, [Richard Chavez] Ortiz trial begins: Defendant
        convinces Judge of mental compentency in hearing before
        proceedings," by Carol Infranca
"Murder retrial ordered for Bryan as adult"
"Maravilla Association to start activity center"
"Board passes English training for Asian in community schools"
"Roybal makes proposals for Mexican border searches"
"Antiwar activities plan July 21–23 UCLA meet"
JUL 23   "KCET-TV portrays Chicano experience August 11"
"Bilingual education bill passes Assembly"
JUL 27   "Jury Takes Seven Hours to Find Ortiz Guilty," by Carol Infranca
"Minority Contractors to Gain Business Tips"
"Federal probe into OEO begins"
"New law enforcement concept set for Maravilla project"
"Second annual Health Fiesta set August 6 at Lincoln Park"
AUG 3   "Health Fair Sunday: ELA Health Task Force sponsors medical
        services"
"Fair Ortiz trial fails says group"
"History, law highlights Franklin High's APEX Program"
"Spanish speaking urged to organize National Council of Spanish
        Speaking Organs."
AUG 10   " 'Yo Soy Chicano' airs Friday"
"Marcha de Mujeres"
"Neighborhood Development plan Funded"
Letter from Alexander M. Mann, Community Analyst, Barrio
        Planners, to Dr. Julian Nava
"UAW Steps up lettuce boycott"
"Mexican-American student problems become course for 300 LA
        teachers"
AUG 17   "Street improvement Project-YALP Reports"
"Consumer Complaint Office Opens"
Joseph Eli Kovner on Boyle Heights clean-up campaign
"Lincoln Heights mobilizes effort against city's urban renewal
        plan," by Eddie Pardo
"Women contribute to Health Fiesta"
"Supports farm workers struggle with ceramics"
"New head librarian appointed"
AUG 20   "Why so many Chicano leaders oppose Edelman plan"
AUG 24   "Aliso angry at poor Rec facilities"
"Las Hermanas group meets to coordinate its program"
"Farmworkers ask support against 22"
Letter from Herminia Ramírez Lewell complaining that there are
        no restrooms at Hazard Park
"MALDF will sue the City Council"
"Court leniency, poor homes blamed for juvenile crime"
Letter from Rafael Flores, director of the National Chicano Survival
        Committee, on urban renewal
"Housing Project in Maravilla," by Al Armijo

"Board approves ouster of Model Cities Chief," by Eddie Pardo

"Isn't impact statement requried?" on Board of Education condemnations

"Minorities to participate in business seminar"

"M.A.Y.O.'s in Charge"

OCT 12 "EYOA fights to stay alive: Employees protesting OEO funding decision," by Eddie Pardo

"UTLA voted to endorse Raul Ruiz, improve student," a letter by Hugh Gottfried, chair of the Political Action Council of Education

"Residents take control of Housing Corp"

"Gang rivalry results in tragic ELA shooting"

"Plans for ELA child care center blocked"

OCT 19 "Many veterans are finding job hunting tougher than service"

"Street project dropped by EYOA"

"Do we need more cops? Yes! Chicano cops . . . ," by Joseph Eli Kovner

"Community style asked for library"

"Snyder opens ELA office"

"S.E.R. Receives 1972–73 training funds"

"EYOA launches 'Operation Eat First' Campaign"

"Attorney Richard Hernandez elected head of Housing Corp."

OCT 26 "New 'Three Day Cooling Off' law will help consumers"

"Religious leaders oppose Prop. 22"

"City threatens Housing Corp. funds"

"Model Cities allocates over a quarter million dollars in scholarship grants to CSULA students"

OCT 29 ELA Medi-screen aims at disease prevention"

NOV 2 "Chavez, Kennedy, King and Cranston all urge No vote on Proposition 22"

"BAPP [Back Yard Alley Park Project] project has been terminated by EYOA"

"Brown Berets disband," by Eddie Pardo

"Roybal intervenes in HDC dispute," by Eddie Pardo

"SER awarded funds"

NOV 9 "Election wins Garcia, Prop 20; Props 14 and 22 defeated"

"Second year of funding for M/C"

"Trouble at ELA Service Center"

NOV 16 "ELA election results misrepresented by press"

"La comision feminil will hold organizing conference Saturday"

"Study slanders Puerto Rican voters," by Eddie Pardo

"Chicano art to be featured at LACC"

"Legislature urged to ban sex discrimination"

"NCHO receives grant for career centers," by National Chicano Health Organization

NOV 23 "Native Americans and Chicanos fasting on 'Day of Mourning'," by Eddie Pardo

"A man of action," by Joseph Eli Kovner

"Accion Chicano"

NOV 30   "Guest editorial: Prison health conditions deplorable, says
        Karabian"
        "Congressman Ed Roybal may enter election race for mayor's
        office," by Eddie Pardo
        "$5 million bilingual education package goes to Gov. Reagan"
        "Accion Chicano studies Siqueiros mural"
        "Aides to Career Education Program approved by Board of
        Education"

DEC 7   "More campus safety steps proposed by B of E"
        "Hearings continue on law student's bid to be lawyer," by Eddie
        Pardo
        "Women's group fights welfare law: Talmadge law hurts poor and
        women most," by Eddie Pardo
        "Open Letter for Survival," by Rafael Flores
        "El Teatro Campesino en el TV canal 4"

DEC 14   "A Chicano Christmas story," by Manuel Cruz
        "Youth-gang conference set today: community organization tackle
        problems now"
        "Urban renewal fears continues [sic] in East-Northeast
        community," by Eddie Pardo
        "Child Care Center Controversy"
        "Congressmen protest Henry Ramirez, Chair for Spanish Speaking
        People"

DEC 17   "ELA H EI wins medical grant"

DEC 21   "New Agency takes over poverty programs in Los Angeles"
        "Law student gets Roybal support; Congressional [sic] and Loyola
        president back Cruz," by Eddie Pardo
        "Chicanos announce Unruh support, candidate defends assembly
        record," by Eddie Pardo
        "Talmadge Protest," by Alicia Escalante
        "Open Letter on juvenile hearings"

DEC 28   "LAPD joins efforts to curtail gang warfare"
        "Anti-delinquent program approved; Outreach Project Ok'd for six
        local schools"
        "Roybal declines to run," by Eddie Pardo
        "Set Award to Kovner Pub for Service"

1973

SMALLER TABLOID FORMAT

JAN 4   "New Year's resolution for East L.A."
        "Maravilla redevelopment is near; Supervisors to decide . . . fate
        Jan. 16," by Eddie Pardo
        "Escalante honored by magazine"
        "Open Letter on grand jury selection process," by Alicia Sandoval
        "MC clerical training skills offered by MAOF"
        "Un millon de dls. para los proyectos de TELACU"
        "Is ELA an Island?"

JAN 11   "Open letter from delinquency committee"
         "Center achieves record placement; trainees being placed in jobs at
              92% rate"
         "Guest Editorial: The Richard Cruz hearing"
         "Deputies brutality slain"
         "Hearings end; bishop, Nava testify for Cruz," by Eddie Pardo
         "We Must Think About Future Goals," by David Sánchez
JAN 18   "Skill Center Enrollment Frozen"
         "Child Care Crisis Conference at ELAC"
         "Human Rights Immigration Confab: Coalition to fight the Rodino
              Bill"
         "Supervisors hear arguments from opponents of redevelopment
              plan"
         "Alatorre to announce Unruh support tomorrow"
         "Gonzales new manager of Staff Builders"
         "Opponents Protest Maravilla Plan"
JAN 25   "Maravilla plan questions arise; Opponents to house meeting
              payments," by Eddie Pardo
         "Dropout prevention program approved for Lincoln High"
         "Phone at City Hall's Office of Latin American Affairs is always
              busy"
         "TELACU Answers Opponents"
         "Open letter to working people of Los Angeles"
FEB 1   "Supervisors approve redevelopment plan for Maravilla," by Eddie
              Pardo
         " 'Los Tres' appeal case Monday"
         "Many will participate in weekend conference"
         "Parent-in-service course set"
         "Roybal opposes freeze on housing subsidies"
         "Justicia organization to become active once again, says president"
         "Study says district is guilty of 'years of educational neglect' "
         "Junta de imigracion"
         "Results of child care conference"
FEB 8   "Supporters demonstrate for 'Los Tres' Rally and march end at
              courthouse where case is appealed," by Eddie Pardo
         "Enrollment freeze ends at ELA Skill Center"
         "Guest Editorial" on welfare for the rich
         Letter from Anthony Alonso, supervising parole agent at the
              Esperanza Community Center, on sponsorship of gang
              symposium
         "La Guerra A La Pobreza Esta Agonizante," by Angel T. Solis
         "Roybal Wants newsmen protected"
         "Chicano librarians wanted"
         "Corky Gonzales Photo-Rally for Los Tres"
         Photograph of National Committee to Free Los Tres
FEB 15   "Welfare Rights, Alicia Escalante," by Eddie Pardo
         "Gang fighting a problem again, Lil Valley Assn. tries to pieces
              after Aranda killing"
         "Indians and their allies rally around free clinic Project"

"Project Ayudate gives free income tax help"
"The President's proposed budget," by Congressman Edward
    Roybal
Letter from Rafael Flores

FEB 22 "Legal aid centers may be closed: Legal Aid in dark about future
    status," by Eddie Pardo
"Dymally on unincorporated area," by Ray Rodriguez
"Chicana resolutions adopted at [National Women's Political
    Caucus] convention"
"Cardoza to head probation program"
"State Task Force formed for MA education"

MAR 1 "Poverty agencies angry: Protesters picket at HUD headquarters,"
    by Eddie Pardo
"President neglects the poor again," by Senator Alan Cranston
"Unruh asks for youth legislation"
"A Community Union: Esteban Torres," by Eddie Pardo
"Desafio A Los Pobres"
"Assembly to consider Garcia bill"

MAR 8 "Operacion Estafadores a success after six months," by Leonard
    Piggot, Los Angeles Police Department, Public Affairs
    Division
"Congressman fights OEO fund cuts"
"Spanish surnamed hired at 20% rate by DOL"
"Avila supports Bradley"

MAR 15 "Farm worker's union files suit against alleged misrepresentation"
"Mike Duran," by Eddie Pardo
"Board seeking bilingual funds"
"Alatorre wants help against drugs"
"Group honors educators"
"Don't let them throw America back"

MAR 22 (Entire issue is missing)

MAR 29 "One Stop Immigration Center has aided 1,235 families"
"El Centro Chicano at USC has new director"
Letter from Rafael Flores on unity
"Propose end to power grab; More military funds allotted than any
    time since WW 2"

APR 4 "Public meeting on ELA Master Plan: Public rally April 10 at
    Belvedere Jr. Hi [sic]"
"Local elementary pupils on education program"
"Racial brotherhood concert at Hollenbeck"
"Rock group on Accion Chicano"
"Premium pay for bilingual city workers"
"ECC protests federal cuts in school support"
"New Chicano police association set"
"You can win in Eminent Domain Cases"

APR 12 "Roybal proposes immigration reforms at house hearings"
"Debs seeks approval of ELA plan: Comprehensive plan sought for
    unincorporated area"
"Roybal criticizes shift of OEO migrant funds"

"Health clinic next Wed. for families"
"Chavez-Ortiz Commemorative march Fri."
"Bilingual skills ordinance passed"
"April 28th meet on Master Plan"
"Chicano Correctional Assoc. honors officers"
"Mother of 13 graduates at Skill Center"
"Anti-Rodino Bill Rally April 28"
"MECHA students outline cannery problems in press confab"

APR 19   "Jose Luis Ruiz; Born and raised in ELA, Ruiz is the producer of
             the farmworkers theatre special 'El Teatro Campesino' "
          "Alatorre criticizes Rodino bill as discriminatory"
          "Guest: Foreign aid for U.S. auto industry"
          "MAPA banquet scheduled for April 28; women to be honored"
          "Officer of the Month—Hernandez"
          "Es inevitable el socialismo"
          "CEP reports 35% increase on job placement of disadvantaged"
          "Collective community workers," by John Marquez
          "Open Letter to Community," by Robert Ramirez, executive
             director of the Aliso-Pico Assoc., Inc., on measures to
             control graffiti

APR 26   "Life style within the Boyle Heights Community," by Raul
             Escobedo
          "MAPA annual banquet April 28"
          "A Statement of Police Re: The Rodino Bill H.R. 962"
          "Probe of Maravilla airs tonight"
          "Committee to Incorporate East Los Angeles," photograph
          "Spectre of Master Plan looms again as 500 People in ELA meet to
             hear master planners"
          "Sandoval takes chairmanship of franchise firm committee"
          "Exec director named for Maravilla Neighborhood Redevelopment"
          "Alatorre keeps his pledge to be available"

MAY 3   "Russell Means arrested in LA," by Julia Luna Mount
          Art Montoya
          "Emergency food drive for United Farm Workers gets underway in
             ELA"
          "La Quebradita holds 6th anniversary sale"
          "Cityhood for East LA"
          "Manzanar Committee honored"
          "Cruz sworn in April 25 as attorney"
          "Talmadge Amendment"
          "Politicians on Accion Chicano"
          "Cinco de Mayo Folklorico at Roosevelt," by Julia Luna Mount
          "Land Grab Scheme!"
          "MECHA Supports Anti-Rodino Bill Fight"

MAY 10   "People worth knowing: Paul Mendoza," by Joseph Eli Kovner
          "Effort made to restore $29 million OEO funds"
          "Teatro Espanol del amo begins in summer"
          "Safe at last! Snyder gets signals on 1st, Utah and Savana"

"Family planning support 100% by ELA residents"
"Alternative school gets B of E endorsement"
"Chicano Assoc. meets"
"City Terrace School plans luau"
"Guanajuato en LA"
"Object to Youth Approach to Causes of Youth Problems"

MAY 17 "Full Support accorded Bradley by Roybal"
"Save the barrio now," by Rosalio Munoz
"Free Los Tres rally May 19"
"50th year feted by ACLU this week"
"Master Plan meeting," by Art Montoya
"Plaza de la Raza gets award"
"Library meeting"
"Open Letter—Reply on Teatro del Amo plans at Cal State"

MAY 24 "MAPA endorses four candidates for May 29"
"Memorial Day Parade in ELA getting community support"
"Free Los Tres rally held Sat."
"Master Plan Meeting," by Art Montoya
"Barrio confab"
"Alatorre to address Femenil Mexican Nacional"
"Evening of love and sharing"
"Tom Bradley como alcalde una real necesidad," by Angel T. Solis
"Bilingual court act introduced by Roybal"

MAY 31 "Bradley Upsets Yorty . . ."
"Preguntada at Belvedere Jr. High Sat."
"Immigration dragnet raid condemned"
"Maymi to head Labor Women's Bureau"
" 'Semana de la Mujer' held at Cal State"
"Spray paint control sought by legislature"
"Apathy," by Rafael Flores

JUN 7 "Energy crisis schizophrenia—no gas, more freeways," by
Congressman Tom Rees
"Tales of Boyle Heights: The nickel . . ." by Joseph Eli Kovner
"Raids on immigrants protested; Grandparent taken away from
babysitting"
"Public meeting tonight on County's MP [master plan] hearings"
"New King of school opens in Montebello"
"Tragedy Hits Boyle Heights"

JUN 14 "Parents unite to halt youth slayings"
"More on Master Plan," by Arthur Montoya
"Senior citizen special activities now at ELA Senior Adult Center"
"Open Letter to the residents and merchants of Boyle Heights," by
the Estrada Court Mural Project managers
"Study of 6,000 elementary pupils in 14 East-Northeast schools
shows reading program"
"Plans Opposed for Widening Streets Near Hazard Park Because of
Environmental Damage," by Herminia Rameríz Lewell
"Integrity," by Rafael Flores, on the police and drugs

"Mothers Fighting for Enrichment Program at Evergreen School"
"UFW move picket line to Los Angeles to world's largest market"
"Property owners meet tonight at Belvedere JH," by Arthur
    Montoya
"Rally at San Ysidro"
"Coast Fed. likes ELA progress"
". . . People Worth Knowing: Henry Diaz. Chicano appointed
    Executive Post with Arizona Department of Economic
    Security"
"Open Letter on ELA Incorporation"
" 'Accion' to investigate Maravilla HP [Housing Project]"

AUG 2   ". . . People worth knowing: Eloy Perez, Parks and Rec"
"Boston Tree Party to Preserve Trees"
"Call for full rights of Chicano"
"Will Bradley Chicano Advisors Committee be able to Impress
    Mayor that they mean business?"
"Protesta Por La Golpiza a Jornaleros De la UFWU"
"Murillo, TELACU, shot"

AUG 9   "Open Letter to Concerned Community Organizations and
    Residents" from the Ad Hoc Committee to Incorporate East
    Los Angeles
"ELA alleys improve," by Ernest Debs
"Mural, murals on Estrada Court's Walls are the fairest of them
    all . . ." by Joseph Eli Kovner
"Roberti scores arrests"
"Chicano Coalition meeting"
"Hollenbeck Div. gets two new captains"
"Film on drugs at Alpha Coffee Hse."

AUG 16 "Roybal hits food price controls as anti-consumer"
"Fight increases on Rodino Bill," by Centro Accion Social
    Autonoma
"Local agency ok's ELA city attempt," by Art Montoya
"Prevention approach to delinquents to continue"
"Teamsters accused of discrimination against Chicano employees"

AUG 23 "Black Mesa Committee heartened by Bradley veto"
"Human rights complaint filed on citizenship exclusion of
    Mexicans"
"El pandillerismo y sus remedios," by Angel T. Solis
"Labor digna da encomio de los pandilleros"
"MAPA women honored"

AUG 30 "People worth knowing . . . Jesse Bojorquez: New Director of
    Business Development and Assistance Div."
"Snyder now in Ramona Gardens Wed. 9–12 Complaints
    welcome"
"Spanish Service Center May Be Discontinued," a letter from
    Hispanic Women's Council of L.A., Inc. to Tom Bradley
"Gang members remove grafitti from Lincoln pool"
"Girls Club forming in ELA"
"Facts . . . not fancy on ELA City," by Art Montoya

"Federal government terminated direct funds to SER/Jobs for Prog."

"Roybal reports waste of fed. funds"

"Chicano [County] Employees bring suit on County"

SEP 6   "Press statement of La Raza Unida Party Aug. 29"

"Court Action on Behalf of Working Moms"

"Rebuttal: KNBC Editorial on ELA Cityhood," by Art Montoya

"[Alfonso] Perez New Administrator Coordinator Area G"

SEP 13   "Guest Editorial: Reapportionment by Assemblyman Alex Garcia"

"Los Angeles is second largest Spanish speaking city in North America," by Joseph P. Busch

"16th of Sept. Fiesta at ELA College"

"Cal State Fiesta de la Raza Sept. 16"

"A New Chevy for Cesar Chavez from Manuel Aragon who won it"

" 'We are definitely open!' SER Will offer same service as in past"

" 'Accion Chicano' concert"

"[Board of Supervisors] Hearings continue," by Art Montoya

"Of Interest to the East Area," by Richard Alatorre

"CASA Invites all to Lincoln Park B-B-Q"

SEP 20   "Guest Editorial: It Happened in Chile!" by John Day

"Guest Editorial: Narcotics Prevention Project—Boyle Heights Center Needs help: City of LA Not Refunding Project," by Frank Lozano

"More Baxter Wards Needed," by Art Montoya

"Un auto para Chavez," by Angel T. Solis

SEP 27   "Alternatives to Grafitti Subject of Research Project"

"Project 'Furlough' to grant LA Senior high school students one-year leaves"

"Feria de los Ninos at Hollenbeck Sun"

"Child care gets funds from B of E"

"I deplore Model Cities Cuts . . ." by Joseph Eli Kovner

"School milk cutbacks 'insane' "

"First Mexican American heads East LA College"

"Bilingual Contract Act passes Senate"

"New law signed on notary public fees"

"20,000 attend Feria de la Raza Cal State LA"

OCT 4   "Community Efforts Curb Crime in East Los Angeles"

" . . . People Worth knowing: Sal Castro—back at Belmont," by Alicia Escalante

"Prohibition of paint intoxicants urged"

"Peace Corps opens drive at Cal State"

"Sheriff guest at next meeting," by Art Montoya

"Roybal calls for National Farmworkers office"

"Farm Labor Violence Committee has initial hearings in October"

"NYC program to continue through Dec. 9 in schools; further funding expected"

"Chicana Service Center Anniversary"

"Un golpe mas al campesino," by Angel T. Solis

OCT 11   "Chavez recommended for Peace Prize: A. Garcia and Mayor
Bradley send recommendation to Sec. of State Kissinger"
"First Mexican American College President in So. Calif.," a
photograph
"Mexican and Latin American resource center to be established at
Plaza de la Raza"
"School bilingual program expanded by $203,470"
"Chavez on 'Impacto' Oct. 13"
"Troubles begin," by Art Montoya
"Notice of Intention on Incorporation Petition," a photograph
"Statewide Confab set for Chicano Social workers"
"Community colleges to expand occupational ed for disadvantaged
students with $214,000 federal grant"
"Job seminar success thanks to community"
"ECO in a Grassroots Community Organization"
"Probation officer honored"

OCT 18   "Blessed are the peacemakers—especially in the East Area," by
Roger M. Grace
"Dial-a-Bus begins this week in E. Los Angeles"
Art Montoya on a KNXT-TV editorial favoring incorporation
"A Week Ago Last Wed. at Estrada Courts," by Joseph Eli Kovner
"Boy fatally shot in search for students with shotgun"
"TELACU Food Stamp Centers mark second year of success"
"Gun incidents on campus reach frightening proportions"
"Minority Affairs Specialist joins OEE at USC"

OCT 25   "Freeway smog is poisoning schools"
"In Interview Bob Archuleta," by Joseph Eli Kovner
Art Montoya on incorporation meeting
"Parents coping with infant mortality to be discussed"
"Chicano Employees Assn. Meet"
"Chicano executive [Dionicio Morales] calls for affirmative action"
" 'Let's Rap' hostess, other personalities in symposium"
"Women aware week at ELAC"

NOV 1   "ELA Chicana Welfare Rights report," by Sra Alicia Escalante
"Bail denied Los Tres"
"Accion Chicano Reports on United Farm Workers," a photograph
"Guest Editorial Alatorre on Immigration Consultants law"
"Incorporation pro and con," by Art Montoya
"Chicano Cause Oppose P.1"

NOV 8   "Captain Rudy De Leon named 'Boss of Year' "
"Bradley coming to Estrada Cts Tues."
"Alcalde to inspect murals," by Joseph Eli Kovner
" 'Los Tres' ordered released on bail"
"Incorporation," by Art Montoya
"Recall Snyder Petition—Pro.—Con."
"Will Mayor Bradley Help Stop Land Grabs?"
"Apoya Moscone el plan de incorporacion"
"Reception for Chicano Commissioners Nov. 15"

NOV 15 "Snyder closer to recall election petitions with 7,500 names filed"

"Comments on defeat of Prop. 1," by Art Montoya

"Republican role in Spanish speaking community to be examined"

NOV 22   "Snyder to meet SC of 14th Dist."

"Guest Editorial 'The Sad Truth'," by Eddie Soto of El Alambre
       M.A.Y.O. de CRC, Corona, California

"What is El Teatro Campesino"

NOV 29   "Coalition meeting at Exposition Park: *Impeachment*: Public
       Action meeting"

"Meeting tonight," by Art Montoya

"Joe Castorena candidate 14th Councilmanic Dist."

"Phil Soto announces appointment"

"La Casa De Los Pobres," by Alicia Escalante de Gandara

DEC 6   "New Condominiums Going Up in ELA . . ."

"Alex Garcia to seek 24th Senatorial seat in '74"

"Motorist taxes," by Art Montoya

"Cutback looms in ELA Library"

"Our Lady of Guadalupe procession Dec. 9"

"Census survey on farm workers"

"Executive of the Week"

"Guest Editorial: 'Slum Land Lords,' " by Francisco Mendoza

"Off to see our mayor . . . ," by Sean Carrillo

"Improve 75 alleys in ELA"

DEC 13   "Veterans Outreach Program Funded"

"California Legislature Showcases Chicano Progress," by Richard
       Alatorre

"Public Invited to ELA College Las Posadas"

"Commission recommends day care"

"Misrepresentation in recall"

"E-NE Dev. Corp. Elects New Officers"

"Master Planning in news again," by Arthur Montoya

"Model Cities' Metropolitan Psychiatric Services—In Search of
       Emotional Tranquility"

"Ramirez dice: censo de Hispanos equivocado por 8 a 10 por
       ciento"

DEC 20   "Ethnic minorities make political moves"

"Cesar Chavez in East LA Mass and March Friday Night"

"A 'Feliz Navidad' from 'Los Tres del Barrio' "

"Master Planning," by Arthur Montoya

DEC 27   "Housing Commission Adopts Emergency Fire Regulation," by
       Fred W. Kline

"Resolution Urges Continued Funding for M/C [Model Cities]
       Programs"

"Police aim for community involvement: reducing crime, dealing
       with tension target of new Grant"

"Recall Snyder petition okayed by court"

"Bilingual-bicultural education program funds sought for ELA"

"Open Letter to Police Dept.," by Rev. Craig Brammer

"Teacher Transfer policy discriminatory against minority"

"To All Members of the Mexican Chamber of Commerce: to the
Public in General"

1974

JAN 3 "Carmen Guzman: 'Ms. Grandmother'"
"5 million youngsters need Bilingual Education and are not getting
it," by Senator Alan Cranston
"Police Lt. to run for 14th D. Council seat"
Art Montoya
Joseph Eli Kovner, an open letter to the Los Angeles City
Councilmen on curtailing of library services to East Los
Angeles
"Edelman endorses ELA incorporation in letter"
"Assemblymen Garcia and Alatorre to work for unity"
"Unemployment to go up 2 per cent [sic] in January"

JAN 10 "Montoya on Incorporation," by Art Montoya
Joseph Eli Kovner on parking meters on Whittier Blvd
Letter from Robert L. Chafee, Director, of DPSS, answering ELA
Chicana Welfare Rights Organization questions

JAN 17 Letter from George E. Chávez to Congressman Edward R. Roybal
on conditions at the General Hospital
Letter from Roybal to Chávez responding to letter on General
Hospital
"People worth knowing . . . Chicana Lib: Yolanda Nava"
Letter from Alicia Escalante de Gándara to Danny Villanueva of
KMEX expressing her dissatisfaction with "Operación
Navidad"
"Executive of the Week"

JAN 24 "Police Rush to Plant Academy in Elysian Park"
Answer to Chávez letter criticizing General Hospital from Ted R.
Estrada, Administrator of ELA Doctor's Hospital
"ELA Master Plan sets off urban renewal fears"

JAN 31 "A Multi-services Seriously Threatened ELA SERVICES
CUTBACKS"
"Update on Yolanda Nava"
"Chicano feminists installation banquet"
"County AF of L CIO Endorses Art Snyder"
"Test taken to clear air," by Dr. David Lopez-Lee
"Master Plan, Incorp., the issues . . . ," by Art Montoya

FEB 7 "Crime reduced 10% in Hollenbeck," by Capt. R. V. DeLeon
"In the 14th Councilmatic District, a Heated Race," by Joseph Eli
Kovner
"Armas Assails Lopez-Lee and Calderon"
"Calderon endorsed by MAPA"
"Chavez endorses Torres, 56th Assembly"
"Independencia Mexicana En Los Angeles," by Angel T. Solis

FEB 14   "Calif. La Raza Unida Party Registration Tops 20,000"
         "Effective representation sought in 56th Assembly Dist."
         "Nat'l Coalition for Fair Immigration confab Mar. 8"
         Letter from Alicia Escalante to Danny Villanueva of KMEX on
               "Operación Navidad"
         "Su Majestad—Las Ganancias"
FEB 21   "Calderon endorsed by Cesar Chavez—County Demo Comm."
         "Judge Takasugi Dismisses 46 Criminal Cases Due to 'Flagrant
               Violation' of Constitutional Rights in East Los Angeles"
         "Latin Media Film and Broadcast Group Backs Cesar Chavez Farm
               Union Boycott"
         Art Montoya on East Los Angeles incorporation
         Joseph Eli Kovner on the CDC Convention
         Art Montoya on the president of the ELA Maravilla-Belvedere Park
               Property Owners Association
         " 'Los Four,' First Exhibition of Chicano Art at LA County
               Museum of Art"
FEB 28   "Mexican American Art Foundation gets 100 HUD houses for low-
               income families"
         "Happy Birthday Hollenbeck Jr. High 61 Years"
         "Art Torres backs ELA incorporation"
         "[Joe] Sanchez Takes Leadership Role in Businessmen for
               Calderon"
         Letter from Lt. Armas asking for justice
         "Richard Calderon gives speech at Mexican C of C"
         "McDonald School seeks roots of Mexican-American Heritage"
MAR 7   "Nat'l Immigration Conference Mar. 8-10"
         "Open Letter to Community . . . Unemployment in ELA," by
               Eduardo Ruiz
         "David Lopez-Lee charges Snyder with influence peddling"
         "Montoya Speaks to Town Hall of Calif.," by Art Montoya
         "Armas calls for multi-service center for seniors"
         "Strikers need food"
         "Class action suit by Espinoso alleges General Motors and
               Standard Oil conspiring to get rid of old Pacific Electric Red
               Car system"
         "Undocumented Workers Need Help—Conference on Immigration"
MAR 14   "Ya Basta! Sra. Alicia Escalante de Gandara"
         "Vote Your Choice Tues."
         Letters on recall and libraries
         "MAPA Plans Hard Get Out the Vote Campaign"
         Art Montoya on the recall strategy
         "Kovner Publications Recommendations Endorsements," by Joseph
               Eli Kovner
         "New Chapter of Feminil Mexicana"
MAR 21   "Teen gang members paint murals at Wabash Center"
         "Recall loses; Snyder stays put"

"Madres contra Drogas"

Letter from George H. Mount, Commissioner of the Mexican
American Education Commission, Los Angeles Unified
Schools, to Mr. Boba, Principal, Sycamore School in
Claremont

MAY 16   "Presentation to Assembly Select Committee on Juvenile
Violence," by Mike Duran

Art Montoya on 2,100 letters by homeowners against incorporation

"MAPA to Hold Testimonial Dinner for Herman Sillas"

"MAPA Fourth Annual Primary Endorsement Convention May
18–19"

Open letter from the National Committee to Free Los Tres

"Natural Birth Discussed Chicana Service Center"

"Incorporation issue reaches impasse"

MAY 23   "ELAC Graduates, Ed Torres, Art Torres, Alex P. Garcia, Richard
Baca, Seeking Political Office"

"Committee to Free Los Tres to Present Program on Political
Assassinations in Sixties"

"MAPA endorsements Sillas, Bugliosi"

Art Montoya on incorporation

Letter from Mrs. Julia Luna Mount Magnolia elementary school
picketing of the United Teachers of Los Angeles building

"Joe Ortega is new director of Law Center"

MAY 30   " 'A new man for a new day' meaningful slogan for Ed Torres"

"Boyle Heights Homeowners & renters to meet Frances Mendoza"

"Educational opportunity program at Cal-State"

JUN 6   Art Montoya on incorporation

"Grafitti bill goes to Reagan"

JUN 13   "Incorporation of ELA public hearing Thurs., June 13"

Art Montoya reviews history of incorporation

"Community Briefs: Committee to Free Los Tres to Present
Program on Political Assassinations in Sixties"

"[Bert] Corona in Unity Rally"

JUN 20   "Hollenbeck reading scores: significant gain," by Whit Rowland

Joseph Eli Kovner

Art Montoya on incorporation

"ACTIELA [Ad Hoc Committee to Incorporate East Los Angeles]
responds to Debs on ELA incorporation"

"A Nuestros Jovenes," by Angel T. Solis

Letter from Alicia Escalante de Gándara on the Chicana Welfare
Rights Organization

JUL 11   "Fire Dept. Activity recruiting Chicanos"

"Discrimination Employment Suit Against State Practices"

"Dept. of Justice Gets Consent Decree Requiring Minority Hiring
by Fire Dept."

JUL 25   "ELA not now capable of incorporation," by Art Montoya

AUG 1   "L.A. Police to promote Latin to command post"

"Wounded Knee Trial of Chicano Activists"

AUG 8   "New Law Means Big Break for Victim of Violent Crime"
          "Is Boyle Heights Worth Saving?" by Raul Escobedo
          Letter from Mermenta Ramirez Lewell on the Friends of Hazard
              Park and Members of Hazard Park Advisory Committee
AUG 15   "600 Mexican-Americans passed up in firefighter test"
          "Boyle Heights Master Plan is Menace, not miracle!" by Arthur
              Montoya
          "ELA is Losing Millions in Retail Sales; Incorporation Will Stem
              Leakage"
          Letter from the Centro Joaquin Murietta
          "El Nuevo Tomo," by Angel T. Solis
AUG 22   "Civil service ups minority recruiters correction 600 out of 1000
              Pass Up Firefighters Test"
          "Undue credit, injustices, broken promises Yet Estrada Murals
              project marches on," by Los Veteranos
          "Minority recruitment for city firemen aided by Los Angeles City
              Schools"
          "E.L.A., Maravilla, Belvedere Property Owners Meet Aug. 27," by
              Arthur Montoya
AUG 29   Letter from Rebecca Reza Grace La Causa de los Pobres and
              Chicana Welfare Rights Organization
          "National Moratorium to Stop deportations and repressions at
              Belvedere Park, Sat. Aug. 31"
          Arthur Montoya
SEP 5   "E.D.C. [East/Northeast Economic Development Corporation] and
              private capital to build City Heights Industrial Plaza"
          "Your dollars are being spent wisely by E/NE-E.D.C.," by John
              Severino, Vice President and General Manager of KABC
          "Maravilla Neighborhood Development is really partial urban
              renewal," by Arthur Montoya
          "Exploring the economic myths about E.L.A. Cityhood"
SEP 12   "Mexican American Community Celebrates 164th Anniversary of
              Mexico's Independence"
          " 'Years of Unity' theme of Feria de la Raza at CSU"
          "Studying 'La Chicana' new State requirement"
          "City Board of Education Approves Nominee to Mexican American
              Education Commission"
SEP 19   "An Emerging Political Force," by Reynaldo Macias
          "Boyle Heights Plan Given Airing at All Nations Tonight"
SEP 26   "Julia Mount endorsed by Jose Gutierrez"
          "E.L.A. Incorporation 'Town Meetings' documentary theme"
OCT 3   "39 Candidates seek office in E.L.A. incorporation move"
          Letter from Richard Polanco, Maravilla Project Administrator,
              taking issue with Arthur Montoya's alleged
              misrepresentation
          "Leader of Farm Migrant Camp Indicted by Federal grand jury"
          "The article about incorporation in the Times," by Arthur
              Montoya

JAN 9   "[Ben Franklin] Library to be built in area"
         "Gang youth aid community"
         "Snyder seeks re-election to office"
         "Garcia files for office"
         "Spanish speaking persons alerted"
         "Food stamp price raise protested"
         "O'Con [sic] to head TELACU"
         "Incorporation negotiation ridicules charge that 4000 votes
              missing," by Arthur Montoya
         "Fenton introduces farmworkers law"
         "Congress fails to extend Spanish speaking unit"
         "[Ed] Avila declares candidacy"
         "Unemployment rate rapidly increasing"
JAN 16   "Hearing on high food prices planned by Human Relations
              Commission"
         "Owners schedule meeting," by Arthur Montoya
         "Chicanas' program[Chicana Service Action Center New] gets
              funds"
         "Suit filed"
JAN 23   "Group parades in front of offices of immigration and
              naturalization consultants," by Carol Clark
         "Program affects local area," by Arthur Montoya
         "Campaign against Gallo underway"
         "Business research specialist appointed to TELACU post"
         "Political happenings"
         "Library compiles history of Boyle Heights area"
JAN 30   "Hayes Moves to Fight Unemployment: Save Juvenile Jobs"
         "Urban Renewal forced," by Art Montoya
         "Too Ornery to Give Up"
FEB 6   "Minorities discuss Bicentennial"
         "Ceremonies scheduled for library"
         "Spanish surname fire fighters hired," by Joseph Eli Kovner
         "Ed Edelman brings more urban renewal," by Art Montoya
         "My love affair with Boyle Heights," by Arthur K. Snyder
         "Garcia proposes new system"
         "Alternative school students achieving"
         "Lizarraga commends legislators"
         "Latin American Secretaries Association plan meeting"
         "Commission president voices Opinion to Chief Davis," by Joseph
              Eli Kovner
         "Snyder opposes food stamp cutback"
FEB 13   "Groundbreaking ceremonies set for new Franklin library"
         "Ed Avila pledges no sniping"
         "Bastidos announces candidacy to council"
         "Benefit, banquet dance planned"
         Arthur Montoya on urban renewal hearings
         "Secret behind library doors," by Councilman Arthur Snyder
         "Mayor appoints Joe Ortega to Council"
         "Hernandez names coordinator of services"

"Butz to cut food stamps"
"Snyder charges disadvantage"
FEB 20 "Urban renewal program boundaries told," by Arthur Snyder
"Former candidate endorses Snyder"
"Group [Madres Contra Drogas] holds meetings"
"Mexican-American lawmakers submit anti-Bracero measure"
FEB 27 "Local librarians transferred, fired amid controversy"
"TELACU Board holds installation"
"Human Relations Commission sponsored public hearing on coping
     with inflation"
"Hearing results told," by Joseph Eli Kovner
"Lawmakers support aliens"
"Surprise party conducted," by Arthur Montoya, on defeat of the
     move to incorporate ELA
"[Edelman] Branch office opens"
"Artists organize union"
"Community action committee announces meeting" on Elysian
     Valley Community Action Committee
"Red Letter day for Boyle Heights," by Councilman Art K. Snyder
MAR 6 "City Council candidates speak at MAPA convention"
"[Joe] Sanchez endorses Dr. David Lopez-Lee"
"Bastidos hits zoning law"
"Armas runs for office"
"Columnist reply to critical letter," by Art Montoya
"CPDC contracts with oil firm a subsidiary of TELACU vapor
     recovery system"
"Hollenbeck to get Rover system," Art Snyder
"Incumbent [Arthur Snyder] endorsed" by the AFL-CIO
MAR 13 "Columnist continues evaluation of letter," by Arthur Montoya
"Ray Escarcega named Board head"
"School system a flop"
"Roybal named to chair housing committee"
MAR 20 "Kovner Publications endorses Alex Jacinto for Trustee"
"MAPA installs officers"
"Owners slate meeting," by Arthur Montoya
"Human Relations at Palo Alto," by Joseph Eli Kovner
"Fire student workers recruitment drive begins"
"Union locals support Avila"
"Lopez Lee questions use of federal funds"
Letters tell of drug and legal problems
Open letter from Councilman Art Snyder to the President calling
     for massive federal funds to curb depression
"President gives books to city"
"Women attend conference"
MAR 27 "Jacinto calls attention to police raid"
"Snyder's record cited by supporters"
"Alex V. Garcia gives away bonus coupons"
"Ed Avila endorsed by leaders"

"Armas gives qualifications"
"Alatorre, Torres vote against bill," by Arthur Montoya
"Hayden assails poor reading scores"
"Speaker meets with Spanish surnamed"
"AFL-CIO supports Snyder"
"Made no endorsement for 14th CC Large field of strong candidates"

APR 3   "Election results in Art Snyder wins; Alex Jacinto in runoff election for trustee"
"Snyder wins re-election to council," by Carol Clark
"Los Tres denied petition for review"
"Edelman meets with residents," by Arthur Montoya

APR 10   Letter gives criticisms of candidates' night
"School week, American Bicentennial," by Art Snyder
"Job program for women set"
"Alatorre response to column," by Arthur Montoya
"Meeting scheduled on violence"
"Two members of Los Tres del Barrio arrested"
"Redevelopment plans called incomprehensible," by Arthur Montoya

APR 17   "Time magazine and the Estrada Court murals," by Joseph Eli Kovner
"Failure of bilingual education," by David Richard Almada, Pd.D.
"Progressive immigration firm—Flores and associates, a blend of service talents"

APR 24   "Claims about farm workers challenged," by César Chávez
"Chicano named to committee"

APR 27   "Minorities join fire department"
"Bilingual education bill introduced"
"Borjorquez attended White House Conference on minority businesses"
"Open house for Chicana Center set"

MAY 1   "Mexican-American community to celebrate Cinco de Mayo"
"Legacy of Cinco de Mayo," by Art Snyder
"Opinion on illegals changes," by Arthur Montoya

MAY 8   "TELACU names top businessmen"
"Food stamp campaign to begin"
"Chicanismo en el arte scheduled"

MAY 15   "Supervisor Ed Edelman to open full-time office"
"Woman named" to the State Development Disabilities Council
"Program to replace grafitti"
"Chicano arts exhibit in planning"
"Program set for library 'Crime Prevention and Justice in the Barrio' Malabar"

MAY 22   "Welfare recipients to get increase"
"Challenges of bi-cultural heritages," by Art Snyder

MAY 29   "Election results in; liberals take control," by Carol Clark
"TELACU opens job development offices"

"Commissioner Joe Sanchez to be honored at dinner"
"MALDEF to celebrate"
"The Doomsayers are wrong," by Art Snyder
"Property owners slate meeting," by Arthur Montoya
"Spanish origin unemployment rises"
"Bilingual education bill approved"

JUN 5   "TELACU sponsors students"
"Angelenos to fete fire commissioner"
"Labor leader [Trinidad Flores] to be honored at banquet,"
"East Los Angeles faced with threat of annexation by Monterey
Park," by Arthur Montoya

JUN 12   "Garcia tells of survey results"
"Drive to stop all annexation underway"
"Assembly ok's bracero bill"
"Schabarum calls for legislation to block welfare loopholes"
"Youth Conference on media set"
Letter of rebuttal to Montoya
Letter on annexation by Monterey Park
"Dr. [Flora Ida] Ortiz to Speak"

JUN 19   "Host of activities await [sic] youths"
"Mural to decorate USC"
"UFW plans rally"
"Mexican-American artist shows work"

JUN 26   "Meeting with L.A. Police Commission," by Joseph Eli Kovner
"From the Flats" Part I
"Measure introduced to penalize employers of illegal aliens"
"115 year old honored as 'father of year' "

JUL 3   "Alternative classroom opens," by Carol Clark
"Meeting with Police Commission," Part II, by Joseph Eli Kovner
"From the flats" Part II
"Annexation proposal," by Arthur Montoya
"Meeting will be conducted"

JUL 10   "Robert L. Lopez: Chairman of E.L.A. Committee for United
Community Action"

JUL 17   "Maravilla resident buys new home"
"ELA citizens municipal council proposed"
"Child care center opens"
"Women's dinner planned"

JUL 27   "Women's program funded"
"Mexico Meeting," by Bertha Marshall
"TELACU announces business division appointments"
"Mi Liberacion, tu liberacion," by Angel T. Solis
"County wide citizens planning council visits ELA"

JUL 31   "Snyder introducing resolution to annex East L.A."
"Grace Montanez Davis named Deputy"
"Women to be honored"

AUG 7   "Unemployment figures released"
"East Los Angeles a political football in community control," by
Arthur Montoya

"Observations on a visit to Mexico," by Bertha Marshall
"La unidad de libertad"

AUG 14   "City Human Relations Commission calls public hearing on
          redlining"
          "County plans to close Gage Fire Station," by Arthur Montoya
          "Minority increase in L.A. schools"
          "La dificil liberacion," by Angel T. Solis

AUG 21   "Commission calls public hearing on redlining"
          "A victory for Sanchez"
          "Bilingual health program saved by override"
          "Snyder urges support of reform bill"
          "La Ley Rodino," by Angel T. Solis

AUG 28   "Mayor visits East L.A."
          "Employment of bilingual persons bill passed"
          "Redlining," by Joseph Eli Kovner
          "New laws are needed to aid citizens, immigrants," by Arthur
          Montoya
          "Proposed bill mandates bilingual personnel"
          "Judges named"
          "CASA to hold press conference on Rodino bill"

SEP 4   "Fifty outstanding youths honored"
          "La educacion del pobre," by Angel T. Solis
          "Understanding the thinking of the people on annexation," by
          Arthur Montoya
          "Dramatic change foreseen," by Congressman Ed Roybal

SEP 11   "[TELACU] Women's banquet sponsored"
          "Thousands of Chicanos to celebrate liberation"
          "Urban renewal creates problems," by Arthur Montoya
          Letters on undocumented workers
          "Gang crimes," by J. S. Gonzales
          "Murals bring national recognition to Boyle Heights," by Arthur
          K. Snyder
          "From stomping to rapping"
          "El Patriotismo," by Angel T. Solis
          Los Angeles East Magazine, September 11, 1975, Vol. 3, No. 1
          Supplement on "Murals of Estrada Courts"

SEP 18   "Chicano named artist in residence"
          "WFM scores some victories," by Arthur Montoya
          "A visit to Mexico," by Bertha Marshall
          "De nosotros depende," by Angel T. Solis

SEP 25   "Injunction invalidates scheme to turn over identities of illegal
          aliens"
          "Moctezuma Esparza and Joe Sanchez host reception for Tom
          Hayden," by Joseph Eli Kovner
          "Chicana center serves"
          "Annexation hearing set," by Arthur Montoya

OCT 2   "TELACU honors 32 women at dinner"
          "Spanish reading program set for publication"
          "Aragon to head committee"

"Franklin library renaming proposed by Art Snyder"
"La libertad como meta," by Angel T. Solis
"Farm workers will get unemployment"

OCT 9   "Unemployment rises despite drop in number of job seekers"
"Community to vote on library name change"
"A golden day," by Joseph Eli Kovner
"Propuestas de Ford," by Angel T. Solis

OCT 16   "Spanish Speaking elderly group gets government funds"
"Montoya speaks out on annexation," by Arthur Montoya
"East Los Angeles Redevelopment: a study in unethical conduct"
"Las soluciones de Ford," by Angel T. Solis
"Low interest loans available," by Arthur Montoya

OCT 23   "On Tom Hayden, Senate race and our historical background," by
          Bertha Marshall
"The Captain's Corner," by Rudy De Leon
"Redlining charged"
"Bilingual education gets grant"

OCT 30   "Manuel Aragon elected to Pitzer College Board"
"TELACU, PUC to conduct franchising seminar"
"La responsabilidad del servidor publico"
"Spanish employees increase"
"Group slates meeting," by Arthur Montoya

NOV 6   "Deputy Mayor says Giveaway expensive"
"Jumping into the fire," by Arthur Montoya
"Roybal library," by Joseph Eli Kovner
"Youth barrios: a community reality," by David Richard Almada

NOV 13   "Boyle Heights preliminary community plan prepared"
"Board member Grace Martinez elected council president"
"Unemployment rate drops"
"Meeting on Annexation plan"
"Farm workers solve problem"
"Second thoughts about annexation"
"California to get $23.5 million in federal aid to schools"

NOV 20   "Garfield High gives two year accreditation"
"Government committee to meet"
"Bilingual conference at school"
"Meeting slated," by Arthur Montoya

NOV 27   "Ed Roybal slated as Parade Grand Marshall"
"Latino democrats approve Organization"

DEC 4   "TELACU to meet with ELA Social Service agencies"
"Armas is an organizer"
"Assemblyman [Art Torres] protests abuses in human
          experimentation"

DEC 11   "Voight to march with UFW"
"Torres opposes ELA annexation"
"Defeat the Rodino Bill," by David Richard Almada
Letter on undocumented workers

DEC 18   "Las Posadas slated for tonight"
          "State Secretary of Health, Welfare visits community jobs
              program"
          "Snyder criticizes annexation"
DEC 25   "Roybal to head political action caucus"

1976

JAN 1   "Murals selected for 'Horizons on Display' "
          "Annexation opposition"
JAN 8   "Vigilance," Joseph Eli Kovner
          "New Branch library set to open in February"
JAN 15   "Unemployment rate drops during December"
          "TELACU, PSE WIN program extended"
          "Chicano [Health] conference scheduled"
JAN 22   "Villalobos honored by Bicentennial Salute"
          "Chicana Center recruiting women"
          "Redevelopment plans of city, county told," by Arthur Montoya
          "30 artists show work featuring Timothy Padilla"
JAN 29   "SB1: a threat," by Bertha Marshall
          "Immigration first hand," by Arthur Montoya
FEB 5   "Chicanos must work together, says Rudy Cervantes"
          "Monterey Park City Council schedules annexation hearing for
              Monday," by Arthur Montoya
          "Joe, Dolores Sanchez to be honored"
          "Sanz announces his candidacy for office of Judge"
          "Even before the plan is approved"
          "Querer es Poder," by Angel T. Solis
FEB 12   "Congressman to seek re-election"
          "Applications sought for area analysis committee"
          "Issue of information wrong," by Arthur Montoya
          "Conference scheduled"
          "El Pandillerismo juvenil," by Angel T. Solis
FEB 19   "RTD Link links seniors with Salazar Park"
          "Oil Wells in Boyle Heights?" by Joseph Eli Kovner
          "[Mexican American Opportunities Foundation] Conference on
              women takes place"
          "Local woman gets honor"
          "Unincorporated areas," by Arthur Montoya
FEB 26   "Mayor moves to save CETA jobs"
          "Benjamin Franklin Library opens to public"
          "Earthquake infor lacking in oil drill ok"
          "[TELACU] Program appeals for more manpower, employees"
          "Urban renewal means disaster for East Los Angeles Residents," by
              Arthur Montoya
          "Assemblyman to seek re-election"
          "La educacion como arma," by Angel T. Solis

MAR 4   "MAPA 56 to hold installation banquet,"
          "Benjamin Franklin library opens new library," by Carol Clark
          "Educational reform forum set slated"
          "Annexation hearing interesting," by Arthur Montoya
          "YCC [Youth Conservation Corps] applications now being taken"
          "Roybal announces new grant"
MAR 11   "Beltran promoted to CPDC [Community Planning and
                  Development Corporation] vice-president"
          "Councilman [Snyder] demands corrections"
          "It happened early one evening," by Arthur Montoya
          "[Chicana Nurses] Organization purpose to be discussed,"
MAR 18   "Borja withdraws from race, endorses Sanz for judge"
MAR 25   "TELACU to start senior citizens co-op"
          "Redlining 'inlawful' in Torres bill," by Joseph Eli Kovner
          "Property owners meet," by Arthur Montoya
          "Bradley to visit East L.A."
          "Groundbreaking for Hills Project slated"
          "Nomination meetings scheduled"
APR 1   "Association [MAPA] installs officers"
          "Chicanos attend conference"
APR 15   "East Los Angeles analysis committee appointed"
          "500 persons attend Sanz fund-raiser"
          "Town meeting scheduled"
          "Public invited to reception"
          "Voting opportunity," by Arthur Montoya
          "Roybal speaks at national conference"
          "CETA program opens"
          "Alatorre blasts amendment"
          "Legislation introduced"
APR 22   "Torres declares special day"
          "CRASH program started"
          "Don't sell your oil leases"
          "Mayor announces summer jobs for youth program"
          "Latino Board member is needed"
APR 29   "Information line for senior citizens now operating in L.A."
          "It should not happen here," by Joseph Eli Kovner, on LAPD and
                  youth
          "Murals add to buildings, bring life to community"
          "[David] Lizarraga elected"
MAY 6   "Cinco de Mayo Marks start of Mexican identity"
          "Fiesta del Grito set for fall"
MAY 13   " 'Ahora' features interview with former political prisoner"
          "Parenthood course for Spanish-speaking"
MAY 20   "Chicanos endorse no on Proposition 15"
          "Proposition 15 should be voted down," by Joseph Eli Kovner
          "Opposition to Proposition 15 announced by Alatorre"
MAY 27   "Plaza de la Raza launches building fund"
          "Jerry Brown to be in ELA," by Joseph Eli Kovner

THE BELVEDERE CITIZEN

1934

MAY 10   "Law's Net Trap Killer's Nephew"
         "Cinco de Mayo Celebration Was Well Attended and Appreciated"
MAY 17   "Two More Entries in Girl's Contest"
MAY 25   "Week's Happenings in the Police Court"
JUN 1   "Many Offenders of County Ordinances Are Found Guilty"
JUN 8   "Corpus Christi Procession Held Altars Visited"
JUN 15   "Ernest Jimenez Cooped for Year"
JUN 22   "Was Field Day at Eastside Airport"
JUL 6   "Wedding Anniversary"
AUG 3   "Story in Nude not Confirmed but Good Yarn"
AUG 10   "Woman's Brother Acted Sentinel for Real Robber"
         "Names of People Adorning Police"
AUG 17   "Free-for-All Was Indulged in on Sunday"
AUG 24   "Dismiss Two Newspaper Men Contempt Cases"
AUG 31   "Girl, 16, Seeks Death by Firing Shot in Breast"
         "All Plead Guilty and Depart Free"
SEP 7   "Second Try to Burn Auto Car Strike Breaker"
SEP 14   "Joe Sandoval and 'Chicle' Are the Same"
SEP 28   "Auto Strikes Pedestrian on Floral Drive"
OCT 5   "Wife Attempts Protect Hubby and Is Nicked"
         "Kicks in Door Dope Thief Is Caught in Act"
OCT 29   "Crazy Mexican Shoots Three, Killing Girl"
NOV 2   "Houser Receives Endorsement of Span-Amer Club"
NOV 9   "Forgot His Date at Jail and Is Doing Full Time"

1935

FEB 1   "Mexican Chamber Is Seeking More Loal Support"
FEB 15   "Gang Shooter Bound Over to Superior Court"
         "Mexican Youths Go on Trial for Lives"
MAR 8   "Lorena Street Is Hostess to Lincoln P-T-A"
MAR 29   "Residents Protest Holding of Noisy Dance"
         "Mad Dog Scare Envelopes the Whole District"
APR 12   "Texas Society Meets Tonight"
         "Another Drunk Causes Bad Accident"
APR 19   "Silver Star Has Election"
MAY 3   "Silver Star Social Club"
         "Cinco de Mayo Celebration on Saturday Eve"
         "Guzman-Fabela Plead Burglar Charge Today"

MAY 17   "Terrace P.T.A. Elect Officers"
MAY 24   "Knife Wielder Attempted the Art of Carving"
JUN 7   "Cold Feet Was Cause of Wife Going to Jail"
JUN 14   "Inhuman Brute Leaves Boy on Street to Die"
          "Belvedere Junior High School Graduates"
JUN 21   "Wife Beater to Road Camp for 6 Months"
          "Catholics in Protest March"
          "Alonso Pena Went Course"
          "Leniency Was Recommended and Granted"
JUL 5   "Danny Vasquez Asked for Six Months, Got It"
          "Hung Jury in Garcia Case Retrial 19th"
          "Latin Post of Am Legion Has New Officials"
AUG 9   "Gilbert Rojo Collected $200 from SERA—Sent Money to Mexico"
AUG 30   "Brave Hombre Rules ESPOSA with Hammer"
          "Cafe Violated Pure Food Act"
          "Gomez Wins Gold Medal Team Trophy"
SEP 6   "Knife Wielder Had Intention to Do Murder"
SEP 13   "Fire Water Down Fall of Lugo Family"
          "Girl Wanders from Parents in Cafe"
SEP 20   "Child Killed as Car Races Down Two Steep Hills"
SEP 27   "Vandalism Runs Rampant in Belvedere"
OCT 11   "PTA/Benefit Friday Night Great Success"
          "Silver Star Social Club"
          "Arrest Pair on Suspicion of Robbery"
          "Rape Case Up to Superior Court"
NOV 1   "Judge Marion Honored by Silver Star"
          "Girl Attacked in Lonely Location Sunday Night"
NOV 22   "Silver Star Club Shows Splendid Steady Growth"
DEC 30   "Black Eyes Exhibited in Court"
          "Men Charged with Deadly Assault"
          "Brass Knuckles Were Used in Fight"

1936

JAN 31   "Wedding Proves Great Magnet Last Sunday"
FEB 7   "Silver Star to Dance Tomorrow Evening"
          "Suicide Attempt Denied and Admitted"
          "A Sizeable Jail for Reckless Driving"
FEB 14   "Albert M. Romero [Commander of American Legion Post 508]
              Passed Away at Hospital"
          "Infant Seriously Burned"
          "Silver Star Club Had Visitors"
MAR 13   "Mexican Chamber of Commerce to Stage Queen Contest and
              Trade Exposition"
MAR 20   "13 Entrants in Queen Crown Contest"
APR 17   "Mexican Industrial Exposition May 2-3-4-5"
APR 24   "Rudy Diaz Must Stand Trial on Felony Charge"
MAY 1   "Trade Exposition Will Open on Saturday"

MAY 15   "11,500 circulation"
            "Another Recall Petition Filed Against Marion"
            "Dolores Perez Held to the High Court"
            "Chacon Arraigned on Felony Charge"
            "Cattle Rustlers Are in Custody"
            "Spanish Classes Attract Pupils of All Ages"
MAY 29   "Effort to Stop the Recall Election"
JUN 5   "Lady of Lourdes School Pupils in Pageant"
JUN 19   "Hoped the Recall Case Will Be Settled"
JUN 26   "Changed Plea to Guilty"
JUL 3   "Spanish Division of Co-ordinating Council"
            "Silva Jury Case Continued for One Week"
JUL 10   "Jimenez Back from Trip to Mexico"
            "Jack Patino Supervises [Spanish] Division [of the Coordinating
               Council of Belvedere]"
JUL 17   "Heinous Offence to Be Heard on 17th"
AUG 21 "All Silvas Were Settled Tuesday"
            "Assault with an Automobile Is Charged"
AUG 28 "Spanish Pre-Election Dinner"
SEP 4   "Sisters Separated for 17 Years Lived within Six Blocks of Each
               Other without Knowing About It"
            "Spanish Paper to Celebrate Double Event"
            "Reopening of Estrada Case and Dismissal"
SEP 11   "Three Young Men Declared Guilty of Vagrancy"
            "Second Attempt at Suicide Failure"
SEP 18   "Marianna School Invites Women Students English for Foreign
               Speaking"
            "Independence Day of Mexico Duly Celebrated"
            "Esquivel-Rios Nuptial Rites Sept. 13"
SEP 25   "American-Latin Legion Post in Drive for Cups"
            "Old Residents of Belvedere Married"
OCT 2   "Young Belvedere Couple United Sept. 26"
            "Catholic Study Club Formed Sept. 24"
            "Garten-Martinez Nuptials Held Sunday"
OCT 23 "Group Discusses Delinquency Situation"
            "Paul Fernandez Convicted of Petty Theft"
NOV 13 "Marianna P.T.A. Planning for Children"
DEC 4   "Juvenile Work by Mexican Chamber"
DEC 11   "Stabbing Is Result of Collision"
DEC 18   "Pablo Gonzales Thanks Friends"
DEC 23   "Prieto Family Mix It with Hit and Run"
            "Marianna"
DEC 30   "Mendoza Held to Answer in Superior Court"

1937

JAN 8   "New Interpreter Made Appearance on Wednesday"
JAN 22   "Brother Charges Theft"

"Marianna"
"Brooklyn"
FEB 5   "Mexicana . . . for Two Days"
           "Young Man Held on Serious Charge"
FEB 19   "Caught with His Hand in Other Man's Pocket"
           "Mexican C of C will Be Hosts February 25"
FEB 26   "Petty larcenist"
MAR 5   "Hit-and-Runner Left Door Handle as Evidence"
           "Attempted to Ride Right in House"
MAR 12   "Coordinator Is Advanced and transferred"
MAR 19   "Investigating Non Citizen Expenditures"
APR 9   "Spanish Fiesta at Meeting"
APR 16   "Cinco de Mayo Celebration Extends Over Five Days. Second
               Annual Mexican Exposition and Food Show Larger, Better
               than Ever"
           "Officers Hold Over for One More Term"
APR 30   "Mexican School Fiesta Tonight at Marianna"
           "Mexican People Preparing for Week of Pleasure at Exposition"
           "Young Drunks Go to Church Services"
           "Grocery Robbers Have All Been Apprehended"
MAY 7   "Three Boys Pleaded Guilty to Murder and Got Life; Valenzuela,
               Rubidoux, Ramirez"
MAY 21   "J. Harmon Caskey [Editor] Passes On"
           "Una Fiesta Ranchera Success"
MAY 28   "City Terrace Organization Holds Meet"
           "Man causes own arrest"
JUN 4   "Mexican Fair Opens Next Sunday: Montebello Stadium Will Be
               Setting for Gorgeous Festivals of Old Mexico"
           "Belvedere Man Wins on Irish Sweepstakes"
JUN 11   "Mexican Fair Is Drawing Big Crowds"
           "Coronation of Saint Last Sunday"
JUN 18   "Plan Permanent Mexican Mission in District"
           "Graduation at Lourdes Last Evening"
JUN 25   "Boys arrested admit Burglary of Store"
           "Population of Belvedere Gains Six"
JUL 2   "Library Benefit Supper Next Friday"
           "Rev. S. M. Ortegon Off to London, England"
           "Two Hundred Forty-two Are Graduated from Belvedere Junior
               High—Fine Program"
JUL 16   "Many aliens to be ousted from relief WPA rolls"
           "Police Team of Mexico City City's Guests"
JUL 23   "Rev. Ortegon Addresses Congress"
JUL 30   "Officers Find Men Beaten, Robbed"
           "A.L. Post No. 508 In Program on August 2"
AUG 6   "Rev. S. M. Ortegon Returns from England"
AUG 20   "Enthusiastic Group form East First Street Business Men's Ass'n of
               Belvedere"
AUG 27   "Mexican Baptist Convention to Close Today"

SEP 3   "Mexico's Great Symphony Orchestra at Hollywood Bowl Next
                Sunday Night"
             "Barbecue Held Saturday in City Terrace"
SEP 10   " 'Spanish Fiesta' Is Scheduled for Parks"
             "Carries Knife Is Arrested"
OCT 8   "Unavoidable Accident"
OCT 29   "M. Romo Charged with Murder"
NOV 5   "Ignacio Gomez Badly Injured in Accident"
             "Return Verdict of Guilty in Ornales' Case"
NOV 12   "Desperately Wounded by Bandit Deputy . . . Holding Own at
                Hospital"
             "Collision Last Sunday Kills Two"
             "Charge Reduced At Preliminary Hearing"
NOV 19   "Noted Editor of Mexico City Is Honored Guest"
NOV 24   "Girl Is Kidnapped and Assaulted by Negroes"
             "Ramirez Bound Over for Trial December 16"
             "Ignacio Morales Progressive Merchant"
DEC 17   "Belvedere P.T.A. Has Christmas Celebration"
DEC 30   "Two Convicted of 2nd Degree Robbery"

1938

JAN 7   "Judge Marion and Helpers Brought Happiness Xmas Day to Many
                Local Homes"
             "Mexican Visitor Honored Guest at Dinner"
JAN 14   "Discuss Zoning Project at Meeting"
FEB 11   "Despicable Act Charged to C. Beaza"
FEB 18   "Spanish Class at Belvedere Eve. High"
MAR 11   "Was Robbed and Beaten by Two Men"
MAR 25   "An Old Mexican Easter Sunday Celebration On"
             "Spoke in Spanish at Meeting"
APR 1   "Rob Maternity Hospital"
             "Playground News"
APR 8   "Mrs. Salazar is Honored on Birthday"
APR 15   "Acosta-Posada Nuptials on April 24"
             "Latin American Pharmacy Set For Easter"
             "New Method of Learning Spanish"
APR 22   "Third Mexican Exposition May 4th"
APR 29   "Serrato Bros. Are Celebrating 2nd Anniversary"
             "Mexican People Preparing to Celebrate Their Great . . . Cinco de
                Mayo . . . Fiesta"
MAY 6   "Permits Granted for Home and Additions"
             "Belvedere P.T.A. Enjoy Good Program"
             "Notice of Appeal in Robbers Case Is Given"
MAY 13   "Cantu Pena Now Occupies New Quarters"
MAY 27   "Mexican Baptist Church Scene of Wedding"
JUN 3   "Young Democrats Hold Meeting"
JUN 10   "Rev. Fr. Sandoval Buried Last Tuesday"

JUN 24   "Young Democrats Select Club Button"
JUL 1   "Porchia-Ulibarri Nuptial on June 26"
JUL 8   "Fine New Branch Mission Near End"
JUL 29   "Eastside Doubles Population in Eight Years"
AUG 12   "Italians, Liberals Endorsement for Marion"
AUG 19   "Trial by Jury for Apodaca Tonight"
OCT 21   "Young Democrats Pledge Loyal Support"
OCT 28   "Women's Democratic Club Issues Invitation to Tea in Montebello
          November 5"
DEC 9   "Police Detail Supplants Curfew"
DEC 16   "Market Now Managed by Juarez"
          "Belvedere Assured of 500 Homes Under Low Cost Housing"
DEC 23   "Frank S. Gonzales Will Receive Fine Gift"

1939

JAN 20   "Property Owners Will Protest Housing"
FEB 3   "Latin American League"
          "Auto Thieves Caught by Deputies"
FEB 17   "Property Owners Will Get Out Injunction"
MAR 3   "Novena at Our Lady of Lourdes"
          "Man Stabbed at East First St. and Alma"
          "Adolfo Luna, Old Resident Died Suddenly"
MAR 10   "Property Owners Will Have Meeting"
          "Would Change Garfield to Jr. College"
MAR 17   "Sheriff's Office Arrests Truck Thieves"
          "Estrellistas Club Sponsors Talks"
MAR 24   "E.L.A. Property Owners Meet March 30"
APR 7   "Debate on Low Cost Housing Tonight"
APR 21   "Lady of Lourdes Parish Social announced"
APR 28   "Fourth Annual Cinco de Mayo to Be Held from May 3 to 5
          Inclusive"
MAY 26   "Latin American Social Last Wednesday"
          "Belvedere Elem. School Gay May Fiesta"
JUN 2   "E.L.A. Property Owners Sign Petition"
          "Building Permits"
JUN 23   "East Belvedere Imp. Ass'n Has Barbecue"
          "Farm Labor Is to Be Discussed at Ambassador"
          "Latin American League Will Hold Social"
JUN 30   "L.A. Citizens Ass. [Latin American Patriotic League] Postponed
          Meeting"
JUL 14   "Benefit Bazaar Given for Church"
          "Mary Erivez Is Sentenced to 20 Days"
          "Mexican Baptist Convention Is Announced"
          "Mr. and Mrs. Prieto Have Gifted Daughter"
JUL 21   "Local Young Men in Old Mexico for Track Meet"
AUG 11   "Latin-American League Meeting Date"

AUG 18   "Tony Leyva, Wife and Guest Will Dig Clams"
         "Sanchez Boy Dies from Bullet Wound"
         "Mexican cafe will stage fiesta"
SEP 1   "Beauty Contest for Mexican Fiesta"
         "Stabbing . . . Lands Youth in General"
SEP 15   "Youth Taken Up by Deputies Kersh & Smith"
         "Wyvernwood Uses Up to Date Gadgets"
SEP 29   "Sanchez Case Must be Retried"
OCT 6   "Ramona Village Plans Are Ready for Bids This Week"
         "Yellow Cars Run Nearly 114,000 Mi. Per Day"
OCT 13   "Catholic Shrine Soon Underway"
OCT 20   "Local Students Make Honorary Societies"
         "Mexicans Being Repatriated in Homeland"
OCT 27   "Shrine Drive to Begin This Sunday"
NOV 3   "Latin American League Meets Tonight"
NOV 10   "Cleland House New and Notes"
         "Guadalupe Group Breaks Ground for Shrine"
NOV 24   "Patriotic League thanks Friends and Members"
         "Chicagoan Is House Guest at Ramirez"
DEC 1   "Building Permits Continue to Mount"
DEC 8   "Latin-American League Held Meeting"
         "David Ramirez Was Married Sunday"
DEC 15   "George Gonzales Met a Tragic Death"
DEC 22   "Local Housing Project Has Met Obstacles in Local Reaction"
DEC 29   "Latin-American League Held Meeting"

1940

JAN 5   "Lourdes Altar Society Gives Luncheon"
JAN 12   "New Homes Are Planned for East L.A."
JAN 26   "Latin-American Young Dems Organized"
FEB 9   "Ramona Project Begins in 30 Days"
         "Legion to Battle Migratory Relief"
FEB 16   "East Los Angeles Property Owners"
FEB 23   "Cum Laudes are Entertained at LACC"
         "Miss Perez Has Opened a New Beauty Shop"
         "L.D.S. Spanish Church Have Conference"
MAR 1   "Mrs. Garcia Warm in Praise of Citizens"
MAR 8   "Meeting of Latin American Young Democrats"
MAR 22   "Joe Chaves Has Office at 127 S. Rowan"
         "Latin Young Dems Present Their Objectives"
MAR 29   "Latin American Young Dems Have Party"
APR 5   "$85,000 Building Increase in March Over Same Month in 1939"
         "Americanization Program at Marianna"
         "Latin-American Young Dems Active"
APR 12   "Latin American Young Dems Meet"
APR 19   "Spanish Dancers for Our Lady of Lourdes Benefit Dinner"

MAY 3   "Latin-American Young Dems Will Meet"
           "Three More Days of the Great Cinco de Mayo Mexican
               Exposition"
           "Lourdes Altar Society Meets Next Week"
MAY 10   "Latin American Young Demos to Give Dance"
           "Carmilita Ruiz Won First at United Artists"
           "Ramona Gardens Is Rapidly Progressing"
MAY 17   "Latin-American Patriotic League"
MAY 24   "Nora Paredes Gets USC Scholarship"
MAY 31   "News from Census Bureau"
           "L.D.S. Conference of Spanish Americans"
JUN 7   "Maria Jiminez [sic] Wins Prize Scholarship"
           "Young Democrats Purge Fifth Column"
JUN 14   "Carmelita Ruiz Wins In contest for Queen at Sheriff's Barbecue"
JUN 28   "Peter Salas as Asset to Belvedere"
           "Brooklyn Avenue School Graduates Seventy-two"
JUL 5   "Latin-American Post Held its Installation"
           "Woman Charged with Assault on Husband"
JUL 19   "Five New Investigators Are Added to East Los Angeles Sheriff's
               Station"
           "E.L.A. Property Owners Meet"
JUL 26   "Artie Fimbres Buys Beauty Shop"
AUG 2   "Democratic Club Organized in Belvedere"
AUG 16   "Latin-American Young Dems. to Meet"
           "Mr. Eddie Quejada Operates Day and Night Garage"
AUG 30   "Introducing the Proprietor of Raquels"
SEP 6   "Meeting That Will Interest All Aliens"
SEP 13   "Americanization Class Starts Monday"
SEP 20   "Catholic School to Be Built by Next Fall Will Cost Nearly
               $60,000"
           "Man Held Answer on Murder Charge"
OCT 4   "Mario Lopez Is Manager of Ball Team"
OCT 18   "Home Owners Will Support Eulia Finn Branin"
OCT 25   "Spanish Group to Hear Jerry Voorhis"
           "Zeferino Ramirez Head of Ramirez Mortuary"
NOV 15   "Democrats of City Terrace Celebrate"
NOV 20   "Californians Should Learn Spanish"
NOV 29   "Many Visitors See Ramona Project"
           "Draftees Left for Headquarters Local Board 203 November 23"
DEC 6   "Lourdes Monthly Social Dec. Twelfth"
DEC 20   "Mexican Baptist Church to Give Program"

1941

JAN 17   "Frank Galindo New Head of Serrato Meats"
           "Enough of Homes in Ramona Gardens"

JAN 24   "Forty-Three Selectees from Belvedere Leave for Military Duty,"
             by Al Diaz
          "Tucson Teachers Visit Local Family"
FEB 7   "Father Enriquez Has Returned to Pueblo of Guadalupe"
FEB 21   "Abe Mendoza Passed Away in Sheriffs Dep. 16 yrs."
FEB 28   "Visitation Night for American-Latin Post"
MAR 7   "Playground Briefs," by Raul Salcido
MAR 28   "Special Service At Mexican Baptist Church"
          "Volunteers and Draftees to Report"
APR 4   "E.L.A. Property Owners Elect Officers"
APR 11   "Draftees of Local 203"
APR 18   "Luncheon by La Soledad Club"
APR 25   "Cinco de Mayo to Be Celebrated at Sixth Annual Dinner"
          "Local Draftees from Board No. 203"
MAY 2   "Cinco de Mayo Celebration to Commemorate Mexican Victory
             Over France"
MAY 9   "Mexican Baptist Church Observes Mother's Day"
MAY 23   "Lourdes C.F.C.M. Will Serve Dinner"
          "Spanish American Baptist Seminary Graduates Eleven"
          "List of Selectees from Board 203"
JUN 6   "Draftees Called by Board 203"
          "Mexican Fiesta at Kern Ave. School"
JUN 20   "Draftee List for Board 203"
          "Lourdes Ladies Give Mexican Dinner"
JUN 17   "List of Draftees for Board 203"
          "Mass Meeting at Belvedere Jr. Hi [sic]" on subject of juvenile
             delinquency
JUL 11   "Draftees Named by Board 203"
JUL 25   "Local Young Men Introduced into the Army"
          "Draftees to Be Inducted for Board 203"
AUG 8   "Draftees Named by Board 203"
          "Lourdes Ladies Announce a Luncheon"
AUG 15   "Organization Formed to Promote Entertainment for Boys on Coast
             First"
          "Aliso Housing Project Under Way"
AUG 22   "Atlantic Council Announces Its New Officers"
          "Fraternity Club Gave Its First Dance Tuesday"
AUG 29   "Association Will Again Discuss Zoning"
          "Spanish Fiesta for Bert Colima"
SEP 5   "In Regard to Zoning on Beverly"
          "Lourdes' Ladies Monthly Social"
SEP 12   "Mexican Dinner at LDS Church 3684 East 3rd St."
SEP 19   "Benefit Fiesta in Guadalupe Patio"
SEP 26   "Eddie Reyes Is Signed Up By Hollywood"
OCT 3   "NYA Aides in Coordinating Youth Groups"
OCT 10   "Fraternity Club Will Get NYA Classes"
OCT 17   "Honor Roll for Belvedere Jr. High"

OCT 24   "List of All Draftees to Report to Board 203"
          "Fraternal Club Dance Invaded by Gang"
OCT 31   "Belvedere Boys Are In the Army Now"
NOV 7   "The Tony Leyvas Rejoice Over Birth of Son"
DEC 5   "New Housing Project to Rise Soon: Bids Will Be Opened on
              December 18 for Work on Mira Villa"
DEC 19   "Pioneer Woman Passed Away Saturday"
DEC 23   "Reverend Ortego [sic] Speaker at Pan American Club"

1942

JAN 15   "NYA Opens New Office on First Street"
JAN 19   "Pair Held in Holdup, Stabbing"

1942 TO MARCH 1943 MISSING

1943

MAR 26   "Alberto Diaz Is Home on Furlough"
APR 9   "Parents' Day Combined with Pan American Day Wednesday at
              High School"
APR 23   "Red Cross Has News for Mrs. Hernandez"
MAY 7   "Cinco de Mayo"
JUN 4   "Mexican Dinner at Santa Maria Center"
JUN 18   "Social at Our Lady of Lourdes"
          "Joe Anda Has New Address"
          "News from Pete Chavez"
          "Zoot-Suit Problem"
          "Earl Gamez Is Prisoner of Japs"
JUL 2   "Lourdes Monthly Luncheon"
          "L.D.S. to Hold Conference"
AUG 13   "Jealous Mate Shoots Wife, Tries Suicide"
AUG 27   "Belvedere Fiesta Planned"
SEP 10   "Soledad Program Broadens"
          Regular news about local servicemen begins and continues
              throughout the war years
DEC 17   "Catholic Procession Held Here"
          "Pvt. Gilbert Reyes Enters Wash. State College"

1944

APR 7   "Sg. A. Elizondo Awarded Air Medal"
APR 14   "Jinx Falkenberg to Star in Pan-American Fiesta"
APR 21   "Latin War Mothers Give Benefit"
MAY 12   "Stress Latin American Culture"
          "Latin Mothers Meet Sunday at 1 P.M."
MAY 19   "Our Lady of Lourdes to Hold Victory Dinner"
MAY 26   "Newly Organized"
          "Latin War Mothers to Meet Sunday"

AUG 4   "Texas Day Picnic August 5"
           "Maravilla Will Organi. ·e Junior Red Cross Unit"
AUG 11   "Fiesta Will Be Held in Belvedere" by the Belvedere Coordinating
           Council
SEP 8   "Irene Duarte to Rule as Queen at Mexican Fiesta"
SEP 15   "Frances Terrazas Joins U.S. Navy Waves"
           "Salute to Mexico Broadcast Over KWKW"
SEP 22   "Civic, Progressive Association to Hold Social"
SEP 29   "Louis Olivarez Killed in Action on Guam"
OCT 6   "Mexican Nationals Aid Labor Shortage in United States"
           "High Court Frees All Defendants of " 'Sleepy Lagoon' "
OCT 20   "Juan B. Paez to Lecture on 'War on Crime' "
NOV 3   "Gala Fiesta to Be Held Sunday"
NOV 10   "Los Caballeros Club to Present Program Today"
DEC 22   "Sgt. J. P. Zamora awarded Air Medal"

1945

JAN 12   "Arrest Trio on Dope Charge"
           "Mexico's Foremost Composer to Conduct Orchestra"
FEB 23   "Pioneer," a photograph of Emilia Camacho, first Mexican "girl"
           to defy tradition and becomes stewardess
MAR 2   "Groups Organize to Oppose Calif. Health Bill"
MAR 16   "U.S. Senate Invites Edward Quevedo to Washington, D.C."
MAR 23   "Sergt. R. A. Diaz Awarded the Silver Star"
           "Three Youths Tear American Flag Arrested"
MAR 30   "Pvt. William Lerma Reported Killed in Action in Germany"
           "Belvedere Coordinating Council Requests Girls' School in East
           L.A."
APR 6   "Luncheon at Our Lady of Lourdes Hall April 12"
APR 13   "Hollenbeck Park to Be Scene of United Nations Rally"
           "Welfare Council of Los Angeles Requests 26,977 Housing Units"
MAY 4   "High Mexico Official to Attend Dedication of Casa Del
           Mexicano"
JUN 1   "S-1 C Encarnacion Nevarez Reported Missing in Action"
JUN 15   "Our Lady of Lourdes School Holds Graduation"
JUL 6   "Director Ingalls Announces Program for East Los Angeles Junior
           College"
JUL 20   "Army Officers Don't Like Race Discrimination"
AUG 10   "Cpl. Rudy Cordova Awarded Silver Star"
           "First Mexican Baptist Church Holds 22nd Annual Convention"
AUG 17   "Death Rate from T.B. Higher Among Latins"
AUG 31   "East Los Angeles College Opens September 4"
           " 'Black and White' Ball to Be Held September 2"
SEP 14   "Viva Mexico—Viva La Independencia; Senor Castillo Najera Guest
           of Honor at Independence Day Fiesta"
           "Death of Sgt. Sandoval Confirmed by War Dept."
SEP 21   "Holifield Appeals for Child Centers to Be Continued"

SEP 28   "S/Sgt. Adolph Robles Killed in Japan September 4"
OCT 5   "Mexican Chamber of Commerce Sponsors Lectures"
          "New Junior College Offers Special Services to Veterans"
OCT 12   "Sgt. Maldonado's Death Confirmed by War Dept."
          "Meeting of Child Care Parents"
OCT 19   "Births Outnumber Deaths in East Los Angeles"
NOV 2   "PTA Leaders and Faculty Welcome Parents"
NOV 9   "East Los Angeles Commended on Nat. Employ. Week"
DEC 21   "Site of New Detention Home Protested"

1946

JAN 4   "Juvenile Delinquency Top for Discussion at Meeting Tomorrow"
JAN 18   "Y2/C.N. Villagrana, Wave, Home on Short Leave"
          "Protest the Erection of Supervisor Smith's Juvenile Hall in
          Belvedere"
JAN 25   "Citizens Arroused Over Proposed Site of Juvenile Hall, Sign
          Protest Petitions"
          "Riggins Ave. School Graduation Program Theme 'Latin-America' "
          "E.L.A. College Women Hold Recognition Awards Banquet"
FEB 1   "Plan Improvements for Local Park in Belvedere"
          "Belvedere Residents Urged to Sign Anti-Juvenile Hall Petitions"
FEB 15   " 'Keep Belvedere Free for Homes—Not Juvenile Halls,' Say
          Petition Signers"
          "Housing Units for Vets in Belvedere to Open Soon"
FEB 22   "Anti-Juvenile Hall Opposition Increases; Petitions Circulate
          Throughout East Los Angeles"
MAR 8   "Editorial: Betrayal in High Places"
MAR 15   "Large Attendance at Business & Professional Association's
          Luncheon"
          "Members of Spanish Church of God in Varied Activities"
MAR 29   "Gala Two-Day Fiesta at 'Parque De Las Magnolias' "
          "Discuss Juvenile Hall Query Tuesday; Residents to Protest"
APR 5   "Supervisors Grant Time Extension on Proposed Juvenile Hall Site
          As Citizens Voice Protests"
APR 12   "Supervisors Accept Compromise Site for Proposed Juvenile Hall"
APR 26   "Leaders Discuss Plans for East L.A. Youth Center"
          "Oscar Apodaca New Chairman of Business & Professional Assn."
MAY 3   "Cinco de Mayo Ceremonies Set Sunday Noon"
MAY 17   "Arthur G. Le Cuyer Claims Oil Concerns Taking Over East L.A."
MAY 24   "Two Men Charged with Violation of Immigration Laws"
MAY 31   "Hold Interesting Program at Casa del Mexicano"
JUN 7   "Beatrice Serrato, Leads Lourdes' Club Queen Contest"
JUN 28   "100 Houseless Vets Move Into Belvedere Housing Project Mon."
JUL 12   "Supervisors' Ordinance Bans Rent Increases"
          "Investigate Klan Activity After Fiery Cross Burning"
          "Roberta Pedroza Elected C.Y.O. Beauty Queen"
JUL 26   "Reporter Finds People Pleased with Local Businessmen's Efforts,"
          by Alberto Diaz

AUG 23   "Rudy Gonzales Elected President of Compolites"
          "Carey McWilliams to Address Latin American Session Friday,
              Aug. 30"
          "Cultural Courses on Mexico Offered at Casa Del Mexicano"
SEP 6   "Announce Plans for Annual 16th of September Fiesta"
SEP 13   "Independence Day Fiesta Opens at Casa Del Mexicano Saturday"
SEP 27   "Large Attendance at Meeting of Business Men's Association"
OCT 4   "Jury Exonerates Deputy Sheriff in Shooting of Boy"
OCT 11   "First Payments Received by East L.A. Oil Lease Holders"
          "Mexican Officials Guests at Business Assn. Gathering"
OCT 18   "Devout Worshippers Witness Dedication Rites of Our Lady of
              Guadalupe Sanctuary"
NOV 15   "Detective Sgt. Earl Dillon Addresses Business Men's Association
              Meeting"
          "Gang War? No! 'Just Quiet Family Feud' Report Says"
          "Garfield vs. L.A."
NOV 22   "Bert Colima Protege to Appear Monday Night at Whittier Arena"
DEC 6   "Hold Ground Breaking Ceremony for Soldiers' Monument
              Saturday"
DEC 13   "Board of Supervisors Seek Local Tract as Juvenile Hall Location"
          "Youth Groups to Sponsor Yule Fest at Maravilla Project"

1947

JAN 24   "Edward R. Royball Seeks Councilman's Post in 9th District"
JAN 31   "Hold E.L.A. Jr. College Graduation Exercises Sunday"
FEB 7   "Graduate Nurse"
FEB 14   "Select Site for E.L.A. Jr. College in Belvedere"
FEB 21   "Sheriff Announces Juvenile Night Patrol to Wage War on
              Delinquency: Will Enforce County loitering Ordinances"
MAR 21   "Police Youth Group Lauded for Work in Curbing Crime"
          "Supervisors Designate Pan-American Day"
MAR 28   "Coordinating Council Plans Health Talk for April Session"
APR 11   "Pan-American Day Program at Business Men's Session Monday"
APR 18   "Mexican Chamber of Commerce Elects New Officers, Directors"
          "Sheriff's Office Holds Man in Accidental Shooting"
APR 25   "Latin Legion Post 500 Auxiliary Installs Officers Sunday"
          "Manuel Rojo, Jr. Hero's Kin, Appointed to West Point"
          "East L.A. Business Women Hold Officer's Installation"
          "CIO Unions Protest Hartley-Taft Anti-Labor Bills"
MAY 2   "Local Groups Observe Mexican Holiday with Parade and Fiesta"
MAY 16   "Begin Evictions at Maravilla Project of Families with Income of
              $3000 or Over"
          "Cultural Group Sponsors Mexican Folk Lore Lecture, Wed. May
              21st"
MAY 23   "Capt. Harry C. Brewster, ELA Sheriff's Station Official Guest at
              Business Men's Session"
          "Roybal Endorses Christiansen for Council Post"

420   COMMUNITY UNDER SIEGE

MAY 29   "Dignataries Attend Mexican-American War Memorial Unveiling
             Ceremonies Today"
         "Group seeks ways, means to forestall possible eviction"
         "E.L.A. Sheriff's Station Operations Outlined by Capt. Harry C.
             Brewster"
JUN 6   "Maravilla Tenants Name Housing Council Leaders"
JUN 13   "Maravilla Project Resident's Council Officials Attend Inter-Project
             Session"
JUN 20   "Maravilla Project Residents Council Seeks Supervisors Aid as
             Eviction Date Nears"
         "Mexican Chamber of Commerce Holds Installation Banquet"
         "Six Local Students Presented Diplomas at ELAJC Yesterday," by
             Bob Barraza
JUL 3   "Sheriff's New Juvenile Facility Opening Set for Mon., July 7th"
         "Commission to Give Decisions on Boyle Heights Oil Drilling"
JUL 11   "Sheriff's New Juvenile Facility Center Opened"
JUL 25   "Dedicate New Mexican Methodist Church Sunday"
AUG 15   "CYO Hq. to Belvedere, Organization Offices Occupy Former
             'Casa Del Mexicano' "
AUG 22   "Offer Youths Mexical Scholarships to Stanford U.: Mexican
             Consul Gives Details of Scholastic Offer"
         "Pro-Belvedere Ass'n. Announces Plans for Fiesta"
AUG 29   "Represents Citizen at 8th Annual 'Black & White Ball' "
         "ELA Jr. College Report Move to New Site Postponed Til Feb.,
             1948"
         "Adopt Loyalty Test for County Employees"
         "ELAJC Grid Aspirants Start Practice At Hazard Playground," by
             Bob Barraza
SEP 12   " 'Viva Mexico! Viva La Independencia' Parade and Fiesta Features
             Celebration: Hold Evening Feat at Belvedere Jr. High School"
SEP 26   "Mexico Flyers in Tribute to World War II Mexican War Dead"
         "Birth, Death Certificate Photo-Copies on File at ELA Health
             Center"
OCT 10   "Survey Shows ELA Residents Health Better Annual County
             Health Dep. Report Filed with Supervisors"
OCT 17   "Catholic Youth Assn. to Hold 'Hornada Social' at Our Lady of
             Guadalupe
OCT 31   "First Of Belvedere's Fallen Heroes Return"
NOV 7   "Arrest 11 in Marihuana Ring Raid"
         "Hold Memorial Rites for Belvedere's Fallen Heroes: Impressive
             Tribute Slated for Sunday Afternoon Nov. 9"
         "Chet Holifield Slated to Speak—Wed. Evening"
NOV 14   "Mexican Chamber of Commerce Holds Ball Wednesday Eve"
NOV 21   "Mrs. Tillie Herebia Girl Born to Daughter Acclaimed Youngest
             Grandmother"
         "Seek Signatures to Place Progressive Party on Ballot"
NOV 26   "Juan Candia Elected President of Mexican American Movement"
         "Mexican Chamber of Commerce Makes Correction Statement"

DEC 5   "Youth Leaders' Talks Feature Groups' Monthly Meeting"
DEC 19   "Thousands Witness Guadalupe Procession"
DEC 31   "Added Police Protection Sought by Business Group"
          "Mexican Chamber of Commerce to Elect New Officers Jan. 6th"

1948

JAN 9   Letter from Oscar Apodaca, Chair of the Belvedere Business and
          Professional Men's Association, sent to the Sheriff asking for
          added police protection
          "Cornelio Camacho Re-elected Head of Mexican Chamber"
JAN 16   "Merchant Says Sheriff Fails to Answer Call as Robbery
          Attempted"
JAN 30   "ELA College Moves to New Location Ceremonies Mark . . . New
          Campus"
FEB 13   "Promise Additional Police aid for Belvedere, Special Deputy
          Assigned to Patrol Belvedere Area"
          "Special Officer Wounded in Shooting Scrape"
FEB 20   "Supervisors OK, Select Juvenile Hall Site"
FEB 27   "Narcotic Suspects Arraigned, Ask for Jury Trial"
          "Special Freedom Program at Belvedere Park"
MAR 12   " 'Unity of Groups Needed' Educator Tells Businessmen"
MAR 19   "Warm Welcome Given New Archbishop on Arrival at ELA
          Station"
APR 2   "Groups Seek Additional Traffic Signals, Improvements"
          "Organize LULAC Post Here"
APR 9   "Give Order for Three New Traffic Signals"
          "Mexican Chamber of Commerce Holds Banquet Thurs., April
          15th"
          "Girls Organize Daisy Club"
APR 23   "Coordinating Council Plans Cinco de Mayo Fete"
          "Appoint Nominating Committee to Name Candidates for Office"
          "LULAC group Denounces Reds"
APR 30   "Mexican Counsul to Be Main Speaker at Celebration Wed. Eve."
          "Casa del Mexicano Benefit Dance at Avalon Ballroom"
          "Latin Vote Registration Doubled Group Announces"
MAY 14   "Cleland House Observes 26th Anniversary with Two-day Fete"
          "Spanish Speaking Protestant Churches Hold Convention"
          "[Joe R.] Chavez Seeks 51st Assembly Dist."
          "Roybal Addresses College Classes"
          "Ibanez for Judge Dance Tonight"
MAY 28   "Manuel Veiga Jr. Named Chairman of Organization"
          "Holifield, Turner Guests of LULAC's"
JUN 4   "Belvedere Child Care Center to Be Retained"
          "Villagran Heads Consular Ass'n."
JUN 11   "Manuel Veiga Jr. to Report on LULAC Convention"
JUN 18   "Discuss Zoning Classification at Business Men's Meet, Zoning
          Clarified," by Manuel Ochoa

JUL 16   "M-1 Zoning for Brooklyn Ave. Discussion Highlights Business
          Men's Session Monday, Neutral Stand Taken by Group on
          Zoning; Seek More Details"
JUL 23   "Julia Chavez to Represent 'Belvedere Citizen' in 'Churubusco'
          Beauty Contest"
          "Plans for 16th Sept. Independence Day Fiesta Discussed by Local
          Group"
JUL 30   "Discuss Additions to ELA Sheriff's Staff"
AUG 13   "Appoint Manuel Veiga Jr. to Head Belvedere-City Terrace's 48th
          Community Chest Fund Drive"
          "Group Plans Annual 16th September Fete: Parade, Special
          Program to Mark Annual Fiesta"
AUG 20   "Special Features to Mark 16th Sept. Parade, Fiesta"
AUG 27   "Annual Affair to Follow Course on Business Streets"
          "C.S.O. in vote Registration Drive"
SEP 3   "Famed Musical Groups Take Part in Sept. 16 Parade"
SEP 10   "Parade & Fiesta Features Sept. 16th Fete: Hold Evening Program
          at Belvedere Park"
SEP 17   "Colorful Parade and Fiesta Mark Annual Sept. 16 Fete"
          "Mexican Consul Addresses Rotary Club Joint Session Tuesday
          Noon"
OCT 1   "Dinner Wed. Eve Marks Opening of 'Casa del Mexicano' Funds
          Drive"
OCT 8   "Slate Socialist Workers Party Meeting Sunday Eve."
OCT 22   "Casa Del Mexicano Benefit 'Nights of Stars' Set for Nov. 4"
          "Andrea Marquez Elected College WAA Treasurer"
          "Rachel Martinez Elected College WAA Historian"
NOV 12   "Dr. Jose Diaz to Address Rotary Club"
          "Mexican-American Press Group Holds Dinner Meeting"
DEC 3   "Mexican Chamber of Commerce Honors Members at Banquet"
          "Annual Our Lady of Guadalupe Procession Set for Sunday, Dec.
          12"
DEC 10   "Hold 18th Annual Guadalupe Procession Sunday; Archbishop to
          Give Blessing"
          "Narcotic Talk Features Council Meeting Wednesday"
DEC 23   "Local Youths Elected to East LA College Body Offices"

1949

JAN 9   "Mexican Chamber of Commerce Meets to Elect New Officers"
JAN 28   "Drive on to Register Latin-American Voters"
FEB 4   "YMCA Invites Men to Form Y's Men's Club"
          "Elect Henry Nava Head of Community Service Organization"
FEB 18   "Belvedere Youths to Attend Guadalupe Coronation in Paris"
FEB 25   "Noted Mexican Artists in Benefit Concert Tonight; Funds aid
          Sonora Flood Victims"
MAR 4   "Approve Plans for Belvedere Swimming Pool, Start Construction
          in April, Project will cost $169,000"

MAR 11   "Return East LA World War II Dead"

APR 22   "Supervisors Reject Proposed East LA Civic Center Site"
         "Report Unemployment Levels Off in East LA; Jobs show
             Increase"

APR 29   "East LA Civic Center Assignment Given to Planning
             Commission"
         "Cinco de Mayo Fete at City Terrace Park"

MAY 6   "F. Fernandez Soliz: Attorney Opens Offices, Established Residence
             Here"

MAY 13   "9th Council District Candidates . . ."

MAY 27   "Hold Memorial Day Ceremonies at Soldiers' Monument Mon.
             Morning; Veteran's Group Plan, Sponsor Observance"
         "Citizen Endorses Bowron for Mayor; Roybal for Council in 9th
             District"

JUN 3   "Bowron, Roybal Elected; Express Thanks to Supporters"

JUN 10   "Belvedere Men at LULAC Convention"

JUN 17   "Hold 23rd Annual Corpus Christi Procession in Belvedere
             Sunday"
         "Mexican-American Group [Mexican American Movement] Meets"

JUN 24   "Dr. F. Bravo Offers Pharmacy Scholarship at U.S.C. to Mexican-
             American Student"
         "Leaders Confer on Juvenile Delinquency"

JUL 1   "Protest Proposed Rubbish Disposal Site in City Terrace: Residents
             File Complaint with Supervisors"

JUL 8   "Property Owners Begin Filing for Assessments Hearings as Board
             of Equalization Convenes"

JUL 15   "Mexican Church of God Installs New Pastor"

JUL 22   "Form New Belvedere Park Business Men's Group Here"

AUG 5   "Dump Site in City Terrace At Standstill: Residents Lodge Protest
             with Supervisors"
         "LULAC Council to Install New Officers Monday"

AUG 12   "Jesse Soto Noe President of LULAC's Install Officers"
         "Zeferino Ramirez Observes 30 Years Community Service"

AUG 19   "Mexican Chamber of Commerce Celebrates Silver Anniversary"
         "LULAC Council 154 Plans Picnic Aug. 28"

AUG 26   "LULAC's Picnic Sun. at Streamland Park"

SEP 2   "FEP Meeting Set for Tuesday Eve."

SEP 9   "Select Area in Belvedere Township as Eligible for House
             Clearance, Community Redevelopment"
         "Four Applicants to Try for Second Bravo Scholarship"

SEP 16   "Mrs. E. Barba to Head Belvedere Chest Campaign"
         "Gay Fetes March Mexico Independence Day; Park Holds Program
             Today"

SEP 30   "Hold Groundbreaking Rites for New Guadalupe Parochial School"
         "Open Mexican Chamber of Commerce Convention Sat."

OCT 9   "Mexican Chamber of Commerce Close Busy Convention"

OCT 18   "Garfield, Roosevelt Renew Grid Rivalry Tonight; Bulldogs Favored
             Overs Teds; Teams Meet for First Time Since 1938"

OCT 21   "M.A.N.A. [México Asociación Nacional Americana] Head to Open
          Founding Convention"
          "Directive Prohibits Discrimination in Armed Forces"

OCT 27   "Maravilla Property Owners Hold Meeting; Hear Regional Planning
          Commission Reports"

NOV 11   "Mexican Chamber of Commerce Sponsors Essay Contest"
          "Youth Groups Formed at Church of God"

NOV 18   "Local Attorney Gives Views on J. Roosevelt as Candidate for
          Gov."

DEC 2   "Belvedere Residents Form Group for Slum Clearance"
          "LAPD Orders All Ex-Convicts, Sex Offenders to Register"

DEC 9   "19th Annual Guadalupe Procession Sunday"
          "Congressman Speaks on Atomic Age and Human Relations"

DEC 16   "Christian Workers Council Install New Officers Here"

DEC 30   "Supervisors Reject Public Housing Plan; Re-affirm Stand for
          Private Low Cost Home Rentals"

1950

JAN 6   "Mexican Chamber of Commerce to Elect New Officers"
          "Supervisors Re-iterate Stand—Won't Act to Obtain Housing Law"

JAN 13   "City Terrace B'Nai B'rith Lodge Installs, New Officers Sunday"
          "Mexican Chamber of Commerce Elects Officials Armando Torrez
          Re-elected Prexy; Name Directors"

JAN 20   "16 Mexico City School Teachers Visit Garfield, Observe
          Instruction Methods"

JAN 27   "Application Blanks for Opportunity Fellowships Available" for the
          John Hay Whitney Foundation
          "Newly Formed ELA Ministerial Asociation Installs Officers"
          "Memorial Planned by Gold Star Mothers"

FEB 17   "Cleland House Club Installs New Officers"

MAR 10   "Install Mexican Chamber of Commerce Officers Tonight"

MAR 17   "Organize New Civic Group Here, Name Temporary Officers"
          "Belvedere Organizing Committee"

MAR 24   "Arthur O. Casas Enters Assembly Race in 5th District"
          "Name Officers of Club Altruism"

APR 7   "A. L. Barney, Citizen Publisher, in Race for State Assembly, 51st
          Dist.," by Alberto C. Diaz

APR 14   "Candidate Held Ineligible for Justice Post"

APR 21   "Hundreds Gather to Mark 25th Anniversary of Garfield High"
          "Maravilla Property Owners Assn. Elects New Officers"

APR 28   "Youth Fellowship Plans Activities"
          "Minority Group Symposium Sunday" on the depiction of
          minority groups on radio and television

MAY 5   "Community Fetes Mark Belvedere Cinco de Mayo Celebrations"

MAY 26   "Sheriff Biscailuz Orders Reserves into Field"

JUN 8   "Assembly Race Undecided as NO Official Count"

JUL 6   "Joe 'Pepper' Gomez Picked as Mr. Muscle Beach of 1950"

JUL 20   "Consideration Given Youth, Minority Groups at Employment
          Office"
          "LULAC's Stage Pation Dance Saturday Eve."
JUL 27   "Meet Lalo Rios, Sensational Star of 'The Lawless'," by Alberto C.
          Diaz
AUG 10   "Msgr. O'Dwyer, Roybla, CSO Oppose Segregated Housing
          Developments"
AUG 24   "City Council Slates Hearing on Proposed Reds Registration Law"
SEP 7   "Art Jurado Acclaimed Role in New Film, 'The Men'"
SEP 14   "Civic Observance, Gay Fiesta, Parade to Mark Mexico
          Independence Anniversary"
          "Local Court Scene of 'Red Registration' Test Case Friday"
          "Belvedere CSO Opens Fall Activity Program"
SEP 28   "CHICANO G.I.'s—BEWARE"
NOV 2   "Belvedere Property Owners Meet Wed." on incorporation papers
          "Robert M. Kenny in Race for Mayor"
NOV 16   "Belvedere CSO to Entertain Shut-ins, Veterans, Orphans"
NOV 21   "Belvedere Property Owners Initiate Many Local Improvements"
          "Discuss Laws of Importance to Women at ELAJC"
DEC 14   "20th Annual Guadalupe Procession Sunday"
DEC 21   "Hear Juvenile Delinquency talk CSO Meeting"
          "Altruista Club Buys Milk for Children"
DEC 28   "Monterey Park Move May Result in Loss of ELAJC; Board of
          Education Issues Protest, Public Hearing Set for Jan. 8"

1951

JAN 11   "Officials Meet to Discuss Fate of ELAJC"
          "Local Residents Oppose Proposed Dump. Protest ELA Jr. College
          Annexation at Hearing. Local Business, Civic Organizations
          Voice Objection"
          "Monterey Park Votes Annexation After Hearing Protests"
          "Planning Commission Hears Complaints on Project Today"
          "Gold Star Mothers Install Officers Mon. Mrs. Moraga, Pres."
JAN 18   "Grant Permits for Dump in City Terrace; Supervisors to O.K.
          Move in Special Session"
          "City Terrace B'nai B'rith Lodge Installs New Officers"
          "Chamber of Commerce Elects New Officials"
          "CSO Mid-Winter Dance Set for Feb. 2"
JAN 25   "Hold Hearing Mon. on Jr. College Injunction, Senate Blocks
          Annex'n"
FEB 1   "CSO To Discuss Proposed 'Dumps' at Session Tonight"
          "Uphold College's Writ of Mandate Against Monterey Park"
FEB 8   "Local Groups Slate Protest Meeting Against Dumps Here"
FEB 15   "Hundreds Attend Dump Protest Meeting here"
          "ELAJC Campus to Serve as Emerging Disaster Shelter"
FEB 22   "C.S.O. Officers Inspect Proposed Dump Site"
MAR 1   "Local Groups Plan Action Against Dump: Mass Meeting Fri."

"Monterey Park Orders Ordinance to Annex 300 Acre Area Where County Plans Dump; New Plan Excludes E.L.A. Jr. College Campus Completely"

"Fisher St. Sidewalk Project assured"

"Recommend Proposal to Set Up Municipal Court Here"

MAR 8   "Two Local Groups in Action Against . . . Dump"

MAR 15   "Propose ELAJC as Site for State College"

"Disclose Plans for Cut-File Dump Temporarily Given Up"

"Welfare Council Forms Mobilization Group"

MAR 22   "Form New Belvedere Teen-Age Group"

"Improvement Council Supervisor on 'Dump Problems' "

"Monterey Park Delays Annexation Plans"

MAR 29   "Manuel Veiga Jr. to Head Group a President"

"Monterey Park Votes to Annex Dump Site Area"

"ELA Business Men Endorse, Support Roybal Re-election"

"Capitol Doings," by William A. Munnell

"Groups Unite Efforts in Fight Against Dump"

APR 5   "Hold Anti-Dump Mass Meeting"

APR 12   "Belvedere Groups Attend City Terrace Dump Protest Session"

"Report Progress on Humphreys-Eugene Sidewalks Project"

APR 19   "Sidewalk Curb Projects to Continue on 50–50 Plan"

"Statement Clarifies Situation on Proposed 'Dump' Here"

APR 26   "Show Movies of Dump Operation at Mass Meeting May 3"

"Cinco de Mayo Fete at Casa del Mexicano"

"Councilman Demands Probe of Pit Where Child Drowned"

MAY 3   "Award Silver Star to Manuel Gutierrez"

"Ralph Tostado Belvedere Marine Wounded in Korea"

"File Suites Against Supervisors in Dump Fight"

MAY 10   "E.L.A. Chapter No. 57 to Install Officers"

"Commend Agencies Aiding L.A. Youth Project"

"Remind Employers Non-Citizen May Be on Defense Jobs"

MAY 17   "3 Local Korean War Dead Arrive in San Francisco"

"Espiritu Latino VFW Post Installs Officers"

"Belvedere Site of Spanish Speaking Evangelical Convention"

"Bertha Villescas to Attend Conference in El Paso, Texas"

"Court Orders Halt Operation of Land Refuse 'Dumps' "

MAY 24   "Supervisor Urges Enlarging Sex, Narcotics Squads"

"Hold 25th Annual 'Corpus Christi' Procession Here Sunday, May 31"

MAY 31   "Coordinating Council Installs Officers at Banquet Tonight"

"7000 March in 25th Annual Corpus Christi Procession"

JUN 7   "Hold Hearing Tonight on Cogan-Kramer Dump Permit at Monterey Park City Hall"

"Ed Fimbres Elected Student Body Prexy at ELA Jr. College"

"Consumer League Speaker at CSO Meeting Tonight"

"Bureau of Adoptions Plans Anniv. Fete; Tell Need of Adoptive Parents for Mexican-American Children"

JUN 28   "Monterey O.K.s Dump in City Terrace"

JUL 5   "City Terrace Mass Rallies Protest Dump"

"Latin-Post 508 Team in Legion's Baseball Championship"

"Supervisors Re-state County Property Non-Discrimination Policy"

JUL 12   "Governor Warren Signs Lower Court Bills; Provides E.L.A. with Two Municipal Courts"

"Latin-Post 508 in Division Play-off Sunday; Dangleis Hurls Shut Out Wins for District Title"

JUL 19   "Gay 'Fiesta' De Las Flores at Belvedere Park Saturday"

JUL 26   "ANMA Opens New Headquarters Saturday"

AUG 2   "Unincorporated Communities May Become Self-Governing Under New Regulation"

"Monterey Park City Council Sets New 'Dump' Hearing Date"

"Veiga-Robison Mortuary Marks Fourth Anniversary of Community Service"

AUG 23   "Monterey Park Grants Zoning for Dump Area"

"CSO to Sponsor Benefit Social Sept. 8"

AUG 30   "Appoint Balt Young Investigator for District Attorney"

SEP 13   "Parade Civic Observances, Gay Fiestas to mark Mexican Independence Anniversary Sat. and Sun."

SEP 27   "Discuss Eugene St. Sidewalk Project Wed."

OCT 11   "Meet Your Business, Professional Men—Oscar Apodaca"

OCT 18   "CSO Meets Tonight at Belvedere School; Show Mexico Films"

"Meet Your Business Professional Men—Atty. Frank F. Solis"

OCT 25   "Hold Military Rites for Two Local Youths"

"Slate Important 'Sidewalks' Meeting for November 2"

"Meet Your Business & Professional Men—Atty. Frank F. Solis"

NOV 1   "Belvedere CSO Holds Meeting Tonight"

"Meet Your Business, Professional Men—Manuel Ochoa"

NOV 8   "Review of Services of Community Chest in East L.A. Area"

NOV 15   "Paul Burke, Bd. of Education Prexy to Address Belvedere CSO Tonight"

"Meet Your Business, Professional Men—Julio Perez"

NOV 22   "Roybal Speaks at B'nai Brith Meeting Wed."

"Meet Your Business & Professional Men—Henry Ybarra"

NOV 29   "Meet Your Business Professional Men"

"Rabbi Bierman to Address CSO Dec. 6"

DEC 6   "Freedom Talk Movie Highlights CSO's Weekly Session"

"Mexican Beneficencia Committee to Hold Stage, Screen Show"

DEC 13   "Hold 21st Annual Our Lady of Guadalupe Procession Sunday"

"Meet Your Business, Professional Men—Agustin Serrato"

DEC 20   "Identify Soldiers from Belvedere Area Held Prisoners by Korean Reds"

1952

JAN 3   "May Close Belvedere Veterans Housing Project Unless More Tenants Apply for Available Rentals; Housing Authority Issues Notice in Answer to Inquiry"

"Meet Your Business, Professional Men—Sal Lopez"

JAN 24   "Sidewalks: Sunol Dr. Property Owners Report at CSO Meet
          Tonight"

JAN 31   "Elect Felix Ontiveros, ELA Business Man, President of Mexican
          Chamber of Commerce"

FEB 7   "Councilman Holland in Public Housing Talk at CSO Meet
          Tonight"
          "Rev. Ruben Saenz to Head Spanish Speaking Ministerial Ass'n"

FEB 14   "Plan Important Activity at CSO Chapter"
          "Meet Your Business, Professional Men—Manuel Alamillo, Auto
          repair and body and fender"

FEB 21   "Agustin Serrato Named to Head Belvedere Red Cross Fund Drive"

FEB 28   "CSO Slates Special Session; Invite Local Groups, Bus. Men to
          attend"
          "Church Federation Official Guest at Installation Service"

MAR 6   "CSO Holds Special Session Tonight; Ask Local Groups, Business
          Men to attend"
          "Tony Ponce Files for Assemblyman's Post in 40th District"

MAR 13   "CSO Hosts Local Business; Group Leaders at Session"
          "Mexican Chamber of Commerce Installs New Officers"

MAR 20   "Bronze Star Medal Cpl. Ed. Ortiz Given Posthumous Award for
          Heroism in Action"
          "Schools, Religious Training Talk at CSO Session"

APR 3   "Trade Union Leader Files for 51st Dist. Assembly Post"

APR 10   "Seeks Reelection to State Assembly in 51st District"
          "Congress Candidates to attend CSO Session Here April 17"

APR 17   "Know Your Community"
          "Congressional Candidates at CSO Meeting"
          "Meet Your Business, Professional Men—John Espinosa"
          "Arthur O. Casas Enters 19th District Congressional Race"

MAY 1   "Know Your Community"

MAY 8   "Eloy Duran Seeks 40th Dist. Assembly Post"

MAY 15   "Office No. 1 Judicial Candidates at CSO Meeting Tonight"
          "Know Your Community; Playgrounds, Community Centers and
          Public Recreation Facilities"
          "Rep. Chet Holifield appoints Daniel Gonzales to Annapolis; Will
          Enter in June"

JUN 5   " 'Health Hints' Talk CSO Meeting"
          "Know Your Community; Transportation Facilities"

JUN 19   "Sgt. Albert C. Robles Presents Gen. Ridgeway with Portrait"

JUN 26   "Discuss Walks with Road Dept. Officials at CSO Meeting"
          "Know Your Community; Tell of Industry, Manufacturing Growth;
          Purchasing Power of District"

JUL 3   "County Road Officials Attend CSO Meeting; Tonight; Discuss
          Sidewalks"

JUL 10   "Espiritu Latino VFW Post Plans Benefit Picnic-Barbecue"
          "Know Your Community; The Belvedere Shopping District"

JUL 17   "Experiences at Camp Aired Tonight at CSO Meeting"
          "Authorization Given Plan for East L.A. Expansion"

JUL 31   "Business Men's Group Holds Session Today; Honor Mike
             Gallardo, Retiring as Bailiff"
AUG 7   "Mexican Consul to Address Rotary Club at Casa del Mexicano
             Wed."
          "Belvedere CSO Holds Important Session"
AUG 14   "Anthony A. Rios Rally Set for Sun.; Will Raise Legal Aid Fund"
AUG 21   "Committee Plans for Annual 16th of September Parade, Zeferino
             Ramirez to Head Local Group Working on Event"
SEP 4   "Discuss Value of One Vote at CSO Session"
SEP 11   "CSO Federation Sponsors Public Session Friday"
          "Sal Gonzales to Head Belvedere CSO"
SEP 18   "Report County Eyes Purchase of Land on Eastside of Fetterly St."
SEP 25   "Stress 'Yes' Vote on Prop. 3 at CSO Meeting"
OCT 2   "CSO Slates Special Program for Tonight's Session"
OCT 30   "Discuss Presidential Election at CSO Meeting Tonight"
NOV 27   "Edward Mehren Speaks on 'Human Relations' at CSO"
DEC 4   "Atty. Joe Scott Speaks at Boy's Club"
          "New Rules in Effect Dec. 23 for Crossing Mexican Border"
DEC 11   "Annual Our Lady of Guadalupe Procession"
DEC 18   "Discuss Controversial Immigration Act at CSO Meeting"

1953

JAN 1   "Grand Jury Asks Women's Prison Be Established in ELA"
          "Seek to Acquire More Property for Civic Center"
JAN 8   "New E.L.A. Municipal Court Set-up to Begin Operation"
          "Councilman Ed Roybal Speaks at Labor School Opening"
JAN 15   "Belvedere CSO Asks Changes in Old Age Assistance Laws"
FEB 12   "Sheriff's Attend Anti-Narcotics School at Biscailuz Center"
          "Business Men Hold Special Confab; Discuss Added Sheriff's
             Protection"
FEB 19   "Start ELA Civic Center in April Acquire Land"
          "ELA Narcotics Workshop in Session Today, Leads Fight Against
             Use of Narcotics"
FEB 26   "Discuss Narcotics Problem, Its Causes at Special East L.A. Anti-
             Narcotic Workshop"
          "Spanish-Speaking People's Eduction Conference at ELAJC"
          "Board of Education Candidates Speak at CSO Session Mar. 4"
MAR 5   "Spanish-Speaking People's Education Conference at ELA Jr.
             College Set for Friday and Saturday"
          "Seek Sidewalks for Residential Streets Here"
MAR 12   "Hold Anti-Narcotics Workshop at CYO Center Today"
          "CSO to Launch Sidewalk, Curb Campaign Tonight"
          "Candidates for Mayor to Speak at CSO Session"
MAR 19   "Discuss Narcotics Problems and Youth at CYO Center"
          "Felix Ontiveros Heads Food Testers Club"
MAR 26   "Second Sidewalks Meeting Set for Tonight"
          "Repeal McCarran Law Rally Set for April 12"
          "Citizenship Meet at Casa del Mexicano Wednesday"

APR 2   "With Your Men in the Service," by David Roque
APR 9   "Bowron, Poulson Face Runoff for Mayor, Final May 26"
APR 16   "New E.L.A. American Legion Post Named for Eugene A. Obregon, Korean Hero"
           "Discuss McCarran Act Special Meeting"
APR 23   "Shift Site of Jail from ELA to Long Beach"
           "Munnell Tells How 'Fringe Area Bill' Affecting Unincorporated Areas Passed by Assembly"
           "Legion Latin Post to Install Officers"
MAY 7   "CSO Sidewalks Meeting Set for Tonight"
           "Richard Tafoya Attending Insurance School in Phila"
MAY 14   "Spanish Speaking Churches Convention Set"
MAY 28   "Poulson Victor Over Bowron . . ."
           "ELA Health Council Slates Forum Friday at Lorena School"
JUN 11   "Corpus Christi Fete Attracts Thousands"
           "Nate Cisneros Receives BA Degree at Pomona"
JUN 18   "Groundbreaking Ceremonies for New East LA Civic Center Set for Monday"
JUN 25   "Mary Lou Valerio to Attend Lutheran Youth Convention"
           "Sheriffs Foreign Relations Bureau Offers Assistance"
JUL 2   "Begin CSO Program of Citizen Classes in Spanish"
JUL 23   "Atty. Wm. Figueroa Joins Firm of Atty. Frank Solis"
JUL 30   "Cpl. Al Gallegos Killed in Action Army Reports"
           "Baptist Churches Hold Annual Convention Here"
AUG 6   "Families Plan Joyous Reunion with Returning Prisoners of War," by Alex Salazar
           "Beneficencia Mexicana Holds Installation Friday"
AUG 13   "CSO Sponsors Garden Party"
AUG 20   "Reds Release Local Soldier from POW Camp"
AUG 27   "Sgt. Omar Serna Released POW, Tells Experience," by Alex Salazar
SEP 3   "Meet Your Business, Professional Men—Joseph Ruiz"
SEP 10   "Belvedere, ELA in 3rd District, John Anson Ford New Supervisor," by Alberto Diaz
SEP 17   "Begin Construction of Eastside Boy's Club"
           "Armando Zamora Freed Korea POW, Returned Home"
OCT 1   "Assemblyman Elliot to Address CSO"
OCT 15   "Deny ELA Zoning Appeal for Sewing Factor"
OCT 22   "Pedro Infante in Benefit Show for Boys Club; Rotary Sponsors Event"
           "Sup. Ford Names New East LA Field Deputy"
OCT 29   "Hollenbeck, Boyle Heights Citizens Meet, Protest Proposed Freeway Link Thru Area"
NOV 5   "CSO Plans Benefit Dance for Citizenship Classes"
NOV 26   "Julio Gonzales Appointed to LAPD Press Relations Post"
DEC 3   "Rabies Epidemic in ELA, Report Six New Cases"
DEC 10   "Hold Annual Our Lady of Guadalupe Procession Sunday; Benediction to Be Held at ELA Jr. College Stadium"

"200 Students Graduate from CSO Citizenship Classes Tonight"
"Ernest E. Debs Candidate for Supervisor"

DEC 17   "10,000 Faithful March in 23rd Annual Guadalupe Procession"
"Unfavorable Publicity by Daily Press Puts Community on Spot,"
      by Councilman Edward Roybal
"Local Youth Car Club Groups Given Sheriff, Police Approval"
"Increase ELA Sheriff Crime Prevention Units"

DEC 24   "Local Groups Battle Delinquency," by David Roque

DEC 31   "Discuss Causes of Juvenile Delinquency," by David Roque

1954

JAN 7   "Mrs. Clemencia Ortiz Oldest Citizen Here 113 Years Young"
"Discuss Youth Car Clubs' Varied Activities," by David Roque
"Coordinating Council to Discuss Car Clubs"

JAN 14   "Sheriff Announces Three-Point Program to Curb Juvenile
      Delinquency"
"[East Los Angeles] Drifters Show Proper Guidance, Nets Results,
      Better Citizens"

JAN 21   "Mourn Death of Fr. Leonard T. Barney"
"Playgrounds, Parks Supply More Than Recreational Facilities," by
      David Roque

JAN 28   "Plan Proposed for Cal Club Sponsors Group"
"Supervisor Ford to Address Mass Meet of Car Clubs"
"Discuss Park, Playground Activities," by David Roque

FEB 4   "Electrical Union Pledges Aid to Eastside Boys Club"
"CYO's Four Point Program Help Combat Juvenile Delinquency,"
      by David Roque

FEB 11   "Order Closing of Belvedere Housing Project by May 1st"
"Richard Gravens for Governor; Ed Roybal for Lt. Governor;
      Samuel W. Yorty for U.S. Senator at Fresno Convention"
"Cleland House Plans Family Approach in Program to Curb
      Delinquency," by David Roque
"ELA Road Knights Hold 'Tardeada' "

FEB 18   "Belvedere Library Designed as County Job Information Post"

FEB 25   "Housing Director Asks Belvedere Vets Project Be Closed by July
      1st," by Alberto Diaz
"Parents Urged to Take Role in Development of Youth Centers,"
      by David Roque

MAR 4   "Philharmonic Orchestra Concert Sunday at ELAJC Auditorium"
"Four Point Program Cy [sic] Santa Maria CYO Center Offers
      Youth Well Balanced Outlet," by David Roque
"Invite Groups to Attend Childhood Youth Conference"

MAR 11   "New Sheriff Substitution for ELA Civic Center"
"Woodcraft Rangers Have Many Varied Activities," by David
      Roque

MAR 18   "Expansion Program Announced for Belvedere Hospital"
"Car Clubs Take Part in Annual Friendship Fete"

AUG 5   "Curtain Comes Down on Youngster's Courageous Fight Against Leukemia"

AUG 12   "Install Rev. S. M. Colunga as Pastor of Belvedere Church of God Sunday"

"1st CSO Class Sworn In Today"

AUG 19   "ELA Drifters Launch Safety Drive Here"

AUG 26   "Supervisors Approve Assessment Petition for Walks . . ."

"Young Democrats Hold Registration Party"

SEP 9   "Airman Joe Salas, Former POW on Way Home"

SEP 23   "A2/c 'Joe' Salas Phones Dad Here of Arrival Sunday"

OCT 14   "CSO Slates 'Meet Your Candidate' Meeting Wed."

"Joe 'Ciro' Salas, Released Prisoner of Reds Home; Relates Experience," by Alex Salazar

OCT 28   "Youth Rally at Soledad Church Sunday Afternoon"

NOV 4   "Knight Elected Governor; Powers Bests Roybal"

NOV 11   "ELA Car Clubs Form Federation Will Aid Needy at Christmas"

"Ed Roybal Thanks Supporters, Suggests Shorter Political Campaign"

DEC 9   "CSO Begins New Spanish Speaking Citizenship Classes"

"Beneficencia Mexicana Plans Teen Hop Sat."

DEC 16   "10,000 Faithful March in 24th Annual Guadalupe Procession"

DEC 21   "Select City Terrace Site for L.A. State College"

"New Probation Office Opens in East L.A."

"ELA Youth Council Meeting Set for Monday, Dec. 27th"

DEC 28   "E.L.A. Car Federation Ends Christmas Give-Away Project"

1955

JAN 6   "Tell Improvements on Belvedere Streets"

JAN 13   "ELA Youth Council Aids Teen-Agers in Securing Jobs"

"Armando Castro Memorial Scholarship Established at ELAJC"

"Dr. Reynaldo Carreon to Head Mexican Chamber of Commerce"

"Honor CYO Workers 25th Anniversary"

JAN 27   "East LA Youth Council Slates Teen-Age Employment Service Panel Discussion"

"Set $1,500 Goal for Castro Scholarship Fund"

FEB 3   "A.L. & Kate S. Barney Retire as Citizen Publishers; Announce Sale of Newspaper"

FEB 10   "Property Owners in Sidewalk Project Session Wednesday"

FEB 17   "Optimist Club to Hear Juvenile Delinquency Talk Tuesday Noon"

FEB 24   "Discuss Fair Employment Practices at CSO Meeting"

"CSO Slates Benefit Dinner Dance Sun"

"Form New East L.A. Car Club—Road Angels"

MAR 3   "Special Car Clubs Meeting Tuesday"

MAR 10   "First St. Parking Meters Sought by Business & Professional Group"

	" 'Espiritu-Latino' VFW Post to Change Name, Stages Vital Session Tomorrow"
MAR 17	"CSO Elects Officers Approves Constitution at National Convention"
	"Supervisors Approve Delinquency Plan"
MAR 24	"Map Plans for 8th Annual Festival of Friendship, May 22"
	"Plan Opening of State College Here in February"
MAR 31	"Mexican-American Student Problems Probed at Confab"
APR 7	"ELA Youth Council Slates Meeting Monday Night"
	"Conduct Citizenship Class for Spanish Speaking People"
APR 21	"ELA Youth Council to Take Part in Youth Conference"
	"Castro Scholarship Fund Nears $5,000 Mark"
APR 28	"Break Ground for New State College Thurs., May 5"
MAY 5	"Dr. Offenberg Appointed to County Housing Commission"
	"Civic Observance, Fiestas Here Mark Cinco de Mayo Celebration"
MAY 12	"Fete Mexican-American Mother of the Year at High Mass Tuesday"
MAY 19	"Improve Belvedere Topic of [East Los Angeles] Civic Association"
MAY 26	"25,000 See Friendship Festival; Crown Gloria Gomez Queen"
JUN 2	"New ELA Sheriff's Office Slated to Open Monday"
JUN 9	"Car Club Group Hold 'Club House' Dance"
JUN 16	"Hundreds Participate in 29th Corpus Christi Procession Sunday"
JUN 30	"CSO to Graduate 300 Persons as New U.S. Citizens"
	"Al Ortega to Head American Legion Post 323"
JUL 14	"ELA Car Club Federation Honors Ray Urata"
	"CSO Appoints New Executive Secretary"
JUL 21	"Julio Gonzales Honored by Group Wins Check Award"
JUL 28	"CSO Sets Spanish-English Panel Discussions on Subject 'How to Grow Old Gracefully' "
	Letter from Fred A. Moore, a Black, who bought house in City Terrace and encountered neighborhood hostility
AUG 4	"Jr. Mexican C of C Holds Initial Session"
AUG 18	"Reveal Effort to Quietly Establish M-4 Zone Here; Citizens Voice Strong Opposition to Proposed Move"
	"Aquinas Club Holds 4th Annual Princesses' Ball Saturday Evening"
AUG 25	"Session to Oppose M-4 Zone Mon. Urge Residents to Sign Petitions"
SEP 1	"Roybal to Discuss Delinquency at Optimist Session"
	"Invite Publico to Annual CIO Labor Day Picnic"
	"Beneficencia [Mexicana] Group Sets Dinner Party"
SEP 8	"Mrs. Pauline Holguin Appointed CSO Executive Secretary"
SEP 15	"Boys' Town Choir of Monterey, Mex., Tours Southland"
	"Mexican-American Art Exhibit at Casa del Mexicano"
	"CSO Advocates New Citizens' Day as Yearly Event"
SEP 22	"Form New Council of Mexican Affairs; Dr. E. Lamar Prexy"

SEP 29   "Eastside Boys' Club to Open October 14"
         "Seize Pair Who Smuggled Baby Into U.S. from Mexico"
         "Latin Dances Taught at Arts Workshop Tuesday"
OCT 13   "Officers Arrest Alleged Witch Doctor in Raid"
         "Inter-Racial Dinner Held at YMCA"
OCT 20   'Hundreds Attend Opening of Eastside Boys' Club, Youngsters
            Begin to Use Facilities"
         "Okay Improvements in Belvedere Area"
         "Spanish-Speaking Ministerial Assn. Makes Plans for Community
            Chest Drive"
         "Newly Formed LEA Coordinating Council Meets"
         "CSO Conducts First Aid Classes Here"
NOV 3   "CSO Collects Donations for Tampico Flood"
         "Public Schools in New Mexico"
NOV 10   "Cantinflas, Many Other Latin Stars Set to Entertain At Huge
            Benefit Show Sun"
         "Supervisors Act on New Juvenile Hall, and Juvenile Facility"
NOV 17   "OK Improvements for Belvedere Park, Award $97,259 Contract"
         "County Opens Senior Citizen Service Club"
         "Students Form New Scholarship Group, 'Casa Collegians' "
         "Educator Speaks at Nazarene Church"
NOV 24   "City Terrace Residents to Protect Dump at Meeting"
DEC 1   "City Terrace Council Slates Immigration Talk Tonight"
DEC 8   "When Is an American, Supreme Court Argue Decision"
DEC 15   "Court Rules Proof Needed to Take Citizenship of Native Born"
DEC 22   "Social, Car Clubs' Federation Aid Needy"
DEC 29   "Beneficencia Mexicana Thanks 'Xmas Donors"
         "Michigan Governor Speaks on 'Civil Liberties' Jan. 3"

1956

JAN 5   "More Than 196,000 L.A. Aliens Begin Annual Registration" as
         required by the McCarran Act
JAN 12   "Reelect Dr. R. V. Carreon President of Mexican Chamber of
         Commerce"
         "Break Ground for New Homes Back of ELAJC"
         "Council Honors Latin Leaders"
JAN 19   "Community Service Organization Opens Annual Membership
         Drive"
         "Belvedere Democratic Club Selects Convention Delegates,
         Alternates"
         "ELA Youth Council to Elect New Officers"
         "Non-Citizen Residents Can Apply for Rental in Housing Projects"
         "Ministerial Ass'n Installs New Officers Rev. Antonio Gamboa to
         Head Group"
         "Council Honors Leaders at Testimonial"

JAN 26   "CSO Slates Meeting Select New Officers"
           "Sam Yorty to Address ELA Democratic Club"
FEB 9   "Dedicate New L.A. State College Campus"
FEB 16   "Mexican Chamber of Commerce Installs New Officers, Directors"
           "Council Sponsors Conference on Education of Mexican-American"
FEB 23   "ELA Youth Council Seats New Officers"
           "CSO Sponsor Hearing Tests for Children"
MAR 1   "New Homes for Mexican-Americans in San Fernando"
           "Magazine Article Tells of Important Significant Role of Mexican
              People in U.S. and California History"
MAR 8   "Council Tells of Housing Discrimination"
           "City Terrace Women's Committee Reports on Dump Situation"
MAR 15   "CSO in Vote Registration Campaign"
           "ELA Youths Attend Student Conference"
MAR 29   "Set Hearing for East LA Zone Change"
APR 5   "10th District PTA Holds Convention Here, 'Youth' Theme of
              Confab"
           "Council Maps Fight Against Dope Problem"
APR 12   "Authorize Oil Drilling at East L.A. Park"
           "Fernando de la Pena Awarded Castro Scholarship"
APR 19   "Keynote Speaker at Youth Conference Here Saturday"
           "Open Long Beach Freeway Link Friday"
           "CSO Annual Dinner to Honor Civic Leaders"
APR 26   "Mexican-Americans Seek Higher School Standards"
MAY 3   "Group Seeks to Halt Housing Discrimination"
           "Ida Lupino to Address CSO Awards Banquet"
MAY 10   "Castro Scholarship Dance May 26"
           " 'ELA Looks Ahead' Conference Set for Saturday, May 19th"
           "Tony Ponce to Head Committee to Elect Elliot"
MAY 17   "Many Groups Here Take Part in 'East LA Looks Ahead' confab"
           "Carlos Teran Heads Mexican-American Affairs Council"
MAY 24   "Political Hopefuls Attend Candidates Nite"
MAY 31   "30th Annual Corpus Christi Procession Sunday"
           "Institute on Mexican-American Problems"
JUN 7   "Albert S. Castaneda Appointed to Better Roads Committee"
JUN 14   "Manuel Martinez: Certified as Attorney Opens Law Offices Here"
           "Give Report on Recent ELA Looks Ahead"
JUN 21   "Council Set Up Employment Service for Youth"
           "CMAA Inducts New Officers: Judge Pfaff to Speak"
JUN 28   "Supervisors Delay FEPC Ordinance Vote"
           "Outline Future of CMAA at Installation"
JUL 5   "Dance Funds to Provide CSO Youth Employment Center"
JUL 12   "Supervisors Approve Oil Survey at Belvedere Park"
JUL 19   "CMAA Opens Funds Campaign"
JUL 26   "East LA Families Obtaining Improved Homes, Realtor Says"
AUG 2   "Youth Employment Service on TV Sun"
AUG 9   "Mexican Youth Band Names Board Members"
           "17th Annual Black and White Ball Sunday, Sept. 2"

"Federation of Spanish-American Voters Group Hears
            Assemblyman Elliot"
AUG 16   "Business Group Today at 12 Noon Plan Formation of Chamber of
            Commerce: Discuss Zoning, Yule Decorations, Hold
            Election"
         " 'Citizen' Correspondent Gives 'On Spot' Report on Democratic
            Convention in Chicago," by Frank Guzman
         "CSO to Assist in Housing Survey"
AUG 23   "Council Seeks Jobs for Youth; Poses Query, Are You Working
            Too Hard?"
AUG 30   "Annual Black & White Ball Set for Sunday Eve at L.A. Breakfast
            Club"
SEP 6   "Mexican Consul to Address Rotary Club"
SEP 20   "September 16 Parade Viewed by 60,000"
OCT 4   "Belvedere Chamber of Commerce New Official; New Group
            Elects Officers, Meets October 15"
OCT 11   "Map Plans for New Welfare Planning Council in East L.A."
OCT 18   "Youth Council to Discuss Yule Job at Meeting"
OCT 25   "Honor Civil Liberties Union Founder Tues."
NOV 8   "Fiesta Raises Funds for Immigration Museum"
NOV 29   "CSO Slates Forum on Health, Officials to Address Public"
DEC 13   "Sup. Ford Joins CMAA Campaign"
         "Panel of Attorneys to Speak at E.L.A. Youth Council Session"
DEC 20   "Protest Ban on Alien Rentals Before Board of Supervisors"
         "Nat'l Officers of G.I. Forum to Visit L.A."
DEC 27   Photograph of Grave Riggers Car Club delivering food baskets

1957

JAN 10   "Councilman Roybal Seeks Re-election"
         "G.I. Forum Banquet Hosts National Chief at Banquet"
         "Name Ralph Guzman Civil Liberties Board"
         "Huge Freeway Building Program"
JAN 17   "Open Public Housing Units to Non-Citizens"
         "County Moves to Acquire Dump Site in Mont. Park"
         "Eastside Boys Club Installs New Officers, Honor Armando
            Torrez"
         "Alianza-Hispano American"
JAN 24   "Freeway Topic of Chamber Meeting Next Monday Noon"
         "East L.A. Committee for Better Civic Government"
         "D.A. Probes 'Brutality Charge' by Two Sheriff's Deputies"
JAN 31   "Man Jailed for Stealing Coffee, Grocer Helps Thief's Family"
         "Sheriff to Enforce Curfew Law, Hold Parents Responsible"
         "Belvedere Chamber of Commerce Investigates Freeway Routes
            Here"
         "Pledge 'Aid to Youth' at [East Central Area Welfare Planning]
            Council Installation"

	"Area-Wide Committee to Discuss Plans for Unsponsored Teen Clubs"
JUL 25	"To Make Area Study Planning Council Acts to Save Public Agencies in E.L.A. Area"
AUG 1	"Area wide Parks Development Group [East Central Area Welfare Planning Council] Formed in East L.A."
	"GI Forum Honors Founder at Dinner Dance"
AUG 8	"Arthur J. Rendon Carries Message of Sympathy to Mexico"
	"Honor Nation G.I. Forum Founder at Special Banquet"
	"Los Caballeros Club Installs New Officers"
	"CSO to Launch Civic Community Improvement Program in East L.A."
AUG 15	"CSO Sponsors House Meetings, Discuss Community Problems"
AUG 22	"Committee Meets to Avert Closing of Day Care Centers in E.L.A."
	"Housing Authority Has Many Rental Units for Elderly Citizens"
	"G.I. Forum Elects State Officers, Frank Paz, Prexy"
	"G.I. Forum National Confab in New Mex."
AUG 29	"City Terrace Residents in Appeal to Close Dump, Meet Tonight"
SEP 5	"City Terrace Residents to Appeal Dump Variance Decision"
SEP 12	"Roybal in Trip to Europe, Mid-East Will Visit Israel"
	"L.A. Texas Old Timers in Horsehide Tilt Sunday"
SEP 19	"Hearing on Freeway Route Through Belvedere: Public Meeting Set for Friday, October 18 at ELAJC Auditorium"
	"Child Day Care Centers Continue Service in ELA"
	"Zambrano Speaks on ELA Civic Improvement"
	"CSO Launches Drive for 1000 New Members"
	"Seek ELA Park Site for Juvenile Facility"
SEP 26	"[East Central Area Welfare Planning Council] Plan Area-Wide Survey on Health Services"
	"Display Freeway Route Map Set Hearing for Oct. 18"
OCT 3	"Group [East Central Area Welfare Planning Council] Meets to Stop Closing of Library"
	"E.L.A. Beautiful Committee Formed by Planning Council"
	"Community Action for Mental Health Services Topic for Meet Set for Oct. 10"
	"Films of Armando Castro Story"
	"CSO Protests The New Driver's License Test"
OCT 10	"Map Showing Freeway Route On Display Here Next Week"
	"CSO Slates Talk On Discrimination in Housing Here Wed."
OCT 17	"Hearing on Proposed Freeway Route Friday at ELAJC Auditorium"
	"CSO Holds Free Membership Barbecue Sunday"
	"Three Citizenship Classes in Session in Belvedere"
OCT 24	"Discuss ELA Area Beautification Plan at Council Session"
	"Order BKK Dump in City Terrace Hills Closed"
OCT 31	"Discuss Police Community Relations at CSO Session"
	"OK Park Area for Girl's Home"

NOV 7   "Health Services Study Discussed by Planning Council Health
         Group"
         "Mexican Artist in One-Man Show"
         "Mental Health Survey Starts Soon in County"
NOV 14   "New L.A. State College Rises on 97 Acre Campus Site in City
         Terrace"
         "Roybal Speaks on European, Middle-East Trip at Rotary"
NOV 21   "Unsponsored Youth Groups Report Due Monday Night"
         "Lancerettes Set Dance for Nov. 23"
NOV 28   "Local Groups Honor Alex Zambrano at Testimonial Dinner
         Monday Night"
         "Roybal Key Speaker at Health Center Dedication Dec. 5th"
DEC 5   " 'It's a Dream,' Says Alex Zambrano at Testimonial Dinner
         Monday"
DEC 12   "ELA Mental Health Committee to Discuss Plans for Survey"
         "Pat Brown Speaks at ELA Democratic Rally Next Month"
         "Henry P. Lopez Candidate for Secretary of State"
DEC 19   "Roybal to Run for Supervisor in John Anson Ford's District"
         "Mental Health Survey Begins in East L.A."
DEC 26   "ELA Group Plan Vote Registration Campaign"

1958

JAN 2   "Attorney Carlos Teran Appointed New East Los Angeles Court
         Judge," by Alberto C. Diaz
JAN 9   "Teran Installed as Municipal Court Judge Here"
         "Judge Teran Ill in Hospital Postpone Banquet"
         Letter from Raul Morin discussing the state of Mexicans in
         California and the GI Forum position
         " 'Pat' Brown in Keynote Speech at Demp Banquet Here"
         "Reelect Planning Commission Chairman" [Arthur J. Baum]
         "County Delays Vote on FEPC Ordinance"
JAN 16   "CSO Opens Vote Registration in East Los Angeles"
         "Honor 'Pat' Brown at Kick off Banquet Here Saturday Night"
         "Judge Teran nominated for President of Welfare Planning
         Council"
         "Narcotics: A Primer on Drug Addiction," by John Ackers, Part I
         "E.L.A. Father Turns in Dope Addict Son"
JAN 23   "Honor Judge Teran at County-wide Banquet Wed. Evening"
         "[ELA Youth Council] Teen-agers Hold Panel Discussion on 'What
         Is a Gang' "
         "Narcotics: A Primer on Drug Addiction," by John Ackers, Part II
JAN 30   "Judge Teran Installed President of Council; Sup. Ford Speaker"
         "Narcotics: A Primer on Drug Addiction," by John Ackers, Part III
FEB 6   "Belvedere Chamber of Commerce Elects Officers, Board
         Members"
         "Narcotics: A Primer on Drug Addiction," by John Ackers, Part IV

"Judge Teran to Install Wabash-City Terrace Council Officers Tonight"

FEB 13 "Narcotics: A Primer on Drug Addiction," by John Ackers, Part V

FEB 20 "Praise Eastside Boys Club for Youth Work at Annual Installation Banquet"

"Narcotics: A Primer on Drug Addiction," by John Ackers, Part VI

"ELA Mexican Band in Concert"

FEB 27 "Raul Morin to G.I. Forum Group"

"Arrest Two in Kidnapping and Murder of ELA Youth"

"Narcotics: A Primer on Drug Addiction," by John Ackers, Part VII

"Campaign Kick Off Dinner for Atty. Henry Lopez Tonight"

MAR 6   "Castro Scholarship Dance Committee Elects Officers"

"Narcotics: A Primer on Drug Addiction," by John Ackers, Part VIII

"Rotarians Hear Talk On 'Youth Accomplishments' "

"Golden State Freeway: Issues Bids on Freeway Between 6th St., Mission Rd. in Boyle Heights"

MAR 13 "Knight Addresses Banquet of L.A. Mexican C of C"

"Discuss Changes on Immigration Law at CSO Meeting"

"Narcotics: A Primer on Drug Addiction," by John Ackers, Part IX

MAR 20 " 'Citizen' Sponsors Dance Contest for Youth Clubs"

"Supervisors Defeat FEPC Proposal"

"Narcotics: A Primer on Drug Addiction: Conclusion," by John Ackers

"Council Honors T. Quinn, Judge Teran at Banquet"

MAR 27 "Coordinating Council Hears Youth Reports"

APR 3   "Benefit Show for ELA Youth Band"

APR 17 "Discuss Future of Mexican-American in Education: Roybal at Roosevelt H.S."

APR 24 "Study Area in Belvedere as Jail Site: Move Would Relocate 460 Families Here if Approved"

"Supervisor and Mrs. Ford Hold Reception for Councilman Roybal"

MAY 1   "Set Final Action on Jail Site for June 10, Property Owners Protest Location of Jail Here or Any Park of East L.A., Ford Suggests Chavez Ravine as Site"

"G.I. Forum Recommends Park Site for Belvedere"

"First Spanish Section"

MAY 8   "Urge $20 Million Neighborhood Center in Boyle Heights Area"

" 'Parks-Not-Prisons' Committee Presents Plan to Supervisor Ford"

"G.I. Forum Slates First Annual Convention Here"

"Anthony Quinn Honorary Chairman of Lopez Committee"

"City Statistics Show Female Far from Being the 'Weaker Sex' "

MAY 15 "Ford Endorses Roybal for Supervisor"

MAY 22 "[East Central Area Welfare Planning Council] Discuss Urban Renewal, Jail Site Monday"

"Mexican American Population Shows 200% Increase in L.A."

MAY 29 "Noted Speakers at GI Forum's Initial Convention"

"Council to Study Urban Renewal Plans, Program"

"Belvedere Streets to Be Improved"

JUN 5   "U.S.-Mexican Colony Pays Warrior Tribute"
           "Judge Teran Picks Planning Council Board Members"
           "Banquet Climaxes GI Forum Confab"
           "Sheriff Investigates Series of Narcotics Seminars in This Area"
           "Democrats Score Election Wins: Roybal and Debs Face Run-off in
              Fall"

JUN 19   "Supervisors Hear Pleas for New Park"
           "Jail Site Danger Grows"
           "Take Homes From Families to Make Room for Prisoners"
           "Citizens Group to Assist in Choice of Jail Site"

JUN 26   "Belvedere-ELA Residents Renounce Jail Site Here"
           "Anthony P. Rios Elected to Fill Post of CSO President"

JUL 3   "County Jail Committee Holds First Session Today"
           "County to Aid Belvedere Street Improvements"

JUL 10   "Jail Advisory Committee Elects Chairman, Tours Jail"
           "Area Planning Council Opposes ELA Jail Site"
           "CSO Elects New Treasurer, Plan July Activities"
           "Board OK's Plans for Girls Detention Home in ELA Area"

JUL 17   "[CMAA] Ask Governor to Form State Juvenile Delinquency
              Commission"
           "Jail Advisory Sub-Committee Issue Report: Recommend
              Centralized County Jail: Tour Jail Sites Today, Including
              Proposed Belvedere Area Location"
           "Select LA as Site for G.I. Forum Convention"
           "Nuevo Servicio Consular En La Casa Del Mexicano"
           "Ayer, Hoy y Manana," by Daniel Estrada

JUL 24   "Annual Fiesta de Las Flores at Belvedere Park Lake Saturday"
           "Property Owners Meet County Jail Site Still Uncertain"

JUL 31   "Select Site for Jail—Not in East LA! Final Decision on
              Committee's Recommendation in Hands of Board of
              Supervisors"
           "Recommend Adoption of Pomona Freeway Thru East L.A."
           "Elect Arthur Rendon Vice-Prexy of City Health Commission"
           "Youth Dies from Stab Wounds Suffered in Fight"
           "[County General Hospital] Outlines Hospital Land Acquisition
              Plans"

AUG 7   "Seek to Raise Water Rates in Belvedere, Set Hearing Sept. 17"
AUG 14   "L.A. Alien Population Shows Gain"
AUG 21   "Honor Henry Lopez at Garden Party, Sat."
           "G.I. Forum State Auxiliary Meets"

SEP 4   "Commission OK's Freeway Route Through Belvedere"
SEP 18   "County Acquires Land for Laguna Park Expansion"
OCT 2   "Present Area-wide Mental Health Survey Report"
           "Teenagers Adult Discussion Groups Begin Sessions Monday"
           "East L.A. Leaders Against Prop. 18"

OCT 9   "Mental Health Survey Report at Welfare Planning Council Session
              Mon. Dr. Louise Seyler to Speak"

OCT 30   "Judge Carlos Teran, Henry Lopez Both Refute Smear Letter
              Statements"

"Citizen Endorses Ed Roybal, Makes Recommendation on County and State Propositions"

NOV 6   "Roybal Tops Debs by 393 Votes In Supervisorial Race"

NOV 13   "Debs Elected Supervisor, Roybal Supporters Demand New Election"

"Editorial" on the Debs/Roybal race

"County to Build Gutters in ELA Streets"

NOV 20   "Grand Jury Turns Down Roybal's Vote Intimindation Plea at Hearing"

"Senator Gonzalez to Address CSO Banquet Sat."

"Planning Council Reviews Committee Progress Reports"

"Editorial: Dead Issue or Live?"

"Citizen's Free Election Committee to Investigate Vote Irregularities"

"Suspect's Cousin Slain, Deputy Hurt in Brawl"

NOV 27   "Adopt 3.5 Miles of Pomona Freeway from Soto St. to Woods Ave."

DEC 4   "Debs, Pitches Take Office, Bonneli New Board Chairman"

"Debs Names Four Deputies"

"Judge Carlos Teran Speaks at G.I. Forum Scholarship Banquet"

DEC 11   "Citizen's Group Charges Intimidation in Election"

DEC 23   "Park Development Committee Sets Area-Wide Session"

"Set Meeting to Discuss Route of Pomona Freeway at ELAJC"

1959

JAN 1   "Welfare Planning Council Plans Annual Meeting"

"Eastside Boys Club Youngsters aid Needy Families"

JAN 8   "Community Council to Discuss Delinquency—Juvenile or Adults?"

"Welfare Planning Council Holds 3rd Annual Conclave"

JAN 15   "Supervisors Back FEPC Measure"

"Reelect A. J. Baum Head of the Planning Commission"

JAN 22   "OK Street Improvements in Belvedere"

"Judge Teran Names Aides for Woodcraft Ranger Campaign"

"C.Y.O. Serves 30,000 Youths in '58"

JAN 29   "Eastside Boys Club Installs New Officers"

"[East Central Area Welfare Planning Council] Study Health Need Services ELA Area"

"Appoint New ELA Area Mental Health Chairman"

FEB 5   "Grant Charter for New Savings and Loan Company in East L.A. Councilman Ed Roybal Heads Association, Local Business, Professional Men on Board"

"Committee [East Central Area Planning Council] Gives Rehabilitation Study Report"

FEB 12   "CSO Elects New Officers, Garcia New President"

"Discuss Community Trends at 3rd Planning Council Banquet Mon."

"Install Judge Teran Council Prexy for Second Term"
"Judge Teran Installed President of East Central Area Planning
    Council"

FEB 19   "Lopez Appointed Inheritance Tax Appraiser"

FEB 26   "Name New Welfare Planning Council Board Members"
"Students Receive Armando Castro Scholarship"

MAR 5   "Drug Firm Official Speaks at Rotary; Elects New Board Members"
"Break Ground for New $150,000 Utah Medical Clinic in East
    L.A."
"Form East L.A. Better Schools Committee"

MAR 12 "Judge Teran Named Presiding Judge of ELA Municipal Court"
"Break Ground for Plaza Community Clinic in East L.A."
"Eugene A. Obregon Name Approved for East L.A. Park"

MAR 19 "Launch Concentrated War on Juvenile Delinquency in County"
"Local Young Democrats at State Confab"
"Assembly OK's Housing Anti-Discrimination Bill"

MAR 26 "Extend 3rd Supervisorial Dist. Boundaries"

APR 2   "Belvedere Chamber of Commerce Sponsors Youth Guitar Groups"

APR 9   "Surprisingly Large Vote Cast in Municipal Election Tuesday"

APR 16   "Highway Officials Discuss Freeways in ELA"
"Appoint James Cruz Central Committee"

APR 30   "Belvedere Chamber Meeting to Feature 'Off-Street Parking' "
"Civic Improvement Group 'Thanks' City Terrace Residents"
"Baile a Beneficio del Mexican-American Youth Band El Sabado"
"Hear Report on Freeway Program in East L.A. Area"
"G.I. Forum Inducts New Officers in Joint Installation"
"Democrats Host Senator Kennedy"

MAY 7   " 'Citizen' Publisher Carl Bigsby Dies"
"Form County-wide Council of Latin American Groups"
"County Plans to Improve Nine East Los Angeles Parks"
"Councilman Roybal to Address Wabash City Terrace Council"
"Capacity Crowd at G.I. Forum"

MAY 14 "Planning Council to Hold Meeting at Juvenile Hall"

MAY 21 "Mexican-American Council Holds Annual Awards Banquet"

MAY 28 "Arthur Alarcon, Deputy D.A., Speaks at Rotary, Hold 'Youth
    Day' "
"School Slate Loses in Citywide Election; Tues, Baca Defeated"
"Mexican-American Affairs Council Presents Awards"

JUN 4   "Castro Scholarship Recipients Boast Annual Dance"
"Incorporation Talk at Chamber Tuesday"
"Seek Incorporation of Belvedere-ELA Area Group Files Petition,
    Sets Boundaries for Proposed City," by Alberto C. Diaz

JUN 11   "CSO to Hold . . . Party"
"Incorporation Talks at Chamber of Commerce Session"

JUN 18   "Supervisor Debs Opens Office in East Los Angeles"
"Fete George Russell on 30th Anniversary at Bank of America"

JUN 25   "Council Approves Dr. R. J. Carreon's Appointment to Police
    Commission"

"Discuss Incorporation Questions at Board Session Monday Eve."
"Incorporation . . . ! Circulate Petitions for Formation of City as
    Same Districts in Area Say, 'Leave Us Out'; Seek to Be
    Annexed"
"G.I. Forum Queen Dance Friday"

JUL 2   "Adopt New Pomona Freeway Route"
"Form Citizens Committee Here For Incorporation of East L.A.
    Area"

JUL 9   "Seek Property Owners' Signatures On E.L.A. Incorporation
    Petitions"
"Editorial: Incorporation or Annexation"

JUL 16   "Incorporation Topic for Chamber Meet"
"G.I. Forum Holds 2nd Annual State Convention Saturday"
"New Members Named to Incorporation Committee"

JUL 23   " 'Balanced Budget, No City Taxes!' Claim Incorporation Backers"

JUL 30   "Hold Hearing on Pomona Freeway"
"City Terrace Holds Meeting Tonight on Incorporation"

AUG 6   "Medal of Honor Heroes GI Forum Convention Guests"
"Report Shows Enough Income to Run Proposed City of ELA"
"Seek Improvements on City Section of Whittier Blvd."
"Mexican Chamber of Commerce Plans Anniversary Fete"

AUG 13   "County Gives Report on Services for Proposed City of East L.A."
"CMAA Installs New Officers Tonight"
"G.I. Forum Opens 11th Annual Convention, Honor War Heroes"

AUG 20   "G.I. Forum Honors War Dead, Elect Officers, Crown Queen at
    Convention"

AUG 27   "Roybal to Speak at CSO Meeting"

SEP 3   "Hold Public Hearing on Freeway Route"
"Roybal Names David Boubion Field Secretary"

SEP 10   "Discuss Incorporation at Council Meeting"
"Freeway Route Not Political Issue Says [Assemblyman William]
    Munnell"

SEP 17   "Colorful Parade Here Climaxes Mexico Independence
    Celebration"

SEP 24   "OK St. Improvements in City Terrace Area"

OCT 8   Photograph of Martin Ortiz, Executive Director of the East Central
    Area Welfare Planning Council
"Disputed Tests Begun in ELA for Ex-Addicts"
"East LA Probation Officer at Narcotic Control Training Program"

OCT 15   "Jose Rodriguez, Top Editor Speaks at 'Newspaper Week' Program"

OCT 22   "Mexican Architecture Exhibit Opens at E.L.A. College Friday"

NOV 5   "OK Contract for City Terrace Park Development"
"Adopt Route for Pomona Freeway"
"City of Commerce Incorporation in Hearing Today"

NOV 12   "Urban Renewal Committee Hears Redevelopment Talk"

NOV 19   "Nominate A. Torrez, A. Rendon for County Grand Jury"

DEC 3   "Judge Teran, Alberto C. Diaz, Citizen Editor to Recieve G.I.
    Forum Awards"
"Welfare Planning Council Names Board Members"

DEC 10   "Sheriff Reports 50% Decrease in Crime in Los Angeles County"
          "GI Forum Awards Banquet Honors Judge, Editor"
          "Form Spanish Speaking Blind Group"
DEC 24   "State FEPC Offices Open Here in L.A., Ford Announces"

1960

JAN 7   "Governor Appoints Judge Teran to Superior Court; Begins Duties"
          "Monterey Park Seeks to Annex Part of East L.A."
JAN 14   "Mexican Chamber of Commerce Elects Officers, Directors"
JAN 21   "*Dangerous Trend* Dr. Paul Sheldon, Occidental Professor, Speaks
              on Drop-outs"
          "Judge Teran Inducted, 300 Attend"
FEB 4   "Editorial of Pride and Prejudice," by John P. Ackers, on Chief
              William Parker
          "File Petition for Belvedere Incorporation"
          "Council Accepts Parker's Explanation on Mexican-Americans,
              Refuses Apology"
          "New Library at Belvedere"
          "Narcotics Council Holds Conference Feb. 11"
FEB 11   "Debs Appoints Felix Ontiveros to Human Relations Commission"
          "New Car Club, 'Road Gems' Elects Officers"
          "Cite ELA Belvedere Incorporation Boundaries"
          "Groups pass Motion to Censure Parker at Meeting"
FEB 18   "Incorporation Backers Foresee No Raise in Taxes for Proposed
              City of East L.A."
          "*Judge Teran Speaks* Brotherhood Week Program at Griffith Jr.
              High Tuesday Night"
          "Invite Public to Judge Teran Testimonial"
FEB 25   "Governor Brown Speaks at Judge Teran Testimonial Tonight"
          "Zeferino Ramirez Death Takes Old Timer Resident Community
              Leader"
          "Council Awards Plaque to Judge Carlos Teran"
          "E.L.A. Incorporation Meeting Set for Monday Night"
          "Muere Don Zeferino Ramirez"
MAR 3   "Cite Advantages; Benefits of Incorporation for E.L.A."
          "Civic, Community Leders Honor Judge Carlos Teran"
MAR 10   "Six File for Judge Teran's Vacated Municipal Court Post"
          "County OK's New E.L.A. City Boundaries"
          "Chamber Backs Incorporation"
MAR 17   "Launch Drive for Signatures to Incorporate ELA"
          "Howard Walshok Appointed Judge of ELA Court"
          "Five Major Goals Outlined by Citizens Incorporation Committee
              for City of ELA"
          "Propose 'No Parole' for Narcotics Second Offenders"
MAR 24   "Chamber General Meeting to Highlight Incorporation"
          "New City of ELA Hopes to Annex Three Adjacent Areas"
          "Ebell Club to Discuss Education of Latin American Citizens"

MAR 31   "Census Begins Nose Count"
          "Castro Scholarship Fund Receives Donations"
APR 14   "Judge Teran Speaks on White House Youth Conference"
          "Welfare Planning Council Forms Senior Citizens Committee"
          "California-Mexico Confab at UCLA"
APR 21   "Issue County Report on East L.A. Incorporation: Cite Income,
              Expense Figures with Initial Surplus of $500,000"
          "CSO Registers 35,589 Latins in Vote Drive"
APR 28   "Atty. A. Alarcon to Head State Narcotics Commission"
          "Mexican-American Political Assn. Elects Ed Roybal Chairman"
          "Atty. Alarcon Speaks at Council Meeting"
          "Panel Discussion Youth Parley"
MAY 5   "Castro Scholarship Committee Sets Date for Annual Dance"
MAY 19   "Three Community Leaders Report on Youth Conference"
          "Draft Plan to Unify Mexican-American Groups"
          "Gov. Brown Hopes Nalline Tests Will End Narcotics Problems"
MAY 26   "Mexican-American Group [MAPA] in Organizing Session"
JUN 2   "Judge Walshok Offers Plan to Curb and Control Narcotics"
          "Sanchez Speaks at Victory Dinner"
          "Walshok, Mizener, Sanchez Judgeship Race to Be Close"
          "Discuss Community Youth Needs at Welfare Planning Council"
JUN 9   "Nixon Leads Gov. Brown, McLain, Sanchez Leads Judge Walshok
              in ELA Municipal Judgeship Battle," by Alberto C. Diaz
          "CMAA House of Delegates Election Meet Tonight"
JUN 16   "Sanchez Tops Walshok by 453 Votes"
          "Elect CMAA House of Delegates Officers"
          "Mexico, California, in Good Neighbor Confab"
JUN 23   "Top Artists Guest at 'Rodriguez Day' Testimonial"
JUN 30   "Supervisors Ask Master Zoning Plan in L.A. County"
JUL 7   "Tell Plans for Model Police Review Board"
          "Mrs. Josephine Sanchez Named to State Democratic Central
              Committee"
JUL 14   "Slate Sanchez for Judge Dinner"
          "G.I. Forum to Honor State Queen July 30"
          "Atty. John Arguellos to Head 'Walshok for Judge' Campaign"
JUL 21   "Community Leaders Back ELA Incorporation"
          " 'Citizen' Backs Incorporation"
          "Sheriff to Enforce Juvenile Curfew"
          "Manuel Sanz to Head Pan-Am. Optimists"
          "Welfare Council Hosts Committee Heads"
JUL 28   "EDITORIAL: Incorporation"
          "File for East L.A. Incorporation Next Week, Committee in Final
              Drive to Secure Additional Support to Assure Incorporation
              Move"
          "State Official Says 'Skilled Minority Workers Have Little Trouble
              Finding Jobs' "
AUG 4   "CSO Lunches Vote Registration Campaign"
          "Mexican-American Affaris Council Set Dinner-Dance"

	"Incorporation Petition Filed with 7000 Names"
AUG 18	"Form Group to Advise Gov. Brown on Mexican-American Problems and to Serve as Liaison on Latin-American Affairs"
	"Sen. Richards Speaks at Mexican American Affairs Council Banquet"
	"East L.A. Incorporation Committee Thanks Citizens for Their Support"
AUG 25	"Judge Teran Accepts Trophy Won by ELA Chest Volunteers"
SEP 1	"Cityhood for East L.A. in Voters Hands; Measure to Go on Ballot, Public Hearing on Incorporation Tuesday Morning"
	Letter from Eugene S. Lowrey pointing out that, until recent years, Mexican Americans were ignored as voters
	"Galeana Head Sanchez' Veterans Committee"
SEP 8	"Supervisors Order Hearing on East L.A. Incorporation Measure for Oct. 20th"
	"Young Democrats to Elect Officers"
SEP 15	"CSO Begins Police Misconduct Survey"
	"Local Leaders on Delinquency Committee"
	"Open Latin-American Headquarters for Nixon in E.L.A."
SEP 22	"CSO Reports More Than 100,000 Register in Vote Drive"
SEP 29	"Council to Fete Governor at Banquet"
	"Arnold Martinez CYO Supervisor"
	"Sanchez-Kennedy Rally in City Terrace"
OCT 6	"Fete New Mexico's Sen Chavez at Luncheon Friday"
	"Supervisors OK Plans for New ELA Court Building"
	"Sanchez for Judge Banquet Set for Oct. 13"
OCT 13	"East L.A. Incorporation Hearing Next Thursday, Supervisors to Hear Opposition to Cityhood"
	"[East Central Area Welfare Planning] Council to Discuss Area Youth Needs"
	"Sanchez Banquet Committee"
OCT 20	"Council of Mexican-American Affairs Honors Gov. Brown at Banquet Tonight"
	"Expect Heated Boundary Dispute at Incorporation Hearing Today, Supervisors to Render Discussion on Cityhood"
OCT 27	"Delay Incorporation Hearing Til December 1st"
	"Public Discussion on Incorporation Set for Wednesday"
	"Otan W. Asa New 'Citizen' Owner"
	"Candidates Speak at G.I. Forum"
	"ELA-Montebello Bar Ass'n Endorse Howard Walshok"
NOV 3	" 'Citizen' Endorses Sanchez for Judge of ELA Municipal Court"
	"Capacity Crowd Packs Stadium for Sen. Kennedy"
	"Sanchez-Walshok Judgeship Race Sparks Local Election"
	"Latin-American Group Supports Nixon"
NOV 10	"Sanchez leads Walshok in race"
NOV 24	"Boundary Hearing on East L.A. incorporation set for Dec. 1st"
DEC 1	"Supervisors Rule on ELA Incorporation Expect heated boundary dispute at Cityhood hearing today"

"California G.I. Forum hold meeting in L.A."

DEC 8   "Decision on Incorporation due Jan. Pros and cons of incorporation
of area presented at hearings by County Board," by Ridgely
Cummings

DEC 15   "State acquires right of way land for Pomona Freeway"

"Gov. Knight to speak on incorporation"

"Monterey Park moves to annex area in East L.A."

"Thousands attend Guadalupe procession here"

"Local leaders head COPE group"

"Roybal Reports on Proposed Improvements in Boyle Heights"

DEC 29   "*Martha Acevedo* Belvedere Coed to Represent Mexico at Model
UN Meeting"

"Alex Zambrano named inheritance tax appraiser"

"Judge Sanchez takes office on January 3"

1961

JAN 5   "Judge Leopoldo Sanchez sworn in office, begins duties at ELA
Court"

JAN 12   "Set Boundaries for Obregon Park, end survey"

"*Moment of Truth* . . . ! Supervisors to decide on East L.A.
cityhood today," by Albert C. Diaz

"Mexican-American residents subject of comprehensive study
survey"

"Roybal draws three opponents for council seat"

"Manuel Q. Sans: Attorney to Mexican Chamber of Commerce"

"*ELA Incorporation* Sup. Frank Bonelli Speaks to Lourdes Holy
Name Society"

"ELA freeway interchange due in March"

JAN 19   "Hold citizens conference on narcotics, Feb. 11, invite public"

"Edward Roybal plans campaign kick-off Monday"

"Death takes Eddie Rodriguez popular radio announcer," by
Alberto Diaz

"Councilman Roybal awaits Kennedy decision on Latin American
Post"

"Supervisors set boundaries for proposed city of East Los Angeles.
Decide election date on Jan. 24, may be 72nd City"

"Arthur Alarcon speaks on narcotics at MAPA dinner"

JAN 26   "Voters to decide ELA Cityhood at Special Election on April 25"

"*Atty. R. Magana* Guest speaker at Judge Sanchez Testimonial
Sat."

FEB 2   "Name discussion leaders for ELA Citizens narcotics confab"

"G.I. Forum fetes Judge Leopoldo G. Sanchez at Testimonial"

"Atty. Joseph Galea speaks at annual CYO dinner"

FEB 9   "President may appoint Teran to envoy post"

"*East L.A. Incorporation Committee* Holds Meeting Tonight Filing
Deadline for Council Today"

"Discuss East LA Narcotics problems at conference Sat."

FEB 16   "Rudy Galeana reelected G.I. Forum Prexy"

"East LA incorporation drive in full swing as 11 file for Council seats," by Alberto Diaz

"John A. Arguelles to head East LA-Montebello Bar Assn."

"500 attend narcotics conference seek ways to solve dope problem"

"Educators discuss defacing property"

"Mrs. Olivia Flores on incorp"

FEB 23   "[National Conference of Christians and Jews] Panel discussion on Mexican-American youth"

"Rev. A. Hernandez installed as area [East Central Area Planning] Council president"

"*East LA Incorporation* Council filing, vote deadline Mar. 2; 14 seek Council seats"

"Writing on walls 'defacing property' topic at meeting"

"Las Palmas School for Girls opens in East L.A."

MAR 2   "*East LA Incorporation* City Council Filing, Vote Registration deadline today, 17 candidates to vie for 5 Council seats," by Alberto C. Diaz

"Meet Candidates For Council"

"Boyle Heights Improvement Assn. meets tonight, Roybal to speak"

"2 hundred attend Roybal campaign kick off session"

MAR 9   "Revise figures on ELA population, assessed valuation"

"Panel to discuss Mexican-American youth problems"

"East L.A. Cityhood in Voters hands, 15 qualify for City Council Elections. Two women, 13 men to be on election ballot"

"Know Your Council Candidates," on Roy J. Derelich and Albert S. Castaneda

MAR 16   "Planning council director speaks to ELA group"

"*Roybal reports* . . . $7 million worth of public works projects for 9th council district"

"Know Your Council Candidates," on Armida Tellez and Robert R. Carbajal

"CSO Delegates hear Governor Brown speak at Convention"

"Giant 'Meet Your Candidates' Rally Tonight"

MAR 23   "Discuss incorporation problems at Civic Ass'n meeting Tuesday"

"Know Your Council Candidates," on Ralph T. Acevedo and Lou Kerpec

"Judge proposes narcotics addict treatment plan"

MAR 30   "300 persons at 'Meet Your Candidates' rally"

"Know Your Council Candidates," on Tim Mestas and Frank F. Solis

"G.I. Forum in stand on political issues"

"Roybal for Councilman"

"Agricultural census lists 4,810 farms in county"

APR 6   "Know Your Council Candidates," on Josephine Woods and Carlos Antuna

"*Roybal wins*: Sam Yorty, Poulson in May runoff"

"Ceremonies Mark Opening 3-mile link of Long Beach Freeway"

"Unincorporated areas pay fair share of taxes"

"Cityhood backers charge union group with 'Bias', AFL-CIO terms charges 'False, Ridiculous', oppose incorporation," by Alberto C. Diaz

APR 13   "*East LA Incorporation* Debate pros and cons of East LA cityhood at public meeting here Friday night. Labor leaders to discuss issue with council candidates at Belvedere Jr. High Auditorium"

"GI Forum installation and awards banquet Friday, Ap. 22 at CYO Hall"

"Know Your Council Candidates," on Manuel Lopez

APR 20   "East LA Incorporation: Voters To Make Momentous Decision Next Tuesday; 15 candidates vie for five City Council seats; Vote registrar predicts 50% turnout as 12,800 eligible to cast ballots," by Alberto C. Diaz

"GI Forum holds awards fete, installation Fri."

"Know Your Council Candidates, Meet Candidate William L. Ramirez"

"[Belvedere Coordinating] Council hears talk on 'Cities and Incorporation Problems' "

"ELA Resident views proposed incorporation with 'great concern' "

"Judge Teran lauds Sal B. Lopez on council"

"Sure, you can Vote for Councilman Even If 'No' on Incorporation"

APR 27   "Defeat East L.A. Incorporation, Voters Fail to Approve Cityhood by 321 Votes"

"Annual Castro scholarship Dance Sunday"

"Incorporation Election . . . a success . . . !"

MAY 4   "Plan youth conference on narcotics"

MAY 11   "Launch Expanded Youth Recreation program"

"Sheriff reports increase in East LA crime"

"FBI narcotics advisor speaks at conference"

MAY 18   "Narcotics youth conference Saturday at Roosevelt High"

"Judge Sanchez to install new Council officers"

"OK improvements for streets in Belvedere area"

"Program aims at curbing juvenile delinquency"

MAY 25   "Memorial Day at Soldiers Monument"

"Dedicate giant ELA Freeway interchange"

"Youth meet on narcotics at Roosevelt acclaimed"

"Vote on State Reapportionment, Belvedere-ELA in 40th, 45th, 51st Assembly Districts; also 19th, 20th, 30th Congressional"

"MAPA holds session Saturday"

JUN 8   "Church 'denounces use of drugs, morally wrong,' says CYO priest"

"Community Progress aid Development aims of Newly Formed Citizens Council"

JUN 15   "MAPA opposes rezoning of area"
         "ELA area rejects Montebello annexation"
JUN 22   "Dedicate Laguna Park Community building"
         "Roybal to enter race for Congress"
JUN 29   "Name ELA Leader to City Police Commission"
         "MAPA acts on rezoning project"
JUL 6   "Discuss Obregon Park Plans at meeting on Tuesday Night"
         "Harold Henry: City Council elects Yorty man president"
JUL 13   "Group to discuss 'narcotic user' symptoms. . . ."
         "Heated Discussions mark meeting on Proposed Obregon Park
            Project, Supervisor Ernest E. Debs presides at session,
            promises 'Fair Deal' for property owners in area," by Alberto
            C. Diaz
JUL 20   "Groups voice opinion on proposed rezoning"
JUL 27   "GI Forum names slate committee chairman"
         "Governor signs pension bill to aid non-citizens"
         Letter protesting article on juvenile delinquency
AUG 3   "Community council tackles East L.A. area problems"
         "G.I. Forum holds convention in Las Vagas"
         "Report shows low rate of major crimes in ELA area"
AUG 10   "Judge Leo Sanchez given outstanding G.I. Forum award"
         "Mexican-American community honors atty. Arthur Alarcon"
AUG 17   "Supervisor Debs Crowns Belvedere Chamber of Commerce
            Queen"
         "Complete appraisal of land for park project"
         "Explain new law granting pensions to non-citizens"
         "CMAA opens fund drive for $50,000"
AUG 24   "Aged non-citizens attend CSO Rally"
AUG 31   "Appoint local man to Mayor Yorty's staff"
SEP 7   "Group forms Spanish-speaking citizens league"
SEP 14   "Gov. Brown to speak at joint Rotary Session"
         "Committee to discuss problems of out-of-school, unemployed
            youths"
SEP 21   "J.C. Cota attends inauguration of Mexico governor"
SEP 28   "Sheriff reports increase in crime conviction rate"
         "Launch planning study of East LA"
         "Mexican-American Voter subject at KNXT telecast"
         "Groups pledge support to aid unemployed youth"
         "Name [Ramona Morin] GI Forum auxiliary chairman"
         "Assemblyman tells GI Forum to unite during elections"
         "Strive to focus needs of Mexican-American groups"
OCT 5   "Name Roybal to represent LA in Madrid"
         "Fete GI Forum head Saturday"
OCT 12   "Fete Nat'l GI Forum commander at reception Sat."
         "ELA community council holds meeting Tuesday"
         "Committee on narcotics sets 3rd conference"
         "Land acquisition to speed-up Pomona Freeway project"
         "Ask Governor for greater recognition"
OCT 19   "Sen. Engle conducts Hearing on Aged at ELA"

OCT 26   "Freeway link due to open December 1"
NOV 2   "Appoint Assemblyman Munnell Superior Court Judge"
          "*ELA Community Council* Meets Tuesday, name representative to
          planning study commitee"
          "Frank X. Paz seeks 48th Dist. Assembly Post"
NOV 9   "Announce consultants, discussion leaders for narcotics
          conference"
NOV 16   "Experts speak at citizens' narcotics confab Saturday, invite
          residents"
          "Henry Gonzales Tex. State Senator to speak at CSO banquet
          Saturday"
          "Propose ELA zoning changes, from R-2 to R-3"
          "Yorty asks federal aid to fight juvenile crime"
NOV 21   "Proposed residential zone changes to be discussed at meeting
          tonight"
NOV 30   "CMAA to climax funds drive with dinner dance"
DEC 7   "Open link of Santa Monica Freeway"
          "Labor federation endorses CMAA funds drive"
DEC 14   "Map of Pomona Freeway on exhibition"
          "Board okays plans for City Terrace swim pool"
          "East Central Planning Committee holds session"
DEC 28   "Board studies supervisorial boundaries"
          "Plan testimonial Banquet for Judge Sanchez"

1962

JAN 4   "Jack P. Crowther: Ex. Roosevelt teacher new superintendent"
JAN 11   "East LA rezoning hearing set for today, seek to change area from
          R-2 to R-3 Zone"
          "Assemblyman Elliot addresses clay workers convention"
JAN 18   "Joseph B. Lopez will run for 51st Dist. Post"
          "Defer East LA zoning action. Will rule on R-2 or R-3 when area
          study completed"
          "East Central Planning Board considers population changes"
JAN 25   "Discuss unemployed youth at conference"
          "Plan major roadway improvements in ELA"
          "Roybal bids for 30th Dist. congress post"
          "M. Viega Jr. to head Boys Club Board"
FEB 1   "40th Dist. MAPA installs officers"
FEB 8   "East Central Planning Committee hears report on transportation
          voice concern over need for special approach to area trans-
          portation and land use"
          "George C. Russell, President East Central Area Welfare
          Announces 1962 Officers'
FEB 15   "CSO Fiesta to honor elderly citizens Sunday"
          "Judge L. Sanchez, elected Chairman of LA GI Forum"
          "Elect Ralph Poblano CMAA president, will succeed Louis Diaz"

FEB 22   "County population increases to 6,332,525"
MAR 1   "Supervisor Debs to seek re-eletion"
MAR 8   "Judge Sanchez files for Superior Court bench"
          "Death takes ELA pioneer, Juan N. Uzette"
MAR 15   "Two 30th District group endorse candidates to convention"
          "Defeated Judge [Howard A. Walshok] claims ELA election illegal,
              Files for full salary, cities ruling as support"
          "Mexican-American Affairs Council sponsors job opportunities
              conference March 31"
MAR 22   "Walshok files petition to regain pay, judgeship"
MAR 29   "Endorse CMAA job confab at Garfield High"
          "Joe Y. Jimenez [Republican] to seek 40th Dist. Assembly seat"
APR 5   "Purchase 50% of land parcels for Obregon Park"
          "*Ray Ceniceroz* ELA resident returns from Venezuela, relates
              experiences"
APR 12   "[East Central Area Welfare Planning] Council slates study of adult
              education needs"
          "Discuss social planning and community renewal"
          "County probes into job discrimination, asks for action"
APR 19   "East Central Planning Committee issues report on housing,
              economic survey"
MAY 3   "Rev. Martin Lugo ordained priest, recites mass here"
          "LA's Latin community to honor Gov. Brown at banquet tonight"
MAY 10   "Youth confab at Stevenson Jr. High, May 24"
          "Name Richard Rubio to head campaign for Atty. Frank F. Solis in
              29th District"
          "CSO honors Maria D. Lang as 'mother of year' "
MAY 17   "Eastside high in population, industry"
          "Name speaker for council youth confab"
MAY 31   "Community Youth confab lists needs of local area"
          "Cranston supports Ed Roybal for Congress"
          "Bueno, Elliot to debate at Roosevelt high group"
JUN 7   "County honors Dr. R. J. Carreon for service"
          "Road projects underway in Eastside area"
          "Rene Tanzel to play at Armando Castro dance"
          "Brown Vs. Nixon As Record Vote Cast, Edward Roybal, George
              Brown Jr. win congressional bids, close assembly races
JUN 14   "Youth agency approved as local council"
JUN 21   "Peace Corps seeks Spanish speaking volunteers in L.A."
JUN 28   "[Armando Castro] Benefit dance Friday provides scholarships"
          "Hearing today to annex ELA-Belvedere properties"
          "Bill Zazueta elected president of Roosevelt high group"
JUL 12   "CMAA to hold banquet, install new officers"
          "Welfare council to hear youth conference reports"
JUL 19   "[Monterey Park] Hearing set for pre-zoning changes in ELA"
          "Park, land swap for vets hospital here stirs debate"
JUL 26   "GI Forum protests park trade"
          "Supervisors modify Pomona freeway plan for local streets"

AUG 2   "Monterey Park approves zone change for 100 acres here"
AUG 9   "City of Commerce moves to annex part of East Los Angeles,
         study eight blocks on Telegraph Rd. industrial area, from
         Atlantic to Kern"
         "ELA Community Council warns of annexation treats here"
         "Billboard alley on ELA freeway"
AUG 16   "*Land important factor in potential of Eastside* Group studies
         residential trends here"
SEP 6   "G.I. Forum Honor first Mexican-American Woman lawyer at
         installation"
SEP 13   "*Family of fourteen* city council honors youth for overcoming
         family hardships"
SEP 20   "Sup. Debs names new field deputy"
SEP 27   "Youth studies group report on findings"
OCT 4   "Monterey Park set to annex 75 acres here"
         "Leadership training series set by East Area Council"
OCT 11   "2nd Leadership workshop set for today"
         "Debs receives council youth conference report"
OCT 18   "*Congressman* Henry Gonzalez to speak at Belvedere Park"
OCT 25   "Planning Committee to study industry development"
         "Discuss group methods at Leadership Workshop"
NOV 1   "Mexican state chambers honor three Latin personalities"
         "CMAA Director to be honored at testimonial fete"
         "Youth agency directors hold conference"
         "Senate candidate promises appointments to Latin Leaders"
         "George Brown backs Kennedy Cuba stand"
         "Rendon reappointed to President's youth committee"
NOV 8   "Democrats win local assembly, congress seats"
NOV 15   "City Council Elections leave two council seats empty"
         "Name LA woman [Eileen Hernandez] to top spot with FEPC"
NOV 29   "Roybal's city council vacancy stirs many would be candidates for
         post"
         "Supervisors in district boundary study"
         "Appoint four to library council here"
DEC 6   "Monterey Park takes final steps to annex area here"
         "Group to discuss new ELA incorporation attempt"
         "Roybal speaks, interviews city council candidates at mass meeting
         Monday," by Alberto C. Diaz
DEC 13   "Discuss 1st steps for East LA cityhood move"
         "Acquire final Obregon land parcels"
         "Planning Council reviews public facilities in area"
         "Elect new officers for council here"
DEC 20   "Councilman Roybal marks final year with City Council"
DEC 27   "Edward R. Roybal resigns City Council Post, Effective December
         31st"
DEC 27   "Mayor lists Human Relations Committee"

1963

JAN 3   "*Beachcomber Review* of community news events of year '62"
JAN 10   "Eleven candidates file for ninth district's City Council seat"
          "*Incorporation* Council elects new vice president"
JAN 17   "Planning committee studies public utilities zoning"
          "Delfino Varela: Humanist award give to Boyle Heights man"
          "Robert Baca to head East LA-Belvedere Democratic Club"
JAN 24   "$500,000 highway projects continue in Eastside area"
          "Know Your L.A. City Council Candidtes—Meet Richard Tafoya"
JAN 31   "Name Lindsay to Roybal's City Council Seat to serve short term.
          Assail council for action in filling vacancies"
          "Know Your L.A. City Council Candidates—Meet Josefa Sanchez"
          "Louis R. Diaz appointed to state post"
FEB 7   "Education and Mexican American Topic of Roosevelt High
          confab"
          "*Council meets Tuesday* Labor leaders support East LA
          Incorporation"
          "*Tafoya Vs Lindsay*? Battle lines drawn for 9th District post"
          "Know Your L.A. City Council Candidates—Meet Anthony
          Serrato"
          "*Assemblyman Song*: Advocates right-to-vote for non-English
          speaking citizens"
FEB 14   "Group claims Latins by-passed for state jobs"
          "[Arthur] Alacon answers committees charges on Latin
          appointments"
          "Welfare Planning Council to install new officers Monday"
          "MAPA fails to endorse candidate here" for 9th Councilmanic
          District"
          "Narcotics panel repeat slated Sunday on KMEX-TV"
          "*Felix Ontiveros* Lindsay names East LA business chief deputy"
FEB 21   "*Planning Committee reviews area guide plan* Predict increase in
          population growth in multiple dwelling units in East Central
          Area"
          "*Slum Renewal* L.A. Co. for Community Improvement"
          "Judge replies on Latin appointments; Answers Governor's aide,
          requests audience with Brown"
          "County Demo group expels R. Carvajal"
          "Song measure gives FEPC right to initiate complaints"
          "Assemblyman Moreno to hold open house, March 2"
FEB 28   "Vote registration in 9th District lowest in city," by David M.
          Barron
          "Solis cleared of fraud charges"
MAR 7   "Mexican-American group, Gov. Brown call truce"
          "Assemblyman Moreno gives support to East Los Angeles
          incorporation movement"
          "Mexican-American Republican group schedules session"
          "Four East LA schools selected for special 'drop out' program"

MAR 14   "*ELA Incorporation* Assemblyman Alfred H. Song officially
                endorses cityhood"
             "Approve pilot 'proposal prevention' program for four East L.A.
                Schools"
             "Assemblyman Moreno introduces bill to ease school districts
                financing"
             "Roybal announces opening of new 30th District office"
MAR 21   "*Citizen of Year* Group honors Manuel Veiga, Jr. hold meeting on
                Monday"
             "Committee reviews East Central Area guide plan, population
                rise"
             "Narcotics, Cityhood topics for Belvedere Coordinating Council"
             "Four persons injured as lightening strikes East L.A. street car
                Saturday"
             "Labor group endorses Tafoya for Council"
MAR 28   "Predict small vote turnout for city council, *Tuesday election.*
                Candidates vie for Council, Board of Education seats"
             "Congressman Roybal backs Tafoya for City Council"
APR 4   "*City Election Results* Tafoya, Lindsay in battle for Ninth District
                Council Seat"
             "Supervisors halt County 'gang' guidance work"
             "Women's night-Leaders of the Mexican American Women's
                League"
APR 11   "Group Guidance continues, order special study"
             "Educator lists problems of non-English speaking pupils"
APR 18   "East area committee urge better planning for intercity zone
                patterns"
             "Roybal urges use of FEPC service"
             "Ed Roybal Reports from Washington"
APR 25   "Ed Roybal Reports from Washington"
             "High officials back Tafoya"
MAY 2   "Tafoya opposes Imposed Program of Urban renewal"
MAY 9   "Ed Roybal Reports from Washington"
             "MARA Group plans projects, special meeting"
             "Moreno to address Demos at CDC endorsing election"
             "Tafoya spells out bold action program for 9th council district"
             "Roybal proposes new move to boost LA development"
MAY 16   "Tafoya urges equal rights for 'all' citizens"
             "Rep. Ed Roybal endorses Tafoya for City Council"
             "Editorial: Urge election of Richard Tafoya"
             "Supervisors re-shuffle district boundaries"
             "*Welfare Planning Council* East LA doctor heads youth committee;
                urges area projects"
MAY 23   "*Tafoya vs. Lindsay* Voters face final decision Tuesday in Ninth
                Council Contest," by David Barron
             "Debs endorses Tafoya for City Council"
             "*Election Tuesday, May 28* Vote for 'Dick' Tafoya"
             "Tafoya issues 10-point challenge in final city council post bid"

MAY 30   "Election Returns Lindsay defeats Tafoya for 9th District Council seat"
          "Castro scholarship chance set dor Breakfast Club June 8"
          "Ed Roybal Reports from Washington"
JUN 6   "Vocational training program studied for East LA youths"
          "Councilman Lindsay, Tafoya issue past election statement, Lindsay blasts Yorty, Debs, Roybal, Unruh"
          "Editorial: The American Way"
          "East LA group spurs incorporation movement, seek immediate action"
          "Plight of Mexican-Americans described at foundation dinner"
          "Ed Roybal Reports from Washington"
JUN 13   "Board to discuss East LA Youth project tonight"
          "Ed Roybal Reports from Washington"
          "*Rep. Brown reports* Congressman tells of new immigration, employment bills"
          "Al Waxman, Eastside Journal founder dies"
JUN 20   "City Council Reorganizes, Asks cut in Mayor's Staff"
          "OK $500,000 Youth Project funds to aid jobless"
          "Ed Roybal Reports from Washington"
          "Chris Ruiz from school 'drop out' to social worker in 20 years"
          "La Beneficencia Mexicana Tiene Elecciones el Martes 25"
          "Community Council elects officers launch East LA incorporation move"
JUN 27   "Swap Hazard Park for Hospital, Plan calls for vet's hospital on park land"
          "Integration Everybody's fight—Roybal"
          "Urge groups to aid youth project"
          "Ed Roybal Reports from Washington"
          "Propose law to safeguard rights of domestic farm workers," by Al Song
          "Open 'Do or Die' ELA cityhood drive; Group names new leaders, discuss boundaries," by David Barron
          "Lawyer's Assoc. installs leaders"
JUL 4   "John Anson Ford FEPC Chief to address rotary club Wednesday"
          "Annexations topic for cityhood group"
          "*Mexican-Americans* ELA medico claims group ignored . . ."
          "Congressmen charge police against 'gang' problem"
          "Ed Roybal Reports from Washington"
          "*Rep. George Brown* Discusses education juvenile crime"
JUL 11   "Approve changes in plans for ELA freeways, streets"
          "Action due on Montebello annexation, Neighboring City moves to take five East LA Areas"
          "Rep. Roybal outlines new plan for Hazard Park, Vets' Hospital, Asks hospital be built here, city to acquire additional land for park"
          "Mexican-American groups to meet in [County Human Relations] Commission parley"

"Ed Roybal Reports from Washington"
JUL 18   *"Hazard Park* Roybal Offers plan to park commission, Proposes
       hospital be built, acquire more land for park"
"Ed Roybal to speak in park trade"
"Study Latin problem at parley"
"Welfare Planning Council backs Roybal's Hazard Park, hospital
       Plan"
"Los Hambriados' Preparan su Feston Anual el 11 de agosto"
"Ed Roybal Reports from Washington"
"*Rep. Brown reports* House Committee works at fair employment
       bill"
JUL 25   "VP Johnson to address Latin confab"
"U.S. Delegate ELA Judge returns from Mexico confab"
"Commission OK's Roybal's Park, hospital plan 'in principle' "
"*Incorporation* Council fails to meet, new group starts"
"Planning Committee reviews ELA Freeway progress"
AUG 1   "*Joe Maldonado* Director named for ELA Youth project"
"Mexican-Americans to host vice President"
"Ed Roybal Reports from Washington"
AUG 8   "*Mexican-American Groups* Host Vice-President . . . Rep. Roybal,
       Brown attend"
"Local physician elected Police Commission officer"
"Community council set to file for ELA incorporation"
"Second edition of book [*Among the Valiant*] due"
"CSO calls for 'rights' meeting"
"Angry crowds attack four lawmen here"
"Ed Roybal Reports from Washington"
AUG 15   "*Vice-President* —Johnson sets conference on Mexican-American
       problems, confab set for November, tells Latins to 'fight
       bias'," by David M. Barron
"CSO Forms Fair Practices Council, here"
"*Educators report* Mexican Americna youth needs help in
       completing education"
"Discrimination in schools discussed at hearing here"
"Ed Roybal Reports from Washington"
AUG 22   "David Arroyo retires from LA Police Dept."
"L.A. Representatives to attend GI Forum National confab"
"Hazard Park: Factions argue over new park location"
AUG 29   "Hear proposal for new park site, study group meet: Hazard Park
       scheduled for Friday"
" 'New Park' topic for association"
SEP 5   "May file for incorporation Friday: ELA Council 'Ready' for
       Cityhood"
"New Playground sites outlined at stormy Hazard Park session"
"*GI Forum* Leaders set political seminar at Fresno"
SEP 12   "File notice of incorporation for East LA"
SEP 19   "*ELA Incorporation* Hearing on proposed city boundaries set"
"Park commissioner goes to Washington for park trade"
"Ed Roybal Reports from Washington"

SEP 26   "*Planning Council* Important to keep up properties"
          "*Martin Ortiz* Named state narcotics authority"
          "Boundary plans ok'd for ELA Incorporation"
          "Discuss plans, goals for East LA Youth job project"
          "Mexican-American 'Ad Hoc' Committee to attend session"
          "CYO Names Jose Vargas division head"
          "*Hazard Park Swap*: Offer substitute site for park development"
SEP 30   "Group seeks property owners ok"
OCT 3   *Vice President Johnson* Sets date for equal opportunities
              conference"
          "ELA Youth job training program opens here"
          ". . . Optimists to view films on gang warfare"
          "Must recognize rights of minority—Ed Roybal"
          "Realtors pledge to seek repeal of Rumford Fair Housing Act"
          "Ed Roybal Reports from Washington"
OCT 10   "*Incorporation* Petition deadline Dec. 6"
          "CMAA awards banquet set for Nov. 2"
          "Lindsay confers with local leaders propose study of Hazard Park
              area"
          "Ed Roybal Reports from Washington: Committee approves strong
              civil rights bill"
OCT 17   "Study standard planning for area communities"
          "Raul Morin elected MAPA Chairman"
          "Ed Roybal Reports from Washington"
OCT 24   "Community Council banquet plans misfire, Judge Marion objects
              to use of his name, Judge informs he'll not attend; Gil Avila
              new chairman"
          "Construction bids for Pomona freeway"
          "Church group takes over White Memorial"
          "Hazard Park: Hospital Plans underway, Seek new location for
              armory on park lands"
OCT 31   "Labor Group backs plan for two Eastside Parks"
          "*Vice President Johnson* invites Latin community leaders to confab
              on equal job opportunities"
          "Present honors Saturday at CMAA awards banquet"
          "Gov. Brown to address annual MAPA convention"
NOV 7   "*LA Convention* Governor, Congressmen to address MAPA
              members"
          "City Terrace woman in protest picket at freeway underpass"
          "*Incorporation* Group spurs East L.A. Cityhood, Richard Rubio,
              Past council prexy declines post"
          "*Equal job opportunities* Minority leaders, U.S. officials set for
              conference"
          "National CSO leaders to meet for L.A. area confab"
          "Congressman attacks extension of Bracero pact," by Congressman
              Ed Roybal
NOV 14   "Political, labor groups pledge support to East L.A. Incorporation
              campaign, Teamsters, MAPA, Demo group back Community
              Council Drive"

"*Vice-President conference* Minority leaders to convene for equal employment confab"

"MAPA parley pledges Mexican-American aid"

"New MAPA leaders elected at convention"

"*Rep. Brown reports*: Congressman supports strong civil rights legislation"

"Urges legislation to halt high school drop-outs," by Alfred Song

NOV 21   "*Incorporation* Seek new petition extension"

"*Dave Boubion* Receives top Peace Corps job in Central America"

"Warns delegates on promoting minorities, Mexican-American leaders attend, voice discontent"

"LA Mexican Chamber celebrates 25th year"

"*KMEX-TV* Spanish telecasts reach over 200,000 homes"

"Mexican-American lawyers host law students tonight"

NOV 28   "*Atty. John Arguelles* Appointed East LA municipal court judge"

"Freeway tunnels: Mothers to continue picketing"

"Arthur Rendon reappointed to President's Youth Committee"

DEC 5   "Guide plan set for East area Development, Publish fifth annual report of planning study"

"Kennedy City? Proposed as name for ELA . . . !" by David M. Barron

"*Governor Brown* Issues report on state employees 'ethnic census' "

DEC 12   "*Kennedy, California?* Short petition extension granted cityhood group"

"Democrats sponsor county-wide minority rights conference"

DEC 19   "Supervisors name Juvenile Delinquency Survey Committee"

"County issues report on proposed city. Lists costs, obligations, revenue of area, tells statistics on total proposed incorporation area," by David M. Barron

DEC 26   "Progress report given on area youth project"

"*East L.A. College.* Mexican-American job problems hearing set"

"Discrimination study in county jobs"

1964

JAN 2   "*East L.A. Incorporation* Deadline nears for cityhood petitions"

"Audrey Kaslow appointed to State FEPC"

"Discuss Fair Housing Act at Council session"

"*Latin job problems* Plans set for subcommittee session at ELAC"

JAN 9   "*East L.A. College* Assembly hearing Friday on Latin job problems"

"Belvedere resident [Edward J. Fimbres] named to top CYO post"

"*Incorporation* OK petition extension; union donates $500"

"County moves to Improve Lights in Freeway Tunnels"

"*Human Relations* Report reviews practices of LA police"

"Elliot Tops labor group vote ratings"

JAN 16   "Congressmen inspect site for Vets Hospital at area park"
"*Joe Maldonado* Appointed executive director of Youth
        Opportunities Board"
"Group reviews Cudhay's city master plan"
"[Belvedere Coordinating] Council to discuss youth job problems"
"Latin job handicaps revealed at hearing"
"Adult education bill attacks illiteracy in U.S."
"New State FEPC head appointed"
"Democratic Party minority conference planned here"
JAN 23   "Political Where . . . Eddie Ramirez to run for 45th Dist. Assembly
        post"
"Atty. Jack Fenton Seeks 51st Dist. Assembly seat"
"Atty. Tony Bueno sets eye on 40th Assembly Dist. job"
"Report $2.5 million increase in East LA youth program"
"Judge Marion 'Citizen of the Year' "
"Area assemblymen lead human rights conference"
"*Dan Luevano* Finance chief to address lawyers"
JAN 30   "*East L.A. Incorporation* Deadline nears for cityhood petitions"
"*$22.6* million Ask funds for VA hospital"
"*Demo minority confab* Mexican American panel asks Legislative
        action"
FEB 6   "*School Drop-outs* Board issues new report"
"*Narcotics pamphlet* coordinating councils to distribute copies"
"Honor new ELA judge [John Arguelles] at Testimonial Banquet"
"Lopez Mateos, LBJ to visit local park"
"CSO launches credit union for members"
"East LA incorporation attempt Fails for lack of filing Petition,
        Required number of signatures short of goal necessary for
        special election," by David M. Barron
"*Demo confab* Plan second meeting for minority rights studies"
"Local businessmen form [Mexican American Business &
        Professional Men's] scholarship association"
"Atty. Rudy Rivas named SBA fee counsel"
"Rep. Ed Roybal reports Civil Rights victory seen in anti-poll tax
        amendment"
FEB 13   "Richard Hernandez Names East LA man to Mayor Yorty's staff"
"Elect Juan Acevedo GI Forum chairman"
"*LA Youth projects* New directors take over duties"
"*Congressman Brown Reports* Legislator reports as House Civil
        Rights Debate"
"*Job office report* Minorities face high unemployment risk"
FEB 20   "Coordinating councils in anti-narcotic drive"
"Youth project names job development head"
"Nominate new officers for [East Central Area Welfare Planning
        Council] Welfare"
"*For Panama Work* Honor Peace Corps Leader"
"Census report tells of low income, jobless here"

"La Colonia Mexicana Lista Para Recibir a Lopez Mateos y L.B. Johnson"

"Political Whirl . . ."

"*Rep. Ed Roybal reports* Explains House passage of new civil rights act"

FEB 27   "Name Dan Luevano Asst. Sec. of Army"

"Jose Castorena appointed to FEPC staff"

MAR 5   "Install Mexican Chamber officers Sat"

"CMMA [sic] sponsors Fair Housing Act debate"

"Average family income in Los Angeles approximates $6,000"

"Arthur Alarcon to be named Superior Judge"

"John Moreno seeks reelection in 51st Dist"

"Political Whirl . . ."

MAR 12   "Congressional vote slated for VA hospital at Hazard Park"

"Launch health project in Eastside, Plan to study health habits of residents"

"Louis C. Diaz renamed to state commission"

"Political Whirl . . ."

MAR 19   "Condemn Hazard Park land for new VA Hospital here"

"Fair housing debate set for tonight"

"MAPA plans endorsing convention set Saturday"

"Montebello to annex East LA area"

"*Once a drop-out!* Education is story of Ernie Sanchez' life"

"Political Whirl . . ."

MAR 26   "Group here seeks additional law enforcement against narcotics," Antonio Canales of the Maravill Housing Project

"Demo, GOP candidates set for Congress, assembly races"

"Political Whirl . . ."

APR 2   "Discuss recreation facilities, Hazard Park land condemnation"

"Mexican-American conference set for next week"

"*MAPA* No endorsement in 40th AD"

"L.A. ranks high resettlement of Cuban refugee families"

"Political Whirl . . ."

"Frank Solis seeks East LA judgeship"

APR 9   "Atty. Gen Mosk to address Welfare Council"

"*Hazard Park* Set Plans to develop park site"

"Francisca Fraide named Mexican Mother of Year," by David M. Barron

"Political Whirl . . ."

"*D.A. Endorsements* MAPA leaders claim candidate violated rules"

APR 16   "*East Area Committee* Report varying population trends"

"Investigate arrest of blind girl, CMAA leader charges mistreatment by ELA deputies"

"*Teenagers Club* Host parents at narcotic conference"

"Youth project counselor set for new post"

"Political Whirl . . ."

APR 23   "*ELA Youth Project* Carlos Borja heads advisory committee"

APR 30 "Plan community forum for Mexican Americans"
    "Political Whirl . . ."
    " 'Backyard group' forms scholarship association"
MAY 7 "Women's club to confer achievement awards"
MAY 14 "Mexican-American forum set at E.L.A.C."
    "Freeway expansion hearing on Tuesday"
    "CSO to honor marching mother's [sic] May 22"
    "Political Whirl
    "*Mexican-American* School group forms new committee"
MAY 28 "Congressman lauds CSO service"
    "Know Your Candidates"
JUN 4 "Arthur Alarcon appointed to Superior Court"
    "*Record Election Vote*! Goldwater wins; Song beats Ramirez,
     reelect Marion, Elliot tops Bueno, Fenton upsets Moreno,
     Roybal, Brown face GOP opposition in November"
JUN 11 "*Bienvenido, Sr. Kennedy*! 5000 residents welcome U.S. Attorney
     General," by David M. Barron
    "Launch plan for ten story Vets hospital in Eastside"
    "Louis Garcia to head San Fernando CYO post"
JUN 18 "*East Central area* Tell need for more parks here"
    "*George Brown Reports* Congressman backs Civil Rights bill"
JUN 25 "Parks commission hears proposals for 'Kennedy Playground' here"
    "*Dr. Julian Nava* Predict peace for future generation"
JUL 2 "*State job office* Minority employment increases"
JUL 16 "Seek employer aid for on the job training program for youths
     here"
    "Is it a hill or a hole or a dirt road? no . . . It's the Pomona
     Freeway . . . !"
    "Task Force set-up by Agency seeks development in area"
JUL 23 "*Mexican-Americans* FEPC report shows they lag in schooling, jobs
     and income"
    "Acquit 3 East LA Men of assault on CHP officers"
    "Approve plans for JFK Playground Hazard Park eight acres
     proposed site"
    "City Council Okays new boundary"
    Map of new council districts
JUL 30 "College training grants . . . youth job project"
    "*Kennedy Playground* Commission accepts Hazard Park Proposal"
    "Issue call for 300 Eastside vote registrars"
    "*Explain functions* FEPC plans meeting with Mexican American
     leaders"
    "New officers of the Mexican-American Lawyers Club"
AUG 6 "*Laguna Park* Dedicate new swimming pool bathhouse"
    "*Henrietta Villaescusa* Name ELA woman to federal post"
    "Black-White Ball to mark Silver Jubilee"
    "CSO launches door-to-door vote registration drive"
    "Dr. Bravo heads Police Board"

AUG 13   "County prepares master plan for East Los Angeles future growth"
          "*Attorney General Kennedy* Endorsement spurs JFK park plan"
          "Union leader heads group against 14"
          "Latin [Dionicio Morales] named to LBJ's civil rights committee"
          "*Rep. Brown Reports* Reviews Viet Nam situation"
          "Congressional candidate propose job training for US-bound
              Mexican immigrants"
          "Congressman names delegates to convention"
AUG 20   "*Mexican Chamber* votes neutral stand on Rumford Act"
          "State resolution recognizes Spanish-speaking citizens"
          "G.I. Forum Discuss Mexican-American job problems here
              tonight"
          "CMAA supports Rumford Act"
AUG 27   "*ELA youngsters at UCLA* Spanish Speaking pupils learn English in
              experimental classes"
          "Judge Arguelles to install new Demo council"
          "*Si - Se Puede* FEPC Booklet encourages young Latins to stay in
              school"
          "Tobias Navarrette passes away here"
          "Congressional action clears way for Vets Hospital, Vote funds for
              Army Reserve Center Here"
SEP 3   "Eastside groups race to register voters as Sept. 10 deadline nears"
          "*Employment aid* Debs proposes youth work training program"
          "*Dr. Max Rafferty* Kiwanis Club hosts State school leader"
          "*UCLA survey reports* Mexican-Americans lack of knowledge of
              Proposition 14"
SEP 10   "[CMAA] Banquet to honor six Mexican-American judges"
SEP 17   "*Mexican-American survey* study attitudes of Latins toward mental
              illness"
          "Job office seeks Spanish-speaking aides"
          "*Oscar Gallegos* New vice principal at Garfield adult school"
          "*Congressman Brown polls voters* Unemployment rated top
              problem"
SEP 24   "CMAA to honor six judges Friday night"
          "Give progress report on Obregon Park"
          "Tell plans for anti-poverty drive"
          "Name Latin [J. J. Rodriguez] to President's panel"
          "FEPC issues report on Bank of America"
          "Youth agencies hear talk on Narcotics"
          "Rumford Act and Proposition 14: 200 hear 'great debate,' " by
              Milton Valera
OCT 1   "Discuss anti-poverty plans for East area, Mayor Yorty, Planning
              Council official addresses citizens," by David M. Barron
          "Political Whirl . . ."
OCT 8   "Judge Sanchez heads East LA March of Dimes"
          "*All land acquired* start construction of Obregon Park"
          "Bill Acosta named YOB project head"

"CAO's Report Advises against city human relations unit"
"Political Whirl . . ."
"The project tops artistic talents of unemployed youth"
"Sub-committee holds hearings on civil service employment"
"OK street improvements in Belvedere-ELA areas"
OCT 15 "Grant Federal Charter for New Belvedere-East L.A. Bank, Dr. Francisco Bravo heads bank board"
"*Equal Employment Foundation* Annual awards banquet to honor Latin leaders"
"Political Whirl . . ."
"Mayor Yorty asks for racial and ethnic survey of city employees"
"[East Central Area] *Planning Committee* Freeways are important to our Eastside Area"
"*Bureau of Investigation* Henry Salcido named to District Attorney's office"
OCT 22 "Know Your Candidates"
"Mexico confers high honor to Dr. R. Carreon"
"*Roosevelt, Garfield* Highs . . . youths join in anti-dropout program"
"Mayor [sic] road projects set in East LA"
"Danny Villanueva named to state post"
"Political Whirl . . ."
OCT 29 "Voters to cast ballots Tues. for national, local election," by David M. Barron
"*Fresno Center* Protest group speaks at commission session"
"LULACS plan benefit fiesta"
"Political Whirls . . ."
NOV 12 "MAPA charges FEPC ignores problems of Mexican-Americans"
NOV 19 "At Harrison School Freeway overpass to replace old tunnel"
"Community meetings slated for discussion of ELA master Plan," by David M. Barron
"*Job projects* Welfare agency calls meeting on poverty act"
"Former East LA man gets key post in YOB research project"
DEC 3 "2.73 million grant awarded L.A.'s anti-poverty program"
"CCAA [sic] honors Carlos Borja appointment [A.I.D.]"
"Richard Calderon seeks City Council post"
DEC 10 "*Key assignments* YOB selects two for ELA project"
"Mexican-American Council to honor Atty. Carlos Borja"
"Master plan report on playground due"
"Court orders State Senate reapportionment"
DEC 17 "Guadalupe procession attracts 15,000"
"*Linda Marmalejo* Peace Corps volunteer serves in Venezuela"
"Supervisors study laws to commit narcotic addicts"
"*Club Latino American* Senior Citizens Install officers"
DEC 24 "State to recruit farm workers here"
"Propose joint city county Human Relations Commissions"
"CMAA holds debate on Bracero laws"

DEC 31   "Peace Corps worker goes to Ecuador"
         "Discuss proposed ELA master plan tonight"
         "*Ninth District* Richard Tafoya declines to run for City Council"

1965

JAN 7   "Coordinating Councils to host sessions on ELA master plan"
         "Welfare council to review area projects"
         "Death takes businessman Oscar Apodaca"
JAN 14   "New group to administer poverty funds, YOB, economic
             federation merged here"
         "Elect Milt Nava Mexican Chamber of Commerce president"
         "Candidates file for city offices"
JAN 21   "*Anti-poverty programs* Special education projects launched in
             Eastside schools"
         "Judge Arguelles heads welfare council group"
         "*Public meeting tonight* Proposed master plan may change face of
             East L.A."
JAN 28   "Approve plans for new East LA Library"
         "*Atty. Carlos Borja* Takes over new post in Latin America"
         "Casa del Mexicano site for session on Poverty Act"
         "Mexican-American supports candidate for school board"
FEB 4   "Angel by the Hand"
         "*Master Plan* May serve as guide for East LA's future"
         "*9th District race* Four candidates to oppose Councilman Gilbert
             Lindsay"
         "GI Forum to host meeting on Poverty Act"
FEB 11   "Planning Council to install new officers . . ."
FEB 18   "Welfare Planning Council honors leaders, Install new officers"
         "Charge indeclared [sic] war in Asia, Congressman Brown hits lack
             of policy in Vietnam"
         "Long Beach Freeway extension completed"
         "*JFK Memorial Park* Public protests was equipment for park, city
             seeks theme for JFK memorial in Hazard Park"
FEB 25   "*Reporter gives views* Behind the scenes 'struggle' for LA's Poverty
             Act funds," by Ridgely Cummings
         "Roadwork continues on major routes, Will cover-up old street car
             rails on East First Street"
         "State Atty. Gen. proposes two civil rights bills"
         "Political Whirl . . ."
MAR 4   "*Eastside Boys Club* Install New officers at banquet, presents
             awards"
         "Veterans Hospital to be built in Eastside, Congress approves bill
             to remove army center from Hazard Park site"
         "Hollenbeck Council Explain Poverty Act effects on East LA"
         "Three key appointments for anti-poverty act war"
         "Poblano sees education as barrier to mobility"
         "GI Forum elects Chairman"

MAR 11   "MAPA endorses Roosevlet, Calderon for city posts"
           "*School board offices* East LA Council set Candidate Night . . ."
           "Launch sidewalk, curb repair project on East First Street"
           "Town meetings discuss ELA 'War on Poverty' "
           "Eastside youth, prep track star, knifed to death"
           "Teachers told problems of Latin Study"
           "Latin Women's league honors social workers"

MAR 18   "Report shows progress on East First Street Sidewalk improvement
              project"
           "CSO explains credit union fund plan at meeting"
           "Alberto C. Diaz selected as 'Citizen of Year' "
           "Mother of slain youth grateful"

MAR 25   "*Welfare planning council* poverty act unit holds first session"
           "*Assemblyman Song Proposes* pre-school English classes for Latin
              children
           "Latin Women's League holds awards fete"
           "Citizens group studies mental health needs"
           "Mayor Yorty says LA convention hall necessary"
           "*Know Your Candidate* Meet Ross Valencia"
           "Political Whirl . . ." on candidates battle for school board posts

APR 1   "Alberto C. Diaz named editor and publisher"
           "Felix Gutierrez elected Cal student prexy"
           "Businessmen near 100% goal on E. First Street sidewalk project"
           "Beachcomber," by Alberto C. 'Al' Diaz, on Ralph Poblano for
              Office #2 of the Board of Education
           "Twelve women honored at Latin League"
           "*Know Your Candidate* Meet Richard Calderon"

APR 8   "Audrey Kaslow appointed to state group"
           "*New judge for East LA!* Supervisors slate hearing on Courts
              merger Tuesday"
           "Mayor Sam swamps foes in record City Election, Lindsay re-
              elected in 9th Council District, Poblano runs fourth"
           "*At long last!* Allocate funds for City Terrace freeway overpass"
           "*150 youths invited* Leadership confab set for Mexican-Americans"
           "*UCLA conference* Discuss cultural values of Mexican-American
              youths"
           "*Planning Council* Slate report on Poverty Act projects here"
           "Off-campus clubs barred at ELA"
           "New anti-poverty agency setup hits smog," by Ridgley Cummings

APR 15   "Approve merger of LA courts"
           "*Add 2 1/2 acres* Expand Fresno playground"
           "Problems of Sr. Citizens topic for new course"
           "Schools send local youths to [Camp Hess Kramer] conference"

APR 22   "*East First Street* Sidewalk, road projects underway"

APR 29   "Supervisors OK oil, gas, drilling lease"
           "Youth shot at City Terrace Park during fight"
           "*Rep. Brown Reports* Survery tells readers views on Viet War"

MAY 6   *"Youth Opportunities Board* Present 'War on Poverty' report here
                 Saturday"
           "ELA Judges Declare War on weapons"
           "Latin Senior citizens Day at Laguna Park"
           "GI Forum installation due Saturday"
           "New senate plan may split ELA; Sen. Rees announces proposal for
                 12 LA senate seats"
           "Franklin library was city's first branch"
MAY 13   "Community program honors senior citizens"
           "J. J. Rodriguez named to state industrial group"
           "Small turn out for YOB session here"
           "Bill Gutierrez named to US Agency"
           "Citizens committee calls for East LA senatorial District"
           "Congressman Reports Brown votes against View war funds"
           "GI Forum installs officers, selects new chapter queen"
MAY 20   *"Poverty funds* Youth Board seeks $15 million grant"
           "MAPA to hold election convention"
           "Reapportionment Latin senate seat bid gains support"
MAY 27   *"City Election* Mrs. Wyman upset, Jones wins board post"
           "MAPA Convention Latin group convenes here, elects officers"
JUN 3   *"New Probation offices* Dedicate $352,000 building Saturday"
           "New plans for Hazard Park Recreation, Privately financed park
                 may be built next to hospital"
           "Save Park group opposes new plan"
           "Discuss proposal for legal aid office tonight"
           "Ex-addicts in anti-dope campaign"
JUN 10   "Judge C. Teran gets Brotherhood Award"
           "Minority committee seeks anti-poverty agency for LA"
           "Battle looms on new park plan"
           "Yorty tells anti-poverty plan"
           "Gonzalo Molina new MAPA chairman"
JUN 17   "Hazard Park meeting on new recreation center picketed here,
                 Opponents hit Roybal on 'land giveaway' "
           "Anti-Poverty War YOB moves to ease LA stalemate"
           "Urban Affairs A. Rodriguez named to school post"
           "Seek Spanish speaking job counselors"
JUN 24   *"Leyes Juveniles* Supervisors issue Laws for Youth booked in
                 Spanish version"
           "Hazard Park hassle continues"
           "Launch new school program in East LA, Thousands of youngsters
                 attend special classes here"
           "White Memorial plans $4.2 million center"
           "Dr. Francisco Bravo resigns from LA Police Commission"
           "LA Police Parker appoints community relations aide"
           "Educators of Mexican descent Unite, elect new officers"
JUL 1   *"Economic Opportunities Projects* Eastside elementary, high
                 schools to open new summer programs"

"*Ratification* needed agreement reached on poverty agency"

"*Summer jobs* city, schools open youth corp [sic] programs"

JUL 8   "*Operation Headstart* Opening remain for pre-school classes here"

"FEPC consultant to hear local complaints"

"Roybal, Brown say officials lost $800,000"

JUL 15   "L.A. Anti-Poverty board merger Plan protested, Pickets hit city approval of plan"

"Master plan for ELA topic of meeting"

"Planning Council continued growth seen for Eastside"

"*Latin Women's League* Schedule constitutional convention for Saturday"

"[Richard] Rubio elected vice chairman of county commission"

JUL 22   "*Fiesta de Las Flores* Three-day festival at Belvedere Park, lakes"

"Youth paint mural for Belvedere Jr. High School"

"County, City, Schools urge 'Anti-Poverty' Action, Approve YOB expansion, $23 million goal"

"*East LA Master Plan* 'urban renewal' charges spurs property owners session tonight"

"Neighborhood Youth Corp job open in LA area"

"Mexican-American Women's League elects officers"

"State employee report shows minorities gain"

JUL 29   "*Council names twelve for anti-poverty board* Group endorses citizens as candidates"

"Over 900 property owners attend 'confused' ELA master plan meeting"

"*Assemblyman Song* Candidate for Senate seat when senate reapportioned"

"*Pre-school classes* 'Operation Headstart' proves huge success"

"LA City to hire 1500 youth corps workers"

"*USC professor says* Negro struggle aids Mexican-Americans"

AUG 5   "East LA site for Congressional hearing on anti-poverty war"

"Release U.S. funds for LA poverty war"

"Plan community-wide meeting on proposed ELA Master Plan"

"*Harrison St. School* Holds session on freeway overpass"

AUG 12   "Demand voice for poverty groups at East LA Congressional hearings"

"Property owners group meets here tonight"

"Funds still available for vets hospital, Federal cutback not affect project"

"Latin educators [Los Angeles County Mexican American Education Committee] elect, install new officers"

"Debs asks poverty area hearings"

AUG 19   "Lindsay asks $100 [sic] to aid Negro"

"CSO opens summer teen program here"

"Plan major improvements for Eastside area parks"

"Councilmen urge human relations unit"

"Aid sought for innocent riot victims"

"Riot over, tension lasts in area"
"Yorty defends police action during rioting"
"Crop pickers needed for lemons, oranges"
AUG 26   "Council OK's Dr. R. Carreon for Commission post"
"Anti-poverty squabble may be settled in LA: Expand board to 25, area to get aid," by Ridgely Cummings
"*Poverty funds* Debs asks 'fair share' for Latins"
"*Mexican-American Adults* Latin Leadership conference announcement"
"East LA committee on aging installs new officers"
SEP 2   "State Assembly to caucus on reapportionment"
"Riots to cost city $2 million"
"Councilman [Billy Mills] asks . . . police study"
SEP 9   "Roybal charges unequal division of anti-poverty funds"
"ELA's Obregon Park plans approved"
"City, County appoint poverty spokesmen"
SEP 16   "$7 million anti-poverty programs"
"Community meeting on Wednesday night, discuss East LA Master Plan"
"Teen Post leaders laud success of proposal"
"Public session due on LA poverty war"
"Name speaker for Latin adult confab"
SEP 23   "Banquet to honor two civic leaders"
"Dedicate first stretch of new Pomona Freeway in East LA"
"Discuss proposed ELA Master Plan, Judge Sanchez moderate special session"
"Mexican American studies foundation announced"
"Felix Gutierrez returns from prexy's conference"
"Reapportionment," by Jack R. Fenton
SEP 30   "VA hospital, armory negotiations stalled"
"Beachcomber," by Alberto C. Diaz, on master plan
"Schools expect $16 million in poverty funds"
"Master Plan opponents to continue fight"
"Debs orders halt to proposed East LA master plan studies, Charge opponents of proposal confused issue"
"Committee drafts candidate for [40th] assembly"
"Poverty projects underway in Mexican-American community"
OCT 7   "*Thirteen projects* Anti-poverty school programs underway in Eastside Schools"
"Monterey Park orders study to annex East LA area. Would entend City limits to new Pomona Freeway"
"Controversy continues on Master Plan"
"Roybal charges favoritism in poverty fund allocations"
"Foundation studies effect of 'Head Start' programs"
"Song predicts committee OK for appointment"
OCT 14   "Unveil grant mural for Pan Am Bank building"
"Civic officials to honor two leaders"

"Retirement banquet honors ELA's Postmaster General [Arthur M. Franco]"

"Youths attend 'Respect for Law' meeting"

"Discuss Latin problems at conference"

OCT 21 "Latins seek bigger slice of anti-poverty funds"

"Break ground for new Obregon Park"

"Bilingual mental health clinic to open here"

OCT 28 "Launch . . . new census of East LA"

"500 pay tribute to Bravo, Carreon"

"*New districts here* Senate apportionment goes wrong"

"OK contract for new freeway overpass here"

NOV 4 "Begins special census here on area dwelling, residents"

"Monterey Park official denies charges of ELA annexation move"

"*Mayor's poverty committee* Peter Diaz elected chairman of local units"

"MAPA starts drive for more registrars"

NOV 11 "Announce $1 million grant for new poverty programs here"

"Open First Link of New Pomona Freeway"

NOV 18 "OK funds for 'teen gang' work"

"*Meeting Tonight* Property owners to continue fight against annexation"

"Launch second phase of census"

"City planner tells problems of area's patchwork planning"

"Roybal reports $2 million grant for job training"

NOV 25 "May name Sanchez to Superior Court"

"Professor [Helen Bailey] to speak about Latin Youth"

DEC 2 "Final stage of census underway, Census workers visit homes"

"*New shopping center!* Ask commercial zone for 3 East L.A. 3 acre site"

"Pueblo Republican Assn. holds kick-off meeting"

"*Latin educators* Lt. Gov. to welcome teacher at San Diego convention"

"Latins don't reap full financial benefits from education"

DEC 9 "County poverty board election set for Feb. 8th"

"McCone riot report issued"

"[Lucky's] Shopping center plan hit hard by opposition," by David M. Barron

"Educators Unit meets to discuss Latin problems"

"Tell of need for teachers of Latin descent"

"Local residents attend Latin teachers Ass'n conference"

DEC 16 "Judge Sanchez named to Superior Court"

"Yorty urges OK for two centers here"

"*$100,000 grant!* Roybal announces approval of new Malabar St. School project"

"Educators [AMEA] urge new study of Latin pupils"

DEC 23 "Peace Corps Spanish speaking volunteers sought here"

"*Dr. Marvin Karno* . . . director for new mental health clinic"

"FEPC names co-chairman at session"
"Younger expands Spanish-speaking staff"
"Claim Mexican-Amer. teachers by-passed"
"MAPA honors education leaders"
DEC 30   "Legal aid office to open in East LA"
"Congressman Roybal tours Job Corps Centers here"

1966

JAN 6   "Open race for Poverty Board"
"Gilberto Soto receives medal for heroic Vietnam rescue!"
"Court has final word on apportionment"
"G.I. Forum Speech Contest announced"
"Sanchez takes Oath for Superior Court"
"El Mercado plans progressing in ELA"
"School hosts confab for Mexican Americans"
JAN 13   "New date for poverty election"
"OK zone change for new area shopping center"
"Veteran's Hospital No Action on Hazard site, says park chief," by
      Ridgely Cummings
"Political reason to open as any candidates prepare for election"
"Latin Women's chamber elects new president"
"MAPA Leader [Bert Corona] named to civil rights unit"
"Educator says schools fail in teaching history"
"*Mexican American Study Project* Immigration History policy
      changes told"
JAN 20   "Assemblyman Song to run for now 28th district senate post"
"Poverty Board elections, funding plan under fire"
"Planning unit Urge better zoning for community growth"
"Latin educators [AMEA] set installation of officers"
"[Equal Opportunities] Foundation to install leaders"
JAN 27   "*Gilbert Avila* Enters Assembly"
"*Salvador Montenegro* Realtor runs for Assembly post"
"*Eddie Ramirez* Pharmacist seeks 45th District post"
"Ben Vega new East LA Judge"
"Anti poverty election set for March 1, City apathy on part of
      Mex.-Americans"
"*Lincoln High* Latin educator to keynote Parents Conference Feb.
      12"
FEB 3   "Final drive for poverty board candidates here"
"*CYO Program* Community development project for Eastside"
"Maravilla Housing Council to discuss area problems"
"Ralph Guzman to speak at educators installation"
"Phil Ortiz enters 51st assembly race"
"Cecilia Pedroza enters Senate race"
FEB 10   "Banquet honors Judge Sanchez"
"Two enter Assembly race in 45th District"

"*Julio Gonzales* Banquet to honor LA policeman"

"Latin group opposes new school bonds"

"CYO appoints Jose A. Vargas asst. director"

"*Mexican-American parents* 1000 expected at Lincoln high confab"

FEB 17   "Eighteen candidates to run for poverty board seats here"

"Opposition blocks Vets hospital. Armory planned for switch to
Rose Hills area"

"*Mexican Americans Parents Conference* Issue 10 point statement
of needs"

FEB 24   "Candidates battle for two district seats in East LA"

"School attendance crippled by flu epidemic . . ." by Dan Moreno

"New Mexico Senator to visit East LA"

"Supervisors to hear case for zone change"

"Dr. Miguel Montes named to state board of eduation"

"Rep. Roybal to file for re-election Monday"

MAR 3   "Low vote turnout for poverty board election"

"CMAA project Pacheco named director of Headstart project"

MAR 10   "Local residents to sit on L.A. Poverty Board"

"Rep. Roybal sees world peace main concern"

"Latin youth leadership confab set"

MAR 17   "Census shows East L.A. income, jobs are down"

"Poverty spokesmen tell goals, issues"

"Job service center opens in East LA"

MAR 24   "Ray Mora named to SBA"

"Supervisor [Debs] comments Latin youth confab"

MAR 31   "Political Whirl . . ."

APR 7   "Yorty asks transfer of armory"

"Latin youths seek answers at conference," by Dan Moreno

"*Miss Opal Jones* NAPP director fired by board"

"Political Whirl"

"Educators report learning English is No. 1 problem"

APR 14   "Commission backs Hazard Park swap"

"List youngsters attending youth leadership conference"

"Councilman Lamport takes issue over EYOA with Dr. H. H.
Brookins"

"Roybal to join LBJ on trip to Mexico"

"*ELA Youth project* Job training center to expand, open second
area location"

"Political Whirl"

APR 21   "Citizens' 'Poverty War' committee forming to represent East LA"

"Welfare recipients training center opens"

"Parents to attend public school week"

"MAPA holds endorsing convention"

"Mexican American groups host conference walkouts"

"Political Whirl"

APR 28   "*Hazard Park Trade* Hearing today on vets hospital plan"

"Youth career conference at Cal State LA"

"Latin woman league presents annual awards"

"[Eddie] Ramirez endorsed by MAPA"

"*Former deputy sheriff* D.A. names first woman investigator"

MAY 5   "City commissioners OK Hazard Park land trade"

"Name [Richard Alatorre] director of new educational program"

MAY 12   "*New ELA agency?* New policy changes announced for anti-poverty war operation"

"Install Jim Madrid new Planning Council prexy"

"New Job training project to begin here"

"State court upsets Prop. 14"

"Political Whirl"

MAY 19   "Call meeting on proposed poverty board for East LA"

"Youth killed in City Terrace Park fight"

MAY 26   "Dedicate Obregon Park tonight"

"John Serrato heads formation of new poverty war board [Eastland Community Action Agency] in East LA"

"CMAA charges police brutality"

"Sheriff says charges untrue"

"Mexican American educators to convene on Long Beach"

"Political Whirl"

"Committee voices support for UCLA Latin Study"

JUN 2   "State Senate, Assembly battles in final stretch"

"Police commission to hold meetings with minority groups"

"Know Your Candidates, 45th Assembly District"

JUN 9   "Gov. Brown edges Yorty, Song, Karabian, win Demos nod, Debs, Sanchez victors"

"Marcos de Leon heads Latin educators unit"

JUN 16   "*Cal State students* Receive grants to tutor pupils, assist local small businessmen"

"White Memorial Hosp. Oked for Medicare, plans major expansion"

JUN 23   " 'Instant jobs' available for 10,000 youths, 16–21, list requirements"

"Announce new plans L.A. Poverty Programs"

"Teen-agers 'Picket for Help' from parents and adults"

"Appoint new East LA Health Educator"

JUN 30   "Hazard Park land swap slated"

"Audrey A. Kaslow named to State Welfare Board"

"Install Frank Serrano president of Latin Educators in ELA"

"*July 5 at Laguna Park* Eastside students to convene, organize community action group"

"*MAPA Convention* Mexican-American political group endorses Gov. Brown"

"*Population-economic trends* UCLA report analyzes East LA problems"

JUL 7   "Oscar Gallegos to direct new job skills center"

"Four groups to takeover [sic] youth training project here"

"Instant jobs for youth called success"
"Seek 5000 volunteers for head start"
"Property owner group to meet"
"Standard Oil to drill on Belvedere Park land"
"Save the Park group to seek injunction if city ok's trade"

JUL 14   "*Veterans hospital* VA official spells out reasons for local site"
"*Sargent Shriver* Poverty war director visits ELA, tours center"
"Young citizens group meets"
"Beachcomber," by Al Diaz; see "Freeways" section

JUL 21   "*Charles Amezcua* Name new manager for YTEP here"
"Poverty Board approves $2.5 million in funds"
"FEPC reports on survey of ELA"
"Calderon picks up 20 votes during recount"
"Latin American Civic Association"

JUL 28   "Okay delay for Hazard Park swap," by Ridgely Cummings
"Rep. George Brown tells why he voted against Federal defense
    bill"

AUG 4   "Linda Marmalejo Peace Corps volunteer coming home"
"Reagan, Brown woo Latin vote"
"Orozco hits Brown's vote on defense bill"
"Beachcomber," by Alberto 'Al' Diaz, on Dr. Bravo and why he
    backed Reagan
"Birth control group campaigns in Eastside"

AUG 11   "Belvedere Businessmen meet today"
"Cool Heads program at Roosevelt High"
"Edgar Perez named to area foundation job"
"Montez urges pre-school for Spanish speaking"

AUG 18   "Poverty agency OK'd for ELA"
"Freeway interchange nears finish, Jan 26 deadline set for new area
    freeway"
"Property owners meet tonight"
"*Mexican Exposition due* Proclaim Mexican-American friendship
    observance week"
"MAPA honors outgoing president"

AUG 25   "Young citizens group plans conference"
"[Mexican American Opportunity] Foundation to open offices in
    East LA"

SEP 1   "Governor to campaign in East LA Friday"
"UCLA's 'Upward Bound' Youth discover new world"
"Mexican Chamber holds annual picnic here"
"*UCLA survey* Report on incomes of Mexican-American"
"Congressman Brown's Viet views rapped by Candidate Orozco"
"Ballet Aztlan, free feature of giant Mexican exposition"

SEP 8   "New group takes over YTEP United Community Efforts, Inc."
"Brown, Orozco lash out with charges"

SEP 15   "Giant Parade to highlight celebrations in East LA"
"Dr. Bravo levels charges against Governor in press statement"

"Scholarships presented by foundation to 17"

SEP 22   "Local business men named to area [Los Angeles Economic]
                Development Agency"

"ACLU opens police 'malpractice' complaint center in Boyle
                Heights"

"Local poverty projects given Federal grants"

"We can have park, hospital says Roybal"

"Roosevelt students tour capital as part of Upward Bound project"

"Committee OK's park land swap"

SEP 29   *Local poverty programs* call for area project report"

"Commission OK's park trade for Vets Hospital"

"Beachcomber, The NAPP and the Mexican-American," by Albert
                "Al" Diaz

"Liberal, peace groups conference in ELA"

"Question on Master plan proposal raised again"

"Luevano tells function of ECAC [Eastland Community Action
                Council] at meeting"

"Group opposes meeting of Liberals here"

"Manuel Real"

OCT 6   "New Mexico's Sen. Montoya to visit ELA"

"Death takes pioneer East LA businessman [Mario Lopez, 57]"

"Richard Tafoya named YTEP director here"

"D. A. Younger appoints new field aide"

"Political forum continues at Cal State LA"

"Beachcomber," by Alberto "Al" Diaz, on master plan

"Mexican-American lawyers Sen. Montoya to speak at installation
                Friday"

"Know your candidates 40th Assembly District: Edward Elliot-
                Peter Diaz"

OCT 13   *"Sal Montenegro* Realtor on Rumford act study unit"

"UCLA study Find Anglos form part of . . ."

"Plan Washington confab in U.S. Mexican-American"

"Welfare Planning Council M. Ortiz resigns as East area director"

"Judge Sanchez to address Catholic women's group"

OCT 20   "Beachcomber," by Alberto "Al" Diaz

"Mexican-American Washington conference, preliminary meetings
                October 20, 26 and 28"

"Prep students attend 'Law and Order' confab"

"Kennedy, Brown visit here Friday, Reagan draws 1800 in East
                LA"

"GI Forum passed resolution," on Opal Jones dispute with Gabriel
                Yanez

OCT 27   "Latins to attend Washington confab"

"John Serrato appointed to youth post"

"East LA businessman [Dr. Francisco Bravo] named to city charter
                study unit"

NOV 3   "National confab set for Mexican Americans"

"Legal aid service helps 4000 people"

NOV 10   "Ya Estuvo! Reagan elected, Geo. Brown defeats Orozco, Song,
Karabian victors here"

"*Dan Luevano* Western OEO chief visits poverty sites"

" 'Poor Power' conference slated here"

"Beachcomber," by Alberto Diaz, on election post-mortems

NOV 17   "Republicans make some gains in area," by David M. Barron

"Brown analyzes slim win in campaign for congress," by Gerald
Stewart

"Report on poor power conference"

"Approve Federal funds for ELA School project"

"New Eastside Corporation announced"

"*Julio Gonzales* School officials honor policeman for activities"

NOV 24   "Foundation to hold rally at Roosevelt High"

"Fund raising dinner Friday night for YTEP"

"School parents protest 'unsafe' completion of freeway overpass"

DEC 1   "City council must decide on 'Hospital for Park' today," by
Ridgely Cummings

"YTEP in ELA comes under fire, local officials here deny charges"

"Picketing, stormy meetings mark 'hospital for park' history," by
Daniel Moreno

DEC 8   "EYOA faces $9 million cut back in anti-poverty programs here"

"Mexican Chamber to elect officers"

"Veterans Hospital for Hazard Park Land swap deal OK'd," by
Ridgely Cummings

DEC 15   "Seek representatives for UCE Board in ELA area"

"*UCLA study project* Mexican-American marriages increasing"

"Yorty signs ordinance on Hazard Park deal"

"Law clerks 'learn the business' in District Attorney's office"

DEC 22   "Ralph Poblano to run for school board"

"Valley link of Pomona Freeway completed"

DEC 29   "Unsafe buildings face demolition in Boyle Heights, central areas,
City Council still to act"

"[Al] Ortega named city commissioner"

"Police complaint center, Pros and cons discussed," by Dan
Moreno

1967

JAN 5   "[State] FEPC opens office for discrimination claims here"

"Propose zone freeze in Boyle Heghs [sic]"

JAN 12   "28 candidates file for School board posts"

"Plan workshops for Sr. Citizens"

"File to halt Hazard Park swap"

"*School Board Race* Mexican-American group to hold super-
endorsing convention Sunday"

"Julia Mount runs for school office no. 3"

"*Assemblyman Karabian* Ben Estrada named administrative aide"

JAN 19   "School report ethnic, racial survey"
          "Dan Reyes new Eastland CAP director"
          "Dr. Bravo to State [Agriculture Commission] post"
          "*School board race* Dr. M. H. Guerra to run despite endorsement
              of Prof. J. Nava"
          " 'Older Latin Americans' Theme for Senior Citizens Conference"
JAN 26   "School report on racial ethnic survey"
          "Mrs. L. S. Baca reelected Planning Commission head"
          "*Hope for EYOA projects* Find possible source for funds"
          "500 at Senior Citizens Confab"
          "Reject zone freeze near vicinity of Hazard Park"
          "Senate bills propose aide for Latins"
          "School Racial, Ethnic Survey"

School	Spanish Surname	White	Black
Roosevelt H.S.			
Pupils	2305	91	195
Teachers	9	100	13
Other certified	0	6	0
Garfield			
Pupils	3324	200	8
Teachers	6	140	10
Other certified	1	5	0
Hollenbeck Jr.			
Pupils	1933	87	301
Teachers	11	64	14
Other certified	1	15	1
Stevenson Jr.			
Pupils	1841	80	22
Teachers	12	61	13
Other certified	0	9	0
Griffith			
Pupils	1743	53	9
Teachers	5	62	4
Other certified	2	16	2
Belvedere Jr.			
Pupils	1875	25	14
Teachers	12	71	5
Other certified	5	26	4
East Los Angeles Community College			
Pupils	3628	7105	964
Teachers	27	459	17
Administrators	0	10	0
Other schools also listed			

FEB 2   "Councilman Lindsay tells of district improvements"
FEB 9   "Tom Reddin appointed new Los Angeles police chief"
           "Local congressman [Ed Roybal] awarded peace medal"
FEB 16   "*Beachcomber* Mexican American White House
                 Conference . . . ¿Quien Sabe?"
           "LA Poverty program given new extension"
           "KMEX-TV Spanish health program beginning second year"
FEB 23   "Roybal calls meeting on proposed Mexican American conference"
           "Civil suit pending to halt Hazard Park swap"
           "EYOA reports new job program due"
           "CSO sponsors meeting with congressman"
MAR 2   "Dedicate Pomona Freeway link in East LA Friday"
           "*UCLA Study* Minority groups pay more for housing"
           "Hazard Park group wins court victory"
           "Debs urges Latin conference"
MAR 9   "*Mexican-American* Youth conference slated"
           "*City Terrace Parents* Protest proposed school bus cuts," by Dan
                 T. Moreno
           "Dinner-dance marks CSO's 20th anniversary"
           "Know Your School Board candidates: Meet Dr. Manuel H.
                 Guerra"
MAR 16   "MAPA endorses School candidates"
           "Candidates hit MAPA endorsements"
           "Latin student group [Mexican American Student Association at
                 East Los Angeles College] formed at college"
           "Job training program planned for ELA in June"
           "Funds assured for legal assistance office"
MAR 23   "*Julio Gonzales* named to state youth authority"
           "CSO celebrate 20th anniversary"
           "Draft policies; How it affects Latin Youths," by David M. Barron
           "*School Board candidates* Meet Dr. Julian Nava"
           "*School Board candidates* Meet Charles Galindo; Meet Ralph
                 Poblano"
MAR 30   "Low-income representative sought for LA Poverty board"
           "Parents confront School Board today on proposed education cuts"
           "East LA area shows increase in population"
           "Supervisor Debs reports White House OK's Plans for Mexican-
                 American confab"
           "Nine Eastside Schools still on double sessions"
           "Beachcomber," on school board race and inflammatory remarks
           "*School Board Candidates* Meet Mrs. Julia Mount; Meet Dr. Robert
                 Docter"
APR 6   "Dr. Nava, Smoot to battle in runoff, Eastside's vote backs Dr.
                 Nava's bid"
           "*Mexican American* Study shows education level up"
           "*For Senior Citizens* Plan referral center in East LA"
           "Jaycees honor Atty. Herman Sillas"

APR 13   "East LA woman named Mexican Mother of Year"
           "Open link of Pomona Freeway here"
           "Four lane expansion planned for freeway in City Terrace area"
           "Youth authority to open project center in ELA"

APR 20   "Police Latin conference set Saturday"
           "Neighborhood councils being formed by ECAC [Eastland
               Community Action Council]"
           "*State Employment Reports* Job training programs boost income of
               unskilled workers"
           "GOP names Dave Gonzales to party post"

APR 27   "*Motivate youths* businessmen to address teens at Career Day"
           "Poverty council chosen for Laguna Park area"
           "Town Meeting group back from Sacramento"
           "New office formed for farm labor recruiting"

MAY 4   "Monterey Park Plans Land grab"
           "*Town Meeting Association* Group to meet with Governor, other
               officials"
           "Leaders, citizens rap news magazine article," on *Time* magazine
               article titled "Pocho's Progress"
           "Montebello GI Forum to install"
           "MAPA contributes to Nava campaign"

MAY 11   "Death takes Raul Morin ELA community leader"
           "Senior citizens invited to Leadership course at Laguna"
           "Vietnam war claims lives of two"
           "Reveal proposal for $1.5 million Latin American center here"
           "Dr. Julian Nava calls for expansion of schools"
           "Open Letter to Governor Reagan"
           "*Adults to listen* Teens discuss social problems at confab"
           "Youngsters give view of career conference"

MAY 18   "Congressman Roybal ask Time apology"
           "*Meeting today* Citizens group plans school board protest"
           "*Electric substation site* Property owners oppose hearing today"
           "YTEP visit highlights Senators tour of area"

MAY 25   "8th Local youth killed in Vietnam"
           "Vietnam war hitting close to home; eight ELA youths dead!" by
               Dan Moreno
           "*Hinges on hospital construction* Federal grant sought to beautify
               Hazard Park"
           "Dr. Nava seeks upset victory"

JUN 1   "Dr. Nava takes early lead over Smoot"
           "Dr. Nava holds 11,000 vote margin"
           "Senate probes Latin education problems"
           "Beachcomber," on politics and AMAE

JUN 8   "Dr. Nava to take Board of Education Seat in July"
           "Hearings begin on Latin problems, Mexican-American rights probe
               at sessions here"
           "ECAC elects three area council delegates"

JUN 15   "*Discuss school needs* At long last, group meets with Governor, as
            tempers flare"
           "Citizens speak out on Civil Rights problems"
           "Schedule Senate hearing on Bilingual Education Bill"
JUN 22   "Charles Samario new president of CMAA"
           "ELA poverty board 'fires' new director," by Dan Moreno
           "George Brown claims high ratio Latins killed in war"
           "Report national progress on Mexican American programs"
JUN 29   "*Mexican-Americans* Senate group hears testimony on bilingual
            education bill, cite many benefits"
           "East LA Skills center celebrates 1st birthday"
           "Supervisors oppose EYOA narcotic addicts' aid plan"
           "*At Laguna Park* First bilingual leadership class in city receives
            diplomas today"
JUL 6   "10th ELA youth dies in Vietnam"
           "*Reverse decision*! County to seek Federal funds for narcotics
            project after all"
           "FHA topic of Cleland House Town Meeting"
           "MAPA to elect new officers at 8th Annual convention Saturday"
           "School board oks $640 million budget," by Ridgely Cummings
           "Property owners group to oppose master plan"
           "Mexican American affairs committee commended"
JUL 13   "Monterey Park pledge, No East LA annexation"
           "Latin community fetes V. Ximenez EEOC official"
           "MAPA Holds state convention this week"
           " 'Morin square' to honor local leader"
           "Three meetings discuss schools, Latin Center plans"
           "Karabian names new field deputy"
JUL 20   "Information center for Senior citizens to open"
           "MAPA plans for national expansion"
           "New East LA Library dedication planned for Thursday, July 27"
           "*Librarian named* Staff appointed for new East LA Library"
           " 'Operation Coolhead' comes to Belvedere Park Saturday"
           "New director named at Hazard Park"
JUL 27   "Group on aging elects new officers"
           "Pickets protest transfer of social worker at area poverty project"
           "Teenagers learn problems of police through new YTEP project"
           "Silver Star medal awarded E.L.A. soldier"
           "Your men in Service"
AUG 3   "$867,000 grant for ELA on-the-job-training"
           "Police chief attends 'hot' youth meeting"
           "Boyle Heights narcotics project awaits formal 'Go Signal' here"
AUG 10   "Peace group preaches anti-war beliefs"
           "Death takes Ed Quevedo Latin Leader"
           "Jobs needed for East LA youths—agency reports"
AUG 17   "Supervisors upset over Obregon Park land under-assessment"
           "Police chief speaks out at Youth session"

"East LA Area target for federally funded work training test plan"
"Congressional promise support for East LA Cultural Center"
"$41 million bill for bilingual education OK'd"
"East L.A. students join work experience programs at UCLA"
"Federal funding may be stopped for project aiding hard core delinquents"

AUG 24   "[Operation SER] Sign $5 million Latin job program"
"Fernando del Rio heads Eastland Action Council"
"Chief Reddin speaks to local youth"
"Board of Education urges passage of Bilingual education bills"
"Report 8,775 deteriorating buildings in East LA area"

AUG 31   "*Heads East LA project* MAOF names Arthur Fregoso job coordinator"
"[MAOF] Sign $million job training contract with Labor Depart, Special project to deal with Mexican Americans"
"Teenagers examine, discuss problems at student confab"
"*Sponsored by Health Department* Teenagers launch information campaign on venereal disease"

SEP 7   "East L.A. job project helps teens, community"
"Sign $1 million pact to aid Latin workers"
"Gala reception honors Dr. Nava"

SEP 14   "ELA paratroopers slain in Vietnam fighting"
"CSO trains Eastside Youth for leadership roles in community"

SEP 21   "Suit seeks ballots in Spanish"
"Name Ed Moreno head of MAOF bilingual project"
"*Manuel Veiga Jr.* ELA Businessman nominated for national service award"
"20% of Vietnam killed are Mexican-American G.I., Nearly 20% of all combat troops slain are Latins, says UCLA report"
"CMAA centralizes offices"
"HUD names new director for Southwest region"
"East Los Angeles woman named to HC Committee"

SEP 28   "SBA grants $1 million loan to "el Mercado""
"Request $1 million new jobs for unemployment"
"Raise minimum wage, Women, minors pay hiked 35¢ an hour"
"College financing for needy students topic of meeting"
"Dr. Nava to tour local YTEP Friday"

OCT 5   "*Mexican-American confab* Discuss Latins future in nation, Cutbacks in poverty program topic of MAPA meeting Friday"
"Local schools to participate in Federal narcotics program"
"Trade, vocational schooling MAOF trainees"
"*Gloria Estrada* Housing authority honors energetic NYC worker"
"*Mike de Anda* Civic leader is also actor"
"Latin actors union join antiwar rally at ELAC"
"Mothers Picket in Support of Euclid School Principal"

OCT 12   "*Dr. Lillian Tallman* Pickets support, oppose removal of Principal"
"Latin position papers reached for White House Conference"

"Roybal states position on Euclid school"

"Peace rally Sunday at ELA College"

"*Dr. Ralph Guzman* Directs $125,000 Economic Community project"

"Latin Lawyers give 'Lex award' to Dr. J. Nava"

"Dan Fernandez joins state Civil Rights unit"

"Former narcotic addicts assist at newly opened Narcotic Prevention Center . . .' '"

OCT 19 "Supervisor calls for investigation of job agency"

"OK Mexican-American parley, discuss programs, El Paso to be site of conference, President, cabinet to participate"

"MAPA boycotts Latin White House confab"

"Human relations workshop at three ELA schools"

"Educators' group honors Dr. J. Nava"

OCT 26 "El Paso hearings begin today on Mexican-American problems, Cabinet offices to hear delegates; varied presentations"

"Huge East L.A. delegation attends White House confab"

"Latin GOP group denounces 'LBJ's' White House conference"

"Dedicate bilingual health center in East LA County"

"Dedicate CMAA Head Start Center"

"MAOF officer spearheads statewide job training unit"

"*Councilman Lindsay* Opposes narcotic centers in Eastside business residential areas"

"Plan growth of LA topic of East Central Area Welfare Planning Council meeting"

"First Mexican-American named PO's Postmaster appeals board"

"Rigo Diaz Appoint Latin to small business advisory council"

NOV 2 "Top federal support promised at El Paso, Discuss specific problems, goals at Latin confab"

"*Supervisor Debs* Federal red tape costly hinderance to poverty war"

"Roybal hails house OK on bilingual teaching bill"

"*Discuss international topics* Four ELA schools send students to human relations confab"

NOV 9 "*Authored by ELA congressmen*, Bilingual, cultural bill wins House approval"

"Debs asks top priority for Latin needs"

"LBJ asks study on Mexican-American needs"

"Roybal raps EYOA cut back in teen posts"

"Discuss poverty war at EYOA community meeting"

"Educational opportunities topic of parent and youth confab"

"*POLARA* Latin Republican group commends school action"

"*Mrs. Aurelia De Anda* ELA woman's job—to help, assist people"

NOV 16 "Gov. Reagan keynotes YOF scholarship dinner dance"

"Vietnam War claims 13th, 14th Eastsiders, Former honor student slain in Vietnam"

"Grassroots audience sought at goals program"

"[SER] Launch job identification drive among Latins next week"

"Educational booths slated for Festival Latino exhibit"

NOV 23   "Vietnam war saddens holiday to two families"
"*In low skill jobs* Educational prejudice hurts Latins"
"Top federal, state officials tour East LA agency Saturday"
"*Educational confab* MAOF director urges citizens to speak out"
"Supervisors act on youths, suggestions"
"EYOA seeks agencies to direct NAPP, tenn [sic] posts programs"
"Eastside GOP rap renewal plan"
"*Ethnic survey* Mexican-Americans 1.3% of UCLA student body"

NOV 30   "Latin affairs minister feted by City Council"
"$100,000 scholarship grant to YOF"

DEC 7   "*Our Lady of Guadalupe* Thousands to march in procession Sunday"
"Education group raps Cal State teacher training"
"New Latin political group organizes, goal to unite votes power at confab"
"*Motivation is Key* Business leader urges teens to prepare now for future jobs"

DEC 14   "Peace group lectures on Vietnam Fri."
"Women's organization honored at luncheon"
"Latin collegiate leaders gather at action confab"
"Job corps continues recruiting drive in East Los Angeles"
"MAPA to award political science scholarship"

DEC 21   "City officials laud passage of bilingual education bill"
"YTEP honors employees advisory council"
"*Literacy law* East L.A. woman, man lose vote case"
"Busca to teach Mexican culture, history to students"
"Headstart aides prove valuable aid to families"
"City school employees enroll in Spanish classes"

DEC 28   "OK $3.1 million Building Program for local schools"
"Commission plans hearings on city charter"
"Information center for narcotics project approved"
"Vote power topic of CSO discussion"

1968

JAN 4   "Two ELA Marines slain in Viet ambush, war dead toll reaches 16 as new year starts"
"Latin political group [Congress of Mexican American Unity] sets plans for endorsing confab"
"*Hire more Mexican-Americans* HUD launches recruit campaign for Latins on college campuses"
"EYOA, Teen Posts compromise funding impasse"
"Six local residents joining NAPP outposts"
"East LA political activists back McCarthy peace slate"

JAN 11   "Former Head Start Chief [Leonard Pacheco] to Garfield education unit"

"Death of 'Coach Galindo' stuns community"
"County assists Spanish speaking job seekers"
"*Rental housing* 7-story complex to rise in City Terrace"
"ELAC students' group lash out at proposed University fee hikes"
"Upward Bound project adds more Latins at UCLA"

JAN 18   "Eastside Vietnam war toll mounts, two more local youth lose
      lives, Reported as 17th and 18th casualties of conflict"
"*In East L.A.* Spokesman for schools tells of unrest"

JAN 25   "Funeral rites today for Vietnam war hero"
"*At Cal State* Latin United Mexican American students stage rally
      over fee plan"
"Beachcomber," on Congress of Mexican American Unity

FEB 1   "*La Ley* Latin police group plans local dinner"
"Yorty's bid for model cities grant includes Eastside areas, Seek to
      improve housing, living conditions"
"[Debs] Ask revision of Federal welfare rules"

FEB 8   "CMAA begins search for project director"
"GOP overlooking Latin delegates for convention, claims
      POLARA"
"37 Candidates file for EYOA Poverty Election"
"[George] Brown names [Armando] Torrez, [Rigoderto] Diaz as
      field aides"
"Mayor urges industrial parks for vacant and undeveloped land"

FEB 15   "CFT president hits school board on ELA condition"
"American-Mexican sought for duty on draft boards"
"Judge Ben Vega elected presiding judge of district"
"Political season opens, candidates file for Office"
"Alex Aviles named specialist for school advisory groups"
"*Dr. Julian Nava asks* College education your goal? Check this
      unusual opportunity"
"Varied discussions highlight teen confab"

FEB 22   "Mexican-American endorsing confab Sunday, Latin groups to
      select, endorse candidates for state, local races"
"Flood of candidates vie for open 40th district seat"
"Vets administration to have office in East LA"
"New health center opens in Maravilla"

FEB 29   "*Mexican-American Unity Congress* Over 500 delegates at
      endorsing convention, Endorse Latin candidates for State
      office, OK congressional aspirants"
"Debs issues progress report of 'Neighborhood Improvement' "
"Teachers group [AMEA] slates 'talk in' Friday night"
"*Congressman reports* Mexican-American Viet War casualties
      high"
"*CMAA* Ask participation of Latins in police relations program"

MAR 7   "Speak-out on school problems set for March 30"
"Better school programs demanded for East LA," by Dan Moreno
"Student walkouts hit East area high schools"

"Bulletin: LAPD tactical alert"
"Rally to protest model cities program called"
"Philip Montez Western Director of U.S. Civil Rights
        Commission"
"Alex Garcia candidate for 40th Assembly"

MAR 14 "*Discuss school walkouts* Invite businessmen, residents to meeting
        at Maravilla Hall"
"Hazard Park case declared mistrial in first day of hearings," by
        Ridgely Cummings
"*CMAA study* Says schools ignored proposals for reform"
"Roybal raps VA on Hazard Park land swap"
"Lawmen, student protestors meet, discuss walkout problems
        here"
"Students confront school board with demands," by Ridgely
        Cummings
"*Pap tests* East LA Health Center offers important service for
        women"
"Federal [Housing] help for Mexican-Americans"

MAR 21 "Candidates in race to place name on ballot. Bill Orozco to oppose
        Congressman Brown, 40th District race attracts many
        candidates"
"Police appeal to 'silent' citizen for aid in murder"
"School walkouts is topic of council meeting today"
"Delegates to ask formation of political arm at state CSO confab"

MAR 28 "School board hears repetition of demands at Lincoln meet,
        Speakers split on tactics by militants," by Ridgely
        Cummings
"Speakout at Belvedere Jr. High Saturday"
"PTA group oppose walkouts"
"School walkout leaders still unhappy with Board," by Danny
        Moreno
"Ask naming of Latin to city housing board"
"*School grievances* Lincoln High meeting aired important issues"

APR 4   "*School board rules* won't select principals on basis of race"
"*Intimidation charged* Teachers rap school board on 'walkouts',"
        by Ridgely Cummings
"Crowther tells students that 'walkouts won't be tolerated' "
"*Judge Sanchez* Voices strong protest against militant leaders at
        speakout"
"*Dr. Tirso Del Junco* CRA [California Republican Assembly] elects
        first Latin in history to presidency"
"TV program on bilingual study feature Ford Blvd. students"

APR 11 "Nava wins one, loses four motions," by Ridgely Cummings
"Include Boyle Heights in model City plan," by Ridgely
        Cummings
"Latin directors to merge manpower under 'umbrella'
        organization"

"AMAE adopts education plans"

"Youth councils confab over summer needs"

"*ELA school protestors* 300 picket B of E meeting, continued demands for action," by Ridgely Cummings

"Introduce bill to protect land for public"

"ELA college to unveil Mexican-American mural"

APR 18   "More 'walkout' demands studied by school board," by Ridgely Cummings

"Citizens group forms ELA advancement council to solve community problems"

"Political Whirl"

APR 25   "*Federal commission* Ximenez calls for labor, community joint action"

"Walk out reprisals charged, Supporters complain to school board," by Ridgely Cummings

"Political Whirl"

"*Audrey A. Kaslow* named to Regional Manpower Advisory Committee"

MAY 2   "*IQ tests discussed* Board continues 'walkout' study," by Ridgely Cummings

"*Mexican-Americans* Education called inadequate," by Jean McDowell

"Political Whirl"

MAY 9   "Walkout opponents due today at school board, Parents hit by four demands by militants"

"UAW plans community project [East Los Angeles Community Labor Action Committee] here"

"Education rally Saturday morning at Obregon Park"

"Political Whirl"

MAY 23   "*Supervisor Debs* Keynote speaker at Senior Citizens confab"

"Board OK's integration proposals," by Ridgely Cummings

"*Wilson High panel* Speakers rap area student 'walkout' "

"Pickets demand teacher ouster at Lincoln"

"Political Whirl"

"Mayor Sam Yorty's youth committee"

"Schools to participate in 'Upward Bound' program"

MAY 30   "Predict light vote for primary election"

"Ask fair share of poverty funds for Eastside"

"School Board members study charges of prejudice," by Ridgely Cummings

"Medical payments Committee hears, charges of discrimination denied," by Ridgely Cummings

"Political Whirl"

JUN 6   "*Kennedy shooting* Police arrest Pasadena man," by Ridgely Cummings

"*Thirteen indicted* Claim walkouts were 'conspiracy'," by Ridgely Cummings

"John Leon to head new ELA instructional center"
"Eastside schools take part in integration programs"
"Closed hearing held on teacher's prejudice charges"
JUN 13   "Hear facts about secret indictments"
"CSO reports activities in East LA area"
JUN 20   "Announce low cost home improvement project here," on HOME
"Condemnation of ELA homes topic tonight"
"CSO reports on clean-up campaign here"
"Rep. Brown to address G.I. Forum state convention"
"*Assembly Bill* aids families displaced by freeway land acquisition"
JUN 27   "*Rep. Brown Says* California draft boards lack Latin
representation"
"Low cost home improvement program gaining acceptance"
"Three student walkout demands approved," by Ridgely
Cummings
"DA issues report on 'walkout' indictments"
"Students hear lectures on Mexican-American"
"Federal funds aid Eastside area educational and work activities"
JUL 4   "*Resolution criticized* Judge Sanchez hits WPC walkout stand"
"Judge Sanchez supports HOME improvement"
"Editorial: School Walkouts, Indictments bring mixed reaction"
JUL 11   "School board considers 3 Demands Favorably, Refer teacher
discipline, pools to committee"
"Dr. F. Bravo raps walkout indictments"
"*Latins still split* New council lines okayed," by Ridgely
Cummings
"*College seminar* Latin politics topic at Mexican-American center"
"*Will not attend sessions* Police advisory group member urges
action"
"*Dr. Nava, Chavez speak* Mexican American series at Cal. State"
JUL 18   "Plan ELA school Math Center"   .
"Housing Dept. officials to speak before town meeting group"
"Immigrant problems topic of meeting"
"Walkout defendants challenge Grand Jury"
"*East LA school issues* School board Okays report on demands,"
by Ridgely Cummings
"Hazard Park case before court today"
JUL 25   "Housing officials to speak at Town Meeting Session"
"Supervisor lists supporters of HOME loan program"
"Mexican-American bid for council area dies," by Ridgely
Cummings
"*Brown Beret warns* 'Advocate hell and you'll all burn'," by
Ridgely Cummings
"200 Eastside youth get YTEP employment"
"Mexican-American seminar concludes"
AUG 1   "Hispanic heritage week passes through House"
"Council approves new district boundary lines"

"Dr. Nava calls for social commitment, Anglos on borrowed time, says educator," by George Stewart
"Brown Berets hold 'open house'"
"CMAA names new Headstart director"
"Council OKs [Jim] Madrid for parks commission," by Ridgely Cummings
"Housing officials to speak before town meeting"
"Senior citizens invited to hear about 'HOME' loan program"

AUG 8   "School board continues study of walkout issues"
"OK purchase of 3.2 acres of land for Roosevelt High"
"Joe Maldonado appointed to top poverty War job"
"Over 200 Senior Citizens endorse HOME program"
"Property owners group hosts 'HOME' meeting"
"*Hazard Park* City wins round in hospital battle"
"CSO plans recognition night, Sunday, Aug. 4"
"Extend East LA narcotics prevention project"
"ACLU files lawsuit over council lines"
"*Social actions, trends* Review Mexican-American seminar activity at college"

AUG 15   "Walkout attorney ask felony charge dismissal Hearing set for Sept. 6 on 10 motions"
"Ximenes defends walk out goals—not tactics"
"*At hearing yesterday* 'Over-policing' is charged by Latin [Carl Vasquez]"
"*Immigrant problems* CMAA leader calls for action in congress"
"KMEX blasts East LA agitators"
"Save Hazard Park group to appeal Judge's decision"

AUG 22   "Property owners group to study HOME program at meeting tonight"
"*Ad Hoc Committee* Group demands review of Eastland Council Actions"
"Poverty area business protest job fund cut-off"
"Elected officials endorse HOME loan program"
"Editorial: Needed Eastside, Bridges of understanding not fences of hatred"

AUG 29   "New agency takes over nine CMAA Headstart centers"
"*ELA attorney* named police examiner"
"*ACLU* Seeks Injunction to halt 'walkout' trial"
"Air charges of police malpractice," by Ridgely Cummings
"Political solution for Hazard Park sought"
"Pastors support HOME loan area program"

SEP 5   "*Sillas takes lead* Return Sal Castro to teaching is demand," by Ridgely Cummings
"*National candidates* MAPA holds endorsing convention"

SEP 12   "Ask dismissal of walkout charges," by Ridgely Cummings
"*MAPA convention* vote no endorsement of Nixon or Humphrey," by J. McDowell; MAPA women, led by Mariana Vidaurri of

Colton, picketed convention, charging machismo and tokenism for women within MAPA

"Supervisors approve HOME application"

SEP 19   "Probe politics; 'chicanery' in 45th District"

"ELA College launches plan to help Mexican-American"

"OEO orders Eastland to reorganize"

"*San Francisco trip* Delegates file request for HOME loan project"

"Mexican-American Opportunities Foundation holds 'open house' "

SEP 26   "*At Lincoln Park* Councilman asks for 'Parque de Mexico' "

"Supervisors back 'grape boycott' "

"Bilingual education bill wins support"

OCT 3   "School Board decision on Sal Castro due today," by Ridgely Cummings

"*Pan American Bank* Announces Mexican-American housing developments, projects"

"CSO sponsors buyers club for families"

"Unity Congress plans 'Dia de la Raza' Fiesta"

"*Disregard intimidation* School board asked to support administration"

"Pickets keep marching at Lincoln High"

"OK changes in freeway expansion program here"

OCT 10   "Midwest conference on Mexican American set"

"*Younger declares.* Eastside majority against boycott"

"*Cancion de la Raza.* Premiere Mexican-American drama"

"*Teachers seek transfers* Chambers hits board reversal on Castro"

OCT 17   "*Federal project* Plan major improvements in East LA Library service"

"Lack of school sit-in ban protected by parent sit in," by Ridgely Cummings

"Must call shots as we see them—Nava," by Charles Cooper

"*Labor Dept. reports* L.A. Mexican American projects top $47 million"

OCT 24   "Defense seeks to quash 'walkout' indictments, Lawyers charge make-up of Grand Jury is illegal," by Ridgely Cummings

"*UCLA sponsored* Committee launches new training seminar"

"$80,000 low cost housing project set for East L.A."

"*Ximenez happy* Spanish surname areas progress"

OCT 31   "Jim Baiz nominated [East Central Area Welfare] planning council prexy"

"Youth training project celebrates Fifth anniversary in East L.A."

"Candidates in final week of election campaign"

"*Walkout 13 case* Grand jury make-up under test in court," by Ridgely Cummings

NOV 7   "New EYOA director appointed, Manuel Aragon Jr. replaces Maldonado"

"Agriculture Association honors Dr. Francisco Bravo"

"Voters return local incumbents to office"

"*Walkout 13 case* Judge rules Latins not kept off jury," by Ridgely Cummings

NOV 14 "Plaza may be built near LB freeway"

"Civil Rights Commission to Study Latin problems"

"LULAC honors councilman [Art Snyder], aide at awards banquet"

NOV 21 "Picket police station over arrest of boy, charge youth was severely beaten"

"Minorities form 46% of students in city schools"

"Drive for Latin identity result of youth revolution?"

"*Walkout cases* Judge will give ruling Monday," by Ridgely Cummings

NOV 28 "*School walkout case* Judge denies notions, indictments stand," by Ridgely Cummings

"Police issue statement on Barba Case"

"Grant Eastside model cities funds"

DEC 5 "$8 million federal grant for HOME loan program in area"

"Walkout case Resume dismissal debate Friday," by Ridgely Cummings

"Mexican-American Unity Congress elects officers"

"Casa Maravilla New Teen Center to open in housing project area"

"Felix Castro, foundation leader, honored by schools"

DEC 12 "Debs defines H.O.M.E. program purpose"

"Dismissal of walkout charges will be sought," by Ridgely Cummings

"Mexican-American Senate hearings on aging problems here on Dec. 17"

DEC 19 "Company awards $2000 to Mexican American foundation"

"*Local leaders speak* Examine problem of Mexican aged," by Ridgely Cummings

DEC 26 "*Charles Semario* CMAA leader honored for service to Head Start"

"Rep Roybal announces new ELA project"

"School walkout trial delayed until Jan. 6," by Ridgely Cummings

"Report on ethnic survey of apprentices"

1969

JAN 2 "County expands Spanish language training program"

"*For Latin youths* Committee meets to discuss drama classes"

"New poverty agency may take over Feb. 1 in ELA"

"East L.A. College to offer Mexican-American courses"

"Mexico border crossing cards to be extended under new rule"

JAN 9 "*Case resumes this afternoon* Lawyer for walkout 13 argue for quashing conspiracy raps," by Ridgely Cummings

"*Temporary Action* EYOA takes over poverty project in Eastland area"

"Black students hold rally at East L.A. College"

"Latin unity group to endorse Jr. College board candidates, Meeting Saturday at Belvedere Jr. High"
"22 candidates eye mayorality post as filing time ends," by Ridgely Cummings
"*Cal State L.A.* Minority studies department for Negroes, Mexican-Americans"

JAN 16 " '*Name calling*' charges School board clears Roosevelt teacher"
"Latin GOP plans state conference"
"*Junior college race* Latin congress backs four candidates," by J. McDowell
"TV film tells story of local youth center"
"Rep. Roybal announces new field representative"
"13 charges dropped in walkout case"

JAN 23 "13 walkout defendants win long trial delay," by Ridgely Cummings
"*East L.A. College* Chris Ruiz to head new Mexican-American Dept."
"Supervisor Debs supports more funds for bilingual education"
"Property owners discuss HOME loan program"
"[Alicía Escalante and Irene Tovar] Discuss problems of Mexican-American women on TV show"
"*Ex-Alcoholico* 'Mi etern gratitud al A. A. Grupo Latino Ameriano' "

JAN 30 "Tony Medina new director of Cleland House"
"Garcia rejects committee assignment, Assemblyman calls urban affairs job a compromise"
"Record rain storm causes 1 death here"
"Bilingual school announces enrollment for new quarter"
"UMAS sets open house"
"Employers hear problems of Mexican-American"

FEB 6 "*City schools project* Children learn English as second language here"
"*C. E. Serrano* Retired Sheriff's captain, Assemblyman's new aide"
"40th District MAPA Chapter to install new officers Feb. 15"

FEB 13 "Funds slashed for YTEP youth trainees"
"East LA group clashed with county supervisors over welfare program," by Ridgely Cummings
"*Free ride on ballot* Gilbert Lindsay assured re-election to council"
"Human relations workshop planned for men and boys in East Los Angeles"
"No 'Good Neighbor Homes' found in East Los Angeles"
"Mexican-American culture courses offered evenings"

FEB 20 "Propose Mexican-American schools study commission, 4 school board votes set to create units," by Ridgely Cummings
"Dionicio Morales heads ARMA, new manpower ass'n"
"*Belvedere Jr. High* Ophelia Flores appointed new girls vice principal"
"Unity group plans conference for endorsement"

"Eastside area crashes 'mess up' freeways"

"*California poll* survey reports favorable response to Latin TV drama"

"HEW chief seeks Latin educator for top U.S. post"

"*For bilingual pupils* School resources center to display new materials"

FEB 27   "Board OK's Eastside Area Education Commission members were picked two months ago"

"36-member panel [Mexican-American Education Commission] created on Latin school problems," by Ridgely Cummings

"Ross Valencia named Garcia's field aide"

MAR 6   "NE Model Cities board members to be named," by Frank Gonzales

"MAPA endorses Tom Bradley for mayor"

"Racial ethnic study on East area schools," by Ridgely Cummings

"Supervisors ask Finch to hold Welfare hearing"

"*Welfare demands!* Christmas bonus among list of 43 requests," by Ridgely Cummings

"MAPA endorses school bond"

MAR 13   "EYOA to run poverty war in ELA, 5 cities," by David M. Barron

"*Equal Opportunities Commission* LA industries report on efforts to hire minorities"

"*Dr. James Shields* New district health officer in Eastside"

"Unity Congress plans to honor 'walkout' leaders"

"Richard Alatorre wins $5000 Ford Fellowship"

"Health Dept. seeks bilingual counselors"

"Labor action group supports Senior Citizen project here"

" 'Model Cities not Urban Renewal,' " So says project directs, asks citizen action," by Frank Gonzalez

"Local labor leader [Esteban Torres] in Venezuela for discussions"

"$400 million for poverty war programs in county"

"Mexican-American history course offered at UCLA"

MAR 20   "*Dolly Zambrano* East LA YWCA chairman youngest to head 'Y' branch"

"School board pledges get through policy"

"No 'bulldozer' approach to model cities"

"*Una Vez Mas!* Panel to discuss Mexican-American problems"

"Brown asks population trend study"

MAR 27   "*Congressman Brown* Reports Mexican-American war deaths decreasing"

"*TELACU* ELA labor union action group has new name"

"Yorty for Mayor, Re-election urged"

"*UCLA UMAS* Seeks community support in demands for Mexican-America"

APR 3   "Bradley Edges Yorty faces mayor in run-off"

APR 10   "*CSO project* Plan 'walk thru' family park in City Terrace"

"School construction 'freeze' hits East LA"

"Barrios unidos meeting given for residents"

"Tommy Enriquez reappointed to Agricultural Commission"

"UMAS, UCLA report on 'Chicano' students"

"[EICC] Issues group attacks school dissent rules"

APR 17   "Sports Heroes City schools to publish booklets on Mexican Americans"

"Property owners group meets tonight"

"Tells steps for EYOA advisory unit at 'Barrios Unidos' meeting tonight"

"*Mexican-Americans* Cal State announces new teacher training project"

"*School Board* Membership in Latin Commission up tonight"

APR 24   "Barrios Unidos sets guidelines tonight"

"40 members ELA Schools' group approved by board," by Ridgely Cummings

"Martin Castillo appointed to Nixon's staff"

"Yorty names 4 to Model Cities board"

"Invite parents, public to narcotics forum at Garfield"

MAY 1   "*Barrio Unidos* Postpone election of local representative," by J. McDowell

"Mexican-American Studies at UCSB"

MAY 8   "*Barrios Unidos* Set election date for poverty representatives"

"City schools increase Mexican-American courses"

"City seeks to expand Malabar project"

"[TELACU] Union opens ELA mattress factory"

"College offers special course of Mexican Americans"

MAY 15   "*Barrios unidos*! Groups meet tonight ask candidates to File," by J. McDowell

"OK appointees to model cities board"

"CSO to honor supporters at dinner-dance"

"*Deb's poll* School unrest blamed on 'organized conspiracy' "

"OK appointees to model cities board"

"Mexican-American Culture Days at Trade Tech College"

"Mexican American law students report on projects"

MAY 22   "*Barrios Unidos* Extend deadline for poverty candidates," by J. McDowell

"Unruh guest at party for Irene Tovar"

"Ralph Guzman speaker at ELA Commencement"

MAY 29   "Congressmen rap decision rejecting bilingual plan"

"Yorty upsets pollsters, elected for 3rd term, Edges Bradley by 55,000 vote margin," by Ridgely Cummings

"Castillo sworn in to federal post [U.S. Interagency Committee on Mexican American Affairs]"

"Congressmen protest cutback of legal services"

"Cal State offers special program for Mexican-Americans"

JUN 5   "Barrios Unidos filing date moved to June 16"

"1970 to identify Latin Americans"

"Castillo, Quevedo named to top federal posts"

"State legislators back East Los Angeles bilingual school program, urge its funding"

"*Board seeks solution* Charge ethnic imbalance in EYOA personnel staff," by J. McDowell

"*Cal State LA* UMAS stirs-up support for nine proposals"

JUN 12 "Councilmen back Bilingual project"

"*Head Start* Centralization plan attracts opposition," by J. McDowell

JUN 19 "UTEP seek jobs for youths, call employers"

"Human relations office opens in Eastside area"

"Barrios Unidos election for anti-poverty posts"

"*Mexican-American students* Slate march, camp-in at Cal State College"

"Tell of HUD influence in L.A. Regional Planning"

JUN 26 "Supervisors ol [sic] split in Eastside poverty districts"

"Latino school officials meet in Washington"

"*Mexican-American* Principals named for Roosevelt, Hollenbeck"

"Protest cuts in Youth Corps"

"*Romana A. Banuelos* Pan American Bank elects woman chairman"

"Conference to discuss problems of ex-convicts"

JUL 3 "Zazueta opposes move to Roosevelt High," by Ridgely Cummings

"Walkout trial delayed pending Court appeal"

"City schools publish book for Mexican-American Studies"

JUL 10 "OK $400,000 for Malabar project"

"Model cities budget wins federal ok"

"UCLA recruitment office opens in East L.A."

"*Brown says* Hazard Park ok as VA hospital site"

JUL 17 "*District Attorney* Spanish speaking deputies assigned to service center"

"Squeaky wheel! Federal official speaks to forum," by Charles Cooper

"Plan major widening of Pomona Freeway"

"Ramona Gardens battles for park"

"ELA school group meets with board, Ferraro, Madirosian argue over Castro," by Ridgely Cummings

"Latin GOP group meets with state officials"

"*Bank of America* Minority home loans hit $11 million in first year"

JUL 24 "*Ramona Gardens wins* State to start sewer projects; park to go up"

"Spanish speaking right-to-vote bill clears final hurdle"

JUL 31 "Decision due this month on Azaueta"

"*For Mexican-Americans* Fund raising banquet for law scholarships"

"Silver Star medal awarded Lt. Zapanta Green Beret"

"*Floyd Manning* Belvedere vice-principal requests reassignment"

"Town meeting group to meet"

AUG 7 "MAOF opens membership drive"

"Dominguez brother now trio of police sergeants"

"CSO not to hire workers for Garden's park project"

"Youth group [Young Adult Leadership Project] battles 'adult' book store"
"Minorities for 17% of apprenticeships"
"Five men in running for Model Cities post"
"Maravilla mothers launch cooperative nursery school"
"Mexican-American studies program at Trade Tech College"

AUG 14 "Teachers, alumni voice support for Zazueta, Principal continues opposition to Roosevelt High appointment," by J. McDowell
"Lou Negrete backs Nixon's OEO proposals"
"Controversy over Sal Castro continues"
"UCLA offers 'Chicano' study course in ELA"
"Labor Dept. OK's program for Mexican-Americans"

AUG 21 "William Zazueta files discrimination charges against LA Unified School Dist.," by Frank Gonzales
"Youth arrest in police death"
"*Improvement project* Ninth home to benefit from Eastside project"
"*Edward M. Davis* New Chief named for Los Angeles Police"
"Debs supports President Nixon's welfare program"
"Yorty, Castillo at sister cities confab in LA"
"EYOA seeks management team to start new . . .'"
"*Rep. George Brown* Announces results of 29th District survey"

AUG 28 "AHORA debuts new series of telecasts"
"HOME officials announce 16th project in area"
"Model Cities boards meet here today"
"Zazueta hearing begins"
"Nixon to declare Hispanic Week"
"EYOA to hold hearings on president's plan"
"Plan 'executive training' seminar for Mexican Americans"

SEP 4 "*Minority group workers* Supervisors adopt new action program for jobs, promotion"
"Dr. R. Carreon re-elected police commission head"
"Sal Castro to appear on ch. 28 AHORA Program"
"KABC-TV to air special on Mexican-American problems"

SEP 11 "City council kills Hazard Park deal, Will still try for West Los Angeles Park"
"First home improved under ELA project"
"Seek Eastside residents for manufacturing plant"

SEP 18 "Lawsuit filed for Castro to halt transfer"
"Zazueta transfer voided by grievance committee"
"David Bubion, new dean of students at Cal State"
"CMAA seeks funds for new area school post"
"*Gov. Reagan* Names Judge Arquelles to Superior Court bench"
"*Oscar L. Gallego* Principal named for new occupational center"
"ELA school commission given new post"
"Sen. Goldwater to address Latin GOP group"

SEP 25 "Arnold Rodriguez named to new area school post"
OCT 2 "*Elementary schools* John Leon appointed East area coordinator"
"East L.A. Schools lowest in city reading, I.Q. exams"

"Castro supporters set 'peaceful' march Monday"
" 'Chicano' studies offered at new East L.A. center"
OCT 16   "Manuel Ruiz named to Civil Rights Commission"
"*Beachcomber* Mexican-American Affairs head speaks to local
      group"
"Mexican-Americans have highest Vietnam death rate, Dr. R.
      Guzman"
"Roybal demands removal of San Jose Judge"
"*East LA College* Report findings of area health research project"
"Annual MAOF Aztec awards dinner Oct. 23"
"KMEX observes Mexican-American Education Week"
OCT 23   "*Adoptions* Mexican-American kids find homes, parents"
"Bilingual health conference to air East Los Angeles problems"
"Model Cities post goes to L. C. Whitehead"
"Local poverty projects battle EYOA for funds"
"Ask School Board to improve reading programs in Eastside"
"Mexican-Americans graduate from executive seminar"
OCT 30   "Dan Lopez named to state manpower post"
"Readings still low but some rise shown," by Ridgely Cummings
"Beachcomber," by Alberto "Al" Diaz
"Herman Sillas named to civil rights unit"
"400 attend health problems conference"
"Seek Mexican-American librarian for Lincoln Heights"
NOV 6   "County to start major road improvements"
"*Head Start leader* bilingual education urged to raise reading
      scores"
"Coalition group launches battle to save anti-poverty funds in
      L.A.," by J. McDowell
"*Mexican-Americans* New committee to probe county hiring
      policies"
"Former convicts organize, seek prison reforms . . ."
NOV 13   "Model cities board plans election of committee here"
"Beachcomber," by Alberto "Al" Diaz
"Health problems here reported at meeting"
"*Mexican Americans* Cal State seeks to interest veterans"
"*Cleland House burns* Launch campaign to rebuild center"
NOV 20   "Danny Villanueva named manager of KMEX Spanish TV"
"Various ELA road projects started"
"Cal State names Alfred Fernandez to Direct Admission position"
"Gil Montano sworn in as SBA head in Los Angeles"
"*Mexican-American* Top health officer to hear areas problems"
"Sal Castro school transfer hearings end"
"Seek Mexican-American women for training in nursery field"
NOV 27   "Describe PTA welfare programs in East area"
DEC 4   "*Thousands march* Annual Guadalupe Procession Sunday"
"Review Funding of E.L.A. poverty projects Thursday," by J.
      McDowell
"Mexican American study courses at ELA UCLA Ctr"
"Set new reading policy for LA city schools"

	"Mexican-American Senior Citizen Club at All Nations Club"
DEC 11	"*Succeeds Judge Arguelles* Carlos Velarde named East LA Court judge"

"Model Cities Program needs citizen action"

"*Parents participate* Workshop on special school problems Sat."

"*Indian-Brooklyn-Alma* Supervisors approve zone change in area"

"*For Mexican-American* Educators' group seeks better schooling"

"Charles Samario reelected to second term as CMAA President"

DEC 18   "Head Start group fetes EYOA President, attends convention"

DEC 25   "*Jail-jobs failure* Government sets get tough policy with manufacturers"

"Council elects officers; heads report on H.O.M.E. program"

"Congress OK's bill to aid Spanish-speaking citizens"

"*Mexican-American* Program Foundation elects officers, cites goals at confab"

1970

JAN 1   "Plan Mexico LA cultural programs"

"*East LA libraries* show special interest films for young adults"

"Model Cities seeks Spanish speaking college graduates"

"*Hollenbeck Hall* Breakground for new 4 story resident hall"

"Councilman warns poverty group not to engage in political activity"

"*Commission says* Mayor should be able to fire, hire without City Council OK"

"Conducts census on consumer buying, Home Improvement plans"

"*In East LA* Despite increase in funds OEO may cut four programs"

JAN 8   "Drug awareness week at Roosevelt, Jan. 12–16"

"Reading improvement plan for local schools approved"

"*Mexican Americans* Marty Castillo speaks on 'Silent Minority' "

"President signs measure to aid Spanish-speaking citizens"

JAN 15   "*Alex Garcia* Assemblyman's bill would lower voting age to 18 . . ."

"Officials predict welfare crisis new year due to increasing number of recipients"

"Students submit 'Bill of Rights' to City Board of Education"

"Math, 'Chicano' study courses at U.C.L.A. East LA Center"

"Name Model Cities deputy administrator"

"ELA representatives testify at U.S. Manpower hearing"

"*ELA Community union* Group seeks Cultural center, offer plans"

JAN 22   "Hearing planned in ELA schools"

"Commission studies plan for plaza, Lincoln Park art, cultural site sought"

"New funds for H.O.M.E. project available"

"Model Cities plan deadline Aug. 31"

"*Manpower agency* Richard Amador heads Mexican-American group"

JAN 29   "Present criteria for Education Commission"
"Seek health aide in East LA for HEW office"

FEB 5   "Discuss Plaza de la Raza at Commission"
"Committee seeks aide for H.E.W. post"
"Narcotics information on clinic Thursday at El Mercado"
"Congress of Mexican-American Unity sets convention dates," by Jean McDowell
"Youth Opportunity Center provides many services"
"Mexican American named to state Veterans Board"
"Mexican-American studies at Immaculate Heart College"
"Ask for Latin Council Districts at hearings"
"*Leadership class* learns about problems by participation, action"

FEB 12   "Assemblyman Garcia's resolution asks impeachment of Judge"
"Alfonso Perez named Roosevelt principal"
"Archbishop Manning visits East L.A."
"Dr. Julian Nava seeks state post"
"Saturday-Sunday Mexican-American Unity Congress sets confab," by Jean McDowell
"Mexican-American builders organize, elect new officers"
"Pete Martinez named to schools' urban affairs post"

FEB 19   "Coroner's inquest on R. Hernandez Thursday morning"
"*LA Schools* Minority group students 48.4% of enrollment"
"Mexican American Unity Congress convention report, CMAA endorses candidates for June election"
"*Catholic Archdiocese* Issue statement, clarifies, defines role in community, government; announce formation of Inter-Parochial council"
"Congressman Ed Roybal seeks re-election"
"Ask U.S. funds to rehabilitate Eastside Homes"
"Richard Calderon candidate in 29th"
"School appeal integration order, Board favors move in 5-2 vote; East LA schools may lose special programs"
"C.S.O. protests on alley lighting"
"*At Lincoln High* Model Cities meeting set"
"TELACU seeks 'Big Brothers' for new program to aid youths"

FEB 26   "*In East LA* Veterans assistance center approved"
"Benefit program at unique Theatre aids LUCHA"
"Enrobing ceremonies for Judge Velarde Friday"
"Manuel Q. Sanz candidate for East LA judge"
" 'Chicano moratorium' march set for Saturday in East L.A."
"*Final Report* Mexican-American Unity Congress convention," by Jean McDowell
"Coroner's jury probes East LA jail death," by Ridgely Cummings

MAR 5   "Brown, Roybal first to qualify for ballot"
"Honor MAPA founders at installation banquet"
"2,500 take part in Chicano Moratorium"

"Telacu mattress plans expansion here"
"Seek 'guarantees' on Model Cities plan," by Frank Gonzales
"Richard Tafoya Montebello City Council candidate"

MAR 12   "*MAPA banquet* Civic officials, many guests attend installation"
"U.S. Census Office opens in Eastside"
"Request $100,000 for Hazard Park improvement"
"CMAU steering unity holds first meeting"
"Noted artists perform at Mexican American Unity Congress show"
"Mayor asks unification of Walls, East LA Model Cities program"
"Student unrest continues for third day at Roosevelt High School"
"*Apprenticeships* Report increase in number of minority youths in programs"

MAR 19   "Sam Cordova on Human Relations Commission"
"Roosevelt High situation quiets down, some students transferred; Parents called in to assist in keeping students in classes," by Margaret Velasquez
"[Southwest] *Council of La Raza* Foundation receives $1.3 million grant"
"*MAPA installation* Honor past leaders, Roybal, Dr. Nava speak," by Jean McDowell
"*Includes East LA* $107,000 grant to train 120 Senior citizens"
"Montebello Board hears talk on H.O.M.E. program"
"College President speaks on 'Minority Students' needs"

MAR 26   "Census Day April 1, forms to be mailed to homes Saturday"
"*Evening of Pride and Unity* Anthony Quinn, Ricardo Montalban, top Mexican stars at benefit"
"TELACU receives $160,000 grant for area economic development"
"MAOF protests police testimony before committee"
"Contract bids for H.O.M.E program street repairs"
"Farm labor offices opens in Eastside"

APR 2   "*Job training Award* $690,000 for new career programs"
"List deputy vote registrars in Eastside, court ruling changes literacy law," by Margaret Velasquez
" '*Pride and unity*' show Top Mexican American artists perform Sat."
"Mrs. A. Escalante named social service post"
"Still time to be counted in 1970 census"
"Hold interviews for bilingual airline stewardesses"
"*Catolicos por la Raza* Seven out of ten defendants acquitted"

APR 9   "*Mexican-American committee* Meets with officials, confer on various EYOA grievances"
"*Roosevelt High* Commission sets school grievance procedures"
"*Ricardo Montalban* Discusses Latin actors, movies on AHORA TV Show"

APR 16   "Supervisors to discuss adding representative of Mexican Americans"
"*From two areas* Elect 14 members to Model Cities council"

"CSO [suit] launched against water conditioning company"
"Mexican-American art on display at Mechicano Gallery"
"Judicial Commission recommends censuring of Judge G. Chargin"
APR 23   "Model Cities appointees announced; Resident councils also name
members"
"Armando Chavez selected new Cleland House executive director"
APR 30   "ELA Model Cities resident council meets first time here"
"*San Bernardino* Widening of freeway to close off East area off
ramps"
MAY 7   "Commission report [*Mexican Americans and the Administration
of Justice*] *in the Southwest* charges abuse of Latins"
"Ernest Sprinkles named to head EYOA Board," by Jean McDowell
"Jury weighs verdict in trial of accused 10"
"*At Laguna Park* Community Health Conference Saturday"
"Roybal endorsed by CMAU, MAPA"
MAY 14   "Psychology of Mexican American Class"
"*Commission report* Legal hurdles limit civil rights of Latins"
"CSO celebrates 23rd anniversary, sponsor dance"
"Hazard Park Assn. celebrated legal victory with picnic Sunday"
"Education commission supports school for suspended students"
MAY 21   "Files complaint charges community improvement program
inadequate"
"Reagan appoints Lopez to State Adult Authority"
"*East LA Health Survey* Improvement key to answer of 'health
crisis' in the barrio; committee reports on survey at press
conference on Monday"
"*LUCHA* Form statewide council for prisoner's rights, reform"
MAY 28   "Name Arthur Raya to HEW Health Post," by Jean McDowell
"Roybal, Lindsay, Garcia attend Aliso-Pico meeting"
"Eddie Ramirez tells why he's a candidate for governor"
JUN 4   "Parents committee seeks education improvement," by Jean
McDowell
"Schools told to help Spanish Speaking pupils"
"MAOF protests use of 'Zapata' in watch ad"
"Work plan approved for Model Cities law, justice phone"
"ELAC recruits students for new educational program"
"*Another Federal Study* Mexican Americans in 'caste system' "
" 'Mexican American' topic of Welfare Council meeting"
"County, HOME make East LA road improvements"
JUN 11   "Raya takes over new Federal health post on July 1"
"*Election Results* Reagan vs. Unruh in Nov. Danielson Wins Demo
nod. Judge Marion edges Sanz in close East LA judgeship
race"
"TELACU receives grant for Eastside home repair program"
"Supervisors back bilingual education program in LA schools"
"*Model Cities* Propose health assistance and referral center"
"Model Cities' task force; session set for next week"
JUN 18   "Roybal asks bilingual election information"

"E.L.A. Health Council to discuss local needs"

"Mexican-American Education Unit granted extended powers by board"

"Chicana Forum meets to discuss identity"

"Anti-Model City rally draws 200 at Lincoln"

JUN 25   "State OK's two acre park for Belvedere"

"Heights men [sic] named head of MC group; Residents Council holds election"

JUL 2   "Mechicano Center, CMAU hold feast to aid artists"

"ELAC receives $200,000 to continue project USTED"

"Younger seeks new trial for 'walkout 13' "

"Arte de los Barrios exhibit now at East LA library"

"Model cities staff restate program goals for area"

"New drug treatment clinic opens in area"

"Hung Jury Reported in Court Case"

"Tree planting project HOME area of Est LA"

JUL 9   "*22 arrested* Youth shot, windows broken on Whittier Blvd."

"*Elected President* ELA's own Dr. Nava heads school board"

"Roadway projects slated by HOME in East LA area"

"*Younger accused* 'Political moves' in Chicano trials cited"

"*Model Cities* Resident council OK's development proposals"

JUL 16   "*Legal Service Unit* Initiates 'police watch' program in East LA area"

"Model cities hears meeting reports"

"*Cesar Chavez* Guest speaker at TELACU anniversary," by Jean McDowell

"Vincent Perez to direct ELAC's Community Outreach Program"

"*Walkout 13* Judge hears motion for charge dismissal"

JUL 23   "*Hearing Monday* Despite election, fete Manual Sanz at dinner Sat."

"Model Neighborhood staff holds community open house July 26"

"*Manslaughter, Assault* Policeman face charge in deaths of unarmed men"

"*Bars prosecution* Court rules for walkout 13"

"Music, art, dance festival to benefit Mechicano Art Center"

"*LA Library* slates fall programs on Mexican Americans"

JUL 30   "*Vayan unidos* . . . Manuel Alcazar returns home with bodies of loved ones [Sanchez cousins]"

"CMAU plans 'peace march' August 29th"

"Spanish speaking Baptists convene"

"*$400,000* Boyle Heights narcotics center awarded grant"

"Council kills motion to reapportion city districts," by Ridgely Cummings

"County seeking Spanish-speaking elegibility workers"

"Case ends with 'landmark' opinion, Dismiss felony complaints, end prosecution," by Charles Cooper

AUG 6   "Judge Meyer B. Marion reaffirmed as judge after recount"

"Police, residents meet Aug. 12, discuss narcotics"

"Chavez signals end of strike, as committee protests union"
"*Measure on ballot* Voters to decide on more councilmen," by
    Ridgely Cummings
"Mexican consul issues strong statement on shootings"
"MAPA rejects GOP, Demos, back Romo"
"Francisco A. Gonzales, letter, on Sanchez cousins"
"Roybal endorses volunteer army, women's rights"
"Plaza de la Raza plans aired Sunday"
"*Mexican-Americans* Dr. Nava's book reviews Past and present"

AUG 13   "Schools report gains in reading"
"Literacy tests not required for voter registration here"
" 'EOP' helps youth enroll, succeed at Cal State LA"
"Assemblyman names legislative summer intern"
"Appoint new ELA school administrators"
"Bomb damages E.L.A. municipal court building"
"Meeting to review model cities action plan"
"CMAU holds Gran Fiesta Aug. 15"

AUG 20   "Court suit halt for two Model City projects, CMAU charges
    inequities in ELA, Watts programs," by Margaret Velasquez
"*$3000 per pupil* Eastside schools benefit from Title I funds," by
    Ridgely Cummings
"Snyder places three under citizen's arrest"
"*Action Plan*! Model Cities Council sets 26 projects"
"MAPA holds special session for membership"

AUG 27   "Launch business agency for Spanish-speaking, $10,000 check for
    Salesian boys club from vice president Spiro Agnew"
"*Law suit threat* Model Cities council okays $12 million in
    programs and projects," by Frank Gonzalez
"Urge minority contractors to bid on housing jobs"
"East LA Chicano Moratorium March scheduled for Saturday,
    Sponsors Predict more than 50,000 to attend Peace Rally,"
    by Margaret Velasquez
"Mexican-American history cultural projects at library"
"*Civil Rights Commission* Issue report on Mexican American
    students, schools"
"Jess Partida aids voter registration drive by COPE"

SEP 3   "Reporter describes incident at Laguna Park melee," by Jean
    McDowell
"Elected officials, candidates comment on Salazar death"
"Ask federal probe of riots, death of KMEX news director," by
    Ridgely Cummings
"Eyewitness account of scene as riot breaks out at park," by Mar
    Pacheco; excellent article and photos
"Pitchess gives view on East Los Angeles riot," by Ridgely
    Cummings
"Ruben Salazar didn't forget community," by Dionicio Morales
"March began with crown in peaceful, joyous mood"
"Business firms close in memory of Ruben Salazar"

"Fire bombs hit stores"

"Moratorium spokesmen express views, policy at press conference"

"$1 million damages to community, War protest march ends in death and destruction," by Frank Gonzalez

"Call for Peace, Unity in East Los Angeles: Editorial"

"Community mourns death of Salazar"

"La tragedia del Easte de Los Angeles como empezo, quienes son culpables"

SEP 10   "Coroner's inquest Thursday on Salazar death"

"Cancel September 16th Parade, Change note of 'El Grito' fete, Pro Parade groups, argue to stage event, committee sets meet," by Albert C. Diaz and David M. Barron

"Federal probe of ELA riot still doubtful," by Charles Cooper

"*Mexican American exhibit* City Central library holds day-long exhibition Sept. 13"

"Ask park renaming for Ruben Salazar"

SEP 17   "*Peace and unity plea* Parade goes on today [Wednesday] with floats, marching unit"

"Model Cities Board raps CMAU lawsuit"

"Approve plans for Belvedere, Maravilla Neighborhood Center"

"*Salazar inquest* Raul Ruiz shows photos, testifies"

"Senior citizens confab planned for Saturday"

SEP 24   "*East LA residents* Air views at Human Relations Commission," by Margaret Velasquez

"*Sept. 16 Parade* Disturbances mar annual fete"

"Arrcola names to Latin-American an education board"

"Civil Rights group asks probe of East Los Angeles Crisis"

"*Salazar Inquest* Witnesses testify on bar incident," by Ridgely Cummings

OCT 1   "$26 million Model Cities program is approved by Los Angeles City Council"

"New principals accept posts at local schools"

"Ray Carrasco appointed HUD area director"

"Police investigate night bombing of Roosevelt High"

"*Salazar hearing* Deputy who fired tear gas shell testifies," by Ridgely Cummings

OCT 8   "Protest Head Start cuts at meeting Sat."

"Model Cities passage topic of meeting Oct. 22"

"Salazar inquest jury is in a 4–3 split decision"

"Student gives views and opinions on Roosevelt High bombings," by Johnny Mosqueda

OCT 15   "Set meeting to protest Head Start budget cuts"

"*Mexican Americans* Reading problems discussion at Malabar library"

"CMAU announces two endorsements"

"Seek Grand Jury probe of 'terrorism' at East LA College"

"Model Cities Board meets this evening"

"County supervisors approve plans for new health facilities in ELA"

"PICA picks problems in education, seeks solutions"

"State prison reforms called for by groups," by Jean McDowell

OCT 22   "Demonstrations shake-up candidates in East LA"

"HUD approval needed to start Model Cities"

"Commission hears report on ELA police relations"

"*Petition* Seek federal riot probe"

"*Salazar death* DA won't prosecute in case"

"Roybal opposes Younger's decision on riot death"

OCT 29   "Know Your candidates"

"ELA Headstart groups protest $1.5 million cut"

"Assembly, house races election ballot Tuesday; Governor race tops political battles here"

"Survivors in Salazar death sue Sheriffs"

"School district reports success of Title I program"

"School teachers to attend workshop on bilingual training"

"Political Whirl," on Mexican American Labor Council endorsement of Younger

NOV 5   "Looks like Reagan, Tunney, Riles, Younger, O'Brien, nip & Tuck"

"Request for injunction on Model Cities dies"

"*Candidates sought* Model Cities seeks residents for boards"

"*$100 million* Law suit charges 'genocide' by law officers"

"Club Sonorense plans coronation dance Sat., Nov. 7"

"Thomas Serrato appointed page to U.S. Senate"

"Suit filed in shooting of Mexican national"

NOV 12   "Political scramble begins for open 27th District Senate post," by Charles Cooper and Frank Gonzalez

"Launch fund drive for Plaza de la Raza"

"Federal program calls for hiring of Spanish speaking"

"Cityhood group forms"

"Model Cities plans third community meeting in Cypress Pk"

"Chief sanitation guest speaker at Task Force confab"

NOV 19   "Manuel Ronquillo assistant dean at Trade Tech"

"Group files petition for recall of Councilman Gilbert Lindsay"

"Launch national campaign for Head Start funds"

"Police community relations group to meet at ELA"

"Mexican-American families with consumer fraud suit"

"County measures call for hiring of Mexican-Americans"

"Richard Ibanez to head LA Lawyers Club"

"Rep. Alex Garicia speaks at MAPA"

NOV 26   "*Martha Ramirez* Elected president of ELA-Montebello realtors"

"*Gloria Guzman* Coed to attend White House confab on youth," by Margaret Velasquez

"Local groups charge 'police harassment' "

"Three file claims against county, plan law suit," by Ridgely Cummings

"Police to expand office to handle more complaints"

"Mexican American heritage topic of Museum programs"

DEC 3   "Secret federal probe into riots, Key witnesses in Salazar death to testify"

"MAPA to elect new officers at meeting Dec. 4"

DEC 10   "City okays $16,000 for Ramona Gardens park"

"Model cities councils meet to discuss law suit . . ."

"Peter Garcia new LA civil service manager"

DEC 17   "Extension planned for East LA sheriff's substation"

"MAPA sponsors caucus to discuss reapportionment"

"*Decentralization* Citizens to attend special meetings"

"Public school desegregation favored, but not busing"

"Congressman Roybal calls for FBI's Chief's resignation"

"City reports 'steady progress' in hiring of minority workers"

DEC 24   "Pitchess, U.S. justice aide discuss riots"

"Model Cities elections set at Roosevelt High"

DEC 31   "*East LA Annexation* Hearing in Monterey Park January 7th on proposals"

"Gloria Guzman attends White House conference"

1971

JAN 7   "Chicano Caucus seeks freedom from poverty agency," by Jean McDowell

"Monterey Park to hear ELA annexation bid"

"East LA residents meet Tuesday to discuss school decentralization"

"$130,000 fire guts HOME headquarters"

"Police helicopter patrol piloted for Boyle Heights," by Frank Gonzales

"Demonstration called to protest LAPD January 9"

"HOME street repairs awared"

JAN 14   "Wind-up hearings on school's decentralization"

"Rudy de Leon appointed police captain"

"*Monterey Park* Planning commission votes against East LA annexation"

"22 testify on annexation"

"Community organizations honor Mexican American women"

"Anti-police rally slated despite weekend violence, Citizens committee marches"

"Museum presents Mexican American programs in Jan."

JAN 21   "Father Luce replies to charges by Chief Davis"

"$25 million awarded to Model Cities, Funds to provide jobs for 1000 L.A. youths"

"Ed Roybal announces $7,276,263 OEO grant"

"Monterey Park council to discuss annexation"

"Eastside residents speak out on decentralization, urge slowdown," by Margaret Velasquez

"Hold final rites for Manuel L. Arechiga at 'Chavez Ravine' "
"Dave Boubion seeks junior college post"
"*Civil Rights Report* Show Mexican-Americans hold few
      government jobs"
"Chicano Caucus reports agencies join group"
"Police Chief Davis claims Latin youths being used by Reds"
JAN 28   "Editorial: Urge peace in community"
"Chicano caucus to discuss ways, and means for direct funding"
"YTEP director reports rise of unemployment in 16–21 age group"
Letters on the protest march
"Review Mexican-American movement since the 1960s," by Ester
      Corral
"Labor Department adopts term 'Hispanos' to identify Latins"
"Richard Amador named chairman of HRD advisory board"
FEB 4   "School ethnic survey shows 'minority' students in majority"
"Riots cost taxpayer $$$$ Estimate damage at $141,000"
"Seven Mexican-American women honored for community
      service"
"1 Dead, fifty injured in moratorium, violence here"
"Reporter gives eyewitness view of rally and riots," by Frank
      Gonzalez
"*Says Pitchess* Deputies didn't shoot to kill during riot"
"LUCHA benefit Sat. to raise funds for reform"
FEB 11   "Sheriff fires three Central Jail guards"
"CMAU to endorse spring candidates"
"Senate hearing Friday on reapportionment"
FEB 18   "Recommend ELA area annexation to city of L.A."
"Monterey Pk City Council to vote in ELA annexation"
"*Reapportionment* Ask Mexican-American representation"
"*Minority survey* Racially diverse LA County population found"
"Msgr. Johnson, Fr. Arzube named auxiliary bishops"
"Advisory council to be appointed for Committee on Spanish-
      Speaking"
FEB 25   "TELACU offers pre-fab units for low-income housing in ELA"
"Elisea Carrillo new MAPA chapter prexy"
"Monterey Park OK's annexation move, County agency to proceed
      with public hearings," by Margaret Velasquez
"Julia Orozco named head East LA librarian"
"Hazard Pk. Assn. opposes proposed V.A. Hospital"
"Franklin Library closed due to quake damage"
"Ask local schools form new district," by Ridgely Cummings
"Model Cities meetings to grow in size, scope; youth included"
"Roybal visits school with bilingual program"
"Board to discuss Sal Castro move, educators protest"
"Planning Council has talk on census topics"
MAR 4   "City Bureau Says Boyle Heights blighted area," by Ridgely
      Cummings
"J. Alex Cota calls for positive ELA programs"

"Local Model Cities money OK'd, See 1000 new jobs in program"

"Expand Mexican American studies programs at UCLA"

MAR 11   "Form [incorporation] committee for East Los Angeles Cityhood"

"Barrio Free Clinic offers medical aid to community"

"Dionicio Morales receives Human Relations award"

"Art walk for Plaza de la Raza, March 28"

"Council OK's defense of three indicted officers"

"Close probe in Salazar death says Atty. General"

"Name two to reapportionment task force"

" 'Immigration and La Raza' topic of conference at ELAC, March 26–27"

MAR 18   "MAPA chapter endorses college, school candidates"

"Grand jury charges Brown Beret leader [David Sanchez] with draft evasion"

"Local seniors selected for pro-White House meeting"

"Immigration laws topic of conference March 26 and 27"

"Mexican-Americans & Indians gain Army land for University"

MAR 25   "*Ramona Gardens* $125,000 grant for recreation project"

"Council to review Model Cities contracts Thurs."

"Garcia warns legislators on reapportionment"

"Unveil Benito Juarez bust at Belvedere Park"

"Immigration laws topic of workshop"

"EYOA opens funding for community projects"

APR 1   "Police helicopter to visit various local schools"

"*Junior College race* 60 vie for five trustee seats," by Ridgely Cummings

"[Antonio F.] Rodriguez named cabinet director"

"Art walk Smashing success for Plaza de la Raza fundraiser," by Jean McDowell

"ELA Cityhood supporters to fight annexation: Abe Tapia to head special committee"

"$99,960 grant for Hazard Park development"

"*Federal aid* Senators hold hearing in LA this week"

"Consecration held for new Bishops, Johnson, Arzube"

"Catholic Welfare Bureau offers immigration aid"

"*Veterans Hospital* Report site will be at USC-County Medical Center"

"Cleland House launches drug information programs"

APR 8   "*Election Returns* Dr. Nava holds 50.9 edge, candidates face run-offs"

"Appoint Robert Medina Sr. Citizen Affairs Chief"

"*East LA* Annexation hearing Wednesday, Incorporation group to oppose move, seek legal support"

"Air problems on unemployment programming at Senate hearings"

"Rule Latins not kept from grand jury duty"

"Garfield begins experimental Mexican-American history units"

APR 15   "*Election Round-up* Dr. Nava thanks voters, Orozco, Lee in run-off"

"Urban Coalition hears views of ELA group"

"[Local Agency Formation] Commission may OK annexation"
"Board commends Boyle Heights narcotics project"
"H.O.M.E. Grant Recipient expresses thoughts on program"
"MECHA club plans school activities"

APR 22   "Commission OK's East LA area annexation, resent boundaries,"
         by Ridgely Cummings
         "*Hearing Friday* Officials conduct probe of Head Start . . .'"

APR 29   "Ask for new unit to do reapportionment, Legislature unfair to
         Mexican-American says Civil Rights Advisory Commission"
         "Group Forms to organize 'Day of the Chicano' "

MAY 6   "*Arnold Rodriguez* ELA educator wins Yale fellowship"
         "Officials probe, seek links in East LA bombings"
         "Authorize 31 Model Cities jobs"
         "College conference Discuss prison reforms, ex-convicts
         rehabilitation"

MAY 13   "Submit Model Cities Projects contracts," by Ridgely Cummings
         "Mexican-American educators sponsor conference at ELAC"
         "EYOA community elections set May 18"
         "HOME program aid totals $6 million"
         "Health official Reports success in Methadone program"

MAY 20   "Name director of Chicano Mental Health Center"
         "*La Raza Unida* Organize new political party"
         "MAPA chapters to endorse candidates"
         "County given ELA Cityhood report, Proposed City covers 6.14
         square miles, numbers 86,490 residents"

MAY 27   "Record 46% vote turnout, Orzco wins Jr. College race"
         "Invite public to reapportionment confab Saturday"
         "East L.A. annexation halted for one year"
         "*Home owner's effort* Improvement project expanded"
         "Elect Chairman Mexican-American studies at ELAC"

JUN 3   "Model Cities school APEX FUNDS ok'd"
         "*Barrio Housing Seminar* Seek ways to build low cost homes for
         residents"
         "*Hearing June 8* Ordinance designates city planning areas"
         "Review election results," by Ridgely Cummings"
         " 'Human Development' Bishop's program has 100 applications
         here"
         "Vikki Carr scholarships awarded to nine students"
         "Convention to discuss job training program for Latins"
         "Laud La Raza task force work"

JUN 10   "Seek support of residents for HOME program expansion"
         "L.A. county to build $11.5 million complex"
         "$226,000 OK funds for Hazard Park, Ramona projects"
         "*Head Start* EYOA cancels local contract"
         "Roosevelt High bombing linked to series of explosions in area"
         Map of area covered by HOME program
         "Research study shows students know constitutional rights, low
         awareness of civil laws"
         "Bill seeks to increase Spanish speaking doctors"

JUN 17   *"27th District* Statewide attention on crucial local race," by
            Charles Cooper
         "Model Cities school programs begin July 1"
         "Taxes, pollution, education major issues in 27th"
         "Veteran educator [Leonard Pacheco] to head ELA schools"
JUN 24   "Roberti, Brophy, Mount in vote run-off," by Ridgely Cummings
         "Investigate burning of youth center"
         "East LA College marks 25th Year"
         "Hilario Pena. New Roosevelt High School principal"
JUL 1   *"For LA Schools* Advisory councils ordered"
         "Four major Model Cities projects go into action"
         "ELA Phone Office Name John Casas as M. Chavez replacement"
JUL 8   "18-year-olds to vote in 27th election"
         "Grant funds to modernize city housing units"
         "East area Human relations council elects new officers"
         "Plaza de la Raza. Projects given official approval for development"
         "East L.A. Committee start endorsement Resolution"
         "OEO grants aid students, study 'poor children' "
         "Funding for EYOA drug programs in ELA approved"
JUL 15   "Bilingual classes to continue at local schools"
         "Bombers hit Pan Am Bank, Post Office"
         "Mexican-Americans Foundation objects to transfer of educators"
         "Luna, Roberti, Brophy battle for local seat"
JUL 22   "Roberti wins 27th Senate election"
         "ELA woman bank official may be U.S. Treasurer"
         "$1.1 million grants to East LA health projects"
         "Dedicate TELACU's low income housing units"
JUL 29   *"OK given* Plan to equalize population in Supervisorial Districts"
         "Set new election date for EYOA Poverty board"
         " *'Operation Brush-in'* Barrio clinic starts dental care program"
         "Aid Latin businessmen Dedicate NEDA [National Economic
            Development Association] East LA regional offices"
         "Name citizens to plan Boyle Heights"
         "Morales hits TV industry on Mexican-American coverage"
         "Trio charged with shooting of officer"
AUG 5   *"Mexican-American* Appointments to high U.S. Posts due shortly"
         "Form textbook 'Task Force', protest school books"
         "Fresno Attorney to head MAPA"
         "Pledge probe of 'police break in' "
AUG 12   "Okay Model Cities scholarship fund"
         "Supervisors OK improvements at Salazar Park"
         "Los Hambriados annual 'Fieston' set for Sunday"
         "Community mourns death of Manuel Veiga, Jr."
         "Ready programs Belvedere Jr. High meets on project refunding
            Wednesday"
         "Disturbance breaks out on Whittier Blvd"
AUG 19   *"Chicano Liberation Front* Group claims bombing credit"
         " 'OLE' sponsors second area health workshop"
         "Assemblyman Chacon asks probe of LA police"

"*Congressman Danielson* seeks probe of job pay-off by aliens"

"*MAPCA* Maravilla Action group sets goals"

"Report fire disturbances on Whittier Bl."

"*Henry M. Ramirez* Named Spanish-speaking Cabinet Committee head"

"Councilmen to hear police complaints"

"*In Lincoln Park* Sign agreement for Latin Cultural center [Plaza de la Raza]"

AUG 26   "*Model Cities* U.S. ok's transit project"

"ELAC drug abuse project receives $41,000 HEW grant"

"$111,000 training grant set for disabled Mexican-Americans"

"Fire destroys garment firm, suspect arson"

"*Ruben Salazar* Mark anniversary of newsman's death"

"Model Cities grants funds to Cal. State"

"*Urban Coalition* Report high jobless rate among minorities"

"Model Cities resident job plan OK'd"

SEP 2   "*Garfield High* Jesus Rodriguez new adult school principal"

"*48th District* Eight seek Assembly seat"

"Few incidents reported on Sunday"

"Slate Feria de la Raza at Cal State College LA"

SEP 9   "*Decentralization* East LA schools have own area"

"New commanders named for Hollenbeck"

"*Mexican-American* Nixon names educator to Cabinet"

" 'School' for priests opens here"

"*Boyle Heights* Protest library services"

"*Drug abuse* Addiction patterns differ in barrios"

SEP 16   "$500,000 improvements due at Belvedere post"

"Youth group protests libraries"

"*Channel 28* 'Chicano movement' topic of television special"

"*No minority history* State board rejects new school books"

SEP 23   "Mrs. Maria Rojas now on EYOA board"

"*Mrs. Romana Banuelos* ELA woman new U.S. Treasurer"

"*Invite Mexican-American* Reapportionment hearings Thursday in Los Angeles"

"Arsonists set fire at Garfield High"

"*Mexican-Americans* Singer, Bishop join reapportionment drive"

"*Spanish-speaking* Cabinet Committee to undergo major changes"

"Yorty proud of city's Mexican heritage"

SEP 30   "Campaigning continues in 48th district race"

"MAPA gives backing to school bonds"

"Roybal calls conference [National Coalition Conference for Spanish Speaking Americans] for U.S. Latins"

"State reapportionment battle looms in East LA"

"Nixon names Latins to U.S. posts"

"*Spanish speaking* Roybal leads battle for more federal jobs"

"TELACU opens food stamp outlet"

OCT 7   "Reapportionment hearing slated"

"Latins walk-off EYOA job officer"

"Park open spaces City seeks funds for northeast area"

OCT 14   "OEO to investigate EYOA"
         "48th Assembly race in final five days"
         "*Underemployment in Barrios* MAOF study sees worsening job
            problems"
         "Second ELA youth dies in gang shooting"
         "*Illegal Aliens* Controversy erupts over arrests at Banuelos plant"
         "Reapportionment Ask East LA Senate Seat"
         "*Planning for Barrios*: Planners to meet at Plaza Center"
         "Model Cities funds to aid young offenders"
         "Bishop Arzube speaks at Catholic Women's Confab"
OCT 21   "*48th Dist. Election* Alatorre, Brophy in run-off," by Ridgely
            Cummings
         "*Mental health project* Launch new barrio training program"
         "Urge Latin Council Dist," by Ridgely Cummings
OCT 28   "Candidates file expenses"
         "Review set of reading programs"
         "Danielson enters battle on hiring of 'illegals'"
NOV 4   "Four battle in 48th Dist. race"
         "*Spanish-speaking* Congressman Roybal sues U.S. for
            discrimination"
         "*Ethnic balance* EYOA ordered to prepare plan"
         "R. Tellez named to U.S. Commission"
         "UNIDO; unity conference program on KMEX-TV"
         "SER project opens new location"
         "Planning Commission to hold night hearings"
NOV 11   "Charges, demonstrations mark lively 48th District election," by
            Charles Cooper
         "*Demand Recount!* Tunney asks census dept. for survey of
            Mexican-Americans"
         "Plaza de la Raza membership drive on"
NOV 18   "*Reapportionment* East LA senate district proposal before
            legislature"
         "OK plans for new play area at Ramona Gardens"
         "EOYA walkout goes on, urge settlement"
         "El Arca sets conference at East LA College"
         "Brophy upsets Alatorre for 48th District seat, Outpolls Alatorre
            by 1500 votes, Ruiz gets 2000"
         "Barrio free clinic gets $9600 grant"
NOV 25   "Expect new changes in state Senate reapportionment plan," by
            Charles Cooper
         "Candidates analyze win, losses in Assembly race"
         "New city hall, police Spanish language phones"
         "Farm workers' benefits bill goes to Reagan"
         "*Local Housing Chief* Low income housing-low priority"
         "Study university relations with Mexican-Americans"
         "Community group asks park improvements"
DEC 2   "*Education Commission* Sets hearings on school punishment
            complaints"

"*Police complaints* Lindsay reports LAPD action on 131 cases"
"Governor may veto state reapportionment proposal"
"Garcia hits congress district plan"
"*Banuelos Appointment* Senators hit alien raid"
"D.A. announces narcotics . . . at Mexico Conference"

DEC 9   "*Open Offices Here* Mexican-American contractors unite"
"Girl dies from shooting at Salazar Park"
"Elect Judge Carlos Velarde ELA Court Presiding Judge"
"Civil rights body finds schools lacking"
"Appoint Dr. Edward A. Aguirre Labor Dept. regional director"
"Mexican Americans sought for city jobs"
"East LA GOP group speaks our [sic] on reapportionment"
"Offer immigration counseling services at Plaza Center"

DEC 16   "Urge census bureau to recount Spanish-Speaking"
"*Edward R. Roybal* Congressman reviews federal programs, visits
      ELA schools"
"Top level meeting on EYOA"
"*First St. Store's* Mural depicts history of Mexican Americans"
"*Letter to Editor* Ex-gang member warns youth"

DEC 23   "Launch campaign to build new library for Boyle Heights"
"Mayor appoints two to EYOA board"
"Commission approves Plaza plans"
"Seek job talks on Spanish speaking"
"*Civil service commissioner* Report on city jobs held by Mexican
      Americans"

DEC 30   "Local youngsters show gains in exams"
"File suit to halt students' I.Q. exams"
"Youth dies in police chase"

1972

JAN 6   "$324,400 financial aid for ELA college students"
"$800 per acre annexation fee dropped by city"
"File suit to test new law on hiring illegal aliens"
"Catholic Agency [Campaign for Human Development] aids
      Mexican American group"
"Reagan vetoes apportionment," by Charles Cooper
"Yorty visits Model Cities projects"
"Health task force head resigns"

JAN 13   "Maravilla group [Association for Progressive Community Action]
      gets $50,000 grant"
"Groups honor East L.A. office district attorney"
"*Model Cities Project* 'One stop' immigration service at new
      center"
"*Jobs of aliens* New law puts onus on employer," by Jerry Lench
"Plan new Maravilla Projects, See townhouse apartments for new
      public housing development"
"Mecha club announces plan for school murals"

JAN 20   " 'Med Ocho' future in doubt, Hospital project may continue
        without Model Cities funds"
      "Favoritism in hiring for project charged"
      "Reader questions facts on city Latin employees"
      "Senior Citizens form area health committee"
      "Set meeting for model cities project"
      "City study tells area past, present," by Ridgely Cummings
JAN 27   "New 30th Congressional District lines announced"
      "Apportionment group continues . . ."
      "*Ethnic Survey* Schools minority enrollment 52.4%; Spanish
        surname 22.7%"
      "Model City forms health clinic council"
      "*Mexican-American* Works in Washington & open up new jobs"
      "*Planners report* Boyle Heights colorful history, Area includes
        incorporated East LA portion," by Ridgely Cummings
FEB 3   "Name director of development group"
      "Seek long time resident for Plaza de la Raza groundbreaking"
      "Openings for Vietnam vets at MAOF"
      "*Alex Avilez* Name Garfield High principal"
      "Informant tells of work for police here"
      "Report complaints against LAPD were 'sustained' "
      "Chicano health conference held"
FEB 10   "Gil Montano new SBA chief"
      "*Hoyo Maravilla* Dedicate new boxing ring Sunday at Obregon
        Park"
      "East LA women risk high cancer danger"
      "EYOA to face La City quiz"
      "Reagan questions minority support for Democrats"
      "*Model Cities* Residents council to review proposals"
      "Ramona Gardens woman honored by EYOA"
FEB 17   "*Drug Abuse Institute* Casa Maravilla man at Washington confab"
      "Census Bureau conducts job, jobless survey"
      "*Garfield High* New principal brings years of knowledge,
        experience," by Anne Burdick
      "Alex Garcia first to file for 40th Assembly seat"
      "Fete Roybal for 25 years of public service"
      "Four new principals at East LA schools"
FEB 24   "Nine East LA gangs declare end to warfare"
      "*Hazard Park* ceremonies mark project completion"
      "MAPA chapter to install new officers"
      "*USC studies* Teachers don't understand pupils"
      "Roybal urges repeal of alien hiring law"
      "Deny federal funds for new library"
      "Lincoln Park Phase I begins for Plaza de la Raza"
      "HUD names Latin coordinator"
      "Stars, officials set for Nosotros fete"
      "*School board* Ethnic Commissions survive vote"
      "Rosalio Munoz freed on draft evasion charges"

MAR 2   "N.E.D.A. Ok $2.8 million for minority business"
         "*Appeals to HUD* Rep Roybal wants low income housing"
         "*Model Cities project* Development Corporation to aid East L.A.
              business"
         "*Improves attitudes* New Program to help teachers"
         "Mechicano Art center celebrates first year"
MAR 9   "Three youths die in separate shootings"
         "Expect Brophy to file for congress, Brophy filing likely today in
              30th race"
         "EYOA fights loss of program contracts"
         "Open nominations for Model Cities council"
         "CSO prepares for 25th anniversary"
MAR 16   "*Invite Nixon* Honor Mexican-American presidential appointees"
         "*40th District* Art Torres enters race for assembly"
         "*Plaza de la Raza* Break ground for new cultural center Tuesday"
         "3.1 million Mexican Americans in California"
         "CSO celebrates 25th year"
         "Roybal backs expanded public works program"
         "New HUD registry to list Latin housing specialists"
         "*Spanish-speaking* Federal agency seeks applicants"
         "Parent teacher confab set"
MAR 23   "*Primary Election* Roybal, Garcia face major opposition June 6"
         "600 attend Plaza Center ceremonies," by Ridgely Cummings
         "*Congressman Roybal* Demands Latin job information"
         "Discuss zoning of central area planning council"
MAR 30   "Propose change in new building here, Businessmen oppose
              modern design for neighborhood center"
         "*UCLA study* Report high teenage jobless rate"
         "*Barrio Planners* Young planners to study visual environment of
              ELA"
         "*Mexican American businessmen* Better Business Bureau seeks
              local help"
         "Fight police academy use of Elysian Park"
         "Lindsay says he backs EYOA"
         "John Chavez gets No. 2 EYOA post"
APR 6   "OK funds for Belvedere Park"
         "Barrio free clinic seeks community aid"
         "Plaza center begins war against vandals"
         "Property owners ask paving of alley"
         "Bilingual classes vital to pupils"
APR 13   "Deputy DA named to East LA office"
         "Federal officials to school, community sites"
         "OK Phase II of Hazard Park work"
         "Nineteen candidates run for Model Cities residents council"
         "Young artists display paintings at festival"
         "Immigration center provides services for community"
         "Lindsay says city should build parks in Eastside"
         "Two Eastside intersections placed on city's critical accident list"

APR 20   "Reagan threatens EYOA fund veto," by Ridgely Cummings
"Model Cities candidates vie for seven council posts"
"Former ELA man [Ricardo Chávez Ortiz] held in skyjacking"
"Anti-drugs rally at ELA College"
"Debs reports HOME program near finish"
"Journalism workshops set for minority students"
"Chicana conference planned for April 29"

APR 27   "*HOME Program* DA protests legal action on homeowners"
"Reveal plan for Maravilla development," by David Barron
"Bilingual program refunding sought"
"*Decentralization* Residents speakout at hearing"
"*Health careers* Youths invited to conference"
"Garcia hits schools for new Title I rules"
"Torres charges Garcia opposed farm labor bill"
"*White Memorial Hospital* Breaks ground for new addition"

MAY 4   "[U.S. Commission on] *Civil Rights Study* Language, cultural ties
handicap Barrio pupils"
"Bibliotecas announce cultural activities"
"Hispanic GOP unit honors Henry Ramirez"
"*Reflecciones* KABC-TV introduces new program"
"John Anson Ford heads Roybal group"
"*Plaza de la Raza* Future Latin cultural center planned"
"Chicanos gain foothold on TV," by David Barron
"Justice battles Latin 'image' in TV, movies"
"Lincoln Heights, El Sereno people handle top community jobs"
"Raza Unida party moving ahead"
"List elected Latin officials"
"Mexican-American Barrio murals tell story of culture"
"*El Arca Project* Build retarded children's center in Lincoln
Heights"
"Cesar Chavez endorses Torres for Assembly"
"Model Cities—New hope for area," by Roger Swanson

MAY 11   "New corporation remodels old homes"
"See early construction of Maravilla housing project"
"Model cities election still undecided here"
"*Roosevelt High* Narcotics prevention program underway"
"*Latin engineers* Launch space information project"
"Model Cities"

MAY 18   "Election tests Area high schools below city wide, national
averages"
"Monterey Park delays annexation action"
"Mobile narcotics display"
"Dedicate Hispanic Center"

MAY 25   "Protest firing of ELA College president, Faculty leaders support
prexy at press conference"
"Proposed Mexican-American Council district"
"Seek NYC slots for Mexican American youth"

JUN 1   "District attorney to probe H.O.M.E. project in East LA"
          "New ELA sheriffs captain [Miguel Gutierrez] announced"
          "Assembly, Presidential race tops election"
          "Youth group works on community murals"
          "City approves minority hiring action program"
          "Set Model Cities meetings"
JUN 8   "McGovern ahead, its Roybal vs. Brophy in Nov."
          "*Maravilla Project* Expect construction to start this summer"
          "Supervisors ask for funds to fight drug abuse"
          "DA after immigration frauds"
JUN 15   "Garcia, Roybal, Brophy win"
          "Mayor addresses ELA Unit"
          "*Belvedere Park* County rejects bids for Phase II Development"
JUN 22   "*Mexican American* women seek unity, advancement in business"
          "*Priest Predicts* Latins to 'possess' California"
          "Armando Morales receives doctorate degree at USC"
          "*Frankling Library* Seek $100,000 for new library"
          "*Art Torres* Defeated candidate forms group"
          "Raza Unida party plans convention"
          "*Mexican-Americans* Offer graduate program for media librarians"
          "Ford tells role of Latins at local plant"
JUN 29   "Approve model care center in East LA, center to care for 600
               children of working parents"
          "Controversy brews over new library"
          "Human relations bureau revived in city budget"
          "Area Councils to decide on poverty funds"
          "PICA slates summer program at Salazar Park"
          "Raza Unida Party sets convention"
          "*Congressman Roybal* Push major reform for U.S. Border Patrol"
          "Labor Dept. honors Latino employer"
JUL 6   "Med Ocho hospital program extended," by Ridgely Cummings
          "City council asks $26 million for Model Cities' second year"
          "Bilingual programs to continue at five elementary schools"
          "Report criticizes EYOA operations"
          "*Census Report* Tell population, facts of status Latin people"
          "HRD opens new job office in Boyle Heights"
          "MAPA chapter to install officers"
          "Latin scholarship group raises $5300"
          "Bill requires school to hire bilingual employees"
          "DA files suit against immigration counsels"
          "Labor Dept. learns needs of minority news media"
JUL 13   "Raza Unida Party tells '72 platform"
          "Ray Andrade charged with setting off bomb"
JUL 20   "Hearing on County Charter Amendments, Session July 25,
               Proposal would increase Board of Supervisors from 5 to 7"
          "OEO money $1.2 million health program for Eastside"
          "Spanish-speaking youths take part in U.S. sponsored project"

"*For Maravilla area* Federal grant for neighborhood facility"
"*Model Cities* OK funds for indoor swim pool at Roosevelt High"
"*East L.A. Residents* group seeks to annex to Monterey Park,
  Grant request to circulate petitions"
"Name Mexican-American to Interstate Commerce Commission"
"Se inicia el Concurso de La Beneficencia"

AUG 3   "Mardiroscian to announce results of special class"
"Supervisors OK $4 million Health Center in East LA"
"Model Cities area councils meet Thursday night"
"Urge EYOA financing for rest of '77," by Ridgely Cummings
"Plaza de la Raza seeks employees"
"*County Commission* Grants time to pursue East LA annexation,
  Despite Vigorous protests, plan to annex 252 acres plus
  college"
"*ELA attorney* appoint Carlos J. Garcia to City Human Relations
  unit"

AUG 10   "Vikki Carr scholarship grants for 19 students"
"Veterans' Hospital in ELA 'A must' says Debs"
"Model Cities second year delay seen"
"The 'New Look' artists . . . paint brushes, murals vs. grafitti"
"Astigmatism prevalent in Mexican-Americans"

AUG 17   "Discuss bids for new Maravilla Project"
"City Council OK's new districts," by Ridgely Cummings
"Boyle Heights Model Cities Council meets"
"MAOF to offer courses for jobs in legal systems, fields"
"Maria Rios . . . a story of courage, inspiration"

AUG 24   "City redistricting due for council vote"
"*More than doubles* Mexican Americans increase in county"
"Mural at hospital honors memory of Ruben Salazar"
"*August 29* Marks anniversary of ELA disturbances"
"$630,000 grant for health task force"
"*Board to hear* Report on school-community advisroy councils
  Thursday"
"Praise G.I. Forum as example of 'Patriotism' "

AUG 31   " 'Chicano Service Action Center' [La Comision Femenil
  Mexicana, Nacional, Inc.] opens Sept. 8"
"*ELA Municipal Court* Enrobing site for Judge M. Gonzalez"
"NE residents protest new district lines"

SEP 7   "*40th district* Raul Ruiz qualifies for election"
"Model cities program ok'd by city"
"*By 12-1 vote* Council approves redistricting plan," by Ridgely
  Cummings
"*Metro MAPA* endorses three candidates for Nov. election"
"Model Cities Social Service task force special election"
"*Plan court action* EYOA takes terminal grant"
"Councilman gives view on restricting," by Art Snyder

SEP 14   "*Reapportionment* Mayor may act on measure today"
"Submit annexation petitions"

"Heckle [Ted] Kennedy at East LA rally"
"Nixon proclaims National Hispanic Heritage Week"
"CSO queen contest Saturday"
"Roybal reports extension of anti poverty projects"
"LULAC Council hosts parade watch"
"Two-day 'Feria de la Raza' at Cal-State U LA"
"Teatro de la Tierra performs at EYOA"

SEP 21   "Reading scores of youngsters in 1st, 2nd, 3rd grades UP!"
"List improved reading scores at local schools"
"Brophy out of race for congress," by Charles Cooper

SEP 28   "Snyder now represents city's 14th Council District"
"L. Whitehead vows to keep Model Cities job"
"Hold public hearing on proposed ELA annexation, session
        Monterey Park City Hall"
"Before election Suit to challenge new district lines"
"ELA Property Owners group elects officers"
"D.A. Joe Busch Seeks funds to reopen Casa Maravilla"
" 'Visual Survey' $60,000 contract for E.L.A. Barrio planners"
"OK $55,000 Redevelopmetn Contract for Maravilla renewal
        project! *218 Acre Area*! Plans call for architectural control,
        commercial, industrial development"
"Change of Barrio Free Clinic, set open house"
"CSO Consumer complaint center"
"1st phase of Plaza de la Raza nears completion"

OCT 5   "OK temporary site for library set public meeting, October 11"
"Monterey Park drops East L.A. annexation! Ad Hoc group to seek
        incorporation"
"Queremos mas Doctores Mexico-Americanos"
"Programa de Ayuda a Drogas-adictos"
"Mexican-American Report more opportunities in health
        professions"

OCT 12   *"In schools* Board gets tough on guns, other arms"
"Board of Grants Votes to oust Larry Whitehead"
" 'Operation Estafadores' topic of 'Focus' KNBC show Sat."
"Local attorney heads National Housing Corp."
"Mrs. Mary Gonzales Mend Directs administrative intern teachers
        project"

OCT 19   "Councilman Snyder reopens Eastside field officer"
"Businessmen to hear talk on incorporation"
"Award contracts to renovate Ramona Gardens"
"MAPA No endorsement for President in election"
"Minority students seek health service careers"
"Release findings on U.S. border procedures"
"Seek film entries from young Chicanos"
"Dinner honors GOP Assembly candidate"
"Bilingual nurses' class to graduate"

OCT 26   *"M.A.O.F.'s* 19th anniversary Aztec Awards honors community
        leaders"

"*New contract* S.E.R. to continue service programs"

"IMPACTO sets Reachout File"

" '*Vida Nueva*' new publication in debut"

NOV 2   "*$2 million* Job training program for Spanish-speaking"

"OK millions for second Cities' year"

"MAOF's Golden Aztec Award to Gil Mejia"

"City council votes to establish new EYOA," by Ridgely
        Cummings

"City Housing May take over Model Cities unit"

"Candidates in final week of Election '72 Campaign"

"Newspapers endorse Dan Nolan, Recommend election of Busch,
        Fenton, Roybal and Garcia"

NOV 9   "Maravilla Neighborhood Development Program, Group elects new
        officers, set meeting dates, progress report"

"Break ground for new 504 unit Maravilla Housing project"

"EYOA is now Community Action Agency (CAA)"

"Nixon landslide win! Record Vote turnout at polls"

"Model Cities begins 2nd Action year"

NOV 16   "Offer seven-step plan to reduce violence in schools"

"*Congressman Roybal* Seeks fair share of poverty funds for
        Mexican-Americans, Wants firm statement of policy"

"Ok plans for 2nd phase of Ramona Park"

"*Election Bound-up* Incumbents win Assembly, Congressional
        posts here"

"Chicano art concepts at college"

"Discuss 'Chicano' music on KLOS"

NOV 23   "TELACU receives $1 million community development grant"

"Nam Pan Am Bank President to SBA Council"

"Ready announcement of East L.A. Health Systems, Officials,
        Board members slate dinner meeting Monday night, outline
        programs"

"Bob Apodaca named Snyder's fieldman"

NOV 30   "Telacu recibe $1 million para desarollo de East LA"

"Invite public to local health forums, Dec. 4–5"

"Sam Cordova to head City Human Relations Unit"

DEC 7   "Name Maravilla Neighborhood Project Committee Members"

"HUD freezes some Model Cities funds"

"*Testimonial Thursday* Honor Arnold Martinez, assist Big
        Brothers"

"*Vikki Carr* Accept applications for scholarships"

Letter from Salvador Barrera deploring injustice to Judge Leopoldo
        Sánchez

DEC 14   "Official cities leadership of ELA Health Task Force"

"Maestros y alumnos del colegio de ELA presentan 'Posadas' "

"Teatro de la Tierra on 'Accion Chicano' "

"TELACU Business Developers at business confab"

DEC 21   "New poverty agency [Greater Los Angeles Area Community
        Action Agency] named to replace EYOA," by Roger Swanson

"Hearings on Maravilla Neighborhood Development Project set for Dec. 28," by Ernie J. Ayala

"Continue 'Barrio Housing seminars' lists programs"

" 'NOSOTROS' elects new '73 officers"

DEC 28   "Maravilla Neighborhood Project hearing set for Thursday Morning, Urge residents, citizens, businessmen group representatives to attend session," by Ernie J. Ayala

"*Maravilla Redevelopment* Barrio Associates hearing delay request denied!" by Ridgely Cummings

"TELACU, PAC attorneys to iron out differences"

"*MAOF offers* Clerical skills training for residents in Model Cities areas"

"*Fiscal mismanagement?* Reddin asks full audit of Model Cities programs"